Hillier's

Fundamentals of Motor Vehicle Technology

5th Edition

Book 1

V.A.W. Hillier & Peter Coombes

T

First published in 1966 by:
Hutchinson Education
Second edition 1972
Third edition 1981 ISBN 0 09 143161 1
Reprinted in 1990 (ISBN 0 7487 0317 9) by Stanley Thornes (Publishers) Ltd
Fourth edition 1991

Fifth edition published in 2004 by:
Nelson Thornes Ltd
Delta Place
27 Bath Road
CHELTENHAM
GL53 7TH
United Kingdom

05 06 07 08 / 10 9 8 7 6 5 4 3 2

A catalogue record for this book is available from the British Library

ISBN 0 7487 8082 3

Page make-up by GreenGate Publishing Services, Tonbridge, Kent

Printed and bound in Slovenia by
DELO tiskarna by arrangement with Korotan - Ljubljana

CONTENTS

PREFACE

Since 1966, many thousands of motor vehicle technology students have relied on *Fundamentals of Motor Vehicle Technology* to successfully complete their studies. Therefore, a large percentage of professional mechanics and technicians owe a debt of gratitude to Vic Hillier for producing the original and updated editions. Whilst serving my apprenticeship with Ford Motor Company Ltd, I was one of those many thousands of former students who made very good use of 'Fundamentals' and I was therefore privileged to be asked to work on the 5th edition of the book.

In just over a century of motor vehicle technology, there has probably been more identifiable change in the last 25 years than in all of the previous years. Whilst the mechanical aspects of motor vehicle technology have gone through an evolutionary process of change over a long period of time, the almost sudden introduction of electronic vehicle systems has enabled and resulted in dramatic changes to the motor car.

Importantly, however, many of the modern electronic systems simply function as enhancements to the same basic mechanical technologies that Vic Hillier wrote about in the first edition of his book. A good example is the use of electronic fuel injection systems, which have completely replaced the carburettor as a means of delivering fuel to the petrol engine; but the use of these modern electronic injection systems has not made a fundamental difference to the basic engine operation or construction. The same is true of virtually every aspect of the motor vehicle, the electronic systems enhance and improve the operation of the mechanical systems, and therefore much of what Vic Hillier originally wrote about in the earlier editions of 'Fundamentals' is still relevant and important for today's vehicles.

Those new automotive technologies are used because of a number of reasons, such as: improving emissions, driver and passenger safety, as well as driver and passenger comfort. Those new technologies are very much dependent on electronics but to be competent with modern electronic systems does not mean that the mechanical systems can be ignored; they do still go wrong and the electronic systems function as an integrated part of the mechanical systems (one does not function without the other). The modern technician must therefore have a very good understanding of the traditional mechanical systems as well as the new electronic systems.

Because the mechanical aspects of the motor vehicle have not changed too much, there was little of Vic Hillier's original work that could be completely eliminated from this latest edition. However, the dramatic increase in the use of 'new' technologies has resulted in the need to produce two books. Book 1 is in fact similar to previous editions of *Fundamentals of Motor Vehicle Technology* but with updated information. Book 1 is also aligned with those topics that students will have to learn about in the earlier stages of their studies.

Book 2 then follows on with greater depth and breadth for modern vehicle technologies and electronic based systems, and Book 2 is therefore appropriate for the more advanced students and for existing technicians who wish to develop their own knowledge of the modern vehicle. Importantly, Book 2 also deals in some depth with diagnosis of modern vehicle systems. The workload of a modern technician embraces a considerable amount of diagnostic work and competence in diagnosis is an essential part of the skilled technician's capabilities.

Books 1 and 2 of Hillier's 'Fundamentals' have been structured to support the NVQ system and the syllabus for the technical certificates. However, the books maintain the tradition of the original Vic Hillier books by providing the reader with a substantial amount of additional information that is not just interesting but it enables a much better understanding of how vehicles and vehicle systems function.

As well as recognising the efforts of Vic Hillier in producing the original content for the 'Fundamentals' book, sincere thanks must go to Ian Gillgrass who has worked with me for a number of years. Ian has provided much of the research information and contributed to much of the content for this latest edition. Thanks must also go to those companies who have allowed us to use information and illustrations within the books.

I hope that students and readers of the 'Fundamentals' Books 1 and 2 get as much benefit, knowledge and pleasure as I did when I used Vic Hillier's earlier editions as a student.

Peter Coombes

ACKNOWLEDGEMENTS

I should like to thank the following companies for permission to make use of copyright and other material:

AE Group plc
Arriva plc
Automotive Products plc
Borg Warner Ltd
Robert Bosch Ltd
British Standards Institution
Champion Sparking Plug Co Ltd
Alexander Duckham & Co Ltd
Dunlop Ltd
Eaton Ltd
EuroNCAP (European New Car Assessment
    Programme)
Ford Motor Company Ltd
GKN plc
Honda (UK) Ltd
Jaguar Cars Ltd
Jensen Cars
Johnson Matthey Incorporated
Lucas Industries

Mazda Cars (UK) Ltd
Perkins Engines Ltd
Porsche Cars (Great Britain) Ltd
Renold Ltd
Rover Group plc
Saab (Great Britain) Ltd
Schrader Automotive Products Ltd
SKF Ltd
SU-Butec
Alfred Teves GmbH
Toyota (GB) Ltd
Volkswagen (UK) Ltd
Volvo Truck Corporation
Volvo Bus Corporation

Although many of the drawings are based on commercial components, they are mainly intended to illustrate principles of motor vehicle technology. For this reason, and because component design changes so rapidly, no drawing is claimed to be up to date. Students should refer to manufacturers' publications for the latest information.

Chapter 1

VEHICLE EVOLUTION, LAYOUT AND STRUCTURE

what is covered in this chapter . . .

- Vehicle evolution
- Vehicle layout
- Vehicle structure
- Routine maintenance

1.1   VEHICLE EVOLUTION

Figure 1.1 An old car (Model T Ford)

1.1.1 Centuries of vehicle development

At a very early stage in human history, it was realized by the more ingenious members of the species that the mobility to mankind provided by nature had some limitations. The human body was severely limited as to the loads it could carry, the distance it could carry them and the speed at which it could travel, even without a load. Furthermore, it is a safe guess that physical exertion was no more enjoyable then than it is today.

Major progress was achieved with the taming and training of suitable animals, which enabled heavier loads to be carried greater distances, often at greater speeds than the human was capable of attaining. There was, of course, the added advantage that most of the effort was provided by the animal, while the human being could travel at his ease, in comfort.

Heavy loads were dragged upon sledges until the next major development occurred, which was when an enterprising but unknown early engineer invented the wheel.

Figure 1.2 A modern car

The wheel made it possible to construct crude carts upon which even heavier loads could be carried more easily. However, the one drawback of wheeled vehicles was (and still is) the necessity of providing a reasonably smooth and hard surface upon which the wheels can run. The development of wheeled vehicles is therefore closely related to the development of roadways or dedicated tracks.

Over the centuries, there was not much in the way of major change other than some improvements in tools, some new materials and a better understanding of the technologies. Together, these changes combined to refine the wheeled vehicle and general mobility, but only within the limitations imposed by the source of power (i.e. the animals) and the basic materials available.

Probably the biggest influence on the development of the wheeled vehicle occurred during the 1800s. During this period, the industrial revolution embraced major developments of known technologies but importantly, new technologies appeared and the understanding of the sciences accelerated at a rapid pace.

Although inventors and scientists did at that time understand the potential for producing 'engines', this potential could not be fully explored because of the materials available. However, production of more suitable materials along with an understanding of how to work and make use of those materials, enabled inventors and scientists to achieve some of their dreams, such as creating engines that used fossil fuels to produce power.

As new materials and manufacturing methods were developed it became possible to make improvements to vehicles. Engines were of prime importance to the evolution of motor vehicles, but every aspect of the wheeled vehicle was improved and developed from the late 1800s through into the next century.

1.1.2 Choosing the right vehicle layout

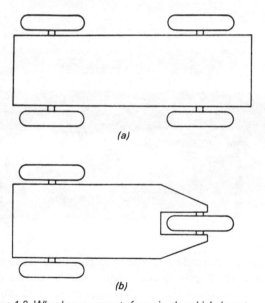

(a)

(b)

Figure 1.3 *Wheel arrangements for a simple vehicle layout*

Motor vehicles were inevitably developed from horse-drawn carriages. In fact, they were called 'horseless carriages', and naturally owed something of their general form and layout to horse-drawn vehicles. For instance, the layout of four wheels arranged one at each end of two transverse axles so that their points of contact with the ground are at the corners of a rectangle (as shown in Figure 1.3a) had been used on carts and wagons from time immemorial. This layout is still by far the most common arrangement on modern vehicles. Three wheels do not provide so much 'useful space' for a given amount of road space occupied by the vehicle (compare Figure 1.3a with Figure 1.3b). However, another important issue is the greater stability provided by a four-wheel layout.

The horse was invariably put in front of the cart to allow the animal to see where it was going, and allow the driver to keep an eye on the horse. The horse was

connected to the cart through shafts that were attached to a front axle, which was pivoted about its centre, thus providing a means of steering. Therefore, when it then came to replacing the horse with an engine, it was natural that front-wheel steering should be retained.

The swivelling axle arrangement is not very satisfactory for powered vehicles. One reason is because a good deal of space must be left for the axle and wheels to swivel, and also because if one wheel strikes an obstruction (such as a large stone) it is extremely difficult to prevent the axle swivelling about its pivot. An alternative arrangement, where the wheels were carried on stub axles (which were free to pivot at the ends of the fixed axle) had already been used on some horse-drawn carriages, and this layout was soon adopted for motorized vehicles.

One other alternative layout for steering the vehicle was tried, and that was to use the rear wheels, or axle, to steer the vehicle. It was soon found that rear-wheel steering had disadvantages which ruled it out for general use. For example, a vehicle steered by its rear wheels would steer to the right by deflecting the rear end to the left, making it impossible to drive away forwards from a position close to a wall or kerb, as illustrated in Figure 1.4.

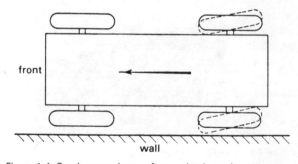

front

wall

Figure 1.4 *One inconvenience of rear-wheel steering*

With a tradition of pulling the vehicle rather than pushing, vehicles generally ended up with the engine at the front. It would have been an ideal solution to then drive the front wheels, which would have shortened the mechanical link (transmission system) to the driven wheels. However, when it came to using mechanical power to drive vehicles, the engineering difficulties of applying power to the same wheels that were used to steer the vehicle were considerable. This explains why, in the past, rear-wheel drive was almost universally adopted.

In addition, when climbing hills or accelerating, the increased load on the rear wheels provides better grip, making rear-wheel drive more attractive. Front-wheel-drive vehicles lose this advantage (even on today's modern designs), so under these conditions the wheels spin more easily. However, improvements in design and changes in the requirements for modern vehicles have progressively resulted in a substantial increase in the number of front-wheel drive vehicles.

The disadvantages of less grip have been reduced and although there is still a mechanical complication when applying the power to the steered wheels, these disadvantages and complications have been very much sacrificed to improve vehicle packaging. Extra space in a small vehicle (which will generally have a relatively low power engine) is much more important to most vehicle owners. Nevertheless, a well-designed front-wheel drive vehicle can now satisfy the requirements for space, power and grip.

If you look at Figure 1.5, you will see that the width between the front wheels is restricted by the necessity for the wheels to swivel for steering purposes.

Although there is a space available between the wheels, which might provide room for one seat, people seem to prefer to sit side by side. There may be much to be said in favour of isolating the driver in the extreme front of the vehicle, but the arrangement is not popular. Fortunately, an internal-combustion engine can be made to fit into this space very conveniently, and although the earliest vehicles had their engines elsewhere, this position was adopted by almost all manufacturers from a very early stage.

Vehicle layout has therefore evolved due to an initial tradition of pulling rather than pushing, but progressively the practicalities of space, grip, stability, engineering issues and of course cost, eventually took over as the dominant issues affecting vehicle layout and design. In fact, if we examine the evolution of every aspect of the motor vehicle, the same would be true.

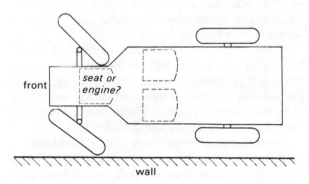

Figure 1.5 One reason for placing the engine at the front

1.1.3 Choosing the right engine

Development of the steam engine began in the 1700s. Improvements to this technology through the 1800s led to its application to the driving of vehicles and, although some of the early attempts were crude and not very successful, several extremely promising carriages were produced.

The heavy steam engine, however, proved less suited to road vehicles than it did to the railway. It was the successful development of the much lighter, high-speed internal-combustion engine (towards the end of the 1800s), which really opened up the way to the power-driven road vehicle, and which made possible the development of the modern motorcar, truck, bus and coach.

The most convenient source of power so far developed for driving road vehicles is the internal-combustion engine, which derives its power from the burning of fuel inside the engine itself. Alternative power units are the steam engine and the electric motor. A steam engine requires a boiler to generate the steam as well as the engine itself, making the complete installation rather bulky. In addition, there are heat losses in the boiler as well as in the engine, so a steam engine is generally less efficient than an internal-combustion engine. During temporary halts, it continues to consume fuel to maintain steam pressure, whereas the internal-combustion engine consumes fuel only when it is actually running.

An electric motor needs a supply of electrical energy to operate. If the electrical supply is to be carried on the vehicle it must be in the form of batteries or accumulators, which are both heavy and bulky in relation to the amount of energy they can store. This limits the range, speed and load-carrying capacity of the vehicle. If an external supply of electrical energy is used the vehicle must be connected to a distant power station by some means such as a system of wires, suspended at a safe height above the road. This system was used for many years to power some buses and trams, and in these cases suitable arms with some form of sliding connection to the wires were mounted on top of the vehicle. Such a system has obvious limitations.

During the latter part of the 1990s and into the twenty-first century, there has been considerable progress on alternatives to the internal-combustion engine. Developments in battery technology and electric motors have resulted in a number of electrically powered vehicles being produced. This new generation of electric vehicles offers very acceptable performance even though the electrical power storage (battery) is located in the vehicle itself.

Alternatives to the internal-combustion engine are continually being researched, such as electric power allied to alternative ways of producing electricity for motor vehicle applications. However, early in the twenty-first century, the internal-combustion engine still dominates.

Alternative fuels are also being explored for the internal-combustion engine because the petrol and diesel used to fuel the internal-combustion engine are refined from crude oil, which is a fossil fuel. Some time in the future the reservoirs of fossil fuels will decline to a level at which alternative fuels will be required to power the motor vehicle. At present, although alternative fuels and power sources are available, they either do not deliver the power required or are not commercially viable to replace the internal-combustion engine under present circumstances.

1.1.4 Transmitting the power

The internal-combustion engine has two characteristics that necessitate certain arrangements in the mechanism that connects the engine to the driving wheels.

Characteristic 1

The internal-combustion engine cannot produce any driving effort when it is not running. The source of energy for the internal-combustion engine (i.e. petrol and air) are of no use until they are mixed, compressed and ignited within the engine. However, a steam engine relies on a separate boiler system to heat the water, thus producing the energy. Assuming the boiler is lit, even when the steam engine itself is at rest, it is necessary merely to admit steam under pressure from the boiler by opening a valve, and the engine will at once start to work. An electric motor also relies on a separate power source, in this case electricity generated from a separate generating system. Therefore, even when the electric motor is at rest, it is only necessary to switch on the electricity supply to the motor. A steam engine and an electric motor can therefore be directly and permanently connected to the driven wheels.

The operating process of the internal-combustion engine does therefore have a small disadvantage compared with a steam engine or electric motor. The disadvantage with the internal-combustion engine is that it must be disengaged from the driven wheels and then started using the starter motor (or other external means) before it will begin to run under its own power and then develop enough power to move the vehicle.

Once the internal-combustion engine is running at a speed where sufficient power is being produced, it has to be connected to the driven wheels. To permit the running engine to be coupled or engaged smoothly, and without shock, to the initially stationary wheels, a mechanism is required that allows progressive engagement of the engine to the driven wheels.

Most vehicles produced over the years have been equipped with a manual gearbox and a device called a clutch. The clutch is a mechanical means of connecting and disconnecting the engine power to the transmission system and thus to the driven wheels. Operation of the clutch enables power from the engine to be smoothly and progressively connected to the driven wheels.

Note, however, that in the USA, and increasingly in Europe and elsewhere, vehicles are equipped with automatic gearboxes. Most automatic gearboxes do not use a conventional mechanical clutch to connect the engine to the gearbox. A fluid-(oil) based system is used which is usually referred to as a 'fluid flywheel' or 'torque converter'.

Characteristic 2

The power developed by an engine depends upon the speed at which it runs. A small engine running at high speed can develop as much power as a larger engine running at low speed. For a high percentage of vehicles, the smaller engine is preferable because the engine

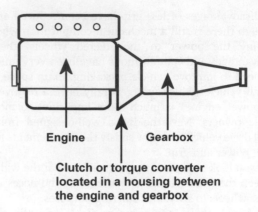

Engine   **Gearbox**

**Clutch or torque converter
located in a housing between
the engine and gearbox**

Figure 1.6 Location of clutch or torque converter

assembly will be lighter and take up less space. Such small, high-speed engines often run at a speed some four or five times greater than the road wheels, so a speed-reducing gear has to be included in the driving mechanism or transmission system that connects the engine to the driven wheels. A speed-reducing gear usually forms part of the rear axle assembly on rear-wheel drive vehicles, or it may form part of the gearbox assembly on front-wheel drive engines.

Unless an exceptionally large and powerful engine is fitted to a very small and light vehicle, another problem arises, which is caused by the fact that engine power is dependent on engine speed. The size and types of engines, which are generally fitted to virtually all vehicles, will not produce sufficient power over the whole engine speed range to provide both acceptable acceleration and top speed.

If the vehicle has a maximum speed of 160 km/h (100 mph), the engine will be operating at a speed where it is producing maximum power. In most cases, the engine is designed so that maximum power is close to the maximum permissible engine speed, which on a modern engine could be around 7000 rpm.

When the vehicle decelerates to a low speed, such as 16 km/h (10 mph), the engine will also have slowed down (in this example to 700 rpm). At such low engine speeds, the engine does not produce enough power to accelerate the vehicle. It would be possible to operate the clutch, thus disengaging the engine from the transmission, and then increase the engine rpm so that sufficient power were developed. However, the clutch would need to be engaged very slowly (slipped for a considerable time) to allow the vehicle speed to increase. The clutch would have to be slipped until the vehicle speed was high enough to match the engine speed, at which point the clutch could be fully engaged. The process of using high engine speeds and slipping the clutch would cause the clutch to wear out very quickly and vehicle performance would not be acceptable. Therefore another method is used to ensure that the engine speed is sufficient to develop the required power when the vehicle is moving slowly.

Virtually every vehicle fitted with an internal-combustion engine will also have a gearbox. The gearbox provides additional gearing options, which can be brought into use or selected, either manually by the driver, or automatically.

What is referred to as the lowest forward gear (first gear) allows the engine to operate at high engine speeds with the vehicle moving at slow speeds. The highest gear (top gear) will allow the engine to operate at high engine speeds when the vehicle is also at high speed.

First gear therefore enables the clutch to be engaged quickly, at very low vehicle speeds, with the engine operating at a high enough engine speed to produce enough power for acceleration, without slipping the clutch.

By including a number of different gears within the gearbox, it is possible to provide good acceleration and general performance at all vehicle speeds. The different gears allow the required engine speed and power to be achieved at all vehicle speeds. It is now common for five

forward gears to be included in a gearbox as well as a reverse gear. Both manual and automatic gearboxes are now being produced with as many as seven forward gears.

In conclusion, to transmit the engine power, it is necessary to have an overall gear reduction to enable engine speeds to be much higher than wheel speeds. Additional gears are required to enable sufficient engine power to be available at all vehicle speeds.

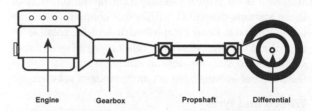

Figure 1.7 Gearbox located behind the engine. Overall gear reduction located in rear axle (on rear-wheel drive vehicles)

1.2   VEHICLE LAYOUT

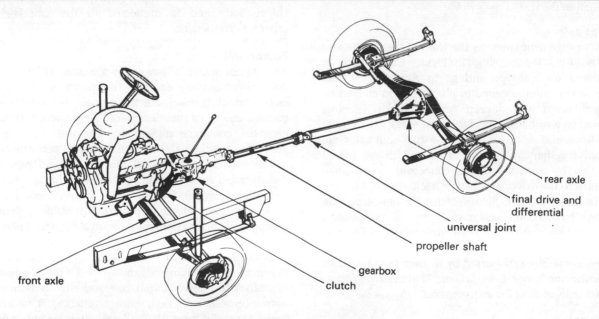

Figure 1.8 Layout of mechanical systems (Simple front engine–rear-wheel drive layout)

1.2.1 Simple layout of mechanical systems

This book primarily covers those vehicles with a laden weight of less than three tonnes and which are generally used either for private transportation or as small commercial or passenger-carrying vehicles. The term normally applied to this class of vehicle is 'light vehicle'.

A wide range of different body shapes and sizes come into this light vehicle category; these range from two-seater cars up to personnel carriers (people carriers and mini-buses) and small trucks (vans). Increasingly, the people carriers and smaller commercial vehicles are derived from normal passenger cars; in effect they make use of similar mechanical components but have bodies that have been adapted for their specific tasks.

Although vehicles are made up of numerous mechanical components, in most cases a number of components will be assembled together, or will work together to form what are generally termed an 'assembly' or 'system'.

Figure 1.8 shows a layout for the various basic mechanical systems used on a vehicle. The layout illustrated is a comparatively simple type used on older generations of vehicles with traditional front engine–rear-wheel drive. The illustration provides a description of a traditional layout for mechanical systems, along with an explanation of the function of those systems described within this chapter. Once this foundation has been established it will be possible to appreciate the finer details of other more advanced and sophisticated systems now in common use, as well as the different layouts used on more modern vehicles.

Wheels and tyres

Most light vehicles run on four wheels, which are usually made of steel or alloy. The wheels are fitted with hollow rubber tyres, which are filled with air under sufficient pressure to support the load they have to carry. The tyres provide contact with the road surface and therefore the grip to the road. The tyres also absorb small shocks caused by minor irregularities in the road surface. Larger shocks are taken by suspension springs and these allow the wheels to move vertically in relation to the rest of the vehicle.

Front axle

This arrangement supports the front of the vehicle and is also used for steering. In Figure 1.8 the axle is mounted on leaf-type springs to form the flexible suspension system needed to absorb shocks created by larger bumps and uneven surfaces. Each wheel is carried on a stub axle; this is pivoted to the extremity of the front axle by a king-pin. The two stub axles are linked together by steering arms, which are joined together by a track rod and connected to a linkage coupled to the driver's steering wheel.

On most modern light vehicles the one-piece axle beam has been superseded by a suspension arrangement that allows each front wheel to rise and fall independently. On the independent systems, each wheel is therefore supported by its own spring without affecting the other front wheel. This arrangement is called independent front suspension.

Rear axle

This carries the rear wheels and supports the weight of the rear of the vehicle. The axle type shown is tubular in section and contains two axle shafts (half-shafts), one for each side, to drive the road wheels.

On the vehicle centre line (or close to the centre line), the axle is enlarged to house the final drive. The final drive system contains a pair of gears which fullfil two functions: the first is to 'turn the drive through 90°', the second is to provide the 'overall gear reduction' which reduces the high engine revolutions to an acceptably lower number of revolutions of the road wheels.

Additionally, the final drive system or assembly will normally contain a sub-assembly known as a differential. When a vehicle turns a corner, its outer wheel rotates faster than its inner wheel. If both road wheels were rigidly connected to one axle shaft, the wheels would not be able to rotate at different speeds, therefore either the inner or the outer tyre would have to slip on the road surface.

Inevitably, the slipping tyre would suffer very rapid wear. However; there is an additional problem caused by rigidly connected wheels. Both wheels would be trying to rotate at the same speed and this has the effect of trying to force the vehicle in a straight line, which would make steering and controlling the vehicle difficult.

These problems are overcome by using the differential gear, a mechanism that allows the wheels to rotate at different speeds when cornering. Although the differential ensures that each road wheel can rotate at a speed that suits the cornering conditions, it arranges for each wheel to receive an equal driving effort irrespective of the speed of rotation of the wheel.

Final drive systems (including the differential) can be located within the gearbox assembly on front-wheel drive vehicles. For those rear-wheel drive vehicles with independent suspension where there is not a rigid axle, the final drive and differential system is mounted on the chassis/body and is connected to the wheels by separate drive shafts.

Power unit

The normal source of power for a motor vehicle is an internal-combustion engine. The petrol or gasoline engine (spark ignition) has traditionally been the most popular due to its superior overall performance. Diesel engines (compression ignition engines) were not generally able to provide the same performance characteristics as the petrol engine, but did provide excellent fuel economy, and better power characteristics for pulling heavy loads.

Due to some of the internal loads within a diesel engine being higher than for an equivalent size of petrol engine, the construction of the diesel engine is usually heavier and stronger and often more expensive. However, the economy advantage of the diesel engine can offset the higher initial cost and slightly reduced output (especially for high mileage vehicles). It has also been generally true that diesel engines are more durable than petrol engines, which has made them ideal for commercial vehicles.

During the latter part of the 1990s, diesel engines benefited from considerable development, which has resulted in comparable performance to the petrol engines. In many countries (especially in Europe), diesel fuel costs a lot less than petrol (lower taxes apply in many countries). The diesel engine is therefore becoming increasingly popular for light vehicles, including executive models.

Transmission

The term transmission can be used to cover the complete driveline between the engine and the road wheels. The complete transmission system therefore includes:

- Gearbox
- Clutch
- Propeller or transmission shaft
- Universal joints
- Final drive and differential system
- Drive shafts (to each of the driven wheels).

However, the term 'transmission' can also be used to describe just the gearbox assembly or system, and applies in particular to the type of arrangement used on a given vehicle, i.e. whether the selection of the gears has to be carried out manually by the driver or whether the gear selection is an automatic process that is performed by the action of mechanical or electronic systems which form part of the automatic transmission (automatic gearbox).

Manual gearbox

A manual gearbox consists of sets of gears that provide different ratios between the engine speed (rev/minute) and the rotation of the gearbox output shaft. The different gear ratios enable the engine speed to be maintained within its power range and ideal working limits, irrespective of the speed of the vehicle. The different gear ratios also have the effect of amplifying or multiplying the torque (twisting force) produced by the engine.

In addition, a gearbox provides a neutral gear in which the engine can run without moving the vehicle, and also a reverse gear, to enable the vehicle to be driven backwards whilst the engine is still rotating in the normal direction.

For most manual gearboxes, a clutch is fitted which allows the engine to be disengaged from the gearbox (see below). The clutch is almost always operated by a foot pedal.

Automatic gearbox

Automatic gearboxes provide the same functions as a manual gearbox except that gear changes are carried out automatically, thus relieving the driver of the task of gear selection. The driver is only required to select the direction of travel, i.e. forward or backward.

Automatic gearboxes are usually fitted with a fluid flywheel or torque converter instead of a clutch. The basic fluid flywheel is now not generally used but the more sophisticated torque converter (also making use of a fluid-based coupling between engine and gearbox) provides a means for disengaging the engine from the gearbox which does not require driver operation. Torque converters provide a smooth re-engagement of the engine to the gearbox, allowing the vehicle to move off or come to rest in a smooth manner without the driver having to do anything other than press the accelerator or brake pedal.

Clutch

The gears in a manual gearbox have to be changed or selected when the vehicle is at rest and being driven. This requires the driver to move a selector lever, which, in turn, either engages or disengages sets of gears. This action should only be performed when the gears are not under load, so a clutch is fitted to meet this need. The clutch enables the driver to disengage the engine from the gearbox.

A sudden connection of the drive from the engine to the transmission would cause a severe jolt and consequent damage to the vehicle. The clutch is designed to avoid this; it allows the driver to accelerate the vehicle away from a stationary position gradually. Also, it enables the driver to disengage the engine from the transmission system and driven wheels temporarily, when road conditions dictate such a need.

Propeller or transmission shaft

The propeller shaft is the long shaft (usually tubular) which links the gearbox to the final drive system on vehicles with rear-wheel drive. Normally an open-type arrangement is used in which the shaft is exposed.

Universal joints

Universal joints are fitted to each end of the propeller shaft to enable the drive to be transmitted through a varying angle. This variation is due to the movement of the axle and final drive system relative to the engine and gearbox.

Even when the final drive system is fixed to the frame and the wheels are independently sprung, the propeller shaft still needs universal joints. This is to allow for the flexing of the frame structure that occurs when the vehicle is travelling over a bumpy surface.

Universal joints can also be fitted to the drive shafts (for each driven wheel) when there is no rigid axle, as is the case for independent suspension systems. Other types of joints are used, such as constant velocity joints on the drive shafts of front-wheel drive vehicles.

Brakes

Understandably, vehicles are required by law to be fitted with an efficient braking system; this usually takes the form of brakes attached to each wheel.

Two types of brake are in general use: disc brakes and drum brakes. Although earlier vehicles used drum brakes on all wheels, disc brakes became more popular for front brakes. Many modern vehicles now have disc brakes on all wheels.

A disc brake consists of an exposed disc, which is attached to, and rotates with, the road wheel hub. On each side of the disc face is a friction pad, held in place by a fixed calliper that is in turn mounted on the end of the axle or stub axle. When the brake pressure is applied, the disc is sandwiched by the friction pads, which slows the rotation of the disc and wheel, or if sufficient pressure is applied prevents the disc from rotating.

Braking is achieved by converting the energy of motion (kinetic energy) to heat energy, so exposure of the disc to the air stream is an important feature of this type of brake. The disc brakes are more effective for repeated stops or for driving at higher speeds or with high vehicle loads. The disc brake does however require high brake pedal effort and therefore some form of assistance (mechanical, vacuum or hydraulic) is usually included in the braking system.

The drum brake system has been in use for many years and is still popular for rear brakes. This is because drum brakes require less effort to achieve effective stopping power. This makes the drum brake ideal for use as a handbrake or parking brake (to keep the vehicle stationary when it is not in use) because the handbrake mechanism is not able to provide the same high levels of force as a foot-operated brake. Drum brakes do however have a tendency to overheat with repeated use or if the vehicle is travelling at high speeds or with heavy loads.

Drum brakes have two brake shoes, which are lined with a friction material, and secured to a backplate fixed to the axle or stub axle. The shoes are contained within a drum that is attached to the rotating hub. Retardation of the drum is achieved by moving the shoes outwards; an expansion which is normally produced by a piston in a hydraulic cylinder.

Light vehicles generally use a hydraulic system to operate the brakes (disc and drum) and will normally have the addition of vacuum servo assistance to minimize the effort that the driver has to apply.

Chassis or frame

The component parts of a vehicle need a structure of some kind on to which they can be attached. Medium to heavy commercial vehicles use a rectangular steel frame made up of two long side members which are linked together by a number of cross members. The assembly, without the body, is called a chassis and the frame alone the chassis frame.

Up until the mid-1950s, most light cars were also constructed using a chassis onto which the body was mounted.

Chassis-less construction

The chassis-less structure is much lighter than the separate chassis construction, so it is now the normal method of construction for light vehicles. The chassis-less system is often referred to as a unitary or monocoque construction.

The unitary construction system uses a specially designed body shell on which all of the transmission system, suspension and engine are mounted. The body shell itself must therefore be able to withstand the various loads of the components and stresses that occur when the car is in use.

Electrical equipment

The modern vehicle has a considerable number of electrical and electronic systems. The *Fundamentals* series of books examines many of these systems, some of which are identified below.

An electric motor is used to rotate the engine, enabling it to start. Vehicles are required by law to be fitted with certain lights, sidelights and headlights for use during the hours of darkness and in poor visibility. Indicators or flashers are used to inform others of the direction in which the vehicle is turning and brake lights that illuminate during the application of the brakes are also required.

Other items are operated electrically, including: windscreen wipers and washers, horns, heaters, audio systems, central locking and various other aids for the comfort of the driver and passengers. The modern motor vehicle uses electronically controlled systems to operate many of these electrical items which were once controlled by simple on/off switches or by mechanical means.

Since the late 1970s, electronically controlled engine systems (for fuel and ignition, as well as other functions) have become increasingly common and it is now essential for vehicles to have such systems to achieve acceptable emissions levels and performance.

Electrical power to operate all of the electrical and electronic equipment comes from a generator, which is driven from the engine. Since certain items may be needed when the engine is not running, a battery (sometimes called the accumulator) is fitted. The generator charges the battery when the engine is running.

1.2.2 Layout for the light passenger vehicle (car)

The engine and transmission layout shown in Figure 1.8 represents that used on most cars up to about 1950. Since then, various developments in technology and changes in lifestyle have meant that the motor vehicle has changed to meet those requirements.

Today, many different layouts are used, with each arrangement offering specific advantages and disadvantages. Variations occur in the location of the engine and the driving arrangement (i.e. driving wheels and how many wheels are driven, and whether these are the back, front or all four wheels).

Front engine

Apart from tradition, there are a number of reasons for siting the engine at the front of a car as shown in Figure 1.9. The large mass of an engine at the front of the car

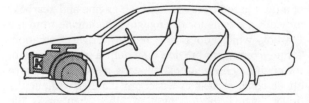

Figure 1.9 Front engine location

gives the occupants protection in the event of a head-on collision; also engine cooling is simpler to arrange. In addition, the cornering ability of a vehicle is generally better (for most drivers) if the weight is concentrated at the front because the weight of the engine is placed over the steered wheels. The engine can be positioned transversely or longitudinally to drive either the front wheels, the rear wheels or all four wheels.

Rear engine

By placing the engine at the rear of the vehicle it can be made as a unit that incorporates the clutch, gearbox and final drive assembly. With such an arrangement it is necessary to use some form of independent rear suspension.

Most rear-engine layouts have been confined to comparatively small cars, because the weight of the engine at the rear has an adverse effect on the handling of the car, making it 'tail-heavy'. The engine mass on a rear-engined car will generally be behind the rear axle line. This creates a pendulum effect during cornering making handling at high speeds more difficult for most drivers. However, a notable exception is the range of Porsche sports cars that have been developed since the late 1950s using a rear engine location. Developments in suspension and other design features have enabled Porsche to achieve good handling with what is generally regarded as an engine location that is not ideal.

Rear located engines also take up a large amount of space that would on a front-engined car be used for carrying luggage. Most of the space vacated by moving the engine from the front can be used for luggage, but this space is usually less than that available in the rear. Although occasionally conventional, vertical engines are used in rear-engined cars, a 'flat' engine, or a conventional engine laid on its side, can provide some additional space for luggage above the engine.

One advantage attributed to a rear-engined layout is the increased load on the rear driving wheels, giving them better grip on the road.

Figure 1.10 shows one of the most famous rear-engined cars – the Volkswagen Beetle. Notice that the front seats are nearer the front wheels than in a front-engined car, and that the floor is quite flat.

When the engine is placed at the rear of the vehicle, it is the rear wheels that are normally driven, although in a few instances all four wheels may be driven.

Central and mid-engine

In general, the central or mid-engine location applies to sports cars. Whereas on a rear-engined car, the engine overhangs the rear axle line, on a mid-engined car, the engine is forward of the rear axle line. This location provides excellent weight distribution that achieves both good handling and maximum traction from the driving wheels. In fact it is often the case that the weight distribution is 50/50 front and rear, which many designers consider ideal.

These advantages, whilst of great importance for sports and special cars, become disadvantages when applied to the more traditional passenger cars. The biggest disadvantage is the fact that the mid-engine location takes up space that would normally be occupied by passengers. Most cars using a mid-engine position are therefore nearly always sports cars fitted with only two seats for the driver and one passenger.

The mid-engined layout shown in Figure 1.11 combines the engine and transmission components in one unit. Mid-engined cars are normally rear-wheel driven.

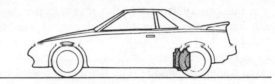

Figure 1.11 Mid-engine location

Rear-wheel drive (RWD)

For the RWD layout, the rear wheels act as the driving wheels, the front wheels are therefore free of mechanical complication other than those mechanical systems necessary for providing steering. In the past, rear-wheel drive was a natural choice because of the difficulty of transmitting the power to a wheel that also had to swivel for steering purposes.

Spacing out the main components in this layout makes each unit accessible but a drawback is the intrusion of the transmission components into the

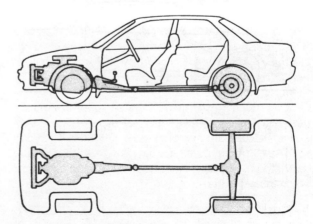

Figure 1.12 Rear-wheel drive layout

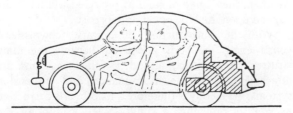

Figure 1.10 Rear engine location

passenger compartment. It is normally necessary to create a large bulge in the region of the gearbox and a long raised bulge (called the transmission tunnel) along the centre of the car floor to accommodate the propeller/transmission shaft.

RWD was favoured by virtually all vehicle manufacturers in the past, because the size of engines, transmission systems etc. dictated spacing out of the systems and components. However, modern design and engineering has achieved reductions in size and weight of the components allowing more compact installations such as front-wheel drive.

Front-wheel drive (FWD)

The compactness of the front-wheel drive layout has made it very popular on modern cars, especially on small cars. FWD is in fact not a new or modern layout; vehicles with FWD were in mass production in the 1930s. However, the engine remained installed in the traditional longitudinal manner, i.e. along the centre line of the vehicle. These early designs of FWD therefore eliminated the need for transmission tunnels but still required a relatively long vehicle front.

In the late 1950s the British manufacturer Austin (with its sister company Morris) launched the Mini, which had the engine mounted across the front of the vehicle (transverse) and additionally, the gearbox was located under the engine. The drive was passed from the gearbox direct to the front wheels. This compact arrangement allowed the Mini to be exceptionally small in overall dimensions but also provided a reasonable amount of space for the occupants. The Mini is generally regarded as the forerunner of modern FWD vehicles.

Although originally introduced for 'baby' cars, the advantages associated with the transverse engine have encouraged the use of front-wheel drive in many medium-sized cars. For space reasons the length of the engine is the limiting factor, but modern designs and engineering have made engines and gearboxes more compact, thus allowing the increased use of more

powerful engines (especially V-type engines) in transverse FWD installations. Accommodating all the main components under the bonnet (hood) in one compartment provides maximum space within the car for the occupants. Also the absence of floor bulges and a tunnel provides more room for the rear passengers.

Four-wheel drive (4WD)

This arrangement, shown in Figure 1.14, is safer because it distributes the drive to all four wheels. The sharing of the load between the four wheels during acceleration reduces the risks of wheel spin.

A further advantage of this layout is shown when the vehicle is driven on slippery surfaces such as snow and mud. On an icy road or driving cross-country (off-highway) a two-wheel drive vehicle soon becomes undrivable because the loss of grip of one of the driving wheels causes the wheel to spin.

Many different types of 4WD systems have been designed and modern 4WD systems make use of sophisticated engineering and electronics to ensure that the power is delivered as required to those wheels that can maintain grip. However, a long-established and relatively simple 4WD design has been fitted to Land Rover vehicles since the 1940s although it had been used before on heavy trucks and all-terrain vehicles.

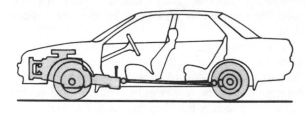

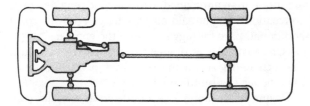

Figure 1.14 Four-wheel drive layout

1.2.3 Body of light passenger vehicle

The main purpose of the bodywork is to provide comfortable accommodation for the driver and passengers, with suitable protection against wind and weather. The degree of comfort provided will naturally depend upon the type of car and its cost.

With the introduction of unitary (chassis-less) construction, the body effectively became the main structure onto which all other vehicle systems are attached (e.g. engine, transmission and suspension systems). The body is therefore a load-bearing structure as well as providing a comfortable location for the occupants.

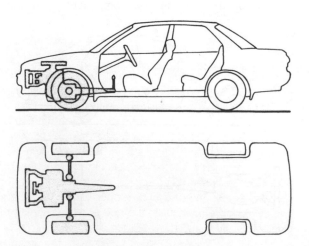

Figure 1.13 Front-wheel drive layout

The majority of mass-produced cars have a pressed steel body, although mass-produced aluminium bodies are being used increasingly due to their lighter weight. Alternatively, when production volumes are low it is not uncommon to construct the body by hand-working aluminium alloy or steel into shape. Another common practice is to mould body panels from GRP (glass-reinforced plastics, often referred to as fibre-glass). Other materials are also now used, such as carbon fibre, to produce body panels and structures. These more exotic and expensive materials are used on almost all F1 racing cars but some expensive sports cars may also use body parts made from these very light but strong materials.

All steel surfaces must be treated and painted. Primarily this is to give protection against rust corrosion; secondly it improves their appearance. External trim, made of stainless steel, chromium-plated brass or plastics, embellishes the body and appeals to the eye by providing a contrast with the plain coloured panels.

Figure 1.15 shows some of the body styles used for cars.

Saloon

A fully enclosed body which is typically able to carry four or more people. Saloon cars generally have either two or four passenger doors. The common shape of body shell is based on three 'boxes'; the front box forms the engine compartment, the centre section the container for the occupants and the rear box a storage space, called a boot (trunk) for the luggage. The three boxes are blended together to give a pleasing appearance and are shaped to enable the car to move through the air with the minimum drag.

For safety purposes the passenger capsule must be suitably strengthened to keep its shape after the car has collided with some other object. Extra safety during front or rear impact can be obtained by arranging for the front and rear regions of the car to fold up in a concertina fashion. This deformation absorbs the shock of impact and although damage to these regions is more extensive, the passenger capsule remains intact.

Estate

The estate body (also known as a station wagon in some countries) has the roofline extended to the rear of the body to enlarge its internal capacity. Folding the rear seats down gives a large floor area for the carriage of luggage or goods. A tailgate (rear door) enables bulky or long objects to be loaded easily. Stronger suspension springs are fitted at the rear to support the extra load.

Hatchback

The hatchback design is generally based on a saloon body but with the boot or trunk area blended into the centre section of the body. The hatchback is therefore halfway between a saloon and an estate car. This type of car is very popular due to its versatility and style.

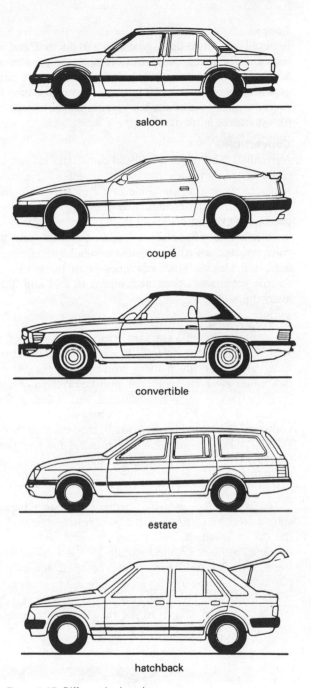

Figure 1.15 Different body styles

Although some hatchbacks are in fact saloon bodies with the boot or trunk effectively removed (usually the smaller cars), many hatchbacks retain the full length of the saloon but the roofline extends down to the rear of the vehicle. As with the saloon bodies, a hatchback can have two or four passenger doors. However, there is a tendency to refer to hatchbacks as having three or five doors because the rear luggage compartment lid (or tailgate) is also referred to as a door on the hatchback bodies. As with the estate, the rear seats fold down to give a flat floor for the transportation of luggage or other objects. When the tailgate is closed, the luggage compartment is normally covered with a parcel shelf.

Coupé

Generally this two-door type has a rigid roof and is intended for two people; a driver and one passenger. Some coupé models are designated '2 + 2'; this generally suggests that the rear seat accommodation is rather cramped for adults but is suitable for children or for occasional adult use.

Convertible

Also called cabriolet or drop-head coupé, this car can be changed into an open car by either removing a rigid roof or lowering a collapsible fabric roof. Prior to the introduction of air-conditioning this type was widely used in hot countries. Many modern convertibles now have what is effectively a rigid roof that can be collapsed and stored in a relatively small compartment behind the seats. Such examples often make use of electric motors or other mechanisms to fold and hide away the roof.

Jacking points

It is sometimes necessary to raise the wheels of a vehicle clear of the ground. It is usually achieved by using a jack, of which there are several types. When jacking up a vehicle great care must be taken to ensure that the jack is on a firm surface and is lifting the vehicle at a point which is sufficiently strong to withstand the concentrated load. Modern cars have special jacking points that are suitable for the jack supplied with the car. Reference to the handbook of the car will show the points at which the jack should be placed.

Jacks, even expensive hydraulic trolley types, should NOT be trusted when a person has to lie under the car or when the collapse of the jack could cause damage, human or mechanical. In these situations some form of rigid prop must be used for safety purposes. The type of prop used is referred to as an axle stand. The use of house bricks or similar objects as axle stands is highly dangerous, as they tend to crumble when placed under excessive pressure.

Apart from securing the jack and stand, precautions should also be taken to ensure that the car cannot roll forwards or backwards; the handbrake should be applied and the wheels should be chocked.

1.2.4 Interior of light passenger vehicle

Internal furnishings and fittings

The quality of the interior fittings and fabrics depends on the amount the purchaser is prepared to pay for the car. The interior finish of modern cars is generally of high quality but the level of luxury generally separates the various models in a given range.

Most cars have individual bucket-type front seats. In the past, a single, one-piece bench-type seat was used because, with this type, three people could be seated side by side. As well as giving greater comfort and safety, the space between the bucket seats allows for the fitting of the gear lever (or selector) and other controls. To allow the occupants to sit comfortably and the driver to obtain a suitable driving position, each seat is carried on rails or runners securely fixed to the floor, with an arrangement that allows the seats to be moved backwards and forwards, (and sometimes up and down) by manual or electrical means.

The rear seat for two or three passengers is normally a non-adjustable bench-type with perhaps a centre armrest to improve comfort when only two people are carried. Extra-large cars or stretched limousines often have extra rear seats, called occasional seats that fold into a division across the car behind the front seats.

Seat materials range from a vinyl to fabric (often referred to as velour), or leather, which was traditional on luxury cars, but is now used on a greater range of vehicles.

Carpets and interior trim

Fitment of a carpet to the floor and the covering of metal body panels enhances the appearance and

Figure 1.16 A car can be raised off the ground using a jack but should then be supported by axle stands

improves the noise level and comfort. A fabric or plastic material is used as a head lining for the roof and for covering other interior surfaces. Panels are fastened to the interior surface of the doors to cover the mechanism for door locking and window winding.

Driving position

Right-hand drive vehicles, where the driver's controls and steering wheel are located on the right, are used in the UK and a few other countries around the world. It is suggested that driving on the left-hand side of the road evolved from the days when a horse rider, who normally carried his sword on the left-hand side of his body, mounted his steed on its left side for obvious reasons. However, in most European countries, the USA and much of the rest of the world, vehicles are left-hand drive and are driven on the right-hand side of the road.

In the case of motor vehicles, where the traffic is keeping to the left side of the road the driver must sit on the right side in order to see that the road ahead is clear before overtaking.

Most countries now drive on the right, so cars sold in these areas have the steering wheel and driving controls situated to give left-hand drive. But note that foot pedals in both right- and left-hand drive systems are normally arranged in the same order with the accelerator pedal on the right.

Controls and instrumentation

As well as the main driving controls, various additional buttons and switches are provided and located within easy reach for the driver to operate. A speedometer, together with other visual instruments provides the driver with information as well as warning indications and messages. These visual instruments are often grouped together but will normally be located on an instrument panel which forms part of the fascia panel that runs across the front of the vehicle interior (often referred to as the dashboard).

Seat belts

Seat belts must be provided by law for the driver and all passengers. It is also compulsory for all occupants to wear seat belts while the vehicle is being driven. The wearing of seat belts minimizes the risk of severe injury if the car is involved in a collision. These belts must be anchored to a substantial part of the vehicle structure in such a way that the anchorages will not be torn out when an accident occurs. On most cars an inertia reel arrangement is used for the attachment of the lower end of the belt. The most popular type of belt used today has three mounting points, which connect with a diagonal shoulder strap and lap belt to restrain the occupant. An automatic, inertia-controlled belt reel attachment is generally preferred because this type allows the occupant to move freely in the seat when the car is stationary or moving normally. When a ball in the mechanism senses that the deceleration (slowing down) of the car is rapid, it rolls forward and locks up a toothed wheel attached to the belt; forward movement of the occupant is then resisted.

Safety restraint systems (SRS)

Many modern vehicles are fitted with additional safety devices to protect the occupants in the event of a collision or accident. There are a number of types of SRS but a commonly used type is the airbag system. Airbags are usually located in the centre of the steering wheel and in the dashboard (for passenger protection). The airbags are designed to rapidly inflate if the forces generated during an accident are above a certain pre-determined level.

Airbags are generally designed to work in conjunction with the seat belts and it is usual practice to provide the front seat belts with a pre-tensioning system, which operates in addition to the airbag function. The pre-tensioning of the seat belts is triggered either by a very strong spring located within a

Figure 1.17 Controls and instrumentation

container or tube, or by a form of pyrotechnic device (effectively a mini-explosion within a container). In either case, the result is that the seat belt will tighten, thus restraining the occupant's body during the accident. The inflated airbag then provides a cushion or restraint for the upper chest and head.

Airbags are now fitted in the sides of seats, in the sides of the roof and in other locations where inflation will provide protection to the occupants.

1.2.5   Light/medium commercial vehicles

Light to medium-sized commercial vehicles are used for the transportation of relatively light goods. They are the type of vehicle used by tradesmen to carry their equipment or by shopkeepers to make local deliveries. Light commercial vehicles are, however, also used for long distance deliveries of light goods as well as for the more local use.

Although in the past a commercial vehicle that was not classified as a 'heavy goods vehicle' was generally referred to as a light commercial, there is now such a wide range of commercial vehicles that there is justification in also using the term 'medium commercial vehicle'.

Light commercial vehicles (car derivatives)

Smaller types of light commercial vehicle are usually derived from a passenger car but with a different body shape to provide increased carrying space. These vehicles are usually called light vans and are typically able to carry up to half a tonne in weight.

Many mechanical components and systems are sourced directly from the car but note that components such as clutches, braking systems and suspension units are often uprated when they are used on commercial versions; this ensures that the parts can withstand the extra stresses. The loads carried by the van may exceed the design limits of the car system, and although stronger components can be used, it is also not uncommon for the rear suspension system of the van to be entirely different in design to that of the car.

Light vans may be fitted with a petrol engine but it is more common for a diesel engine to be specified by the purchaser.

Because the front half of a light van is often identical, or very similar to, the car from which the van is derived, there is usually seating for the driver and a passenger. Car-derived comfort systems can also be included in a light van, such as air conditioning etc.

Medium-sized commercial vehicles

Larger vans or medium-sized commercial vehicles are usually unrelated in general design to a passenger car. Although the engine and transmission may be sourced from a passenger vehicle, the structure and size of the medium van is usually much larger than most passenger cars and it is often the case that specially designed or adapted engines are used. Since low cost operation is an essential factor, most of these vehicles are fitted with a diesel (compression-ignition) type engine.

The general construction of the medium sized van is either a unitary construction or it may be constructed using a chassis onto which the body is attached. Manufacturers normally offer a number of different body shapes and sizes to suit the buyer's needs. The enclosed type of body may be offered in different lengths and heights (Figure 1.19). When a vehicle is required for the transportation of bulky equipment (e.g. materials carried by builders and decorators) an open body is often preferred. A light vehicle having this type of body is called a pick-up and an example of this type is shown in Figure 1.20.

Figure 1.19 Medium-sized van

Figure 1.18 Car-derived light commercial vehicle (light van)

Figure 1.20 Pick-up body mounted on a chassis

Suspension systems can be derived from car systems but due to the weights carried by the vans, they are more usually of a design specific to the vehicle. It is also common for the rear axle to have twin wheels at each side, again to better support heavy loads.

People carriers or mini-buses

The term mini-bus was traditionally used to describe vehicles that carried up to 13 people including the driver. In recent years, vehicles carrying from five to eight people have usually been referred to as people carriers, with the term mini-bus now referring only to larger passenger carriers.

As is the case with light commercial vehicles, people carriers also fall into different categories. Many of the recent, smaller sized people carriers are in fact a passenger car platform onto which a different body shell has been attached. However, larger people carriers and mini-buses are more closely related to the medium-sized vans.

The larger people carriers are generally of unitary construction but with very little sourced from passenger cars, apart from possibly the engine and transmission. Mini-buses can be of unitary construction but as is the case with the larger vans, chassis-based designs are also available.

Diesel engines are again a common feature of mini-buses and people carriers due to the fuel economy and pulling power they offer.

Figure 1.21 Small and large people carriers

4 × 4 recreational and executive vehicles

This type of vehicle is generally regarded as having originated in the early 1970s with the Range Rover, a luxury version of the long established Land Rover.

The Land Rover had evolved from military requirements of the 1930s and 1940s. It was a very spartan vehicle with four-wheel drive, intended for agricultural use and other applications where the four-wheel drive system enabled excellent traction and grip on rough or loose surfaces.

The Range Rover made use of the four-wheel drive technology developed from the Land Rover, which was still mounted on a traditional chassis frame. However, a more luxurious body was mounted on the chassis and the comfort levels within the Range Rover were more like those of a luxury car than the Land Rover. The engines used in the Range Rover are also generally much more powerful than those traditionally mounted in the Land Rover.

During the 1990s, many manufacturers launched competitors to the later versions of the Range Rover. These competitors, along with the latest Range Rovers are now very sophisticated vehicles that retain the four-wheel drive capability but are in effect luxury vehicles in most cases. They are classed as being recreational vehicles and have the capability to go 'off-road'.

Construction of recreational vehicles is either based on a chassis frame with the body and mechanical systems attached to the chassis, or they are unitary in construction. Engines are usually the same as (or adaptations of) engines used in passenger cars, with diesel engines becoming more popular.

Figure 1.22 A 4 × 4 recreational vehicle

1.2.6 Heavy goods vehicles, coaches and buses

Heavy goods vehicles

Although this book concentrates mainly on light vehicles, a review of some heavier vehicles is included for comparison purposes.

Heavy commercial vehicles or trucks are in fact generally referred to as heavy goods vehicles (HGVs).

For long-distance transportation of goods a truck is used and these come in various shapes and sizes. A heavy vehicle has a load-carrying capacity in excess of about three tonnes. Note that some slightly lighter trucks are produced which have similar construction to the heavy vehicles but they have been built at a lower weight for licensing reasons.

A large, flat platform is needed to carry larger and heavier loads, and because this can generally only be provided above wheel height, no special effort is made to lower the chassis frame. The chassis frame usually consists of two straight and deep side-members joined by several cross-members. The frame supports the main components of the vehicle as well as the platform that forms the basis of the body. The driver sits in a cab at the front of the vehicle, with the engine either forward of the driver or, in most cases on modern heavy vehicles, the drivers cab is actually on top and slightly forward of the engine.

The engine is usually a large capacity diesel, often making use of turbo charging. The main requirements for the engine are an ability to produce high levels of pulling power (generally referred to as torque), reliability and low fuel consumption.

To carry heavy loads the rear wheels either have twin tyres, fitted side-by-side, or special wide-section single tyres. Vehicles exceeding a certain total loaded weight are required to have six wheels carried on three axles, whilst even heavier vehicles are required to have eight wheels, two on each of four axles. These legal requirements are laid down in Construction and Use Regulations drawn up by Parliament. They are constantly liable to revision, so readers seeking further details of maximum permitted weights and dimensions of vehicles are advised to consult the regulations currently in force. Figure 1.23 shows a four-wheeled truck.

Figure 1.24 A three-axle – six-wheel HGV (note that the twin wheels on the rear axles are classed as a single wheel)

but not always, driven, but no provision is made for steering them. Eight-wheelers have two front axles (steered but not driven), and two rear axles (driven but not steered).

HGVs are allowed to tow a trailer on which an additional load can be carried. There is, in addition, a type of vehicle that consists of two parts: a four- or six-wheeled tractor unit (which does not itself carry any load) to which is attached a semi-trailer having two or four wheels at its rear end. The tractor unit is attached to the semi-trailer by a special turntable coupling (sometimes referred to as a fifth wheel). With this arrangement, the tractor supports some of the weight carried by the semi-trailer.

The combination of tractor and semi-trailer is called an articulated vehicle. The trailer has retractable wheels on which its front end can be supported: this enables the tractor to be uncoupled and used with another trailer while its former trailer is being loaded or unloaded. An example of an articulated vehicle is shown in Figure 1.25. Many haulage companies use articulated vehicles, as this type of vehicle is capable of carrying large and heavy loads over long distances.

Figure 1.23 A two-axle – four-wheel HGV

When six wheels are used, the two extra wheels may be carried on an additional axle at the rear of the vehicle, as shown in Figure 1.24. These extra wheels are usually,

Figure 1.25 An articulated HGV

Buses (omnibuses)

These vehicles are designed to transport numbers of passengers, up to about forty of whom may be carried on a single floor or deck. Figure 1.26 shows a single-decker bus, which has its entrance to the front, where the driver can observe passengers boarding or alighting from the vehicle. The doors are normally power-operated by the driver to prevent passengers getting on or off when the bus is moving.

In towns and cities there are usually short distances between stops, and speed of loading and unloading passengers is very important. The entrance to the bus is about 300 mm above ground level, an easy step up from the edge of the pavement. From this platform another step up leads up to the deck of the bus.

To make room for the front entrance and to help reduce the floor height, the engine and transmission are placed at the rear of the vehicle.

A double-decker bus capable of seating about sixty passengers is shown in Figure 1.27. Construction and Use Regulations stipulate a maximum height for the vehicle and a minimum ceiling height for both upper and lower decks. This means that the floor of the lower deck must be fairly close to the ground; the engine and transmission are once again situated at the rear of the vehicle.

In older designs of double-decker bus the entrance was placed to the rear of the vehicle, the disadvantage

Figure 1.27 A double-decker bus

of this arrangement is that the driver is unable to see passengers getting on and off except with the aid of mirrors, which do not give an adequate view of people on the platform or those running to catch the bus. By placing the platform at the front the driver can have a direct view of passengers boarding and alighting, as in the case of the single decker bus shown in Figure 1.26. Exit doors can be placed in the centre of the bus which permits the entry and exit of the passengers at the same time, allowing a shorter stop to pick up and drop off passengers.

Coaches

Vehicles of this type are designed to carry between thirty and forty passengers over fairly long distances in greater comfort than is generally provided by buses. Speed of loading and unloading is less important, but a large amount of luggage space is required. Modern coaches are used for many purposes and therefore the design and specification to which the coach is built varies from a low level to a high level, and can even include a toilet. The entrance is either at the front or behind the front wheels.

Some buses and coaches are made with the body structure forming the main frame; although this is not very common it has the advantage of reducing overall weight.

Figure 1.26 A single-decker bus

Figure 1.28 A coach

1.3   VEHICLE STRUCTURE

1.3.1 Requirements of the vehicle structure

Conflicting requirements

The structure of a vehicle has to fulfil a number of requirements, some of which have conflicting objectives. As an example, a stronger structure would be able to withstand general use more reliably and also provide a safer environment for the occupants. However, stronger structures mean more weight and expense for the materials, thereby representing a conflict for which designers and manufacturers must find a compromise.

Compromises can be achieved more easily now than in the past due to the use of different materials than were available at a realistic cost a few years ago. Additionally, computer-aided design provides the designer with greater capability to make structures stronger, lighter and less expensive.

However, there are some primary requirements that a vehicle structure must satisfy and these are detailed below.

Locating the vehicle systems

The prime purpose of a vehicle structure must be to provide a location for all the necessary vehicle systems and components such as the engine, suspension and transmission.

The purpose of the vehicle (passenger, HGV, etc.) will dictate the size and weight of the vehicle systems and components and therefore the structure will be designed accordingly. A small passenger vehicle generally makes use of a lightweight unitary construction (combined chassis frame and body) that is able to locate the relatively light vehicle systems and components, and provide sufficient space for the occupants. However, heavy goods vehicles (HGVs) usually have a very strong separate chassis frame to locate its heavier, bulkier vehicle systems and components. There then needs to be a separate body to accommodate the driver and provide sufficient space to carry and protect the loads that will be carried.

Locating the occupants

Passenger vehicles (cars) have another prime requirement, which is to provide sufficient space and comfort for a driver and passengers. Irrespective of whether the car is a two-seat or six-seat vehicle, there are some general requirements that nearly always apply, such as location of comfort systems (e.g. heating) and the need to provide safe and comfortable seating etc. Luggage space is also required, the amount of space depending on the type of passenger vehicle. A sports car is not normally expected to have as much luggage space as a large saloon car.

Safety

Although safety was not a major issue in the earlier days of vehicle design, modern vehicles must pass many stringent safety checks and consumers expect safety to be a fundamental design consideration.

In the past vehicle structure relied to a large extent on strong materials to provide safety in accidents. Modern vehicle structures rely on clever design to achieve better results. Some parts of the vehicle structure (especially the front sections) are designed to collapse or deform in accidents, thus absorbing some of the impact forces. The centre section containing the occupants is, however, designed to maintain its original shape thus protecting the occupants from the injury that would occur if the centre section collapsed.

In this way modern designs achieve high levels of safety protection with a much lower weight of materials than was the case with older vehicle designs.

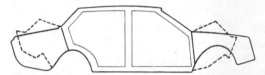

front and rear crumple zones absorb shock of impact

Figure 1.29 Collapsible vehicle structure

Weight

All vehicles are now built with weight as a major consideration. Apart from more weight usually meaning more material and therefore greater cost, heavier vehicles require more power to achieve the required performance. More power requires more fuel and this results in increased emissions. Emissions and fuel consumption are therefore a prime motivation to reduce the weight of a vehicle.

Reduced weight helps to reduce wear on components such as tyres, but also all of the main vehicle systems (e.g. engine, transmission and suspension) will be under less stress and strain. If a component or system is under less stress or strain, it too can be made lighter. If all the vehicle systems can be made lighter, then the net result is lower build costs and a further reduction in fuel consumption and emissions.

Aerodynamics and style

Most modern cars are built with an integral chassis frame and body. With such a structure many of the load-bearing elements are likely also to be visible. Body styling is obviously important if vehicle manufacturers and designers are to achieve sales. However the body styling must be achieved alongside the requirement to maintain strength and safety.

Figure 1.30 Examples of an aerodynamic body and non-aerodynamic body

Body style is also influenced by the need to achieve good aerodynamics. An aerodynamic body shape requires less power to maintain any given speed, thereby helping to reduce the amount of fuel used (especially at higher speeds) and also contributing towards improved emission levels and performance.

1.3.2 Chassis frame construction

The chassis frame
Most modern cars do in fact combine the frame with the body. This integral or unitary construction produces a stronger, lighter vehicle unit which is cheaper to produce when a large number of similar units are made. However, for heavier vehicle applications (such as trucks) and some vehicles where limited numbers are produced, the chassis frame is a separate structural member to which the main components, such as the engine, transmission and body, are attached, i.e. it forms the 'skeleton' of the vehicle.

Whether in a car or a truck, a vehicle structure has to withstand various static and dynamic loads. The deflections of a simple rectangular frame, consisting of two side-members connected together with two cross-members, are shown in Figure 1.31 These deflections are caused by the following forces:

1 The weight of the components and passengers gives a bending action; this causes the frame to sag as in Figure 1.31b.
2 Road shocks, caused by vehicle motion or impact with an obstacle, produce two types of deflection in the frame:

- *Lozenging*, the term used when the rectangular frame is pushed into a parallelogram shape as in Figure 1.31c.
- *Twisting* due to a deflection at one corner of the frame as in Figure 1.31d.

The body and frame must be as light as possible, yet offer maximum resistance to these deflections.

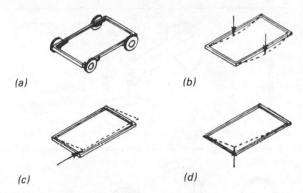

(a)   *(b)*

(c)   *(d)*

Figure 1.31 a–d Distortion of a simple frame

Frame sections
The ideal frame section has a good resistance to bending and torsional effects. The three main forms shown in Figure 1.32 are in general use:

- Channel
- Tubular
- Box.

When a beam bends, the material is subjected to a tensile and a compressive stress. Figure 1.33a shows the top layers of the material being compressed, while the bottom layers are extended. The mid-layer is not subjected to tension or compression, and is known as the neutral axis. Some idea of the amount of stress can be given by referring to the cross-section of the beam shown in Figure 1.33b; the length of each horizontal line represents the stress suffered by that layer.

From the above it will be seen that a slightly deeper channel or box section can give the same resistance to bending as a much heavier solid, rectangular section. In a similar manner, the distance between the top compression member and the lower tension member is the main factor governing the strength of the tubular frame shown in Figure 1.33c.

Whenever a hole has to be drilled in a chassis member, either to reduce weight or to attach something, it should be positioned in a low-stress region, e.g. along the neutral axis.

When a force is applied to the centre of a beam (see Figure 1.33d) there is a tendency for the material to break at its centre. This is because the stress is greatest at this point, as shown in the diagram. In order to resist this stress, either the beam must have the same deep section throughout its length, or a varying section of a depth proportional to the stress suffered. The latter design would be much lighter.

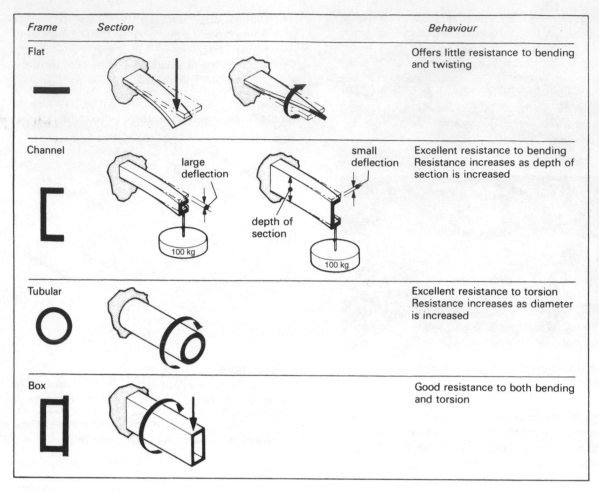

Frame	Section	Behaviour
Flat		Offers little resistance to bending and twisting
Channel	large deflection small deflection depth of section 100 kg 100 kg	Excellent resistance to bending Resistance increases as depth of section is increased
Tubular		Excellent resistance to torsion Resistance increases as diameter is increased
Box		Good resistance to both bending and torsion

Figure 1.32 Frame sections

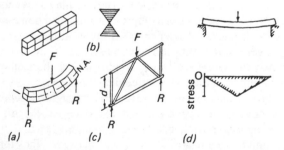

Figure 1.33 a–d Effect of load on frame members

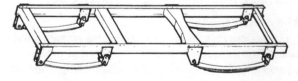

Figure 1.34 Frame for a light truck

Frame design

Figure 1.34 shows a pictorial view of a frame suitable for a light truck or minibus that uses a non-independent suspension system. It consists of two channel-shaped side-members, which are held apart by a series of cross-members. These are positioned at points of high stress and are cold-riveted to the side-members. The depth of the channel section must be sufficient to minimize deflection. Most frames used on light vehicles are made of low-carbon steel with a carbon content of 0.15–0.25%.

Since the load at each point of the frame varies, a reduction in weight can be achieved by either reducing the depth of the channel, or having a series of holes positioned along the neutral axis in the regions where the load is not so great.

Lozenging of the frame is prevented by fitting gusset plates to reinforce the joins between the side- and cross-members, or by adding X–type (cruciform) bracing between two or more of the cross members.

The frame shown in Figure 1.34 has a very poor resistance to torsion, so the body has to fulfil this role. Often the body is not designed to resist these stresses, and problems will therefore occur; these include movement between doors and pillars producing creaks during vehicle movement, broken windscreens and cracking of the body panels.

Body jigs for pressing integral bodies are very expensive, so it is common to use a separate chassis frame when the production of a given model is on a fairly small scale. Since most cars constructed in this way have independent suspension, the frame needs to be extremely rigid at the points where the body and main components are attached. This is achieved by using box-section members welded together and suitably reinforced in the regions of high stress (Figure 1.35).

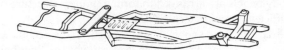

Figure 1.35 A box section frame

A backbone frame, as shown in Figure 1.36, is an alternative construction to the conventional rectangular frame. This consists of two longitudinal, box-section members welded together at the centre and separated at the front and rear so as to accommodate the main components. A series of outrigger frame members are welded to the spine to support the floor of the body.

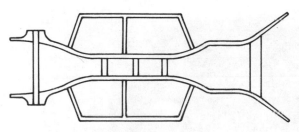

Figure 1.36 A backbone-type frame

Energy-absorbing frame

In the past it was considered that safety for the occupants of a car involved in a collision could be improved by making the chassis frame very stiff. This is untrue because on impact a 'tank-like' structure subjects the occupants to an extremely high deceleration. As a result the forces acting on the human body as it smashes into a hard surface are likely to cause death or serious injury.

Most modern frames overcome this problem by constructing the front and rear ends of the frame in a manner that allows them to absorb the main shock of the impact. Body panels in the vicinity of these crumple zones are generally damaged beyond repair when they suffer a substantial impact, but this is a small price to pay for occupant safety.

Figure 1.37 shows the principle of a frame designed to absorb the energy of front and rear end impacts.

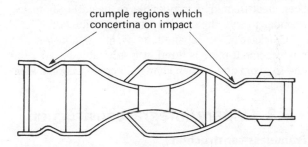

Figure 1.37 An energy-absorbing frame

Frame repairs

Whenever a vehicle has been involved in a major collision, it is necessary to check its frame alignment. A visual check generally reveals major misalignment, but if this is not obvious a frame check will be required. This is conducted as follows (also see Figure 1.38):

a **Wheel base check** Set the front wheels in the straight-ahead position and check the wheel base on each side.

b **Alignment** After checking to verify that the rear wheels are parallel with each other, hold a cord or straight edge against the rear wheel, then turn the front wheel until it is parallel with the cord and note the clearance (if any) between the wheel and cord. This should be the same on both sides.

c **Plumb-line check** Drop a plumb line from the outside of each fixed shackle of the spring to give eight chalk marks on the floor. Connect up the points as shown; all diagonals should cross the centre line if the frame is correctly aligned.

The tolerance for each check depends on the size of frame, but 6 mm is often laid down as the maximum permissible deviation.

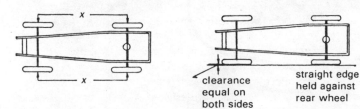

(a) Wheel base check

(b) Alignment check

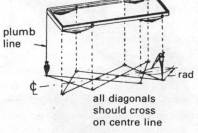

(c) Plumb-line check

Figure 1.38 a–c Checking chassis alignment

The vehicle is normally placed on a vehicle jig (Figure 1.39), which is specifically designed to hold it when carrying out these measurements. It is critical to ensure these measurements are accurate; any inaccuracy during repair can affect the way the vehicle drives after the repairs have been carried out. Modern vehicle jigs use laser measurement tools to ensure this accuracy is achieved.

Frame straightening is carried out using jacks and chains, and is a specialized repair. Unless the frame has been heat-treated it is possible to heat the damaged member to ease the straightening operation.

Cracks can be repaired by welding, and when a reinforcement plate is fitted, it is advisable to taper the end to avoid any sudden change in cross-sectional area.

1.3.3 Unitary/integral construction

Frameless construction

In the previous section dealing with chassis frames, it was stated that the body shell helps to resist the torsional movement of a simple frame, but defects in the construction soon show up because the shell is not designed to withstand these stresses. In the 1930s, the development of the all-steel body made possible the elimination of a separate frame. A suitably designed body shell was found capable of withstanding the various frame stresses. This frameless or integral arrangement gives a stiff, light construction, which is particularly suitable for mass-produced vehicles, and since the late 1940s and early 1950s nearly all light cars have been built with this construction.

Figure 1.40 shows some of the forces that act on a car body and the general manner in which the various body panels are arranged to form a unitary structure of sufficient strength to resist these forces.

The diagram shows that the weight of the occupants causes a sagging effect which is resisted by the floor and roof panels. Since these two members are widely spaced, thin sheet metal can be used to form a box-like structure that is both strong and light in weight.

Torsional stiffness of the body is achieved by strengthening the scuttle at the front and by using cross-ties, or fitting a ribbed metal panel behind the rear seat squab.

The thickness of the material used depends on the stress taken by the panel. Structural members such as sills, rails and pillars are often about 1.1 mm (0.045 inch) thick, whereas panels such as the roof are

Figure 1.39 A vehicle mounted on a vehicle jig

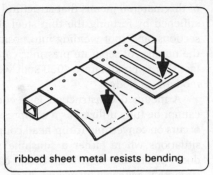

ribbed sheet metal resists bending

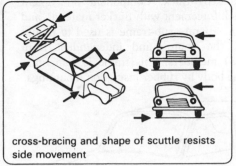

cross-bracing and shape of scuttle resists
side movement

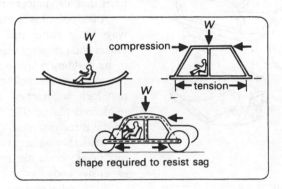

compression

tension

shape required to resist sag

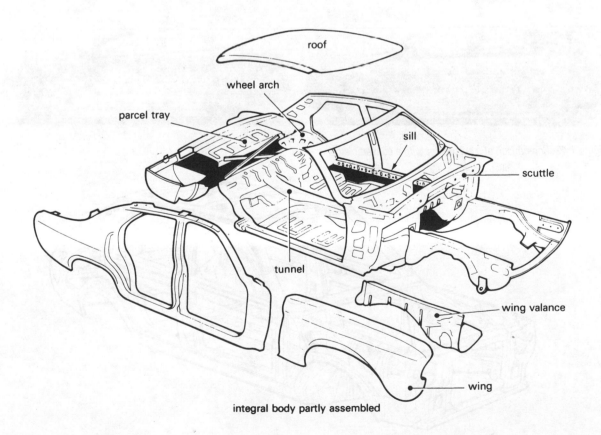

roof

wheel arch

parcel tray

sill

scuttle

tunnel

wing valance

wing

integral body partly assembled

Figure 1.40 Integral body construction

0.9 mm (0.035 inch) thick. Component attachment points require reinforcement with thicker material, and in some cases a separate sub-frame is used to mount such items as the engine and independent front suspension (IFS) members. This frame is sometimes connected to the body by rubber insulation mountings.

Figure 1.41 Separate sub-frames

Since extremely good ductility is essential for the pressing of the panels, a very low carbon (0.1%) steel is required. The low strength (278 MN m^{-2} or 18 tonf in^{-2})

of this material means that structural members must be stiffened by forming the thin steel sheet into intricate sections, and spot welding into position. Some idea of the number of separate pressings can be gained by the fact that approximately 4000 spot welds are used on a modern car body.

A modified construction is needed when the roof cannot be fully utilized as a compression member. This occurs on convertible (drop-head coupé) models, and in situations where either a sunshine roof, or very thin door pillars are used. In these cases the required strength is achieved by using a strong underbody frame. In addition, extra stiffness is given to the body-shell parts that are subject to torsion.

A body-shell is normally constructed in one of two ways: it is either made by spot-welding the panels, pillars and pressings together so as to form a strong box, or by building a space frame (Figure 1.43). The latter structure gives a skeleton of high structural strength on to which is attached the steel, aluminium or glass-reinforced plastic (GRP) body panels, doors, roof, etc. Of the three materials used, steel is the most common for vehicles made in high volume; this is because production costs are lower once the initial outlay on expensive body jigs and robots has been recovered.

To avoid vibration of the panels, which gives an objectionable noise called drumming, a sound-damping material is stuck on the inside of the panels.

Figure 1.42 Comparison of a saloon car with a convertible car

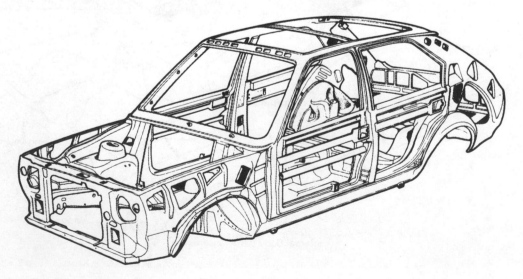

Figure 1.43 Space frame

Safety in the event of an accident

The safety of a modern car is improved by enclosing the driver and passengers in a rigid cell. At the front and rear of this safety compartment are attached sub-frames; these are designed to concertina on impact as shown in Figure 1.44. The crumple zones of the body are intended to absorb the shock of a collision and, in consequence, reduce the rate of deceleration that is experienced by the occupants.

Before vehicles can be sold, at least one vehicle in a model range must be submitted to an approved centre for an impact test. To pass this severe, destructive test, the level of safety of the occupants must reach a given standard. In addition the doors must remain closed during impact and must be capable of being opened after the test. The inclusion of this test feature shows why special 'anti-burst' locks are now in common use.

On modern vehicles safety belts must be provided for the driver and all passengers. Seat belts act as a primary restraint and must be securely anchored to suitable strengthened parts of the body. They reduce the risk of front and rear seat occupants being thrown through the windscreen, or thrust against the body fittings, when the car slows down faster than its occupants.

Many of today's vehicles are fitted with supplementary restraint systems (SRSs) which include seat belt pre-tensioners and airbags. If the vehicle system sensors detect a sudden serious impact, the airbag (or airbags) inflate to prevent serious injury to passengers within the vehicle, and the seat belt pre-tensioners help to restrain the passengers within their seats.

Internal body trim, fittings and controls must all conform to safety standards, and changes during recent years in the design of parts such as steering wheels, control knobs, and even seat construction, have materially reduced the risk of human injury.

Extra protection for the occupants during roll-over of a drop-head model car is given by incorporating in the body structure a strong tubular bar to take the place of the metal roof panel. This tube, set across the car, can be either fixed rigidly or made to move to its protection position automatically when roll-over of the car is sensed.

Figure 1.44 Crumple zones

Figure 1.45 Impact testing

Body shape

Body shape is dictated by a number of factors. The shape must appeal to the buyer, and should have a good performance in relation to the ease with which it passes through the air.

The aerodynamic shape of cars is expressed as a drag coefficient. The lower the value of this coefficient, the easier the car slips through the air, as a result of which fuel economy is improved. Today fuel cost and environmental impact are important, so greater attention is paid to the air resistance of a car. Manufacturers now use wind tunnels during the design process to ensure that the optimum aerodynamic shape is achieved.

Air resistance

Under normal conditions the power required to drive a vehicle through the air consumes most of the engine energy, so ways of reducing this energy drain need to be sought.

Air resistance is given by the expression:

Air resistance $=$ Drag coefficient $\times$ Area $\times$ Velocity^2

This expression shows that the air resistance increases with the square of the velocity of the vehicle relative to the air, so the resistance becomes very great when the vehicle speed is high (Figure 1.46). Compared with the resistance at 50 km/h, the resistances at speeds of 100 km/h and 150 km/h are four and nine times as great respectively.

Wind tunnel tests enable the air resistance of a vehicle to be measured. Since the cross-sectional area of the vehicle and its velocity relative to the air are known, it is possible to calculate the aerodynamic drag constant (C_d). When a vehicle is designed with the aid of computer software, this calculation is used to obtain the optimum aerodynamics before a dummy vehicle is placed in a wind tunnel.

A low C_d is obtained when the body is streamlined to enable it to pass through the air with the minimum

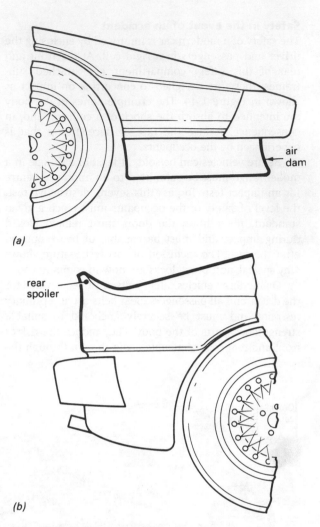

(a)

(b)

Figure 1.47 Air dam and spoiler

disturbance. Since much of the resistance is caused by the low-pressure region at the rear of the vehicle, the aim is to return the air to this region with the minimum of turbulence after it has flowed over the body.

Resistance is directly proportional to the cross-sectional area, so a low and sleek sports-type car performs well in this respect.

Various refinements are made to the body to reduce air drag. These include the recessing of protruding items such as door handles, and the shaping of the body below the front bumper to form an air dam (Figure 1.47a). Although it can be seen that protruding items are shaped to reduce air resistance, much of the under body is also streamlined to ensure a smooth airflow. Many vehicles now have plastic shields fitted to their undersides, particularly around the engine and transmission areas. Many of these small components may seem insignificant but reduce the C_d value and can dramatically improve the stability of the vehicle at high speeds.

Airflow control devices are sometimes fitted by car manufacturers (or owners) to the rear of the vehicle. According to their shape and position, these devices

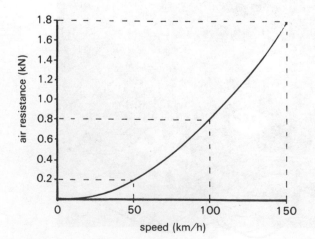

Figure 1.46 Force required to overcome air resistance

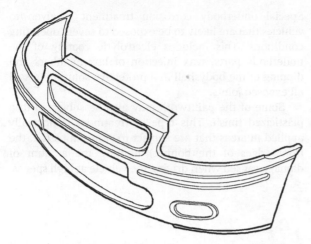

Figure 1.48 Moulded bumpers

Figure 1.50 Indication of air flow over a car in a wind tunnel

either smooth out the air flow to reduce the disturbance, or act as a spoiler to deflect the air upwards so as to increase the adhesive force acting on the rear wheels (Figure 1.47b). Although these arrangements are beneficial on racing cars and high speed sports cars, on many production cars they may be regarded just as 'image creation' embellishments.

Older generation vehicles were often fitted with bumpers made from metal that was chromium-plated to provide an attractive finish to the component. Although referred to as a bumper, they offered limited protection if the vehicle was involved in an accident. Bumpers fitted to the front and rear of the vehicle of a modern car are

made from a plastic material, which is easily moulded into a shape that provides a low resistance to the air flow, and also enhances the appearance of the vehicle.

These bumpers often form the majority of the front and rear of the vehicle and therefore little (or in some cases no) further body panels are required to form the front or rear of the vehicle. Such bumpers are also referred to as 'pedestrian friendly', since if a car collides with a pedestrian at a very low speed, the injuries sustained by the pedestrian will hopefully be very minor.

Paintwork

When bare metal is exposed to the atmosphere, it soon corrodes. In the case of steel, the surface becomes pitted and the strength of structural parts rapidly decreases as the rust 'eats' into the sound metal.

One way of reducing corrosion is to coat the surfaces with paint; this acts as a barrier between the metal and oxygen in the atmosphere.

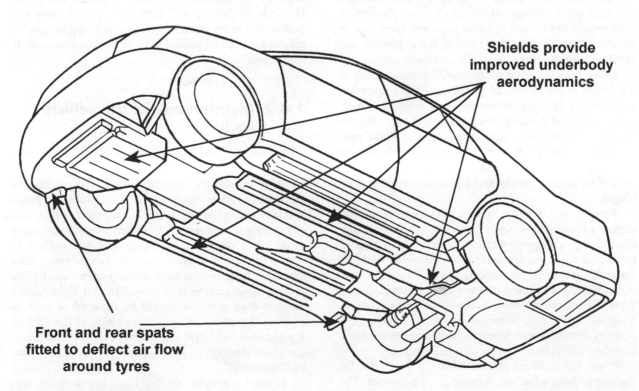

Shields provide improved underbody aerodynamics

Front and rear spats fitted to deflect air flow around tyres

Figure 1.49 Underbody aerodynamics

Corrosion also occurs when two dissimilar pieces of bare metal are joined by water. In this case the action is similar to that of a battery; the passage of electricity from one 'plate' to the other 'plate' (in this case the two metals) causes an electrolytic action that corrodes the metal. Salt, mixed with the moisture that connects the two metals, increases the electrical flow; this is the reason why corrosion is accelerated in winter.

The car owner regards paintwork as an embellishment of the bare metal, so the manufacturer selects a colour, finish and texture to anticipate the personal preferences of the potential customer.

Special underbody corrosion treatment is given to vehicles that are likely to be exposed to severe operating conditions. This includes electrolytic coating of the underbody parts, wax injection of box members and dipping of the bodyshell in a protective solution to seal all exposed joints.

Some of the paintwork may also be subjected to a plasticized finish. This type of treatment is normally applied in areas that are subject to stone chips (i.e. the front edges of the bonnet) limiting the amount of damage caused when driving the vehicle at high speeds.

1.4   ROUTINE MAINTENANCE

1.4.1 Maintenance of vehicle systems

This book deals primarily with mechanical and electrical/electronic vehicle systems. Each of the individual chapters and sections within the book cover the vehicle systems and also detail any maintenance requirements. General body maintenance is not covered in detail within this book, so a brief account is included here.

It is important to remember that it is only in recent years that virtually all vehicle systems (for light passenger vehicles) have become almost maintenance free. The modern light passenger vehicle requires maintenance that is restricted to oil and filter changes and occasional changes of the spark plugs. Inevitably, consumable items such as brake pads and tyres require occasional replacement due to wear, but in general, the vehicle systems require very little routine maintenance.

Older vehicles, even some models produced late in the 1960s required regular greasing of the suspension and steering systems. Wheel bearings required regular adjustment and greasing along with oil changes for the engine, gearbox and final drive, often at 3000 mile (4800 km) intervals. Batteries required a regular top-up of distilled water and a range of other items were also subject to routine checks and maintenance, even door hinges.

Possibly the biggest change, however, relates to engine maintenance. Apart from the routine oil and filter changes, engines required regular adjustment of valve clearances, adjustment to the carburettor and fuel system, as well as spark plug changes and adjustment/replacement of other ignition components. Typically, an engine service would be carried out at 3000 or 5000 mile intervals on older vehicles, or possibly at twice yearly intervals. Different oils may also have been specified for summer and winter use.

It was still common practice as late as the 1970s, for engines to have what was referred to as a de-coke. The build-up of carbon on the intake and exhaust valves in the intake and exhaust ports and on the combustion chambers would require removal, which was usually achieved by removing the cylinder head and manually removing the carbon deposits. Whilst the cylinder head was removed, it was also common practice to regrind the valves and valve seats to ensure a gas-tight seal of the combustion chambers. A de-coke may have been an annual event up until the 1960s but improvement in fuels, oils and engine design have progressively eliminated the need for regular de-cokes.

Vehicle maintenance has been dramatically reduced in recent years, to a situation where an occasional inspection and oil changes are virtually all that is required. The distance covered by a vehicle, along with the style of driving will affect the life of tyres and brakes, but many modern vehicles only require routine maintenance on an annual basis or at longer intervals in some cases.

1.4.2 Maintenance of the vehicle body

The modern vehicle requires little bodywork maintenance except regular cleaning to ensure that any corrosive substances (such as salt) do not corrode the metal body panels. Many of the body panels are either specially treated or made from rust-resistant materials so the body should remain free from corrosion for many years. Since the vehicle body is no longer subject to corrosion, many vehicle manufacturers now offer extensive long-term anti-corrosion warranties. During routine maintenance it is essential that if bodywork damage does occur, it should be repaired as soon as possible to prevent premature corrosion of the vehicle. If a repair is not implemented or does not conform to the manufacturer's guidelines, the warranty can become invalid.

In use, especially during high speed travel (i.e. motorways) bodywork is continually subject to flying debris from other road users; small stones are often picked up in tyre treads and then fly out whilst the vehicle is being driven. To prevent such occurrences, many of the front panels of vehicles (i.e. front bumpers) are made from a plastic material which tends to deflect such objects without damage. If the paintwork is chipped, the material used to form the panel (often a form of plastic), is unaffected by corrosion, although it may be necessary to have the paintwork repaired for cosmetic reasons.

Routine maintenance should also include the inspection for any sharp edges that could cause injury to pedestrians that walk past the vehicle. If a sharp edge is noticed, the component should be repaired or replaced before the vehicle is returned for public highway use.

Repair of vehicle bodywork damage usually requires the skills of several craftsmen: a panel beater to repair the dent and a paint sprayer to apply the paint to a finish that matches the existing paintwork. Although many bodywork repairs still require these processes,

advances in bodywork technology have meant that many small repairs can be carried out using a 'smart' repair procedure, limiting the repair to a very small area, reducing the time of repair and also the cost. Many small dents can be repaired without the need to repaint the damaged area.

Underbody damage can usually only be seen when the vehicle is placed on a vehicle lift. It is therefore essential that when a vehicle is serviced, the underside of the vehicle is examined for body damage as well as component damage.

It has already been stated that many modern vehicles are fitted with underbody aerodynamic components. During the servicing of the vehicle it may be necessary to remove these panels to gain access to some of the engine components such as the engine sump plug to enable the oil to be drained, or the oil filter to aid replacement. If any of these components are removed for the purpose of servicing, the technician should remember to refit them afterwards using the appropriate fixings.

Chapter 2

ENGINES

what is covered in this chapter . . .

- The internal-combustion reciprocating engine
- Working principles of the four-stroke and two-stroke engine
- Torque and power
- Single-cylinder and multi-cylinder engines
- Crankshafts
- Connecting rods
- Pistons, piston rings and gudgeon pins
- Intake, exhaust valves and valve springs
- Valve operating mechanisms
- Intake manifolds
- Air cleaners and filters
- Exhaust systems, silencers and catalytic converters
- Engine lubricants
- The engine lubrication system
- The engine cooling system
- Supercharging and turbocharging (forced induction)
- The petrol four-stroke cycle in detail: valve and ignition timing
- Combustion and combustion chambers
- Intake manifold design – petrol engines
- The requirements of a fuel delivery system
- The fuel supply system
- Electronic petrol injection – multi-point
- Electronic petrol injection – single point
- Mechanical petrol injection
- The simple carburettor
- Constant-choke carburettors
- Variable choke – constant-depression carburettors
- Ignition systems
- Engine management
- Vehicle emissions
- The diesel four-stroke cycle in detail
- Diesel combustion
- Diesel engine combustion chambers
- Main components of the diesel engine

- Mechanical aspects of the diesel fuel system
- Electronic diesel fuel system
- Diesel emissions
- Routine engine maintenance
- Routine maintenance of the petrol fuel system
- Ignition systems – routine maintenance
- Routine maintenance of the diesel engine
- Alternative types of engine and fuel

2.1   THE INTERNAL-COMBUSTION RECIPROCATING ENGINE

2.1.1 A practical solution for the automobile

In Chapter 1, reference was made to the steam engine, which had been around since the 1700s. Although the steam engine was evolving and becoming increasingly efficient, it had limitations related to its size and weight. The main problem was the separate boiler assembly, required to produce steam from water. Once the steam was produced it was transferred under pressure to a cylinder containing a piston. The steam pressure then pushed the piston down the cylinder and a mechanical linkage converted the linear movement of the piston into a rotary movement (in most cases).

Some designers realised that an advantage would be gained if the process of creating pressure could be integrated into the same assembly as the cylinder and piston. As detailed in the following section, some attempts were made to use coal gas, which was actually ignited within the cylinder thus creating a high enough pressure to push the piston. The coal gas engine was an internal-combustion engine and in many ways this type of engine was an improvement on steam engines of the time, but it still failed to make the major leap forward that designers were trying to achieve.

While the burning of coal gas did create an increase in pressure within the cylinder which moved the piston, other fuels could be used that would create much higher pressures when they were ignited and therefore provide a much more powerful force on the piston. By combining a mixture of air and fossil fuels (refined oils), and igniting the fuel mixture within the cylinder, much greater pressures were achieved. It was, however, necessary to achieve higher temperatures within the cylinder to achieve ignition and combustion of the fuels.

Although an electric spark could be created within the cylinder, it was not hot enough to ensure effective combustion of the fuel mixture. However, it was realised that by compressing the mixture within the cylinder, the effect would be to raise the temperature of the mixture thus making ignition and combustion much

easier. The compression process is similar to pumping up a tyre with a hand or foot pump; compressing the air generates heat.

In an internal-combustion engine, the fuel mixture contains a high percentage of air (which is a gas) and the compression process therefore causes the temperature of the air to increase. Adding a spark to the already hot mixture causes a small part of the mixture to ignite. The mixture starts to burn and, as with any burning process, the flame will then spread to the remainder of the fuel. During the combustion process of the internal-combustion engine, the flame spreads very rapidly to the remainder of the mixture. Therefore, by compressing the mixture, the temperature increases and it is then only necessary to add a spark at the right time to create full ignition and combustion.

In fact, as detailed later, some engines do not even require the additional spark because the temperatures reached during compression are sufficient to ignite the fuel mixture. These engines are known as 'compression-ignition engines' (commonly referred to as diesel engines).

In both types of engine (spark ignition and compression ignition), once the fuel has started to burn (combustion) it generates a substantial increase in temperature. The increase in temperature causes the mixture to expand, and because it is contained within the cylinder, this results in a rapid and substantial increase in pressure. It is this increase in pressure that forces the piston down the cylinder producing the power.

There has always been argument as to whether the combustion process is in fact an explosion or just a very rapid burning process, and no attempt is made to resolve that argument within this book. However, the combustion process is without question very rapid; when an engine is operating at 6000 revolutions per minute (rpm), the time taken to ignite the fuel mixture and force the piston from the top to the bottom of the cylinder is in the region of four thousandths of a second (4 milliseconds), with the main burning process only taking a small part of that time.

The internal-combustion engine therefore gained favour with designers because it enabled high power outputs to be achieved in a compact and integrated assembly. The steam engine did, however, remain popular where exceptionally high power was required and size was perhaps less of a problem. For this reason, steam locomotives remained in use pulling trains through to the early 1960s.

As previously mentioned, development of the internal-combustion engine was largely related to use of fossil fuels. Although petrol and diesel fuels are both extracted from crude oil, their characteristics are different when used in an internal-combustion engine. The differences between petrol and diesel engines are explained later in this chapter but the most obvious difference is that diesel fuel is ignited using only the heat generated by compression. In a petrol engine, although heat is created by the compression process, an appropriately timed electric spark is used to provide the additional heat to start ignition of the petrol/air mixture.

Petrol engine history

A Frenchman, Etienne Lenoir, made the first commercially successful internal-combustion engine in 1860. It ran on coal gas, but worked on a cycle of operations, which did not include compression of the gas before ignition: as a result it was not very efficient. In spite of this it was in some respects superior to small steam engines of the time, and a great many were sold and did useful work driving machinery in factories. In 1862 Lenoir made a 'horseless carriage' powered by his engine and possibly drove it on the roads, but he lost interest in this venture and nothing came of it. In fact, a method of carrying out the cycle of operations using compression of the gas, was described in a patent dated 16 January 1862 taken out by a French civil servant, M. Beau de Rochas. Since he did not have the means to develop the patent himself, the patentee offered it to Lenoir who, failing to realize its importance, turned it down.

However in Germany, Dr N. A. Otto started the manufacture of gas engines around 1866. Although the first Otto engines were extremely noisy, they were quite effective. Around 1875 Otto took out a patent describing a method of carrying out the cycle of operations, which was in fact identical with that of Beau de Rochas' thirteen years earlier (it is however, most unlikely that Otto had heard of the Frenchman or his patent). Otto's new engine was an immediate success. It was much more efficient than Lenoir's and was very quiet, a characteristic which led to its being named 'Otto's silent gas engine'.

Lenoir, realizing his mistake, began to manufacture engines working on the same principle. Otto, of course, sued him for infringing his patent rights, but Lenoir had no difficulty in proving that his engines were made under the earlier patent of Beau de Rochas, which had by now lapsed. The court proceedings at last brought poor Beau de Rochas the fame he deserved, and he was awarded a sum of money by the Academy of Sciences in Paris in recognition of his invention. Even so, the method of operation, which he was the first to describe, and which is the one used in most modern engines, was for many years (and sometimes still is) known as the Otto cycle.

Compression-ignition (diesel) engine history

The compression-ignition type of engine is often called a 'diesel engine'; the name is derived from the German engineer Dr Rudolf Diesel, who in 1892 took out a patent (No. 7241) on an engine, which relied on the heat generated during compression to ignite a fuel of coal dust. This fuel was blasted into the cylinder by air pressure when the piston was at the end or the top of its stroke. The aim of the design, which was successfully applied to an engine five years later, was to achieve a higher thermal efficiency or improved fuel consumption by using a compression ratio higher than that employed on petrol engines. In those early days, pre-ignition (ignition before the spark) occurred in a petrol engine if the compression ratio exceeded a given value. In fact, this problem can still occur on modern engines if the compression is too high.

Many authorities do not recognize Diesel as the inventor of the engine, which was the forerunner of the modern compression-ignition engine. They state that the patent (No. 7146), which was taken out in 1890 by a British engineer (Herbert Ackroyd-Stuart), and put into commercial production two years later, contained all the fundamental features of the modern unit. This patent, which was the result of practical development work on low-compression oil engines, included the induction and compression of air, as well as the timed injection of a liquid fuel by means of a pump.

To avoid taking sides in this controversy, the terms 'compression-ignition' (CI) or 'oil engine' are often used.

2.1.2 The reciprocating engine

In Chapter 1 we saw that the internal-combustion engine has evolved to become the dominant automobile power source. Although there are variations on the internal-combustion engine such as the Wankel engine, the 'reciprocating' engine is by far the most common type used. This chapter therefore deals in great detail with the reciprocating–type engine but it does also briefly examine the Wankel engine.

The reciprocating engine is defined by its use of pistons that reciprocate within a cylinder, i.e. the pistons move up and down to complete the cycle of operation, including the power stroke (see Figure 2.1). The pistons are connected via connecting rods to a crankshaft, which is rotated as the pistons move up and down. The crankshaft then transmits the power to the gearbox and transmission system.

Although the above paragraph identifies the essential components for creating and delivering power from the engine, there are numerous other components and systems that are required to make the whole process work. These components and systems are dealt with in great detail in the following sections.

Petrol and diesel reciprocating engines: the main differences

The reciprocating engine can be divided into two main types, depending on the fuel used: petrol and diesel. Although there are fundamental differences between the two types, they share many common principles of operation and many common components. The main differences relate to fuel supply and ignition.

Note: The petrol and diesel types can also be divided into two sub-types, depending on which operating cycle they use, i.e. two-stroke or four-stroke. Because these two sub-types are both commonly used, they are covered separately within this chapter, but note that the four-stroke operating cycle is the most popular and is therefore generally used as the starting point in the explanation process.

Diesel engines require fuel to be delivered under very high pressures with very accurate timing of the fuel delivery, and have therefore traditionally made use of high-pressure pumps, which meter and time the fuel delivery. A petrol engine, however, is not as critical with regard to the timing of fuel delivery and delivery pressure, so simple devices known as carburettors were (until relatively recently) the main means of metering and delivering fuel.

A diesel engine makes use of heat created by the compression of a fuel and air mixture to ignite the fuel. The compression ratio and pressures within the cylinder are therefore high. A petrol engine however, does not generally have so high a compression ratio and so requires the addition of a spark or arc to ignite the fuel.

In recent years the petrol engine has been the subject of much change because of exhaust and other emissions legislation. This has resulted in the simple carburettor being replaced by fuel injection systems, which are now electronically controlled. Additionally, the simple-type ignition systems have been replaced by more advanced, electronically controlled systems. In fact, as well as fuel and ignition control, many other aspects of petrol engine operation are precisely managed by a computer (electronic control). Such control is referred to as 'engine management'.

Since the end of the 1990s, diesel engine design has also been influenced by emissions legislation, and the latest diesel fuel systems are much more closely related to the petrol injection systems. The diesel engine does still require higher fuel injection pressures and still relies on heat generated by compression to ignite the fuel. However, today's diesel engine has engine management-type controls, very similar to those fitted to petrol engines. However, the basic differences between petrol and diesel engines remain.

Because the petrol and diesel engines share many common design features and components, the initial

sections of this chapter cover both types of engine. Any differences between diesel and petrol engines are identified where appropriate and later sections deal with issues specific to petrol and diesel systems.

2.1.3 The main components of a reciprocating engine

Figure 2.1 shows the main parts of a reciprocating engine.

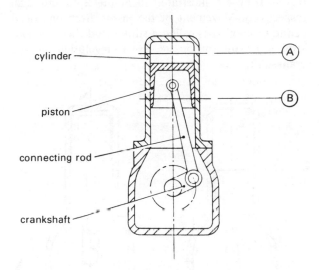

Figure 2.1 The main parts of an engine

1 **The cylinder**, in its simplest form is a circular tube, which is closed at one end.
2 **The piston** fits closely inside the cylinder. Ideally it would be perfectly gas-tight yet perfectly free to move up and down inside the cylinder.
3 **The connecting rod** connects the piston to the crankshaft. At the piston end of the connecting rod is a swivel pin called the 'gudgeon pin'. The gudgeon pin is fitted into holes in the piston and the connecting rod, thus coupling them together.
4 **The crankshaft** is the main shaft of the engine and is carried in bearings in the crankcase. Offset from the main part of the shaft is the crankpin to which the connecting rod is fitted and is free to turn.

The arrangement is such that rotation of the crankshaft causes the piston to move up and down inside the cylinder. Lines A and B in Figure 2.1 indicate the limits of travel of the top of the piston. As the piston moves upwards the space between its top surface and the closed end of the cylinder is reduced, i.e. the gas trapped in this space is compressed. As the piston moves downwards the space above it is increased, i.e. the gas in this space expands.

The crankshaft can be rotated by pushing the piston up and down in the cylinder. Starting with the position shown in Figure 2.1, the crankshaft rotates clockwise as the piston is pushed downwards until the piston reaches the lowest point of its travel. At this point the crankpin will be directly under the centre of the crankshaft, and the centres of the gudgeon pin, crankpin and crankshaft will all lie in a straight line. In this position pressure on the piston will have no turning effect on the crankshaft, and this position is therefore called a 'dead centre'. Another dead centre occurs when the piston is at the extreme top of its travel.

These two dead centres, which are known as bottom dead centre (BDC) and top dead centre (TDC) respectively, mark the extreme limits of the piston's travel. They are illustrated in Figure 2.2a and 2.2b respectively. Movement of the piston from one dead centre to another is called a stroke, and there are two strokes of the piston to every revolution of the crankshaft.

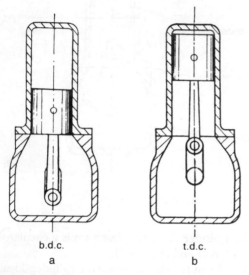

b.d.c.   t.d.c.

a   b

Figure 2.2 Top and bottom dead centres

Engine size

The usual method of indicating the size of an engine is to state the volume of air and fuel taken into the engine during each complete cycle of operations. In effect, this is the usable volume within the cylinder between the TDC and BDC positions of the piston.

The volume of a cylinder can be calculated by using the following formulae:

(a) $V = \pi r^2 h$

where V is the volume of the cylinder, r the cylinder bore radius and h the stroke (between TDC and BDC). Note that π (pi) = 3.142

(b) $V = \pi d^2 h/4$

where V is the volume of the cylinder, d the cylinder bore diameter and h is the stroke (between TDC and BDC). Note that π (pi) = 3.142

The internal diameter of the engine cylinder is called the bore, while the distance the piston moves between TDC and BDC is called the stroke.

Since this is the volume displaced or swept by the piston, it is called the displacement volume or swept volume of the cylinder. If the engine has several cylinders, as most have, the total swept volume of the engine equals the swept volume of each cylinder multiplied by the number of cylinders.

Example 1: using formula (a) $\pi r^2 h$

Cylinder bore	d = 68.2 mm (6.82 cm)
(Cylinder radius)	r = 34.1 mm (3.41 cm)
Stroke	h = 68.2 mm (6.82 cm)

π (3.142) $\times r^2$ (3.41 $\times$ 3.41) = 36.535
36.535 $\times$ (h 6.82) = 249.17 (cubic centimetres) cc

If the example is a four-cylinder engine, then the total capacity of the four cylinders = 4 $\times$ 249.17 = 996.68 cc. This engine would be referred to as a 1 litre (1000 cc) engine.

Example 2: using formula (b) $\pi d^2 h/4$

Cylinder bore	d = 68.2 mm (6.82 cm)
(Cylinder radius)	r = 34.1 mm (3.41 cm)
Stroke	h = 68.2 mm (6.82 cm)

π (3.142) $\times d^2$ (6.82 $\times$ 6.82) = 146.14
146.14 $\times$ (h 6.82)/4 = 249.17 (cubic centimetres) cc
for each cylinder.

Note that when the bore is equal to the stroke (as in the above example), the engine is called a 'square engine'. In a similar way, when the bore is larger than the stroke the engine is called 'over square', or if the bore is smaller than the stroke it is called 'under square'.

Compression ratio

An important feature of the dimensions of an engine is a comparison between the swept volume (as described above) and the space into which gas is compressed. When the piston is at TDC, there is a small space above the piston, which is called the clearance volume. When the piston rises, it compresses the gas into this space. The clearance volume will be much smaller than the swept volume of the cylinder and therefore the gas will be compressed into a much smaller space.

If for example the swept volume (volume swept by the piston from BDC to TDC) is 100 cubic centimetres (100 cc – for practical purposes identical to 100 cm³) and the clearance volume is 10 cc, the total volume above the piston when the piston is at BDC is 110 cc. In effect, the cylinder could be filled with 110 cc of gas or air.

If when the piston rises to TDC, the 110 cc of gas is now compressed into only 10 cc of clearance volume, the gas has been compressed to one eleventh of its original volume. Because 10 cc is one eleventh of 110 cc the relationship or ratio of total volume to clearance volume is 11:1.

With reference to Figure 2.3:

$$\text{Compression ratio} = \frac{\text{Total volume}}{\text{Clearance volume}}$$

$$= \frac{\text{Swept volume} + \text{Clearance volume}}{\text{Clearance volume}}$$

$$= \frac{\text{Swept volume}}{\text{Clearance volume}} + 1$$

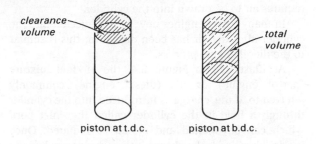

Figure 2.3 Cylinder volume and compression ratio

2.2 WORKING PRINCIPLES OF THE FOUR-STROKE AND TWO-STROKE ENGINE

2.2.1 Basic operating process

As mentioned previously, the piston is pushed down the cylinder by the pressure on its upper surface. The pressure is produced by the principle that if a gas is heated it will expand. However, if the gas is held in a confined space then when the gas is heated, there is no room for expansion. The result is that the heated gas suffers an increase in pressure and forces the piston down.

The greater the amount of heat passed to the gas, the greater its expansion. If, however, there is no room for expansion, then the greater the amount of heat passed to the gas, the greater its pressure will be. In an engine, the air is heated to a very high temperature and therefore a correspondingly high pressure is created inside the cylinder. The high pressure is used to exert a considerable force on the piston.

If the piston is at the top of its stroke, pressure above the piston can only push it downwards. There may still be some pressure left when the piston reaches the bottom of its stroke and this must be released before the piston is moved back to the top of the cylinder again. The pressure is released by opening a hole in the cylinder called the exhaust port. Because of the rotation of the crankshaft, the piston is then able to pass back to the top of the stroke without much opposing pressure.

It would be possible to heat the air inside the cylinder by applying a flame to the outside of the cylinder. To reach the air however, the heat would have to pass through the cylinder wall. Much of the heat would be lost by heating the cylinder and the air outside it, so this would be an inefficient process.

A more efficient method is to directly heat the air inside the cylinder, and this can be achieved by a burning process inside the cylinder. To achieve this, a suitable combustible fuel is mixed with the air then ignited and burnt within the cylinder. The cylinder will of course still absorb a good deal of heat, and arrangements must be made to prevent it getting too hot, but the contents can be raised to a much higher temperature and so develop a correspondingly higher pressure.

Engines that use heat produced by burning a fuel to develop mechanical power are called heat engines. An engine where fuel is burnt internally is referred to as an internal-combustion engine. Internal-combustion engines can use any one of a variety of fuels, but in most cases for automotive applications, petrol or diesel fuels are used. Note that some engines are now fitted with conversion systems to enable them to operate on Liquid Petroleum Gas (LPG).

Petrol is a liquid refined from crude petroleum, and is particularly suitable as a fuel for motor vehicles. It is clean to handle and relatively cheap. At normal temperatures, petrol is a liquid, which can be carried in a vehicle in quite a small tank. However, petrol gives off a flammable vapour even at quite low temperatures thus enabling ignition and burning of the vapour to take place even within a cold engine with little difficulty.

Diesel fuel is also refined from crude oil and has similar properties to that of petrol (relatively cheap, easy to handle and is a liquid at normal temperatures). Diesel differs from petrol in that it gives off a flammable vapour less readily and therefore requires a different ignition process to enable the fuel to be burnt.

2.2.2 Cycle of operations

Before petrol or diesel can be burnt they must be mixed with a suitable quantity of air to enable them to burn. Many fuels require a specific amount of oxygen before they will ignite and burn efficiently. In a petrol engine, the fuel has traditionally been mixed with the air outside of the cylinder and then drawn into the cylinder as a mixture. In the diesel engine, the fuel is introduced (injected) directly into the cylinder, and therefore requires air to be drawn into the cylinder.

In many petrol engines now, fuel is injected into the cylinder after the air has been drawn in; this is similar to the diesel engine process.

As illustrated in Figure 2.4, the air/fuel mixture (petrol engine) or air (diesel engine) commonly referred to as the 'charge' is introduced into the cylinder through a hole in the cylinder called the 'inlet port' which can be opened and closed as required. Once inside the cylinder the charge is then compressed by the upward movement of the piston before burning. If the charge is already compressed before it is ignited and burnt, this greatly increases the pressure after burning.

In the case of the petrol engine, ignition is achieved by an electric arc or spark, which is made to jump across the small gap of a sparking plug. The sparking plug is located so that the spark is exposed to the mixture thus enabling ignition. Sparking plugs are generally screwed into the top of the cylinder (cylinder head). Note that the spark must occur at precisely the correct time to ensure good combustion of the fuel/air mixture and thus achieve good power.

In a diesel engine, the piston compresses the air to a higher pressure than in a petrol engine. This compression process creates a considerable amount of heat, resulting in a very high temperature within the cylinder. When diesel fuel is injected into this high temperature air, the temperature is high enough to ignite the fuel. As with the petrol engine, the start of the combustion process must occur at the correct time and this is achieved by precisely timing the injection of the fuel.

Burning of the fuel creates heat, thus causing a substantial pressure rise, and so pushing the piston down the cylinder (the power stroke). The burned gases and any remaining pressure are then released through the exhaust port.

During the compression stroke and the power stroke, both the inlet and exhaust ports are closed off by valves. The valves are opened (usually by a mechanical system) when the fresh charge is drawn into the cylinder and when the burned gasses are released from the cylinder. The timing of opening and closing the valves and ports is critical and the valve operating mechanism is designed so that the valves open and close at precisely the correct time. Valve mechanisms are covered in greater detail later in this chapter.

The running of the engine involves the continuous repetition of four operations that make up what is called the cycle of operations. These operations are continuously repeated (as long as the engine is running) in the following order:

1 The space in the cylinder above the piston is filled with the charge (either a mixture of petrol vapour and air or just air for the diesel engine and some petrol engines). The mixture or air is able to enter the cylinder when the piston moves down (this is generally referred to as the **induction stroke**).
2 The charge is compressed into the top end of the cylinder (called the combustion chamber) thus raising its temperature. This is achieved by the upward movement of the piston (this is generally referred to as the **compression stroke**).
3 For petrol engines, the petrol vapour is ignited by an electric spark and burned. For diesel engines, the injection of diesel fuel into the heated charge causes ignition and burning of the fuel. The resulting increase in pressure drives the piston down the cylinder (this is referred to as the **power stroke**).
4 The burned gases are expelled from the cylinder. This is achieved by the upward movement of the piston (**exhaust stroke**).

Note: The four cycles coincide with four strokes of the piston (top to bottom or bottom to top of piston travel), therefore the cycle of operations is referred to as the four-stroke cycle. However, a two-stroke cycle engine is also common in motor vehicles (mainly motor cycles) and although there are major differences in the details

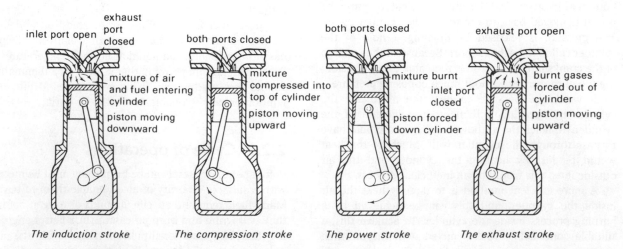

The induction stroke   The compression stroke   The power stroke   The exhaust stroke

Figure 2.4 The operation of an engine on the four-stroke cycle

of the way the four-stroke and two-stroke types work, the principle of induction, compression, ignition and exhaust remain applicable to both types. Four-stroke and two-stroke cycles are dealt with in later sections in this chapter.

Notice that the gas helps the piston to move only during one of these cycles of operations (the power stroke). The remaining operations provide no power or help to the movement of the piston. The induction and exhaust strokes, and more especially the compression stroke (where energy is required to compress the air or mixture), require energy to move the piston. The energy needed to complete the induction, compression and exhaust strokes is actually opposing the rotation of the crankshaft.

Flywheel effect

To assist in keeping the crankshaft rotating between power strokes and thus enable the induction, compression and exhaust strokes to be performed, a flywheel (a large weight or mass) is attached to the end of the crankshaft.

Note: The flywheel is effectively a weight that when turning helps to keep the crankshaft rotating. This is no different to spinning a pushbike wheel or a car wheel when it is free of the ground; the more energy used to initially spin the wheel, the longer the wheel will rotate. Also, the heavier the wheel the greater the amount of energy it can store and therefore it will rotate for longer. When a single cylinder engine operates at a very slow speed, there is a relatively long time between power strokes of the piston; the flywheel action helps to maintain the crankshaft rotation until the next power stroke.

The energy provided by the flywheel to keep the crankshaft turning is therefore not simply used to push the piston back up the cylinder. It is also necessary for the flywheel energy to keep the crankshaft rotating against the opposing forces created by the compression, induction and exhaust strokes.

Note that for multi-cylinder engines there are a greater number of power strokes per turn of the crankshaft, one provided by each of the cylinders. The amount of flywheel action needed is therefore not so great. A twelve-cylinder engine is much less dependent on a flywheel than a four-cylinder engine for example.

2.2.3 The four-stroke cycle

The four-stroke cycle for the petrol engine (spark ignition) is very similar in principle to that of the diesel engine (compression ignition or CI). The following explanation for the working operation of an internal-combustion engine highlights the four-stroke cycle; for further details on the operation of the spark ignition and compression-ignition engines and their fuel systems, refer to the relevant petrol or diesel engine section within this book.

During the four-stroke cycle (Figure 2.4), one complete stroke of the piston (from top to bottom or bottom to top of the stroke) is used to carry out each of the four operations which comprise the complete cycle of operations. To complete the cycle, four strokes of the piston are needed, hence the term 'four-stroke cycle'.

To allow the fresh charge (fuel mixture or air) into the cylinder and to allow the burnt gases to exit the cylinder, inlet and exhaust ports are provided. Valves are located at the end of the ports where they meet the cylinder. The valves are closed for most of the cycle but open at the appropriate time to let in the fuel mixture or let out the burnt gases. Valves are generally opened by a mechanical system and closed by a spring, although some variations do exist.

Starting with the piston at TDC, as the crankshaft rotates, the next four strokes of the piston will result in a number of different processes and actions taking place:

First stroke (induction) When the piston moves down the cylinder, the inlet port is open and the exhaust port is closed, a fresh charge is drawn into the cylinder. Most petrol engines draw in a mixture of air and fuel, however a diesel engine draws in a charge of air only. At the end of the stroke, the inlet port closes.

Second stroke (compression) The piston moves up the cylinder with the inlet and exhaust ports both closed. The charge is therefore compressed and forced into the combustion chamber which is located at the top end of the cylinder.

Third stroke (power) Towards the end of the compression stroke, the highly compressed charge is hot due to being compressed.

For a petrol engine, an electric spark or arc is provided by a sparking plug and ignition system. The spark ignites the air/fuel mixture, which then burns.

For a diesel engine, the diesel fuel is injected at high pressure into the hot compressed air and mixes to form a combustible air/fuel mixture. The heat of the air ignites the fuel mixture, which then burns.

In both petrol and diesel engines, the air/fuel mixture burns very rapidly within the confined cylinder, which heats the gas to an even higher temperature and considerably increases its pressure. Both the inlet and exhaust ports are closed off by the valves, so the ignited mixture cannot escape and its pressure therefore forces the piston down the cylinder.

Fourth stroke (exhaust) The rotation of the crankshaft causes the piston to return up the cylinder. The inlet port remains closed but the exhaust port is now opened. The movement of the piston towards the top of the cylinder therefore forces the burnt gases out of the cylinder via the exhaust port. At the end of the exhaust stroke, the exhaust port closes and the inlet port re-opens for the next induction stroke, which follows immediately.

By referring to the above explanation and to Figure 2.4 it is possible to note the relationship between the position of the pistons on the different strokes and the opening/closing of the inlet and exhaust valves.

Petrol four-stroke

For petrol engines (spark ignition), the air and fuel mixture enters the cylinder via the inlet port. In most petrol engines the fuel is mixed with the air before entering the cylinder, although there is an increasing trend to inject fuel into the cylinder after the air has been drawn in.

The amount of air or air/fuel mixture allowed into the cylinder is usually regulated by some form of valve located in the intake port system. The valve operation is controlled by the driver and is usually referred to as a throttle valve or throttle butterfly.

In most modern petrol engines, the petrol is delivered via a fuel injection system, by which fuel is delivered under relatively low pressure into the inlet ports via injectors. However, there is an increasing use of direct injection, where fuel injectors deliver the fuel direct into the cylinder (at a relatively high pressure). The throttle butterfly regulates the amount of air passing through to the cylinders and the fuel injection system regulates the amount of fuel injected, thus ensuring that the mixture of petrol and air is correct.

Note: Until the early 1990s most engines made use of a carburettor to mix the air and fuel into the correct proportions. The carburettor was located at the outer end of the inlet port, and the mixture would therefore pass from the carburettor via the inlet ports to each of the cylinders. The inlet ports for each of the cylinders generally joined together and this assembly was referred to as an inlet manifold.

Diesel four-stroke

If the engine runs on diesel fuel (compression ignition), air is drawn into the cylinder through the intake ports and manifold, but fuel is injected into the cylinder at very high pressure via a fuel injector.

2.2.4 The two-stroke cycle

It has always been considered a disadvantage of the four-stroke cycle that there is one working stroke but three 'idle' (non-working) strokes.

Between 1878 and 1881 a Scotsman, Dugald Clerk, developed an engine in which the cycle of operations was completed in only two strokes of the piston, thus providing a power stroke for every revolution of the crankshaft. However, this engine used a second cylinder and piston to force fresh mixture into the working cylinder. The second piston therefore acted as a pump to force the charge into the working cylinder.

In 1891 Joseph Day invented a modified form of Clerk's engine, in which he dispensed with the second cylinder but made use of the space in the crankcase underneath the piston as a pumping chamber. Additionally, Days' engine also avoided the use of valves to close the inlet and exhaust ports by making use of the piston to cover or uncover the ports.

Although petrol and diesel two-stroke engines are similar in operation, it is necessary to describe them separately.

The two-stroke petrol engine

Instead of using valves to open and close the inlet and exhaust ports, two-stroke engines generally make use of ports located at strategic positions along the length of the cylinder. As the piston rises and falls within the cylinder the ports are covered and uncovered. There are generally three ports: an inlet port, an exhaust port and a transfer port (which connects the lower chamber beneath the piston to the upper chamber above the piston).

The operation of the two-stroke engine, which is illustrated in Figure 2.5, is as follows.

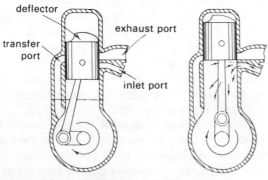

1 Piston rising, compressing mixture above, decreasing pressure below. All ports closed

2 Piston passing t.d.c., mixture above piston ignited, fresh mixture entering crankcase

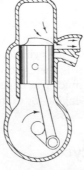

3 Piston moving downward. The fresh mixture in the crankcase has been compressed. The piston has just uncovered the exhaust port, and is about to uncover the transfer port

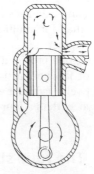

4 Piston passing b.d.c. exhaust and transfer ports open. Fresh mixture entering cylinder via transfer port, directed to top of cylinder by deflection on piston, driving out burnt gas through exhaust port

Figure 2.5 The operation of an engine on the two-stroke cycle

1 Beginning with the piston about halfway on its upward stroke, all three ports are covered. The upward movement of the piston compresses a fresh charge in the top of the cylinder, but at the same time the upward movement of the piston causes the pressure underneath the piston to fall below atmospheric pressure (note that this lower chamber underneath the piston is sealed). Near the top of the stroke the lower edge of the piston has risen sufficiently to uncover the inlet port, and because the lower chamber pressure is lower than atmospheric pressure, a fresh charge is forced or drawn into the lower chamber.

2 Just before the piston reaches the top of the stroke, the charge above the piston is ignited in the same manner as in the four-stroke engine, and with the same result: the high pressure of the burned gases drives the piston down the cylinder. When the piston is then on its way down the cylinder, at a point which is a little below TDC the piston re-covers the inlet port thus blocking of the lower chamber or crankcase. Further downward movement of the piston then compresses the charge in the crankcase. Near to the bottom of the stroke, the top edge of the piston uncovers the exhaust port, and because the burnt gases in the cylinder are still at a relatively high pressure (higher than atmospheric pressure), these gases flow out of the cylinder.

Slightly further down the stroke, the top of the piston uncovers the transfer port. The charge that is compressed in the lower chamber below the piston flows into the upper chamber above the piston, where it is deflected upwards by the specially shaped piston top. This deflection prevents the charge shooting straight across the cylinder and out of the exhaust port.

As the piston rises on its next stroke the transfer and exhaust ports are re-covered and the cycle of operations begins again.

In modern engines of this type the deflector on the top or the crown of the piston has been dispensed with, and the transfer port or ports (there are usually two) are shaped and aimed so as to direct the fresh mixture towards the top end of the cylinder away from the exhaust port.

Two-stroke engines might be expected to develop twice the power of a four-stroke engine of the same size, but unfortunately this is generally not the case. Two-stroke operation is generally less efficient than the four-stroke and despite the deflector on the piston, mixing of the fresh charge with burnt gas cannot be avoided: there is usually some loss of fresh mixture through the exhaust port and incomplete scavenging of burnt gas from the cylinder. The main advantages of the two-stroke engine, therefore, are its greater simplicity and smoothness. It is commonly used for smaller motorcycle engines but two-stroke engines are seldom used for motorcars.

Note however that modern developments of the two-stroke engine have helped to improve efficiency as well as emissions levels.

Two-stroke diesel (compression-ignition) engine

Although the two-stroke compression-ignition engine is not so popular as the four-stroke unit, some manufacturers regard the two-stroke engine's smoother torque delivery, simpler construction and smaller unit size as supreme advantages.

Originally, this type was restricted to low-speed industrial and marine applications, but higher-speed units are fitted to commercial vehicles. The great disadvantage of the two-stroke petrol engine, i.e. the loss of fuel to the exhaust when both ports are open, does not apply to the compression ignition variants because the lower and upper chambers only contain air until the moment that the diesel fuel is injected into the upper chamber. Therefore, any fresh charge that might mix with the exhaust gas cannot contain any fuel, so the two-stroke cycle is most suitable for compression-ignition operation.

Figure 2.6 shows the sequence of operations for a simple two-port valveless form of CI engine.

Figure 2.6a indicates the piston descending to BDC, during which time air enters the cylinder through the inlet port, and 'burnt' gas flows out through the exhaust port.

Figure 2.6b indicates the piston ascending, the inlet and exhaust ports are both covered by the piston to provide the compression stroke. After the air has been compressed to a compression ratio of between 12:1 and 16:1, the high temperature of the compressed air ignites the fuel when it is injected into the cylinder, which then forces the piston down and produces the power stroke, Figure 2.6c.

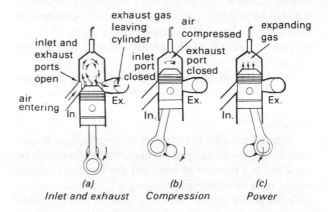

Figure 2.6 Two-stroke cycle – valveless form

Automotive vehicle applications using a compression-ignition two-stroke engine normally employ a more positive method of ensuring that a fresh charge of air is forced into the lower chamber. What is referred to as a blower (or supercharger) is used to pressure-charge the cylinder with air, but it is possible to utilize the pressure waves or pulses in the exhaust system to induce the 'new' air into the cylinder.

Figure 2.7 shows a Uniflow-type of two-stroke engine, which is fitted with an exhaust valve and pressure-charged with a Roots-type blower. This arrangement gives excellent cylinder evacuation and recharging, which is claimed to give double the power output of a four-stroke engine of the same capacity.

Opening the exhaust valve before uncovering the circumferential air-ports allows the remaining burnt gas, which is still under a relatively high pressure, to start pumping out through the exhaust port. However, the air-ports are then uncovered by the piston, thus allowing the pressure-charged air (which is approximately 30% greater in volume than the cylinder capacity) to enter the cylinder, which not only scavenges the remaining burnt gases from the cylinder, but also helps cool the cylinder.

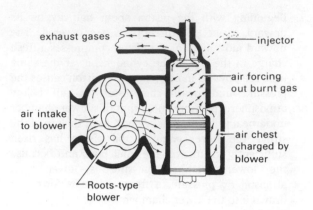

Figure 2.7 Uniflow-type two-stroke engine

2.3   TORQUE AND POWER

2.3.1 Producing torque and power

When engines are discussed, there are usually two terms used to indicate how 'powerful' an engine is: torque and power. Although there is a relationship between torque and power, they are in fact different measurements of what an engine can achieve. The values of torque and power provide indications of the performance that can be expected from an engine.

Torque is generally associated with strong pulling power, which would be typically required in a vehicle that has to pull heavy loads such as a large commercial vehicle or heavy goods vehicle. A light car that is used to pull a caravan would ideally have a high-torque engine.

Power is generally associated with engines that are intended to produce high vehicle speeds. Racing cars and sports cars would generally have high-power engines.

It is not unusual for engines to produce high torque and high power outputs. This combination can be achieved in a number of ways but the simplest example would be a large capacity engine, e.g. a six litre eight-cylinder petrol engine, which is able to produce large torque values at low engine speeds as well as high power output at higher engine speeds. Small petrol engines do not normally produce high torque levels but they can be designed to produce relatively high power outputs.

Diesel engines generally provide slightly lower power than an equivalent sized petrol engine but they do normally produce more torque than the equivalent

petrol engine, which is one reason why diesel engines are popular for light and heavy commercial vehicles.

Petrol engines are normally able to operate at higher engine speeds which enables higher power outputs to be produced (as will be explained later).

2.3.2 Torque

Torque, by definition, is a twisting force. It is generally quoted as a force acting against a lever of a given length. The force can be expressed as that applied by a given weight, e.g. kilograms force (or pounds force if using Imperial measurement). The length of the lever can be expressed in metres or feet. An example of a torque specification is 10 kg m which means that ten kilograms of force are acting on a lever which is one metre long.

Let's use tightening a wheel nut as an example (Figure 2.8). If a short lever is used on the socket to turn the wheel nut, then the amount of force acting on the lever to tighten the wheel nut is quite high. If, however, a long lever is used then the force required is lower. Assuming that the wheel nut must be tightened to a specified value, then when the short lever is used it will require a greater force to be applied by the technician to tighten the nut to the specified value than if the long lever is used.

The *work* done to tighten the nut is in fact the same whether the lever is short or long. The difference is the amount of force being applied.

Let us assume that the short lever is one metre long and the long lever is two metres long. If the force

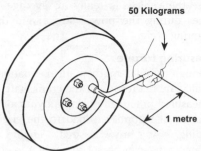

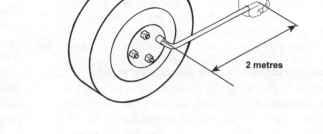

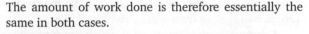

Figure 2.8 Tightening a wheel nut with a short and a long lever

required to tighten the wheel nut using the short lever is 50 kilograms force, then the force required using the long lever would be half, i.e. 25 kilograms force.

However, both the long and the short levers apply a twisting force to the wheel nut and the final result is the same in both cases. Therefore, a short lever can apply the same twisting force to the wheel nut as the long lever but a greater force must be applied to do so.

With the short lever 50 kilograms force is applied to a one-metre lever; the twisting force could be quoted as 50×1 kg m. With the long lever, 25 kilograms force is applied to a two-metre lever, which could be expressed as twisting force of 25×2 kg m, which is the same as 50 kg m.

Torque is therefore the product of the length of a lever and the force applied to it.

It should be noted that when the long lever is used, the technician's hand would move through twice the distance compared with when the short lever is used (Figure 2.9). This means that the 25 kilogram force is applied by the technicians hand but over twice the distance of the 50 kilograms force using the short lever.

The amount of work done is therefore essentially the same in both cases.

Torque in an engine

For an engine, a torque value is an indication of the twisting force available at the crankshaft. Figure 2.10 shows the piston and connecting rod assembly which is forcing the crankshaft to rotate. The force applied by the piston is being created by the combustion process above the piston. The greater the expansion of the gases above the piston, the greater the force acting on it.

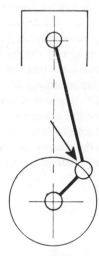

Figure 2.10 Piston and connecting rod applying force to the crankshaft

When the force of the combustion process pushes the piston down it applies the force directly to the connecting rod and crankshaft. The connecting rod applies the force to a crankpin on the crankshaft, so the distance between the centre of the crankpin and the centre of the crankshaft can be regarded as the lever. It is often referred to as the 'crankshaft throw'. As previously mentioned, torque is the combination of the force acting on the end of the lever so as the force applied by the piston increases so will the torque.

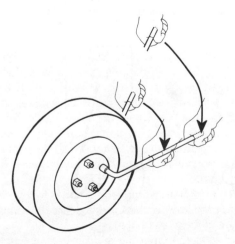

Figure 2.9 Work done tightening the wheel nut

Additionally, if the force remains the same but the length of the lever (crankshaft throw) is increased, the torque will increase.

Torque is created at every power stroke of a piston but not during the induction, compression or exhaust strokes. A single cylinder four-stroke engine will therefore only produce torque once every two crankshaft revolutions.

Torque variation during the power stroke

In reality the torque at the crankshaft is not constant. When combustion occurs and the gases start to expand, the pressure on the top of the piston increases. This pressure rise continues while the gases expand. However, the piston moves down the cylinder, which increases the volume above the piston, thus tending to reduce the pressure, which in turn reduces the force acting on the piston and crankshaft. This means the torque will change during the power stroke.

A second factor is the angle at which the connecting rod meets the crankshaft, as this also changes as the crankshaft rotates. Figure 2.11a shows the piston moving down at a position just after TDC. The angle between the connecting rod and the crankshaft is such that it is difficult to turn the crankshaft. Figure 2.11b shows the connecting rod and the crankshaft at right angles, which is a more effective angle to transfer the force. Figure 2.11c shows the piston almost at BDC where the angle between the connecting rod and the crankshaft again makes it difficult to turn the crankshaft.

It must also be remembered that the force acting on the piston is only produced during the power stroke, which means that on a four-stroke engine, the induction compression and exhaust strokes do not produce torque at the crankshaft. The flywheel effect (energy stored in the flywheel) keeps the crankshaft rotating between power strokes and contributes some energy but the torque available at the crankshaft will vary during the four strokes of the cylinder.

The 'effective torque' available at the crankshaft to move the vehicle is really an average of the torque values during the power stroke and the rest of the operating cycle.

Measuring torque

Although complex mathematical equations can be used to calculate the torque at the crankshaft, engine torque is measured practically using a dynamometer, which is a device that applies a load to the engine while it is running. At any desired engine speed, the dynamometer can be set to apply a load which can be progressively increased or decreased.

If the engine is operated at full throttle, and the load applied by the dynamometer prevents the engine speed from increasing above a certain speed (e.g. 3000 rpm, this represents the maximum effort the engine can provide at this speed. If the load is increased, the engine speed reduces; if the load is decreased the engine speed will increase.

In effect, the load being applied by the dynamometer acts as a brake, and the term 'brake dynamometer' has also been applied to these devices.

Because the load being applied by the dynamometer can be set to a known value, it is possible to calculate or measure the torque being provided by the engine. Note that the engine power (section 2.3.3) is also measured using a dynamometer.

There are various types of dynamometer. Engine manufacturers usually use a type that allows the engine to be mounted on a frame, with the crankshaft (flywheel) directly connected to the device that applies the load. Load is often provided using a water-based system, where the water acts as a resistance. A paddle wheel is driven by the engine and water is allowed to flow onto the paddle wheel. By increasing or decreasing the flow of water, the load can be increased and decreased. Other dynamometers use electricity and magnetism to create the load. Electric systems use a principle similar to that of a generator, by altering the

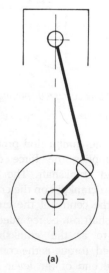
(a)

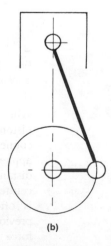
(b)

(c)

Figure 2.11 Torque variation due to different angles between the connecting rod and the crankshaft

Figure 2.12 Vehicle rolling road dynamometer for measuring power and torque © MAHA

magnetic field strength within the generator assembly to regulate the load being applied by the generator when it is connected to the engine.

To summarise, a dynamometer is able to apply known loads to an engine and thus allow the twisting force (torque) available at the crankshaft to be measured at different engine speeds.

A different method of testing torque and power is available, in which measurements are taken from the vehicle's driven wheels. This type is referred to as a 'rolling road dynamometer'. The principle of operation is the same as for an engine dynamometer, but the vehicle is driven onto the dynamometer so that the driving wheels rotate on a set of rollers. Although most rolling road dynamometers now use an electrical system to create the load, some water-based dynamometers are still used.

Maximum torque

It has been explained that torque at the crankshaft is produced by the force acting on the piston during the power stroke, which is then applied to the connecting rod and crankshaft. The greater the force acting on the piston, the greater the torque. Because the force acting on the piston is a result of the pressure rise created by combustion of the air/fuel mixture the more efficient this combustion process the greater the force acting on the piston. Also, providing a greater volume of air and fuel in the cylinder should result in a greater force from the combustion process.

Larger cylinders can theoretically accommodate more air and fuel, and so produce more torque than smaller cylinders. However, an engine is of limited size and weight for many practical reasons; the task is to achieve maximum torque for a given size of engine or cylinder.

Efficiency and engine speed

There are many factors which affect how much air and fuel can be drawn into a cylinder of a given size. When the inlet valve opens while the piston is passing down the cylinder this creates low pressure in the cylinder, which 'sucks' the air into the cylinder.

When an engine is operating at very high speed, although the low pressure caused by the downward piston movement is very fast, there is very little time for air to enter the cylinder. This results in the cylinder not being completely filled with a fresh charge of air or air/fuel mixture. The air speed through the intake system (manifold and inlet ports) is however also high, which helps to maintain a reasonable flow of air into the cylinders.

At slow engine speeds, the slow piston speed results in a correspondingly slow air speed through the intake system which can again mean that the cylinder is not entirely filled with a fresh charge.

At medium engine speeds, the piston speed and air speed are relatively high and a reasonable time is available for refilling the cylinder.

Therefore, at medium engine speeds, the cylinder usually receives the largest charge of air or air/fuel mixture, and this results in a higher pressure being created from the combustion process. This in turn provides a greater force to the piston and produces greater torque.

Many engines produce their maximum torque value at a medium engine speed. Figure 2.13 shows a typical torque curve for a petrol engine; note that the torque increases until the engine reaches approximately 3500 rpm, then reduces, although the engine speed continues to increase. This indicates that the cylinder is receiving the largest charge of air (or air/fuel mixture) at 3500 rpm, thus producing the greatest force on the piston and torque from the power stroke.

As mentioned previously, there are many factors affecting engine design and also how much air and fuel enter the cylinder. One critical factor is the timing for the opening and closing of the inlet and exhaust valves.

Ideally, valve timing should be varied to suit different engine speeds, and devices are now common on many modern engines to achieve variable valve timing. However, in the absence of such sophistication the general trend (for petrol engines) was for maximum torque to be achieved at around 50% to 60% of maximum engine speed, e.g. maximum torque at 3500 rpm for an engine with a 6000 rpm maximum speed (see Figure 2.13).

For engines with variable valve timing (and perhaps other relevant engine design features), it is not uncommon to have a consistently high torque value from low through to high engine speeds, although maximum torque is still often produced at just over 50% of the maximum engine speed. Figure 2.14 shows a torque curve from an engine fitted with variable valve timing; note the improvement in torque at low engine speeds compared with the curve in Figure 2.13.

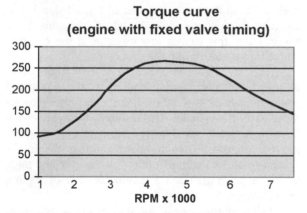

Figure 2.13 The torque curve from a petrol engine

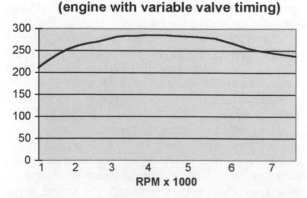

Figure 2.14 The torque curve from a petrol engine with variable valve timing

Quoting torque values

Torque can be thought of as a 'twisting force', a force acting against a lever. For many years different units of torque were used in different countries. In Britain and America (and other countries that used Imperial units) the 'pound foot' (lb ft) was used. This uses the force measured in pounds and the length in feet to give the unit, for example 200 lb ft. However, force can be expressed in kilograms force (kgf) or any other unit of weight, and length could be in metres (m).

There is, however, now a general agreement to use a unit of force called the newton (N) and to measure length in metres (m). So torque is now usually quoted in 'newton metres' (Nm).

2.3.3 Power

The power output of an engine is usually defined as the work it does (energy converted) over a period of time.

Work, power, force and torque are all different, measurable aspects of the way in which a machine functions, and each tells us something different about the process going on in the machine, in this case an engine.

An example of the difference between force, torque, work and power can be illustrated by the example of a cyclist riding a push-bike. Force is applied by the rider's legs to the pedals and the pedal cranks. The torque at the crank centre will depend on the force applied by the rider and the length of the pedal cranks. A considerable amount of torque is required to move the push-bike away from rest, especially if the bike is going up a steep hill. However, when the pedals move the rider is beginning to do work. After one minute of cycling the bike will have travelled some distance. The greater the distance the greater the amount of work done, and if this work is divided by the time taken to do it, the result is the power developed. The faster the same amount of work is done, the greater the power developed.

Another example is a horse that is harnessed to a heavy cart. If the horse provides just sufficient force to tighten the rope, but not sufficient to move the cart, then no work is done. If, however, the horse applies a greater force the cart will move, which means that work is being done. The further the cart moves, the greater the amount of work done.

Because the horse was the most common source of power for many years, engine power was traditionally quoted in horsepower, (1 horsepower = 33,000 ft lb per minute or 746 watts). A commonly used measurement for power is the kilowatt (1000 watts). So 1 horsepower = 0.746 kilowatts.

Other measurements used for power include 'PS' a German unit similar to the traditional horsepower rating (PS is an abbreviation for horsepower in German) where 1 PS = 0.986 horsepower.

Engine power

It has been previously identified that torque is produced during the power stroke. However, the amount of work done during the power stroke would be an indication of the power.

If a single cylinder four-stroke engine is operating at 1000 rpm, it will produce a certain amount of torque at the crankshaft (combustion creating pressure and force on the piston which then acts on the crankshaft). The same torque will be created during each of the individual power strokes but each power stroke would move the vehicle only a short distance.

However, when the engine has turned through 1000 rpm, there will have been 500 power strokes, which would have moved the vehicle over a relatively long distance. The distance moved by the vehicle in one minute could be an indication of the power. Therefore, in theory, the faster the engine turns, the greater the number of power strokes and the greater the total power. It could therefore be said that each power stroke produces the torque at the crankshaft, but the greater the number of power strokes results in increased power.

However, one factor that affects both torque and power is the force that is applied to the piston on the power stroke. A lower force will result in less torque, which would then not be able to move the vehicle very quickly. This would mean that the vehicle would not move so far in one minute, i.e. less power.

Therefore, the greater the amount of air and fuel (in the correct proportions) that can be drawn into a cylinder, the greater the torque and power.

It has already been highlighted that the amount of air and fuel (fresh charge) drawn into the cylinder will vary with engine speed. This typically results in an engine achieving the best torque value at a mid-range engine speed. Because the fresh charge will get smaller as the engine speed increases beyond the mid-speed range, less torque is produced. However, although each power stroke will therefore not be as strong when the engine speed is higher, there will be a greater number of power strokes due to the increased engine speed.

If, for example, the volume of fresh charge drawn into the cylinder remained the same, no matter what the engine speed, then if the speed doubled thus giving twice the number of power strokes, the power would also double. Note that the torque produced at each power stroke would remain the same.

If, however, the volume of fresh charge reduced slightly when the engine speed increased (which is the normal trend above mid-engine speeds), then even if the engine speed doubled, there would not be twice as much power.

As an approximate example, if the fresh charge and therefore the torque produced are at their maximum at 3000 rpm, an engine may be producing 100 PS of power. If, when the engine is then operating at 6000 rpm, the fresh charge and torque are only three quarters of the values (75%) produced at 3000 rpm, then each power stroke would be three quarters as

powerful. Although the engine speed has doubled, which should in theory now give 200 PS of power, the force on each power stroke is only three quarters which means that the power will be three quarters of 200, i.e. 150 PS.

Figure 2.15 shows a typical torque and power curve for a petrol engine. Note that the torque is low at low engine speeds but gradually increases to a maximum at 3500 rpm. The torque then reduces as the engine speed gets higher due to a smaller fresh charge being drawn in. However, although power is low at low engine speeds, it increases with the increase in engine speed and continues to increase through to around 5500 rpm. At the high engine speeds, the fresh charge is becoming much smaller, and although there are many power strokes at high engine speeds, each power stroke is weaker and therefore total power is reducing.

In conclusion, engine power is dependent on the amount of charge that can be drawn in or introduced to the cylinder. The greater the amount of charge, the greater the power (and torque). However, if the engine speed is increased there will then be a greater number of induction and power strokes which will result in greater power.

The greater the total amount of air (or air/fuel mixture) that can be drawn into an engine (or consumed by the engine) during a given time, e.g. 1 minute, the greater the quoted power output.

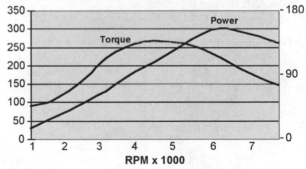

Figure 2.15 Torque and power curves for a petrol engine

2.3.4 Altering the power and torque characteristics of an engine

Increasing torque at any particular speed requires an increase in the size of the fresh charge. Different valve timings will also have a great effect on the size of the charge at different engine speeds. Intake port design, valve size and many other factors also affect the speed at which maximum torque is achieved.

It is often the case that designing the engine so that maximum torque is achieved at higher engine speeds results in lower torque at mid-range engine speeds.

Designing an engine to achieve the desired characteristics for its application is a compromise. A Formula 1 race car engine can provide in excess of 800 PS at engine speeds in the region of 19,000 rpm. However, the low speed torque from a Formulae 1 engine would not be suited to pulling a caravan at low speed up a steep hill.

As previously mentioned, modern engines can be fitted with variable valve timing and other devices that enable high torque values to be produced at low and high engine speeds, which means improved power across a wider rpm range. Although these engines are much more efficient over a wide range of engine speeds, there still need to be some compromises to match the application of the engine.

2.4   SINGLE-CYLINDER AND MULTI-CYLINDER ENGINES

2.4.1 Limitations of the single-cylinder engine

With the exception of some motorcycles, virtually all motor vehicle engines have more than one cylinder. To understand the reasons for this it is necessary to consider the limitations of the single-cylinder engine and the ways in which multiple cylinders overcome these limitations.

Irregular torque output

The torque (twisting force) exerted upon the crankshaft of a single-cylinder engine fluctuates widely during each cycle of operation. As shown in Figure 2.16, the torque reaches its maximum value during the power stroke, however, during the exhaust, induction and compression strokes some effort has to be applied to the crankshaft to keep it turning.

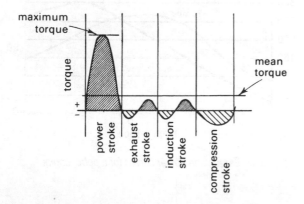

Figure 2.16 Torque fluctuations in a single-cylinder engine

The energy necessary to keep the crankshaft turning is provided by the flywheel, which has stored some of the energy created during the power stroke.

Although the maximum torque developed may be high, its average or mean value is very much lower. (The mean torque is that steady value of torque, which would do the same amount of work per minute as the actual fluctuating torque.)

The driving effort developed by the engine (especially a single-cylinder engine) is therefore rather jerky, especially at low speeds: a heavy flywheel is therefore necessary to give acceptable smoothness and ensure sufficient energy is available to maintain crankshaft rotation between power strokes (primarily at low engine speeds). Also, the transmission system must be capable of transmitting the maximum torque developed (not just the mean or average torque), and is therefore undesirably heavy in relation to the mean torque.

Figure 2.17 shows that if four cylinders are used and they are working in succession, the mean torque is only a little less than the maximum torque. If a single-cylinder engine is replaced by a four-cylinder engine where the four cylinders have a total capacity which is the same as the single cylinder, each of the four cylinders individually produce a lower maximum torque value than the large single cylinder. However, the mean torque of the four cylinders is probably greater than that of the equivalent single-cylinder engine, and torque delivery will be smoother. This increased mean torque can be transmitted by the same transmission system as was needed for the single-cylinder engine which had a high maximum torque.

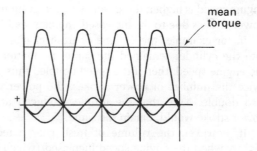

Figure 2.17 Torque fluctuations in a four-cylinder engine

Power output and engine speed

The power that an engine can develop is determined by the amount of air it can consume per minute, i.e. its swept volume or cylinder capacity, and the speed at which it runs (the greater the speed, the greater the number of induction and power strokes). However, the inertia forces on the reciprocating parts of the engine limit the maximum engine speed, and these forces depend upon the mass of these parts and their acceleration.

As mentioned in section 2.3, the higher the engine speed, the greater the power that can be developed. But engine speed is limited by the weight (mass) of its moving parts.

For a given swept volume the bore and stroke of a multi-cylinder engine are smaller than those of a single-cylinder. As an example, a single-cylinder engine of 1 litre, which has an equal bore and stroke of the same dimensions, would have a bore and stroke of approximately 108.4 mm. However, a 1000 cc four-cylinder engine would have four cylinders each of approximately 250 cc; each cylinder would have a bore and stroke of approximately 68.2 cm (assuming that the bore and stroke were again equal).

For the four-cylinder engine the size and mass of each piston will therefore be smaller and the stroke shorter. Therefore, at the same engine speed the inertia forces on the reciprocating parts of a multi-cylinder engine will be considerably less than those in a single-cylinder engine. The multi-cylinder engine can safely run at higher speed, develop greater power and have longer life.

Balance

The inertia forces, which are caused by the acceleration of the reciprocating parts of the engine, tend to cause vibration. To balance these forces and neutralize their effects, equal and opposite forces must be introduced. This can only be done by additional reciprocating parts making similar movements but in the opposite direction.

While a single-cylinder engine cannot be perfectly balanced, it is much easier in multi-cylinder engines to neutralize much of the imbalance by having sets of pistons, connecting rods and crankpins moving in opposite directions during crankshaft rotation. On a four-cylinder engine, it is traditional for two pistons to be travelling in the opposite direction to the other two pistons, thus providing opposing forces which almost cancel out each other.

2.4.2 Number of cylinders and arrangement

Engine shape

The shape of a single-cylinder engine cannot be altered very much, and its size will depend upon its swept volume, bore and stroke. This does not leave the designer much scope for making the engine compact so as to fit it into a smaller space in the vehicle. When several cylinders are used the designer has a choice of several different cylinder arrangements, by means of which the engine shape can be varied to suit the space into which it must fit.

Limitations on cylinder numbers

The advantages resulting from the use of more than one cylinder are not gained without some sacrifices. One of the chief objections to the multi-cylinder engine is the greater cost and complication due to the increased number of parts that have to be made and assembled. Other difficulties arise in connection with fuel and ignition systems. For these reasons the majority of motor vehicles use engines having four, six or eight cylinders. A few small vehicles have used two-cylinder engines, while some large cars have used 12 or even 16 cylinders, but these are exceptional cases.

Cylinder arrangements

There are three main arrangements that are commonly used for the cylinders of an engine.

1 **In-line** The cylinders are arranged in a single row, side by side and parallel to one another. They may be vertical, horizontal or inclined at any convenient angle. In-line engines usually have four or six cylinders but five- and three-cylinder engines are used, with a few eight-cylinder in-line engines produced in the past.
2 **Vee** The cylinders are arranged in two rows at an angle to one another. For the two-, four- and eight-cylinder engines, the V-angle is usually 90°. For six- and twelve-cylinder engines it is usually 60°, occasionally 90° or 120°. There are, however, exceptions to this, for instance some V4 engines use a V-angle of 60°. In each case the crankpins are suitably offset in order to equalize the firing interval impulses. Some twelve-cylinder engines are arranged with a 65° V-angle and again the crankpins will be suitably offset to equalize firing pulses. Note that vee engines are now being produced with ten cylinders (five cylinders on each bank).

    There are also some 'narrow angle' vee engines with a total of five cylinders. The angle is so narrow that the engine is almost an in-line engine.
3 **Opposed** This could be regarded as a V-type engine in which the V-angle is 180°. The cylinders are usually placed horizontally. Note that the opposed cylinder arrangement may also be referred to as a 'flat or 'boxer' engine.

Cylinder numbering

The cylinders of an engine are identified by giving them numbers. When there is only one row of cylinders they are usually numbered from one end towards the other, but in the case of other arrangements there is considerable variation in practice.

The cylinders of in-line engines are usually numbered 1, 2, 3, etc., commencing from the 'free' or non-driving end. Note that some exceptions have existed where the driving end cylinder has been regarded as number 1.

In the case of vee or opposed engines, each group of cylinders is usually numbered in the same manner, but groups of cylinders are identified by letters A, B, etc.

More often they are identified as L and R for the left and right cylinder banks. Sometimes one group of cylinders contains even numbers and the other odd; sometimes one group of cylinders is numbered consecutively, followed by the cylinders in the other group.

2.4.3 Firing order

The cylinders of a multi-cylinder engine are arranged to have their power strokes in succession, and the order in which the cylinders work is called the 'firing order' of the engine. For smoothest running, the power strokes should be spaced at equal intervals, each interval being equal to the number of degrees per cycle of operations (720° for a four-stroke engine) divided by the number of cylinders. For a four-cylinder engine the interval will be 720°/4 = 180°; for a six-cylinder, 720°/6 = 120°.

The firing order of an engine is primarily determined by the disposition of the cylinders and the cranks on the crankshaft, i.e. whether the engine is in-line, vee or opposed. This determines the possible firing orders.

Firing orders for some of the common types of engine are discussed in a little more detail in the following pages.

Four-cylinder in-line engines

Figure 2.18 shows a simple line diagram of the arrangement of cylinders and cranks in four-cylinder four-stroke engine. Power strokes occur at intervals of 180° of crankshaft rotation and the pistons move in pairs, 1 and 4 forming one pair, 2 and 3 the other.

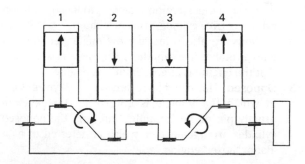

Cylinder no.	1	2	3	4
1st stroke	P	C or E	E or C	I
2nd stroke	E	P or I	I or P	C
3rd stroke	I	E or C	C or E	P
4th stroke	C	I or P	P or I	E

P – power stroke   E – exhaust stroke
I – induction stroke   C – compression stroke

Figure 2.18 Arrangement of cylinders and crankshaft for a four-cylinder in-line engine

Suppose piston 1 is commencing its power stroke; piston 4 will move down its cylinder on its induction stroke. Piston 2 will move upwards on either its exhaust or compression stroke, and piston 3 on either its compression or exhaust stroke. We can now make up a table showing the four strokes made by each piston during one cycle of operation (Figure 2.18).

From this table in Figure 2.18, we see that there are two possible firing orders for a four-cylinder engine. These are '1243' and '1342'; both 'are in common use.

In addition to taking the firing impulses, the crankshaft also has to resist the forces caused when the pistons change their direction of movement. The arrows in Figure 2.18 indicate these inertia forces and the circular arrows show the effect on the crankshaft. By arranging the crank throws so that the two circular arrows oppose each other, it is possible to achieve reasonable balance of the engine as a whole.

The high speed and power produced within a modern engine makes the load applied to the crankshaft and centre bearing very high. Extra main bearings are provided between each crank throw to stiffen the construction. Figure 2.19 shows a typical crankshaft for a four-cylinder engine with five main bearings.

Six-cylinder in-line engines

Figure 2.20 is a line diagram of the cylinder and crank arrangement for a six-cylinder in-line engine: (a) and (b) show alternative crankshaft arrangements as viewed from the front.

In arrangement (a), commencing with pistons 1 and 6 at TDC, the next pair to come to TDC will be 3 and 4, followed by 2 and 5, and then 1 and 6 again. If piston 1 is commencing its power stroke, the next power stroke will occur in either of the cylinders 3 or 4, and the following one in either of the cylinders 2 or 5. There are thus four possible firing orders:

132645, 135642, 145632, 142635

In the first three of these, all three cylinders in one half of the engine fire during one revolution and the three in the other half fire during the next revolution. In the last pattern, cylinders in opposite halves of the engine fire alternately. This arrangement is generally preferable as it helps to obtain good 'distribution' of the air/fuel mixture. It is the only one in common use, although others have been used in rare cases.

If the cranks are arranged as shown in (b) the pistons come to TDC in the order 1 and 6, 2 and 5, 3 and 4, followed by 1 and 6 again. In this case the four possible firing orders are:

123654, 124653, 154623, 153624

Once again only in the last option are cylinders in opposite halves of the engine firing alternately, and this is the one in common use.

Both alternative crank arrangements are used, and there are thus two alternative firing orders in common use for a six-cylinder engine – 142635 and 153624.

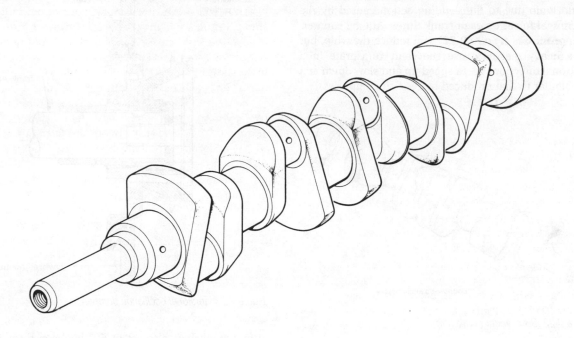

Figure 2.19 Crankshaft: four-cylinder, five-bearing

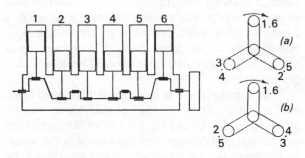

Figure 2.20 Arrangement of cylinders and crankshaft for a six-cylinder in-line engine

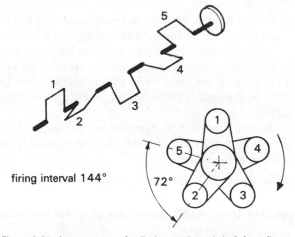

firing interval 144°

Figure 2.21 Arrangement of cylinders and crankshaft for a five-cylinder in-line engine

Five-cylinder in-line engines

There are obvious manufacturing advantages to using similar-sized parts in the various engines offered by a vehicle producer. When this policy is adopted, there are occasions when a given vehicle requires an engine with a power output and smoothness factor mid-way between that of a four- and a six-cylinder unit; this is achieved using a five-cylinder layout. Similarly there are cases when a six-cylinder in-line unit is too long and a V6 is too heavy.

Figure 2.21 shows the throw layout of a five-cylinder crankshaft. The angle between the throws is 72°, the firing interval is 144° and a typical firing order is 12453.

Torsional oscillation

A six-cylinder crankshaft is long and slender. One end is attached to a flywheel, which rotates at a near-constant speed, whereas at the front end, the firing impulses cause the shaft to wind-up and then unwind.

If the shaft were made in the form shown in Figure 2.20, the rate at which the shaft vibrates would be very high. As the firing impulses occur at a slower rate, no problem would arise from this vibration, but the shaft would whip due to the bending action caused by the centrifugal forces on each crank throw. Adding counter-balance masses (Figure 2.22) will reduce the whip, but these heavy masses cause the shaft to vibrate in a rotational direction, i.e. to speed up and slow down at a rate similar to that produced by the firing impulses.

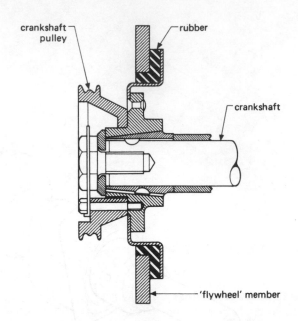

Figure 2.23 Torsional oscillation damper

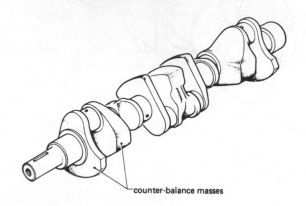

Figure 2.22 Six-cylinder crankshaft

At speeds where this occurs, the oscillation becomes severe and at these times the irregular movement of the front end of the shaft can cause problems with valve timing gears, general vibration of the engine and in severe cases, breakage of the shaft due to fatigue.

A torsional oscillation damper is fitted to prevent the build-up of vibration at the speeds at which vibration is severe. The damper shown in Figure 2.23 consists of a small flywheel member, bonded by rubber to a hub attached to the front end of the crankshaft.

At times when oscillation occurs, the constant speed of the flywheel member opposes the winding up and unwinding of the shaft. The extent of the vibration movement is reduced by means of the energy-absorbing rubber.

Torsional oscillation dampers are not required on engines having short, stiff shafts such as those used on four-cylinder engines.

V6 engines

The diagrammatic sketch in Figure 2.24 shows two banks of three cylinders set at an angle of 60° with a six-throw crankshaft also set at 60° between throws. The firing interval is 120° and the banks are fired in the order R-L-R-L-R-L. The 240° angle moved by the crank between adjacent cylinders in any one bank being fired gives good distribution. It will be seen that the cylinders in each bank fire in the order: front, centre, rear.

V8 engines

Figure 2.25 shows the arrangement of cylinders for a V8 engine. The earliest engines of this type used a crankshaft similar to that used in the in-line four-cylinder engine, as shown in (a). Later the crank arrangement shown in (b) was adopted because it gives better balance.

Power strokes occur at intervals of 90° in both cases, and the 'pairs' in which the pistons move are, for arrangement (a), 1A and 4A, 1 B and 4B, 2A and 3A, 2B and 3B, giving eight possible firing orders. In the case of arrangement (b) the 'pairs' are 1A and 2B, 1B and 3A, 3B and 4A, 4B and 2A, also giving eight possible firing orders. An interesting exercise is to calculate all of the possible firing orders for V8 engines for crankshaft arrangements (a) and (b).

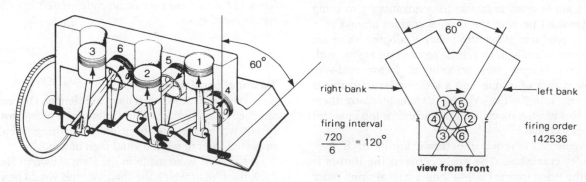

Figure 2.24 Cylinder and crank arrangement for V6 engine

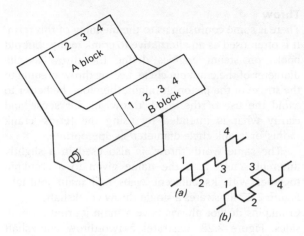

Figure 2.25 Cylinder and crank arrangement for a V8 engine

V12 and V10 engines

Today many manufacturers use engines with more than eight cylinders; V12 and V10 engines. These engines, often in the region of four or five litres in capacity, are used in many luxury and sports vehicles.

Determination of firing order

It is necessary to know the firing order of an engine to be able to connect up the sparking plug leads correctly, or to connect test equipment to the ignition system. There are several methods by which it may be found. It is sometimes marked on the engine, or on a plate on or near the engine. It is invariably given in the workshop manual. If the engine is not marked and the workshop manual is not available the following method can be used:

1 Remove the valve gear covers and note which are the inlet valves and which the exhaust.
2 Rotate the engine in the direction in which it runs and watch the order in which one set of valves, inlet or exhaust, operate. This will give the order in which the inlet strokes or exhaust strokes occur, and the power strokes occur in the same order.

An alternative method is for the technician to position his thumbs and fingers over the plug holes (or fit corks in the plug holes suitably secured to each other): rotate the engine and note the order of cylinder 'compressions' as they occur.

2.5 CRANKSHAFTS

2.5.1 Crankshaft main features

The crankshaft converts the reciprocating motion of the pistons into a rotational movement, which is then used to power, in the case of a motor vehicle, the transmission and wheels. The large forces caused by the combustion pressures are transferred to the pistons and the connecting rods through to the crankshaft, which then rotates at very high speeds. On multi-cylinder engines the crankshaft harnesses the power from individual cylinders and converts it into a single rotational force. The length of the crankshaft dictates the length of the cylinder block.

The crankshaft of an engine is formed of a number of 'sections' such as that illustrated in Figure 2.26.

The main journals (a part of a shaft which rotates in a bearing is called a journal), which are located through the centre line of the crankshaft, rotate in the main bearings.

The crankpin or crank journal, to which the connecting rod is fitted, is offset from the main journals by a distance called the crank radius.

The webs of the crankshaft connect the main journals to the crankpin. Where the journals join the webs a fillet or radius is formed to avoid a sharp corner, which would be a source of weakness. This is of vital importance in crankshafts that are subjected to particularly heavy loads.

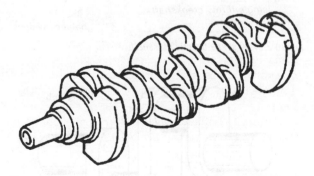

Figure 2.26 Example of a crankshaft fitted to a multi-cylinder engine

Balance masses

In some cases the webs are extended to form balance masses, which are used in certain types of engine. These masses help to ensure that the rotating parts are balanced as effectively as possible and so cause as little vibration as possible while the engine is running. It is not possible to balance completely the rotating parts of all types of engine; this is, for instance, one of the objections to the use of single-cylinder engines, which are impossible to balance perfectly, though they can be made satisfactory for certain purposes.

In some engines in which the rotating parts are perfectly balanced, masses similar to balance masses may still be used: centrifugal force acting on the crankpins causes heavy loading of the adjacent main bearings at high speeds, and by extending the webs to form balance masses a counter-centrifugal force is applied in opposition to that on the crankpin, thus reducing the bearing loading. Masses used in this way are more properly known as counterbalance masses.

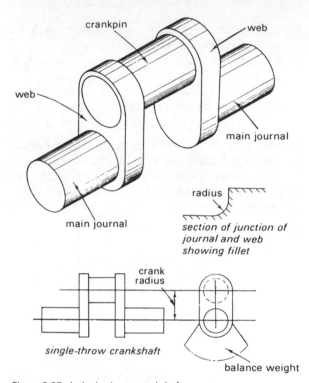

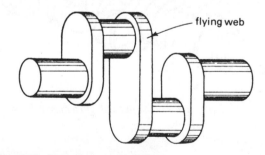

Figure 2.27 A single-throw crankshaft

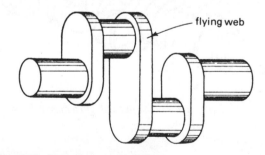

Figure 2.28 A two-throw crankshaft

Throw

There is some confusion as to the meaning of this term. It is often used as an alternative to crank radius, but old books on steam engines define the throw as the diameter of the crankpin circle, i.e. the throw is equal to the stroke of the piston. It might, therefore, be better to avoid the use of the word 'throw' in this sense and clarify what is intended by using the terms 'crank radius' or 'crank circle diameter' as appropriate.

The same word 'throw' is also used in a slightly different sense: it is the name given to a crankpin together with its adjacent webs and main journals. Figure 2.27 illustrates a single-throw crankshaft. Crankpins do not always have a main journal on both sides. Figure 2.28 illustrates a two-throw crankshaft having only two main journals, the crankpins being connected together by a flying web. However, on most modern engines, a crankpin usually has a main journal at each side. Figure 2.29 shows a four-cylinder engine crankshaft with five main bearing journals.

Flywheel attachment

The flywheel is usually attached to the rear end of the crankshaft. The attachment must be perfectly secure, and it should be possible to assemble the flywheel in one position only. This is because the crankshaft and flywheel, besides being balanced separately, are also balanced as an assembly, and if the flywheel is not fitted in the same position as that in which the assembly was balanced, some imperfection of balance may arise that can cause vibration.

Note: It is possible that the crankshaft itself may be balanced within the limits permitted, but not perfectly; the flywheel may also have a small but 'tolerable' imbalance. Should the crankshaft and flywheel be assembled so that the imbalance of the crankshaft and the imbalance of the flywheel are 'added' this would cause severe vibration. The problem could, however, be solved by turning the flywheel through 180° on the crankshaft.

Another reason to only allow securing the flywheel to the crankshaft in one position is that a reference point on the flywheel may also be used as an indication of TDC for number 1 cylinder (the reference point is detected by a sensor). This is common practice when an engine management system is used that requires an accurate reference point to TDC of number 1 cylinder.

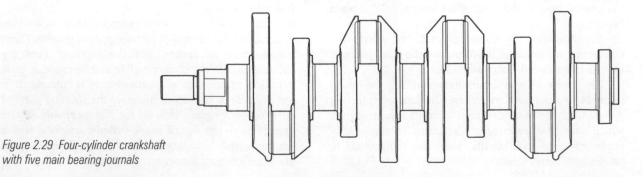

Figure 2.29 Four-cylinder crankshaft with five main bearing journals

Figures 2.30 and 2.31 show a common method of attaching the flywheel to the end of the crankshaft. A flange is formed on the end of the crankshaft which is a close fit into a counter-bored hole in the centre of the flywheel. The flywheel is secured by a number of bolts, which pass through holes drilled axially through the flywheel face, and screwed into threaded holes in the crankshaft flange. One or more dowels are usually fitted to relieve the screws of shearing loads, and the dowels, or bolts, are often unevenly spaced to permit assembly in one position only. A suitable locking arrangement is provided for the nuts or screws.

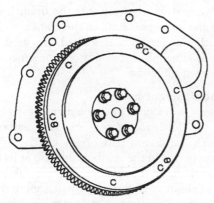

Figure 2.30 Flywheel bolted at rear of crankshaft

Oil-ways

Engine lubrication systems are dealt with in section 2.13 in this chapter, but it is necessary to mention the method by which oil is supplied to the crankpin journals and main bearing journals. Oil is delivered under pressure to the main bearings (from an oil pump), where it is fed into a groove running around the bearing at about the middle of its length.

A hole is drilled through the crankshaft (as shown in Figure 2.32) running from the main journal, through the web to the surface of the crankpin. The main journal end of the drilled hole is positioned so that it ends at the groove in the main bearing; therefore, as the shaft rotates, a continuous supply of oil is able to pass from the groove through the drilled hole and along to the crankpin.

Some large crankshafts have their crankpins and journal bored out to reduce weight and therefore reduce

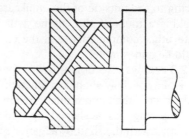

Figure 2.32 Oil-way drilled through crank web

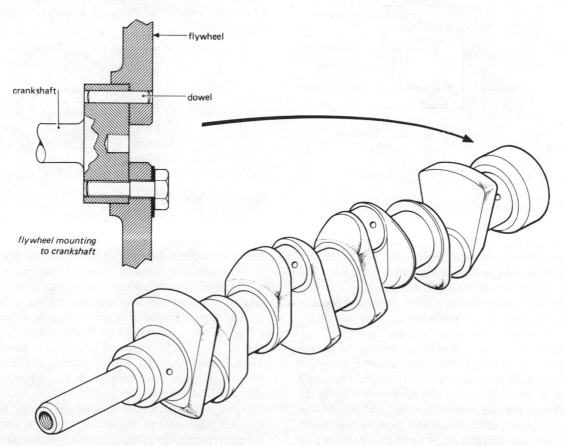

Figure 2.31 Crankshaft; four-cylinder, five-bearing and flywheel mounting

the forces created when the crankshaft is rotating. The ends of these hollow pins and journals are usually closed by caps or plugs held in place by bolts (see Figure 2.33) to prevent the escape of oil.

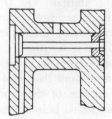

Figure 2.33 Method of sealing hollow journals

Oil retainers

The crankshaft projects from the rear end of the crankcase, and some of the oil which is pumped into the rear bearing to lubricate it will escape from the rear end of the bearing to the outside of the crankcase. The oil, besides making a mess of the engine, will invariably contaminate other components (e.g. the clutch plate) which would be undesirable.

Figure 2.34 shows a section of a 'lip-type seal'. The seal consists of a specially shaped synthetic rubber ring supported by a steel shell and fitting into a recess in the crankcase. The ring has a shaped lip which is held lightly in contact with the shaft by a 'garter spring'.

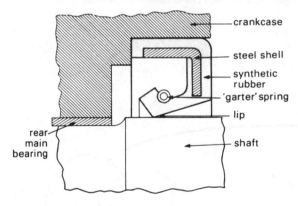

Figure 2.34 Section of a lip-type seal

Figure 2.35 shows two other methods of preventing oil escape from the crankshaft. Immediately behind the rear journal a thin ring or fin of metal can be formed around the circumference of the shaft. Oil reaching this ring from the rear bearing is flung off by centrifugal force as the shaft rotates, and is caught in a cavity from which a drain hole leads the oil back inside the crankcase.

Behind this 'flinger ring' a square-section, helical groove or scroll, rather like a coarse screw thread, is machined onto the surface of the shaft. The outer surface of the shaft has a small clearance inside an extension of the rear bearing housing, and any oil that reaches this part of the shaft will tend to be dragged round with the shaft but at the same time held back by the stationary housing. As a result the oil is drawn along

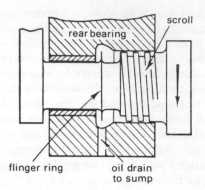

Figure 2.35 Scroll-type oil retainer

the groove and directed towards the drain hole, thus allowing the oil to pass back to the crankcase. In most cases both the methods described are used on the crankshaft, although sometimes only one method may be considered sufficient.

Clutch shaft spigot bearing

The power developed by the engine is transmitted through the clutch to the gearbox. The gearbox shaft, onto which the driven part of the clutch is fitted, is usually supported in the gearbox and also at its forward end in a bearing in the rear end of the crankshaft. The bearing in the rear of the crankshaft (referred to as a 'spigot bearing') is often a roller-type bearing. Other spigot bearings may be simple bronze bushes pressed into axial holes in the rear end of the crankshaft (see Figure 2.36).

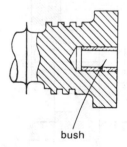

Figure 2.36 Clutch shaft spigot bearing

Front end or nose of the crankshaft

For most engines, the front of the crankshaft is used to drive other components and mechanisms. Importantly, the camshaft (which is the mechanism used for opening and closing the inlet and exhaust valves) is usually driven from the front end of the crankshaft, although in a few cases it is taken from the flywheel end. The front end of the shaft is extended beyond the front main journal, the extension being parallel or sometimes stepped, i.e. the forward part is of slightly smaller diameter than the rear part.

Onto this extension is pressed the timing gear or sprocket (chain-driven system) or timing pulley (belt-driven system). The timing sprocket or timing pulley then drives a timing chain or timing belt, which in turn drives the camshaft. An additional pulley (or pulleys) are then attached in front of the timing gear or timing pulley. The additional pulleys are used to drive other belts that in turn may drive the cooling fan, the water pump and alternator or other devices such as a power steering pump.

A common method for locating the sprocket and pulleys on the crankshaft is with a 'Woodruff key'. The key locates in a slot in the crankshaft nose and also in a slot in the gear or pulleys. The key transfers the drive from the crankshaft to the sprocket and pulleys. The sprocket and pulleys are then secured by a nut or screw threaded into the end of the shaft.

If a timing chain is used to operate the valve mechanism, the timing sprocket is enclosed inside a cover called the timing case, with the additional pulleys being outside of the timing cover. Oil retaining arrangements on the timing cover are similar to those at the rear of the crankshaft, although the oil flinger is usually a separate part, gripped between the timing gear and pulley bosses.

Note that some engines may use a train of gears to drive the camshafts. The first gear in the train will be the crankshaft timing gear, located on the nose of the crankshaft. All of the gears will be contained within the timing cover.

If a timing belt is used instead of a timing chain, the timing pulley will also be external (not enclosed within an oil-tight timing cover). A simple cover will, however, be provided to protect the belt.

Figure 2.37 shows the arrangement for locating a timing sprocket and the additional pulley, as well as showing the timing cover and a lip-type oil seal retained in the timing cover. The lip of the seal should be smeared with oil before fitting the pulley onto the crankshaft.

Crankshaft materials

Crankshafts are made of high quality steel or iron. These materials are processed by either forging or casting.

Forging gives greater strength, but stiffness is of more importance than strength alone. Most modern shafts have large journals and relatively short throws that allows the crankpins to overlap the journals when viewed from the end of the shaft. This feature allows the shaft to be cast, which results in a lighter shaft and is cheaper to manufacture because it requires less machining. In addition modem nodular irons are exceptionally strong and, when ground to a fine finish and then surface-hardened, provide an excellent bearing surface. In this case the term 'nodular' applies to the inclusion of minute rounded lumps of graphite, (carbon). These particles are not combined with the base material so their existence in a free state classifies the material as iron and not steel.

Following the initial forming, the shaft is ground to give a very smooth and accurately dimensioned surface of the journals and crankpins. Often the webs are not machined, but in the case of a high-performance engine the shaft would be machined all over to reduce oil drag.

Unless special precautions are taken, the repeated load applied to the shaft and the continual torsional flexing of the shaft while the engine is running, especially in the region of the rear journal fillet, causes the shaft to fracture. This fatigue can be minimized by 'fillet rolling' (Figure 2.38).

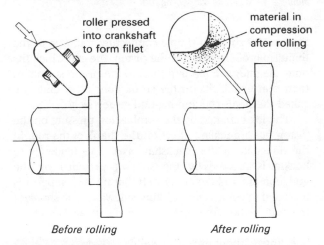

Figure 2.38 Fillet rolling

For long life there must be a large difference in hardness between the shaft and the bearing surfaces. Many modern engines use a comparatively hard bearing, so the journals and crankpins must be hardened. The hardening of the bearing surfaces is achieved by either nitriding or an induction hardening process. The former process involves heating the complete shaft to a temperature of about 500°C in an atmosphere of ammonia gas for several hours. During this period the steel absorbs nitrogen from the ammonia and forms a hard surface of iron nitride. Induction hardening is an electrical process.

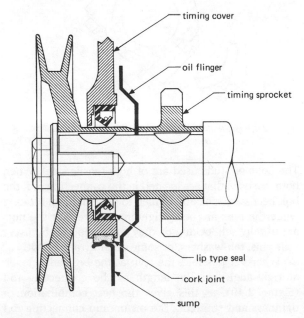

Figure 2.37 Mounting of crankshaft pulley and timing chain sprocket

2.6 CONNECTING RODS

2.6.1 General design

The connecting rod or 'con rod' (Figure 2.39), connects the piston to the crankshaft. The connecting rod is therefore subject to the high forces exerted on the piston by combustion pressures. When combustion pressure forces the piston down the cylinder, the connecting rod must transfer the force through to the crankshaft, which is then made to rotate.

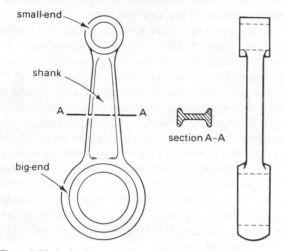

Figure 2.39 A simple connecting rod

Figure 2.39 shows a simple connecting rod. Due to the limitations of space inside the piston, the end which fits onto the gudgeon pin and then to the piston is smaller than that which fits on the crankshaft; these ends are called the small-end and big-end respectively.

The load created by the combustion pressure on the piston has a buckling effect on the shank of the rod, in the direction of the crankshaft axis. This tendency to buckle is resisted by the support provided by the gudgeon pin and the crankshaft, but no such support is provided to counteract buckling sideways. The shank of the rod is therefore generally made in an H-section, which gives the greatest possible resistance to sideways buckling, without excessive weight.

2.6.2 The big-end

The simple connecting rod shown in Figure 2.39 has a one-piece or 'solid-eye' big-end. This can only be used if the crankshaft is of built-up construction, i.e. if the shaft is made in sections assembled and suitably fixed together, allowing the big-end to be slipped over the end of the crank pin before the shaft is assembled. While this practice was once common in single-cylinder motorcycle engines and has even been used in a few multi-cylinder car engines, it is much heavier and more expensive than the usual one-piece crankshaft

construction illustrated in Figure 2.26 (section 2.5). Built-up crankshafts are therefore very rarely used in car engines.

To fit a connecting rod to a one-piece crankshaft, the connecting rod must be manufactured with a split big-end. The split is usually created across the centre of the crankpin region of the big-end, the two halves of the big-end are then assembled around the crankpin and bolted together (Figure 2.40).

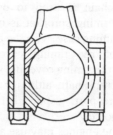

Figure 2.40 A spilt big-end cap

The detachable portion is called the 'big-end cap'. The big-end cap can be fixed to the connecting rod with either nuts and bolts, or with nuts that screw onto studs that are fixed into the connecting rod. Big-end caps may also be secured using bolts that screw into the connecting rod (Figure 2.41).

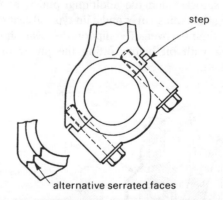

Figure 2.41 Big-end split obliquely

The bolts or studs used are of high-tensile steel. When bolts are used that are located in the connecting rod, the bolt heads are specially formed to prevent them rotating while the nuts are being tightened. Note that the nuts are usually self-locking or they can be locked by using split-pins, tab-washers, or some other arrangement.

Wherever possible, the split at the big-end is made at right-angles to the length of the connecting rod (Figure 2.40), as this gives the best combination of tightness and strength. The piston and connecting rod are usually assembled together and this assembly is then placed in position in the engine, normally by passing the connecting rod through the cylinder from the top end, or alternatively entering the piston into the cylinder from the lower end (crankshaft end). The removal of the piston and connecting rod assembly is made in the reverse way.

If the crankshaft is already in position it is usually impossible to get the piston past the crankshaft, especially if the shaft has balance weights. Although it would be quite practicable for the engine manufacturer to insert the pistons and connecting rods before fitting the crankshaft into its bearings, it is often necessary during repair work to remove one or more pistons; if the crankshaft also had to be removed just for this, a great deal of extra work would be needed.

On many modern high-speed engines the size of the crankpins required to give the crankshaft the necessary stiffness makes the big-end so large that it is impossible for the connecting rod to be assembled or withdrawn through the cylinder if the big-end is split at right angles to its length. In such cases, the difficulty is overcome by splitting the connecting rod at an oblique angle (see Figure 2.41).

At high engine speeds large inertia forces act on the piston and impose loads on the connecting rod particularly when the piston changes direction of travel. This causes tensile stress when the piston has reached TDC and compressive stress around BDC. When the big-end is split perpendicularly (Figure 2.40), the inertia forces around TDC impose high tensile loads on the big-end bolts. On the other hand, when the rod is split obliquely (Figure 2.41), the forces also tend to slide the cap sideways across the rod, and impose heavy shearing loads in addition to the tensile loads on the screws securing the cap. To relieve the screws of these shearing loads the joint faces of the rod and cap have steps machined in them (see Figure 2.41). Alternatively the joint faces may be doweled or serrated.

Big-end bearing

To provide a suitable bearing surface for the connecting rod to run on the steel crankpin, the inside surface of the big-end eye is lined with a thin coating of a special bearing metal. It is, however, normal practice to use a separate bearing shell (which is also made in two parts). The shell fits inside the big-end eye and its surface has the special bearing coating, which will then contact the crankpin. The bearing and material is described in Chapter 8.

2.6.3 Small-end

The construction of the small-end of the connecting rod varies according to the method of securing the gudgeon pin (refer to section 2.7), which may either be fixed in the small end (semi-floating) or free to move (fully-floating). In the latter case a solid-eye small-end is used, and this is generally lined by a bronze bush which is pressed in. A bushed, solid-eye small-end is shown in Figure 2.42.

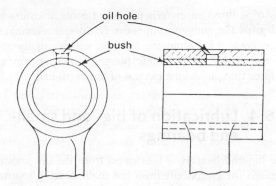

Figure 2.42 Connecting rod small-end for fully-floating gudgeon pin

If the gudgeon pin is fixed in the small-end it is usually done in one of two ways as illustrated in Figure 2.43. The screw is arranged so that a small groove must be made in the surface of the gudgeon pin to allow the screw to be fitted. This provides positive endwise location of the pin independently of the clamping action of the screw, besides ensuring correct assembly.

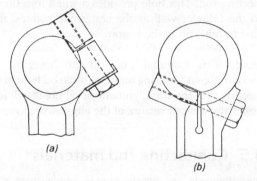

Figure 2.43 Method of clamping a gudgeon pin in a small-end

The screw is locked after tightening by some method such as the tab-washer as illustrated in Figure 2.43a.

An alternative method of securing the semi-floating gudgeon pin is by making the pin an interference fit in the un-bushed solid-eye of the connecting rod small-end. Assembly is usually carried out by either pressing the pin from the piston using a suitable press and specialized tools (Figure 2.44), or by heating the small-end of the rod, which causes it to expand and allows the gudgeon

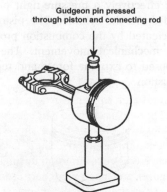

Gudgeon pin pressed through piston and connecting rod

Figure 2.44 Adaptors used for pressing out a gudgeon pin

pin to be fitted easily. When the rod cools, it contracts and grips the gudgeon pin securely. Special techniques are necessary for removing the pin, which usually rely on mechanical or hydraulic presses which act on an adaptor that pushes the pin out of the small-end.

2.6.4 Lubrication of big- and small-end bearings

The big-end bearing is lubricated from the oil passing through the crankshaft from the main bearing journal through to the big-end bearing journal.

If the small-end is of the semi- or fully-floating design, an oil hole is normally drilled through the centre of the connecting rod, from the top of the rod (small-end) to the big-end. The engine oil under pressure passes through to the connecting rod when the oil hole in the big-end of the crankshaft aligns with the hole in the connecting rod, therefore oil is only passed to the connecting rod once every crankshaft revolution. In some cases a second oil hole is drilled through the connecting rod. This hole provides a small injection of oil to the cylinder wall as the crankshaft rotates, thus helping to lubricating the piston.

Note: Whenever the crankshaft bearings are replaced, it is essential that the oil holes in the crankshaft big-end bearing align with the oil hole in the connecting rod; the misalignment of oil holes will lead to premature wear or seizure of the engine components.

2.6.5 Connecting rod materials

Connecting rods are nearly always made from steel forgings, accurately machined where necessary. In high-performance engines they are often machined all over

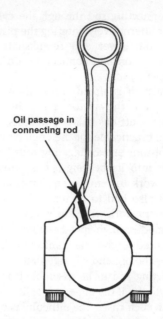

Oil passage in connecting rod

Figure 2.45 Oil passage in the connecting rod

to reduce weight to the minimum, and polished to remove surface scratches, which might lead to fatigue failure.

Some exotic and expensive alloys or steels are now used in high-performance and racing engines; these materials provide reduced weight with increased strength but at a high cost.

In a few cases where aluminium alloy is used for the connecting rods, although the main advantage is reduced weight, a further advantage is that aluminium is a good material for bearings, and aluminium rods can be used without any bush in the small-end.

2.7   PISTONS, PISTON RINGS AND GUDGEON PINS

2.7.1 The main features

The piston is effectively a pressure-tight plunger that slides up and down the cylinder. The piston converts the pressure created by the combustion process into a reciprocating mechanical movement. The piston is therefore exposed to extreme forces and temperatures during combustion.

Figure 2.46 Example of a typical piston

By connecting a reciprocating piston to a crankshaft with a connecting rod, the reciprocating movement is converted into rotational movement of the crankshaft.

Figure 2.47 shows the main features of a piston. The crown forms the upper surface on which the combustion pressure acts. The force created due to combustion is equal to the cross-sectional area of the cylinder multiplied by the gas pressure. This force, which acts along the centre-line of the cylinder, is transmitted through the structure of the piston to the gudgeon pin bosses and thence through the gudgeon pin to the connecting rod.

During the greater part of the power stroke the connecting rod operates at an angle to the centre-line of the cylinder. This causes a side force to be applied by the piston to the cylinder wall (Figure 2.48). It is

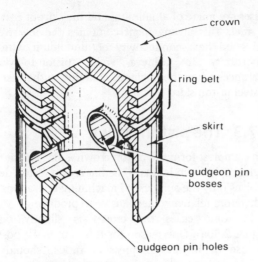

Figure 2.47 Main features of a piston

therefore necessary to provide bearing surfaces on the piston to carry this side force: these bearing surfaces are formed on the piston skirt.

To allow the piston to move freely in the cylinder, the piston must have a small clearance (Figure 2.49). Unfortunately, this clearance allows gas to leak from the combustion chamber past the piston. Because the greatest leakage occurs when pressures are highest and the gas is hottest (combustion and power strokes), much of the oil film lubricating the piston will be burnt away or carbonized. After combustion, the gases contain water vapour, carbon dioxide and probably small amounts of sulphur dioxide, which can contaminate the lubricating oil and lead to corrosion of the engine parts.

To reduce the leakage as much as possible, piston rings are fitted into grooves formed on the piston just below the crown. The rings are usually made of selected steel materials and they have a characteristic similar to springs, i.e. the rings will tend to expand out so that they closely contact the cylinder wall (refer to section 2.7.5).

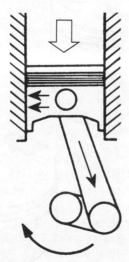

Figure 2.48 Side-thrust of piston caused by the angle of the connecting rod

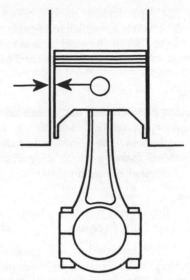

Figure 2.49 Clearance between the piston and the cylinder

The crown of the piston is directly exposed to the extreme temperature of the burning gases during combustion. These gases remain extremely hot during the power and exhaust strokes. The piston absorbs a great deal of heat from these hot gases and will reach a very high temperature unless heat is removed from the piston quickly enough to keep its temperature within reasonable limits. The piston can pass this heat on to the cylinder walls through the piston rings and skirt, and it can do this better if the material from which the piston is made is a good conductor of heat.

Most metals expand with a rise in temperature, and since the piston gets hotter than the cylinder (which can be cooled more effectively), under running conditions the piston will expand by a greater amount and the clearance between cylinder wall and piston will become smaller as the engine parts heat up. Therefore the clearance allowed when the engine is assembled must be large enough to allow for the decrease in clearance that occurs at running temperature, and the material used for the piston should preferably have a low coefficient of thermal expansion.

However, large clearances, especially when the engine is cold, allow excessive side-to-side movement of the piston. This movement is usually at its greatest when the crankpin passes the top and bottom dead centres (when the connecting-rod angle changes), and this causes a noise called piston slap, which is objectionable and can result in premature wear of the piston and cylinder wall.

2.7.2 Materials

Early engines had pistons made of cast iron. Cast iron has good strength and hardness at operating temperatures and forms a good bearing surface against the cylinder wall. However, cast iron is relatively heavy, rather brittle and liable to develop cracks. Additionally, cast iron is not a particularly good conductor of heat. However, cast iron has a coefficient of expansion which is comparable to that of the steel or iron cylinder thus allowing quite small clearances to be used between the piston and cylinder.

Aluminium

In its pure state aluminium has a high coefficient of thermal expansion, is relatively soft and low in strength. The addition of about 12% silicon and small quantities of other elements makes a strong alloy that has a low coefficient of thermal expansion.

Advantages

The main advantages resulting from the use of aluminium alloys for pistons are:

1   Improved thermal conductivity (passes the heat away quickly), which makes for lower piston crown temperatures. The lower piston crown temperature reduces the heating of the fresh mixture during the induction stroke, which results in a fresh mixture that is cooler and denser, leading to improved engine power output.
2   Reduced mass of the piston due to the lower density of aluminium, thus permitting the engine to run at a higher speed and develop more power.
3   Because of its lower melting point it can be cast in steel moulds or dies. This gives greater accuracy of casting and reduced production costs if the pistons are made in large numbers.
4   Aluminium alloys are usually softer than cast iron and are easier to machine.

Disadvantages

The main disadvantages resulting from the use of aluminium alloys for pistons are:

1   Greater coefficient of thermal expansion. This necessitates the use of larger clearances when cold, resulting in piston slap. Piston slap can be minimized by special construction of the piston skirt and by the use of alloys which have a relatively low coefficient of expansion.
2   Aluminium is not as strong as cast iron, particularly at high temperatures. It is therefore necessary to use a greater thickness of material to avoid piston distortion under load. Although the thicker material is not ideal because it adds weight, the weight is still lower than a cast-iron piston.
3   Aluminium is also softer than cast iron, especially at high temperatures; this may lead to excessive wear of the ring grooves. Improved alloys have been developed and in some cases other methods have been adopted to overcome this difficulty.
4   Aluminium is more expensive than cast iron, though this is to some extent offset by its greater ease of casting and machining.

Some pistons have been produced with a 'composite construction'. The composite pistons resulted in a two-piece construction in which the crown and gudgeon pin

bosses are made of aluminium and the skirt of cast iron or steel. This arrangement combines the low weight and good heat conductivity of aluminium with the opportunity to achieve small piston-to-cylinder clearances when the engine is cold due to the cast iron or steel piston skirt.

2.7.3 The piston crown

In its simplest form the piston crown is flat and at right angles to the cylinder axis. The flat crown piston design involves only the simplest of machining operations and is therefore relatively inexpensive to produce.

In some cases the crown is slightly dished (Figure 2.50a). One reason for this is to make possible the use of higher compression ratios, should this become desirable, simply by reducing or eliminating the 'dish'. It is sometimes done to provide a particular form of combustion chamber. Certain designs of combustion chamber require the piston crown to be made a particular shape, such as the domed crown (Figure 2.50b).

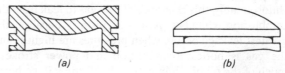

Figure 2.50 (a) Concave or dished piston crown
(b) Domed piston crown

Although these relatively simple piston crown designs have been used in many engines, modern engines usually have piston crowns that are more complex to enable improved combustion and emissions. Figure 2.51 shows more complex piston crown designs.

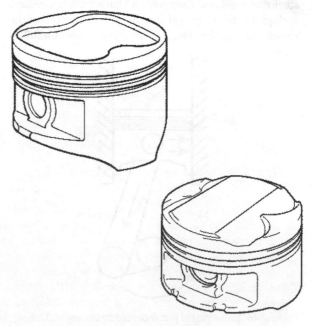

Figure 2.51 Complex piston crown designs

2.7.4 The ring belt

The ring belt is a series of grooves machined into the piston, into which are fitted the piston rings. It is most important that this part of the piston is accurately made. In particular, each ring groove should lie in a plane at right angles to the cylinder axis. The ring belt is generally given more clearance in the cylinder than the skirt and does not normally bear against the cylinder wall. The ridges, which separate the ring grooves, are called 'lands'.

There are usually three of these grooves above the skirt, and sometimes there is an additional ring groove in the skirt below the gudgeon pin.

2.7.5 Piston rings

Compression rings

It was mentioned earlier that the purpose of the piston rings is to prevent gas leakage through the clearance between piston and cylinder walls, but so as to also allow the piston to move freely up and down the cylinder.

The piston rings described in this particular section are fitted for the purpose of preventing gas leakage and are normally referred to as compression rings, pressure rings or gas rings. Two compression rings are generally fitted to a piston, located in the top two grooves. The compression rings also assist in transmitting the heat from the piston through to the cylinder walls.

Figure 2.52 shows the main features of a piston compression ring: it is generally rectangular in section. Its 'nominal diameter' is the diameter of the cylinder into which it is to fit.

Note: The nominal diameter is measured on the ring with the gap closed, using a steel tape that is passed around the ring and pulled tight.

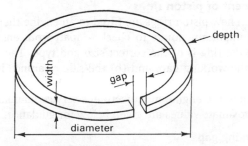

Figure 2.52 Piston ring dimensions

A radial cut is made in the ring so that it can be placed in position in the groove on the piston. When in position in the cylinder the gap between the ends of the ring, (called the working gap) needs to be large enough to ensure that the ends of the ring do not actually touch, however hot the ring may get. When out of the cylinder, because the ring material has a natural tendency to spring outwards, the actual diameter of the ring is larger than its nominal diameter. The gap (now called

the free gap) is also larger than the working gap. The free gap ensures that when in position in the cylinder, the ring will exert an outward pressure against the wall of the cylinder along its whole circumference.

Figure 2.53 shows a section of the ring in position in its groove and filling the clearance between the cylinder wall and piston. The depth of the ring should be slightly less than the depth of the groove, to ensure that side forces acting on the piston are transferred to the cylinder via the bearing surfaces on the skirt and not through the piston rings, and also to ensure that the clearance between the inner surface of the ring and the bottom of the ring groove is not less than the correct piston clearance.

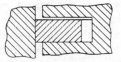

Figure 2.53 A plain rectangular-section piston ring

The width of the ring must also be slightly less than the width of the groove to ensure that the ring is perfectly free to move about in its groove. If the ring is too close a fit in its groove it is liable to become stuck due to the build-up of by carbonized oil, which will collect on the groove and the ring surfaces.

Figure 2.54 shows that rings are not always of a true rectangular cross-section and that they may be slightly modified, typically in one of three ways:

1 (Figure 2.54a). The outer surface of the ring is given a slight taper towards the top (about 1°). The purpose of this is to speed up the 'bedding-in' process when the ring is new.
2 (Figure 2.54b). The top inner corner of the ring is cut away, leaving the cross-section of the ring like a thick letter L. This serves the same purpose as the taper-faced ring.
3 (Figure 2.54c). The top outer corner of the ring is cut away. This ring should be used when new top rings are fitted to worn cylinders. The cut-away portion avoids contact with the ridge that develops at the upper limit of ring travel in a worn cylinder. Some manufacturers name this ring a 'ridge dodger'.

Many other compression ring designs exist that are in detail different to the standard rectangular ring. However, the basic function of these rings remains the same, i.e. to prevent gas leakage past the piston.

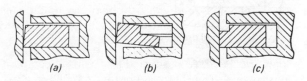

Figure 2.54 Special types of compression ring

Oil-control or scraper rings

The compression rings so far described are fitted to prevent the escape of gas through the clearance that exists between cylinder and piston.

Other types of piston rings are fitted, designed to control the oil film on the cylinder wall. They are designed to permit adequate lubrication of the piston against the cylinder wall, without excessive quantities of oil getting past the piston and into the combustion chamber. When oil enters the combustion chamber it would be decomposed and partly burnt, forming deposits of carbon on the combustion chamber walls and causing smoke and harmful emissions in the exhaust gas.

Special types of ring have been developed to prevent excessive oil passing the piston and entering the combustion chamber. These rings are intended to glide over the oil film as the piston moves upward, but to scrape off all but a very thin film of oil on the downward stroke, and are thus known as 'oil-control rings'.

Holes at the back of the ring groove can allow the oil collected by the scraper ring to return to the underneath of the piston. Alternatively, a chamfer is machined onto the lower edge of the ring groove and the drain hole is placed at the chamfer. The combination of the chamfer and the shape of the ring (Figure 2.55) causes the oil to collect at the chamfer and then pass through the drain holes.

Figure 2.55 shows sections of several types of oil-control rings and their grooves. The bevelled scraper is the least severe in its action; the grooved type the most severe.

The proximity of the piston to the oil being discharged from the crankshaft bearings, combined with cylinder distortion, has demanded that a scraper ring exerts an outward pressure of approximately 3150 kPa (4501 lbf in^{-2}): this is about twenty times as great as the standard type of piston ring.

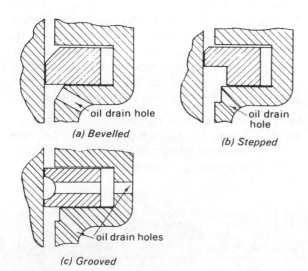

(a) Bevelled

(b) Stepped

(c) Grooved

Figure 2.55 Types of oil-control ring

Figure 2.56 shows a steel oil-control ring. It consists of two narrow steel rails separated from each other by a specially shaped spacer. Large outward pressure is obtained by fitting an expander spring behind the ring. To avoid incorrect assembly, some designs combine the various ring elements into one unit.

Figure 2.56 A steel oil-control ring

Piston ring materials

The most important properties of the material used for piston rings are:

1. **Wear resistance** – especially in the case of the compression rings which operate with limited lubrication.
2. **Elasticity** – to ensure that the ring will maintain sufficient outward pressure against the cylinder wall and maintain contact with the surface of the cylinder.
3. **Temperature tolerance** – the temperatures to which the ring is subjected to in use must not adversely affect the above properties.

The material, which most nearly fulfils these requirements is cast iron. In some cases the wear resistance is improved by chromium-plating the outer face of the ring using a special process or adding another substance to the cast iron such as nickel to form an alloy. In some oil-control rings, the material used is steel, generally chromium-plated on the edges which bear upon the cylinder wall.

Fitment of piston rings

When new piston rings are fitted to an engine there are two important points to check – apart from ensuring that the ring is of the correct size and type. These are (a) the working gap, and (b) the side clearance in the ring groove. The correct figures for these are usually given in the engine manufacturer's service manual, but approximate values are given below for guidance.

Working gap

Water-cooled engines 0.003 × bore diameter
Air-cooled engines 0.004 × bore diameter

Side clearance in groove

0.04 mm (0.0015 in)

For example, a ring fitted to a water-cooled engine of bore 82 mm could have a gap clearance of 0.246 mm.

Measurement of working gap

This gap is measured by putting the piston ring, removed from the piston, into its cylinder and 'squaring it up' by pushing it up against the end of the piston, also placed inside the cylinder. The gap between the ends of the ring is then measured using feeler gauges. If the cylinder is worn, the ring should be in the least worn part of the bore when this measurement is made. Too small a gap can be rectified by carefully filing or grinding one end of the ring, preferably in a special jig which ensures squareness of the ring ends.

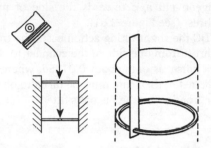

Figure 2.57 Measuring the working gap

2.7.6 Gudgeon pins and pin bosses

Gudgeon pin bosses
The gudgeon pin bosses are normally formed as part of the piston casting or forging. The bosses must be designed and formed in such a way that they can withstand the loads transmitted from the piston crown (due to combustion pressure) through to the gudgeon pin without any possibility of the piston distorting. Additional loads created when the piston changes direction at TDC and BDC are also transmitted through the gudgeon pin bosses. The bosses are usually formed with substantial struts or thick webs to improve their strength.

It is important that the gudgeon pin holes are bored accurately and with an extremely fine surface finish.

Gudgeon pins
There are two main types of gudgeon pin depending upon the method of locating them in position in the connecting rod small-end and in the piston. To provide the strength necessary to carry the high loads imposed upon them by gas pressure on the piston, and a wear-resistant surface, they are made of steel, usually alloyed with 3–4% of nickel to increase toughness, and then case-hardened to obtain a wear-resistant surface. Clearly, the ends of the hardened pin must be prevented from rubbing against the cylinder wall – otherwise it would soon score deep grooves in the cylinder surface. Gudgeon pins are usually made tubular to reduce weight.

The two types of gudgeon pin used are:

1 **Semi-floating** (Figure 2.58). These are securely fixed in either the piston or the connecting rod. Although it was at one time common practice to fix the gudgeon pin in the piston by means of a screw threaded into one of the gudgeon pin bosses, this

practice has been discarded in favour of fixing the pin in the connecting rod.

Alternatively the gudgeon pin may be an interference or press fit within the connecting rod small-end. Movement is therefore confined to oscillation of the pin in the piston.

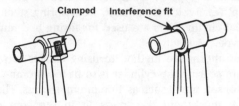

Figure 2.58 Semi-floating gudgeon pin

2 **Fully-floating** (Figure 2.59). This type of gudgeon pin is free to turn in both piston and connecting rod, and is generally used in modern engines in which the loads are particularly high. The pin is shorter than the cylinder diameter and is normally prevented from contacting the cylinder by the fitment of circlips at either end of the piston, as illustrated in Figure 2.59.

Figure 2.59 Fully-floating gudgeon pin and snap rings (circlip retaining rings)

Figure 2.60 shows two different types of circlip. The method shown in (a) consists of a spring-steel ring, which is sprung into a groove inside the piston hole after the gudgeon pin has been fitted.

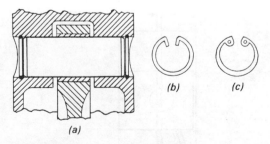

Figure 2.60 Location of gudgeon pin by circlips

The circlip is sometimes made of round-section steel wire and may have its ends bent inwards as shown in (b) to make it easier to fit and remove with pointed-nose pliers.

Some circlips do not have the bent-in ends; in this case the ends of the gudgeon pin are slightly chamfered as shown at (a) (this helps to prevent the circlip being forced out of its groove by endwise forces), and small notches are cut in the piston so that a pointed instrument can be inserted behind the circlip to remove it.

Another type of circlip often used is the 'Seeger circlip' (c), which is stamped from spring steel sheet. Special circlip pliers are used for fitting and removing this type.

An alternative method to using circlips to prevent the pin scoring the cylinder is to fit mushroom-shaped pads of soft metal such as aluminium or brass. The stem of the mushroom is a press fit in the bore of the gudgeon pin. This method is seldom used in modern engines.

Gudgeon pin fit

The gudgeon pin is usually made a tight push-fit in the piston when cold; this eases off slightly when the piston reaches normal running temperature. You must not use force to remove a tightly fitting pin unless you do it very carefully, and great care must be taken to ensure that no force whatever is applied to the connecting rod, to avoid the risk of bending it. If possible, heat the piston in hot water or oil; if the piston cannot be immersed in oil or water, you can wrap rags soaked in hot water round the piston, after which the gudgeon pin can be pushed out easily without risk of damage.

Offset gudgeon pins

The skirt clearance needed for a solid-skirt alloy piston has increased the occurrence of piston slap when the engine is cold. This noise can be reduced by offsetting the gudgeon pin axis towards the side of maximum piston thrust (see Figure 2.61).

At TDC the slight tilting action eases the transfer of piston thrust from one side of the cylinder to the other. Since the offset is only about $0.0125d$, where d is the piston diameter, then care must be taken to observe the marking 'front' when the piston is fitted.

2.7.7 The skirt

The simplest form of this is illustrated in Figure 2.47. Here the skirt forms a downward tubular extension below the ring belt. This arrangement is called a 'solid skirt'. It is the strongest form of skirt and is often used for engines where the loads on the piston are particularly great.

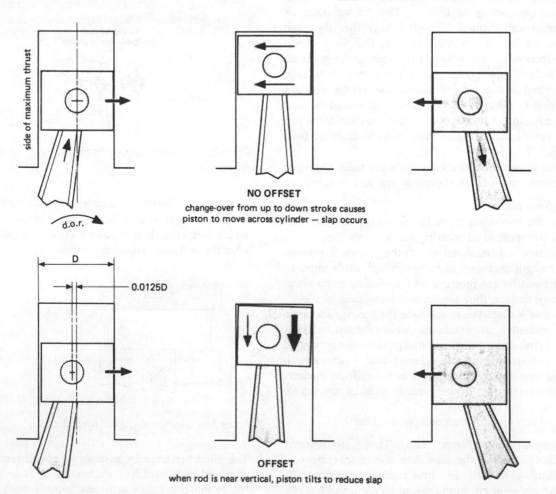

Figure 2.61 Effect of an offset of gudgeon pin

To permit the use of small clearances with aluminium alloy pistons when cold, special types of skirt construction are used which involve some degree of flexibility of the skirt. For example, the skirt may be almost completely separated from the ring belt, except at the gudgeon pin bosses, and split down one side (Figure 2.62). This allows it to fit in the cylinder with very little clearance when cold; expansion of the skirt due to the rise in temperature is taken up by the split, which gets smaller as the skirt expands. The split usually extends the full length of the skirt and is at a slight angle, to avoid leaving a wear ridge on the cylinder.

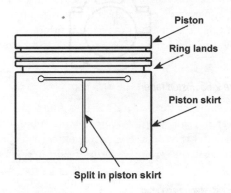

Figure 2.62 A split skirt piston

When assembling split skirt pistons onto the connecting rod it is important that the side of the piston without the split in the skirt (the stronger side of the piston) is bearing against the cylinder wall during the power stroke. This is because the thrust against the piston is highest during the power stroke and requires the strongest part of the skirt to take these high loads.

The high piston load of a modern engine has meant that the split skirt has been superseded by low expansion, solid skirt pistons such as the thermal slot or link strut types.

Thermal slot piston

Cutting a lateral thermal slot (Figure 2.63) at the bottom of the ring groove on the thrust and non-thrust sides of the piston directs the heat from the hot (250°C) piston crown to the gudgeon pin boss regions. In some designs these slots are extended axially downwards into the skirt and terminate with a circular hole (Figure 2.62). Thermal expansion of the crown and bosses, combined with the effect of the gas load, pulls in the thrust faces and allows the piston to be fitted with a small clearance. To compensate for this action the piston is oval when cold.

Link strut piston

Link strut pistons (Figure 2.63) have special alloy steel (Invar) plates cast into the skirt. This material has an extremely low coefficient of thermal expansion, so the resistance given by these plates limits the expansion of the skirt.

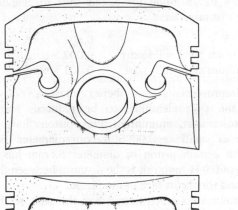

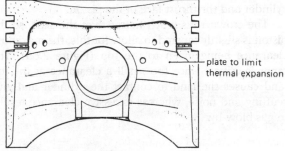

Figure 2.63 Thermal slot and link strut pistons

The piston skirt is forced against the cylinder wall during the power stroke due to the side thrust exerted on the piston. To prevent the piston skirt seizing against the cylinder wall a special finish is usually applied to the skirt referred to as a 'striation finish', which may make the skirt of the piston look as if it has been poorly finished (Figure 2.64). Some manufacturers may even apply to the piston skirt a thin coat of resin or a coating of iron and tin to reduce friction between the cylinder wall and the piston skirt.

Figure 2.64 Piston skirt surface finish

Piston clearance

The clearance left between the cylinder and piston when the engine is assembled will depend on the piston material, piston design and the operating temperature of the engine. Too small a clearance is likely to cause seizure, whereas excessive clearance results in gas blow-by, noise and high oil consumption.

For a particular engine the manufacturer's manual should be consulted to obtain the actual clearances. In the past, a rough guide for piston skirt to cylinder clearance was taken as:

Cast iron	$0.001 \times$ bore
Aluminium alloy, solid skirt	$0.002 \times$ bore
Aluminium alloy, split skirt	$0.001 \times$ bore

Design improvements and better materials have allowed the skirt clearance to be reduced. Many modern solid skirt, aluminium alloy pistons have a clearance as small as $0.0005 \times$ bore diameter. For example, a certain piston of diameter 82 mm has a clearance of 0.041 mm; this is the distance between the cylinder and the thrust face of the piston.

The crown runs much hotter than the skirt, so the piston is slightly tapered to allow for this, the maximum clearance being given to the top (Figure 2.65). The taper is critical since too small a clearance at the top land causes the land to contact the cylinder and give scuffing and noise, whereas excessive clearance results in gas blow-by.

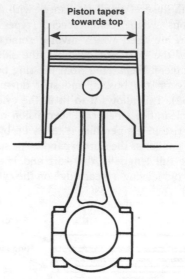

Figure 2.65 Piston taper

2.8 INTAKE, EXHAUST VALVES AND VALVE SPRINGS

2.8.1 The function of valves

It has been previously described that air or air/fuel mixtures enter the cylinder via the intake ports and after combustion the burnt gases exit through the exhaust ports. However, the intake and exhaust ports must only be open for the period when the intake air or mixture is being drawn in (intake port) or when the exhaust gases are being expelled (exhaust port); at all other times, the port must be closed off. If the ports are not closed at other times, then the compression stroke, combustion and the power strokes cannot take place.

A valve is therefore fitted to each of the inlet and exhaust ports on a four-stroke engine; the valves open and close at appropriate times using some form of operating mechanism (usually mechanical). Note that two-stroke engines also have ports that are opened and closed, although for the simplest two-stroke engines, this is often achieved by the position of the piston in the cylinder, which covers and uncovers the ports as the piston rises and falls.

The way valves operate is subject to the following important considerations. Valves must:

1 make a completely gas-tight seal in the ports when closed
2 offer the minimum of resistance to the flow of gases when open
3 require the simplest possible mechanism to operate them
4 operate with the minimum of friction
5 operate with minimum wear.

There are many other design requirements for valves that vary, depending on the type of engine to which they are fitted. Engine speed and temperature as well as the required power output of the engine are important factors in valve design. Together these factors influence the shape, material and number of valves used for each cylinder.

2.8.2 Types of valve

Although one particular type of valve, the poppet valve, is totally dominant on four-stroke engines, there have been a number of different types of valve that have been used with varying levels of success.

The following list covers the four main types of valve that have been used on internal-combustion engines.

1 **The poppet valve.** This was already in use on steam engines before successful internal-combustion engines were developed. It has proved so successful that its use has continued and it is almost the only type to be used in modern engines.
2 **The slide valve.** This too was very commonly used on some early internal-combustion engines, but proved less satisfactory than the poppet valve and is now obsolete.
3 **The sleeve valve.** Several versions of this type of valve have been used. The two most successful were the Knight and the Burt–McCullum.
The Knight-type valve originated in about 1905 and consisted of a sleeve free to slide inside the cylinder

with a second sleeve free to slide inside it, the piston moving within the inner sleeve. The sleeves were moved up and down inside the cylinder, and ports cut in the sleeves were arranged to uncover the cylinder ports at the correct times.

This valve was used by the Daimler Company from about 1909 until about 1933: it was also used by a number of continental manufacturers such as Panhard, Minerva, Voisin, Peugeot and on a few Mercedes models.

The Burt–McCullum sleeve valve consisted of a single sleeve which was given a combination of up-and-down motion and part-rotary motion inside the cylinder, ports in the sleeve uncovering the cylinder ports at the appropriate times. It was developed in about 1909 and was first used in the Argyll car in 1911. It has also been used in a few other cars, but its greatest success has been in aircraft engines, chiefly the large engines made by the Bristol Aeroplane Co. beginning about 1935. It was also used in the famous Napier 'Sabre' engine, a twenty-four-cylinder engine developing about 3500 hp, and in the last of the Rolls-Royce piston-type aero-engines, the 'Eagle', also a twenty-four-cylinder engine developing over 3000 hp.

Although these types of valve seemed to have many advantages over the cruder poppet valve they have not survived in motor-vehicle engines. Their main drawback was relatively high oil consumption and a smoky exhaust allied to complex operating mechanisms.

4 **The rotary valve.** Several types of rotary valve have been developed and some have given very good results. They consist of rotating 'plugs' fitted across the ports, having holes, which at the correct times, uncover the ports and allow gas to pass.

Note that the only type of valve at present in common use in four-stroke motor vehicle engines is the poppet valve and this is the only type which is described here in detail.

2.8.3 The poppet valve

Figure 2.66 shows the installation of poppet valves on a modern engine. A poppet valve, with its immediate attachments, is shown in Figure 2.67. The valve itself consists of a disc-shaped head having a stem extending from its centre.

The edge of the head on the side nearest the stem is accurately ground at an angle of typically 45° to form the face but sometimes other angles (e.g. 30°) are used.

When the valve is closed, the face is pressed into contact with a similarly ground seating at the inner end of the port. Beyond the seating the port curves smoothly away clear of the valve.

The condition of the face and seating is of vital importance in ensuring the gas-tight seal between the valve and the valve seat. The valve face and the valve

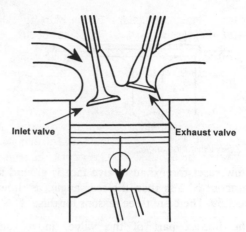

Figure 2.66 Example of poppet valves with the intake valve open

seat are ground on special machines, and each valve face is sometimes lapped into the valve seat with a very fine abrasive. Whether this is necessary or even advisable if the grinding is sufficiently accurate is often in dispute but lapping the valve into the valve seat has been common practice for many years, especially when overhauling engines.

After a considerable period of use, it is possible that the condition of the valve face and seating will have deteriorated and may allow gas leakage; this would then dictate that the valve and seat are reground or lapped together. Special grinding machines have been developed for this purpose although it should be noted that there are some valve designs and materials in use which should not be subjected to re-grinding, and then component replacement is the only permissible option.

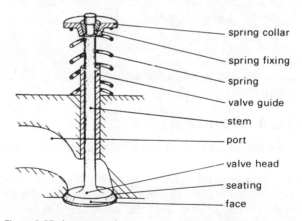

Figure 2.67 A poppet valve

Figure 2.68 shows the face and seating in more detail. The seating is narrower than the face, to reduce the risk of trapping particles of carbon between face and seating, and to ensure a surface contact pressure great enough to provide a gas-tight seal. The thickness of the head indicated by the arrows is most important: a sharp edge, particularly in the case of the exhaust valve, is liable to become excessively hot and may cause pre-ignition (ignition of the mixture inside the cylinder before the spark occurs).

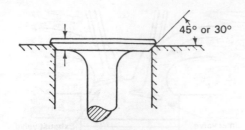

Figure 2.68 Valve face angles

In a few cases the exhaust valve face is ground to an angle about ½° less than the seat angle, as shown in Figure 2.69. There are three reasons for this:

1 The hottest part of the valve under running conditions is the stem side of the head, and the additional expansion on this side makes the face and seat angles equal at running temperatures.

2 The exhaust valve gets very hot (often red hot when the engine is running at full throttle) and is then less strong. Under these conditions the load applied by the valve spring (used to close the valve) tends to cause the head to dish slightly, which can lift the inner edge of the face (nearest the combustion chamber) clear of the seating if the angles are the same when cold.

3 It reduces the risk of trapping carbon between face and seating. In this case the face and seating cannot be lapped in.

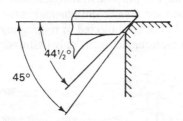

Figure 2.69 Valve face angle different from seat angle (exaggerated)

2.8.4 Valve seats

The valve seat has to be made of a material that can withstand the impact of the closing valve, will not wear or corrode and can withstand the operating temperatures during engine operation. If the cylinder head is made of cast iron, the valve seat can be cut directly into the cast iron.

If the cylinder head is made of a softer material such as an alloy, the valve seat has to be hardened to ensure that it can withstand the engine operating conditions. A valve seat insert is therefore usually fitted to an alloy cylinder head to ensure that the seat will not wear too quickly. These inserts are normally an interference fit with the cylinder head although other processes have been used such as screwing the insert into the cylinder head. The fitting of inserts requires a special process of either heating the cylinder head or lowering the temperature of the valve seat to an extreme

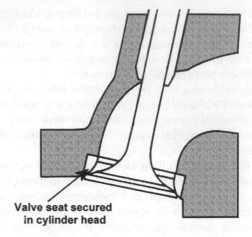

Figure 2.70 A valve seat insert

temperature and then pressing it into the cylinder head's aperture.

2.8.5 Valve guide

The valve slides in a hole in the cylinder or cylinder head called the 'valve guide'. The guide must be perfectly true with the seating, and a small operating clearance is allowed between the valve stem and the guide. The clearance allows lubrication of the valve guide and prevents any possibility of the valve sticking in the guide. Excessive clearance may lead to the valve seating being worn oval, and in the case of the inlet valve, it can allow additional air as well as oil to leak into the mixture entering the cylinder.

The guide is usually made in the form of a detachable sleeve to permit easy renewal when worn, but in some cases (typical of cast iron cylinder heads) the guide can be machined into the head casting (integral), which assists the transfer of heat from the hot exhaust valve to the cooling system. In this case, wear is rectified by boring or reaming out the guide slightly and fitting a valve with an oversize stem.

It is normal practice to fit valve guide oil seals to the intake valve guides (refer to Figure 2.71). The seals prevent excess oil passing between the valve stem and

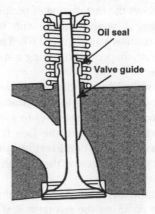

Figure 2.71 Valve guide fitted with an oil seal

valve guide, which could occur on the intake stroke due to the vacuum in the intake port which could draw in oil. Oil entering the engine would then burn during combustion causing blue smoke from the exhaust and unwanted exhaust emissions. Seals can be fitted to the exhaust valve guides but this is not generally common practice; because of the exhaust stroke there will be a higher pressure inside the chamber as opposed to a vacuum. The higher pressure will not permit oil to pass down the guide into the port and cylinder.

When the guides are detachable they sometimes have a shoulder formed on them (Figure 2.72a). The guides are interference fit in the cylinder head and are pressed into the head until the shoulder is firmly seated onto the head casting. Guides without shoulders are easier and cheaper to make; when fitting these types of guide, a portion of the guide protrudes from the cylinder head (Figure 2.72b). The length of the protrusion will usually be indicated by the vehicle manufacturer's information.

The protrusion allows for a longer guide to be produced, which helps to ensure that the valve operates correctly and seats properly onto the valve seat. Therefore, it is also normal to see a protrusion even on integral valve guides (Figure 2.72c).

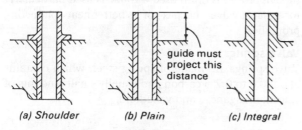

Figure 2.72 Types of valve guide

2.8.6 The valve spring

The spring rapidly returns the valve to its seat after it has been opened, and then holds it closed (assisted by gas pressure during the compression and power strokes) until the valve is next opened.

The spring must be strong enough to close the valve quickly at maximum engine speeds. The spring strength needed depends upon the weight of the valve and any other part of the valve assembly that moves with the valve (the greater the weight, the stronger the spring required).

The maximum engine speed and typical operating speeds also influence the strength required for the valve spring. Design of valve operating mechanisms used to open the valves will also affect the valve spring design and spring strength.

If the force exerted by the spring is insufficient the valve will be late in closing at high rev/min and so limit maximum engine speeds.

Valve springs are usually of the helical coil type, as shown in Figure 2.73, with a typical installation shown in 2.74.

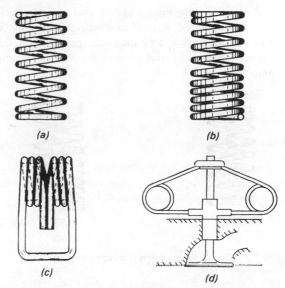

Figure 2.73 Types of valve spring

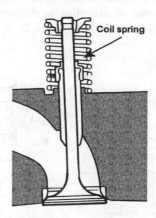

Figure 2.74 Typical installation of a helical (coil) valve spring

Another type of spring occasionally used is the hairpin spring shown in Figures 2.73c and 2.73d. Hairpin springs are liable to surge (as described below), and are more difficult to fit into the space available and are therefore not commonly used.

Helical or coil springs are liable to 'surging' at certain engine speeds, when the centre coils vibrate in a direction parallel to the valve stem. In extreme cases this can lead to breakage of the springs, and can also allow the valves to bounce off their seating after closing. This may be overcome in several ways:

1 The springs are designed so that, when the valve is fully open, they are compressed until adjacent coils almost touch, so preventing the building up of excessive surging.
2 The coils are spaced closer together at one end than the other (Figure 2.73b). Springs of this kind must be fitted with the 'close' coils nearest the cylinder head.
3 Two (or occasionally three) springs are used, one inside the other (refer to Figure 2.75). This does not prevent surging, but the two springs will not both

surge at the same engine speed, and 'valve bounce' will be prevented. Also, if one spring should break, the second spring will maintain pressure on the spring attachment and prevent the valve dropping into the cylinder.

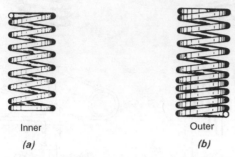

Inner   Outer

(a)   *(b)*

Figure 2.75 Double valve springs (shown separated)

Valve spring fixing
Several different methods have been used to attach the spring to the end of the valve stem. Some commonly used methods are shown in Figure 2.76.

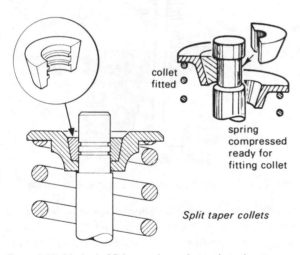

collet fitted

spring compressed ready for fitting collet

Split taper collets

Figure 2.76 Method of fixing a valve spring to the valve stem

2.8.7 Valve materials

Exhaust valve
The exhaust valve head is exposed to the full heat of the burning gas during combustion, and when the hot gases are released from the cylinder they sweep past the exhaust valve head. The exhaust valve is the hottest part of the engine, and it is estimated that under full power conditions it reaches a temperature of around 700°C. A special high-tensile steel is required for the exhaust valve to operate satisfactorily for long periods; alloys have been developed for this purpose containing varying amounts of manganese, silicon, nickel and chromium.

The exhaust valve is cooled by passing on the heat in two directions:

1 Along the stem and through the guide into the cylinder head.
2 Directly into the cylinder head from the face to the seating when the valve is closed. For extreme operating conditions the valve stem is sometimes made hollow and partly filled with sodium, which is a very soft metal having a melting point of 98°C. Under engine operating conditions the sodium becomes molten, and in splashing from end to end of the valve stem it assists the transfer of heat from the hot head. This is an expensive form of valve construction and is only used when absolutely necessary.

Some valves are coated with aluminium to improve the heat transfer from the valve to the seat and to also prevent corrosion to the valve seat. 'Aluminized valves' cannot be reground in the normal manner because the surface coating is comparatively thin.

Inlet valve
The inlet valve is also made of high-tensile alloy steel usually containing nickel, chromium and molybdenum.

Valve guides
Detachable valve guides are usually made of cast iron, though bronze is often used. Bronze is used particularly for exhaust valves, because of its better heat-conducting properties.

Valve springs
Valve springs are made of spring steel, which contains about 0.6 to 0.7% carbon and usually small amounts of silicon, manganese and vanadium.

2.8.8 Valve location

The position of the valve in the cylinder head depends upon the design of the combustion chamber which is discussed later in this chapter. It is sufficient for the present to list the possible positions of the valves:

1 **Side valve or L-head**
   Both valves are at one side of the cylinder; valve heads are uppermost with the stems approximately parallel to the cylinder axis. To accommodate the valves in this position the combustion chamber is extended sideways from the top of the cylinder forming a shape similar to an inverted letter L (Figure 2.77a). This arrangement is not used on modern engines.
2 **Side valve or T-head**
   This is similar to a standard side valve arrangement except that inlet and exhaust valves are fitted at opposite sides of the cylinder. This arrangement, though common on early engines, has been obsolete for many years.
3 **Vertical overhead valves**
   Both valves are fitted over the top of the cylinder (within the cylinder head) with their stems

approximately vertical and parallel (Figure 2.77b), usually in a single row.

4 **Overhead inlet and side exhaust or F-head**
The inlet valve is arranged as an overhead valve, and the exhaust as a side valve (Figure 2.77c). This arrangement is not used on modern engines.

5 **Inclined overhead valves**
Both valves are fitted over the top of the cylinder head, but in two rows inclined at an angle to one another (Figure 2.77d).

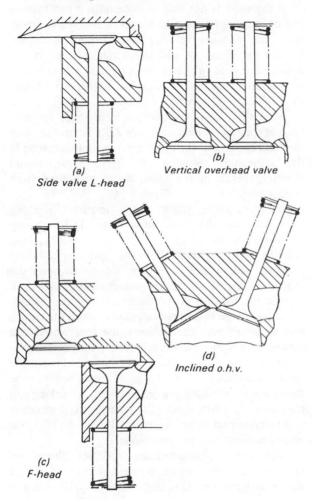

(a)
Side valve L-head

(b)
Vertical overhead valve

(c)
F-head

(d)
Inclined o.h.v.

Figure 2.77 *Valve locations*

2.8.9 Basic valve-opening mechanisms

It has already been explained that the valves are moved to the closed position and then held closed by the valve springs. However, opening of the valves is almost universally performed using a mechanism, which relies on a cam. Cams are carried upon one or more camshafts, which are driven (rotated) by suitable gearing (or drive mechanisms) from the crankshaft.

The cam is simply a device that has a high point and a low point. When the cam is rotated, the high point pushes the valve open.

The cams do not usually act directly on the valves since their rotary motion would impose a side force on the end of the valve stem. To combat this side force cam followers are interposed between the cam and the valve. These followers may take one of two forms:

1 Tappets or cam followers, which rest upon the cams and are guided so as to move in a straight line.
2 Rockers (or levers), which rock upon fixed pivots.

If the cams are placed close to the ends of the valves, no additional mechanism may be needed, but in the case of overhead valves this involves a long and possibly complicated driving gear between camshaft and crankshaft.

Older engines generally made use of a camshaft, which was located reasonably near the crankshaft (in the engine cylinder block), so that a short and simple driving gear could be used. In such cases the motion of the tappets was conveyed to the valves through pushrods and overhead rockers.

Most modern engines do in fact use overhead camshafts along with a longer or more complex mechanism to transfer the drive from the crankshaft to the overhead camshaft. The use of overhead camshafts is largely dictated by the need to provide accurate and positive valve control to assist with good combustion and low emissions. Valve locations on modern, highly efficient engines, are not easily operated with pushrod systems. Additionally, modern belts and chains are less expensive to produce and more reliable than in the past, and combined with operating performance of the overhead camshafts mechanisms, overhead camshaft systems are now preferable to pushrod systems.

Figure 2.78 *Typical camshaft appearance*

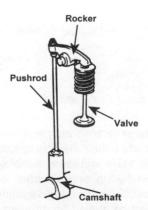

Figure 2.79 *Layout of a pushrod-operated overhead valve system with rocker shaft*

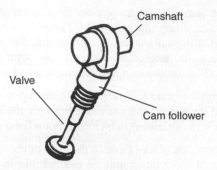

Figure 2.80 Layout of a direct-acting overhead camshaft system (the cam acts directly on the follower, which in turns acts on the valve stem)

Valve clearance

A valve is closed when its face is pressed into contact with the seating by the full force of the valve spring.

Figure 2.81 shows a simplified arrangement of valve, tappet (cam follower) and cam, and in (a) the valve is shown in the fully open position. As the cam rotates, the valve is then forced to close due to the action of its spring (not shown). At (b) a condition is shown in which the tappet/cam follower has reached the base of the cam before the face of the valve has come into contact with the seating. Since the tappet cannot move upwards any further the valve cannot completely close.

At (c) the tappet is shown in the same position on the cam, but the valve face has reached the seating before the tappet has reached the base of the cam, leaving a gap or clearance between the end of the valve and the tappet. This is called 'valve clearance' or 'tappet clearance', and it is clear that in this case the tappet cannot prevent the valve from closing properly.

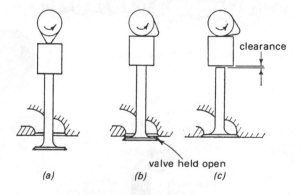

Figure 2.81 The need for valve clearance

There must always be a working clearance in the valve-operating gear when the valve is in its closed position to ensure that the valve will close completely. When the clearance is checked, allowance must be made for the fact that under different running conditions the amount of clearance will be altered by different temperatures. The valve, cylinder block, cylinder head and valve operating mechanism will all expand at different rates.

Depending on the design and type of valve actuation (e.g. pushrod system, overhead camshaft system etc.) the working clearance increases or decreases with changes in engine temperature and operating conditions. Additionally, wear of the valve face, cam and follower (and also the pushrod) will result in a change to the working clearance. If the clearance is too large, this will result in excessive noise and component wear. If the clearance is too small, the valve may not be able to close fully.

If the valve is not able to close fully, it can cause a loss of pressure in the cylinder and burnt valves (more often the exhaust valves). The burning is caused because one of the paths for the escape of heat is cut off if the valve does not close properly, and gas at a very high temperature will be forced at high speed through the gap between valve face and seating.

Note that on many overhead camshaft systems, such as the type shown in Figure 2.80, when the valve face and the end of the valve stem wear, this results in the clearance reducing. Excessive wear would therefore result in the valve being prevented from closing fully.

Another major effect of an incorrect working clearance is that the valve timing is altered (the opening and closing of the valve). Referring to Figure 2.80, if the working gap between the cam and the follower increases, when the cam then rotates towards the follower, the cam would not contact the follower until later in the rotation of the camshaft. This means that the valve would open later. Similarly, when the cam is moving away from the follower, the cam would lose contact with the follower much sooner, thus causing the valve to close sooner. Taken together this means the valve would not be open as long as would normally be the case if the working gap were correct. A working gap that is too tight would have the reverse effect. Incorrect valve timing and valve duration will have an effect on engine performance and emissions.

The engine manufacturer specifies the valve clearance and the engine conditions under which it should be measured (i.e. engine hot or cold) and it is most important that the clearance should be correct under the specified conditions.

On older designs of engine, valve operating systems usually have provision for adjusting the valve clearance during assembly and for maintenance. On some mechanisms this is achieved by the fitment of an adjusting screw. Other mechanisms make use of pre-sized shims or spacers which are inserted between the cam follower and the valve stem. In most cases, on systems where adjustment is possible, the clearance should be checked at specified intervals to ensure that it has not been altered by wear.

It is often assumed that valve clearance decreases as the engine becomes hotter, but this is by no means always the case. It is suggested that students should themselves check the valve clearances of a number of engines both hot and cold, and note the results.

Many modern engines now use a hydraulic cam follower mechanism, which automatically provides the correct clearance between the cam follower and the valve stem (refer to section 2.9.4).

Valve rotation
In order to keep the valve face and seat clean of carbon deposits or any other particles that may adhere to the surfaces while the valve is open, the valves on modern engines are made to rotate as they open and close. This also has the effect of slightly reducing wear marks that could occur in one position if the valve did not rotate.

The valves can be rotated using either of two methods:

1   The collets that retain the valve spring become loose when the valve is opened by the action on the camshaft or by a rotator that is fitted between the valve spring and the valve.
A rotator is fitted between the top of the valve and the valve spring. When pressure is applied to open the valve by the valve mechanism, the pressure also acts on the rotator and the valve rotates slightly.

Note that the greater the engine speed, the greater the speed of valve rotation.

2   A second method of rotating the valve is achieved on systems where the cam acts directly onto the follower. By slightly offsetting the cam and the cam follower, as the cam strikes the follower, it causes the follower to rotate slightly. Because the follower is acting on the top of the valve stem, this also causes the valve to rotate slightly as it opens.

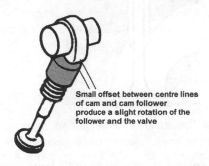

Small offset between centre lines of cam and cam follower produce a slight rotation of the follower and the valve

Figure 2.82 Method of rotating the valves

2.9 **VALVE OPERATING MECHANISMS**

2.9.1 Cams and camshafts

In section 2.8, it was highlighted that valves are used to open and close the intake and exhaust ports; also that most four-stroke engines rely on a cam system to open the valves (section 2.8.9). Cams and camshaft based systems have been used since the very earliest internal-combustion engines and have only really changed significantly in the method used to transfer the lift of the cam to the valve, and the way in which the camshaft is driven.

A cam is a component, which is shaped so that when it rotates on the shaft it causes another component (which is in contact with it) to move in a different manner. There are very many types of cams in use in all manner of machines but with regard to inlet and exhaust valves, the rotating cam causes the valve to move in a linear way, which enables the valve to open and close the ports.

The type of cam used to operate the valves of a motor-vehicle engine is a relatively simple one such as that illustrated in Figure 2.83.

As previously described in (section 2.8.9), the cam does not normally act directly on the end or stem of the valve; a cam follower (sometimes referred to as a tappet) follows the profile of the cam as it rotates (Figure 2.84). The follower then transmits the

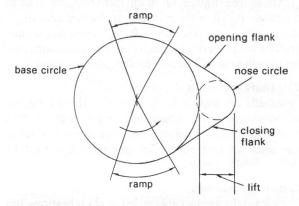

Figure 2.83 Details of cam

movement to the valve (either directly or via a pushrod or rocker mechanism).

The cam follower remains stationary during that part of the cam's rotation when it rests upon the base circle, and its 'lift' begins at the point where the opening flank joins the base circle. At the peak of the cam (highest point of the cam lobe) the lift is maximum, and the follower then falls as the closing flank passes beneath it. When the follower is again in contact with the base circle it will have returned to its original position.

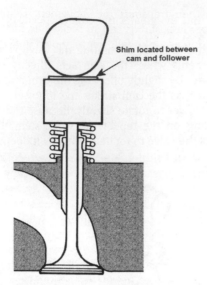

Figure 2.84 Cam acting onto a cam follower

In some engines there may be fairly large variations of clearance under different running temperatures. To ensure quiet operation, even when the clearances are large, the flanks are joined to the base circle by ramps, which extend over about 30° of cam rotation. When checking valve clearances it is most important that the cam follower should be resting on the base circle of the cam (refer to Figure 2.83). One way of ensuring this is to turn the engine to the position where the applicable valve is at full lift, and then turn the crankshaft one complete revolution.

On simple engines, all of the cams required to open the valves for all of the cylinders are formed on a single shaft called the camshaft. It is, however, normal practice on modern engines to use two camshafts; one for the inlet valves and one for the exhaust valves.

Camshaft materials
Camshafts are usually made of steel, either by forging or casting, with subsequent machining. Forged camshafts usually have the cams case-hardened, while the cams of cast shafts are generally hardened by chilling during casting.

Camshaft bearings
The camshafts are usually carried in plain bearings, but in some cases ball or roller bearings may be used. In many engines the shaft is moved into position from the front end of the engine (either into the cylinder block or cylinder head) and must therefore pass through the bearing holes. To enable this to be done the bearings must be larger than the cams.

2.9.2 Camshaft location

Side-valve engines
Earlier designs of engine located the camshaft in the cylinder block, often just to one side and slightly above the crankshaft. This location was very convenient on

older engines that had side valves; each of the cams was effectively located just beneath the valve stem and therefore only required a cam follower to transmit the cam movement to the valve stem (Figure 2.85).

The location of the camshaft, which was close to the crankshaft, allowed the use of a short chain and sprocket system to drive the camshaft, although some engines used gears to transmit drive.

Due to the inefficiency of side-valve engines, vehicle manufacturers no longer use this layout.

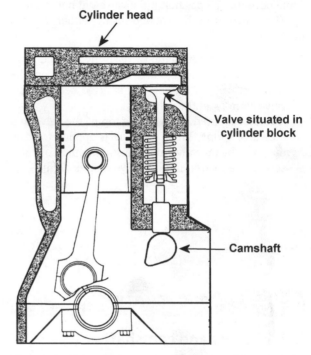

Figure 2.85 Side-valve layout showing location of the camshaft

Overhead-valve (OHV) engines with pushrods
To improve engine efficiency and allow greater power outputs, engine designs progressively made use of overhead-valve layouts, where the valves were located in the cylinder head. However, many overhead-valve engines were based on the original side-valve designs and therefore retained the camshaft in the cylinder block. It was therefore necessary to use a pushrod and rocker shaft system to transfer the movement of the cam to the valve (Figure 2.86).

Although the pushrod and rocker system added some complication to the valve-operating mechanism, the camshaft remained conveniently located in the cylinder block, which allowed the simple drive mechanism of the side-valve engines to be retained and allowed engine height to be kept to a minimum.

Overhead camshafts (OHC)
Further developments in engine design resulted in a trend towards overhead camshafts. The advantages include more accurate control of valve operation, especially at higher engine speeds, which could not be reliably achieved with the pushrod system.

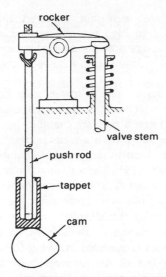

Figure 2.86 Simple overhead valve system using pushrods and rockers. The camshaft is located in the cylinder block

Many overhead camshaft designs retain the use of a rocker to transmit the cam movement to the valve, the cam usually acting directly onto the rocker, which in turn moves the valve. Many variations exist for overhead camshaft designs; Figure 2.87 shows a commonly used simple, overhead, camshaft system using a rocker.

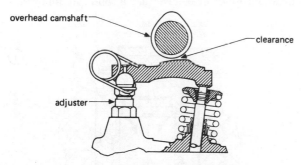

Figure 2.87 Simple overhead camshaft and rocker layout

2.9.3 Cam followers

Cam followers and tappets
The term 'tappets' has long been associated with the component that immediately contacts the cam, i.e. where the cam lobe taps the component to move it. On older engine designs (e.g. a side-valve engine) the term tappet was universally applied to these components, which often contained some form of adjuster to set the working clearance of the valve. In general, however, these components are now referred to as 'cam followers' on all engines, but reference is made to tappets within this book with regard to those components that were originally referred to as tappets.

The purpose of cam followers
As mentioned previously, cam followers are used to follow the movement of the cam as it rotates. The follower then transmits the movement to the valve, directly or via pushrods and/or rockers. In fact, a rocker can function as a cam follower as shown in Figure 2.87.

By using a cam follower, the stem of the valve is only forced to follow a linear (up and down) motion. If, however, the stem of the valve is in direct contact with the cam it is also forced *sideways* by the cam, which can result in the valve binding on the valve guide and accelerated wear of the valve stem and guide.

Overhead and side-valve tappets/cam followers
Figure 2.88a shows a type of tappet typically made of cast iron. The bottom surface that rubs against the cam would be chilled in the casting process to provide a hardened surface. These tappets, which sit in a machined bore, are hollow and may have 'windows' which help to reduce weight and assist lubrication. This type of tappet operates directly in the cylinder block and would be used in side-valve engines. The valve stem sits in the top of the adjuster, which is used to set the working clearance. Figure 2.88c shows a slightly different type of side-valve tappet.

Figure 2.88b illustrates a tappet/cam follower that is used in an OHV pushrod-type engine. The pushrod sits in the top of the follower and an adjuster forms part of the rocker. The location and construction are the same as for the side-valve type tappet.

Figure 2.88d shows a tappet or cam follower, which has a roller that makes contact with the cam lobe. This type of cam follower is no longer in common use but was in the past effective on lower speed engines.

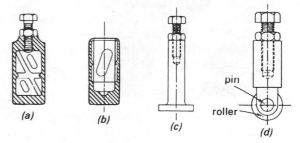

Figure 2.88 Types of tappet

Most tappets/cam followers used on pushrod or side-valve engines have a flat base, and are used with cams that have convex flanks. Some cams have straight flanks, and these operate on followers with curved ends.

Flat-based tappets are usually allowed to rotate in their guides; in fact the design promotes rotation because this reduces the rubbing speed between cam and tappet and spreads the wear over the whole of the tappet base. Rotation of the tappet is encouraged by offsetting the tappet from the centre-line of the cam or by grinding the cams with a very slight taper (about 1°) in which case the foot of the tappet is ground very slightly convex, forming part of a sphere of large radius.

Overhead camshaft type cam followers

For overhead camshaft engines where the cam is directly in line with (or above) the valve stem, the cam follower is located in a machined bore and sits between the cam and the valve stem. The followers are usually made of steel and arranged so that they sit over the valve and valve spring (Figure 2.89).

Traditionally, a pre-sized shim or spacer is inserted between the top of the valve stem and the internal face of the follower. The thickness of the shim selected during manufacture dictates the working gap. When wear occurs, which results in too large or too small a working gap, different thickness shims need to be inserted to obtain the correct working clearance. Note that some cam followers of this type included a tapered adjusting screw that screwed into the follower from the side and effectively replaced the shim. By adjusting the tapered screw, the working clearance could be altered.

Other types of overhead camshaft systems make use of rockers that act as cam followers. Figure 2.87 shows a typical example.

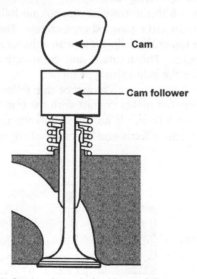

Figure 2.89 Overhead camshaft with cam follower

2.9.4 Hydraulic cam followers

It has been previously identified (section 2.8.9) that a working clearance is required to ensure that the valve can fully close and is not held slightly open by the cam. On the valve-operating systems examined so far, a means of manual adjustment is normally provided to enable the correct clearance to be obtained.

An automatic means of adjusting the clearance is achieved using 'hydraulic cam followers'. In fact this type of cam follower provides what is effectively a zero working clearance at all times and at all temperatures. The hydraulic follower allows the valve to fully close but does not then allow any additional clearance.

Hydraulic cam followers have been used for many years and have been fitted to pushrod operating systems and to overhead camshaft systems. Although

earlier designs were not favoured for high-speed engines, modern high revving sports and even some racing engines are now fitted with hydraulic followers.

A typical hydraulic cam follower is shown in Figure 2.90.

The hydraulic cam follower body (1) contains a plunger (2), which is formed into two chambers: a feed chamber (3) and a pressure chamber (4). Oil from the main engine lubrication system is passed to the feed chamber and then to the pressure chamber via a one-way ball valve (5). The oil flow from the pressure chamber is controlled by the amount of clearance between the follower body and the plunger. By accurately setting this clearance, a given amount of oil is allowed to escape up the side of the plunger each time the tappet is operated. A spring (6) tends to force the plunger out of the follower body and therefore eliminate any clearance that may exist, but although this spring reduces the valve clearance to zero, it does not have the strength to operate the engine valve.

Figure 2.91 shows the operation of the hydraulic follower.

When the cam rotates and begins to open the valve, (Figure 2.91a) oil in the pressure chamber is trapped, since the ball valve will not allow it to return to the feed chamber. As a result, the upward movement of the tappet body pressurizes the oil and causes the plunger to be moved a similar amount. During this stage the hydraulic follower behaves like a solid cam follower.

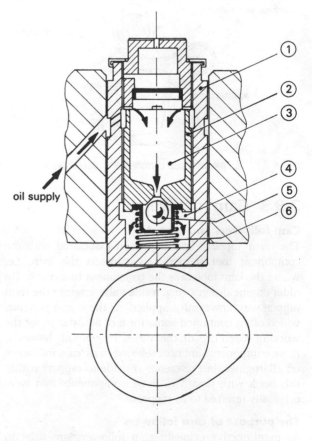

Figure 2.90 A hydraulic cam follower

Further rotation of the cam allows the valve to close (Figure 2.91b); the small leakage up the side of the plunger during the time that the oil was pressurized will mean that the pressure chamber requires more oil to make up for the oil loss. Additional oil is provided by allowing fresh oil from the feed chamber to pass the ball valve until the chamber is filled.

During engine warm-up the engine valve expands and this decreases the volume of oil in the pressure chamber needed to take up the clearance between the cam and the engine valve. This occurs over a period of time and is compensated for by the slight oil loss from the pressure chamber that occurs every time the tappet is operated. Consequently, zero valve clearance and correct seating of the valve is achieved irrespective of the temperature of the engine.

Figure 2.92 shows a hydraulic cam follower installed on an overhead camshaft and rocker system. The adjusting nut enables a base setting to be achieved for the zero clearance; once this is initially set, the hydraulic follower maintains the zero clearance. On direct acting overhead camshafts (without rockers), a hydraulic follower can directly replace the standard follower.

Slight oil loss from the hydraulic follower can occur when the engine is unused for a period of time and this can cause the followers to rattle for a short time after the engine is initially started. Although modern

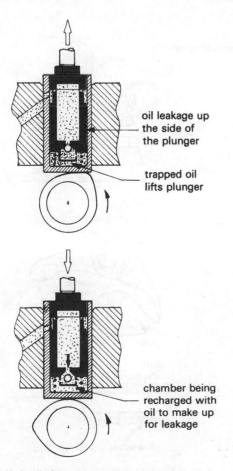

Figure 2.91 Hydraulic follower operation

- oil leakage up the side of the plunger
- trapped oil lifts plunger
- chamber being recharged with oil to make up for leakage

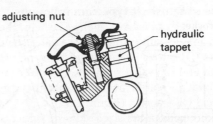

Figure 2.92 Overhead camshaft with hydraulic follower

- adjusting nut
- hydraulic tappet

hydraulic follower designs and modern oils have now virtually eliminated this problem, wear in the follower or incorrect oil can cause rattle. Engine oil that has not been changed at the specified intervals can also affect hydraulic follower operation.

2.9.5 Pushrods, rockers and overhead camshaft systems

Although the different methods of operating the valves have been identified in section 2.8 and within other parts of section 2.9, some additional details are worth covering related to the pushrod-based systems, the overhead camshaft systems and the use of rockers.

Pushrods and rockers

Many engines have been produced with overhead valves operated by a camshaft that is located in the cylinder block (crankcase), close to the crankshaft. This arrangement necessitates the use of pushrods to then transmit the motion from the cam followers or tappets from the cylinder block up to the valves (located in the cylinder head).

However, the positioning of the valves does not allow the pushrods to directly contact and move the valves; therefore, a rocker arm is used which is the link between the top of the pushrod and the valve.

A typical pushrod and rocker arrangement is shown in Figure 2.93a. This arrangement is suitable for overhead valve engines where all the valves are arranged in a line along the length of the cylinder head, with the valves set vertically (or almost vertically).

The rockers pivot on a common rocker spindle or shaft, which is supported by pillars attached to the cylinder head. The rockers are spaced apart on the spindle by distance pieces, or springs, or both. Each of the individual valve clearances can be adjusted by a hardened, ball-ended screw in the end of the rocker; the ball then fits into a small cup formed in the top end of the pushrod. The cup in the end of the pushrod retains oil to ensure lubrication at this point. The lower end of the pushrod is ball-ended and is located in a cup formed in the tappet.

For those overhead valve engines where the valves are arranged at angles or inclined, a different and more complex arrangement of pushrods and rockers is required (Figure 2.93b). For engines where the valves are inclined, it is usually preferred to use an overhead camshaft arrangement.

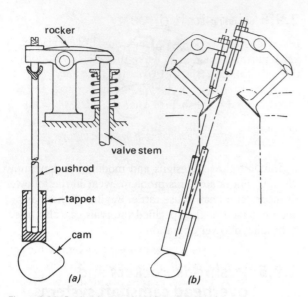

Figure 2.93 Pushrod operation of overhead valves

Rockers used to affect valve lift

The rocker system provides an opportunity for the designer to use a cam profile that has a relatively small amount of cam lift, which is then amplified by the rocker action to provide a larger movement at the valve. The rocker is used as a simple lever and by placing the pivot point of the rocker more towards one end of the rocker arm, instead of in the centre, a different leverage ratio can be obtained.

Figure 2.94 shows an exaggerated example of using the rocker arm leverage ratio to obtain a larger valve movement from a relatively small cam lift. Although such extremes of leverage would not be used on an engine, using a leverage ratio on the rocker allows designers to utilize softer or lower cam profiles that

may produce less noise and wear to the cam followers but still achieve the required valve movement.

Pushrod and rocker arm construction

The pushrod may be a solid steel rod, the two ends suitably 'formed' from the rod itself. Alternatively, the pushrod may be tubular, of either steel or aluminium alloy, with separate hardened steel ends pressed on.

The rocker is usually made from a steel forging, but is sometimes formed from a steel pressing, and some are made in a special type of cast steel.

Overhead camshafts and rockers

Rockers are sometimes used on overhead camshaft engines, and in these arrangements, the rocker also functions as a cam follower. Figure 2.95 shows two examples.

For the example shown in Figure 2.95a, the valve clearance can be adjusted using the screw at the pivot. The spring at the end of the rocker is used to secure the rocker to the pivot point.

In the arrangement shown in Figure 2.95b the eccentric bush is a close fit in the rocker, but can be rotated in the rocker by a hexagonal flange at one end. The other end of the bush is threaded, and the bush is locked in the rocker by tightening a nut on this threaded end. To adjust the clearance, slacken the nut, rotate the bush to give the correct clearance, and then re-tighten the nut.

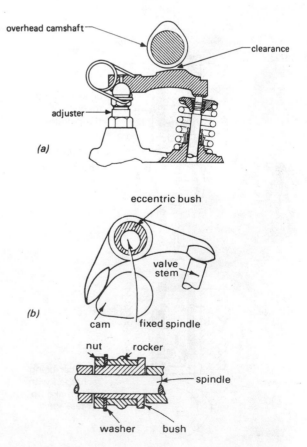

Figure 2.95 Valve rocker with overhead camshaft

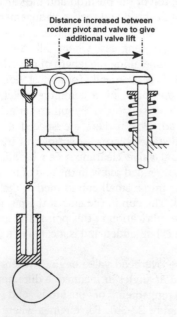

Figure 2.94 Example of using a rocker arm leverage ratio to obtain greater valve movement

Figure 2.96 shows an overhead camshaft arrangement for use on an inclined valve layout. A single camshaft is used with rockers acting as cam followers and transferring the cam lift to the valves.

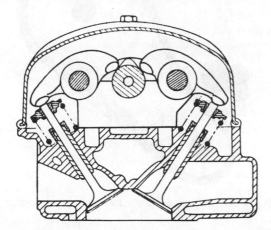

Figure 2.96 Overhead camshaft and rockers operating inclined valves

Direct acting overhead camshaft systems

When the valves are arranged in an inclined manner as shown in Figure 2.96 (typical of a pent roof combustion chamber design), it is often preferred to operate the valves using a camshaft situated directly over each row of valves, as illustrated in Figure 2.97. This arrangement is referred to as a double overhead camshaft (DOHC) system.

The cam lobe acts directly on the cam follower, which acts directly on the valve stem; this ensures accurate and positive valve operation. The DOHC layout has a minimum of moving parts (i.e. no pushrods or rockers) thus reducing the weight of moving components and also allowing very high engine speeds to be achieved. The DOHC arrangement is therefore used on modern engines where high engine speeds and high power outputs along with low emissions are the primary requirements.

It is now common for hydraulic cam followers to also be used on DOHC layouts; the hydraulic follower simply replacing the standard follower.

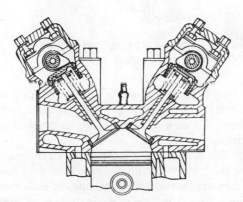

Figure 2.97 Double overhead camshaft arrangement (DOHC)

2.9.6 Camshaft drives

In an engine working on the four-stroke cycle each valve must be opened once for every two revolutions of the crankshaft, which makes it necessary for the camshaft to rotate at half-crankshaft speed, i.e. the speed ratio of crankshaft to camshaft is 2:1.

Chain drives (timing chains)

When the camshaft is situated near to the crankshaft, a short chain connects the crankshaft sprocket to the camshaft sprocket; the camshaft sprocket having twice as many teeth as the crankshaft sprocket (Figure 2.98).

The timing chain is either a single row type or a duplex with a double row of rollers. However, unless special provision is made, camshaft drive component wear will cause the chain to lengthen and a rattling noise will be heard as the irregular rotation of the camshaft slaps the chain against the timing cover.

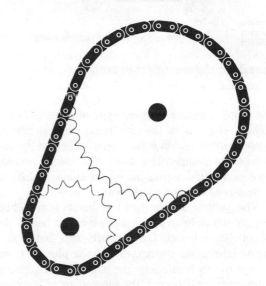

Figure 2.98 Simple chain drive for the camshaft

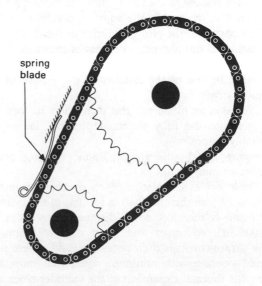

spring blade

Figure 2.99 Spring blade chain tensioner

Compensation for wear is achieved by fitting an automatic adjuster to rub on the non-driving (slack side) of the chain. Figure 2.99 shows a spring blade adjuster, which relies on the spring tension of the blade to push on the slack side of the chain.

Hydraulic adjuster for timing chains

Figure 2.100 shows a hydraulic type of automatic adjuster, which is used in conjunction with a fixed slipper made of a plastic material; the slipper damps chain 'flutter'.

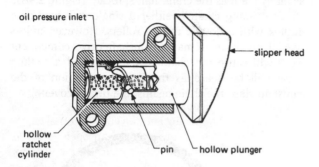

Figure 2.100 Hydraulic-type chain tensioner

The plunger in this compact type of adjuster is forced against the chain by hydraulic oil pressure to compensate for chain wear. A ratchet resists the return travel of the plunger. This non-return feature overcomes the need for undue pressure on the chain, which would cause power loss and extra wear.

The rubber slipper head is bonded to a hollow plunger, which has a peg that engages in a helical slot in the ratchet cylinder. Oil pressure, supplied from the engine lubrication system, acts on the plunger to assist the spring in tensioning the chain. When chain or component wear occurs, the movement of the plunger causes the peg to push on the smooth face of the helical slot in the hollow ratchet and rotate the ratchet a small amount. Oil, trapped in the adjuster, acts as a damper and seepage past the plunger lubricates the chain.

Return of the plunger, in excess of that required to allow for thermal expansion, is resisted by the peg engaging in one of the notches in the groove of the hollow ratchet.

Provision is made for the technician to lock the plunger into the fully retracted position, for engine assembly purposes.

Figure 2.101 shows a hydraulic adjuster acting against a timing chain.

Chain drives are also used on overhead camshaft engines (where the camshaft is located in the cylinder head and is therefore some distance away from the crankshaft). A longer and more complex camshaft drive arrangement is then necessary. The system used should operate with minimum noise and must also allow for thermal expansion of the cylinder block and head.

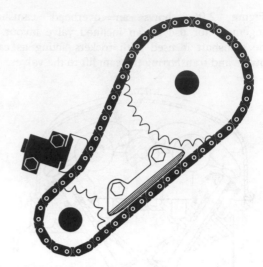

Figure 2.101 Hydraulic adjuster acting against a timing chain

Figure 2.102 illustrates a typical layout of drive chain for an overhead camshaft engine. The illustration shows a chain drive to a camshaft, which then drives a second camshaft via gears. On a single overhead camshaft engine, the chain drive would be similar to the system illustrated but without the gear drive to the second camshaft. The gear drive for a second camshaft is one method of providing a drive to an engine with double overhead camshafts (DOHC).

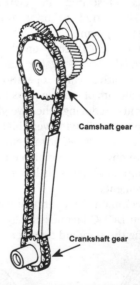

Figure 2.102 Chain drive to an overhead camshaft. Also showing a gear drive to a second camshaft

The chain is long, so a guide is provided for it on the drive side (right-hand side in this example). A hydraulic tensioner acts on a tensioner blade on the slack side of the chain.

On DOHC engines, a chain drive arrangement can still be used, but the chain will pass from the crankshaft and then across two sprockets, one on each camshaft (Figure 2.103). This type of chain drive is still used but is more suited to smaller engines where the chain is

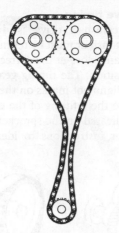

Figure 2.103 Chain drive arrangement for a double overhead camshaft engine

likely to be relatively short. A chain tensioner would be required, as is the case with single overhead camshaft systems, and also a chain guide may be fitted.

Some older designs of DOHC engines (notably the Jaguar XK engine, which was produced for over 40 years from the late 1940s) used a complex chain drive arrangement due to the size of the engine. Its layout is shown in Figure 2.104.

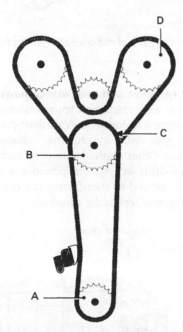

Figure 2.104 Complex chain drive for double overhead camshaft engines

Gear drives

When the camshaft is fitted close to the crankshaft a gear layout similar to that in Figure 2.105 can be used. Spur gears (straight cut teeth) are noisy, so helical teeth are generally used. Sometimes the large gearwheel is made of a plastic or other non-metallic material and, in some cases, an idler gear is fitted where the distance between the crankshaft and the camshaft is large.

Belt drives

Many modern overhead camshaft engines use a rubber timing belt to drive the camshaft or camshafts. The belt is notched to form equally spaced teeth, which maintains the correct valve timing. An example of a single overhead camshaft engine with a timing belt drive is shown in Figure 2.106.

Belt drives provide a relatively cheap, very quiet and efficient way of driving a camshaft when it is mounted far away from the crankshaft (e.g. OHC). A timing belt does not require lubrication and can therefore be located on the outside of the engine. In fact, timing belts are manufactured of rubber and similar materials, which if contaminated with oil can lead to premature failure.

Because a timing belt can be located on the outside of the engine, it enables the camshaft drive to be easily disconnected when the cylinder head has to be removed or when the belt needs to be changed.

Breakage of the timing belt can cause internal engine damage if the piston were to strike an open valve. An arrow printed on the timing belt indicates the direction of rotation to be fitted. If a timing belt is to be removed and refitted during engine repairs, the direction of rotation should be noted before the removal of the belt.

The timing belt is usually constructed using reinforced belt materials such as glass fibre strands or similar flexible cords. The reverse side of the belt is backed by smooth rubber, which provides a surface for the tension to be applied to the belt with a tensioner pulley. The timing belt may also drive a water pump and balancer shafts. For some timing belt applications it

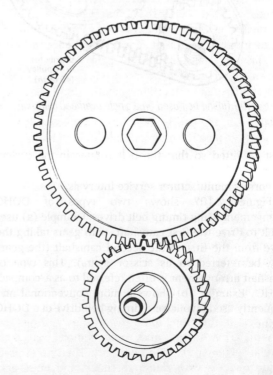

Figure 2.105 Camshaft gear drive, suitable when the camshaft is located in the cylinder block close to the crankshaft

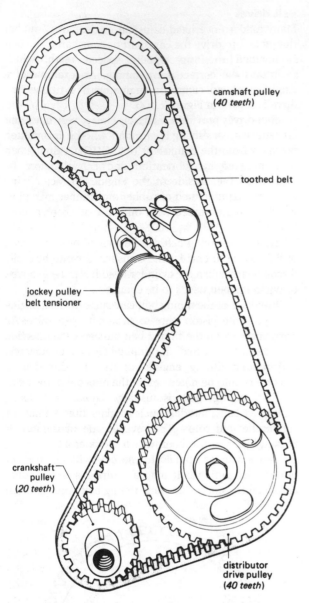

Figure 2.106 Timing belt used on a single overhead camshaft engine

must be fitted so that the belt rotates in the correct direction. The timing belt should always be replaced at the correct manufacturer service intervals.

Figure 2.107 shows two types of DOHC arrangement using timing belt drives. Example (a) uses a belt to drive the first camshaft, with gears taking the drive from the first to the second camshaft (the gears may be referred to as scissor gears). This type of camshaft arrangement is often referred to as a 'compact DOHC'. Example (b) shows a more conventional and frequently used layout for a timing belt drive of a DOHC engine.

Setting the valve timing

Whenever the camshaft drive is disconnected, the crankshaft and camshaft must be retimed to ensure that the valves open and close at the correct time in relation to the piston position. The timing gears and sprockets normally have alignment marks on them, which should be aligned before the refitting of the camshaft drive. If no marks are indicated on the sprockets always refer to the manufacturer instructions to identify the correct procedure.

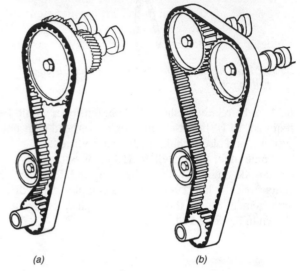

Figure 2.107 Two types of belt drive arrangement for a DOHC engine

Camshaft sprocket and gear attachment

As is the case with crankshaft sprockets and gears, it is common practice to locate the camshaft drive sprocket or timing gear wheel onto the camshaft with a Woodruff key. Other methods are used such as splines but the Woodruff key system provides a simple and inexpensive method of transferring the drive from the sprocket or gearwheel to the camshaft.

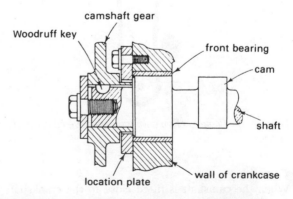

Figure 2.108 Attachment of camshaft timing gear

2.10   INTAKE MANIFOLDS

2.10.1   Function of the intake manifold

Put as simply as possible, the function of the intake manifold is to distribute the fresh charge (air/fuel mixture with petrol engines, or air charge with diesel engines) to the individual cylinders.

A single-cylinder engine would simply require a small length of pipe to guide the airflow into the intake port, the airflow probably originating at an air filter. On a multi-cylinder engine it is possible to have separate intake pipes for each cylinder and separate air filters at each pipe (many racing engines have used this arrangement). However, most mass production engines have a single air filter with a manifold or pipe-work that allows the airflow from the filter to be distributed to the individual cylinders.

To a certain extent, the traditional manifold arrangement evolved due to the way in which petrol and air were mixed and supplied to the cylinders on older types of petrol engine. Until the early 1990s, the majority of petrol engines made use of a 'carburettor' which is a device for mixing petrol and air in the correct proportions (refer to section 2.25 later in this chapter). In most cases cost and simplicity dictated the use of a single carburettor. Therefore, a mixture of petrol and air from a single carburettor had to pass to each of the cylinders; this was achieved using what we now term the 'intake manifold' or inlet manifold. The carburettor was mounted onto the manifold with the air filter either directly fitted to the intake of the carburettor or connected to the carburettor by a suitable hose or pipe.

Note that modern petrol engines use fuel injection systems, which deliver the fuel to the intake port (usually at the very end of the manifold where it meets the intake port) or in an increasing number of cases, direct to the cylinder. The modern intake manifold therefore only distributes the air from the air filter to the intake ports.

It is important to note that petrol engines (with a few exceptions) make use of a throttle valve or butterfly valve to control the volume of air passing to the engine; this allows the driver to control the engine power. Carburettors usually had the butterfly valve located within the carburettor body. Modern petrol engines fitted with fuel injection still require a throttle mechanism and therefore a butterfly valve is fitted to the intake manifold; the butterfly valve assembly is usually referred to as a 'throttle body assembly'.

On diesel engines, because the diesel fuel is delivered direct to each cylinder, the intake manifold simply functioned as a means of distributing air from the air filter to the intake ports for each cylinder. Traditionally, most diesel engines relied on controlling the volume of fuel delivered as a means of controlling engine power so a butterfly valve or throttle mechanism was not used. Modern diesel engines do, however, tend to make use of throttle systems so there is a similarity with the petrol engine in that a throttle body may form part of the manifold system.

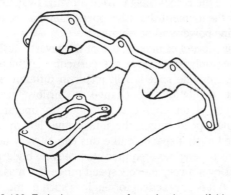

Figure 2.109 Typical arrangement for an intake manifold with a single carburettor

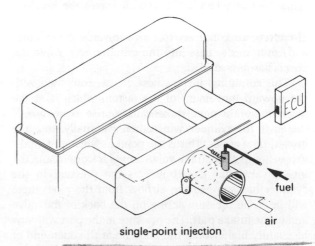

multi-point injection   single-point injection

Figure 2.110 Typical arrangement for a manifold on a petrol injection engine

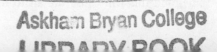

2.10.2 Intake manifold design

Manifold design is covered in greater detail in section 2.19, but this section provides a general understanding of the essential design features.

There are several difficulties to be overcome in designing a satisfactory induction manifold, difficulties so complex that the designer of a very famous engine has remarked that 'a certain amount of what can only be termed witchcraft is apparent' in the development of the induction manifold.

Many intake manifolds were originally developed on a basis of trial and error to provide the best design that suited the engine. Today, intake manifolds are designed by computer programmes to provide the optimum configuration, although some adjustments to these designs are often made once a manifold has been manufactured. Some of the difficulties in designing what appears, on the surface, to be a relatively simple component will be considered in this section. Other demands on the design of the intake manifold will be considered in the relevant petrol and diesel sections.

Airflow and reverse airflow

If a single, straight and very long, open-ended pipe is connected to the intake port of a single-cylinder engine, and the engine is then driven by an electric motor, the engine will draw air through the pipe during its induction stroke (piston moving down the cylinder and the intake valve is open). The moment the piston moves down the cylinder and starts to create a low pressure (vacuum), air will begin to flow from the pipe into the cylinder. Air will, however, also be flowing at the open end of the pipe and along the length of the pipe towards the cylinder; this is because there is a lower pressure in the cylinder than at the open end of the pipe. It is no different to sucking on one end of a straw, which causes air to flow through the straw.

When the piston reaches BDC it is no longer creating the suction or vacuum and in theory, the airflow in the pipe should stop. In reality, the air already moving along the pipe will have some momentum (in much the same way as when a cricket ball leaves the bowler's hand it maintains movement because of momentum). Therefore, air continues to move towards the cylinder and continues to pass into the cylinder even when the piston has passed BDC.

This continued inward flow of gas, combined with the upward movement of the piston, which is at the beginning of the next stroke, causes a rise in pressure of the air in the cylinder, which then eventually stops the inward flow of gas. This is the point at which the intake valve should close. If the valve timing is 'correct' and the intake valve has closed just as the pressure in the cylinder has stopped the airflow from the pipe, there will be some pressure acting on the back of the valve and in the intake port. The pressure in the port will now be slightly higher than the pressure at the open end of the pipe, and this will cause the air to rebound away

from the valve and port thus causing airflow along the pipe *away* from the closed valve.

If the valve closes too late the build-up of pressure in the cylinder will already have caused this 'reverse flow' before the valve closes. If the valve closes too early, the momentum of the air will cause it to build up pressure at the valve end of the port still further, producing the same result – a reverse flow.

During reverse flow, the gas again acquires momentum (in a direction away from the valve and port), which will cause the flow to continue until the pressure at the port end of the pipe falls below atmospheric pressure (the pressure at the open end of the pipe). This low pressure at the port end then results in another reversal of airflow from the open end of the pipe back towards the valve and intake port. These reversals of airflow in the pipe will continue for some time if there is little or no opposition to flow, the time for one complete oscillation depending upon the length of the pipe.

By carefully selecting a suitable length of pipe, it is possible to arrange that, at the moment the intake valve opens for the next intake stroke, the gas in the pipe is already moving towards the cylinder because of the oscillations in airflow from the previous intake stroke. The result is that more gas will enter the cylinder than would be the case if the gas were moving away from the port at the moment the valve opened, and a useful gain in engine power will be obtained.

This process of making use of the reverse airflow is, however, only effective at one particular engine speed. Different engine speeds will result in different speeds for the oscillations of change in airflow direction. Therefore, if an engine is intended to operate at a particular speed range, the intake pipe length can be matched to that speed. While this can be very usefully applied to engines required to deliver high power outputs over a very narrow speed range (such as racing engines) it is impractical for engines such as those used in ordinary motor vehicles, which are expected to give good results over a wide range of speeds.

For those engines used in normal road vehicles, the intake pipe should not be too long, and a compromise has to be obtained in the pipe length to ensure good power delivery at low and high engine speeds. The length of pipe between the throttle butterfly and each cylinder intake port should be as near equal as possible.

Manifolds compared with single pipes

Although a manifold is a convenient way of passing air from a single air filter, or from a single carburettor, to each of the different cylinders, it can provide a means of overcoming a problem with reverse airflow.

If a single pipe were used for each cylinder, when the airflow is reversed away from the engine it would pass out through the carburettor, which would result in petrol being drawn *out* of the carburettor along with the air. This would waste petrol and is, in fact, dangerous. However, if it is remembered that the reverse airflow is caused by a rise in pressure at the time the intake valve closes (or the piston is moving up the cylinder), then this increase in pressure could be matched to the opening of an intake valve on another cylinder. By connecting all of the individual intake pipes of a multi-cylinder engine together, thus forming a manifold, it is possible to divert the reverse airflow towards another cylinder, thus preventing air and petrol passing out through the carburettor.

Note that on many older engines, especial racing engines, it was very common for the reverse airflow to occur at low engine speeds, which would cause air and fuel to pass out of the carburettor. This was often referred to as 'spit back' and was simply due to the intake pipe length and valve timing not being suited to low engine speeds.

It is common on modern engines to connect all of the intake pipes or tracts with a chamber, usually referred to as the plenum chamber. The chamber provides a means of absorbing or damping the pressure pulses created by each of the cylinders (when the intake valves close). The high and low pressures caused by the continual reversals of airflow (oscillations) do not then have such a large effect when the pipe lengths are not matched to the speed at which an engine is operating.

It is also increasingly common on modern engines to make use of variable length induction tracts to suit the engine speed and load (covered in greater detail in Book 2 in this series). By varying the effective length of the tract at certain engine speeds, it is possible to provide a more suitable length intake tract, thus increasing the engine torque and power across the operating speed range of the engine.

Even distribution to all cylinders

One essential requirement of the intake manifold is to ensure that the airflow is the same to each of the cylinders. This requirement was especially important on engines that made use of a carburettor to provide the petrol/air mixture.

A typical problem was in the design of an intake manifold for a six-cylinder in-line engine ('straight six cylinder') with a single carburettor. Figure 2.111 shows a layout for a six-cylinder engine with the carburettor located centrally between the ends of the engine. The intake pipe lengths for the middle two cylinders is much shorter than for the end two cylinders.

The first problem encountered is that the maximum and minimum reverse airflow effect would occur at different engine speeds for the outer cylinders compared with the inner cylinders and compared with the other two cylinders.

Another problem is that the intake pipe leading to the middle two cylinders is relatively straight, while the pipes leading to the outer cylinders have bends. If the bends in the pipes are too severe, this can restrict the airflow, which reduces the power of the outer cylinders compared with the inner cylinders.

Additionally, on carburettor engines, the petrol and air formed a mixture that passed from the carburettor and along the intake pipes to the intake ports and cylinders. Because petrol is heavier than air, when the mixture passes around a bend or sharp corner, the petrol tends to separate from the air (the air goes round the corner but the petrol tends to travel straight on). Although the separated petrol is eventually drawn into the cylinder, it will no longer be mixed with the air.

The mixture that does reach the cylinder will therefore be 'weak' (less petrol, than ideal), which results in poor combustion. The separated petrol will not burn because it is not mixed with air and therefore passes out of the exhaust pipe as unburned fuel which is a pollutant.

To overcome the problem it was necessary to calibrate the carburettor so that extra petrol was mixed with the air to ensure that the outer cylinders had an acceptable mixture of petrol and air. However, if the engine had only one carburettor feeding all cylinders, this resulted in the centre cylinder having too much fuel ('rich mixture'), which again causes high levels of harmful emissions and wastes fuel. None of the cylinders received the correct mixture of air and fuel, the power developed by the different cylinders was not consistent and the emissions and fuel wastage was high.

By redesigning the manifold so that a longer pipe length is achieved for the centre cylinders, a better balance of mixture and power is achieved across the cylinders and the engine operates more smoothly and efficiently.

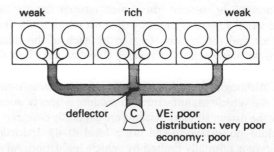

Figure 2.111 Design for a six-cylinder intake manifold which has poor distribution to the cylinders. Note that a deflector is used to assist in making the distribution more even across the cylinders

2.11 AIR CLEANERS AND FILTERS

2.11.1 Air cleaning/filtering systems

When an engine is running, it takes in a considerable volume of air, which may contain a large proportion of dust. This dust will find its way into the engine cylinders and mix with the lubricating oil to form an abrasive compound which will cause premature wear of pistons, cylinders and bearings. In an attempt to reduce such wear, a filter or filters are generally fitted to the air induction system to clean the air by removing the dust particles.

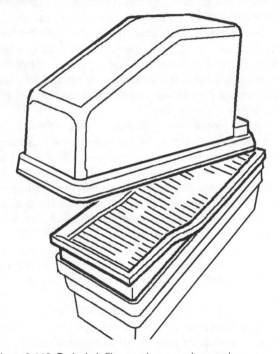

Figure 2.112 Typical air filter used on a modern engine

Air filters are often combined with silencers designed to eliminate or reduce the noise created by the air induction system (caused by the restrictions to the flow of air and the pulsing created by each of the intake strokes along with the reverse flows of air when the intake valves close).

Although the induction noise is sometimes 'tuned' by the vehicle manufacturer to produce a 'sporty' sound for the driver, silencer systems are generally designed to reduce noise levels. The noise level of the induction system is normally limited by vehicle legislation. An air filter housing fitted to a modern engine which is fitted with a fuel injection system may have more than one silencer or resonance chamber to help reduce the induction roar.

Figure 2.113a, illustrates the construction of one type of simple air cleaner and silencer. Air first passes through the filtering element (1) that collects as much of the dust as possible. The air then passes down the central tube (3), and into the intake system (or carburettor) through the connection (4). Some of the

sound waves or pulses are absorbed in the resonance chambers (2).

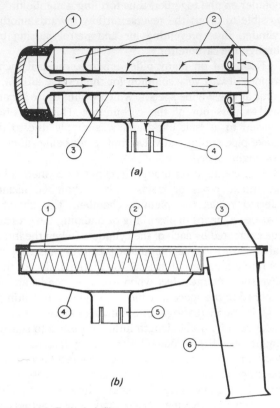

(a)

(b)

Figure 2.113 Typical air filter
a Air cleaner and silencer
b Paper element air cleaner

The filtering element shown in this diagram consists of a tangled mass of fine wire, which is lightly coated with oil. As air threads its way through the wire mesh, dust sticks to the oil and the cleaned air passes on. Periodically (more often in very dusty conditions), the element should be thoroughly cleaned in a suitable cleaning solution, e.g. paraffin, to remove the trapped dirt. After drying, it should be dipped in clean oil and drained; this leaves a thin film of oil adhering to the wire mesh to collect more dirt. The oil-coated types of air filter are now very rarely used on general motor vehicles.

Nearly all air filters are now of the paper element type. The filtering element is composed of a special grade of paper through which the air passing to the engine is drawn. A considerable area of paper surface is necessary to avoid restriction to the airflow, and the necessary area is provided within a filter of reasonable size by making the paper into a large number of fine pleats as shown at (2) in Figure 2.113b. This paper filtering element is surrounded by either a pressed-steel or a flexible rubberized frame and fitted into the lower part of the filter casing (4), and is enclosed by the cover

(3) which is held in place by clips or screws. Air enters through the tube (6), passes through the paper element (2) and then to either the intake trunking or manifold (or carburettor on older fuel systems) through the connection (5). A silencing action is produced partly by the form of the tube (6) and also by the absorption of sound waves from the carburettor by the paper element itself. An additional advantage of this type of filter is its small overall height.

Some cylindrical-type air cleaners (often used with diesel engines) are fitted with vanes that promote cyclones within the air filter casing as the air is drawn in. The cyclones generated within the casing tend to separate the dust particles from the air before the air reaches the filter element, therefore increasing the interval before the filter requires replacing. The air filter casing should always be cleaned during the replacement of the air filter element.

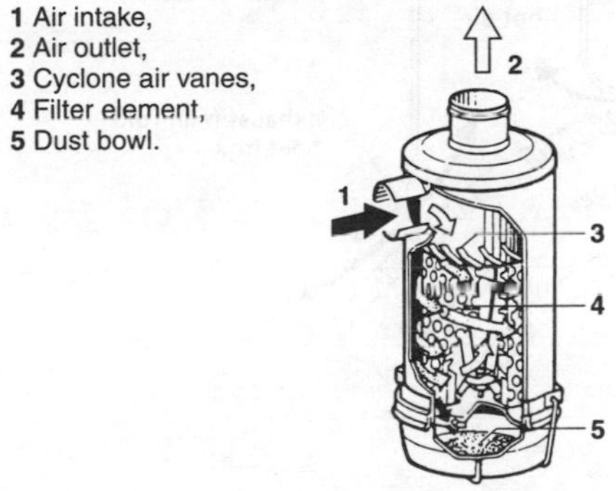

1 Air intake,
2 Air outlet,
3 Cyclone air vanes,
4 Filter element,
5 Dust bowl.

Figure 2.114 Air filter with cyclone vanes fitted

Other materials used for filtering elements are cloth and felt. These, like paper, cannot normally be cleaned and should be replaced at the intervals specified by the vehicle manufacturer. It is normally advised on a service schedule that a vehicle operating in a dusty environment should have the air filter replaced at shorter service intervals.

2.11.2 Air cleaner intake temperature

Engines operate in various climatic conditions; the air drawn into the induction system will be at a temperature that depends on the ambient air temperature. Ideally, fuel systems require that the air drawn through the air intake system be at a suitable temperature for mixing with the fuel.

Although the issue of appropriate air temperature is applicable to engines fitted with fuel injection, it is very critical for older engines that used carburettors which mixed the air and fuel within the carburettor body. The carburettor body may not always benefit from the heat of the engine and this could lead to cold intake air not mixing effectively with the petrol.

Additionally, carburettors could suffer 'icing' of the carburettor body and internal bore due to cold air passing through the carburettor absorbing heat from the carburettor body. The carburettor body temperature then fell to a level where moisture would freeze, restricting the flow of fuel through the fine ports or jets within the carburettor assembly.

To overcome the problems of cold air in the intake system, some air cleaners have an intake tube, (6) in Figure 2.113b, which is adjustable to suit summer and winter conditions. Hot air helps fuel vaporization and also prevents ice forming in the carburettor venturi. The intake would be set to take in air from the region of the exhaust manifold during the winter season.

In summer the air is already warm, so further heating would result in low power due to poor volumetric efficiency. To avoid these problems, the intake tube entrance should be sited in a cold-air region.

Automatic hot air intake systems

Good vaporization of the fuel is necessary if the vehicle is to conform to emission control regulations, so an automatic control is often fitted to ensure that the air intake temperature is correct under all normal operating conditions.

With automatic hot air intake systems, the air cleaner assembly has two intake tubes; one sited to take in cold air, the other set to receive hot air preheated by the exhaust manifold (Figure 2.115). Selection of the proportion of hot and cold passing to the air cleaner is by an air control flap valve, which is moved by a vacuum-operated diaphragm connected to the induction manifold.

A thermo-valve mounted in the air stream in the air cleaner senses the temperature of the air entering the engine. When a given temperature is reached, (e.g. 25°C) the thermo-valve opens and bleeds air into the vacuum pipe. This destroys the depression in the diaphragm chamber and moves the valve towards the 'cool' position.

During slow-running and cruising conditions, the high manifold depression (e.g. above 500 mbar) lifts the diaphragm against the spring and moves the air control vent to select hot air.

2.11.3 Air cleaner construction

Air cleaners and filter systems, although simple in function, are designed as a fundamental part of the induction system. As previously stated, the filter may be contained in a chamber that assists with the damping of sound waves, but the chamber will also affect the action of the airflow and reverse airflow (refer to section 2.10). The whole intake system is therefore designed so that each part assists in some way towards engine performance, economy and emissions control.

It is not unusual for engine performance to alter if the air filter is blocked or removed. For unmodified engines, it is therefore advisable to retain the filter elements and filter casing/chamber to ensure that engine performance is maintained.

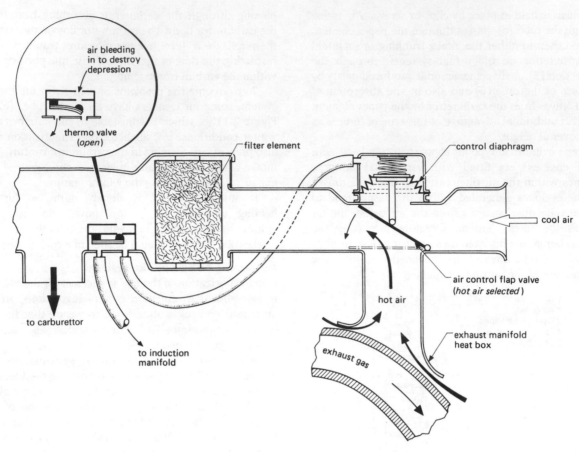

Figure 2.115 Automatic hot air intake system

2.12 EXHAUST SYSTEMS, SILENCERS AND CATALYTIC CONVERTERS

2.12.1 Exhaust systems

The exhaust system consists of three main parts, with a fourth part that functions as a means of reducing emissions:

1 **The exhaust manifold** which collects the exhaust gases from a number of cylinders and leads them to an exhaust pipe.
2 **The exhaust pipe** conducts the exhaust gases to a suitable point before discharging them into the air. This point is usually at the rear of the vehicle, but certain special types of vehicle (such as petrol tankers) may be required by law to discharge their exhaust gases at some other point.
3 **The silencer** reduces the noise of the high-pressure pulsations of the hot exhaust gas.
4 **The catalytic converter** promotes a chemical/thermal reaction of the exhaust gases to reduce the level of unwanted emissions (pollutants).

2.12.2 Exhaust manifolds

The exhaust manifold is the component used to collect the exhaust gases from each cylinder and then distribute those gases to a pipe or pipes. In effect, the exhaust manifold performs a similar task to the intake manifold but in reverse. The design of an exhaust manifold is therefore critical to the way in which an engine performs and different designs have certain advantages and disadvantages.

Temperature

When an engine is running at full throttle, the temperature of the exhaust gases may reach 800 °C or more. When an engine is operating at full load, the exhaust manifold can often be seen to glow 'red hot', especially if there is insufficient cooling air flowing around the manifold. To withstand such temperatures, exhaust manifolds are generally made of iron castings or fabricated from steel pipes and plate by welding.

Exhaust manifold design

The main problem in the layout of an exhaust manifold is possible interference between cylinders. Consider the manifold shown in Figure 2.116, which is fitted to a four-cylinder engine having the firing order 1-2-4-3. Ideally, when piston 1 is approaching TDC at the end of its exhaust stroke, the momentum of the gas moving along the exhaust pipe should be helping to scavenge the burnt gas from the cylinder. However, in the example, the exhaust valve of cylinder 2 would now be open and also discharging a cylinder full of high-pressure burnt gas into the manifold. The shape of this manifold will clearly result in some of the gas discharged from cylinder 2 entering cylinder 1, or certainly blocking the flow of the final gas from cylinder 1. This will result in an unduly large proportion of burnt gas remaining in cylinder 1 when its exhaust valve closes.

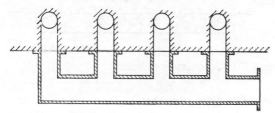

Figure 2.116 A simple exhaust manifold

The manifold shown in Figure 2.117 is an improvement on Figure 2.116, since the entry of each port into the manifold is curved so as to maintain an outward flow from each port rather than permit one port to blow back into another.

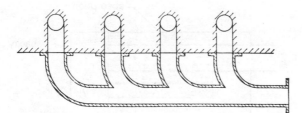

Figure 2.117 Improved exhaust manifold

Exhaust ports are sometimes 'siamesed' to simplify and cheapen the cylinder head casting. A common arrangement is shown in Figure 2.118. Note the shaping of the end branches of the manifold to avoid interference between cylinders, and also that this cannot occur between the cylinders served by the siamesed ports since, on a four-cylinder engine, exhaust strokes occur in these cylinders one revolution apart.

Interference can be completely avoided by having a separate pipe for each cylinder, but for ordinary cars and commercial vehicles this arrangement is too bulky and expensive. Furthermore, it is possible to use the gas pulsations from one cylinder to assist the flow of gas from another at certain engine speeds. This is done by

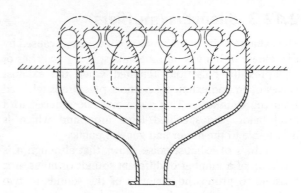

Figure 2.118 Exhaust manifold for a four-cylinder engine, one pair of exhaust ports siamesed

joining selected separate pipes from each cylinder, first in pairs thus making two pipes, which are then joined into one. The lengths of the various sections of pipes are important, depending upon the engine speed at which the greatest benefit is desired; in a four-cylinder engine (with a typical firing order of 1-3-4-2) the pairs of pipes joined are 1 and 4, 2 and 3. Therefore, when performance is an important consideration, a pipe layout similar to that shown in Figure 2.119 is used for a four-cylinder engine.

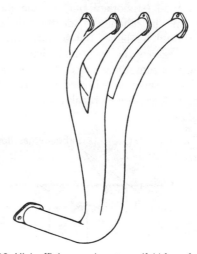

Figure 2.119 High efficiency exhaust manifold for a four-cylinder engine

For six-cylinder engines the cylinders which should be paired in this manner are 1 and 6, 2 and 5, and 3 and 4, but this is much more difficult to arrange compactly and neatly than in the case of a four-cylinder engine. It is, however, easy and convenient to use two manifolds, one for cylinders 1, 2 and 3, and the other for cylinders 4, 5 and 6, each group having cylinders with equally spaced firing intervals. The pipes from these two manifolds usually join at some distance from the cylinder head, but in a few cases two completely independent exhaust systems are used, one for each group of three cylinders.

2.12.3 Silencers (mufflers)

The exhaust noise of an 'unsilenced' engine is caused by the release of hot gas into the atmosphere in a series of high-pressure pulsations (created when the exhaust valves open and exhaust gas under pressure is released from the cylinders). This noise must be reduced to a level below the specified legal limit and which is acceptable to the driver and general public.

Analysis of exhaust noise shows that although it is made up of a number of different sounds or notes, it is possible to group the majority of the sounds in two main frequency bands:

1 Low frequency – caused by the air pumping action of the engine. This sound is also produced when the engine is motored over without combustion taking place.
2 High frequency – caused by the release and rapid expansion of very hot gas at a temperature of 800–1000°C.

To dampen these frequencies, two silencers are needed: a capacity-type to treat the low frequencies and an absorption-type to treat the high frequencies.

Capacity-type silencers

Figure 2.120 shows a capacity type silencer. It consists of a large chamber in which the regular gas pulsations can be damped (smoothed out) by the bulk of gas contained in the chamber. Ideally this expansion chamber should be large, but because the available space often restricts the size, more than one capacity-type silencer is sometimes fitted. The damping of the low-frequency waves is achieved by fitting baffles to create a turbulent zone to break up the flow of gas in the silencer.

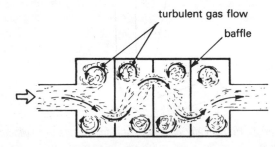

Figure 2.120 Capacity-type silencer

Baffles reduce the free flow of gas, so a poor design could cause a build-up of pressure in the exhaust system. This backpressure reduces engine power because any exhaust gas that is allowed to remain in the cylinder (residual exhaust gas) will occupy space that would otherwise be filled with the fresh charge. In this way the volumetric efficiency of the engine will be reduced. The engine power suffers both from the loss of cylinder volume occupied by the exhaust gas residual, and from the heat of the burnt gas. The presence of this very hot gas heats the new charge as it enters, lowering its density and reducing its mass.

Absorption-type silencers

The construction of this type, also called a Burgess silencer, is shown in Figure 2.121. It consists of a straight-through perforated tube, which is surrounded by a sound-absorbing material such as glass fibre. Damping of the high-frequency sound waves is achieved by the material, which causes a slight retardation in the wave. When the wave returns from the outer chamber it is out of phase with the vibration of the gas passing through the perforated tube, so the opposing action of the two waves smoothes out the high frequency peaks.

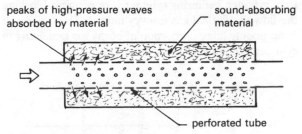

Figure 2.121 Absorption-type silencer

Composite-type silencers

This type of silencer, shown in Figure 2.122, is a combination of the capacity and absorption types. This combination is attractive, assuming space or ground clearance is sufficient for its installation.

Some silencers have a number of tubes and/or chambers to produce out-of-phase sound waves that vibrate in sympathy with the main frequencies of the gas passing into the silencer; hence the term 'resonator' that is sometimes used to describe this type of silencer.

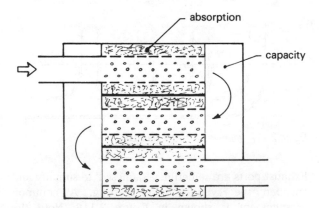

Figure 2.122 Composite-type silencer

Silencer material

Steam is one of the products of combustion. When the exhaust system is cold, the steam condenses to form water that either drips from the tailpipe or collects in the silencer until the system heats up. The combined effects of water and acids from combustion, high-temperature gas, and water from the road, produces a highly corrosive action which would rapidly attack a normal low-carbon steel exhaust system. This corrosion can be resisted by coating the steel with aluminium or by using a more expensive material such as stainless steel. To prevent the build up of water in the silencer, a small hole at the lowest point of the silencer allows the water to drain thus preventing premature corrosion.

2.12.4 Exhaust pipes

An exhaust pipe is a simple means of distributing the exhaust gases from the engine to an exit point (to the atmosphere). However, the exhaust pipe also functions to support the silencers and catalytic converters. Therefore the exhaust pipe must have sufficient strength and durability to carry the hot gases and take the weight of other components.

Pipes are made of steel tubing, which is in some cases protected against corrosion and oxidation by being coated with aluminium by a metal-spraying process.

Since engines are usually carried on flexible mountings, provision must be made for their movement relative to the frame. In some cases, there is either a flexible joint or a length of flexible exhaust piping between the exhaust manifold and the exhaust system, which allows for some movement of the engine. The exhaust is normally supported on the frame by flexible attachments, usually incorporating bonded rubber blocks.

Exhausts made of steel tubing corrode after a while. They corrode externally due to climatic conditions such as rain and due to the salt used on the roads. The engine, even when operating efficiently, produces a large quantity of steam (H_2O) and other corrosive chemicals which are the products of incomplete combustion and these corrode the steel tubing internally. Some exhaust systems are manufactured from stainless steel, and although more expensive than 'aluminized' steel, they reduce corrosion and increase the life of the pipe.

The complete exhaust pipe and silencer assembly, along with the catalytic converters is generally referred to as the exhaust system.

Exhaust system design

A well-designed, or finely tuned, exhaust system can improve engine power by using the negative and positive pressure pulses which travel back and forth along the front exhaust pipe to start the new charge flowing into the cylinder during the valve overlap period. An ideal pipe length gives a negative pressure pulse in the cylinder at the instant the inlet valve opens. The assistance given by the exhaust is only achieved at certain engine speeds, so the design should be tuned to give its support at the time when extra engine power is required.

High performance engines may be fitted with a 'variable length exhaust system', using a similar principle to that found in variable induction manifolds; the length of the exhaust being altered by valves within the exhaust system.

In reality, most variable length exhaust systems have two different routes through which the gases can flow, the route being controlled by the opening or closing of the valves. The different routes provide different lengths for gas flow travel as well as the potential for different silencers, back pressures, etc.

At low to medium engine speeds the length of the exhaust is tuned to provide maximum engine power through the use of the positive and negative pressures that exist in the exhaust. The extra length of the exhaust system can also accommodate additional silencers that may help to reduce the noise of the exhaust at low engine speeds. When the engine reaches a high speed, the valves within the exhaust system open, allowing the exhaust system to shorten in length, thus providing the best tuning of the exhaust system at high engine speed. Shortening the exhaust length also reduces the number of silencers, which restricts the flow of exhaust gas through the exhaust system at high speed.

2.12.5 Exhaust catalytic converter

To comply with emission regulations, most modern petrol engines, are fitted with a catalytic converter. The catalyst converts the harmful gas produced as a result of the combustion process into less harmful products (refer to section 2.30 within this chapter).

The catalytic converter is located in the exhaust system either as an integral part of the exhaust manifold (often referred to as 'close-coupled') or just before the first silencer. This enables the catalyst to reach a high temperature even when the flow of exhaust gases is low, i.e. engine at idle. The appearance of the catalytic converter is similar to that of an exhaust silencer. The casing of the catalytic converter is usually made from stainless steel to improve its durability.

If a catalytic converter is fitted to a petrol engine, a sensor is normally fitted upstream of the catalyst, between the exhaust ports and the catalyst. This sensor, referred to as an oxygen sensor, monitors the oxygen content in the exhaust. The information is passed to the fuel system computer (ECU), which controls the fuelling of the engine. This process is necessary because a catalytic converter only operates efficiently if the

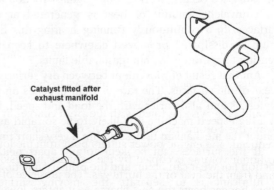

Catalyst fitted after exhaust manifold

Figure 2.123 Exhaust catalyst fitted to an exhaust system

correct amount of oxygen is present in the exhaust gas. The computer monitors oxygen levels (which will alter with changes in the fuel quantity or air /fuel ratio) and then adjusts the fuel quantity accordingly.

Note that modern fuel systems may also use a second oxygen sensor, located after the catalytic converter, which is used by the ECU to monitor the performance of the catalyst, i.e. the efficiency at which

the converter reduces the pollutants. It is typical to fit a single catalytic converter to four- or five-cylinder engines (especially in-line engines). Engines with a greater number of cylinders normally require two or more catalytic converters. This is due to the design of the exhaust layout and also to prevent the catalyst restricting the flow of exhaust gases. Further details on catalytic converter operation are given in section 2.30.

2.13   ENGINE LUBRICANTS

2.13.1 The need for lubrication

The internal-combustion engine has many sliding and rotating components, which are in constant contact with one another. If a lubricant were not used these components, which are made from various materials, would soon seize, and in some extreme cases even melt, due to the friction and heat generated by the components rubbing against each other. To prevent seizure and reduce the friction between components an oil lubrication system is used.

Friction and heat
When two surfaces are in contact, there is an opposition to relative movement between them, which is called friction. If the surfaces are clean and dry, the force needed to overcome friction depends on:

1   The materials from which the surfaces are made.
2   The surface finish, i.e. whether rough, smooth or polished.
3   The load pressing the surfaces together.

For any one pair of clean dry surfaces it can be shown by simple experiments that the ratio::

$$\frac{\text{Resistance to movement}}{\text{Load pressing surfaces together}}$$

is a constant number. It is called the 'coefficient of friction' for those surfaces.

When friction is overcome and movement between two surfaces occurs, work is done against friction and an equivalent amount of heat is generated at the surfaces. In a continuously running bearing this heat must be dissipated or moved elsewhere to keep the bearing temperature within reasonable limits.

Another result of movement between dry surfaces is wear of the surfaces. The rate of wear depends on the materials and also varies with the load and speed, but in a high-speed machine it is likely to be so rapid as to render the mechanism useless within a very short time.

If the surfaces can be kept totally apart neither friction nor wear can occur, and the primary function of a lubricant is to separate the moving surfaces. Lubricants may be solid, liquid or gaseous, but liquids

are by far the commonest and are almost universally used in motor vehicles.

As well as separating the surfaces of the components, a liquid lubricant can function as a means of cooling a component. As stated previously, heat is generated due to friction and although the lubricant reduces the friction and generation of heat, heat is still generated within all parts of the engine.

A liquid lubricant, which is usually oil, can in fact be pumped around the engine. The flow of oil passing through the engine bearings and other components is therefore able to absorb heat from those components and carry it away. When the oil returns to a reservoir, it then passes the heat to the rest of the oil and then on to the reservoir container (an oil tank or 'sump' at the base of the engine). The reservoir or container then passes the heat to the atmosphere. Note that it is increasingly common to fit an oil cooler to modern engines, especially high performance engines. The oil cooler is effectively a radiator which is exposed to airflow; the heat within the oil being passed to the radiator body and then on to the air passing across the radiator.

2.13.2 Viscosity

When moving surfaces are completely separated by a film of liquid lubricant, the only resistance to motion is due to the viscosity of the lubricant. Viscosity is the property of fluids which causes them to resist flow: the greater the viscosity the greater the resistance. Thus the 'friction' in a well-lubricated bearing depends upon the viscosity of the lubricant. But the viscosity also influences the rate at which the lubricant is squeezed out from between two surfaces when load is applied, so the greater the lubricant's viscosity, the greater its ability to withstand load. Hence the lubricant should have a high enough viscosity to withstand the maximum load to be carried without causing excessive resistance to movement.

The rating introduced by the Society of Automotive Engineers (SAE) is universally adopted to classify oils according to their viscosities. This method uses a number to represent the viscosity (e.g. SAE 20). The higher the SAE number, the higher the viscosity, or to use a more common expression, 'the thicker the oil'.

Whereas engines in the past used a comparatively thick oil, such as SAE 50, the need to reduce both fuel consumption and cold-cranking loads has brought about the common use of thin oils, e.g. SAE 10. An even better economy can be achieved with the very thin oil, SAE 5, but this can only be used on engines having extra-close fitting bearings. Suitability can only be determined by seeking manufacturers' advice.

Viscosity index

The viscosity of lubricants decreases with increasing temperature; the extent of this change is measured by the viscosity index. A high index indicates a relatively small change in viscosity while a low index indicates a large change. The lubricant used should have a suitable viscosity at its normal operating temperature in the engine. This means that when the engine is cold, the viscosity will be unnecessarily high, leading to poor circulation of the lubricant and excessive friction ('oil drag'), possibly even to the extent of making the engine difficult to start.

Multi-grade oils

In the past the high viscosity oil used in engines during the summer made engine cranking difficult in winter, so different grades were specified for the two seasons. Nowadays special additives that reduce the change in an oil's viscosity with temperature are often used, and this has meant that the same grade can be used throughout the year. These oils are called multi-grade or cross-grade, or given trade names that suggest the viscosity remains constant. They can be recognized by the special SAE rating; this has two numbers separated by the letter 'W'. A typical oil is 'SAE 5W 40'. In this case the oil is equivalent to SAE 5 when tested at a sub-zero temperature, (the 'W' indicates winter conditions) and has a viscosity of SAE 40 at the normal rated temperature.

Oiliness

This property is the ability of an oil to 'cling' or be attracted to a metal surface. The effect of this property is seen when a spot of oil is applied to a clean piece of metal; the oil film spreads out over the surface and resists being removed when wiped with a cloth.

Degree of oiliness varies with the type of oil. Vegetable-based oils are excellent in this respect.

2.13.3 Oils

The lubricant used for motor vehicle engines – and most other components – is oil. Oils are obtained from three main sources:

1 **Animal:** purified and suitably treated animal fats, such as tallow and whale oil, are used for certain purposes, but decompose too readily to be suitable lubricants in modern motor vehicle engines.

2 **Vegetable:** these also decompose too readily to be satisfactory, though one example, castor oil, was used quite extensively at one time. Its chief merit is ability to lubricate under arduous conditions, but after a fairly short time treacle-like deposits are formed, so today it is seldom used.

3 **Mineral:** oils of this type are refined from natural crude oil and are far more stable than other types. They form the basis of practically all modern lubricants, and though by no means perfect, they can be improved by the addition of certain chemicals known generally as additives.

Synthetic oils

Although standard mineral oils have been in general use for motor vehicle engines for many years, synthetic oils have increasingly been specified since the 1990s. Synthetic oils are based on natural crude oil (as are conventional mineral oils) but they have been 'chemically engineered' to improve performance. In simple terms, non-synthetic mineral oils are produced using natural crude oil as the raw material or base product, from which suitable fractions are extracted and refined to produce the modified mineral oil. With synthetic oils, the same base product is used but the extracted fractions are modified or changed chemically. Additives are also used (see below) as is the case with conventional mineral oils, with the end result that synthetic oils have benefits over conventional mineral oils.

Synthetic oils generally have improved performance over a wider temperature range compared with mineral oils, including a generally lower viscosity. Importantly, synthetic oils do not 'break down' as readily as mineral oils at high temperatures. Because modern engines usually operate at higher temperatures than older designs, synthetic oils assist in ensuring better lubrication and the anti-wear properties of synthetic oils extend engine and component life.

It is important to note that not all engines will benefit from the use of synthetic oil. This is especially true of engines that were designed before synthetic oils were in general use. It is always advisable to refer to a vehicle manufacturers specification for engine oil, or to consult an oil manufacturer prior to using synthetic oil in an engine that was originally designed for conventional mineral oils.

Additives

Additives are used in most oils to improve oil performance. Different additives have different properties and characteristics. Amongst the most important additives for use in engines are:

a Oxidation inhibitors

At high temperatures mineral oils tend to oxidize (combine with oxygen), forming hard deposits on the hottest parts with which they come in contact (e.g. the underside of the piston crown,) and varnish-like deposits on parts that are not quite so hot (e.g. the piston skirt). Other products of oxidation may be carried in the oil and deposited in other parts of the engine. If they settle in oil passages, they may eventually reduce the oil flow to a dangerous extent. Nowadays, oxidation inhibitors (or anti-oxidants) are added to the oil to reduce oxidation.

b Detergents

In general use, oil becomes contaminated with oxidation products and with burnt or partly burnt products of combustion which escape past the pistons. These usually consist of extremely small and relatively soft particles which will not harm the bearings, but which tend to settle out and block up oil passages. Around piston rings they become baked hard and restrict the free movement of the rings, eventually sticking them completely in their grooves.

The function of detergent additives is to keep these oxidation products in suspension in the oil so that they are not deposited inside the engine. The oxidation products are then removed from the engine with the dirty oil when the oil is changed.

c Viscosity index improvers

Certain chemicals have the property of reducing the change in viscosity of mineral oil caused by change in temperature.

d Anti-foam agents

Some engines suffer from the formation of foam or froth in the oil, and suitable additives are used to reduce this tendency.

2.13.4 Types of oil-based lubrication

Boundary lubrication

This form of lubrication relies on the oiliness property of an oil to coat the surfaces and fill the cavities of low-speed rubbing components to ensure that metal-to-metal contact and resulting wear are avoided.

Boundary lubrication is used in an engine for all sliding components other than the highly loaded bearings that require a pressure feed. The supply of oil for the boundary lubrication film is provided by splash; this comes from the oil thrown out from the crankshaft bearings.

Hydrodynamic lubrication

The bearings of a modern engine must withstand great loads and high rubbing speeds. If the surfaces are to be adequately held apart when subjected to these arduous conditions, the quantity of oil supplied must be sufficient both to fill the space between the shaft and bearing and to make up for the oil squeezed out from the bearing as it rotates. To ensure these requirements are met, the bearing is force-fed with oil at a pressure sufficient to maintain the supply at all times the engine is running.

Highly loaded bearings rely on 'hydrodynamic lubrication' to separate the surfaces. This is achieved by

using the natural movement of the oil (hence the term hydrodynamic) to create an 'oil wedge' to lift and centre the shaft in the bearing.

Figure 2.124 shows the principle of this method of lubrication. The bearing is made larger than the shaft to the extent governed by the type of oil to be used and the expected thermal expansion.

When the engine is stationary the shaft rests on the bottom of the bearing and is supported only by a thin oil film (Figure 2.124a), This boundary film provides lubrication when the engine is started.

Initial rotation causes the boundary layer of oil on the shaft to move around with the shaft owing to its oiliness property. This movement, together with the inherent resistance of the oil particles to shear (viscosity), forces the oil between the surfaces to create a 'wedge' (Figure 2.124b). This wedge lifts and centres the shaft in the bearing (Figure 2.124c). This diagram also shows an indication of the pressure variation and its relationship to the oil wedge that is generated by the hydrodynamic oil film.

To achieve effective lubrication in the bearing, an adequate supply of good quality oil at a suitable pressure must be provided to maintain an oil wedge.

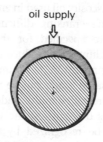

oil supply

(a) Shaft stationary

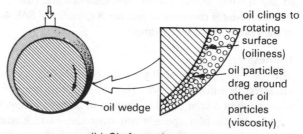

oil clings to rotating surface (oiliness)

oil particles drag around other oil particles (viscosity)

oil wedge

(b) Shaft starting to rotate

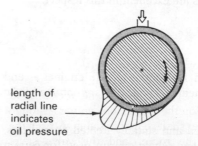

length of radial line indicates oil pressure

(c) Shaft rotating at high speed

Figure 2.124 Bearing lubrication – the oil wedge principle

2.13.5 Oil as a coolant

In modern engines, oil helps to cool such parts as pistons and bearings. In its passage around the engine, the oil picks up heat from the hot parts with which it comes in contact. To prevent excessive oxidation and loss of viscosity the oil itself must be cooled. In most normal types of engine the circulation of air around the engine and the oil reservoir (normally the sump) is sufficient for this purpose. Many vehicles today are fitted with an oil cooler, which helps to reduce the temperature of the oil when the engine is placed under high load. Vehicles such as high performance cars are normally fitted with oil coolers in the form of a small radiator, which is placed in the air stream. The flow of cool air passes across the radiator fins, and this lowers the temperature of the oil as it passes through the radiator. Many engines are fitted with an oil cooler that simply passes engine coolant around the oil filter housing. The hot engine oil passing through the oil filter housing is cooled by the engine coolant which, although it is not cold, is cooler than the oil.

2.14   THE ENGINE LUBRICATION SYSTEM

2.14.1 Main features

The function of the lubrication system of an engine is to distribute lubricant to all the surfaces requiring lubrication. In the earliest motor vehicles, crude lubrication systems were considered quite satisfactory.

As early as 1905 Lanchester used a system in which a pump forced oil under pressure into the crankshaft bearings, and this has developed into the typical system, of which an example is shown in Figure 2.125. Figure 2.126 shows the same system in the form of a diagram, omitting all components not included in the lubrication system.

The oil is carried in the sump ((16), in Figure 2.125), in which the level must be high enough to cover the pump inlet but not so high that the crankshaft dips into the oil. A dip-stick (6) is a simple means of checking the level of oil in the sump, though other means, such as a float indicator or an electric gauge, may be used. A mechanically driven pump (15) draws oil from the sump and delivers it via the main filter (18) to the main oil gallery (7). A rather coarse strainer (17) is fitted over the pump inlet to protect the pump from small hard objects, which would cause damage.

From the main oil gallery, oil is supplied to the main crankshaft bearings. A feed is also taken from the main oil gallery, through an oilway in the cylinder block and cylinder head (3) to the camshaft bearings. Note that another feed is taken from the camshaft feed across to the rocker spindle (2) to lubricate the rocker shaft bearing. Depending on the design, oil can pass through a drilling in the rocker shaft so that it is able to reach the contact points of the rocker and the valve stem. Additionally, oil can be fed to the contact point between the rocker and the cam lobe, although on some designs oil can be pressure fed direct to the cam lobes via drillings in the camshaft.

When the oil has seeped out of the camshaft bearings and the rocker bearings, it is splashed about the camshaft chamber to lubricate valve stems etc. This oil eventually drains back to the sump via tubes or channels cast into the cylinder head and engine block. Again, depending on the design, restrictors may be used on the feed to the rocker shafts and even to the camshaft bearings, which may not require the same high pressures that are provided for the crankshaft bearings. An excess of oil could result in too much oil passing onto the valve guides and into the combustion chambers, therefore the restrictor can also function as a means of reducing oil flow. It is also usual to have oil seals fitted to inlet-valve stems to prevent oil being drawn into the combustion chambers through the inlet ports.

Holes (10) drilled through the crankshaft convey oil from a groove (12) round the main bearing to the big-end: the groove is supplied from the main gallery (7) via the oil way (11), so that there is an uninterrupted supply to each big-end.

A small hole (9) drilled in a suitable position in the connecting rod allows an intermittent jet of oil to spray onto the cylinder walls, and in some engines a hole (shown in dotted lines) is drilled through the shank of the connecting rod to take an intermittent supply to the small-end bearing.

Oil splashed off the crankshaft lubricates the remaining parts, and eventually drains back to the sump.

The quantity of oil delivered into the system by the pump depends upon the pump capacity and the speed at which it is driven. Exactly the same quantity must escape from the system, and this can normally happen only through the bearing clearances.

As engine speed increases, the pressure in the system increases in order to force a greater quantity of oil through the constant bearing clearances. The pressure must be sufficient to ensure an adequate flow through the bearings at relatively low speeds. Therefore, at higher speeds, the pump will deliver higher volumes and generate higher pressures, which would be unnecessarily high, and risk bursting joints and causing excessive power loss in driving the pump. The pressure in the system is therefore limited using a pressure relief valve (14).

1   rocker spindle .
2   oilway to rocker spindle
3   pipe to rocker spindle
4   oilway to gudgeon pin
5   camshaft bearing
6   dipstick
7   main oil gallery
8   outlet from pressure filter
9   oil jet to cylinder wall
10 oilway to big end
11 oilway to main bearing
12 groove round main bearing
13 passage from pump to filter
14 pressure relief valve
15 pump
16 sump
17 inlet strainer
18 main filter

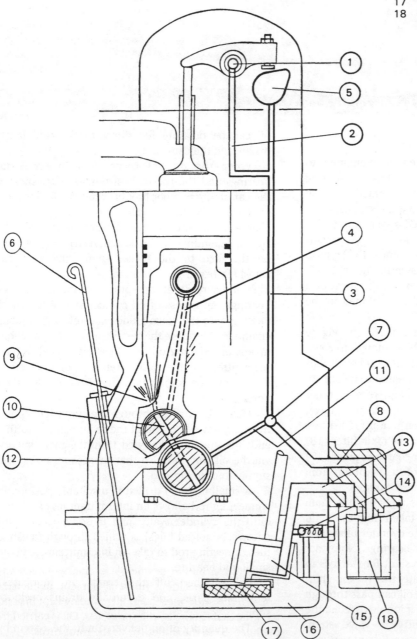

Figure 2.125 A typical basic lubrication system

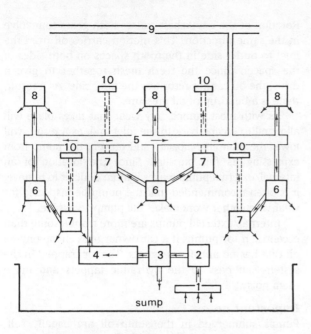

1 suction strainer
2 pump
3 pressure relief valve
4 main filter
5 main oil gallery

6 main bearings
7 big-end bearings
8 camshaft bearing
9 rocker shaft
10 gudgeon pins

Figure 2.126 Block diagram of a lubrication system

2.14.2 Oil pumps

Several types of pump are used:

Gear-type pump (Figure 2.127)

For many years this type was almost universal, and it is still in use. Gear-type pumps consist of a pair of gear wheels meshing together in a casing (1), which fits closely around the tips of the teeth and the ends of the gears. One gear (2) is fixed to the driving spindle (3) and drives the other gear (7), which rotates idly on a fixed spindle (6). Inlet (4) and outlet (5) ports are cut

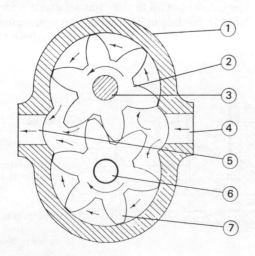

Figure 2.127 A gear-type oil pump

in the casing on either side of the meshing point of the gears. When the gears rotate they carry oil from the inlet to outlet ports in the spaces between the teeth. As a tooth of one gear moves out of mesh with a space between two teeth of the other gear, oil flows in through the inlet to fill the void left. On the outlet side, oil is displaced through the outlet port as a tooth of one gear moves into the space between two teeth of the other. Note particularly the direction of the oil flow and the direction of rotation of the gears, shown by arrows.

Eccentric rotor-type pump (Figure 2.128)

The casing (1) has a cylindrical bore in which is fitted the outer rotor (2). The outer surface of this is cylindrical, but a number of lobes are formed on its inner surface. The inner rotor (3) has lobes formed on its outer surface, one fewer than the number on the outer rotor. It is fixed on the driving spindle (4) and mounted eccentrically in the casing so that each of its lobes makes contact with the inner surface of the outer rotor, dividing the space between the rotors into a number of separate compartments of varying size. The size of each compartment varies as the rotors turn. Inlet and outlet ports are cut in the end plate of the pump, and positioned so that the pumping compartments sweep over the inlet port (6) as they increase in size and over the outlet ports (5) as they decrease. The pump is shown assembled at (a) while sketch (b) shows the rotors removed to reveal the ports more clearly.

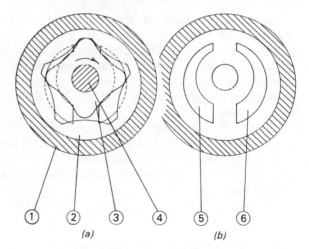

Figure 2.128 An eccentric rotor-type pump

Eccentric vane-type pump (Figure 2.129)

The earlier form of this pump is shown in Figure 2.129a. The casing (1) has a cylindrical bore in which is fitted the rotor (2) mounted on a shaft eccentric to the casing bore and touching it at one place. Spring-loaded vanes (4) are a close-sliding fit in a slot cut diametrically through the rotor, their outer edges being kept in contact with the casing bore by the spring (3). Oil is carried from the inlet (5) to the outlet (6) as the rotor turns.

A later version of this pump used on some modern engines is shown in Figure 2.129b. This has two one-piece vanes, each with a diametral slot, the two at right angles to one another. Each vane is cut away as shown at (7) and the bore of the casing is not truly cylindrical but shaped so that each vane touches the bore at both ends in all positions.

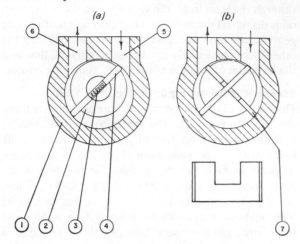

Figure 2.129 An eccentric vane-type pump

Internal/external-type pump (Figure 2.130)

This type was primarily introduced on automatic gearboxes. However, its compact size and ease in which it can be driven without the need for a separate drive shaft, has made the pump popular for use on some engines.

Normally two flats on the 'front' end of the crankshaft are used to drive the inner gear (1); this meshes with and drives the outer gear (2), which is positioned off-centre. The outer gear is supported in a casing (3) and the wide region between the gears is filled with a crescent-shaped spacer (4) which projects from the casing.

At one end of the pump two ports are formed in the casing to allow oil to flow to and from the pump. On the front face of the pump a flat plate is fitted to blank off the gears and ensure that the only path for the oil is via the gear teeth.

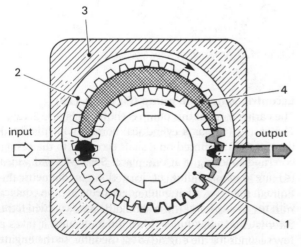

Figure 2.130 An internal/external-type oil pump

Rotation of the crankshaft causes both gears to revolve in the same direction. This motion carries oil from the inlet to outlet side in the tooth spaces on both sides of the spacer. Since the teeth mesh together to give a drive, the oil cannot return to the inlet side. As a result, there is a build-up of oil pressure.

As with most pumps, any wear that takes place will allow oil to escape back to the inlet and, as a result, will lower the pumping capacity and prevent the pump from expressing its full pressure. Since the location of an internal/external pump makes it more difficult to remove, it is often recommended that the pump be inspected for wear when other work makes the pump accessible.

Internal/external pumps are more troublesome than eccentric rotor pumps if a car owner uses cheap engine oil that has no anti-foam agents. The air trapped in the system can pass to the hydraulic tappets and make them noisy.

Important note

Pumps submerged in the sump oil are usually self-priming. This means that the oil level causes the oil to flow into the pump so as to wet the gears and bridge the clearances.

However, some pumps are mounted above sump level. This type of pump must be primed by filling it with oil from a convenient external point. This operation is essential if, for any reason, the pump becomes dry, a condition sometimes created when the engine is assembled or when the engine has been allowed to stand unused for a considerable time.

To avoid drain-back of oil from the pump, some systems incorporate a valve between the intake filter screen and the pump.

2.14.3 Oil pressure relief valves

Figure 2.131 illustrates a simple type of pressure relief valve, which consists of a ball held by spring pressure over a hole drilled into the main oil channel leading from the pump to the bearings.

The pressure of oil in this channel exerts a force on the ball (5), tending to lift it off its seat against the load of the spring (3). The spring load is adjustable by screwing the cap (1) in or out, and locking it in the

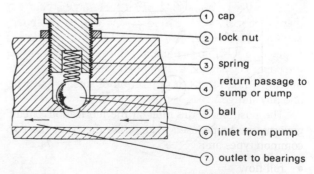

Figure 2.131 A ball-type oil pressure relief valve

correct position by the lock nut (2). When oil pressure is great enough to lift the ball off its seat, oil is allowed to escape from the main oil channel, thus relieving the pressure and preventing further rise. Oil escaping past the valve returns either to the sump or the pump inlet valve via the passage (4).

Figure 2.132 shows an alternative type of valve in which a plunger (4) replaces the ball, and an alternative method of adjustment is shown. In this case the spring load is adjusted by adding or removing shims (2) above the spring.

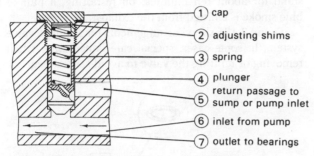

1. cap
2. adjusting shims
3. spring
4. plunger
5. return passage to sump or pump inlet
6. inlet from pump
7. outlet to bearings

Figure 2.132 A plunger-type oil pressure relief valve

2.14.4 Oil filters

The purpose of the filters in a lubrication system is to remove from the oil abrasive particles that would cause rapid wear of the bearings. If a fluid containing solid particles is passed through a porous material (the filter) particles will either be too large to enter the pores, will become lodged in the tortuous passages of the pores, or will pass completely through, depending upon the relative sizes of the pores and the particles. Clearly, the finer the pores the smaller the particles the filter will remove from the fluid, but its resistance to the flow of fluid will be correspondingly greater. Thus a very fine filter will need to have a very large surface area if the flow of oil to the engine bearings is not to be restricted.

A rather coarse wire mesh strainer is usually fitted at the pump intake to protect the pump against the occasional large objects that could enter into the engine, or hard objects large enough to damage the pump. On the pressure side of the system a much finer filter is used.

The modern replaceable filter consists of about four metres of resin-impregnated paper; this is pleated to expose a large external surface area to the oil and is retained in a cylindrical metal canister. The porosity of the paper is designed to trap nearly all particles over 25 microns (0.025 mm), a proportion of smaller particles and any sludge.

The position of the filter in the lubrication 'circuit' governs the name used to describe the type; the two common types are:

- full-flow
- by-pass.

Figure 2.133 shows a schematic layout of the two arrangements:

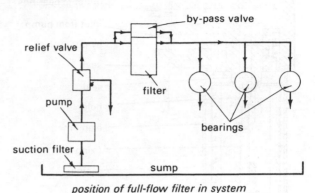

position of full-flow filter in system

Figure 2.133 Position of oil filter in system

A full-flow filter treats all the oil delivered to the bearings provided the filter is clean and the oil is not excessively viscous.

A by-pass filter is fed only a proportion of the oil delivered by the pump. Although this filters out finer particles than the full-flow filter, it only cleans the proportion of oil passing into the filter; the oil passing to the bearings is unfiltered. For this reason most engines today use full-flow filters.

Full-flow filters

In addition to the filter material, this type incorporates a by-pass valve that opens when the pressure drop across the filter exceeds about 1 bar (15 lbf in^{-2}). This valve opens when the filter is clogged, or when the oil is cold, to avoid oil starvation of the bearings.

Although this arrangement gives limited protection to the engine, the continued use of a filter that is not changed at the recommended time will eventually cause damage to the bearings owing to the supply of unfiltered oil.

The replaceable full-flow filter is made in two forms:

- element-type
- cartridge-type.

Element-type

Figure 2.134 shows the construction of this type of filter. The assembly is mounted directly on the side of the crankcase by a pad, which overcomes the need for troublesome external piping. Today most filters use a paper element, but in some cases a felt element, carried on a wire mesh frame and convoluted to give a large surface area, is occasionally fitted to suit other conditions.

The filter should be changed at the recommended service intervals and this is carried out by removing the bolt at the base of the filter casing. This type has a number of seals and these should be renewed when the filter is changed. After renewing the element it takes a few seconds for the engine to fill the filter, so the engine should not be accelerated during this time.

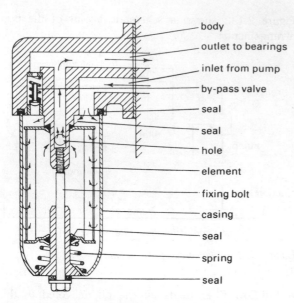

Figure 2.134 A full-flow oil filter

Cartridge-type

This type, shown in Figure 2.135, is also called a 'spin-on filter'. It is a throw-away filter designed to simplify the task of removing and refitting.

The canister unit, either screwed directly onto the side of the engine crankcase or onto the oil pump housing, is sealed with a synthetic rubber ring. The cartridge-type oil filter houses a paper filter element and by-pass valve. The cartridge-type oil filter is used on modern engines.

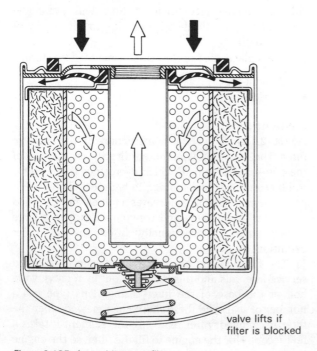

Figure 2.135 A cartridge-type filter

2.14.5 Valve stem sealing

An overhead valve mechanism, using either rockers or an overhead camshaft, needs a good supply of oil. This requires the valve stems to be fitted with effective seals to stop the oil trickling down the valve guides by gravity and, in the case of the inlet valve, being drawn in by the manifold depression. Although this oil leakage is beneficial as regards stem wear, the oil consumption and exhaust smoke make sealing necessary.

Ineffective valve seals and worn guides can normally be diagnosed by allowing a warm engine to stand for about ten minutes: on restarting, a puff of blue smoke is emitted from the exhaust.

Figure 2.136 shows arrangements for sealing a valve system. In some cases, special care is necessary when removing or refitting the valve to avoid seal damage.

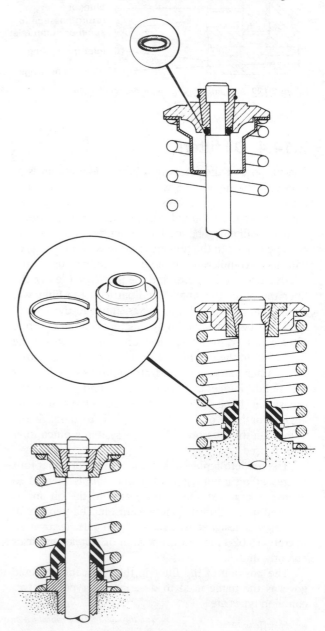

Figure 2.136 Valve oil sealing arrangements

2.14.6 Crankcase ventilation

If ideal conditions prevail within the engine, the air spaces in the crankcase, rocker cover and timing cover would be filled with a fine oil mist that coats all working parts. Unfortunately, this is not the case, especially when the vehicle is used for short journeys. The main problems are:

- Blow-by of the pistons carries unburnt fuel, corrosive gases and steam into the crankcase.
- Steam coming into contact with cold surfaces, such as the camshaft and sump covers exposed to the cold air stream, causes condensation. Water produced in this way mixes with the oil to form an emulsion called cold sludge, a dirty, black, smelly mess that causes corrosion and obstructs oil flow.

The ill effects of these problems can be minimized if the air can be made to circulate around the inside of the engine. In the past this was achieved by providing a 'crankcase breather' for clean air to enter the crankcase and a vent pipe to expel the dirty fumes into the atmosphere. Sometimes the end of the vent pipe was fitted with an airflow detector to lower the pressure and 'draw out' the fumes. Systems such as this were effective, but caused air pollution, especially if the engine was worn.

Positive crankcase ventilation (PCV)

PCV is necessary to conform to emission control regulations. The system uses a 'closed crankcase ventilation' arrangement to prevent partially burnt fuel and fumes being discharged to the atmosphere. Instead the fumes are returned to the induction system for burning in the combustion chamber.

Figure 2.137 shows the layout of a typical closed ventilation system. In this arrangement the oil filler cap contains a calibrated passage and regulator valve that

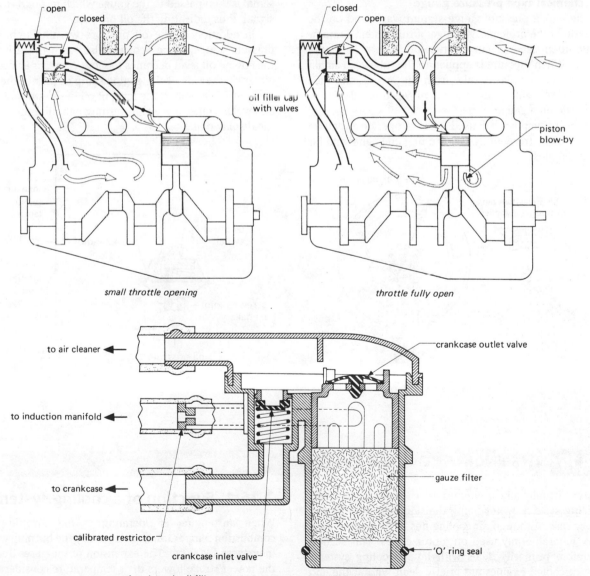

small throttle opening

throttle fully open

section through oil filler cap which incorporates ventilation valves

Figure 2.137 *Closed engine ventilation system – positive crankcase ventilation*

allows air to enter the crankcase only when the throttle is less than half open. At full throttle the two hoses connected to the air cleaner and manifold convey the fumes to the induction system for burning in the engine.

To allow the engine to function correctly, especially during slow running, air must not be allowed to enter the system at points other than those designed for entry. The crankcase should therefore be sealed during the operation of the engine; components such as the oil dip stick and oil filler cap must be effectively sealed to prevent escape of the crankcase fumes.

2.14.7 Pressure indication

An indication of the oil pressure can be signalled to the driver by either a pressure gauge or a low-pressure warning light.

Mechanical type pressure gauge

In the past a pressure gauge system was based on the Bourdon tube principle. A gauge of this system contains a Bourdon tube; a curved tube as shown in Figure 2.138. When pressure is applied to the tube via a small-bore copper or plastic tube from the engine, the tube tends to straighten out and this moves a needle across the scale on a gauge.

This principle is still used today to operate a vacuum gauge, an instrument used for tuning an engine and for fault diagnosis.

Electrical type pressure indicator

Modern vehicles use electrical/electronic systems (usually an oil warning light), to indicate to the driver when the oil pressure drops to a 'dangerous' point or use an illuminated display to show the actual oil pressure.

Figure 2.139 shows a low-pressure warning light system. The pressure switch is normally fitted on the side of the engine block and connected to the main oil gallery. When the oil pressure is low (e.g. the engine is not running), the switch contacts are closed and the light is illuminated in the display panel. When the engine is started, oil pressure in the main gallery applies pressure to the pressure switch. When the pressure is sufficient to overcome the switch spring pressure, the electrical contacts are separated, which extinguishes the warning light.

Many vehicles are fitted with electronic pressure gauge systems. A sensor is located so that it measures the pressure in the main oil gallery, and an electrical signal is then passed to the gauge which responds to the signal, thus indicating the oil pressure.

In addition to the oil pressure warning light and pressure gauge, some vehicles also warn the driver if the engine oil level becomes too low. A sensor is located either on the side of the engine sump or part of the dip stick, which monitors the level of oil in the sump. If the oil level becomes too low a warning light illuminates on the display panel.

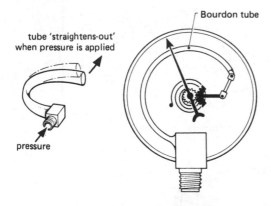

Figure 2.138 Pressure gauge – Bourdon type

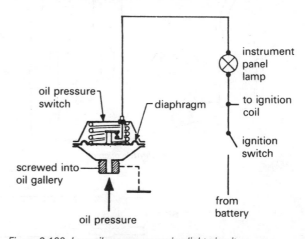

Figure 2.139 Low oil pressure warning light circuit

2.15   THE ENGINE COOLING SYSTEM

Note: Virtually all car engines are cooled using a liquid cooling system, water being the liquid used in almost every case. Although air cooling has been used on cars, it is generally only used on motor cycles. This section therefore primarily deals with liquid cooling systems but air-cooled engines are briefly dealt with at the end of the section.

2.15.1 Function of a cooling system

When an engine is operating at full throttle, the combustion temperatures produced by the burning gases may exceed 2000°C. The expansion of the gases during the power stroke lowers their temperature considerably, but during the exhaust stroke the gas temperature may still be not far short of 800°C (Figure 2.140). All of the engine parts that come in contact with the hot gases will absorb heat in proportion to the gas temperature, the area of surface exposed and the duration of the exposure; this heat will raise the temperature of the engine components. The temperature of the exhaust gases is above 'red heat' and much above the melting point of such metals as aluminium. Unless steps are taken to limit the temperature of the engine components, a number of problems will arise:

1 The combustion chamber walls, piston crown, the upper end of the cylinder and the region of the exhaust port are exposed to the hottest gases and will reach the highest temperatures. The resulting thermal expansion of these parts will distort them from their correct shape, causing gas leakage, loss of power, valve burning, and possibly even cracking of a cylinder or head.

2 The oil film, which should lubricate the piston and cylinder walls, will be burnt or carbonized causing excessive wear and even seizure of the piston.

3 Engine power will be reduced due to the heating of the fresh air/fuel mixture entering the cylinder, which reduces its density. The increased temperature of the fresh gas will also increase the liability to detonation, thus making a reduction in compression ratio necessary.

4 The surface of the combustion chamber may become hot enough to ignite the fresh gas before the spark occurs. This is called 'pre-ignition', and will result in serious damage to the engine if it persists.

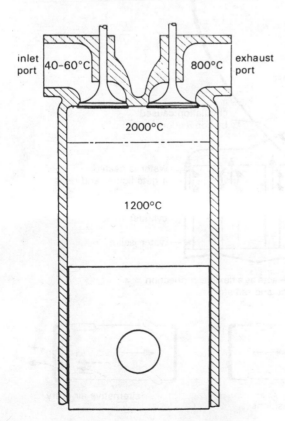

Figure 2.140 Approximate gas temperatures in engine

The function of the cooling system is to remove heat from the engine components at a high enough rate to keep their temperature within safe limits and so avoid these troubles.

It is, however, important not to overcool the engine, or other problems will arise:

1 Heat is necessary to assist in vaporizing the fuel inside the cylinder during the compression stroke. Unvaporized fuel will be deposited on cold cylinder walls, and besides being wasted it will dilute the lubricating oil and destroy its lubricating properties.

2 Water vapour formed during combustion will condense on the cold cylinder walls, forming a sludge with the lubricating oil and corroding engine parts. The rate of wear is considerably greater when the engine is cold than when hot for this reason.

Experience suggests that the temperature of the cylinder head must be kept below about 200–250°C if overheating is to be avoided.

A correctly designed liquid cooling system removes different amounts of heat from different parts of the engine. As an example, the region around the combustion chamber and the exhaust valves will be exposed to much greater temperatures than the base of the cylinder. Therefore the cooling system must be designed to remove large amounts of heat from the area surrounding the combustion chambers and exhaust valves, but there will be less heat to remove away from the base of the cylinder.

Circulation of the liquid is controlled so that in different parts of the engine, the flow of water will be different. The various galleries or tubes through which the liquid flows are different in size to selectively regulate the flow of water.

2.15.2 Liquid coolant

The liquid used to carry heat away from the cylinders and heads is almost invariably water, to which may be added certain chemicals. The chief advantages of water are:

• It has a high specific heat capacity, i.e. a given amount of water, heated through a given temperature range, absorbs more heat than almost any other substance.

• It is readily available in most parts of the world at little or no cost.

Water has, however, certain disadvantages:

• It boils at a temperature somewhat lower than is desirable for best possible engine performance, especially at heights much above sea level (the boiling point of water falls as altitude increases because pressure falls with the increase in altitude).

• It freezes at temperatures often encountered during winter in many parts of the world. Since ice expands with fall in temperature, there is a considerable risk of cracking the cylinder blocks if freezing is allowed to occur.

- It may tend to corrode some of the metals with which it comes into contact.

These objections can be wholly or partly overcome in the following ways:

- The temperature at which the coolant boils can be raised by operating the system under pressure. The way this is achieved will be described later, but the boiling temperature is raised by about 1°C for every 4 kN m⁻² (0.6 lbf in⁻²) that the pressure is increased.
- The freezing temperature of the coolant can be lowered by adding an antifreeze chemical. The one most commonly used is ethylene glycol, and a solution containing about 20% of this in water is sufficient to give complete protection in Britain. The strength of the solution can be checked by means of a suitable hydrometer.

- The risk of corrosion can be reduced or eliminated by the addition of suitable chemicals. These are usually included in the antifreeze solution.

2.15.3 Thermo-syphon system

The coolant is made to circulate around the cooling system so that heat absorbed by the coolant from the cylinders can be dissipated in a radiator. The simplest method of producing this circulation relies upon convection currents in the coolant. These result from the reduction in density caused by expansion of the coolant with increase in temperature. A system using this method of circulation is known as a 'natural circulation system', or a 'thermo-syphon system', and is illustrated in Figure 2.141.

The basic system consists of a water jacket, which is connected by a synthetic rubber hose to a header tank.

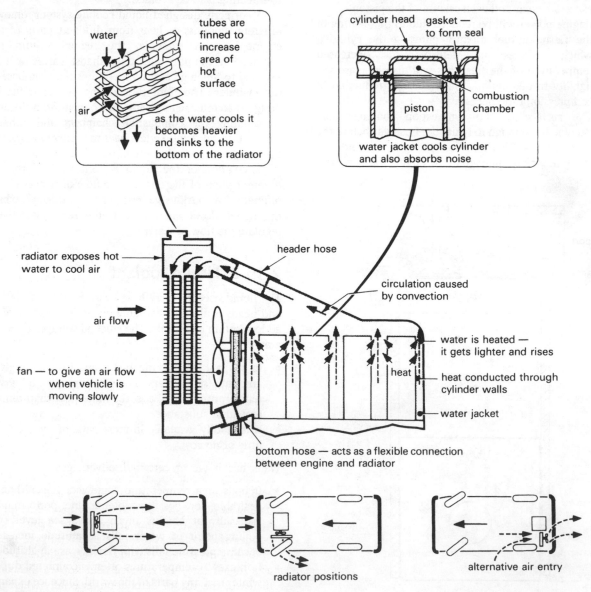

Figure 2.141 A simple type of liquid cooling system

This tank forms part of the radiator, which is a heat exchanger made by connecting two tanks (header and lower) with a number of finned tubes to provide a large surface area for the disposal of unwanted heat. Airflow over the tubes and fins carries away the heat radiated from the hot coolant and so lowers the temperature of the coolant as it passes down the tubes. A bottom hose connects the lower tank to the engine water jacket to provide a return path to the engine for the coolant.

When the engine is running and the vehicle is either stationary or travelling slowly, the airflow through the radiator is insufficient to give adequate cooling. At these times overheating is avoided by using a fan to act as an air pump. Energy to drive the fan is supplied by a vee-belt from the crankshaft, or alternatively the fan can be driven directly by an electric motor.

The principle of operation is based on the three means of heat transfer: conduction, convection and radiation. Cooling of the engine takes place in this sequence.

Conduction

Heat flows from a hot substance to a cold substance. The hot internal parts of the cylinder pass the heat from one metal particle to the next through the walls to the comparatively cool outer surface. Coolant in contact with the metal surface receives the heat and carries it away.

Convection

This is based on the principle that as the temperature of water rises from 4°C, it gets lighter, i.e. its density decreases as the temperature increases.

Coolant in the water jacket becomes heated, and since it becomes lighter it rises to the top of the jacket and flows through the header hose to the radiator. The

hot water in the jacket is replaced by colder water fed in from the lower tank of the radiator. When the flow is combined with the upward flow in the jacket, a natural circulation of the coolant is achieved which is called 'convection'.

Circulation due to the thermo-syphon action can only take place if the coolant level in the header tank is above the level of the header hose.

Radiation

Heat travels through air in a wave form similar to light. Radiated heat can be felt if your hand is placed close to a hot surface.

The purpose of a radiator is to transfer the heat from the coolant to the air. The air must move because, if it is stationary, the air temperature will soon become close to the coolant temperature and heat transfer will be very slow. To avoid this problem, cold air is continuously supplied to the radiator through vehicle motion or using a fan, and thus heated air is also carried away.

2.15.4 Pump circulation systems

Modern vehicles do not rely on the thermo-syphon system for engine cooling. This is because the body line of the vehicle prevents the use of a tall radiator and the large quantity of coolant required is too heavy to be carried around. When these disadvantages are combined with the slow cooling action and long delay before the engine reaches its optimum running temperature after cold starting, it is apparent why a more positive and compact cooling system is required. Systems using a pump to move water through the cooling system provide one important solution to the problems of the thermo-syphon system.

Figure 2.142 shows the main features of a pump-assisted cooling system. The layout is based on the simple thermo-syphon system but uses a pump, generally belt-driven, to promote circulation of the coolant. The increased rate of flow of coolant given by a pump system allows a smaller radiator to be used, and where necessary this can be mounted lower relative to the engine. Mounting the pump directly onto the cylinder block is common practice; this overcomes the need for an outlet hose between the pump and engine. The alternative is to make the pump a separate unit, which is convenient when the pumping capacity has to be increased to suit hot climates.

Unless special attention is given to the outlet flow of coolant from the pump, those cylinders at the end of the engine farthest from the pump will operate at a much higher temperature than those at the front. This is because the coolant will gain heat as it flows to the rear of the engine. Besides causing the rear cylinders to wear at a higher rate, the reduced heat flow to the coolant increases the risk of detonation especially when these cylinders are operating on a weaker air/fuel mixture

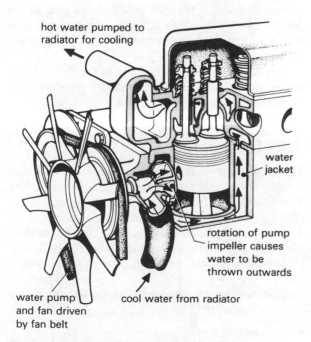

hot water pumped to radiator for cooling

water jacket

rotation of pump impeller causes water to be thrown outwards

water pump and fan driven by fan belt

cool water from radiator

Figure 2.142 Pump-assisted circulation of coolant

than the remaining cylinders (which was not uncommon with older carburettor engines).

One method of minimizing this problem is to incorporate in the cylinder head a tube that runs from front to rear of the engine (Figure 2.143). Holes (2) formed in the tube (1) direct jets of relatively 'cold' coolant around the outside of the exhaust valve seats and any other parts of the combustion chamber that need extra cooling. Holes in the cylinder head gasket allow convection currents to carry away the heat from the regions where the heat is less intense.

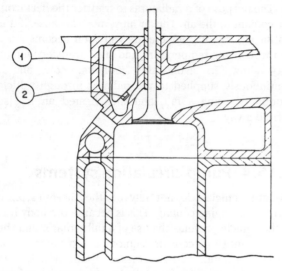

Figure 2.143 Water distribution tube in cylinder head

The cooling pump

Figure 2.144 shows a typical water pump. The body of the pump is generally a cast iron or light alloy casting which carries a double-row ball bearing pre-packed with grease and sealed for life. The bearing must be robust because it has to withstand the radial load caused by the driving belt.

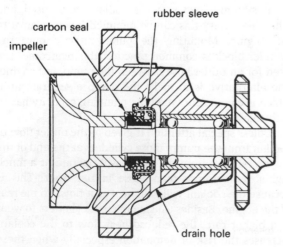

Figure 2.144 A water pump

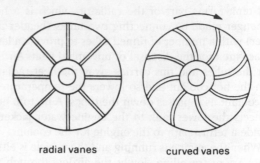

Figure 2.145 Face of water pump impellers

Mounted on the spindle, and retained in position by an interference fit, is the impeller. This has either radial or curved vanes as shown in Figure 2.145, which act as the means either to pressurize the coolant or to agitate the fluid sufficiently to produce a given flow. Various materials can be used for an impeller; it can be cast iron, stamped in steel or moulded in plastic. The stamped impeller is very cheap but has a low pumping efficiency and as a result the energy consumed lowers the fuel economy of the engine. A moulded impeller is more efficient but since this type suffers from bearing rotation and creep at the fixings, the cast impeller, shrouded in a manner to give a flow about three times greater than the stamped type, is favoured.

One of the most important parts of the pump is the seal between the impeller and casing. This is intended to prevent coolant entering the bearing, which would cause noise and rapid wear. The seal shown in Figure 2.144 is retained in the casing and is a spring-loaded carbon type; this is bonded to a synthetic rubber sleeve fitted to allow for the difference in expansion between the carbon and the casing. An annular groove in the casing, on the bearing side of the seal collects any coolant that might pass the seal A drain hole at the bottom allows coolant to drip from the pump, a sign that the pump seal is defective and the pump needs replacing.

Normally the pump is situated at the 'front' of the engine and is driven at about crankshaft speed by a vee or notched belt.

2.15.5 Radiators

The radiator is a liquid-to-air heat exchanger that consists of two tanks and a core or matrix from which heat is radiated from the coolant to the air. To be effective the hot coolant contact area exposed to air moving through the core should be as large as possible. Also, it should offer minimum resistance to the flow of air to ensure that the hot core is exposed to the coldest air.

The core can be constructed in various ways; two common forms are:

- tube and fin cores
- cellular or film-type cores.

Tube and fin cores (Figure 2.146)

The tubes through which the coolant flows are of a flattened oval section and made of brass about 0.125 mm thick. They are arranged in three or four rows and pass through a series of thin copper fins. The whole assembly is dipped in solder to bond the tubes and fins together. Modern radiator cores are generally constructed of aluminium.

At each end of the radiator core are tanks. If the core is made from brass these tanks generally are also made of brass and soldered to bond the units together. The tanks fitted to modern aluminium cores are made from plastic. An outlet tube is fitted to each tank, which provides a connection point for the synthetic rubber hoses that supply and receive the coolant from the engine.

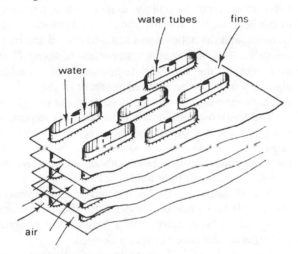

Figure 2.146 Tube and fin radiator construction

Cellular or film-type cores (Figure 2.147)

Two forms of strip are used in this construction.

The waterway strip is a shallow trough with corrugated flanges. Two of these strips are placed together to form a water space similar in shape to a well flattened tube.

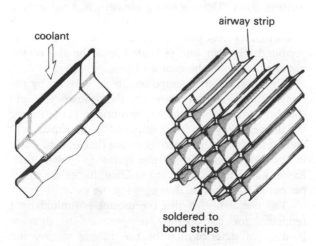

Figure 2.147 Cellular film-type radiator construction

The airway strip is deeply corrugated and is placed between the water tubes to increase the hot surface area.

After arranging the strips to form a matrix and fitting a tank to each end, the assembly is dipped in a solder bath to bond the strips and seal the waterways.

Flow direction through the radiator

The coolant flow through a radiator can be from either top to bottom or side to side, called vertical-flow and cross-flow radiators respectively.

Vertical-flow

This is the oldest type of radiator and is designed to use the downward flow caused by natural convection as the water cools on passing through the radiator. The increased speed of circulation given by the pump overcomes the dependence on natural circulation, but the direction of flow is unchanged.

Modern radiators are much wider and shorter than earlier designs, the actual shape being governed by the available space. To ensure the system is completely filled with coolant, a filler cap, combined with a vent that also acts as an overflow, is fitted at the highest point of the radiator.

On some cars with automatic transmission an oil cooler is used. This can be incorporated in the main radiator by mounting the oil cooler under the engine-cooling radiator.

Cross-flow

Lower bonnet lines used in the last few years have meant that a wide, short radiator, often placed lower than the engine, is needed. This requirement is achieved with the cross-flow pattern. Used in conjunction with a pump, the system cools the water as it flows across the radiator. The two main engine hoses are connected to the end tanks; normally the 'hot' inlet to the radiator is situated higher than the outlet.

Figure 2.148 shows the layout of a typical cross-flow arrangement. This uses a separate reservoir that is often made of a transparent material, allowing the coolant level to be easily checked. This reservoir also performs two other duties: it acts as an expansion chamber to allow for the change of coolant volume with temperature, and as a degas tank to condense the steam that collects at the highest point of the engine, the region under the filler cap, A.

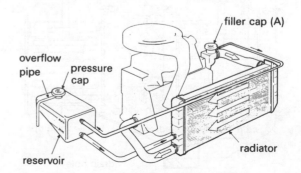

Figure 2.148 A cross-flow cooling system layout

Normal topping up of the system is made at the reservoir, but whenever the engine is drained, the system must be refilled at point A to avoid an air lock.

2.15.6 Temperature control of the cooling system

The cooling system must be capable of keeping the engine temperature within safe limits under the most arduous conditions, such as when climbing long, steep hills at full throttle in hot climates. Since these conditions represent a very small proportion of the running time for most vehicles, it is clear that the cooling system will overcool the engine most of the time unless some method of reducing its effectiveness is adopted when necessary.

There are two ways in which this may be done:

1   By controlling the circulation of the water. This is the commonest method and is achieved by a temperature-sensitive valve called a thermostat.
2   By controlling the airflow through the radiator using shutters or blinds.

Thermostats
There are two types in use:

The bellows-type thermostat (Figure 2.149)
The operating element is a sealed, flexible metal bellows (8) partly filled with a liquid, which has a boiling point somewhat lower than the boiling point of water (such as alcohol, ether or acetone). Air is excluded from the bellows, which contains only the liquid and its vapour, so that the pressure inside the bellows is due to the vapour pressure of the liquid. This varies with temperature, being equal to atmospheric pressure at the boiling temperature of the liquid, less at lower temperatures and greater at higher temperatures.

The lower end of the bellows is fixed to a frame (7) which is attached at its upper end to a circular flange (4), by which the thermostat is supported in its housing

(9) which is usually formed in the outlet from the cylinder head to the radiator. A poppet-type valve (3), attached by a stem (5) to the top of the bellows, controls a circular opening in the flange to regulate the flow of water. A flat spring blade (6) holds the stem in light contact with a V-shaped groove in a cross member of the frame which supports the stem, and provides sufficient friction to prevent flutter of the valve.

At low temperatures the pressure inside the bellows is lower than the atmospheric pressure outside it and the bellows then contracts, holding the valve closed and preventing water circulating through the radiator.

As the water temperature increases, hot water will collect around the thermostat (which is usually in the engine outlet connection), heating the liquid in the bellows and so increasing the pressure inside the bellows. At about the boiling temperature of the liquid in the bellows, the internal and external pressures will be equal, and the bellows will begin to extend and open the valve. This occurs at a temperature of about 70 to 80°C and by the time the temperature has reached about 85 to 90°C the internal pressure in the bellows will have extended it sufficiently to open the valve fully.

The thermostat therefore performs two important functions: (a) it shortens the time required to get the engine warmed up after a cold start, and (b) it prevents the temperature falling below about 70°C when the engine is running at light loads.

A small hole (2) drilled in the valve acts as a vent to prevent air being trapped underneath the valve when the system is being filled, and a loosely fitting 'jiggle-pin' prevents this hole becoming clogged.

The 'free length' of the bellows is such that when internal and external pressures are equal, the valve is open; thus, should the bellows develop a leak, the valve will remain open, so the thermostat is fail-safe.

The wax element-type thermostat (Figure 2.150)
The operation of the wax element-type thermostat depends upon the considerable change in volume, which occurs in certain types of wax at around their melting point. The operating element is a substantial metal cylinder or capsule (7) filled with wax into which is inserted a thrust pin (2). A flexible rubber sleeve (8) surrounds the pin and is seated into the top of the capsule to prevent the escape of wax.

The thermostat is supported in its housing by the flange (5) in a similar manner to the bellows-type, and the thrust pin (2) is attached to a bridge (1) spanning the flange. The valve (3) is attached to the capsule (7) and closes against an opening in the flange, being held in the closed position by the spring (6) when cold. Expansion of the wax during melting, forces the thrust pin out of the capsule, thus opening the valve.

The useful life of this thermostat is limited by a tendency for its opening temperature to increase because of deterioration of the rubber sleeve, but typically the wax-type thermostat is claimed to last for

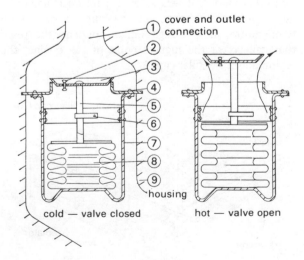

cover and outlet connection

① ② ③ ④ ⑤ ⑥ ⑦ ⑧ ⑨

housing

cold — valve closed   hot — valve open

Figure 2.149 A bellows-type thermostat

in excess of 100,000 km. It is much more robust than the bellows type so that sudden and complete failure is extremely unlikely. This is just as well since failure would generally cause the valve to remain closed, resulting in overheating of the engine. If, however, a leak develops in the rubber sleeve (8) below the thrust pin, the valve will stick open.

The hole (4) serves the same purpose as the hole (2) in the bellows type (Figure 2.149), and usually has a jiggle-pin also.

The opening temperature of wax element-type thermostats is unaffected by coolant pressure, so this feature makes it suitable for use in most modern cooling systems.

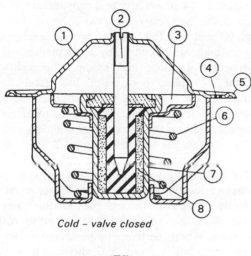

Cold – valve closed

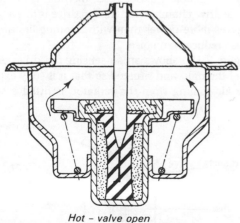

Hot – valve open

Figure 2.150 A wax element-type thermostat

Radiator blinds

A very simple arrangement for controlling the airflow through the radiator is illustrated in Figure 2.151. A spring-loaded roller blind (4) is carried at the lower end of a rectangular channel section frame secured to the front of the radiator. A cable control enables the blind to be raised to blank off as much of the radiator as may be necessary to maintain the required temperature. The end of the cable is taken into the driving compartment of the vehicle and incorporates some means of fixing

the blind at a suitable height. It is desirable that a temperature gauge should be fitted to indicate to the driver the temperature of the cooling water.

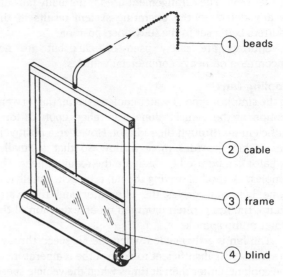

Figure 2.151 A simple radiator blind

Radiator shutters

This rather more complex arrangement for regulating the airflow through the radiator is illustrated in Figure 2.152. A rectangular frame fixed to the front of the radiator supports about twelve horizontal rods, each of which carries a metal strip about 40 mm (1.5 inches) wide. When these strips are all vertical they blank off the airflow through the radiator, but by turning them through 90° a free passage for air is provided.

Small levers fitted to one end of each spindle are connected to a vertical strip, which may be raised or lowered to open or close the shutters. This may be operated manually as in the case of the blind, but the short movement necessary makes possible the use of a

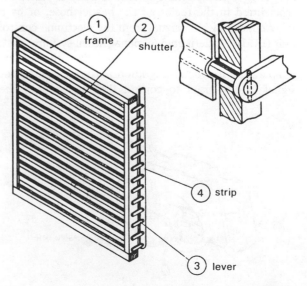

Figure 2.152 Radiator shutter arrangement

thermostat device. Shutters such as these were once fitted to some of the more expensive types of car and operated by a thermostat immersed in the radiator header tank. The arrangement used is normally fail-safe as any defect in the operating system results in the shutters being set in the fully open position.

Shutters are rarely used on cars but are not uncommon on heavy commercial vehicles.

Cooling fans

In the simplest type of water-cooled system, the forward motion of the vehicle alone was relied upon to force sufficient air through the radiator. However, a positively driven fan provides more airflow so that a smaller radiator can be used to dissipate the required heat. The simplest method of driving the fan is by belt, usually the same belt that drives the alternator and the water pump; the fan is often mounted on an extension of the water pump spindle.

The fan is only needed when the air speed through the radiator is insufficient to control the temperature of the coolant. Other than at times when the vehicle speed is low (as in heavy traffic or hill climbing,) the energy required to drive the fan continuously robs the engine of power and increases fuel consumption.

Energy saving is achieved by aerodynamic shaping of modern plastic fan blades, compared with the pressed steel blades used in the past, and the modern vehicle achieves a better economy still by using a drive system that cuts out when fan operation is not needed.

Two common fan systems are:

- electric drive
- viscous drive

Electric fan (Figure 2.153)

The fan is driven by a separate electric motor which is only switched on when the cooling water reaches a predetermined temperature (e.g. 90°C).

The electrical circuit for the motor is controlled either by a thermostatic switch, usually a bimetallic type, fitted in the region of the header hose, or by a relay energized by a signal from the electronic control unit (ECU). Modern engine management systems use a coolant temperature sensor to monitor the engine temperature for fuelling/ignition purposes. The sensor signal is also used to control the operation of the cooling fan. When the engine has reached a predetermined temperature the engine management ECU provides a control signal to the cooling fan relay.

Viscous fan (Figures 2.154 and 2.155)

This type of drive has a disc-shaped clutch plate that is placed in a container of silicone fluid. The viscous drag of the fluid, caused by its resistance to shear, provides a non-positive drive that is designed to slip at an increasing rate as the engine speed rises.

Viscous drives for fans are made in two forms: torque-limiting and air temperature-sensing.

The torque-limiting fan drive, as the name suggests, is capable of transmitting to the fan a maximum torque that depends on the viscosity of the fluid.

Figure 2.154 shows a typical construction. A clutch disc is sandwiched between the two halves of the casing, which is fitted with fluid seals to prevent leakage of the silicone fluid. Aluminium alloy is normally used as a material for the disc and casing. This lightweight material is chosen because it has good thermal conductivity for dissipating the heat generated by the shearing action of the fluid. Fins on the outside of the casing also aid heat transfer from the coupling to the air.

The two graphs shown in Figure 2.155 show the performance characteristics of this type of drive.

The air-sensing fan drive, as well as being torque limiting, varies the fan speed to suit the temperature of the air that has passed through the radiator. It does this by controlling the amount of fluid in contact with the drive plate. When the temperature sensor detects that the coolant is below about 75°C, the fluid is evacuated from the drive chamber and the fan drive is disengaged. This saves more power than with a torque-limiting fan and also reduces fan noise.

Figure 2.156 shows an air-sensing fan drive. At the front of the unit, and situated so that it is fully exposed to the air coming from the radiator, is fitted a spiral-

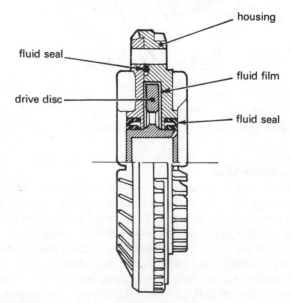

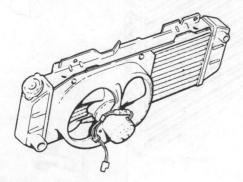

Figure 2.153 Electric cooling fan

Figure 2.154 A viscous fan drive

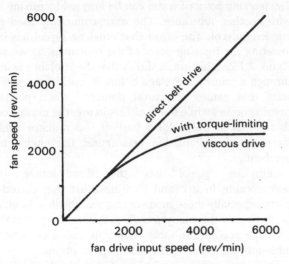

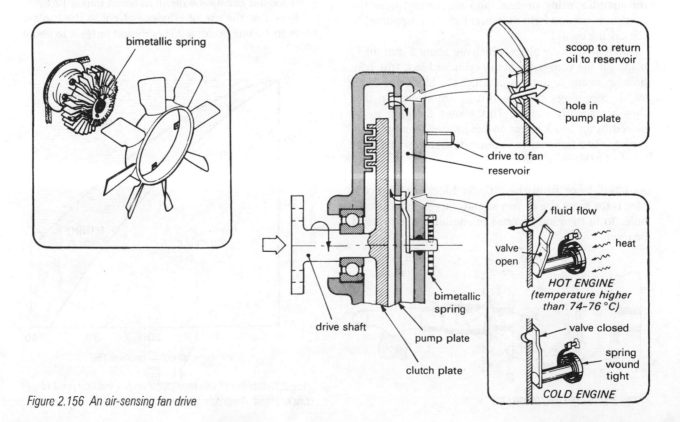

Figure 2.155 Viscous fan performance characteristics

shaped bimetal sensor. This sensor controls a valve arm, which is made to rotate through a small angle as the temperature changes and either cover or uncover an inlet port in the pump plate.

The fan is not needed at low radiator temperatures, so the sensor causes the valve plate to close the inlet port. This action stops the flow of fluid from the reservoir to the drive chamber. Since the existing fluid in this chamber is being pumped back to the reservoir continuously by a combination of centrifugal action and

scoop movement, and no fluid is entering the chamber to take its place, the chamber soon empties and the drive disengages.

At high radiator temperatures the thermostatic coil moves the valve arm and uncovers the inlet port; as a result fluid flows from the reservoir to restore circulation between the reservoir and drive chamber, and drive to the fan is restored.

Figure 2.157 shows the performance characteristics of an air-sensing fan of the type fitted to light vehicles.

Figure 2.156 An air-sensing fan drive

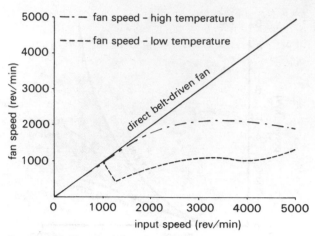

Figure 2.157 Characteristics of an air-sensing fan

2.15.7 Use of antifreeze mixtures

One of the disadvantages of water as a coolant is the fact that in many parts of the world temperatures may drop to freezing during the winter months.

Water is peculiar in that its maximum density occurs at a temperature of 4°C and from this point it expands with either rise or fall in temperature. So long as it remains liquid this has no serious consequences, but solid ice expands on cooling and will transfer its expansion to its container. If this happens to be the brittle cast iron cylinder block, it is likely to crack and this results in a very expensive repair. A less drastic effect occurs when the expansion of the ice forces out the cylinder block core plugs. The holes are the result of the manufacturing process, and are holes where the sand core, used to form the water jacket, is supported in the casting mould.

Welch-type core plugs, which are about 2 mm thick, blank off the core holes in the cylinder block (the core holes exist due to the way in which the block was cast). Welch core plugs, prior to fitting, are shaped so that they are slightly convex. This allows the plug to be placed in the block recess and expanded by tapping its centre with a hammer to increase its diameter and form a tight fit (Figure 2.158).

Most modern core plugs are a cupped shape and are an interference fit in the cylinder block, i.e. the core plug is the same size or very slightly larger than the core hole. To fit the plugs, a press or similar process should be used.

The freezing point of water can be lowered by mixing it with another substance. The most commonly used is ethylene glycol. The effect that ethylene glycol has in lowering the freezing point of the coolant is shown in Figure 2.159. This graph shows that the coolant passes through a 'mushy ice' stage before it reaches the solid state that causes structural damage. When partial freezing occurs while the vehicle is in use, the mushy ice that forms in the coldest part of the radiator tank interrupts the circulation and causes the engine to overheat.

Ethylene glycol has the disadvantage of decomposing in use and forming acids that corrode parts, especially those made of aluminium alloy. To give protection to the many metals that come into contact with the coolant, suitable chemicals called corrosion inhibitors are added to the antifreeze solutions.

Modern antifreeze solutions remain in the cooling system for the whole year rather than being drained at the end of the winter. In view of this, a reputable make of antifreeze should be used to give the engine all-year protection from corrosion. The antifreeze solution may lose some of its antifreeze and corrosion properties over a period of time. Some manufacturers recommend that the coolant be changed at certain service intervals to ensure that the engine has full protection from freezing as well as corrosion.

In the UK a coolant mixture containing 25% antifreeze (one part antifreeze to three parts water), is often recommended to suit the conditions experienced during a normal winter. This proportion gives protection against ice damage down to minus 25°C and gives coolant circulation down to about minus 12°C.

Note that the use of ethylene glycol in the coolant raises its boiling point; a 25% solution raises it to about 103°C.

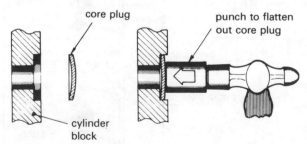

Figure 2.158 Core plug fitting

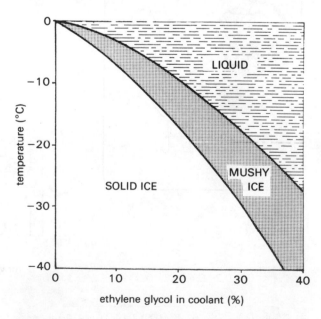

Figure 2.159 Effect of ethylene glycol on the freezing point of coolant

Since the specific gravity of ethylene glycol differs from that of water, it is possible to check the proportion of antifreeze in the engine coolant by using a special hydrometer together with a thermometer.

Ethylene glycol is toxic and care should always be taken when handling such chemicals and ensure that all antifreeze is disposed after use in the correct manner. Many antifreeze manufacturers are now using different chemicals to ensure that the antifreeze is environmentally friendly. Some antifreeze solutions are composed of propylene glycol because it is less toxic to humans and animals while others are organic-based products, typically phosphate and silicate free. When adding antifreeze to a cooling system, always ensure that the fresh antifreeze is compatible with the antifreeze already in the cooling system. If unsure always drain the cooling system, flush and refill with fresh antifreeze.

2.15.8 Pressurized cooling systems

Another disadvantage of water as a coolant is the fact that its boiling point is lower than the most efficient engine operating temperature, and to prevent boiling and the formation of steam pockets around exhaust ports and sparking plug bosses, it is necessary to keep the temperature of the water leaving the cylinder head below 85–90°C.

The temperature at which a liquid boils rises as the pressure on it increases. In the case of water, the variation of boiling point with pressure is shown in Figure 2.160.

Pressure can easily be imposed on the water in a cooling system by sealing it off from the atmosphere, so that any steam formed by the boiling water will raise the pressure and suppress further boiling until the temperature has risen still further. There is obviously a limit to the pressure that a radiator and rubber hoses can withstand, and a pressure relief valve, such as that illustrated in Figure 2.161, is necessary. The one illustrated is incorporated into the header-tank filler cap. Starting from cold, the header tank will contain some air above the water at a pressure approximately that of the atmosphere. As the water is heated it expands, compressing the air, and if the temperature rises sufficiently for boiling to begin, the steam formed will raise the pressure still further. This suppresses the boiling until the pressure in the header tank rises sufficiently to lift the pressure valve (8) against the loading of the spring (3), whereupon air and steam will escape through the vent pipe (5). By this means the system may be operated without boiling at a temperature slightly below that corresponding to the pressure needed to lift the valve.

The operating pressure that can be used with a cooling system is governed by the strength of the radiator and hoses. When the manufacturer has calculated this, the appropriate radiator pressure cap is fitted. For information purposes the 'blow off pressure' is stamped on the cap; typical values range from 0.5 bar (7 lbf in^{-2}) to 1.0 bar (15 lbf in^{-2}).

When the engine is stopped and cools down, condensation of vapour and contraction of the water reduces the pressure in the header tank. Should this pressure fall appreciably below atmospheric, there is a risk of the hoses and even of the header tank collapsing. To prevent this, a vacuum valve (4) is fitted in the centre of the pressure valve and acting in the opposite direction. This means it is closed by a spring (7) assisted by positive pressure inside the header tank, but opens against the spring loading if header tank pressure falls about 7 kN m^{-2} (1 lbf in^{-2}) below atmospheric.

The advantages to be gained by using a pressurized cooling system are as follows:

1 Elimination of coolant loss by surging of the coolant during heavy braking.
2 Prevention of boiling during long hill climbs, particularly, for example, in regions much above sea level.

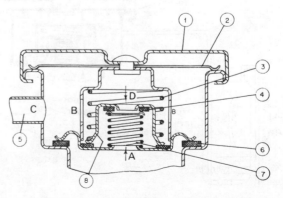

Figure 2.161 Pressure cap for coolant

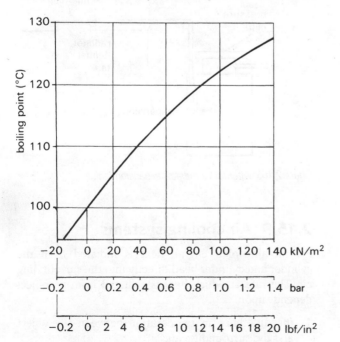

Figure 2.160 Variation of boiling point of water with pressure

3 Raising the coolant working temperature improves engine efficiency.

4 It allows a smaller radiator to dissipate as much heat as a larger one operating at a lower temperature.

Never remove the cap when the coolant temperature is above 100°C, since the release of pressure will cause the water to boil violently and the resulting jet of steam and water from the open filler can cause serious scalds. At temperatures below this the cap should be released slowly. It is designed so that the spring disc (2) (which is rivetted between the cover (1) and the frame which contains the valves) remains seated on the top of the filler neck until after the seal (6) has lifted, so allowing pressure to escape through the vent pipe (5) before it can escape from the main opening.

Since bellows-type thermostats are sensitive to pressure changes, they are unsuitable for use in pressurized cooling systems. The wax element-type does not have this disadvantage.

Sealed cooling systems

A further refinement of the cooling system consists of an arrangement whereby the system is kept completely full of coolant, expansion of the coolant being accommodated by providing an expansion tank into which the displaced coolant can pass and from which it can return to the system as the coolant in the system contracts on cooling. There are several variations of the arrangement, of which two are briefly described here.

Figure 2.162 shows an addition to the pressurized system already described, the modification consisting of leading the vent pipe from the filler neck to the bottom of an expansion tank. A vent pipe is fitted to the top of the expansion tank, which may (though it is not necessary) have a drain tap and a filler cap.

The pressure cap differs from that shown in Figure 2.161 only in having a sealing gasket fitted between the filler neck and the spring disc (2).

The system is completely filled with coolant up to the top of the radiator tank filler neck and the cap is then fitted. As the engine warms up the coolant expands, lifting the pressure valve off its seating, and

some coolant passes into the expansion tank. Air displaced from the expansion tank escapes through the vent pipe. The expansion tank is seldom more than about half full under normal conditions.

As the engine cools down after stopping, the coolant in the system contracts, withdrawing coolant from the expansion tank back into the system through the filler cap vacuum valve – hence the necessity for the gasket under the spring disc.

A variation of this system uses a plain, airtight filler cap on the header tank, the pressure and vacuum valves being contained in a small housing permanently attached to the header tank.

Figure 2.163 shows an alternative system in which the pressure cap is fitted on the expansion tank, which is connected to the top of the header tank by a small pipe. The filler neck on the header tank is sealed by a plain filler cap. The radiator header tank is completely filled with coolant and a small amount of coolant is also added to the expansion tank. As the cooling system warms up, coolant expands into the expansion tank, which in this case is under pressure. As the system cools down coolant from the expansion tank is drawn back into the radiator header tank.

The advantages claimed for a sealed system are:

- It eliminates coolant loss by expansion.
- It eliminates the need for periodic topping up, and prevents possible engine damage by neglecting to top up.
- By excluding air from the main system it considerably reduces corrosion of the components in the cooling system and deterioration of the antifreeze additives.

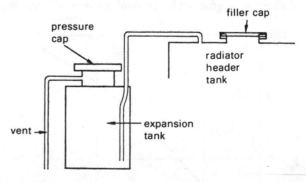

Figure 2.163 Alternative radiator expansion tank

2.15.9 Air cooling systems

For an air-cooled engine heat is radiated from the cylinder and cylinder head directly into the surrounding air. The rate at which heat is radiated from an object depends upon:

1 the difference in temperature between the object and the surrounding air.

2 the surface area from which heat is radiated.

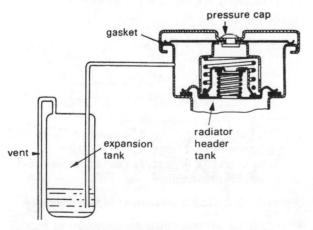

Figure 2.162 A radiator expansion tank

Since (1) must be limited, the surface area of the cylinder and head exposed to the air must be increased, and this is achieved by forming fins on their external surfaces (Figure 2.164).

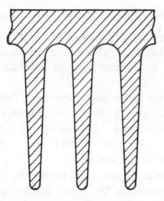

Figure 2.164 Section of air-cooled fins

It is also necessary to remove the heated air from around the cylinder and deliver a constant supply of cool air around and between the fins. This means that the cylinders must be sufficiently widely spaced to permit a suitable depth of finning all around them, and the engine must be placed in an exposed position where the motion of the vehicle can provide the necessary supply of cool air. If it is necessary or desirable to enclose the engine, for the sake of protection or appearance, a fan must be used to supply the air, with suitable cowls to direct the air where it is needed.

The volume of air required to conduct a given amount of heat away from the cylinders of an air-cooled engine is about 2000 times the volume of water necessary to remove the same amount of heat. To provide the necessary airflow around the cylinders of an enclosed engine, a powerful fan is essential. Figure 2.165a shows a fan of the simple curved blade type, known as an axial-flow fan because the direction of airflow is parallel to the axis of the fan spindle. This type of fan is sometimes used, but the radial-flow (or centrifugal) fan, shown in Figure 2.165b, is more often used since it is more effective and a fan of smaller diameter can be used for a given airflow. This type of fan consists of a number of curved radial vanes mounted between two discs, one or both having a large central hole.

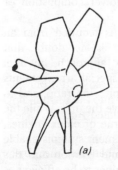
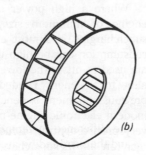

Figure 2.165 Types of fan

When the fan is rotated, air between the vanes rotates with it and is thrown outwards by centrifugal force.

Figure 2.166 shows a simple air-cooled system for a four-cylinder in-line engine. A centrifugal fan (4), driven at approximately twice crankshaft speed, is mounted at the front of the engine and takes in air through a central opening (5) in the fan casing (6). From the fan the air is delivered into a cowl (3), from which it passes over the fins on the engine cylinders (1). Baffles (2) direct the airflow between the fins, from which the air picks up heat, so cooling the cylinders.

The in-line type of engine shown is not the most suitable for air cooling, since the cylinders have to be placed further apart than would otherwise be necessary, in order to allow enough air to flow between them. Vee-type engines, or horizontally opposed types, are better in this respect since the cylinders have to be spaced far enough apart to leave room for the crankshaft bearings and this allows a good airflow between the cylinders while keeping the total engine length short.

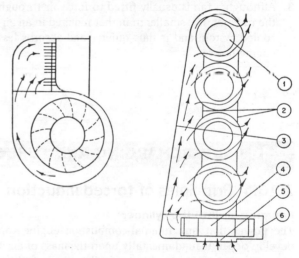

Figure 2.166 Air-cooling system for a four-cylinder in-line engine

2.15.10 Comparison of air- and liquid-cooled systems

Air-cooled system

Air cooling has several points in its favour:

1 An air-cooled engine should generally be lighter than the equivalent water-cooled engine.
2 The engine warms up to its normal running temperature very quickly.
3 The engine can operate at a higher temperature than a water-cooled engine.
4 The system is free from leakage problems and requires no maintenance.
5 There is no risk of damage due to freezing of the coolant in cold weather.

However, air cooling has a number of disadvantages:

1 A fan and suitable cowls are necessary to provide and direct the airflow. The fan is noisy and absorbs a

fairly large amount of engine power. The cowling makes it difficult to get at certain parts of the engine.

2 The engine is more liable to overheating under arduous conditions than a water-cooled engine.

3 Mechanical engine noises tend to be amplified by the fins.

4 The cylinders usually have to be made separately to ensure proper formation of the fins. This makes the engine more costly to manufacture.

5 Cylinders must be spaced well apart to allow sufficient depth of fin.

6 It is more difficult to arrange a satisfactory passenger compartment heating system.

Liquid-cooled system

The main points in favour of liquid or water cooling are:

1 Temperatures throughout the engine are more uniform, thus distortion is minimized.

2 Cylinders can be placed close together and the engine made more compact.

3 Although a fan is usually fitted to force air through the radiator, it is smaller than that required in an air-cooled system and is thus quieter and absorbs less engine power.

4 There is no cowling to obstruct access to the engine.

5 The water and jackets deaden mechanical noise.

6 The engine is better able to operate under arduous conditions without overheating.

The main disadvantages of water cooling are:

1 Weight, not only of the radiator and connections but also of the water. The whole engine installation is likely to be heavier than an equivalent air-cooled engine.

2 Because the water has to be heated, the engine takes longer to warm up after starting from cold.

3 If water is used, the maximum temperature is limited to about 85 to 90°C to avoid the risk of boiling away the water.

4 If the engine is left standing in very cold weather, precautions must be taken to prevent the water freezing in the cylinder jackets and cracking them.

5 There is a constant risk of leaks developing.

6 A certain amount of maintenance is needed, e.g. checking water level, anti-frost precautions, cleaning out deposits, etc.

2.16   SUPERCHARGING AND TURBOCHARGING (FORCED INDUCTION)

2.16.1   Principles of forced induction

Pumping air into the cylinder

The power that any internal-combustion engine can develop depends fundamentally upon the mass of air it can consume per minute. The normal method of filling or charging the cylinders of a four-stroke engine consists of allowing the pressure of the atmosphere to force air into the combustion chambers. The downward movement of the piston on the intake stroke creates a partial vacuum, which is a lower pressure than that of the atmosphere. The amount of air entering the cylinder therefore depends on the difference in pressure between the atmospheric pressure and the lower pressure (vacuum) in the cylinder.

If, however, air is forced into the cylinders under a pressure that is higher than atmospheric pressure, a greater mass of air will enter the cylinder and the engine will be 'supercharged'. Forcing the air into the cylinders can be achieved by using some kind of air pump. Such a device is called a 'supercharger'.

Reducing the compression ratio

It should be noted that a supercharger would cause the fresh charge to enter the cylinder at a much higher pressure than on a conventional (un-supercharged) engine. This increased fresh charge pressure would then

cause a much higher pressure to be created on the compression stroke. If pressures during the compression stroke are too high, this will increase the charge temperature, which can lead to premature or pre-ignition of the fuel mixture.

To overcome the problem, when an engine is supercharged, the compression ratio is usually reduced compared with a 'normally aspirated' (un-supercharged) engine. Unfortunately, lower compression ratios usually result in lower combustion efficiency, which usually increases fuel consumption.

Although combustion efficiency may be slightly lower, with regard to engine power, the advantage of having a much greater volume of air in the cylinder outweighs the disadvantage of lower combustion or thermal efficiency.

Where a high power output is required from an engine of minimum size, there is no doubt that supercharging is a most effective approach, but fuel consumption can be high unless special arrangements are used to offset the lower compression ratio, and to allow for the energy needed to drive the unit. While the previous statement is generally true of older engines, modern electronic engine management systems enable very precise control of fuelling and ignition and this therefore allows supercharged engines to be efficient as well as powerful.

Position and drive arrangements of the supercharger

The position of the supercharger in the induction system depends on the fuel system used. On early spark-ignition engines the supercharger (or blower as it is often called), forced the air into the carburettor where it then mixed with the petrol and passed into the engine. Many later designs for carburettor engines favoured an arrangement where the supercharger was fitted between the carburettor and the engine, therefore the supercharger pulled the petrol and air mixture from the carburettor and pumped the mixture into the engine.

With the advent of petrol injection, the arrangement has reverted to a system in which the supercharger only pumps the air; the petrol is delivered independently by the injectors.

A supercharger can be positively driven by belt, chain or gears from the engine crankshaft.

Turbocharger

A different type of supercharger, referred to as a 'Turbocharger' is driven by energy contained within the exhaust gases as they flow from the engine. The turbocharger, has gained favour over recent years (although not universally), because it uses the energy in the exhaust gas instead of directly robbing the engine of some of its power.

It is sometimes claimed that the turbocharger is the answer to emission problems as well as present day demands for better fuel consumption. However improved fuel efficiency is difficult to obtain from a spark-ignition engine unless the turbocharger is very carefully matched with the engine. This reservation is based on the fact that thermal efficiency (or fuel economy) depends on the compression ratio, and to avoid detonation, the ratio must normally be lowered slightly when a supercharger is fitted. However, as stated earlier, modern engine management systems do now allow higher compression ratios to be used on supercharged and turbocharged engines, than formerly.

Supercharged compression-ignition engines (diesel)

Supercharging is not limited to spark-ignition engines; compression-ignition engines may also be supercharged and in some ways are more suitable for supercharging and turbocharging.

A typical example of the introduction of a supercharger into a CI engine is where there is a need to raise maximum engine power to meet a legally permitted increase in the load carried by a vehicle. Instead of fitting a larger engine, many manufacturers have uprated the power of the existing engine by using a turbocharger.

In general, the CI engine is already constructed and designed to work at very high cylinder pressures with diesel fuel. The combustion chamber design and fuel delivery systems are therefore designed to reduce as far as possible the potential for pre-ignition. The

compression ratio problem does not therefore apply to CI engines. The following gives a rough guide to the advantages gained by turbocharging a CI engine:

1 A four-cylinder turbocharged engine gives the power output of a six-cylinder normally aspirated engine.
2 A six-cylinder turbocharged engine gives the fuel consumption of a four-cylinder normally aspirated engine.

Two-stroke engines

Note that a two-stroke engine does not have an induction stroke created by the downward movement of the piston, but relies upon air being forced into its cylinders by some kind of pump (usually the lower chamber beneath the piston). The two-stroke engine is therefore not supercharged unless the pressure of the air filling the cylinder is above atmospheric pressure.

A two-stroke engine is normally 'pressure-charged' (as opposed to supercharged) either by using by using the underneath of the working piston in the lower chamber or by using a separate cylinder as a charging cylinder. However, two-stroke engines have been supercharged using separate air pumps such as a Roots-type blower (covered in section 2.16.2).

Strictly, a two-stroke engine cannot be supercharged unless the exhaust ports are arranged to close before the inlet ports close.

2.16.2 Types of direct drive superchargers

The Roots blower

This device was patented about 1865 by F. M. and P. H. Roots in America and was used for a number of purposes including (in very large sizes) ventilating mines. Figure 2.167 illustrates the construction generally used for engine supercharging. Depending on the size of engine for which the blower is to be used, the width of the casing would be about 150–300 mm (6–12 inches).

It can be regarded as a form of gear pump in which each gear (called a rotor in the Roots blower) normally has two teeth or lobes. (Some Roots blowers have rotors with three or even four lobes.) The rotors have a small clearance inside the casing and are carried on shafts, which are geared together outside the casing; each rotor shaft is supported by a bearing at either end. One shaft is driven at approximate engine speed and drives the other at the same speed.

The Roots blower is an 'air displacer' and not a compressor. The air is not compressed within the blower but simply carried round from inlet side to outlet side in the spaces between the lobes and the casing. The pressure at the output side depends upon the relative swept volumes of the blower and the engine, and the speed at which the blower is driven.

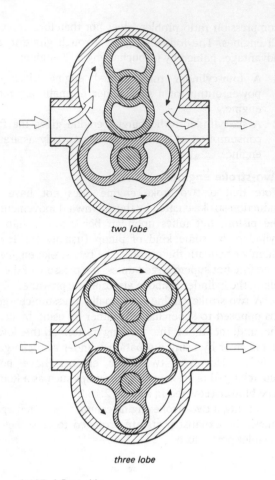

two lobe

three lobe

Figure 2.167 A Roots blower

The rotors operate continuously against the full delivery pressure and thus more power is absorbed in driving this device than would be required if compression took place within the blower. At low pressures this disadvantage is small, but it increases rapidly as pressure rises.

Owing to the rotor clearance there will be some back leakage of air, which increases as delivery pressure rises but this decreases as engine speed increases. Therefore, this type of supercharger is mostly used for high-speed engines and relatively low supercharge pressures.

The operation of a Roots-type supercharger fitted to a modern engine is normally controlled by an electronic control unit (ECU). The ECU controls the operation of the supercharger by a magnetic clutch, which is fitted to the supercharger drive pulley. The supercharger is driven by the crankshaft, typically using a rubber belt. When the clutch is disengaged the supercharger is not driven; when the ECU operates the magnetic clutch, the drive is engaged and the supercharger then operates. The magnetic clutch is operated when the ECU senses that the throttle is open and the engine is also under load, such as during acceleration.

To prevent the rotor gears from seizing they are supplied with oil. The oil level in the supercharger should be checked or renewed during routine maintenance.

The vane compressor

In its simplest form a vane compressor consists of a cylindrical casing in which is mounted eccentrically a cylindrical rotor carrying protruding vanes. The vanes divide the space between the rotor and the casing into a number of compartments, which vary in volume as the rotor turns.

In Figure 2.168a, the compartment shown shaded is in the position of maximum volume and the vane (1) has just cut off communication between this compartment and the inlet port. In Figure 2.168b the rotor has turned to the position where the vane (2) is just about to open the compartment to the outlet port, and it can be seen that the volume of the compartment is now smaller than it was in Figure 2.168a, which results in the air being compressed. The position of the leading edge of the outlet port dictates the amount of compression; this leading edge positioning would normally be arranged to correspond with the required delivery pressure for the engine to which the compressor is fitted.

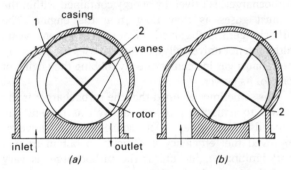

Figure 2.168 Principle of the vane compression

Figure 2.169 shows one practical form of this device, which has, at various times, been marketed under the names of a Centric, Arnett and Shorrocks compressor.

The vanes are mounted on a shaft, which is placed centrally in the casing, each vane being carried on two ball bearings so that the vanes are always radial to the casing. The vanes pass through slotted rods or 'trunnions' carried in the rotor and there is a very small clearance between the tips of the vanes and the casing. The rotor is driven at approximately engine speed by a belt, chain or gears.

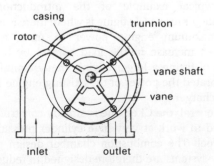

Figure 2.169 The trunnion-type radial vane compressor

One minor disadvantage of the vane compressor is the necessity for lubrication due to the sliding of the vanes in the rotor. While this is fairly easy to arrange it is undesirable because the oil mist carried into the engine may cause combustion difficulties, particularly in compression-ignition engines.

The centrifugal blower

If the Roots blower can be likened to a gear pump the centrifugal blower can be simply described as a glorified water pump (as used in an engine cooling system). The impeller is more carefully designed and made than the corresponding part of the water pump and is driven at considerably higher speed.

Figure 2.170 illustrates the construction. The driving shaft is driven at some five to six times engine speed. Air is drawn in through the air inlet (intake), carried round between the vanes of the impeller and thrown outwards by centrifugal force into the volute casing; it exits via the outlet port, from which it passes to the inlet manifold.

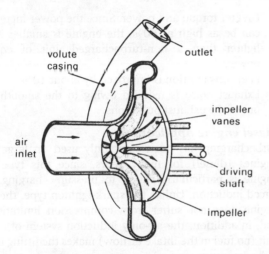

Figure 2.170 A centrifugal blower

The advantage of this type of blower is that a small size of blower can deliver a considerable quantity of air. It has two main disadvantages for automobile use. The first is the very high speed at which it must be driven (which introduces problems in the drive arrangements during rapid acceleration and deceleration) and the second is that it is only efficient over a very narrow impeller speed range.

2.16.3 Turbo-type supercharger (turbocharger)

The difficulties of driving a centrifugal blower at very high speeds, and the loss of up to 35% of the engine's power to provide this drive, can be overcome by using the energy contained in the exhaust gas to drive a centrifugal blower or compressor. A turbine on one end of a shaft is driven by the flow of exhaust gas; on the

other end of the shaft is the centrifugal compressor. The combination of centrifugal compressor and an exhaust-driven turbine is called a turbo-supercharger or turbocharger.

Attempts to apply this principle to engines have been made from time to time since the early 1900s, but only within recent years has the method been successfully applied to motor vehicles. The blades of the turbine have to operate at the high temperature (about 1000°C) of the exhaust gases, so only when a reasonably priced material became available for the blades was it possible to make an economical unit.

Normally a turbine of the radial flow type is used to drive the compressor. It has a similar construction to a centrifugal blower but the gas flow through the unit is reversed (Figure 2.171). A special material, such as nickel or nickel–chromium alloy iron, is used for the turbine; this is necessary because of the high temperatures. A cast iron casing, formed like a snail's shell to feed the exhaust gas on to the periphery of the turbine blades, encloses the turbine. A flange on the part of the casing that forms the gas passage to the turbine connects the unit as closely as possible to the exhaust manifold of the engine. A connection to the gas outlet at the centre of the turbine casing allows the exhaust gas to be passed to the normal exhaust system.

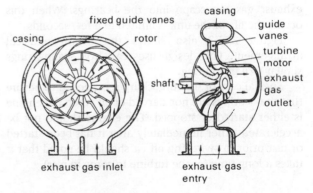

Figure 2.171 A radial flow turbine

When the unit is in operation, the exhaust gas expelled from the engine cylinders at high temperature and velocity is delivered into the casing and the gas is then directed to the turbine rotor. Before the gas flows from the casing to the turbine it first has to pass through either specially shaped passages or a ring of guide vanes; these ensure that the gas strikes the outer tips of the turbine blades tangentially so that the turbine can be driven in the required direction. As the gas flows towards the centre of the turbine, the blades slow down the gas velocity. This action extracts energy from the gas and causes the turbine to spin at a high speed. This can be in excess of 100,000 revolutions per minute under engine conditions in which the temperature and/or velocity of the exhaust gas is high.

The exhaust-driven turbine is supported by a shaft, which transmits the drive to the centrifugal compressor.

The casings of aluminium alloy and cast iron for compressor and turbine respectively are bolted together to form a single unit; it is this assembly that is called a turbocharger or 'turbo' for short (Figure 2.172).

In view of the high speed of operation, two plain floating bearings (often made of cast iron) are needed to support the shaft (Figure 2.173). This type of bearing requires a pressurized supply of clean oil to resist wear and an adequate flow of oil to keep the bearings cool. The bearings are supplied with oil by a pipe connected to the engine's lubrication system. After passing through the bearings the oil is collected in a cavity, formed in the casing between the compressor and turbine, from where it is allowed to drain back naturally into the engine sump.

Gas and oil sealing are very important. Oil must not enter the compressor and exhaust gas must not pass to the bearings. The onset of either condition soon becomes apparent to the driver. Oil passing the compressor seal, especially when it is being pumped through by exhaust gas that is escaping from the turbine, produces a vast quantity of blue smoke. Any defect in the turbocharger that disturbs the action of the seals, such as shaft movement caused by worn bearings, soon shows up. Poor lubrication, caused by a lack of pressure or dirty oil, is a common cause of rapid bearing wear; this is accelerated when the shaft movement allows hot exhaust gas to escape into the bearings. When this occurs the life of the unit is limited to a few seconds.

Figure 2.173 also shows the bearing-and-seal arrangement. This design uses cast iron sealing rings similar to a piston ring.

Special care of the turbocharger is needed to ensure that the bearings are not starved of oil when the engine is either started or stopped. The engine should not be accelerated either immediately after it has been started or just prior to switching off (it should be noted that it takes a long time for the turbine to come to rest).

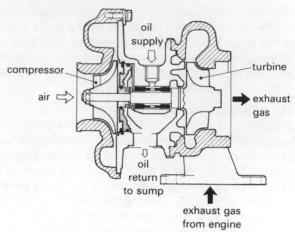

Figure 2.173 Section through a turbocharger

Turbocharging for diesel and petrol engines

Fitting a turbocharger to an engine, which originally was normally aspirated, gives the following advantages:

1 Greater torque and power. Since the power increase can be as high as 60%, the engine is smaller and lighter than a non-turbocharged unit of equal power.
2 Fuel consumption is improved by about 10%.
3 Exhaust noise is reduced owing to the smoothing out of the exhaust pulsations.

Diesel engine applications

Turbocharging has been commonly used on large CI engines (diesel) for many years, since this type of engine is particularly suited to pressure charging or forced induction. Unlike the spark-ignition type, the CI engine does not suffer from compression limitations and, in addition, the air-only induction system of a CI unit (no fuel in the intake airflow) makes the fitting of a turbocharger much easier.

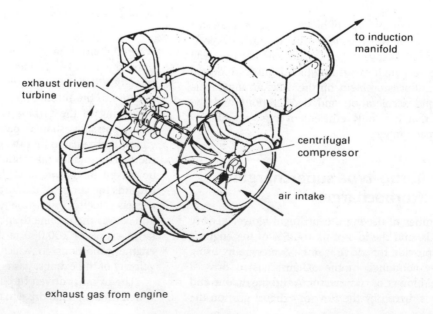

Figure 2.172 A turbocharger

More recently, diesel engine cars with small and large capacity engines have become increasingly popular across Europe and other markets. Due to the advances in diesel engine management systems, turbocharging has proven to be an extremely efficient way of producing high power outputs along with excellent fuel economy. Even some sports saloons are now fitted with turbocharged diesel engines.

Petrol engine applications

A car fitted with a 'turbo' is generally associated with top-of-the-range models designed to give a performance, especially acceleration in mid-range, far above the normal levels of non-turbocharged engines. Engines that are suitable for turbocharging conversion must be structurally strong to withstand the extra load and higher speeds. Also if the turbocharged engine was originally designed as a normally aspirated engine, it will probably require a lowering of the compression ratio to avoid mechanical damage caused by combustion problems such as detonation.

Virtually all modern petrol engines are fuel-injected, and this suits the process of turbocharging. The complexity of turbocharging carburettor engines restricted the use of turbochargers, but fitting turbochargers to fuel-injected engines is a relatively simple arrangement. Careful matching of the turbocharger to a given engine ensures that the maximum boost (pressure above atmospheric) is limited to about 1.5 bar, i.e. the maximum pressure in the inlet manifold is 1.5 times atmospheric pressure.

Boost limitation and boost control

The exhaust gas temperature of a petrol engine is much hotter than that of a diesel engine, so this places extra stress on the turbocharger. Furthermore, current emission regulations relating to the discharge of NO_x (oxides of nitrogen – refer to section 2.30 in this chapter) mean that the boost may need to be reduced at times when this pollutant would normally be produced in unacceptable quantities. This occurs at high engine speed and/or at certain load conditions.

To meet emissions requirements and also to minimize the risk of engine damage, a boost-limiting valve is fitted (Figure 2.174). Under high load conditions, this poppet-type valve, often called a 'waste-gate', is opened mechanically so as to allow some of the exhaust gas to by-pass the turbine, which therefore reduces its pumping action.

Modern engines use an electronic engine management system to set the ignition timing and control fuelling and it is therefore logical to use the same engine management system to monitor and regulate the boost pressure. Such systems can control the boost pressure very accurately throughout all engine speed and load conditions, and this allows the boost pressure to be maintained at the optimum value with regard to power, economy and emissions.

The electronically controlled waste-gate systems make use of engine vacuum and boost pressure to

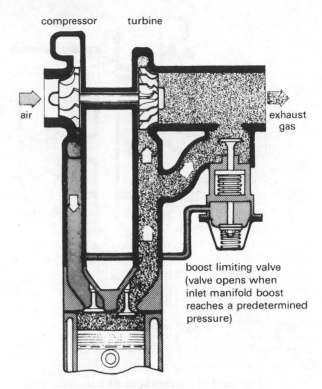

compressor   turbine

air

exhaust gas

boost limiting valve (valve opens when inlet manifold boost reaches a predetermined pressure)

Figure 2.174 A turbocharger with boost limiting valve

actuate the waste-gate, as illustrated in Figure 2.174. However, an additional valve is positioned in the pipe, which passes the boost pressure to the waste-gate. The valve is controlled by the engine management computer, which is able to sense the boost pressure via a signal passed from a pressure sensor. The computer or ECU is then able to control the valve, which in turn regulates waste-gate operation.

An alternative method of limiting boost pressure is to use a pressure relief valve in the induction manifold; this opens when the boost reaches a predetermined maximum and allows air in the manifold to bleed to the atmosphere. This type of system is now not so widely used due to the superior efficiency of electronically regulated waste-gate systems.

Charge-air coolers (intercoolers)

Compression of the charge and its passage through a hot turbocharger raises the temperature of the air; this results in a reduction of the density of the charge as well as increasing the chance that premature detonation will occur.

To overcome the problem, some petrol and diesel engines have a heat exchanger fitted between the turbocharger and engine (Figure 2.175). This unit, often called an 'intercooler', is generally an air-to-air heat exchanger, although some systems use a separated portion of the cooling system radiator as a means of dissipating the heat from the intake air. By lowering the air temperature to around 50–60°C volumetric efficiency is improved and detonation tolerance is increased.

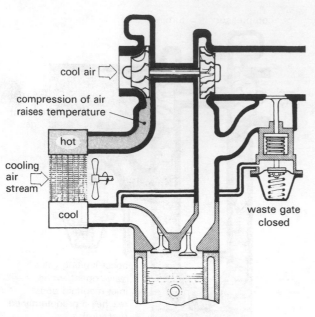

Figure 2.175 A turbocharger with an intercooler

Advantages and disadvantages of turbocharging petrol engines

The advantages of turbocharging petrol engines include:

1 Higher torque for acceleration from low speed.
2 Lower exhaust noise and emission.
3 Better fuel economy due to a reduction in the pumping energy expended during the induction stroke. (This advantage is seldom achieved in practice because many drivers alter their driving technique to take full advantage of the extra power of a turbocharged engine.)

The main disadvantages of a turbocharged petrol engine (apart from the extra hazards created when inexperienced drivers attempt to demonstrate the extra performance) are:

1 The higher initial cost of turbocharger and allied equipment.
2 The higher repair and servicing costs especially when other engine components are damaged by a defective unit.
3 At low engine speeds, a delay in engine response after depressing the accelerator. Since the turbine takes a time to reach its effective speed, an acceleration delay occurs with older type units often referred to as 'turbo-lag'.

Variable-geometry turbos

A turbocharger is associated with turbo-lag, noise and high emissions, especially NO$_x$. With advances in engine technology and computer-controlled engine management systems it has been possible to alter the geometry within the turbocharger during engine operation. The variable-geometry turbo provides lower

emissions, improved engine power and torque with lower fuel consumption. A variable-geometry turbo (Figure 2.176) is normally used in conjunction with a diesel engine or with high performance petrol engines.

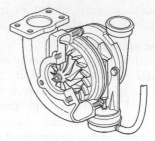

Figure 2.176 A variable-vane turbocharger

By altering the flow of the exhaust gases at the inlet port of the exhaust turbine, it is possible to optimize the speed of the turbine during low and high engine loads. During low engine loads, the vanes of the turbo nozzle are closed (Figure 2.177), which directs a minimal flow of exhaust gas across the turbine impellor. The turbine spins relatively slowly producing very little turbo charging effect in the inlet manifold.

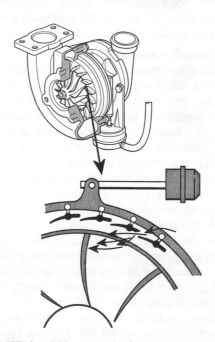

Figure 2.177 A variable-vane turbocharger at low load

When the load applied to the engine is high, the flow of exhaust gas at the turbine inlet port is also high. The nozzle vanes are opened by the ECU via the operation of the actuator (Figure 2.178) and flow of high-speed exhaust gases passing over the turbine, driving the impellor at high speed. The high speed of the turbine drives the compressor, which provides a high boost pressure in the inlet manifold.

The engine management ECU monitors engine operating conditions, such as engine speed and engine load using information from sensors, and the ECU then controls the position of the nozzle vanes via the actuator.

Variable geometry turbochargers provide a faster response to throttle opening, reducing the effect of turbo-lag. The ECU can accurately control the turbo boost pressure using a variable-geometry turbocharger; a traditional poppet valve waste-gate is no longer required to reduce or regulate the boost pressure. When boost pressure is too high, the nozzle vanes are closed thus reducing the speed of the turbine, resulting in a reduction of boost pressure.

The ECU controls the nozzle actuator with the use of either a solenoid-operated vacuum valve or electrical stepper motor.

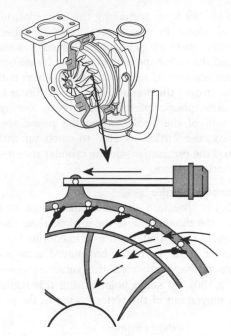

Figure 2.178 A variable-vane turbocharger at high load

2.17 THE PETROL FOUR-STROKE CYCLE IN DETAIL: VALVE AND IGNITION TIMING

Note: In section 2.2 (especially 2.2.3), the general principles of operation of an engine on the four-stroke cycle was described. The following section provides further detail on the four-stroke cycle in relationship to the petrol engine, particularly in connection with ignition and valve timing, and the opening and closing of the inlet and exhaust valves.

2.17.1 Valve operation and the four-stroke engines

The first point to be appreciated is that it is not possible for a valve to move from closed to fully open (or vice versa) instantaneously. The opening and the closing movements are each spread over a considerable angle of crankshaft rotation. Thus, if a valve is required to be effectively open at the beginning of a stroke (TDC or BDC) it must begin to open before the dead centre. Similarly, if a valve is required to be open at the end of a stroke, it must not close completely until after the dead centre.

Even if the valves could be opened and closed instantaneously, the dead centres would not be the best points at which to open and close them, except at very low engine speeds. The engine gives its best performance when the greatest mass of air and fuel is passed through the combustion chamber and burnt effectively.

Consider an engine running reasonably fast; the most suitable point at which to open the inlet port depends upon conditions at the end of the exhaust stroke, and we will begin our study with the piston moving down the cylinder on the induction stroke and the inlet port already wide open (Figure 2.179).

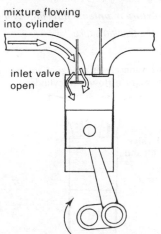

Air/fuel mixture entering cylinder during induction stroke

Figure 2.179 Induction stroke

Induction stroke

The downward movement of the piston reduces the pressure inside the cylinder so that the pressure of the atmosphere (or supercharge pressure) forces air through the air filter and along the inlet pipe, i.e. the flow of air along the pipe is accelerated. The inertia of this air (its resistance to change of speed) causes it to lag behind the piston movement, so that by the time the piston has reached its maximum speed (about half-way down the stroke) the pressure inside the cylinder is well below atmospheric pressure. However, during the second half of the stroke, when the piston speed is decreasing, the airflow is able to catch up with the piston and the pressure inside the cylinder rises towards atmospheric pressure.

Compression stroke

At BDC the direction of piston movement reverses. However, the momentum of the airflow along the inlet pipe towards the cylinder causes it to continue entering the cylinder, until the piston has moved some way up the next stroke – provided the valve remains open (Figure 2.180). At some point during this stroke, the upward movement of the piston increases the pressure

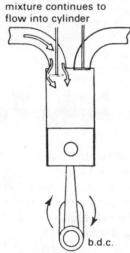

Momentum of mixture maintains flow into cylinder at b.d.c.

Figure 2.180 End of induction stroke

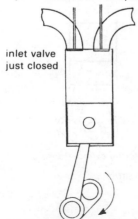

Inlet valve closing point

Figure 2.181 Compression stroke

inside the cylinder sufficiently to stop the inward flow of air. This then begins to force air out of the cylinder and the greatest possible amount of air will be trapped inside the cylinder if the inlet valve closes at this point (Figure 2.181). The inlet valve will therefore ideally always close just after BDC – how much after will depend upon engine design which must account for the typical engine speed range, the length and diameter of the inlet pipe, and throttle opening.

Power stroke

At about the end of the compression stroke, the compressed air/fuel mixture is ignited. The time at which the ignition occurs ('ignition timing') will depend on the engine speed and the ratio between the air and fuel. The mixture burns once ignited, which increases the gas pressure even further and the piston is therefore forced down the cylinder on its power stroke. During the downward movement of the piston, the increasing volume lowers the pressure of the gas within the cylinder, but if the exhaust valve remains closed the pressure will still be well above atmospheric when the piston arrives at BDC.

The pressure that exists at the bottom of the power stroke offers some resistance to the upward movement of the piston during the exhaust stroke, even though the exhaust valve may now be open. Moreover, as the piston approaches BDC, the leverage or effort exerted by the connecting rod on the crankshaft decreases rapidly because of the angle between the connecting rod and crankshaft. The pressure on top of the piston therefore has a rapidly reducing effect on the rotation of the crankshaft.

By opening the exhaust valve early (i.e. before the piston reaches BDC) a good deal of the burnt gas is allowed to escape before the piston begins its upward exhaust stroke. Therefore the pressure remaining in the cylinder is much lower and consequently the opposition to the pistons upward movement is very much reduced (see Figure 2.182).

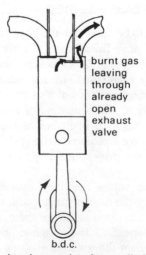

Burnt gas already escaping from cylinder at b.d.c.

Figure 2.182 Start of exhaust stroke

The point at which the exhaust valve opens must be carefully chosen so as to sacrifice as little as possible of the effect of the pressure in driving the piston downwards during the power stroke, while ensuring that as much gas as possible will escape before BDC to minimize the opposition to the piston's upward movement during the exhaust stroke.

Exhaust stroke

If the exhaust valve is opened before BDC on the power stroke, then the exhaust gas is already moving out of the cylinder and along the exhaust pipe before the piston starts the exhaust stroke. When the piston is actually on the exhaust stroke, the rising piston then increases the gas velocity along the exhaust pipe.

As the piston approaches TDC and its upward velocity decreases, the pressure in the cylinder which is forcing out the exhaust gas progressively reduces. Additionally, the momentum of the gas that is already rushing along the exhaust pipe actually creates a lower pressure or partial vacuum inside the cylinder.

Because there is now a low pressure or vacuum in the cylinder, if the inlet valve is now opened, fresh mixture will begin moving into the cylinder (assuming that the cylinder pressure is lower than the atmospheric pressure or supercharge pressure. The opening of the inlet valve can usually occur before the piston has reached TDC on the exhaust stroke. So by opening the inlet port before the exhaust port has closed, the momentum of the exhaust gas can be used to start the flow of fresh gas into the cylinder without any help from the piston (Figure 2.183).

Fresh gas entering the cylinder will, of course, be drawn towards the exhaust port thus helping to displace the exhaust gas. Placing the valves on opposite sides of the combustion chamber makes the fresh gas sweep right across the chamber on its way from inlet port to exhaust port. This ensures that the combustion chamber is thoroughly 'scavenged', or cleared of exhaust gas and filled with fresh gas. If the ports are very close together it is possible for fresh gas to reach the exhaust port without displacing all the burnt gas from the cylinder.

The correct moment to close the exhaust port is the moment the fresh gas reaches the exhaust port. Thus the opening point of the inlet valve and the closing point of the exhaust valve depend upon:

1   The flow velocity of exhaust gases along the exhaust pipe. This in turn depends upon engine speed, throttle opening, the length and diameter of the exhaust pipe and the restricting effect of the silencer.
2   The pressure in the intake manifold, which is dependent upon engine speed and throttle opening.
3   The position of the ports in relation to the combustion chamber and to each other.

The inlet valve usually opens a little before TDC and the exhaust valve remains open a little after TDC. Thus, for some angle of crankshaft rotation around TDC both valves are open at the same time. The opening of the inlet valve overlaps the closing of the exhaust valve. This is called the period of 'valve overlap'.

While a large valve overlap may be beneficial at high engine speeds if the ports are arranged on opposite sides of the combustion chamber, it will be difficult for the engine to idle or run slowly at light load. At low engine speeds and small throttle openings the pressure in the inlet manifold is well below atmospheric pressure (a vacuum gauge connected to the manifold will show a high vacuum/low pressure under these operating conditions).

At light throttle settings and low speeds, the quantity of gas exhausted from the cylinder is small and moves slowly. Therefore, the exhaust gas will have very little momentum and will not have the effect of significantly reducing the pressure in the cylinder below that of atmospheric pressure. Under these conditions, opening the inlet valve before the exhaust valve has closed will result in a rush of exhaust gas into the inlet manifold. Therefore, on the following induction stroke the fresh charge drawn into the cylinder will include exhaust gas. This will certainly result in a lowering of the efficiency of the combustion process because a proportion of the charge will be exhaust gas instead of the required air/fuel mixture. The ignition and burning of this contaminated mixture will be difficult and will result in loss of power and misfires. The greater the percentage of exhaust gas contaminating the fresh charge, and the lighter the load (lower the volume of fresh charge) and the slower the engine speed, the worse the situation is likely to be.

If the engine is never required to run slowly, e.g. a racing engine, this may not matter, but all engines used in normal motor vehicles must be able to idle smoothly and reliably, and for such engines the amount of valve overlap must be strictly limited.

momentum of gas flowing
along exhaust pipe draws
fresh mixture into combustion
chamber

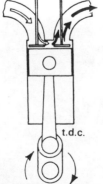

t.d.c.

Opening of inlet valve overlaps
closing of exhaust valve

Figure 2.183 End of exhaust stroke

To sum up, therefore:

1 The inlet valve remains open after the piston has passed BDC at the end of the induction stroke (inlet valve closing lag).
2 The exhaust valve opens before the piston reaches BDC at the end of the power stroke (exhaust valve opening lead).
3 The exhaust valve usually remains open after TDC at the end of the exhaust stroke (exhaust valve closing lag).
4 The inlet valve usually opens before the exhaust valve has closed (valve overlap) and usually before TDC (inlet valve opening lead).
5 The amount of lead (or lag) of valve opening or closing points, and the amount of overlap will depend upon the design of the engine – particularly the port arrangement and inlet and exhaust systems – and upon the performance characteristics the engine is required to have.

The opening and closing points of the valves in relation to piston and crankshaft position are called the 'valve timing', and the correct timing for an engine (that selected by the engine manufacturers) is given either in the form of a table or by means of a valve timing diagram. Some examples of valve timing tables and diagrams are given in Figure 2.184, together with brief details of the engine to which they refer. Students should make similar tables and diagrams for other engines.

2.17.2 Variable valve timing and valve lift

It should be noted that fixed valve timing has been a standard feature of virtually all engines until relatively recent times. The valves opened and closed at a fixed period in relation to crankshaft rotation at all engine speeds and loads. However, there is increasing use of mechanisms that provide variable valve timing. The variable valve timing systems alter the valve timing (while the engine is running) to suit engine speed and load conditions. Although there have been purely mechanical-based systems, most modern systems make use of the engine management computer to regulate the mechanical actuation of changes to the valve timing.

A petrol engine has to operate at varying engine speeds from idle, typically 750 rpm through to high speeds, up to 7000 rpm and above. When the inlet and exhaust valve timing is fixed (the valve timing occurs at a fixed time in relation to the crankshaft angle at all engine speeds) the timing is not suitable for all engine operating speeds and loads. The engine will therefore have a valve timing that is most suitable to just one particular engine speed, which is generally at around 50% to 60% of the engine's maximum speed. The chosen valve timing will result in the greatest combustion efficiency (and therefore greatest torque) at the selected engine speed.

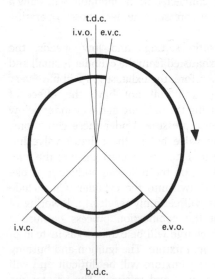

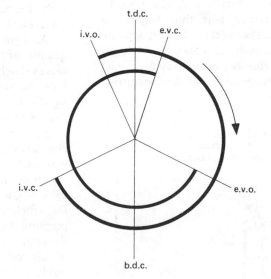

4 CYL. o.h.v. ENGINE
SWEPT VOLUME 848 cm³
COMPRESSION RATIO 8.3 : 1
MAX. TORQUE – 62 Nm AT
                          2900 REV/MIN
MAX. POWER – 31.3 kW AT
                          4500 REV/MIN

4 CYL. o.h.c. ENGINE
SWEPT VOLUME 1955 cm³
COMPRESSION RATIO 9.2 : 1
MAX. TORQUE – 151 Nm AT
                          3500 REV/MIN
MAX. POWER – 72 kW AT
                          5200 REV/MIN

i.v.o. – inlet valve opens
i.v.c. – inlet valve closes
e.v.o. – exhaust valve opens
e.v.c. – exhaust valve closes

Figure 2.184 Valve timing diagrams

Slow engine speeds

At slow engine speeds (e.g. at idle), if the inlet valve timing is altered so that it is retarded or opens late (opens when the piston is at TDC at the beginning of the induction stroke), all of the exhaust gas would be expelled through the exhaust valve and the cylinder would fill with fresh, uncontaminated mixture. A fresh mixture will result in a good burn of the gas during the next power stroke and therefore the engine will be stable when at idle. If the engine speed were to be increased but the retarded valve timing retained, it will be impossible to fill the cylinder with a correct amount of fresh mixture and so reduce the power output at high speed. Therefore retarding the inlet valve timing is good for engine idle speeds, but poor for high performance.

High engine speeds

At high speed, if the inlet valve timing is advanced (the inlet valve opens before the piston reaches TDC, before the beginning of the induction stroke) the fresh mixture can be drawn into the cylinder by the depression caused by the flow of exhaust gas through the exhaust valve. The flow of exhaust gas will therefore improve the gas flow through the cylinder at higher engine speeds. Advancing the valve timing at high engine speeds increases the volumetric efficiency of the engine and therefore improves power and torque output.

If, however, the engine has fixed valve timing, there has to be a compromise between advancing or retarding the valve timing, as most engines used for everyday purposes operate in the low to mid speed range. The engine will be fairly stable at idle, but will lose the high performance that the engine could produce if the valve timing were to be advanced. If the vehicle is to be used as a sports car, the engine speed is likely to be high, so the valve timing could be biased towards the advanced side. The engine will have good high engine performance but will be less stable at idle speed.

With the introduction of engine management systems and advances in engine technology, it has been possible to achieve a method of varying the valve timing depending on engine speed and load. Variable valve timing allows the valve timing to be retarded at low engine speeds (i.e. idle speed) and advanced at high engine speeds. By varying the valve timing while the engine is running, it is possible to achieve the optimum valve timing for all engine operating conditions. It is also possible by varying the valve timing, to lower the emission levels from the engine during certain driving conditions.

Valve opening period

The valve opening period is dictated by the profile of the cam lobe, which is constant with conventional valve operating gear. When the engine is at low to medium speeds, the valve opening period allows sufficient fresh mixture into the cylinder to provide good engine performance. At higher engine speeds, the volumetric efficiency of an engine will increase if the opening period of the valve is increased. It is possible to increase the valve opening period by increasing the valve lift (cam lobe profile). Increasing the valve lift (or opening period) at high engine speeds provides an increase in the volume of fresh mixture drawn into the cylinder, resulting in an increase in engine power.

A number of different systems now exist that control valve lift, valve opening duration and valve timing. These systems are examined in greater detail in Book 2.

2.17.3 Ignition timing

In describing the cycle of operations (section 2.2), it was stated that the mixture was ignited 'at about the end of the compression stroke', and that after ignition, the mixture 'burns very rapidly' and causes the rapid pressure rise within the cylinder. It is clear that the rate at which the mixture burns must be very high, because if it is not, the piston will have moved most of the way down the cylinder before maximum pressure is developed.

To achieve the maximum effect, the maximum pressure should occur approximately 10° after TDC Since, however, the mixture does take some time to burn and develop maximum pressure, the spark, which initiates the combustion process must be timed to occur before the piston reaches TDC, i.e. the timing of the spark must be in advance of when the maximum pressure should occur. This is referred to as the 'timing advance'.

The amount of advance necessary to give best results varies with engine speed and throttle opening, and it is usual practice to fit automatic devices such as an engine speed advance mechanism and an engine load mechanism to regulate the ignition timing in accordance with engine conditions (refer to section 2.28 within this book). With the old type contact breaker (points) systems and some earlier electronic ignition systems, it was necessary to set a base timing (i.e. time the ignition) correctly. This then allowed the automatic timing advance systems to alter the timing as necessary when the engine was running under different operating conditions.

As an example, a base timing setting could be 10° before TDC. If the initial timing is set at this point (usually set at around idle speed), the advance mechanism will then advance the timing as the engine speed increases. This is due to the fact that the speed at which combustion takes place, and therefore the time taken to reach maximum pressure within the cylinder, will not change significantly. If the engine speed were therefore to increase, there would be less time for combustion to take place. The timing must therefore be advanced ahead of the base timing to allow sufficient time for the combustion and pressure rise to occur.

However, under certain load conditions (when the throttle opening is increased), the cylinder pressures will increase due to the higher volumes of air able to enter the cylinder. Additionally, the air/fuel ratio will be richer with fuel than when operating under light load conditions. Along with other factors, the higher cylinder pressures and richer mixture will speed up the combustion process. If the ignition timing is advanced too far, this could result in the maximum pressure occurring too soon. It could result in the pressure attempting to force the piston down the cylinder before it had actually reached TDC on the compression stroke. The advanced timing would cause early detonation which can lead to engine and component damage.

To overcome the problem, a timing retard mechanism is used that responds to engine load (often using the intake manifold vacuum as an indication of load). When the load increases, the timing can then be retarded slightly.

To summarize, then, there is usually an engine speed-related advance mechanism and a load-related retarding mechanism.

Mechanical advance and retard mechanisms were common until the early 1990s but modern systems use electronic control, which ensures very precise and accurate timing for all operating conditions (refer to section 2.28 within this chapter).

2.18 COMBUSTION AND COMBUSTION CHAMBERS

2.18.1 Combustion

The spark ignition combustion process starts when the arc at the sparking plug ignites the fuel/air mixture and continues while the flame propagates through the mixture. It finishes when the mixture has completely burnt (ideal combustion) thus forcing the piston down the cylinder. The end result of the combustion process is that the rise in pressure created by the expansion of the gases forces the piston down the cylinder, which is the power stroke.

The combustion process occupies only a small amount of the total four-stroke cycle but combustion efficiency is very dependent on a number of factors and operations that take place during the remainder of the four-stroke cycle. Importantly, good combustion is achieved when the pressure within the cylinder (resulting from the compression stroke) is at the desired value. The temperature of the air/fuel mixture is raised during compression and if the temperature and pressure are correct, this results in good ignition of the mixture and an efficient burning (combustion) of the mixture.

Figure 2.185 indicates the pressure rise and fall within the cylinder during the compression stroke, through combustion and the power stroke.

If no combustion takes place within the cylinder at the end of the compression stroke, the pressure in the cylinder will rise during the compression stroke as the piston rises and compresses the gas inside the cylinder; the pressure will then fall again as the piston passes back down the cylinder.

The compression pressure attained will depend on the compression ratio, i.e. a low compression ratio results in a low compression pressure.

First phase of combustion
When a spark occurs in the cylinder as the piston reaches TDC at the end of the compression stroke, the mixture ignites and a flame propagates through the mixture. Combustion raises the temperature and this results in expansion of the gases.

Because the combustion process takes place within the restricted upper part of the cylinder (combustion chamber), the gas expansion causes a rapid and substantial pressure rise that is much greater than the pressure achieved from the compression stroke only (Figure 2.185).

The time between the spark occurring and the increase in cylinder pressure above the normal compression pressure is referred to as the 'ignition delay period'. The ignition delay period will depend on a number of factors.

1 the quality and timing of the spark
2 the air/fuel ratio
3 the mixing of the air/fuel mixture
4 the temperature of the mixture inside the cylinder (as a result of being compressed on the compression stroke)
5 the pressure within the cylinder (created during compression).

The ignition delay period is constant in time so the ignition point has to be advanced with increased engine

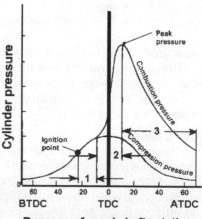

Figure 2.185 Cylinder pressures during compression, combustion and the power stroke

speeds in order to achieve the peak combustion pressure at the correct time, e.g. approximately 10° after TDC (top dead centre).

Second phase of combustion

The second phase of combustion is the rapid rise in pressure from the normal compression pressure to the peak combustion pressure. A rapid rise in cylinder pressure occurs as the flame propagates through the air/fuel mixture in the combustion chamber. The rate at which the flame propagates through the mixture depends on a number of factors that exist within the combustion chamber.

Assuming that the first phase is correct, the combustion pressure depends on a number of other factors including:

1 The air/fuel ratio – correct ratio provides the best combustion and therefore greater pressure.
2 The mixing of the air/fuel mixture – poor mixing will give a mixture that cannot burn completely and this will result in a lower pressure.
3 The atomization of the fuel within the air – if the fuel does not atomize, this will also result in a mixture that cannot burn completely and a lower pressure.
4 The shape of the combustion chamber – a good shape will ensure consistent speed of flame propagation and burning across all of the mixture, thus providing the best pressure.
5 The position of the sparking plug within the cylinder – a correctly placed sparking plug within the chamber will help to ensure that the flame starts at a point where it can spread evenly across all of the mixture and provide a consistent burn and pressure rise.
6 The swirl/turbulence within the combustion chamber – this ensures that the mixture maintains movement within the chamber and so aids flame propagation.

Third phase of combustion

The third phase of combustion is the pressure reduction from the peak pressure through to when the exhaust valve opens and the mixture is expelled through the open valve. During this third period, if all applicable factors for phase 1 and phase 2 are correct (including the air/fuel mixture and ignition), the flame will have propagated to the furthest point within the combustion chamber and cylinder as the piston descends. Due to the descending piston and the extinguishing of the flame, the cylinder pressure will fall rapidly from the peak combustion pressure.

2.18.2 Timed ignition, detonation and pre-ignition

One important aspect of creating combustion is the heat required to ignite the air/fuel mixture within the cylinder.

A diesel engine operates using a high compression ratio that results in high temperatures being produced during the compression stroke. The heat generated during compression is then sufficient to ignite the atomized diesel fuel as soon as it is injected into the cylinder (directly into the combustion chamber).

When petrol is used as the fuel in an engine, the compression ratio is usually lower than for a diesel engine, which means that the temperatures reached during compression are also lower. However, the compression stroke raises the temperature of the petrol/air mixture to a level where the addition of a hot arc (provided by the sparking plug) is then sufficient to easily ignite the fuel.

For a petrol engine, therefore, there is a careful balance between creating enough heat during compression to ensure that the arc can easily ignite the mixture, and not creating too much heat, which could cause premature ignition of the mixture.

There are two main problems that can occur, which are caused by some form of premature ignition of the mixture or premature ignition/combustion of a pocket of mixture. These problems are referred to as detonation and pre-ignition.

Detonation (Figure 2.186)

Detonation causes high velocity shock waves to be reflected around the combustion chamber and is often identified by a metallic knocking noise heard from the engine, which is commonly referred to as 'pinking'.

As the flame front moves through the combustion chamber it progressively ignites the mixture ahead of it. Note also that as the mixture starts to burn, which creates the pressure increase, the additional heat of the burning mixture and additional heat due to increased pressures, further raises the temperature of the remaining unburned mixture. In reality this increase in temperature means that the unburned mixture is now closer to its ignition point and should therefore ignite more easily when contacted by the flame front.

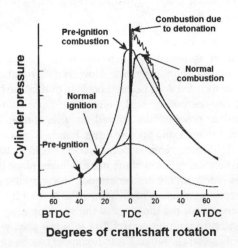

Figure 2.186 Cylinder pressures caused through detonation and pre-ignition

If the combustion chamber is well designed, the flame should spread evenly from the start point (sparking plug) in all directions and therefore evenly ignite all of the mixture. Assuming that the sparking plug is in the centre of the mixture, this would result in an even movement of the flame front throughout all of the mixture, which would produce progressive combustion.

Now imagine that the combustion chamber is shaped like a long thin tube; the flame travels progressively along the tube and ignites the mixture ahead of it, but the heat created (as the mixture burns and the pressure increases), is more likely to pass through the unburned mixture more rapidly than the flame front. This could then result in the unburned mixture at the far end of the tube suddenly igniting due to exposure to the heat, before the flame front has reached it. This sudden combustion of unburned mixture can set up shock waves. In fact, the problem can be exaggerated if more than one pocket of mixture were to suddenly combust thus creating more than one set of shock waves that then meet, thus creating a more severe set of shockwaves.

Although the above explanation somewhat simplifies the problem, less efficient combustion chambers and other problems can allow pockets of mixture to suddenly combust prematurely causing shockwaves. If a combustion chamber design creates pockets of air that are some distance away from the sparking plug, although in normal driving conditions there may not be any problem, under certain conditions where the combustion temperatures are higher, detonation could occur.

The pocket of mixture that has caused the shockwaves due to its sudden combustion, also generates a lot of heat very rapidly. The heat is transferred from the ignited mixture to the combustion chamber walls (along with the shockwaves), and on to other protrusions within the combustion chamber. This can result in overheating and damage to combustion chamber walls, piston crown, sparking plug and head gasket, etc.

Pre-ignition (Figure 2.186)
Pre-ignition is similar to detonation in that ignition occurs earlier than intended. However, detonation is usually associated with isolated pockets of mixture being ignited by excessive heat, *after* the normal timed combustion process has started in the conventional manner. Pre-ignition, on the other hand, is associated with the whole combustion process being started prematurely, i.e. ignition of the mixture takes place in the cylinder before an arc has occurred at the sparking plug. This premature ignition of the mixture is started by some other means, not the timed arc at the sparking plug

Premature ignition occurs due to a hot spot within the combustion chamber. These hot spots can be caused by the heating up of sharp edges of components, e.g. head gasket, sparking plug centre electrode, poorly seated valves or even carbon that has built up within the combustion chamber over a period of time. Even excessive intake air temperatures or overheating of the engines can cause pre-ignition because the mixture in the cylinder will be at a higher temperature and so closer to the ignition point. Any hot spots then act as the final means of igniting the mixture ahead of the sparking plug arc.

Due to pre-ignition, the cylinder temperature and combustion pressure increase before the piston reaches TDC and sooner than would normally occur. This premature pressure rise puts added stress on engine components and also leads to engine 'knock', loss of power and overheating. If the cylinder operates at a higher temperature due to the pre-ignition, the hot spot may become even hotter and the pre-ignition occurs even earlier, eventually leading to engine damage.

2.18.3   Octane rating and anti-knock

The octane rating of petrol is a measure of the fuel's anti-knock characteristics, that is its ability to burn without detonation or combustion knock in a spark ignition engine. The higher the octane rating of a fuel the less likely the fuel is to cause knocking in an engine. Two methods are normally used to measure the fuels ability to burn; the research method and the motor method. The research method is widely used and the octane number given to the fuel is referred to as the 'research octane number' and the abbreviation given is normally 'RON'.

Compression ratio and detonation
In general, if an engine design were prone to knocking due to detonation, and a higher octane petrol was not available, the engine would have to be produced with a slightly lower compression ratio. This would result in lower compression pressures and temperatures, which would reduce the tendency for detonation. Another option is to set the ignition timing to a slightly retarded value, which would again reduce the tendency for detonation and knocking. Unfortunately, older type mechanical ignition advance systems were not accurate enough to enable the exact timing to be achieved under all of the different operating conditions, so it was therefore necessary to adjust the base timing setting so that the timing was retarded over much of the engine's operating range.

Anti-knock additives
In the past, a lead-based additive (more precisely 'tetraethyl lead' and/or 'tetra methyl lead', TEL and TML) was added in very small quantities to the fuel to help raise the octane rating of petrol. In basic terms, the lead (which does not burn or combust) acts as a form of retardant to the speed of combustion. This helps to prevent the rapid combustion of the mixture or pockets of mixture that could cause detonation. It was thus possible to use higher compression ratios (which

produce higher compression pressures and temperatures). Engines could be produced with higher compression ratios, to improve combustion efficiency and power, with a much-reduced tendency to knock.

The disadvantage of lead is that it is a pollutant. Since 1972 there has been a progressive reduction in the amount of lead used in petrol. Since the early 1990s, most cars have been fitted with catalytic converters (to aid emission reductions), and these converters are damaged by lead. Lead-free fuel is now the normal petrol used in modern engines.

To help maintain the required octane numbers for the petrol used in modern engines, petrol suppliers now use additives other than lead. The standard or regular petrol in Europe has a 95 RON rating. It should be noted that the old, leaded petrol had ratings as high as 100, which was necessary for higher compression engines, especially those fitted to sports cars.

Importantly, modern engines actually have much higher compression ratios than in the past, with sports car engines having ratios as high as 11/1 compared with a typical value of around 9.5/1 in the 1970s. The high compression ratios on modern engines are necessary to achieve more efficient combustion, which enables a reduction in overall exhaust emissions (required by law). However, there is inevitably the potential for detonation with such high compression ratios.

Engine timing control reducing detonation
Fortunately, as well as the modern lead-free additives used in petrol, electronic control of ignition and fuelling have helped to resolve the problem. Ignition timing can be altered while the engine is running within tiny fractions of a second. The electronic computer is able to monitor engine operating conditions and adjust the ignition timing to the exact value required, which is usually just below the threshold that would cause detonation. If necessary the fuel mixture can also be altered very rapidly as another means of reducing the tendency to knock.

Many engines have a 'knock sensor' which detects when knock or detonation starts. The computer is then able to rapidly alter timing and/or fuelling to prevent further knocking occurring.

Note 1: Higher octane fuels have become more readily available in Europe due to further improvements in refining of fuels and different additives. 98 RON is a commonly available rating for petrol and may be more suited to very high performance engines, or those engines with very high compression ratios.

Note 2: The lead used in the past as anti-knock additive also acted as a type of lubricant or protection for certain parts of the engine. Valve seats were offered considerable protection to pitting, which is caused by heat and the hammering action of the valve when it opens and closes. Valve guides are also quoted as having protection from wear due to the lead forming a protective barrier on the valve stem/valve guide surface.

Without lead in the petrol, it has been necessary to use different materials for valve seats and guides to overcome the pitting and wear problems. Also note that older vehicles that were designed for operation with leaded petrol may require modification or restricted use if they are to operate on unleaded fuel.

2.18.4 General principles of combustion chamber design

The power that can be obtained from an engine depends upon:

1 The amount of air that can be passed through the engine per minute, called its volumetric efficiency.
2 The efficiency with which the air can be mixed with fuel and burnt to release heat, called its thermal efficiency.
3 The efficiency with which the energy released by the burning fuel can be converted into mechanical work at the driving end of the crankshaft, called its mechanical efficiency.

Although the design of the combustion chamber can have little direct influence on mechanical efficiency, it has a great deal to do with both the volumetric and thermal efficiencies. It has, however, an indirect influence on the mechanical efficiency.

Requirements for high volumetric efficiency
The chief requirements for high volumetric efficiency are:

1 Large and unobstructed ports offering the minimum obstruction to the flow of gases.
2 The most suitable valve timing for the engine speeds and throttle openings at which the engine will most often be required to operate.
3 A mixture temperature which is as low as possible at the moment the inlet valve closes. Due to thermal expansion, the cylinder will hold a smaller mass of mixture if the temperature of the mixture is hot.

Requirements for high thermal efficiency
The chief of these are:

1 The highest possible compression ratio that can be used without knocking (detonation).
2 The minimum loss of heat to the combustion chamber walls. This depends upon the temperature difference between the hot gases and the walls, and upon the wall surface area. Since a high temperature is necessary to produce high pressure it is important to reduce the surface area, that is to make the combustion chamber as compact as possible. This compactness has a further benefit – it reduces the time taken by the gas to burn, by reducing the distance the flame has to travel. It can be assisted by placing the sparking plug as near as possible to the centre of the combustion chamber.

Possibly the most important consideration in the use of a high compression ratio is the anti-knock rating (octane number) of the fuel used. Since high-octane fuels are expensive, a compression ratio must be chosen which balances thermal efficiency against fuel cost, bearing in mind the purpose for which the engine is to be used.

Note: Although a high compression ratio results in lower fuel consumption for a given amount of work done, any gain may be entirely offset by the extra cost of the high-octane fuel necessitated by the high compression ratio. If running cost is of no importance, the fuel with the highest octane rating available may be used with a correspondingly high compression ratio.

The design of the combustion chamber can also contribute to the suppression of knocking. The risk of detonation is greatest in the last part of the air/fuel mixture to burn, called the 'end gas'. The risk of detonation in the end gas can be reduced in two ways:

1   By getting the gas burnt as quickly and as evenly as possible by ensuring that the flame front travel is as short a distance as possible. It should be noted that if the gas burns much too quickly due to temperatures being too high, this could also result in some detonation.
2   By arranging that the end gas is burnt in the coolest part of the combustion chamber. It is easier to do this by placing the sparking plug near to the exhaust valve (which gets very hot), therefore starting combustion in the hottest part. The end gas is therefore likely to be closer to the inlet valve, which is much cooler, and so less likely to cause detonation.

Turbulence
The rate at which the flame travels through stagnant gas is much too low to be of use in a high-speed engine, and it was realized many years ago that a violent agitation (turbulence) of the mixture is necessary to help spread the flame rapidly throughout the mixture of air and fuel. There are two ways of creating turbulence:

1   By arranging the inlet port so that the mixture enters the cylinder obliquely and at high velocity, thus setting up a swirling motion that persists during the compression stroke. This is known as 'induction turbulence', and although helpful, it is not by itself sufficient.
2   By designing the combustion chamber so that at TDC the piston approaches part of the cylinder head very closely, thus displacing mixture from this region with some violence. This action has been given the very descriptive name of squish, and turbulence created during the compression stroke is known as compression turbulence.

Mechanical efficiency
The positioning of the valves is one consideration in the design of the combustion chamber, and depending upon this, the valve operating gear will be either more

or less complicated. The greater the complication of the valve gear the more friction is absorbed in operating the valves. This will also influence the cost of manufacturing the engine, and the maintenance it is likely to need.

Exhaust emission (also refer to section 2.30)
Many countries, along with Europe, have regulations that specify the maximum amount of undesirable exhaust products that may be discharged. When considering combustion chamber shape, the exhaust pollutants that influence the design are:

1   **Carbon monoxide (CO) and hydrocarbon (HC)**. CO is produced if the fuel mixture is partially burnt, hydrocarbon if the fuel remains unburnt.
2   **Oxides of nitrogen (NO_x)** These gases are formed when the combustion temperature exceeds a given value.

To achieve a 'clean' engine, the designer must produce a combustion chamber that does not generate high pollutant levels. Additionally, for modern vehicles the design must incorporate a catalytic converter in the exhaust system to convert the harmful gases remaining in the exhaust into less harmful gases. However, even with modern combustion chamber design and catalytic converters it is virtually impossible for an engine to emit totally harmless exhaust gases, therefore most vehicles have other devices that are used to control these harmful emissions (including electronic ignition and fuel control).

In general the effects of the shape of the combustion chamber on the pollutants are as follows:

Unburnt or partially burnt fuel
The chamber shape should be as compact as possible. Long narrow chambers such as those used in the past on some OHV, over-square engines gave a 'dirty' exhaust due to the difficulty of completely burning all of the charge in the short time available. This effect was very pronounced when the idling speed was low or under conditions of over-run when the ignition timing was unsuitable.

NO_x (certain combinations of nitrogen and oxygen)
Many high performance engines of the past used a high compression ratio in conjunction with a very compact chamber. This gave a very high flame speed, which produced excessively high combustion temperatures. Although the power output was exceptional, the percentage of NO_x far exceeded what is acceptable today. Flame speed is the controlling factor, so the chamber shape must achieve a compromise in flame speed – too fast causes NO_x, and too slow results in some of the charge being unburnt (high HC).

A further difficulty arises when the effect of engine load is considered. An engine set to give a 'clean' exhaust when idling or cruising often exceeds the NO_x limit when full throttle is applied. To overcome this problem, some engines have an arrangement that recycles some of the exhaust gas back into the induction manifold: the system is called 'exhaust gas recirculation' (EGR). The burnt gas (which is no longer able to burn again) mixing with the new charge acts as a retardant and therefore slows down the rate of burning and so reduces the NO_x to an acceptable level. Valves controlling the flow of recirculated exhaust gas should only allow recirculation under certain engine operating conditions, i.e. only at times when excessive NO_x would be formed.

Unleaded fuel

By not allowing the use of lead additives in petrol a high anti-knock (octane) rating cannot be obtained so economically. This originally meant that the compression ratio of engines could not be so high as to cause combustion knock. For a given fuel the ratio that causes the onset of this fault depends on the chamber's resistance to knock, together with many other factors such as timing, mixture quality and temperature. The chamber shape selected for an engine must enable the engine to use a lower octane fuel and produce a high power output together with good fuel economy – a difficult task for a design engineer. However, modern electronic control of ignition and fuelling, together with good combustion chamber design has allowed higher compressions to again be used.

2.18.5 Combustion chamber shapes

With the previously mentioned requirements for a combustion chamber taken into consideration, it is worth examining some of the different shapes used for combustion chambers.

The L-head combustion chamber

Volumetric efficiency is not particularly high in this design (Figure 2.187). The arrangement of the valves on one side of the cylinder restricts valve size to about half cylinder diameter or less, and there are sharp bends through the ports and into the cylinder.

The chamber is not very compact, but there is a good deal of freedom in the choice of sparking plug

position to obtain the best results. The compression ratio is limited to about 7:1, as it is necessary to leave sufficient space above the valves to allow them a reasonable lift.

By bringing the surface of the head down close over the piston at TDC, leaving a suitable passage between the offset combustion chamber and the cylinder, both induction and compression turbulence are improved. It is in fact easy to get too much turbulence causing rough running through excessively rapid combustion.

The position of the valves makes possible the use of the very simplest valve operating gear, and mechanical losses are consequently low.

Though popular at one time, this combustion chamber is now obsolete in vehicle engines on account of its low volumetric efficiency and restriction on compression ratio.

The 'bathtub' combustion chamber

The valves are placed vertically over the top of the cylinder (Figure 2.188), giving a better port shape leading directly into the cylinder. The gas flow (and thus the volumetric efficiency) are much better than with the L-head design.

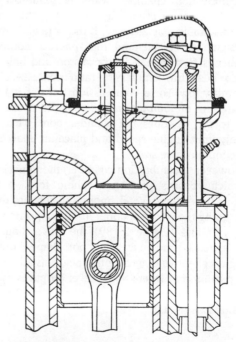

Figure 2.188 Bathtub design

The valves are arranged in-line, slightly offset from the cylinder centre, and the sides of the combustion chamber form a shape like an inverted bath (from which the name derives). Almost the only position for the sparking plug is the one shown, but this happens to fit in well with requirements, and the plug can be slightly nearer the exhaust valve than the inlet.

The chamber is reasonably compact, and in some cases the bathtub shape is somewhat bent to make the chamber roughly heart-shaped when seen from below.

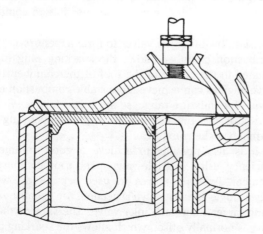

Figure 2.187 Side-valve design

There is little induction turbulence, but this is made up for by the very good compression turbulence produced by the squish effect. The squish area, as it is called, is placed on the side of the combustion chamber opposite to the sparking plug, to ensure a thorough sweep of fresh gas over the sparking plug as the piston approaches TDC.

The valves are often inclined to the port side of the cylinder head, to give a slightly reduced bend to the ports. This also gives a wedge-shaped combustion chamber, which makes for more effective control of flame speed. The sparking plug is fitted at the thick end of the wedge, thus giving a large area of flame front during the early stages of combustion, and speeding up the first part of this process. As combustion proceeds, the flame area is reduced, thus reducing somewhat the speed of the final stages of combustion and minimizing the risk of detonation.

The hemispherical combustion chamber

It is commonly believed that the ideal shape for a combustion chamber is a perfect sphere. This belief is based upon the fact that the sphere has the smallest surface area per unit volume and thus the heat loss to the combustion chamber walls is reduced to the minimum. In most other ways, however, this shape is most unsuitable. For instance, if the bore and stroke of the engine are equal, and the spherical combustion chamber is formed half in the piston and half in the cylinder head, the compression ratio is only 2½:1, which is absurdly low. For a compression ratio of 8:1 and a similar form of combustion chamber the stroke would need to be 4⅔ times the cylinder bore. This would severely limit engine speed and place an unacceptable restriction on valve size.

However, a combustion chamber, the upper surface of which consists of a hemisphere formed in the cylinder head, has several important benefits to offer. By inclining the valves at about 45° on opposite sides of the centre-line (Figure 2.189) the valve diameter is much increased and an excellent port shape is obtained, giving excellent volumetric efficiency. This advantage is so important that where high power output is the main consideration this type is excellent, but high NO_x emission is a great disadvantage.

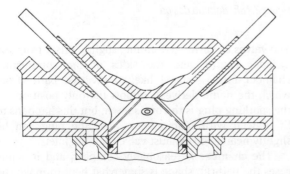

Figure 2.189 Hemispherical design

To obtain a high compression ratio the piston crown must be domed, giving the combustion chamber a shape like the peel of half an orange and having a high surface area per unit of volume, quite the opposite of the 'ideal' spherical shape. However undesirable this may be, it is of little importance compared with advantages gained.

Induction turbulence can be arranged by having the inlet port at a slight angle to a cylinder diameter, and compression turbulence can be obtained by a suitable shape of piston crown.

The chamber is of a shape easy to machine all over, giving accurate control of compression ratio. Although the sparking plug cannot be fitted in the ideal position, it can be placed near the centre of the cylinder head, where good results are obtained.

The greatest drawback to this type of combustion chamber is undoubtedly the complication necessary in the valve operating gear. The best method is twin overhead camshafts, one directly over each row of valves, but this is also the most complicated and expensive (refer to section 2.9.2 for illustrations).

Alternative arrangements are:

- a single overhead camshaft with rockers
- a double side camshaft, pushrods and rockers
- a single side camshaft, pushrods and rockers.

With improved designs, materials and lubrication, the objections to the use of the hemispherical head are less important, and the increasing emphasis on engine power output, even for 'production' cars, has resulted in the use of the twin overhead camshaft layout (which has been used for practically all racing-car engines since about 1912).

The four-valve combustion chamber

A large-diameter valve is needed if good volumetric efficiency is to be achieved, but it is difficult to blend a large valve into a compact combustion chamber. This problem is minimized by using four valves, two inlet and two exhaust.

Figure 2.190 shows a typical four-valve chamber. Since the total port area of two inlet valves is greater than that given by one valve, it is possible to combine good breathing and economy with low exhaust emission. Inclining the valves to form a 'pent roof' type combustion chamber allows the sparking plug to be situated in the centre of the roof of the chamber. Four valve engines can achieve more stable combustion over a wide fuel mixture range, so are suited for the weaker lean-burn designs as well as engines operating on normal or richer mixtures.

It is also possible to achieve a good volumetric efficiency using a triple-valve pent roof combustion chamber. Two inlet valves are used per cylinder while only a single exhaust valve is needed, the exhaust valve being larger than each inlet valve. The single exhaust valve is normally offset, which allows the sparking plug to be positioned centrally in the combustion chamber.

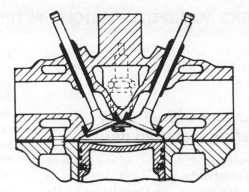

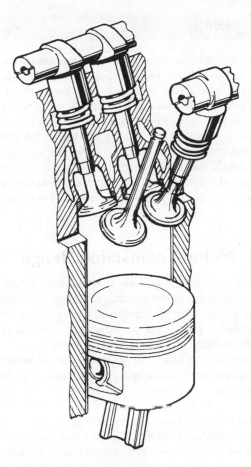

Figure 2.190 A pent roof combustion chamber

The cross-flow, bowl-in-piston combustion chamber

In this design (Figure 2.191) the underside of the cylinder head is flat and a bowl in the piston forms the combustion chamber. The effect of having a machined chamber in the piston gives close control of the shape and capacity, so compression ratio variation between cylinders is minimized. A high ratio could be used if emission restrictions did not apply.

The flat head allows the large valves to open direct into the cylinder so good breathing and scavenging is possible; this can be improved still further by increasing the bore/stroke to oversquare.

Squish action around the chamber is obtained by the small piston-to-head clearance around the piston crown. In some engines, recesses are cut in the piston to prevent contact between piston and valve.

The term cross-flow applies to the port arrangement; the inlet and exhaust manifolds are fitted on opposite sides of the engine. This feature gives space to use better manifold shapes, which further improves volumetric efficiency and exhaust scavenging.

(See section 2.30.5 later in this chapter.)

Figure 2.191 A cross-flow, bowl-in-piston design

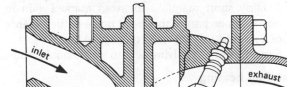

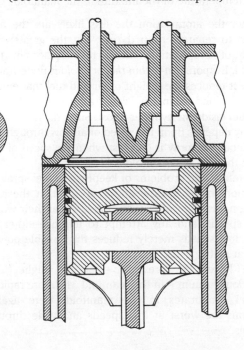

2.19 INTAKE MANIFOLD DESIGN – PETROL ENGINES

Note: Also refer to section 2.10 for additional information on intake manifolds.

2.19.1 Behaviour of fuel spray dictating manifold design

With the old carburettor fuel systems, air and fuel were mixed at the entry point of the inlet manifold (within the carburettor), and then drawn into the cylinder via the inlet manifold. It is the presence of the fuel spray in the air passing along the manifold that is responsible for most of the difficulties. Since liquid fuel is much denser than air it has a much greater disinclination to change either its speed or direction, so that where changes of speed or direction occur in the manifold the air responds to these changes much more quickly than the fuel.

Unless the speed of the flow of mixture along the manifold is kept at a fairly high level the fuel spray tends to settle out on the floor and walls of the manifold, and fuel will then not reach the cylinders in a form in which it can easily be vaporized.

The cross-sectional area of the manifold (bore size) must therefore be small enough to ensure that the flow of mixture through it is sufficiently rapid to maintain the fuel spray in suspension in the air, even at low engine speeds. This is contrary to what is required to obtain the best filling of the cylinders.

There are three other factors that influence the extent to which the fuel remains in suspension in the air stream. These are:

1 the fineness of atomization of the fuel
2 the pressure (or depression) in the manifold
3 the temperature of the mixture in the manifold.

The finer the atomization the less likely are the fuel particles to separate from the air, but the greater the amount of evaporation which takes place in the manifold. Evaporation *within the manifold* is undesirable because it reduces the weight of air and fuel that enters the cylinder, and the internal cooling due to vaporization of the fuel inside the cylinder is lost. Since the fineness of the spray depends upon the speed of airflow through the choke tube, the spray is coarsest when the speed of the mixture through the manifold is lowest.

Therefore, the problems of keeping the fuel spray in suspension in the airflow and ensuring that the fuel spray remains fine rather than coarse are at their worst at low speeds, and any attempt to improve either or both at low speeds merely reduces the possible power output at high speeds.

The lower the pressure – or the higher the depression/vacuum – in the manifold, the more rapidly the fuel evaporates in the manifold. Here again, conditions are worst at low speeds and wide throttle openings.

Heating of the mixture encourages evaporation in the manifold and so helps to keep the fuel in suspension in the air, but it also reduces the possible power output, for the reason stated above and because it reduces the density of the air. In this case, however, conditions are rather better. Provided the heating is applied via the walls of the manifold, because the faster the mixture travels through the manifold the less time it has to absorb heat, the mixture will pick up more heat under those conditions when it will be most helpful, i.e. at low speeds.

2.19.2 Features of manifold design

Enough has been said to indicate that manifold design is so complex that it is not possible to design one that gives satisfaction under all conditions, so it is only to be expected that a great deal of variation in manifold design will be found on motor vehicle engines.

For what may be called the 'normal' types of motor vehicle engines, smoothness and economy are of more importance than just power. The manifold will be designed to provide the best possible distribution of mixture, both as to quantity and equality of air/fuel ratio among the individual cylinders. Features that contribute to smoothness and economy rather than power include:

1 A relatively small bore size to maintain reasonably high mixture speeds at low engine speeds.
2 Sharper corners rather than gentle bends where changes in direction occur. The turbulence created at these sharp corners assists in keeping the fuel in suspension in the air (unfortunately sharp corners can cause separation of petrol and air at high engine and air speeds).
3 A fairly short manifold to avoid marked gain in power at one part of the speed range at the expense of a marked loss at some other speed.
4 Some means of applying heat to the manifold walls.

Manifold heating

Applying heat to the manifold and using this heat to vaporize the fuel is essential if the fuel mixture is to be evenly distributed to all cylinders then easily ignited and completely burnt. Moderate heating is required because excessive heat, as used in the past (when the exhaust gases were made to come into contact with the inlet manifold at a hot spot), lowers volumetric efficiency, i.e. it reduces the ratio of the mass of air induced into a cylinder per cycle compared to the swept volume of the cylinder.

Heat is transferred to the manifold in two ways:

1 conduction from the cylinder block through the manifold gasket
2 conduction from the coolant circulated through a jacket that surrounds the inlet manifold.

This conducted heat is absent until the engine warms up, so in addition to being provided with an extra-rich mixture (with its associated pollution problems), many engines are fitted with electrical heating devices to warm the air during the initial period of cold running.

Figure 2.192 shows a water-heated manifold.

Water from the coolant system is piped to a jacket adjacent to the carburettor and then returned by another pipe to the coolant system.

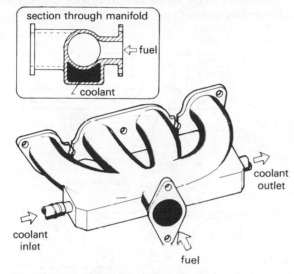

Figure 2.192 A water-heated manifold

Electric manifold heaters

Fuel vaporization is very poor during both cold starting and the warm-up period; this results in low power output, poor economy and high exhaust emissions.

To overcome the problem, many engines are fitted with some form of electric heater to preheat the air and fuel as it passes through the inlet manifold. Figure 2.193 shows two forms of heater, which automatically come into operation when the engine is below a set temperature and remain in use until the engine has warmed up.

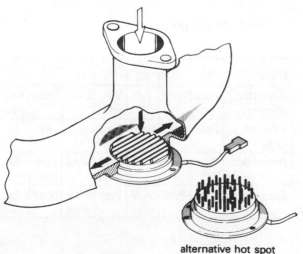

alternative hot spot
(hedgehog type)

Figure 2.193 Manifold heaters

2.19.3 Typical manifolds

Various aspects of manifold design can be illustrated by studying some of the layouts used in recent years.

Four-cylinder in-line

The layouts shown in Figure 2.194 indicate various manifold arrangements that can be used for a four-cylinder engine.

Figure 2.194a is the cheapest arrangement and it was commonly used for the more basic types of engine. Since the inlet valves for cylinders 1 and 2 and cylinders 3 and 4 are adjacent to each other the inlet ports in the cylinder head can be joined together, or siamesed. This simplifies the head casting and allows a two-branch manifold to be used. Aluminium alloy is used because the excellent thermal conductivity of this material allows the manifold to warm up quickly; also it is a lightweight metal. However, the siamesed arrangement has two serious limitations:

1. poor volumetric efficiency due to the restriction of the gas flow caused by the number of bends
2. severe induction robbery due to the overlap of induction strokes that occur in adjacent cylinders.

Power produced by an engine depends on the quantity of gas that can be charged into the cylinder during the induction stroke. For this reason a high volumetric efficiency (VE) is a prime objective when designing an inlet manifold. Since sharp bends in the tract reduce gas flow, an ideal manifold from a VE aspect should have gas paths as straight as possible. This does, however, contradict the use of sharp bends, which can be used to promote turbulence to improve mixing of the air and fuel.

'Induction robbery', as the name suggests, means that some cylinders do not get their full share of new gas. Consequently the total power output from the engine is low and the variation in power from the cylinders reduces the smooth running of the engine.

One of the two robbery periods can be seen by considering an engine with siamesed ports and a firing order of 1-3-4-2. Bearing in mind that each inlet valve opens early and closes very late, there is a large crank angle when the inlet valves of cylinders 3 and 4 are open simultaneously. Towards the end of the induction stroke of cylinder 3, at high engine speeds the gas will be flowing freely into the cylinder at a very fast rate. Opening the valve in cylinder 4 will not induce the gas to change its direction, so cylinder 4 will be starved of fuel until the valve in cylinder 3 has closed. This action is repeated for cylinders 2 and 1, so robbery occurs in two crank positions of the cycle. Firing orders used on this design of manifold give similar robbery effects.

The carburettor used on a multi-branch manifold should have its throttle spindle parallel with the engine axis to avoid one branch being starved of mixture during part-throttle operation.

Figure 2.194b uses twin carburettors and owing to the straighter air passages, the VE is raised, especially at high engine speeds. Robbery is still a problem here, and the irregular airflow through each carburettor requires a slightly richer mixture than before. The two separate manifolds are normally interconnected by a 'balance pipe', which gives smoother idling by equalizing the depression in each manifold.

The cylinder head layout used in Figure 2.194c can be fitted with many different manifold arrangements. These options were often used by manufacturers to provide a range of engines, each with different power characteristics to suit their intended purpose, e.g. sports car engine or light commercial vehicle engine. The elimination of the siamesed ports overcomes the problem of robbery as long as the individual tracts of the manifold are of adequate length.

Ideally each cylinder should receive the same amount of air, the ratio of petrol and air should be identical and the additives contained in the fuel should not vary in quantity between the cylinders. The term distribution is used to describe the ability of a manifold to meet these requirements, so the layout shown in Figure 2.194c gives a better distribution than the first layout.

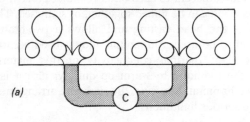

(a)

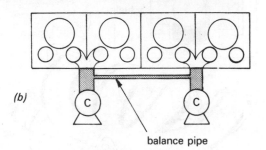

(b)

balance pipe

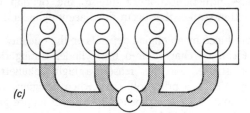

(c)

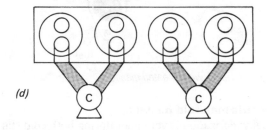

(d)

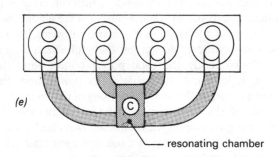

(e)

resonating chamber

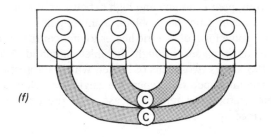

(f)

C = carburettor

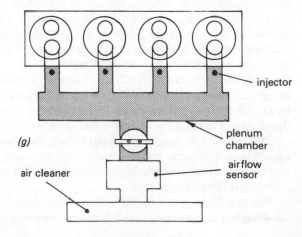

(g)

injector

plenum chamber

air cleaner

airflow sensor

Layout	(a)	(b)	(c)	(d)	(e)	(f)	(g)
Volumetric efficiency	Poor	Good	Fair	Very good	Good	Good	Very good
Induction robbery	Poor	Poor	Good	Good	Ex	Ex	Ex
Distribution	Poor	Fair	Fair	Very good	Good	Very good	Ex
Economy	Poor	Poor	Very good	Poor	Very good	Good	Ex

Figure 2.194 Manifold layouts – four-cylinder engines

Six-cylinder in-line engines

The problems associated with four-cylinder manifolds are accentuated with long manifolds as fitted to six-cylinder engines, so the power output and economy of this type of engine can be changed dramatically by altering the manifold layout. This point is illustrated by the two manifolds shown in Figure 2.195.

The siamesed port arrangement shown in Figure 2.195a uses a single carburettor and a three-branch manifold which gives very poor air/fuel distribution although fitting a deflector improves the distribution.

The use of twin carburettors and a manifold layout as shown in Figure 2.195b gives a more costly arrangement but with much better distribution and a higher VE. In this case the use of twin carburettors improves the economy because the airflow through the carburettors is regular and the mixture does not have to be set rich to satisfy the end cylinders.

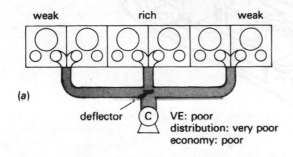

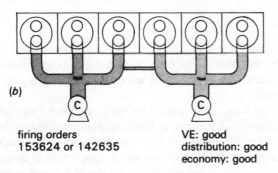

Figure 2.195 Manifold layout – six-cylinder engines

Vee engines

Compared with in-line engines, the vee arrangement gives a much shorter manifold, which reduces the mixture variation between cylinders.

In V6 and V8 engines, more than one cylinder will be on induction at the same time, so mixture robbery will take place if a single-manifold system is used. To overcome this problem, vee engines are normally fitted with a manifold cast as one piece but formed into two separate tracts.

Figure 2.196a shows a V6 layout with two tracts. Applying the firing order to the cylinder numbering system used shows that the banks fire: right, left, right, left, right, left. The interval between firing strokes in a given bank means that there is a similar interval between induction strokes.

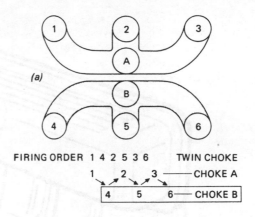

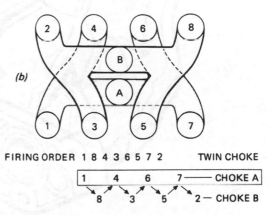

Figure 2.196 A vee engine inlet manifold

A V8 manifold is shown in Figure 2.196b and once again the firing order and manifold shape are arranged to use each tract alternately to minimize the robbery caused by overlapping induction strokes.

The restricted space between the two banks makes the twin-choke carburettor most suitable for vee engines.

Fuel injection system manifolds

To overcome poor fuel distribution between cylinders and to improve VE on multi-cylinder engines, multipoint fuel injection is used. Placing the injectors near to the inlet port allows for precise fuel delivery for each cylinder and robbery from other cylinders is eliminated. The inlet manifold provides each cylinder with filtered air, and the fuel is then mixed with the air near the inlet port, either at the very end of the manifold tract or within the cylinder head inlet port.

The throttle butterfly is located in the throttle housing at the beginning of the inlet manifold. The air enters a large reservoir within the manifold often referred to as the plenum chamber. The large volume of air stored in the plenum chamber dampens the pulsations in the manifold caused through the opening and closing of the intake valves.

To meet the very strict emission regulations now imposed on motor vehicles, multipoint fuel injection systems are used on all modern engines.

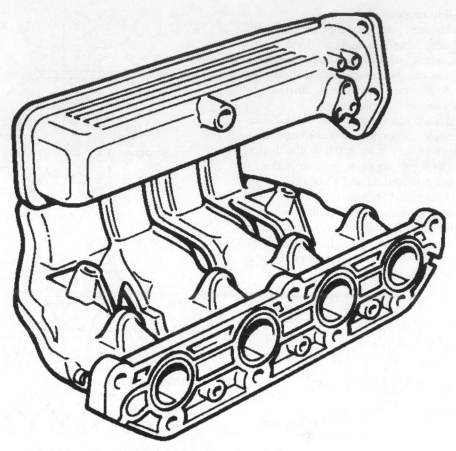

Figure 2.197 Fuel injection inlet manifold with plenum chamber design

Note that electronic single-point injection systems mixed the fuel with the air at the beginning of the inlet manifold and were in this respect similar to the carburettor. These single-point injection systems were therefore subject to those distribution difficulties similar to that of a carburettor fuel system.

Variable induction manifolds

To obtain the highest VE an engine's cylinder must be filled with the maximum volume of air/fuel mixture possible when the inlet valve is open. The maximum volume of the gas can only be drawn into the cylinder if the airflow in the inlet manifold is moving towards the cylinder when the inlet valve opens. The airflow in the inlet manifold oscillates due to the opening and closing of the inlet valve during the induction stroke resulting in pressure waves in the inlet manifold. If the flow of air towards the cylinder is timed to the opening of the inlet valve it is possible for the maximum volume of air to be drawn into the cylinder. It takes a specific period of time for the air to pass through the inlet manifold tract for a given engine speed. By selecting a suitable inlet manifold length and diameter, oscillations in the manifold can be arranged so that the airflow in the manifold is moving towards the cylinder when the inlet valve opens. Selecting the correct length and diameter of the inlet manifold tract provides the maximum

volume of gas drawn into the cylinder increasing the VE, however if a fixed length and diameter inlet manifold tract is used this will only occur for one engine speed.

A long inlet manifold tract provides excellent cylinder filling at low to medium engine speeds while a shorter inlet manifold tract provides excellent cylinder filling at higher engine speeds. A compromise is usually made with a fixed length of inlet manifold tract, which provides good engine power over a wide range of engine speeds.

By altering the length of the inlet manifold tract with engine speed, it is possible to increase the engine power and torque at both low and high speeds. A variable inlet manifold tract also provides lower emissions levels. With the use of modern technology and electronically controlled systems it is possible, via valves within the manifold, to alter the length of the inlet manifold tract while the engine is running. The electronic control unit monitors engine speed and engine load and controls the position of the valves within the inlet manifold to suit the engine's operating conditions.

The ECU usually controls the position of the valves with an electronic vacuum regulator valve. The ECU may also monitor additional engine operating conditions such as engine and air temperature.

2.20 THE REQUIREMENTS OF A FUEL DELIVERY SYSTEM

2.20.1 Introduction

It has been seen in previous sections that the power produced from an internal-combustion engine is the result of high pressure from the heating of a gas (burning of a fuel mixture) inside the engine cylinder.

During one complete engine cycle (induction, compression, power and exhaust), the pressure acting on the piston varies widely, but it has an average value which is called the 'mean effective pressure' (MEP). The effort exerted by the engine is clearly proportional to the MEP), which depends upon the engine design, compression ratio, and the temperature to which the gas is heated by combustion.

2.20.2 Combustion of petrol

Petrol is a fuel that is particularly suitable for use in internal-combustion engines, especially light motor vehicles. It is a clean liquid, which is easily stored and flows freely. Petrol gives off a flammable vapour at quite low temperatures and when burnt produces a large amount of heat. A disadvantage of petrol is its highly flammable qualities and reasonable precautions against fire are needed.

Before petrol can be burnt it must be vaporized and mixed with a suitable quantity of air. Combustion is a process involving the chemical combination of a fuel with oxygen.

Crude petroleum, from which petrol is produced, is a mixture of various compounds of hydrogen and carbon (called hydrocarbons). Petrol consists of these constituents of crude petroleum which have boiling points between the temperatures of, roughly, 30°C and 200°C.

2.20.3 Calorific value

The amount of heat generated by the complete combustion of a unit mass of fuel is called the calorific value of the fuel. Note that for an average sample of petrol, the calorific value is about 44 MJ kg^{-1}.

2.20.4 Mixture strength

The mixture strength is the proportion of air that is mixed with the fuel required to produce the engine's power. It should be noted that the mixture strength is always quoted by the weight of the air and fuel, not their volume.

Example: an air/fuel ratio of 14:1 indicates 14 g of air mixed with 1 g of fuel.

It has already been noted that for perfect and therefore complete combustion to occur during the power stroke, the air/fuel ratio supplied to the engine is 14.66:1 (called the chemically correct mixture or stoichmetric mixture). This is usually referred to as 14.7:1.

A mixture having a greater proportion of fuel to that of air, is referred to as a 'rich mixture' (e.g. 10:1).

A mixture having a greater proportion of air to that of fuel, is referred to as a weak or 'lean mixture' (e.g. 20:1).

Both rich and lean mixtures will burn, but will produce different results and levels of power.

2.20.5 Influence of air/fuel ratio

Mixtures having uniform air/fuel ratios of less than about 8:1 or more than about 22:1 cannot normally be ignited in the cylinder of a petrol engine. Within this air range the mixture strength has a considerable influence on the engine's power output, drivability and emission levels.

It should be emphasized that the mixture strengths referred to are those in which the fuel is completely vaporized and thoroughly mixed with the air so the proportion of air and fuel is the same throughout the mixture in the cylinder. Unfortunately, this is rarely the case in an engine which is running.

It may be expected that the chemically correct mixture should give optimum results, but this is not always correct. As an example, it is impossible, under normal engine operating conditions to ensure that the fuel is evenly distributed throughout the air. During some engine conditions, the fuel may not be completely vaporized when combustion occurs.

The main effects of a variation in air/fuel ratio are observed on:

1 The mean effective pressure (MEP)
The MEP reaches a maximum value with a slightly rich mixture (excess fuel). The upper curve in Figure 2.198 provides some idea of the way in which the MEP varies with changes in air/fuel ratio.

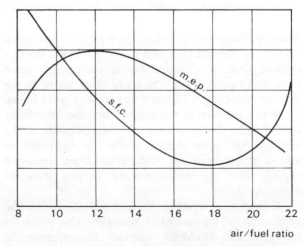

Figure 2.198 Effect on the MEP with changes in air/fuel ratio

2 The rate of combustion

The speed of the flame travelling through the mixture varies in a manner similar to the MEP. The speed of the flame is high with a slightly rich mixture and slows down markedly as the mixture is weakened, and to a lesser extent as the mixture is enriched. One result of this is a tendency for the engine to run hotter if the mixture is weak.

3 The rate of fuel consumption

This is called the specific fuel consumption (SFC) and it is found to be lowest with mixtures that are slightly weaker than the chemically correct mixture, as shown by the lower curve of Figure 2.198.

4 Exhaust gas emissions

If an engine is supplied with the chemically correct mixture, it should result in carbon dioxide (CO_2), water (H_2O) and nitrogen (N_2) being emitted from the exhaust (Figure 2.199). These substances are regarded as harmless to the environment but note that CO_2 contributes to the 'greenhouse effect'. The chemically correct mixture is called the stoichiometric air fuel ratio.

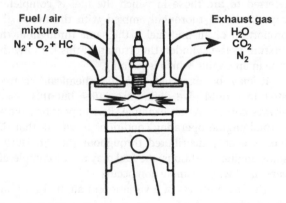

Fuel / air mixture
$N_2 + O_2 + HC$

Exhaust gas
H_2O
CO_2
N_2

Figure 2.199 Complete combustion

Unfortunately, the internal-combustion engine is not 100% efficient, therefore additional substances are produced during the combustion process. These include carbon monoxide (CO), hydrocarbons (HC), oxygen (O_2) and oxides of nitrogen (NO_x).

If the mixture is made richer, the proportion of carbon dioxide in the exhaust gas decreases while the amount of carbon monoxide increases, and a small amount of unburnt hydrogen is also found. As the rich mixture limit of combustibility is approached, some unburned carbon appears as sooty black smoke in the exhaust gases; this is always a sign of excessive richness.

If the mixture is weakened from the chemically correct ratio, the proportion of carbon dioxide in the exhaust gas again decreases. Carbon monoxide is almost absent once the mixture has been weakened slightly, but the proportion of oxygen increases accordingly.

A change in mixture strength will also affect the proportion of the oxides of nitrogen. The oxides of nitrogen are produced due to the increase in temperature during combustion.

These changes in the composition of the exhaust gases can be used to estimate the air/fuel ratio on which the engine is running. A sample of exhaust gas can be analyzed chemically, though this is impracticable in a motor vehicle workshop. An alternative check is available in the form of an item of workshop equipment referred to as an 'exhaust gas analyser'. The analyser detects the proportions of the gases by electronic means and indicates the air/fuel ratio on a display. The workshop technician uses the exhaust gas analyser reading to check the operation and efficiency of the engine, fuel and ignition systems.

2.20.6 Vaporization

It should be noted that it is the petrol vapour, and not the liquid, which burns. It is therefore important that the petrol supplied to the cylinder is vaporized before combustion occurs.

2.20.7 Atomization

Generally the time is too short to vaporize the liquid fuel completely before combustion, so additional means must be provided to break up the fuel mechanically into small particles by a process called atomization. The liquid fuel is broken up by either subjecting it to a turbulent airflow, or by pumping the fuel into the air stream through small holes in an injector. This action not only aids the production of a fast burning mixture but also helps to mix the air and fuel evenly, i.e. it aims to produce a homogeneous mixture.

2.20.8 Carburation systems

In the past, the bringing together of the petrol and air was usually carried out using a carburettor. The carburettor mixes the air and petrol in the correct air/fuel ratio to obtain the performance desired from the engine.

Figure 2.200 illustrates, in simple form, a carburation system to mix the fuel with air drawn into the engine.

During the delivery of the fuel into the intake system the carburettor also atomizes the petrol to give good combustion.

When a liquid changes state into a vapour it absorbs heat (called latent heat), from the surroundings. If petrol were to be vaporized in the carburettor, the latter would be chilled by the heat taken from it to vaporize the petrol. As a result any moisture in the air passing through the carburettor would be condensed, deposited on the throttle and choke tube, and frozen. In this way the passage through the carburettor would become blocked by ice and the engine would stop.

To prevent the formation of ice, the carburettor is usually supplied with hot air, which is drawn from the

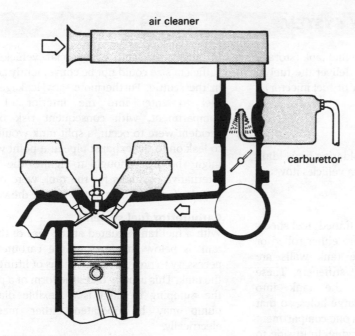

air cleaner

carburettor

Figure 2.200 A carburation system

region around the exhaust manifold. However, overheating the air should be avoided because it reduces power output. Since petrol vapour occupies a considerably greater volume than the equivalent quantity of liquid, if the petrol is in vapour form rather than liquid, a much smaller mass of air/fuel mixture can be drawn into the cylinder.

If the petrol can be vaporized inside the cylinder, the heat absorbed during fuel vaporization will have a beneficial cooling effect on the inside of the combustion chamber, particularly when the engine is developing full power.

Therefore the best results are obtained if the fuel can be introduced into the cylinder in liquid form, but provided all of the fuel can be vaporized before combustion occurs. Since vapour is given off from the surface of a liquid, the rate of evaporation can be increased by breaking up the liquid into a fine spray of minute droplets.

2.20.9 Fuel injection systems

Most modern engines now use a petrol injection fuel system to mix the petrol and air. The injection system ensures the precise delivery of fuel into the intake system under all engine operating conditions. A modern injection system is usually electronically controlled although during the development of the systems a few mechanical injection systems were tried. Providing the precise quantity of fuel to the cylinder allows the engine to:

- produce low emission levels
- develop an increase in engine power and performance
- be more fuel efficient.

Figure 2.201 shows a multi-point fuel injection system (one injector delivers the fuel for each cylinder). Note that the injector is located near to the inlet valve, the fuel becomes atomized as it is injected into the air stream, which is then mixed with the air that is drawn into the cylinder of the engine.

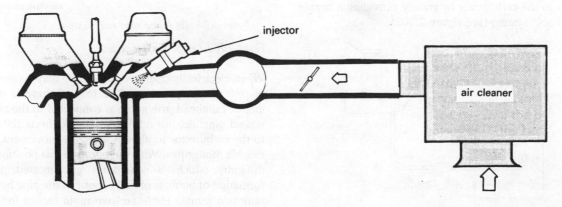

injector

air cleaner

Figure 2.201 A fuel injection system

2.21 THE FUEL SUPPLY SYSTEM

The fuel supply system consists of the fuel tank (storage tank) and a pump, which is used to deliver the fuel to the fuel metering system (carburettor or fuel injector).

2.21.1 The fuel tank

Most fuel tanks are constructed by soldering or welding pressed metal, although many modern vehicles now use plastic moulded tanks.

Soldered tanks

The walls of the tank are made from tinned steel sheets cut and bent to shape. The seams are either rolled or rivetted before soldering, and the tank walls are internally supported at intervals by stiffeners. These consist of sheets which divide the tank into compartments but are pierced with large holes, so that although they allow fuel to pass from one compartment to another they prevent the fuel 'surging' from side to side of the tank.

Welded tanks

This construction uses steel pressings for walls and stiffeners, with joints and seams welded. The tank is often coated inside, and sometimes outside also, with tin or lead.

Plastic tanks

Most fuel tanks today are constructed from a plastic material. Materials such as high-density polyethylene can be easily moulded into irregular shaped tanks to fit into spaces situated away from accident impact zones. Extra protection against impact and exhaust heat can be given by using steel plates.

2.21.2 Location of the fuel tank

It was at one time common practice on small and some medium-sized cars to fit the tank as high as possible in the scuttle (between the engine bulkhead and the base of the windscreen). With the carburettor mounted fairly low at the side of the engine, the fuel could be allowed to flow to the carburettor by gravity, providing a simple and reliable system (see Figure 2.202).

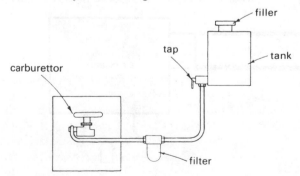

Figure 2.202 Gravity fuel systems

In large cars and commercial vehicles, a tank of sufficient size could not be conveniently accommodated in the scuttle. Furthermore, any leakage would allow fuel to enter into the interior of the driving compartment, with consequent risk of fire. If an accident were to occur, a split tank would allow petrol to leak on to the exhaust pipe at a point where the pipe might be hot enough to ignite the fuel. Various alternative positions for the tank were tried, the most popular for cars being at the rear of the vehicle.

Carburettor fuel systems

With a fuel tank situated at the rear of the vehicle, the tank is below the level of the carburettor and it is necessary to provide some means of lifting the fuel from the tank. This usually takes the form of a pump in which the pumping element is a flexible diaphragm. The pump may be operated either mechanically or electrically.

When mechanically operated, it is mounted on the engine and worked by a special cam on the engine camshaft. As the engine is carried on flexible mountings, it is necessary to include a length of flexible piping in the pipeline connecting the pump to the tank, as shown in Figure 2.203a.

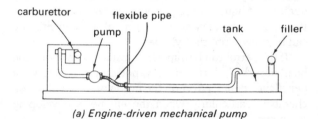

(a) Engine-driven mechanical pump

(b) Pump-feed fuel system

Figure 2.203 Layout of a fuel system

When electrically operated, the pump may be mounted in one of two positions. The first of these is on the engine bulkhead: the pump is connected to the tank by a rigid pipeline, but a flexible pipe connects the pump to the carburettor to allow for engine movement on its flexible mountings. With the pump in this position, one difficulty which is sometimes encountered, is the formation of bubbles of fuel vapour in the pipe between tank and pump. There are two main causes for this – heat and reduced pressure. If the fuel pipe is heated by passing near the exhaust pipe it should be relocated, but if the heating is merely due to hot weather little can be done. The trouble is aggravated by the fact that the pipeline between tank and pump, being on the suction side of the pump, is operating under a pressure less than atmospheric, a condition that encourages the formation of vapour. Thus the alternative position for an electric fuel pump is close to the tank so that the main length of the pipeline is under pressure and the formation of vapour is discouraged. Both these positions are shown in Figure 2.203.

Petrol injection fuel systems

Engines that use an injection system to deliver the fuel are usually fitted with an electric pump. The pump is fitted near to, or submerged in, the fuel within the tank. The pump assembly required to draw the fuel from the tank may also be used to supply the fuel direct to a fuel injection system but on some systems a separate pump can be used.

2.21.3 Mechanical fuel pumps

The constructional features of a mechanical pump are shown in Figure 2.204. The upper part of the body (16) contains the inlet connection (1), the inlet valve (2), the outlet valve (3) and the outlet connection (4). The circular diaphragm (5) (made of fabric impregnated with synthetic rubber) is clamped around its edge between the upper (16) and lower (15) parts of the body. It is also clamped at its centre between two dished circular plates attached to the upper end of the diaphragm pull rod (6). A spring (7) fitted between the lower diaphragm and the lower body pushes the diaphragm upwards. The pump is bolted to the wall of the crankcase. The lever (8) passes through an aperture to bear against an eccentric (9) on the engine camshaft, the end of the lever being pressed lightly against the

eccentric by the spring (12). The lever pivots on a pin (10) on which is also pivoted a section link (13), the other end of which engages the lower end of the diaphragm pull rod.

When the engine is running, the lever (8) is rocked on its pivot. Movement of the lever towards the pump causes the step (11) on the lever to engage the link (13), which it moves about the pivot (10), so pulling the diaphragm and compressing the diaphragm spring (7). Movement of the lever (8) away from the pump allows the diaphragm to be moved upwards by the spring (7).

Downward movement of the diaphragm increases the volume of the pumping chamber above the diaphragm, holding the outlet valve (3) on its seat, opening the inlet valve (2) and drawing fuel from the tank through the inlet connection into the pumping chamber. On the upward stroke of the diaphragm, pressure is applied to the fuel in the pumping chamber by the spring (7), closing the inlet valve but forcing the outlet valve off its seat and delivering fuel through the outlet connection (4) and a pipe to the carburettor.

When the carburettor is full of fuel a valve in the carburettor closes, preventing the entry of any more fuel, and consequently fuel is now unable to leave the pump. The diaphragm will thus be held in its lowest position by the fuel in the pumping chamber under the loading of the spring (7), although the lever (8) will maintain contact with the eccentric (9) through the influence of the spring (12).

The pressure at which fuel is delivered to the carburettor is determined by the force exerted by the spring (7). This force in turn depends upon the dimensions of the spring and the extent to which it is compressed when the diaphragm is in its lowest position. Within limits, this may be varied by selecting a suitable thickness of packing to place between the pump mounting-flange and the engine crankcase; a greater thickness reducing the pressure slightly and a lesser thickness increasing it.

Should the diaphragm develop a leak, fuel can escape through a number of drain holes (14) drilled through the wall of the pump body.

Maximum fuel pressure at inlet and outlet points depends on the pump model but typical values are:

Inlet: vacuum of about 150 mm (6 inches)
Outlet: 21–35 kPa (3–5 lbf in^{-2})

2.21.4 Electric fuel pumps

Note: Electric fuel pumps used for petrol injection fuel systems are detailed in section 2.22.

Although electric fuel pumps have been extensively used in the past, the mechanical pump was preferred with carburettor fuel systems because of its low cost. Also the mechanical pump operates only when the engine is running, so fire risk is reduced when the vehicle is involved in a crash.

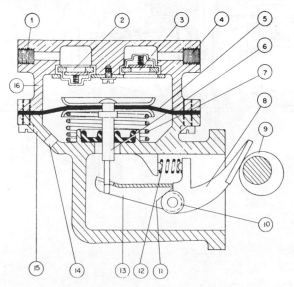

Figure 2.204 A mechanically operated diaphragm fuel pump

The electric pump (Figure 2.205) consists of two parts: the pumping section, which is similar to the corresponding section of a mechanical pump, and the electrical unit, which operates the diaphragm.

Movement of the diaphragm (9) is effected by energizing an electromagnet and attracting an iron armature (8). At the end of the stroke during which the fuel is entering the pump, the pushrod (7) moves the toggle-spring assembly and clicks open the tungsten contacts (1). This interrupts the electrical supply to the magnet coil (2), allows the spring (3) to return the diaphragm and forces the fuel through the outlet valve to the carburettor. When the diaphragm reaches the end of its travel, the contacts close and the cycle is repeated.

This action will continue until the carburettor is full of fuel, when the diaphragm will be unable to make its return stroke, holding the contacts open until the carburettor requires more fuel. The pressure at which the fuel is delivered to the carburettor is governed by the strength of the spring (3).

Reference was made to the fire risk following a crash. To minimize this hazard, some vehicles have an 'inertia-actuated cut-off switch' connected in the electrical supply to the fuel pump. A deceleration greater than 5 G (49 ms^{-2}) causes the switch contacts to open.

2.21.5 Filters

All fuel injection and carburettor fuel systems have many passages and small holes through which petrol must flow. Tiny pieces of dirt can obstruct the flow and prevent the correct functioning of these systems. Water in the fuel system causes corrosion to system components, which is detrimental to precision-made parts of the fuel system.

The petrol companies take a great deal of trouble to ensure that the petrol delivered by their pumps at filling stations is clean. It is possible for dust and dirt to enter the tank of the car whenever the filler cap is open, even for short periods. Air also contains moisture, which will condense inside the fuel tank.

A coarse gauze suction filter is normally fitted to the 'pick up' pipe inside the fuel tank. It is a sensible precaution (with fuel injection systems a necessity) to fit one or more filters in the fuel system to trap dirt and water.

Fuel filters fitted to fuel injection systems are fitted between the fuel pump and the fuel injector/s. Filters are usually made of either fine nylon meshing or pleated paper; the latter is typical of fuel injection system filters. The pleats allow the largest filtration area possible within a given space. These types of fuel filters are sealed and must be replaced as an assembly.

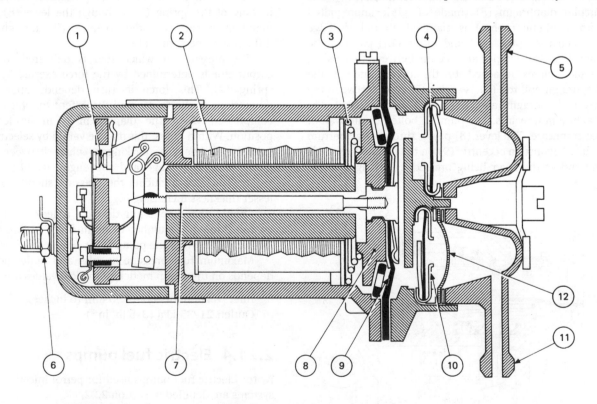

1	contact breaker points	7	pushrod
2	magnet coil	8	magnet armature
3	return spring	9	diaphragm assembly
4	outlet valve	10	inlet valve
5	outlet connection	11	inlet connection
6	electrical supply connection	12	filter

Figure 2.205 An electrically operated low pressure fuel pump used on carburettor systems

Fuel filter

1 Paper filter, **2** Strainer, **3** Support plate.

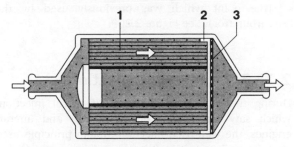

Figure 2.206 Section through a fuel filter

Filters used in conjunction with carburettor fuel systems may be fitted in one or more of the following positions:

1 around the outlet from the fuel tank
2 at the fuel pump inlet
3 at the carburettor or injection system inlet
4 at any convenient point in the pipeline connecting the tank to the fuel delivery system.

Fuel filters for carburettor purposes may consist of brass wire gauze of a mesh sufficiently fine to trap those particles of dirt that are large enough to cause trouble in fuel pumps and carburettors, and of an area large enough to pass more than the maximum fuel flow. If previously damped with petrol such filters will also trap water.

Replacement of filters

To prevent clogging of the filtration element, the filter assembly should be replaced at the specified service intervals as indicated by the manufacturer. When replacing the fuel filter it is important that the fuel flow is in the correct direction, arrows marked on the filter casing normally indicate the direction of fuel flow through the filter.

2.21.6 Pipelines

For many years the pipes used to convey the fuel from tank to carburettor were made of copper, a metal of great flexibility, which enables it to be easily bent to shape, and possessing good resistance to corrosion. Copper, however, is relatively expensive and has been almost entirely replaced in modern vehicles by plastic or steel.

Engines are supported on flexible mountings, which permit fairly extensive movement of the engine relative to the frame, to prevent vibration being transmitted to the bodywork and passengers. It is therefore necessary to include a length of flexible piping in the fuel pipeline. Plastic petrol piping, even when reinforced with braiding to improve strength, becomes soft and melts when exposed to excessive heat. In view of this, the pipes should be kept clear of the exhaust system.

2.21.7 Fuel pipe connections

Where pipes are connected to tanks, pumps, filters and carburettors, some form of secure but easily detachable connection is required.

Fuel injection systems operate using high pressures, so to prevent fuel leaks from the connections, screw type unions are used, such as those shown in Figure 2.207. Illustration (a) shows a fuel filter connection, of the banjo bolt type which is sealed with the use of two fibre washers. Illustration (b) shows how the end of the pipe is flared to mate with a suitable conical seating in the filter housing union.

Figure 2.207 A fuel filter connection

Modern fuel injection systems use 'quick release' connectors. These connectors allow fuel system components to be replaced very quickly during routine servicing without the need for special tools.

A very simple connection is used with carburettor fuel systems, in which the end of the plastic pipe is simply pushed on to a tightly fitting tubular extension on the component (Figure 2.208). The hose is usually secured to the component with a retaining clip. Occasionally a petrol-proof adhesive is used to secure the hose to the extension tube.

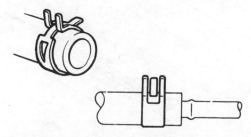

Figure 2.208 A push-fit fuel pipe connection

2.22 ELECTRONIC PETROL INJECTION – MULTI-POINT

2.22.1 Introduction

The term 'petrol injection' is used to describe any system in which pressurized fuel is forced out of a nozzle in an atomized state to mix with a supply of air.

Modern systems are controlled electronically because this form of control enables the fuel quantity to be accurately set to suit the engine operating conditions. Strict emission control regulations have demanded precise metering of the fuel, and although petrol injection systems are more expensive than carburettor fuel systems, they are now used to control the fuelling on all engines. Most petrol injection systems are integrated with the ignition system into an engine management system.

A petrol injection system that delivers the correct quantity of highly atomized fuel gives the following advantages:

- lower exhaust pollution
- lower fuel consumption
- higher power output
- smoother engine operation due to an even power output from each cylinder
- automatic adjustment of the air/fuel ratio to suit all operating conditions.

2.22.2 Injector positions

Injection systems can be classified into two main groups, multi-point and single-point. This classification is based on the number and position of the injectors:

1 **Multi-point injection** – individual injectors are used for each cylinder. An injector is positioned near to the inlet valve of each cylinder, Figure 2.209.
2 **Single-point injection** – one injector discharges fuel into the air stream before the throttle butterfly (the point which was previously used by the carburettor). See Figure 2.209.

2.22.3 Multi-point injection

During the development period of petrol injection, which saw many uses on two-stroke and aircraft engines, the well-tried injection system principle used on compression-ignition (diesel) engines was applied to spark-ignition engines.

On most of these trial applications the injector sprayed fuel into the combustion chamber, but this 'direct' injection system required high fuel pressures, and unless the injection commenced in the early part of the compression stroke, vaporization was poor.

'Indirect' injection is now preferred (Figure 2.210) although with the increase in engine and electronic technology together with stricter emission controls, a number of vehicle manufacturers are developing and fitting direct injection petrol systems. With an indirect injection system, an injector, operating at a relatively low fuel pressure, (e.g. 2–3 bar or 30–44 lbf in^{-2}), is fitted to spray the fuel downstream into the air as it passes the inlet valve of the engine.

The fuel is pressurized to a comparatively low pressure, so a simple injector construction can be used to deliver the fuel. The injector, either a continuous flow injector or an intermittent injector, sprays fuel into the inlet manifold. The opening action of the injector atomizes the fuel, which is then drawn into the cylinder with the airflow in the inlet manifold.

Injection of petrol can be timed or continuous. In the former, fuel is sprayed into the airstream, usually just before induction stroke is about to commence.

The air induction system provides the location for the air filter and throttle valve housing. The inlet manifold

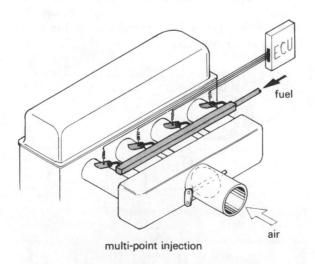

multi-point injection

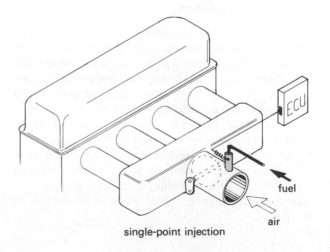

single-point injection

Figure 2.209 Multi-point injection and single-point injection

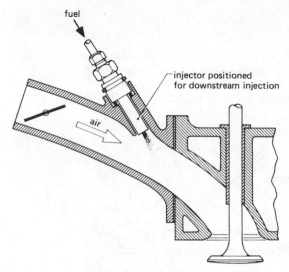

Figure 2.210 Indirect petrol injection

(previously detailed) provides a large reservoir of air, often referred to as the plenum chamber.

2.22.4 Metering methods

An ideal injection system must supply to the engine a quantity of atomized fuel, which is correct to suit the engine operating conditions (speed and load). The system must also vary this quantity to allow for alteration in engine temperature and changes in air density caused by ambient temperature and altitude variations.

The multi-point injection system can be separated into two main types, either 'mechanical' (continuous injection) or 'electronic' (intermittent injection). This section details the operation of the electronic system, later sections of this book detail the mechanical systems.

2.22.5 Electronic petrol injection system

The first full electronic system was introduced by Bendix in the USA in 1950. Seventeen years later a similar unit was made by Bosch and was fitted to a Volkswagen model. Since that time electronic fuel injection (EFI) has been a common system for both sports type and luxury category cars. Today, it is necessary to fit electronic petrol injection systems to comply with emission regulations.

The full electronic system uses a solenoid-operated fuel injector. The injector is opened at set times in the engine cycle, hence the term 'intermittent'. The injector is held open for a period of time proportional to the quantity of fuel that is required.

A number of variations exist for electronic injection systems. The main differences relate to the method of calculating or measuring the amount of air entering the cylinder (which then dictates the amount of fuel required). The main variants are:

1   Indirect – Pressure/vacuum sensing systems.
2   Direct – Airflow or air-mass sensing systems.

Pressure/vacuum sensing systems (speed/density)
This system uses a manifold absolute pressure (MAP) sensor to measure the manifold depression. Signals from the MAP sensor are passed to the ECU and, after taking into account the information received from the other sensors, the ECU provides a control signal for the injector to open for a set period of time, proportional to the mass of air that the engine is receiving.

An example of a pressure-sensed system is the Bosch D-Jetronic system. The 'D' refers to 'druck', which is the German word for pressure.

The mass of air induced into the engine for a given throttle opening depends on the manifold pressure. The manifold pressure is monitored by a MAP sensor, which passes an electrical signal to the ECU to indicate the quantity of air entering the engine. The MAP sensor signal is processed by the ECU and is used (in conjunction with other sensor information) to determine the period of time that the injectors should remain open.

Commencement of injection is triggered by an engine speed signal supplied from either the ignition distributor or an engine speed sensor, situated adjacent to the flywheel or crankshaft pulley. On earlier generations of electronic injection such as the D-jetronic system, all injectors were opened/closed at the same time (simultaneously) on four-cylinder engines, with six-cylinder engines having the injectors triggered in two groups of three. However all injectors were triggered twice for every engine cycle (once every crankshaft revolution). Later systems operate injectors individually in sequence (sequential).

Also on earlier generations of electronic injection, if additional fuel is required for cold starting, the fuel is supplied from a cold start injector.

The 'brain' of the electronic system is the electronic control unit (ECU). The ECU receives information from a number of sensors (Figure 2.212), and compares sensor information with data programmed into its memory, to provide control signals to the injectors to open them as required. Injector valves are opened once per crankshaft revolution and fuel quantity is governed by the period that the injector is held open by the solenoid.

Figure 2.211 indicates additional system components that are used to sense engine operating conditions and provide additional control for the injection system.

The 'throttle position switch' passes a signal to the ECU to identify when the throttle is either in the idle position or when the throttle is wide open. With the engine at idle, a slightly richer mixture is required. At wide-open throttle the engine requires full load power enrichment.

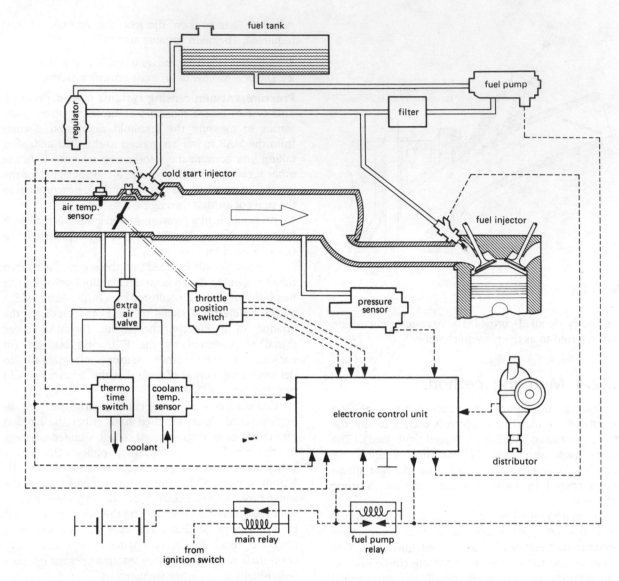

Figure 2.211 Electronic petrol injection fuel system – pressure-sensed airflow – Bosch D-Jetronic

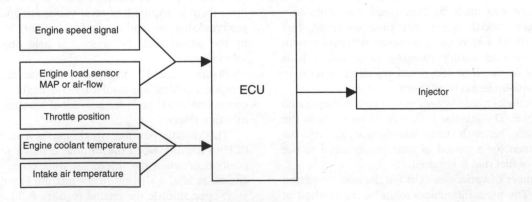

Figure 2.212 Input and output signals of an electronic fuel injection system

Fuel pressure, produced by an electrically-driven fuel pump, is maintained at a constant pressure (approximately 3 bar) with the use of a fuel pressure regulator.

Airflow and air-mass sensing systems

This type of petrol injection system measures the volume or mass of air flowing into the engine by either:

- An airflow meter (vane or flap type)
- An air mass meter (hot wire).

Both of these sensors produce an output signal voltage, which changes as the volume of airflow increases. The signal voltage is passed to the ECU and is used (in conjunction with other sensor information) to determine the period of time that the injectors should remain open.

Vane or flap metering

Figure 2.213 shows the layout of a system similar to a Bosch L Jetronic. The 'L' refers to 'luft', which is the German word for air.

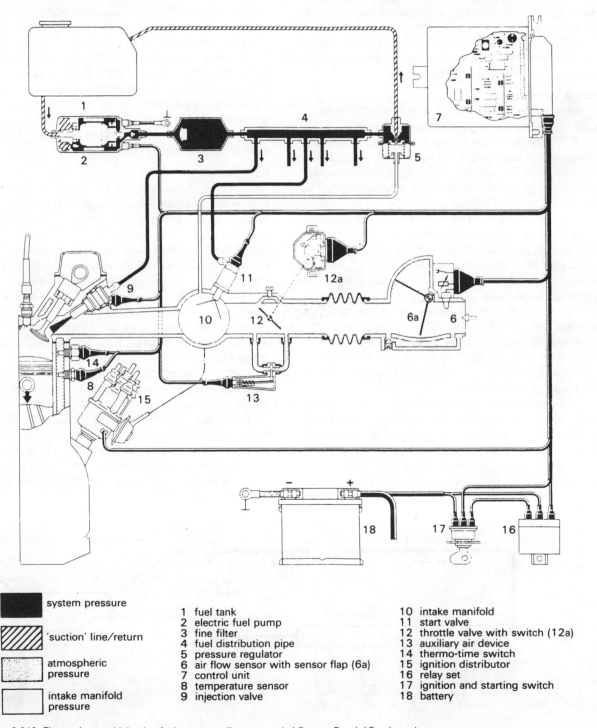

system pressure	
'suction' line/return	
atmospheric pressure	
intake manifold pressure	

1 fuel tank
2 electric fuel pump
3 fine filter
4 fuel distribution pipe
5 pressure regulator
6 air flow sensor with sensor flap (6a)
7 control unit
8 temperature sensor
9 injection valve
10 intake manifold
11 start valve
12 throttle valve with switch (12a)
13 auxiliary air device
14 thermo-time switch
15 ignition distributor
16 relay set
17 ignition and starting switch
18 battery

Figure 2.213 Electronic petrol injection fuel system – direct-sensed airflow – Bosch LE – Jetronic

The action of the flap sensor is similar to a sprung-loaded door, which is exposed to a movement of air. When the air speed (or volume) is increased, the force on the door also increases and will move it through an angle to a point where the force of the air is equal to the reaction of the spring.

The position of the vane is monitored using a potentiometer. The potentiometer signal voltage is passed to the ECU. The ECU can therefore sense the volume of air induced into the engine from the signal voltage. The dampening chamber within the sensor prevents the vane oscillating due to the pulsations in the inlet manifold.

Other than the arrangement for sensing the airflow, the basic injection system is similar to that previously described with the use of a MAP sensor.

Hot-wire metering

Both the Bosch LH Jetronic and some Lucas EFI systems used this method of measuring 'mass' airflow.

The principle of the system is based on the cooling action of air blown over a hot surface. The rate of heat transfer depends on the rate of airflow – easily demonstrated when you blow on a hot substance to cool it, e.g. a cup of hot tea.

The sensor has a hot wire element, which is heated by an electric current sufficient to maintain it at a constant temperature. When airflow is increased, the cooling action is greater, so the current through the wire filament has to be increased to maintain it at the constant temperature. The voltage required to provide this current provides an indication of the air mass entering the system. The sensor signal voltage is processed by the ECU and is used (in conjunction with other sensor information) to determine the period of time that the injectors should remain open to provide the correct quantity of fuel.

Changes in air temperature will alter the density or mass of the air entering the engine. To provide air temperature correction, a compensating resistor (sensor) is placed in the airstream near to the hot wire. A change in air temperature causes the sensor to alter its resistance and this compensates for the effect of air temperature on the hot wire. The ECU can maintain the required air/fuel ratio to compensate for variations in atmospheric temperature and pressure. This feature is especially significant when the vehicle has to operate at different altitudes.

2.22.6 Fuel supply system

Although there are various electronically controlled fuel supply systems in use by vehicle manufacturers, the basic fuel system and the supporting electrical circuitry is often similar. The following description of a typical system is intended to show the basic principle of the main fuel supply system components.

The fuel supply system provides the injectors with adequate fuel at a pressure sufficient to allow the injectors to give good atomization. The quantity of fuel injected is dependant on the fuel pressure, so the pressure must not vary.

Figure 2.214 shows the main components of the fuel system; they include the following:

Fuel pump

Normally a roller-type rotary pump driven by a permanent-magnet electric motor (Figure 2.215). Rotation of the pump moves the rollers outwards and seals the spaces between the rotor and casing. As the fuel is carried around with the rotor, a combination of the rotor movement and the decrease in volume of the pumping chamber causes an increase in pressure.

Fuel from the pump passes through the motor, which aids the cooling of the internal components of the pump. More fuel is supplied than is required, the excess fuel is recirculated back to the tank and this reduces the risk of vapour-lock problems.

Two ball valves are fitted in the pump, a pressure relief valve, which limits the maximum pressure, and a non-return valve at the outlet of the pump.

Pump operation is controlled by the ECU via a fuel pump relay. Note that on a few systems, the current supplied to the pump is passed through a ballast resistor to reduce the supply voltage. The resistor is by-passed when the engine is cranked to compensate for the lower battery voltage.

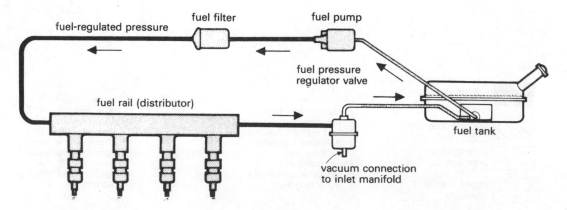

Figure 2.214 Fuel system

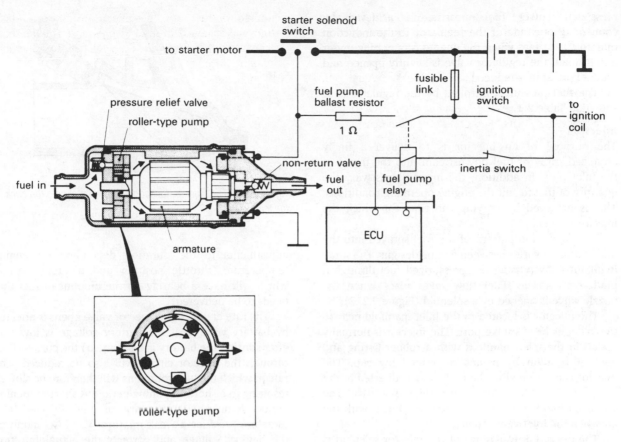

Figure 2.215 Fuel pump and electrical supply circuit

On switching on the ignition, the pump motor runs for a short period of time to initially pressurize the fuel system. After this initial period the pump is stopped until the engine is cranked.

Some systems feature an 'inertia switch'. For safety reasons the switch is fitted in the electrical supply line to the fuel pump or relay. In the event of a collision, the switch contacts open and the pump ceases to operate. The switch can be reset by pushing down a protruding plunger.

Fuel pressure regulator

The pressure regulator controls the operating pressure of the system and is set to maintain a constant pressure difference (e.g. 2.5 bar or 36 lbf in^{-2}) between the fuel in the fuel rail and the inlet manifold, irrespective of throttle opening. It consists of a spring-loaded diaphragm and ball valve (Figure 2.216).

Manifold depression depends on throttle opening (e.g. engine load) so when the opening is small the high

depression encourages more fuel to leave the injector. To compensate for this, the fuel system operating pressure is lowered when the manifold depression is high (high depression or high vacuum equals a low

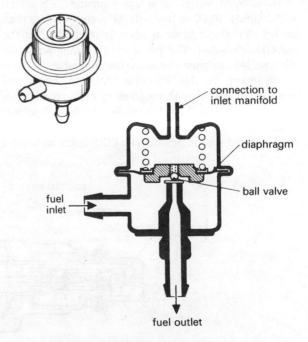

Figure 2.216 A pressure regulator

Table 2.1 Regulator control pressure

Engine condition	Manifold depression	Typical operating pressures
Idling	Very high	1.8 bar (26 lbf in^{-2})
Full throttle	Very low	2.5 bar (36 lbf in^{-2})

pressure). Lower fuel pressure is achieved by connecting one side of the regulator to the induction manifold. At times when the engine is operating under a light load, the regulator valve is slightly opened and the fuel pressure is reduced.

The fuel pressure controlled by the regulator is as shown in Table 2.1.

Injectors

The purpose of an injector is to deliver a finely atomized spray of fuel downstream into the throat of the inlet port. In addition, the injector must vary the quantity of fuel to suit the engine operating conditions. This is achieved by varying the time for which the injector is open.

The shape and pattern of the fuel sprayed into the inlet manifold varies between engine designs. The spray is obtained by passing the pressurized fuel through a pintle-type nozzle. Fuel flow takes place when the nozzle valve is opened by a solenoid (Figure 2.217).

The injector is located in the inlet manifold near to the cylinder head intake port. The injector is normally sealed in the inlet manifold with a rubber O-ring and held in position by means of a retaining clip. The injector is positioned so the fuel spray is directed at the back of the closed inlet valve (Figure 2.218). The atomized fuel is then drawn into the cylinder with the air when the inlet valve opens.

The operation (opening) of the injector solenoid is controlled by the ECU. The injector is normally supplied with battery voltage from a relay and the earth circuit is controlled by the ECU. When the ECU completes the earth circuit, the solenoid operates and the injector valve opens allowing fuel to be sprayed into the inlet manifold. Movement of the valve is limited to about 0.15 mm (0.006 inch) and the period of time that the valve is open varies from approximately 1.5 to 10 milliseconds (0.0015 to 0.0100 second). The time period that the injector is open is referred to as the 'injection duration'. The pressure of a spring acting on the needle valve then closes the injector valve.

Variation in the injection duration alters the quantity of fuel that is supplied to each cylinder per engine cycle. The ECU determines the basic injection duration from the volume (or mass) of airflow and the engine speed sensor signals. The ECU makes additional

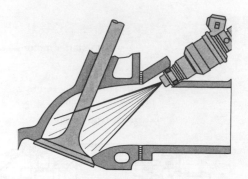

Figure 2.218 Fuel injector location; spraying fuel onto the back of the inlet valve

adjustments to the duration depending on engine temperature, throttle position and air temperature, which will have a bearing on the amount of fuel that needs to be delivered.

The rate at which the injector valve opens is affected by battery voltage. If the battery voltage is low (i.e. after starting the battery is discharged) the current flow through the injector circuit will also be reduced. The rate at which the injector opens will therefore be slower, resulting in a shorter opening period. A shorter opening period reduces the quantity of fuel injected and therefore provides a weak mixture. The ECU monitors the battery voltage and corrects the actual injection duration accordingly.

On earlier generations of electronic injection, all injectors were opened/closed at the same time (simultaneously) on four-cylinder engines, with six-cylinder engines having the injectors triggered in two groups of three but also simultaneously. Later systems operate the injectors sequentially (in the same order as the cylinder firing order. The injectors can be opened twice for every engine cycle (only half the volume being delivered each time the injector is opened), but many later systems only open the injectors once every cycle (the total required fuel quantity being delivered each time an injector opens).

When the engine is started from cold, additional fuel must be injected which is provided by either increasing the frequency of injection or increasing the injection opening time (injection duration).

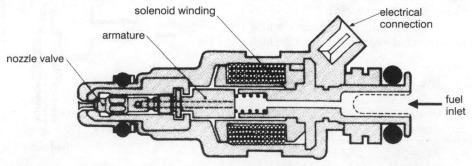

Figure 2.217 Fuel injector

2.23 ELECTRONIC PETROL INJECTION – SINGLE POINT

2.23.1 Single-point injection

Single-point injection (SPI) is also often referred to as 'throttle body injection' (TBI) because it uses a single injector to spray fuel at a point on the air intake side of the throttle butterfly; injection of fuel is at the point where a carburettor would normally be situated.

The single-point injection system loses some of the merits of multi-point fuel injection, especially the advantages associated with good fuel distribution, but its value should be assessed against a carburettor fuel system.

The call for better atomization of the fuel, especially at low engine speeds, more precise control of the air/fuel ratio to meet emission regulations, and additional demands to meet modern requirements for cold starting and warm-up, forced many manufacturers to abandon the lower cost option, a carburettor.

Where the higher cost of multi-point injection does not warrant its use on some vehicles, a single-point system is a compromise. A single-point injection system is often easier to control electronically than a carburettor, and because electronic systems are more sensitive in operation, the single-point system becomes an attractive proposition.

Figure 2.219 shows a typical TBI layout, the single solenoid-operated injector situated centrally in the air intake.

Fuel supply is a pressurized system similar to that used in a multi-point layout, although the fuel pressure is usually considerably less, typically 1 bar.

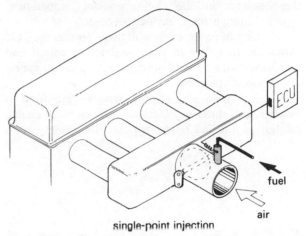

single-point injection

Figure 2.219 Single-point injection

Mono-Jetronic schematic diagram

1 Fuel tank, **2** Electric fuel pump, **3** Fuel filter, **4** Fuel-pressure regulator, **5** Solenoid-operated fuel injector, **6** Air-temperature sensor, **7** ECU, **8** Throttle-valve actuator, **9** Throttle-valve potentiometer, **10** Canister-purge valve, **11** Carbon canister, **12** Lambda oxygen sensor, **13** Engine-temperature sensor **14** Ignition distributor, **15** Battery, **16** Ignition-start switch, **17** Relay, **18** Diagnosis connection, **19** Central injection unit.

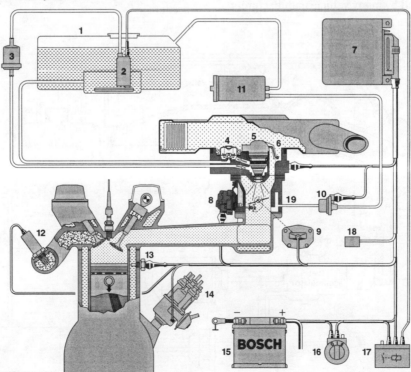

Figure 2.220 Bosch Mono-Jetronic electronic throttle body injection system

Injected fuel is directed into a venturi-shaped region around the throttle, so the increased air speed at this point is used to further break up the fuel.

The volume of air is usually monitored with a MAP sensor although various methods have been used, including a throttle position sensor that accurately monitors the precise throttle angle and rate at which the throttle is being operated.

Many of the other sensors used in a multi-point fuel system are used with a single-point injection system; these sensors include engine coolant temperature, intake air temperature, engine speed, etc.

Working in conjunction with these sensors the ECU varies the fuel flow to give deceleration cut-off and enrichment during cold start, warm-up, acceleration and full-load operation.

Many of these single-point systems were fitted to vehicles with three-way catalytic converters. To enable catalyst to function efficiently, the fuel system has to provide the air/fuel mixture to the engine at the ideal ratio (i.e. 14.7:1). To achieve this, the fuel system is fitted with an oxygen sensor to accurately monitor the oxygen content in the exhaust before the catalyst. The ECU monitors the oxygen sensor signal voltage and responds accordingly by either reducing the quantity of fuel delivered (weakening the mixture) or increasing the fuel quantity (enrichening the mixture).

The disadvantage of single-point injection, like carburettor fuel system, is that the air/fuel mixture cannot be evenly distributed to the cylinders through the inlet manifold. Because it is not possible to balance the distribution of the air/fuel mixture evenly to each cylinder the emissions are higher than those with a multi-point system. Due to stricter emission legislation and new regulations it has been necessary for vehicle manufacturers to replace these low cost, single-point systems with multi-point systems.

2.24 MECHANICAL PETROL INJECTION

2.24.1 Mechanical systems

The Bosch K-Jetronic system is described in this section. Although there have been a few mechanical petrol injection systems used, the K-Jetronic has been the most popular and was used by many vehicle manufacturers.

The mechanical injection system uses the principle of 'continuous-flow' fuel injection, with airflow sensing to meter the fuel.

Figure 2.221 shows the basic mechanical injection system. Its operating principles are detailed in this section.

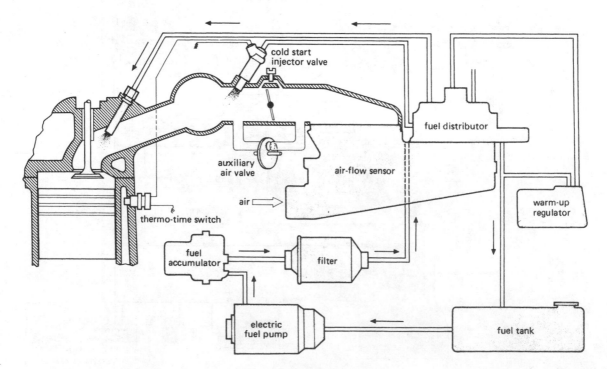

Figure 2.221 Bosch K-Jetronic continuous-flow fuel injection with airflow measurement

Fuel pump

The fuel pump uses a permanent magnet electric motor to drive a roller-type pump. The pump pressurizes the fuel sufficiently to provide the required supply pressure to operate the injectors. Maximum pressure in the fuel primary circuit is limited to 4.7 bar (about 70 lbf in^{-2}) by a pressure regulator valve, and excess fuel from this valve is returned to the tank.

Accumulator

The spring-loaded diaphragm which forms an 'accumulator':

1 maintains the pressure in the line to aid hot starting
2 reduces the build-up of pressure on starting
3 smoothes out pulsations and reduces pump noise.

Fuel distributor and airflow sensor

This unit controls the quantity of fuel delivered to the injectors. The air sensor (Figure 2.222) consists of a venturi (1) in the induction pipe into which is fitted a movable disc (2). Attached to the disc is a counter-balanced lever (3), which acts on a control plunger (4). Mounted around the plunger are a number of diaphragm valves (5), one for each injector. The purpose of these valves is to provide a fuel supply to the injectors which is proportional to the movement of the control plunger.

When the engine is stationary, the disc (2) is resting in a closed position in the venturi. The lever (3) and the control plunger will be in the lowered position so no fuel passes from the waist of the plunger to the chamber above the diaphragm, and no injection can take place.

On starting the engine, the air movement through the venturi lifts the disc – the extent of the movement is governed by the quantity of air flowing through the venturi. When the disc has lifted a set amount, the lever will raise the control plunger (4) and open a slit to allow fuel to the chamber.

Although fuel pressure now acts on both sides of the diaphragm, the force of the spring moves the diaphragm downwards and opens the valve at the centre of the diaphragm to release the fuel to the injector. The flow of fuel from the chamber slightly lowers the downward force on the diaphragm, so a valve-open position is reached which corresponds to the amount that the control plunger is moved.

Opening the throttle gives a greater airflow, so the disc (2) will rise further, which, in turn, will raise control plunger (4) and allow more fuel to pass to the chamber. This extra fuel flow will more than make up for the fuel that is 'escaping' past the valve to the injector, so the extra downward force produced by the fuel pressure lowers the diaphragm, opens the valve further and increases the quantity of fuel going to the injector.

From its description it can be seen that the diaphragm unit acts as a differential pressure valve. It regulates the pressure drop on each side of the diaphragm to a constant value of 0.15 bar (about 2 lbf in^{-2}) irrespective of supply pump pressure, nozzle opening pressure or fuel flow.

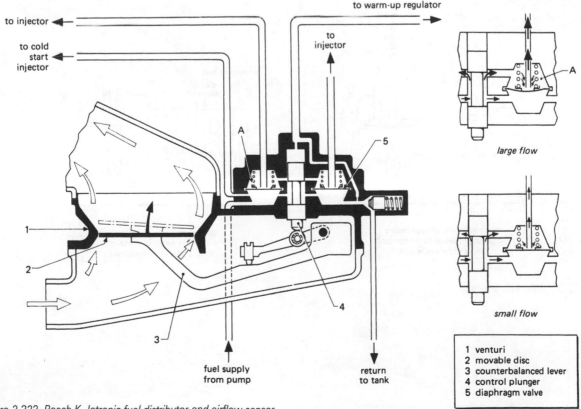

1	venturi
2	movable disc
3	counterbalanced lever
4	control plunger
5	diaphragm valve

Figure 2.222 Bosch K-Jetronic fuel distributor and airflow sensor

The air/fuel ratio given by this system can be altered by varying the control pressure which acts on the end of the control plunger. Reducing this pressure allows the sensor plate to move a greater amount for a given airflow and results in a richer mixture.

Warm-up regulator

This controls the mixture enrichment during the cold running and warm-up periods (see Figure 2.223). It consists of a valve, operated by a bimetallic strip, which lowers the control pressure acting on the end of the control plunger when the engine is cold.

Cold-start injector

The layout of the system (Figure 2.222) includes a cold-start injector positioned downstream of the throttle. This electrically operated injection valve, together with the auxiliary air device, comes into operation when the thermo-time switch senses that the engine is cold.

2.14.2 Mechanical system with electronic control

Closer matching of the mixture to meet changing loads and operating conditions, and the introduction of stricter emission control regulations induced the manufacturers to modify the K-Jetronic system. The modified system is called Bosch KE-Jetronic; the letter E signifying 'electronic' control of the fuel system.

Precise control of the mechanical system with electronics allows the air/fuel mixture to be more accurately controlled. The ECU, with the information from the additional sensors, is able to vary the mixture to suit a wider range of operating conditions.

Comparing the Bosch KE-Jetronic system shown in Figure 2.224 with the basic K system, the following items represent the main differences:

Primary-pressure regulator

More precise control of the system pressure is obtained by using a modified regulator valve which senses the inlet manifold depression.

Electro-hydraulic pressure actuator

The unit functions as a fine mixture adjustment control to vary the air/fuel ratio slightly to suit all engine operating conditions, including operation during warm-up, acceleration and at full load.

Electronic control unit (ECU)

The ECU acts as the brain of the KE-Jetronic system. It monitors the signals it receives from the various sensors, which include the throttle valve switch, airflow potentiometer, engine speed and temperature sensors. The ECU analyses these signals and passes an output signal to the actuator, which controls the air/fuel mixture.

In addition, other features are included to allow fuel cut-off during over-run. The KE-Jetronic ECU also controls the mixture accurately by monitoring the oxygen content in the exhaust gas using an oxygen sensor signal ('closed-loop fuel system').

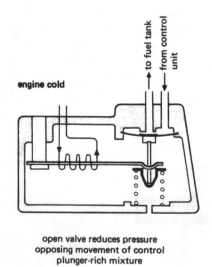

open valve reduces pressure opposing movement of control plunger-rich mixture

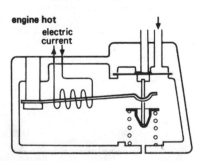

during warm-up, electrical current heats bi-metal strip and gradually closes valve

Figure 2.223 Warm-up regulator

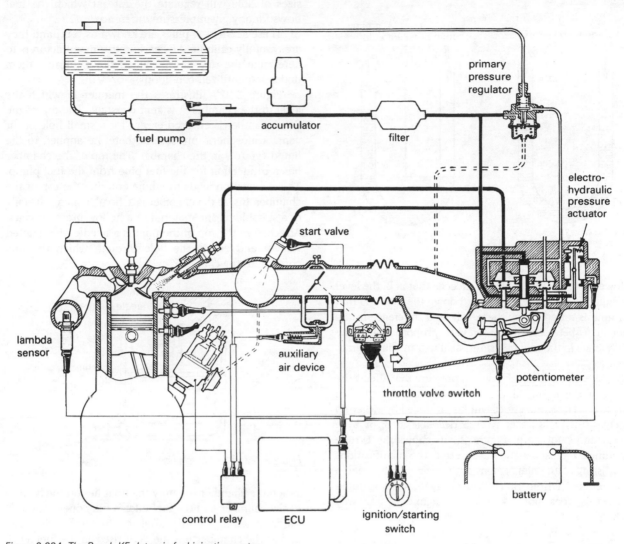

Figure 2.224 The Bosch KE-Jetronic fuel injection system

2.25   THE SIMPLE CARBURETTOR

The term 'simple carburettor' refers to the basic type of carburettor. While it might be suitable for certain types of engine, it will not provide the correct fuelling for an engine fitted to a motor vehicle. Modifications to this simple type of carburettor are necessary to allow it to provide the correct fuelling for an engine over the entire operating range.

A carburettor consists essentially of two parts:

1   A component that provides a small reservoir of fuel and also regulates the volume of fuel delivered to the carburettor by the fuel pump. The volume of fuel delivered is dependant upon the rate at which the fuel is used by the engine. The part is usually referred to as the 'float chamber'.

2   A component that atomizes the fuel, mixing it with the correct amount of air for the engine operating conditions. This part is known as the 'mixing chamber'.

Although these two parts are identified separately, they are not necessarily separated from one another.

2.25.1 The float chamber

The action of this is based upon the principle of the simple U-tube, illustrated in Figure 2.225.

Diagram (a) shows a U-tube partly filled with liquid. Providing the pressure acting at A and B are equal, the levels of liquid in the two limbs of the tube will be at the same height.

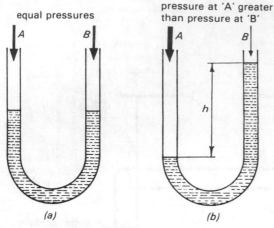

Figure 2.225 A simple U-tube

However, if the pressure at A exceeds that at B, the level of liquid in limb A will be forced down the tube and that in limb B raised. Thus there will be a difference in the height *h*, between the two levels, proportional to the difference in the two pressures, as illustrated in diagram (b).

Note that it is not the actual pressure that affects the level of the liquid in the tubes, but the *difference* in pressure. The same effect will be produced by either an increase of pressure at A or a decrease at B, or by a combination of both. Figure 2.226 shows the U-tube modified for use in the carburettor, the modifications consisting of an enlargement of the size of limb A, and a shortening of limb B. (It can easily be demonstrated that this does not affect the principle in any way whatsoever.)

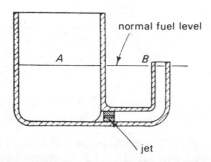

Figure 2.226 Modified U-tube as used in a carburettor

Under normal conditions the limb (or chamber) A is open to the pressure of the atmosphere. The chamber remains full of fuel, to the level of the top of limb B or slightly below. If this level can be kept constant and limb B subjected to a pressure lower than that of the atmosphere, fuel will be drawn out from B at a rate which depends upon the difference in pressures and the opposition (restriction) which the liquid encounters in flowing from A to B.

It is a simple matter to provide the necessary restriction to fuel flow by fitting, at any convenient point in the tube B, a plug with a small hole. Different

sizes of hole will regulate the rate at which the fuel flows for any given pressure difference.

These small hole plugs are known as 'jets', and they are carefully calibrated by carburettor manufacturers to determine the rate at which fuel flows through them under standardized conditions.

Figure 2.227 illustrates the manner in which the level in the chamber A is kept constant. The top of the float chamber is encased except for a small hole or air vent. Atmospheric pressure is therefore applied to the liquid (petrol) in the chamber. The top of the chamber has a connection for the fuel pipe from the fuel pump. This connection leads to a hole entering the top of the chamber. Inside the chamber is a 'float', which is usually of a suitable plastic material or a hollow brass pressing. Attached to the top of the float is a needle, the pointed (valve) end enters the hole through which the fuel comes into the chamber.

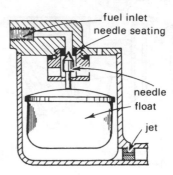

Figure 2.227 A float mechanism

When the chamber is empty the float lies on the bottom of the chamber and the fuel inlet is fully open. The fuel pump, when in operation, delivers fuel to the chamber, and as the chamber fills the float rises on the fuel level. When the chamber is full, the action of the float brings the end of the needle valve into contact with a seating at the end of the fuel inlet hole. Contact of the needle with the seat prevents any further entry of fuel. When some fuel is used from the chamber and the fuel level falls, the needle valve reopens to allow more fuel to enter the chamber. The maximum height of fuel in the chamber is arranged to be slightly below the top of the discharge nozzle.

2.25.2 The venturi

This device consists simply of a tube of which the bore diminishes gradually to a 'throat' and then gradually enlarges to its original size, as illustrated in Figure 2.228.

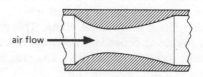

Figure 2.228 Venturi

Gas flowing along this tube will increase in speed, just as it passes through the throat. The result of this is that the pressure of the fluid is reduced as its velocity increases, and will rise again as the velocity falls once the fluid has passed the narrow portion of the tube.

The increase in the gas flow through the venturi can be demonstrated by the apparatus shown in Figure 2.229. This consists of a series of glass tubes, whose ends are dipped into a trough of coloured water. A blower (like a vacuum cleaner) is used to pass air through the venturi, the level of water in the tubes is noted when the blower is switched on.

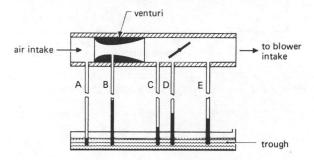

Figure 2.229 Demonstration of air pressure variation in a carburettor

When there is no air flowing through the venturi, the level in all tubes is equal, but when air is moving through the venturi, the level in tube B will be higher than that shown in the other tubes. This indicates that the air pressure in the 'throat' of the venturi is less than that which exists on each side of the restriction. Increasing the air speed through the venturi causes a greater drop in pressure. In a similar way if the throat of the venturi is made smaller, the drop in pressure for a given air speed will be greater.

Whenever the air pressure is lower than the atmospheric pressure, the term 'depression' can be used. Therefore the venturi used in this example increases the air speed and forms a depression.

The mixing chamber of a carburettor is the region centred around the venturi. It is situated in the induction pipe that supplies the engine with air. Fitted at the throat of the venturi, which is also known as the choke tube, is an outlet from a pipe or drilling that conveys petrol from the float chamber.

The combination of the depression created by the air passing through the venturi and the petrol supply from the float chamber allows the petrol to mix with the air. Since the depression intensifies as the volume of air passing through the induction pipe increases, the amount of petrol supplied to mix with this air will also increase.

2.25.3 The complete carburettor

Figure 2.230 shows a simple carburettor. The only component not mentioned so far is the throttle valve (or butterfly). The purpose of the throttle valve is to

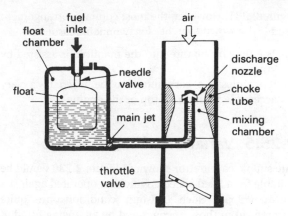

Figure 2.230 A simple carburettor

regulate the engine power by controlling the flow of air entering the engine.

The action of the carburettor is as follows:

When fuel is supplied to the carburettor by the fuel pump, fuel enters the float chamber through the inlet connection, and rises in both the float chamber and also the fuel discharge nozzle. As the level rises, the float also rises, and lifts the needle into the needle seating which cuts off the entry of fuel when the level is just below the top of the discharge nozzle.

When the engine is rotated, air is drawn in through the air intake and choke tube (venturi), producing a pressure drop or depression inside the choke tube. The depression created in the venturi draws fuel from the float chamber via the passage and jet into the mixing chamber. The rush of air through the choke tube will, if its velocity is great enough, atomize the fuel as it passes through the discharge nozzle.

The mixture of air and atomized fuel is drawn into the engine at a rate which depends upon engine speed and the extent of opening of the throttle valve. The driver controls the position of the throttle valve by the position of the accelerator pedal.

As the rate of airflow increases, because of either an increase in engine speed, a wider throttle opening or both, the depression in the choke tube also increases, thus drawing more fuel through the jet.

The size of the choke tube is selected so that the air velocity through it is sufficient to atomize the fuel at the lowest speed at which the engine is required to run. The desired mixture can be obtained by using a jet of a predetermined size, which allows the correct amount of fuel to flow and join the air stream.

2.25.4 Attitude of choke tube

In Figure 2.230 the axis of the choke tube shown is vertical. The angle of the choke tube does not affect its function, so long as the float chamber remains vertical. Carburettors are made with the choke tube horizontal, vertical, or at some intermediate angle, as shown in

Figure 2.231. However, the most common arrangement used is the 'downdraught', for two main reasons:

1 The flow of mixture into the manifold is assisted by gravity.
2 It enables the carburettor to be fitted in a very accessible position on top of the engine.

2.25.5 Variation of air/fuel ratio

The simple carburettor shown in Figure 2.230 would be suitable for a fixed-speed engine that operated against a constant load. Such constant conditions are quite different from those encountered by an engine fitted to a motor vehicle.

When the load and/or speed of an engine fitted with a simple carburettor is increased, the mixture strength supplied by the carburettor becomes richer, i.e. the air/fuel ratio decreases as the speed or load is increased (Figure 2.232).

The increase in mixture strength is overcome either by incorporating a 'compensation system' into the carburettor design or by using a carburettor design which employs the 'constant depression' principle.

The difference in construction that is used to overcome the mixture variation problem enables carburettors to be classified as either:

- Constant – choke carburettors
- Constant – depression carburettors.

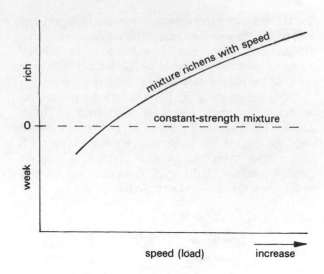

Figure 2.232 *Mixture variation with a simple carburettor*

The former have a fixed size of venturi and incorporate a compensation system to maintain a near-constant air/fuel ratio.

Constant-depression carburettors have a variable choke, which enlarges as the engine speed and load increase. Externally the shapes of the carburettors are quite different, so identification is simple.

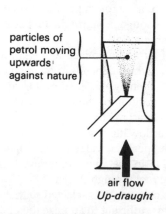

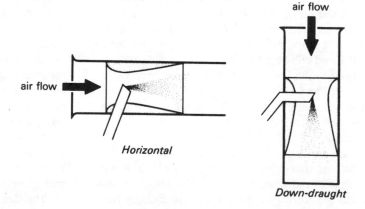

Figure 2.231 *Attitude of the choke tube*

2.26 CONSTANT-CHOKE CARBURETTORS

2.26.1 Constant choke or variable depression

Constant-choke carburettors are also known as 'fixed-choke', or 'variable-depression' carburettors because the depression in the fixed-size venturi varies when the engine speed changes. This variation in engine speed must be balanced by the fuel flow if weakness or richness of the mixture is to be avoided.

2.26.2 Need for mixture compensation

The change of mixture strength supplied by a simple carburettor is due to the fact that the carburettor is attempting to meter two different components, air and petrol. Air is a gas, which flows very easily, whereas petrol is a liquid that opposes flow. In addition, petrol has a tendency for its particles to stick together as well as to the walls of the passage through which it flows.

By selecting suitable sizes for the choke tube and jet, it is possible to obtain the correct air/fuel mixture to suit a specific engine speed, but when the speed is increased, the subsequent increase in the depression would promote an excessive flow of petrol. This enrichment with an increase in speed and/or load is prevented by incorporating a compensation system in the carburettor.

2.26.3 Compensation systems

A compensation or correction system is necessary to maintain a near-constant air/fuel ratio. Accurate matching of the jets to the system is necessary to avoid under- or over-correction; the former implies that the mixture becomes richer, and the latter weaker as the speed or load increases.

2.26.4 Air-bleed compensation

This method of correction is the most commonly used. The constructional details of the system vary between different makes of carburettor, but the principle remains the same.

The arrangement shown in Figure 2.233 consists of an air jet that bleeds air into an emulsion, or diffuser tube, in the side of which are drilled a number of small holes. Petrol is supplied to the well via a main jet and the outlet from the well is situated in the venturi.

When the main jet is not in use, the petrol levels in the well and float chamber are similar, but when the venturi depression is sufficient to cause fuel to discharge from the outlet, the level in the well falls. This drop in level increases as the throttle is opened and

when full throttle is reached the fuel level in the well is very low.

This opening of the throttle would cause a simple carburettor to supply a mixture that becomes richer as the speed increases. A correction system overcomes this problem by using the drop in fuel level in the well to expose air holes in the emulsion tube. When the mixture strength shows a sign of becoming rich, a hole is uncovered and air is bled into the system. This reduces the depression, which is felt on the main jet and, as a result, restores the correct mixture strength.

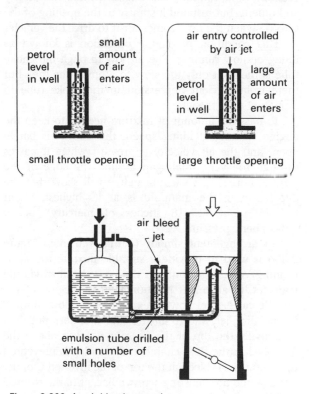

Figure 2.233 An air-bleed correction

2.26.5 Idle systems

A decreased airflow into the engine results in a reduction in air velocity at the venturi, and consequently the pressure at this point rises nearer to atmospheric. If the carburettor is properly corrected this will not alter the mixture strength, but it will result in a progressive coarsening of the spray owing to the reduced velocity of the airflow. Also, as the airflow is reduced, the velocity will eventually become insufficient to maintain the fuel droplets in suspension, owing both to their increased size and the low air velocity in the manifold. There is, therefore, a speed below which the engine will not run, and this depends primarily upon the size of the choke tube and, to a lesser extent, the diameter and length of the inlet manifold. The conditions necessary for good low-speed operation are quite unsuitable for developing reasonably high power at high speeds, and there is obviously a limit to the extent to which power at high speed can be sacrificed to obtain good low-speed operation.

The extreme condition of low air velocity through the choke tube occurs when the engine is running but not driving the car. It then has merely to develop sufficient power to overcome its own internal friction. This is the case whenever the vehicle is stationary, but may be required to move at any moment, as, for instance, when halted in traffic or at traffic lights. For economy and comfort, the engine should run slowly and quietly, but respond instantly to the opening of the throttle when the time comes for it to drive the vehicle.

This condition of engine operation is known as idling or slow-running. The airflow through the choke tube is then not only too slow to atomize the fuel, but there is insufficient depression in the choke tube to draw fuel from the jets.

To pass the amount of mixture needed to keep the engine running at idling speed, the throttle is barely open, and the air velocity is greatest where it passes through the very small gap around the edge of the throttle butterfly. A vacuum gauge will show that the depression in the manifold is at its highest, about 380–450 mm (15–18 inches of mercury) below atmospheric pressure.

An arrangement similar to that shown in Figure 2.234 is used to provide a suitable mixture for slow-running. A passage connects the float chamber, via the main jet, to an outlet positioned in the region of the throttle valve. Fuel flow is regulated by a slow-running jet or idling jet, and to ensure that fuel does not flow continually the top of the passage is taken above the fuel level in the float chamber. Siphoning is prevented by having an air bleed at the top of the inverted U of the passage and an adjusting screw adjacent to the throttle enables the volume of emulsified fuel entering the engine to be regulated to suit the condition of the engine. The speed at which the engine runs is determined primarily by the extent of the throttle opening; normally this is set by a throttle stop adjusting screw on the throttle linkage.

When the engine is idling a strong depression exists on the engine side of the throttle, causing fuel to be drawn from the idling system. This fuel mixes with the air spilling past the edge of the throttle butterfly.

2.26.6 Mixture strength for idle speeds

At idle speed, only a very small quantity of fuel is required for the engine to run. Under these conditions the cylinder contains a comparatively large quantity of exhaust gas. The exhaust gas dilutes the new charge, so in order to provide an ignitable mixture, a charge that is

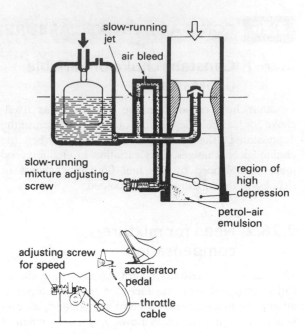

Figure 2.234 A slow-running (idle) system

slightly richer than normal is provided during slow running. The enrichment of the mixture is strictly limited because any unburned, or partially burnt fuel causes the exhaust emissions that pollute the atmosphere. Many engines are fitted with carburettors which will not idle at a speed less than about 900 revolutions per minute.

2.26.7 Acceleration from idle

Opening the throttle from the idling position causes more air to pass the throttle. This lowers the depression (raises the pressure) and reduces the fuel discharge from the slow-running outlet. At the same time, the airflow through the choke tube causes the main jet system to come gradually into operation. The changeover does not always occur smoothly, with the result that any deficiency in the fuel supply is accompanied by a sudden drop in engine power.

To avoid this 'transfer flat spot' the arrangement shown in Figure 2.235 is used. At a throttle position where the flat-spot would normally occur, one or more holes are drilled adjacent to the edge of the throttle valve to provide additional fuel discharge outlets. Fuel

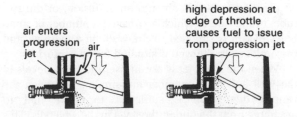

Figure 2.235 Two-hole idling system

discharge from the upper hole is controlled by an interchangeable jet called a progression jet.

When the engine is idling a high depression on the engine side of the choke causes petrol to discharge from the lower drilling. During this phase the progression hole will be above the throttle, so air will enter this hole, pass through the progression jet and bleed into the slow-running mixture to assist in the emulsifying process. As the throttle is opened, the rush of air past the edge of the throttle will create a depression in this region and will cause fuel to discharge from the progression outlet.

2.26.8 Idle speed adjustment

To meet emission regulations, final adjustment of the slow-running mode requires a tachometer to set the engine speed accurately and an exhaust gas analyser to measure the quantity of carbon monoxide and hydrocarbons present in the exhaust gas.

The slow-running adjustment varies with different engines and carburettors, but the main points are as follows:

1 Check that the ignition system is serviceable and that the ignition timing is correct.
2 Warm up the engine to its normal operating temperature.
3 With the engine running, adjust the throttle stop screw to obtain the recommended idle speed.
4 Adjust the volume control screw until the highest and smoothest speed is found.
5 Set the exhaust emission level to the manufacturers specification.
6 Reset the throttle stop screw to make the engine slow-run at the recommended speed.

2.26.9 Emission control

To meet emission regulations, the slow-running system of a carburettor is designed to take into account the following:

- **Tamper-proof adjusting screws**
Screws provided for mixture adjustment are arranged so that non-qualified personnel are deterred from altering the mixture. The adjusting screw is normally hidden in a recessed hole, which is sealed by a metal or plastic plug.
- **Carbon monoxide (CO), hydrocarbon (HC) content in the exhaust gas**
An exhaust gas emission test, taken after the idle speed has been set, should show that the CO and the HC content is below the value specified by the manufacturer.
- **Running on**
When the ignition is switched off the driver expects the engine to stop immediately. Sometimes an engine

continues to run very erratically for a period of time or until it is stalled by the driver. During this running-on period combustion is initiated by a hot-spot within the combustion chamber, such as a valve or sparking plug electrode. The extraordinary high temperature of a component is often produced when the engine is operated on the weak mixture required to meet the emission regulations.

Various arrangements are used to overcome this problem. The method shown in Figure 2.236 is an electric solenoid which cuts off the slow-running mixture when the ignition is switched off. The system is often referred to as an 'anti-run-on valve' or 'anti-dieseling valve'.

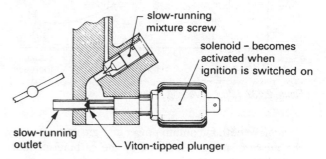

Figure 2.236 Anti run-on valve

2.26.10 Economizers and power systems

Under ideal conditions a carburettor that supplied a chemically correct mixture (approximately 15:1) would cause the engine to produce maximum power and economy at all speeds and loads. In practice the physical problems associated with correctly vaporized fuel distribution to each cylinder makes it impossible to achieve this ideal. Even if it could be achieved, the difficulty of bringing each particle of fuel into intimate contact with the correct amount of oxygen needed to burn it completely to carbon dioxide (CO_2) and water (H_2O) makes the ideal unachievable.

Varying the mixture strength supplied to an engine that is operating under load at a fixed speed causes the engine performance to change as shown in Figure 2.237. The graph plots the 'fuel used per unit of power' against the 'torque output'.

When the air/fuel mixture is weak the fuel economy is very poor and the torque output is low. As the mixture is enriched both the economy and torque improve, but after the lowest point of the curve (maximum economy) has been reached, further enrichment produces a slight increase in torque at the expense of economy. Continuing to enrich the mixture past the maximum torque point produces a drop in torque and a considerable rise in fuel consumption.

Three points on this graph should be noted:

1 The chemically correct (CC) mixture strength gives neither maximum economy nor maximum power.

2 Maximum power (P) requires a mixture that is slightly rich.

3 Maximum economy (E) requires a mixture that is slightly weak.

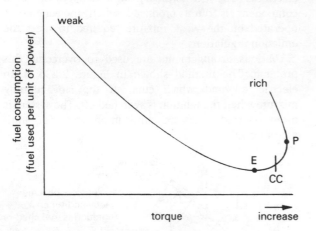

Figure 2.237 Effect of varying air/fuel ratio

To achieve both maximum power and greatest economy the mixture strength supplied by the carburettor must be varied to suit the operating conditions, i.e. it must provide a slightly rich mixture for power and slightly weak mixture for economy. Emission regulations normally prevent the use of mixtures richer than 15:1, because they do not fully burn during combustion, so the engine power output at 15:1 is the maximum and the operating mixture range is on the weak side of this value.

The devices used in a carburettor to vary the mixture strength to suit either the power or cruising conditions are called 'economizer or power' systems.

In all cases the weak cruising mixture is obtained by reducing the petrol flow through the main jet system. This can be achieved either by using a smaller jet or by reducing the pressure difference across the jet.

Restoration of the air/fuel ratio to 15:1 for power is achieved either by providing an additional path from the float chamber to the choke, or by exposing the main jet to the normal pressure difference. This is achieved through the use of a mechanically operated or vacuum-operated 'power valve'.

2.26.11 Acceleration pumps

Whenever the throttle is plunged open, there is a sudden weakening of the mixture. One of the reasons for this is the delay caused by the reluctance of the fuel to respond compared with the fast action of the air. If the carburettor is already delivering a slightly weakened mixture to provide maximum economy, the further weakening that occurs when the throttle is opened causes a delay before the engine responds (in some cases it will cause the engine to misfire) resulting in a flat spot.

Whereas a carburettor without an economy system has small reserves of fuel on the outlet side of the main jet to allow for sudden increases in speed or load, an economy-type carburettor generally needs an 'acceleration pump'. The pump delivers fuel into the mixing chamber when the throttle is plunged open.

There are two main types of acceleration pump, mechanical and vacuum-operated.

Mechanical acceleration pumps

The mechanical pump shown in Figure 2.238 is controlled by a linkage connected to the throttle. This linkage acts on a diaphragm, which draws fuel via a one-way valve from the float chamber and pumps it past a delivery valve fitted in the outlet passage. A separate jet, or restriction, in the passageway regulates the flow of fuel delivered by the pump.

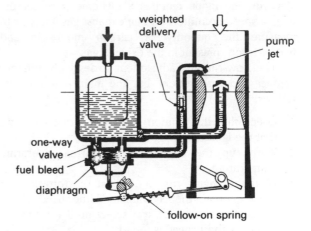

Figure 2.238 A mechanical accelerator pump

When the fuel outlet pipe terminates in a region where the pressure is lower than atmospheric there is a risk that fuel will discharge continuously, so a device such as a weighted valve is used to prevent this flow.

Most pump designs use a spring in the pump operating linkage to increase the time that the fuel in the pump chamber is being discharged. This additional fuel also improves exhaust emissions and economy.

Vacuum acceleration pumps

The pump shown in Figure 2.239 operates using the sudden change in manifold pressure that occurs when the throttle is suddenly opened. The pumping action is produced by the diaphragm spring, which is compressed when a high depression acts in the vacuum chamber. A sudden collapse of this depression allows the spring to discharge fuel into the mixing chamber.

2.26.12 Cold starting

Provisions in the fuel system are necessary to start a cold engine, as the low cranking speed of the engine is insufficient to allow the venturi to create an adequate depression. In addition, the slow-moving air entering the engine causes a large amount of fuel to be deposited

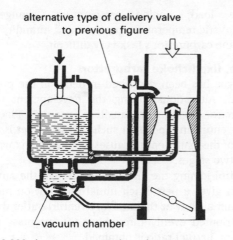

Figure 2.239 A vacuum-operated accelerator pump

on the walls of the inlet manifold. Since the manifold and cylinders are cold, very little vaporization of the fuel takes place, so ignition of the charge under these conditions is very difficult.

Note: Petrol consists of many different hydrocarbons (HC) and the fractions (types of HC) that make up the fuel have different boiling points in the range 85 to 220°C. A light-fraction fuel boils (vaporizes) at a low temperature whereas a heavy-fraction fuel does not boil until the temperature approaches 220°C.

The provision of extra fuel during cold starting ensures there is an adequate supply of light-fraction fuels that are able to vaporize in the cold engine. If the quantity of gas formed by this vaporization is sufficient, it is possible to ignite the gas and produce enough heat to drive the engine over, even though the cold oil is causing a large drag.

Cold-starting systems used with fixed choke carburettors are normally of the 'strangler' type.

A strangler-type cold-starting system

Figure 2.240 shows the principle of a strangler. It consists of a flap valve which is positioned at the air entry point of the carburettor. When the valve is closed,

the strangulation of the air supply intensifies the depression felt at the venturi. As a result, extra fuel is supplied to provide a very rich mixture (typically 8:1).

Once the engine has started, the richness of the mixture must be reduced to a point where the engine runs smoothly. This reduces the risk of rapid cylinder wear caused by fuel washing the oil film from the top part of the cylinders. Excessive fuel also 'fouls' the sparking plugs and prevents them functioning in the normal manner.

For historical reasons the strangler is sometimes called the 'choke', which is the reason why this is occasionally marked on the driver's control knob. The control cable acts on the strangler valve, the first movement of the 'choke' control opens the throttle a small amount to give a 'fast idle' to allow for the extra drag on the engine when it is cold.

The driver must not 'over-choke' the engine, because this action 'floods' the engine with fuel vapour and starves it of air. Combustion cannot occur under these conditions and this becomes apparent when a driver attempts to start a hot engine after it has not been used for a few minutes. During this time the fuel in the manifold vaporizes and drives out the air. So when the starter is operated, the engine will not fire until sufficient air has been induced. If the driver misreads the temperature condition and pulls out the 'choke', the result will be that the engine becomes flooded and most probably the plugs will be fouled. To clear the over-choked condition, the driver should push in the 'choke' and then keep the throttle fully depressed as the starter is operated. This action allows the engine to start after a few seconds unless the sparking plugs have been flooded with petrol.

To minimize the problems associated with over-choking, the strangler normally incorporates some arrangement to weaken the mixture as soon as the engine starts. Figure 2.241 shows an offset strangler valve that allows the moving air to act on the valve and partially open it after the engine has started.

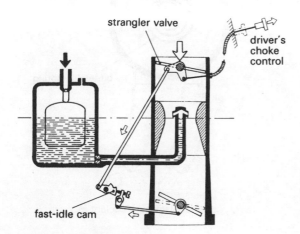

Figure 2.240 A simple strangler system

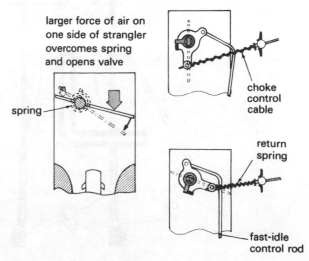

Figure 2.241 Offset strangler

Automatic strangler

Incorrect use of the choke by the driver, especially the delay in returning it to the 'off' position during driving, causes emission problems as well as those drawbacks previously outlined. To overcome these problems, the automatic choke was introduced.

Figure 2.242 shows the principle of one system, which uses a bimetallic strip to sense the temperature of the coolant. When the engine temperature is less than about 15 °C the bimetal strip pulls the strangler to the closed position.

After the engine has started, the strangler is partly opened by the diaphragm in the vacuum chamber; this is activated by the high depression created in the inlet manifold.

As the engine warms up, the rise in coolant temperature causes the bimetallic strip gradually to reduce its pull on the strangler. Due to the rate at which the bimetallic strip heats up, the richness and the fast-idle action are slowly changed to suit the engine temperature.

2.26.13 Constructional features for later types of carburettor

The importance of emission control has meant that a carburettor must supply air and finely atomized fuel which is evenly distributed in the proportion needed to suit the engine operating conditions.

These requirements can be met fairly easily if the engine operates at one constant speed, but wide speed limits coupled with other variable factors (such as engine load, engine temperature, changes in atmospheric temperature, pressure and humidity, etc.), make the carburettor's task very difficult.

Single, fixed-choke carburettors

This type has been described in detail in the previous section. Alterations during the development of the carburettor include an 'auxiliary venturi'. Placing a small venturi in a position such that its outlet is in the waist of the main venturi causes the fuel to mix with the air in two stages.

Petrol joining the air flowing through the auxiliary venturi gives a petrol-rich initial mix, but on meeting the main airflow at the auxiliary venturi outlet the fuel is distributed evenly throughout the air mass and a constant air/fuel ratio is obtained.

Twin-choke carburettor

Engines such as V6 and V8-types normally require two carburettors. The two carburettors are effectively joined together to share a common float chamber.

Normal practice is to arrange the manifold so that one venturi system supplies one set of cylinders and the other venturi the remaining cylinders. Each venturi requires a system for cold starting, slow-running, cruising and power.

The two throttle valves are interconnected and should be synchronized to give the same opening at all engine speeds.

Twin-barrel sequential carburettor

To obtain fuel economy, good atomization of the fuel is required. In a fixed-choke carburettor this can be achieved by using a comparatively small-diameter

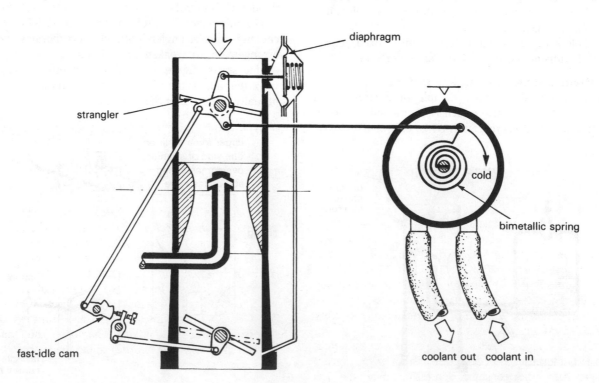

Figure 2.242 An automatic choke

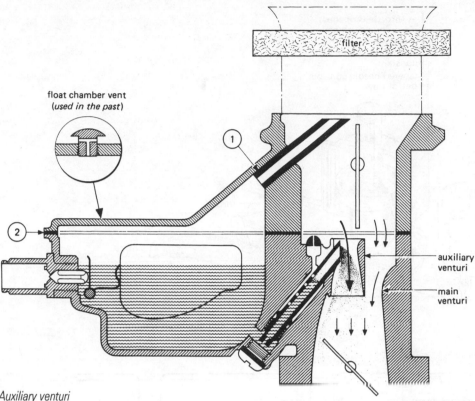

Figure 2.243 Auxiliary venturi

venturi. Unfortunately the restriction to airflow of a small venturi gives poor volumetric efficiency and results in reduced maximum power.

When both economy and high maximum power are required, a multi-barrel, sequential-type carburettor is often fitted.

The two throttle valves are coupled together in such a way that the secondary throttle remains closed until the primary throttle has opened about two-thirds. When

the primary throttle opens past this point, the linkage moves the secondary throttle so that both throttles reach the fully open position together.

This sequential movement allows the primary barrel to supply all cylinders with a slightly weak, well-atomized mixture for cruising conditions. When power is required, the secondary barrel provides extra fuel and a good supply of air to meet the engine's fuel requirements.

2.27   VARIABLE CHOKE – CONSTANT-DEPRESSION CARBURETTORS

2.27.1 Constant-choke limitations

The varying depression which acts on the jet of a constant-choke carburettor makes it necessary to fit some form of compensating device to prevent mixture enrichment with increase in engine speed. Also, the size of the venturi (choke) is a compromise that gives neither maximum economy nor maximum power.

Carburettors which operate using a 'variable choke' or 'constant-depression' principle do not suffer these drawbacks because the size of the choke alters to keep the air speed through the choke constant.

The air speed can therefore be set to that required for good atomization of fuel over the full engine speed range. Also, the constant depression over the jet overcomes the need for a compensating system.

2.27.2 Principle of the constant-depression carburettor

Figure 2.244 indicates the basic construction of a constant-depression carburettor (which is also known as variable-choke and variable-venturi carburettor).

The venturi (choke) is formed by a movable piston which alters the size of the venturi to suit the quantity of air being drawn in by the engine. An air vent maintains atmospheric pressure in the space below the piston and a communicating passage transfers the depression from the mixing chamber (the space between the choke and throttle) to the space above the piston.

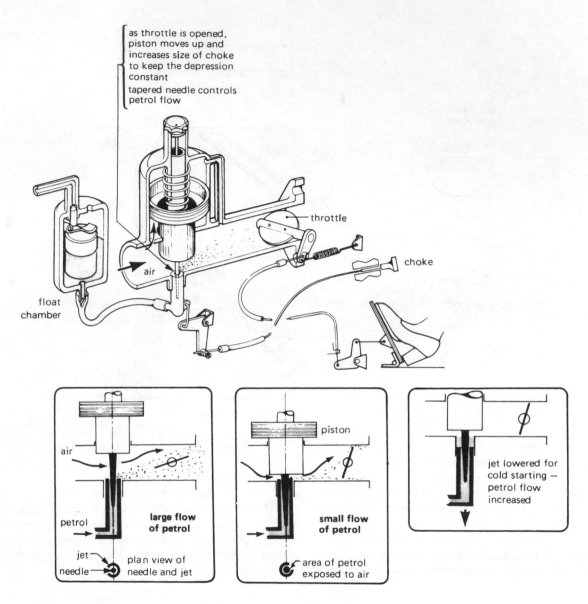

Figure 2.244 Principle of the constant-depression carburettor

When air is flowing through the carburettor, there is a difference in pressure between the air intake and the mixing chamber. This difference in pressure acts on the piston and gives an upward force to oppose the downward force caused by the piston weight and the light spring.

When the upward force due to air pressure difference is increased by opening the throttle, the piston rises and the choke area enlarges. Similarly, when the throttle closes, the mixing chamber depression reduces, the piston falls and the choke area decreases.

Whatever the airflow, the piston assembly always takes up a position that maintains a constant air speed through the choke to ensure that the petrol jet is acted upon by a constant depression – hence the name given to this type of carburettor.

A tapered needle is attached to the piston, the rise or fall of the piston will therefore vary the effective area of the petrol jet. By altering the taper of the needle, it is possible for the carburettor manufacturer to vary the fuel flow to suit the quantity of air being supplied at any speed.

2.27.3 SU-type

Figure 2.245 shows a section through an SU constant-vacuum set in the cruising position. The main features of its operation are:

• **Slow-running**
The piston will be lifted very slightly from the lowered position and the depression caused by the air rushing over the petrol jet will give a small fuel supply to suit

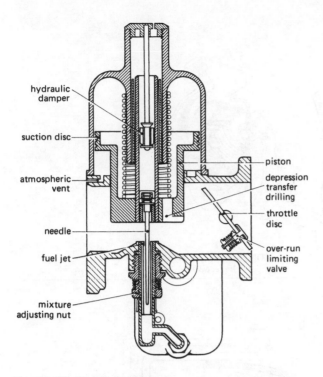

Figure 2.245 The SU carburettor

the conditions. A separate slow-running jet system is usually unnecessary unless emission restrictions are strict.

- **Throttle opening**

When the throttle is opened, the mixing chamber depression is increased. The increase in depression causes the piston to rise to a point where the mixing chamber depression is just sufficient to support the piston. The higher the piston moves, the larger the area of the jet and the greater the flow of petrol.

- **Cold starting**

A lever, operated by a cable control, lowers the fuel jet in relation to the needle. This enlarges the jet opening and increases the amount of fuel which is mixed with the air. The initial movement of the control cable also slightly opens the throttle to give 'fast idle' action.

- **Mixture adjustment**

An adjusting nut acts as a stop to limit the upward movement of the jet. Unscrewing the nut lowers the jet and richens the mixture throughout the entire speed and load range of the engine. Note that later SU carburettors were fitted with a mixture-adjusting screw located on the side of the body of the carburettor. This adjusting screw acted on the jet.

- **Hydraulic damper**

The damper restricts the rate of upward movement of the piston during acceleration. This provides a slight enrichment of the mixture. The damper also reduces piston flutter caused by the irregular flow of air through the induction systems.

- **Over-run limiting valve**

The valve (poppet valve) which is spring-loaded, is situated in the throttle butterfly. When the vehicle is

decelerating (i.e. road wheels drive the engine) with the throttle closed, the valve opens to supply a fuel mixture, which helps to reduce exhaust pollution.

2.27.4 The Zenith–Stromberg constant-depression (CD) carburettor

This is a very similar carburettor to the SU type, but whereas the SU type uses a solid piston, the Zenith–Stromberg CD carburettor has a synthetic rubber diaphragm (Figure 2.246).

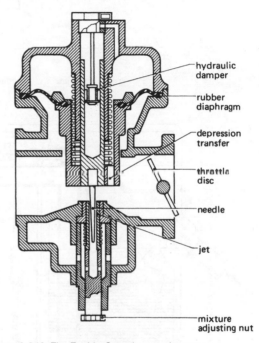

Figure 2.246 The Zenith–Stromberg carburettor

2.27.5 Ford Variable-Venturi (VV) carburettor

The addition of the Ford VV carburettor to the range of variable-venturi carburettors introduces many features which help to reduce harmful exhaust emissions. It also overcomes the two main disadvantages of the fixed-venturi type: the need for mixture correction devices and the choke air speed problem that gives poor atomization of fuel at low engine speeds and breathing restriction at high engine speeds.

Figure 2.247 shows a diagram of this type of carburettor. An air valve, operated by a diaphragm, is used to vary the area of a large, fixed venturi. A tapered needle, attached to the air valve, fits into a main jet to control the petrol flow.

The operating principle of the Ford VV carburettor is similar to that of other variable-venturi carburettors.

In Figure 2.247 the carburettor is shown in the cruising position. A depression in the mixing chamber

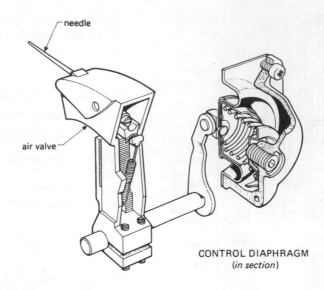

CONTROL DIAPHRAGM
(*in section*)

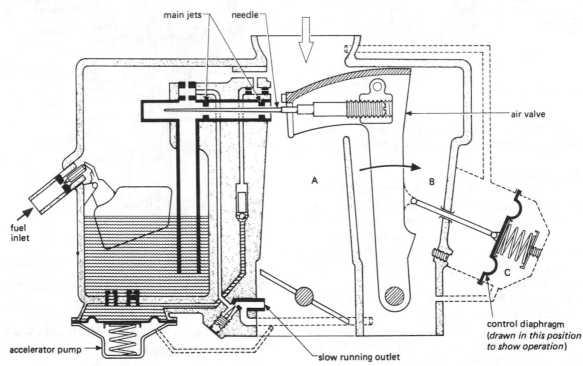

Figure 2.247 Ford variable-venturi carburettor (shown in diagrammatic form)

(A) is communicated through the air valve chamber (B) to the diaphragm (C). When engine load is steady, the difference in air pressure on the diaphragm balances the force given by the diaphragm spring.

When the throttle is opened a given amount, the following events take place in quick succession:

1   Depression will become more intense in the mixing chamber (A) because insufficient air passes the air valve. This depression is transferred to the diaphragm chamber (C).
2   Atmospheric pressure now pushes the diaphragm against the spring. As the diaphragm deflects, the linkage will move the air valve and increase the venturi opening. This prevents the venturi air speed

from increasing and will restore the depression in the mixing chamber (A) to the original value. At this point the various forces on the diaphragm are again balanced.

Closing the throttle gives a reverse action – the depression in regions (A) and (C) diminish and the spring closes the air valve to prevent a decrease in the venturi air speed. Operating in this manner, the air valve will keep the venturi air speed constant irrespective of throttle opening.

Idle speed

Due to stricter emission legislation, carburettors were required to provide improved atomization and a better distributed idle mixture. The VV design achieves this by using a separate slow-running system. This is similar to that used in constant-choke units except that in the VV carburettor the slow-running system only supplies about 70% of the total mixture; the remainder is provided by the main jet.

Acceleration

A slightly rich, well-atomized mixture is obtained by using a vacuum-operated accelerator pump. The mixture provided by this pump compensates for the sudden drop in venturi air speed caused by the rapid opening of the air valve.

Cold starting

When the engine is cold either a manual or automatic choke, in the form of a miniature auxiliary carburettor, supplements the mixture provided by the main system. The choke control acts on a needle in a fuel jet which opens when the engine is cold. Fuel from this jet is mixed with air and the resultant mixture is discharged into the main system at a point beneath the throttle valve.

2.27.6 Electronically controlled carburettors

With the introduction of increasingly stringent emissions legislation, a provision for improved fuelling was required to provide lower emissions and an increase in fuel economy.

These two requirements can only be met by a fuel system that is able to accurately monitor the engine's operating conditions, and so provide a near-ideal air/fuel mixture. Such a system must be very sensitive and quick to react; electronic control systems were used in conjunction with the carburettor to meet these requirements.

The features covered here applied to a constant-depression carburettor, but many aspects considered also apply to other types of carburettor.

Figure 2.248 shows the layout of a typical electronic control system fitted to a constant-depression carburettor. In this system four sensors are used to monitor the engine and ambient (surrounding) conditions that affect the operation of the carburettor.

Electrical signals from these sensors are passed to a computer called an electronic control unit (ECU), in effect the 'brain' of the system. From these input signals, the ECU responds to the given set of conditions and provides output signals to various components (actuators). This enables the carburettor to operate efficiently over a wide speed and load range.

The electronically controlled fuel system provides:

- mixture for cold-starting
- idle speed
- fuel cut-off when the vehicle is on over-run or the ignition is switched-off.

Cold starting

Accurate measurement of ambient and engine temperature conditions via electronic sensors ensures that the mixture supplied during cold-starting is set to suit the engine temperature.

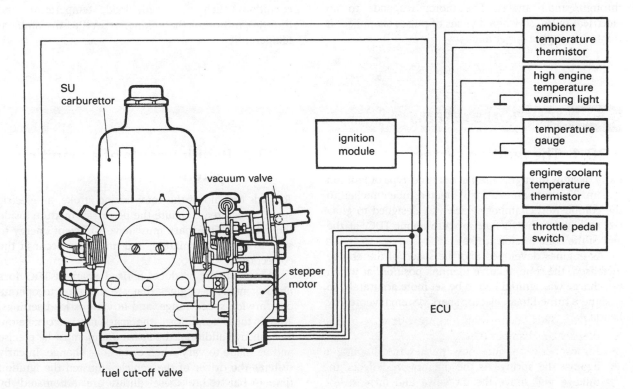

Figure 2.248 SU carburettor with electronic control

Figure 2.249 shows a carburettor with an auxiliary starting system that is brought into operation when the cylindrical 'choke' is rotated by an electrical stepper motor.

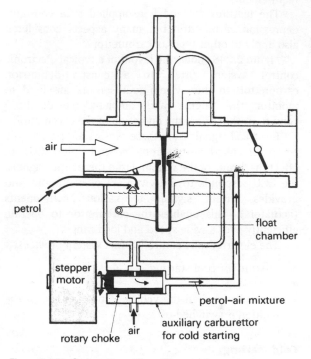

Figure 2.249 Carburettor with auxiliary starting system

This type of rotary motor has a range of about three revolutions and is capable of rotating in either direction through small angles. The motor responds to an electrical pulse, so when a series of pulses is applied, it rotates through a larger angle.

The diagram shows the choke in operation and supplying an extra-rich mixture to supplement that delivered by the main system. Air that enters the starting carburettor flows around the rotary choke and mixes with fuel coming from the float chamber. The quantity of air/fuel mixture is determined by the position of the rotary choke, which in turn is controlled by the stepper motor. As the engine warms up, the associated movement of the rotary choke gradually reduces the mixture supplied by the system until the fuel and air ports are eventually cut off and the auxiliary fuel system closes.

Idle speed control
Many modern generation carburettors use a stepper motor to control the idle speed or engine slow-running. The stepper motor acts directly on the throttle linkage and effectively 'jacks' open the throttle when the ECU detects that the engine speed is too low when at idle. The engine idle speed can be set lower without the engine stalling when this type of control system is used.

Fuel cut-off
Economy can be improved by cutting off the fuel supply when engine power is not required. The fuel cut-off can be achieved by using an electrical solenoid valve to reduce the air pressure in the float chamber.

Mixture control
Elaborate compensation systems that are required on constant-choke carburettors can be eliminated with variable-choke designs by using an electronic system to control the mixture strength.

The system sets the air/fuel ratio to suit operating conditions such as speed, load, temperature and throttle position of the engine, as well as the ambient temperature.

2.28   IGNITION SYSTEMS

2.28.1 The ignition system

Early designs of engine used a 'hot tube' type of ignition system. This was an externally heated tube attached to the combustion chamber, which was designed to glow red and ignite the fuel-air mixture about TDC, at the end of the compression stroke.

As engines developed and the speed of the engine increased, the time, relative to crank position, at which the charge was ignited had to be set more accurately, so designers turned to an electric spark system invented by Lenoir.

2.28.2 Requirements of an ignition system

Towards the end of the compression stroke, an electric spark is required to ignite the petrol/air mixture inside the cylinder. The spark must have sufficient energy to start to ignite the mixture, and must also occur at the correct time.

A system that produces a 'fixed' spark at TDC does not suit modern engines that are designed to operate over a wide speed range, and at various load settings. To suit these conditions, the spark must occur before TDC and, in addition, the spark timing must be precise and be made to vary when conditions change. In early systems the driver of the vehicle adjusted the ignition timing, but today these duties are automated by mechanical or electronic means.

Altering the timing to make the spark occur earlier in the operating cycle is described as 'advancing' the ignition. Conversely, the term 'retard' is used when the timing is changed to make it occur later.

To obtain a high power output from an engine, the maximum cylinder pressure should occur at 10° after TDC, irrespective of engine speed and mixture/load conditions. Since it takes a comparatively long time for the burning mixture to build up to its maximum pressure, the spark must be set to allow for this time period.

The angle of advance is enlarged when the load is decreased or if either the air/fuel mixture ratio or engine speed is increased. The change in timing is necessary because the crankshaft moves through a larger angle during the extra time taken by the gases to build up to the maximum pressure.

2.28.3 Production of high voltage

Although early designs used a comparatively low voltage 'trembler' arrangement, the introduction of the 'high-voltage, timed spark system' considerably improved engine performance.

The voltage needed on a high-voltage system to produce a spark depends on the size of the sparking plug gap and on the gas pressure within the cylinder. A normal gap is about 0.6 mm (0.024 inch), and although only a small charge of about 600 volts is required to produce a spark across this gap in the open air, it will take 10–50 times this voltage to fire a sparking plug that is under combustion pressure in a cylinder.

The combustion pressure should be taken into account when an ignition system is being tested – a spark produced at a plug outside the cylinder does not guarantee that it will spark when it is subjected to cylinder pressure.

A high-voltage spark can be generated by a 'magneto' or 'coil-ignition' system.

Magneto

This is a small, self-contained ignition unit which generates pulses of high-tension current and distributes them to the appropriate cylinders at the correct time.

Some motorcycles and small single-cylinder engines still use this system, but it is not used on modern vehicles.

Coil ignition

This system uses electrical energy produced by a battery or alternator to supply the low-tension ignition current. The ignition coil transforms the low voltage (battery voltage) to that required to produce a high-voltage spark (several thousands of volts). Compared with a magneto system, the coil-ignition system makes engine starting much easier. It is also simpler to control the maximum voltage to suit conditions.

2.28.4 Coil-ignition systems

The conventional battery-inductive ignition system was introduced by Kettering in 1908, but it was not until the mid-1920s that the system was accepted as a successor to the magneto for use on cars.

Until recently, the main layout of a coil-ignition system, as it is commonly known, did not change, but the current need to design cleaner, more efficient engines has demanded ignition systems that produce a higher energy spark that is timed far more accurately. Electronically controlled coil-ignition systems of the 'breakerless' type meet these requirements. To avoid confusion, the conventional breakerless system will be called the 'Kettering-type'.

The Kettering-type coil-ignition system

Figure 2.250 shows the layout of a basic system that has been in use for many years. Although more modern electronic ignition systems appear more complicated (with the introduction of electronic control modules) the principles remain the same. The main components are:

Ignition coil

The ignition coil produces the high voltage necessary to cause a spark at the sparking plug. It transforms the battery voltage of 12 V to a low-current, high-voltage charge that is required to jump the plug gap. Inside the case of the ignition coil there are two windings connected to three external electrical terminals:

1 Low tension (LT) to the battery via the ignition switch.
2 Low tension (CB) to the contact breaker.
3 High tension (HT) to the sparking plug via the distributor. This lead, often referred to as a 'king lead' must be highly insulated to prevent loss of the HT current.

Contact breaker

A high-tension current is produced by the ignition coil, when the low-tension circuit from the battery through the coil to the earth connection (vehicle frame) is interrupted.

The contact breaker is a mechanical switch consisting of two contact points, a fixed contact, screwed down to a base plate, and a movable contact that is insulated from the metal parts that surround it. A cam, normally driven by the engine camshaft, operates the movable contact against the reaction of a strip-type spring. The number of lobes on the cam matches the number of cylinders (e.g. a four-cylinder engine has four lobes) so one revolution of the cam will give a spark for each cylinder. On a two-stroke engine, one spark per engine revolution per cylinder is required, so the cam is driven at the same speed as the crankshaft instead of half crankshaft speed as required by a four-stroke unit. A spark at the plug occurs at the instant the contacts open, so the assembly is set (timed), in relation to the crankshaft, to give a spark at the correct time.

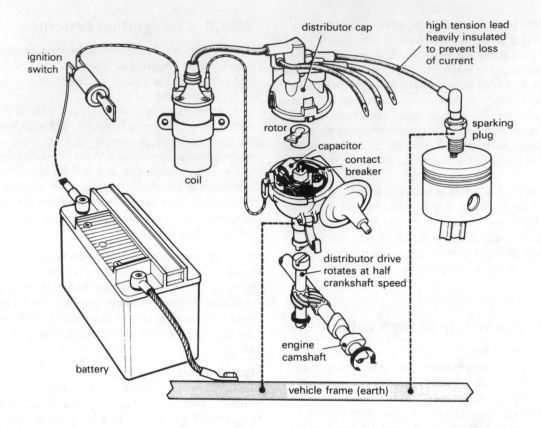

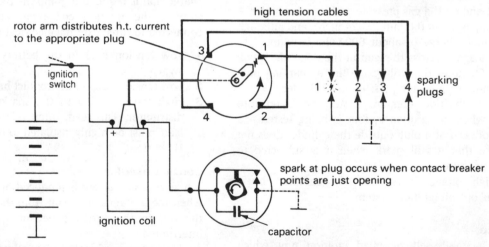

Figure 2.250 A coil-ignition system of the Kettering type

Capacitor (often referred to as a condenser)
The capacitor is connected in the circuit across the contacts, (i.e. in parallel). The condenser reduces arcing of the contacts and in consequence gives a rapid interruption of the LT circuit.

Distributor
On a single-cylinder engine the HT lead from the coil is connected directly to the sparking plug. A multi-cylinder engine has a number of sparking plugs and each one of these has to be connected to the ignition coil when the high-voltage charge is supplied to the plug. The HT switch used to select the appropriate cylinder's spark plug is called a 'distributor'.

It consists of a hard plastic distributor cap, inside which is a rotor arm, which is rotated at half crankshaft speed by the shaft that drives the contact breaker cam. The HT lead (king lead) from the coil fits in the centre of the cap and a carbon brush rubs on the rotor to transmit the electrical charge through to the rotor arm. At the instant the points open and the spark occurs, the rotor arm is set to point to the 'segment' in the cap that is connected to the correct cylinder sparking plug that requires the high voltage charge.

The distributor cap, rotor, contact breaker assembly and automatic advance systems are all incorporated in one unit, which is referred to as the 'distributor unit'.

High-tension lead

Highly insulated with PVC or thick rubber, the HT leads connect the ignition coil to the distributor and to the sparking plugs.

Electrical interference is reduced by using 'suppression' leads. These leads have a high electrical resistance. The conductor used for the HT lead is either carbon impregnated cotton or glass fibre. These leads are generally made up in a set to suit the suppression requirements of the particular vehicle.

Sparking plug

The plug consists of a highly insulated centre electrode, and an earth electrode, which is welded to the metal body of the sparking plug. A typical gap of 0.6 mm (0.024 inch) between the electrodes enables a spark to be produced when a high voltage is delivered to the plug.

2.28.5 Magnetism and induction

To help you understand the operation of the ignition, and other systems, consider the following.

Figure 2.251 shows a conductor passing through a piece of paper, on to which are scattered some iron filings. When current flows through the conductor, the iron filings arrange themselves in a series of concentric circles. The iron filings arranged in this manner indicate the presence of a magnetic field. If the process could be slowed down, you would see that on making the circuit, the field moves outwards from the conductor. When the flow of current is interrupted, the reverse occurs – the field collapses from the outer edge.

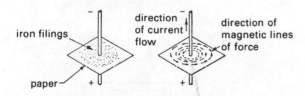

Figure 2.251 Demonstrating a magnetic field using iron filings

Figure 2.252 shows a length of wire wound in the form of a coil. On closing the switch, the magnetic field surrounding each turn of the coil combines with other fields to produce a larger field. A soft iron core, mounted in the centre of the coil concentrates and intensifies the field.

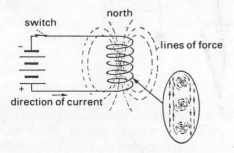

Figure 2.252 Production of a magnetic field using a conductor

This core becomes a magnet when current is flowing through the coil (2.253). The strength of the magnet is governed by the amount of current flowing, and the number of turns on the coil.

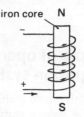

Figure 2.253 Generation of a field by an electromagnet

Figure 2.254 shows another coil, termed a 'secondary winding', which is wound around, or placed near, the 'primary winding'. A galvanometer (an instrument used for detecting small electrical currents) is connected in the secondary circuit. The switch is then operated.

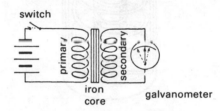

Figure 2.254 Inducing current in a secondary winding

On closing and opening the switch, the galvanometer needle momentarily flicks one way on switching the circuit on, and the opposite way on switching the circuit off. This was first discovered by Faraday, and from his experiments it was concluded that when a magnetic line of force cuts a conductor (or vice versa), an electro magnetic force (EMF) is induced in that conductor. The magnitude of the EMF, depends on:

1 the rate of change of the magnetic field
2 the number of turns on the coil.

In the apparatus shown in Figure 2.254, the build-up of the field around the primary winding causes the lines of force to cut the secondary circuit, therefore an EMF is induced in the secondary circuit. Since the build-up is slower than the collapse, a much higher EMF is induced when the circuit is broken.

If the secondary circuit contains more turns than the primary winding (2.255), it is possible to obtain a higher voltage in the secondary circuit. For example if the secondary contains 100 times the number of turns wound on the primary winding, the EMF will be 100 times greater than the EMF in the primary, assuming the efficiency is 100%. This increase in voltage in the secondary circuit is balanced by a proportional *decrease* in the *current* of the secondary circuit.

Figure 2.255 Stepping up EMF with more turns on the secondary coil

2.28.6 Principle of operation of a coil-ignition system

The layout of an earth-return ignition system is shown in Figure 2.257. The system consists of two circuits: primary and secondary.

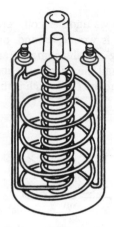

Figure 2.256 Internals of a coil indicate the primary/secondary and core

Primary circuit
Wound around a soft iron core are several hundred turns of comparatively heavy enamelled wire. This is arranged in series with a battery, ignition switch and contact breaker. A capacitor is connected in parallel with the contact breaker.

Secondary circuit
A secondary coil winding, consisting of several thousand turns of fine enamelled wire, is wound under the primary coil. One end of this winding is joined to the contact breaker terminal, the other end is connected in series with the distributor and sparking plugs. A 'return path' from the plug, via the earth electrode, passes through the battery and primary winding, and so EMF induced in the primary winding is added to the large EMF produced in the secondary winding. This gives the coil a higher efficiency.

When the ignition is switched on and the contacts are closed, the current flowing in the primary winding sets up a magnetic field around the iron core of the coil.

Opening the contacts interrupts the current flowing in the primary circuit, and causes the magnetic field to collapse. During this collapse, the lines of force cut the secondary winding, and induce an EMF in the secondary circuit. A higher EMF than that acting in the primary is obtained, since the secondary coil contains more turns. The HT current is conveyed from the ignition coil to the rotor arm. The rotor arm should be pointing to the correct distributor segment, which is connected to the sparking plug of the cylinder that requires the ignition HT charge.

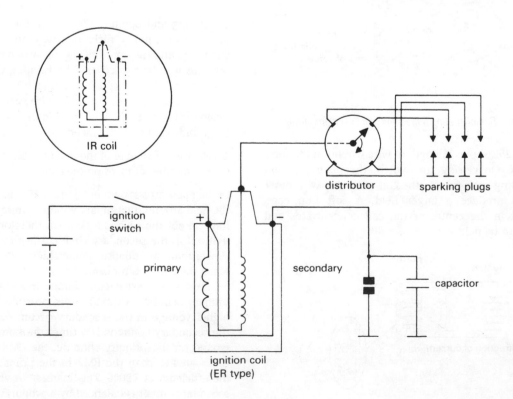

Figure 2.257 An earth-return coil – ignition system

Capacitor

A capacitor is fitted for two reasons:

1 It reduces arcing of the contacts.
2 It ensures a quicker collapse of the magnetic field.

It consists of two sheets of foil or metallized paper, which are separated from each other by at least two sheets of insulating material such as waxed paper. These are wound into a cylinder shape, and inserted into a metal container. One sheet is joined to the earthed container, and the other sheet is connected by a wire or metal strip to the insulated side of the contact breaker.

When a voltage is applied to the terminals, a current can be made to flow into, but not through, the capacitor. The voltage charges the capacitor to a value equal to the supply voltage, and when this point is reached, the flow of current ceases.

If the supply is now disconnected, the charge will be retained for a time, but will gradually 'leak away'. When a charged capacitor is connected to a circuit, the charge produces a current flow in the opposite direction to the original supply current.

In order to understand the function of the capacitor, consider the operation of an ignition system which has the capacitor disconnected. When the contacts open, the lines of force cut the primary winding as well as the secondary, and therefore an EMF is also induced in the primary winding.

The build up of EMF is sufficient to cause a spark to jump the small contact points gap. Arcing maintains current flow in the primary circuit, and thereby prevents the rapid collapse of the magnetic field, as well as causing serious burning of the contacts.

The action is in many ways similar to the hydraulic analogy shown in Figure 2.258. Water flowing along a pipe at great speed will produce a sudden pressure rise if the tap is shut off quickly. The surge of pressure may lead to the discharge of an amount of water through the 'closed' tap, by lifting the tap washer off its seat.

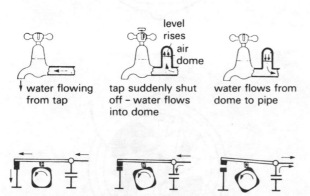

Figure 2.258 Action of a capacitor

Fitting an air dome (as illustrated) to the system allows the water to flow into the dome as the tap is suddenly shut off, but after a short time the air forces the water back into the pipe.

The capacitor must perform a duty similar to the buffer action of the air dome. When the contacts open, the capacitor absorbs the self-induced current, and by the time the capacitor is fully charged the contacts have opened sufficiently to prevent a spark occurring at the contact breaker points.

Ignition coil output

The voltage needed to produce a spark sufficient to ignite the air/fuel mixture is increased when the engine compression pressure is raised or if the mixture strength is weakened.

To meet modern engine requirements various refinements are made to the ignition system.

Oil-filled coil

Immersing the windings in oil gives the following improvements:

- Provides better insulation and greater resistance to moisture.
- The primary winding operates at a lower temperature, so the lower resistance allows more current to flow.
- Reduces corona (glow of light) effect.

2.28.7 Distributor

Figure 2.259 shows the construction of the complete distributor assembly, which comprises the distributor, contact breaker assembly and automatic advance mechanism.

A rotor arm, mounted above the cam and driven at half engine speed, is contacted by a spring-loaded carbon brush. The brush allows the rotor arm to rotate but still maintain an electrical contact with the HT terminal at the centre of a moulded 'Bakelite' distributor cap. Cables from the cylinder sparking plugs connect, in the engine firing order, with segments held in the cap. These are positioned so that there is a small gap between the rotor arm and the segment.

Contact breaker

The contact breaker consists of two tungsten contacts, a fixed earth contact and a movable insulated contact. The insulated terminal is linked by its return spring to a terminal on the side of the main body (Figure 2.260).

A cam with four lobes (four-cylinder) or six lobes (six-cylinder) opens and closes the contacts as the cam rotates. Elongated holes through which the contact breaker clamping screw passes, allows for adjustment of the contact gap. The gap is set to provide the correct ignition coil charge time, (if in doubt refer to manufacturer information).

A capacitor, earthed by a fixing screw to the contact base plate, connects with the insulated screw on the side of the main body.

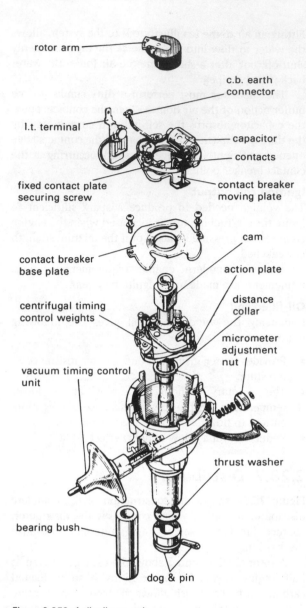

Figure 2.259 A distributor unit

2.28.8 Ignition timing advance

Maximum cylinder pressure should be developed just after TDC, which generally means that the spark must be produced before TDC, since a period of time elapses while the gas builds up to its maximum combustion pressure. The time factor is fairly constant, but the angle moved by the crankshaft during this time varies in proportion to the engine speed. This means that, as the engine speed is increased, the timing of the spark must be advanced.

Alteration of the ignition timing to suit speed and load conditions is performed by two automatic advance and retard mechanisms. These are:

- **Centrifugal** – advances the spark as the speed increases (i.e. engine speed sensitive)
- **Vacuum** – uses induction manifold depression to advance the spark during light load (cruising) conditions (i.e. engine load sensitive).

To advance the timing of the spark, either the cam is turned in the direction of rotation (DOR) or the base-plate is moved against the DOR.

Centrifugal advance

The advancement of the distributor cam in the arrangement shown in Figure 2.261 is produced by two fly-weights (bob-weights). These are pivoted on a baseplate, which is rotated by the distributor shaft. A contoured face on the driving side of each flyweight acts against a camplate. The camplate is integral with

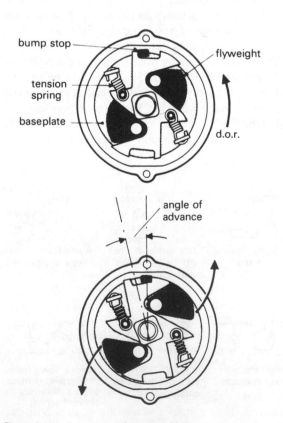

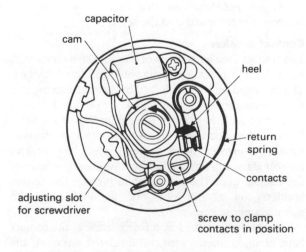

Figure 2.260 The contact breaker assembly

Figure 2.261 Contact breaker assembly

the cam so that when the flyweights move outwards due to centrifugal force, the cam is rotated in the DOR.

The flyweight movement produced by a given increase in engine speed is determined by the strength of the two tension springs fitted between the baseplate and camplate. By carefully matching the spring strength and flyweight contour to the ignition timing requirement, good engine performance can be obtained. A typical advance curve for a 'mechanical system' is shown in Figure 2.262.

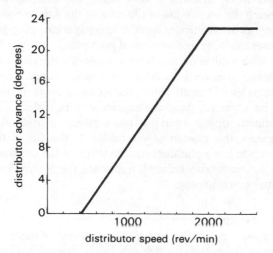

Figure 2.262 Typical advance curve of a centrifugal advance

On some engines the rate of advance in the low speed range has to be greater than at speeds greater than about 1000 rpm. This can be achieved by using springs of unequal strength with the stronger spring fitted slack on its post.

Vacuum timing control
The normal centrifugal mechanical advance mechanism is sensitive to speed, but cannot sense the degree of load on the engine. This means that maximum advance must be restricted to avoid engine 'pinking'. The condition is particularly severe when a weaker mixture is produced. Weaker mixtures and slow burning of the fuel during part-load conditions demand a greater ignition advance than that used for maximum engine load. To overcome this problem, a vacuum control unit is often incorporated in the distributor unit.

The main construction is illustrated in Figure 2.263. The inlet manifold pressure is monitored at a drilling, generally in the vicinity of the throttle butterfly, which is communicated to a 'vacuum' chamber. The vacuum chamber is fitted with a spring-loaded diaphragm, and linked to the distributor body.

During cruising conditions, a high depression (vacuum) acts on the diaphragm to give maximum ignition advance.

When engine load is increased (acceleration), the depression in the inlet manifold decreases, and the vacuum chamber rotates the distributor to a position giving less advance.

Vacuum-advance control valves
Providing the precise ignition timing is essential if the engine is to meet the emission limits imposed by legislation. Control of the vacuum-advance is often used to meet these requirements and this has meant that additional control valves (such as a spark delay valve) have been fitted in the vacuum pipe between the inlet manifold and the vacuum-advance unit. These valves provide additional advance control via the vacuum-advance unit. A further development has been the introduction of dual-diaphragm chambers; these are more sensitive to the variation in load on an engine.

Note: It may be necessary to either leave or disconnect the vacuum unit when checking or adjusting the ignition timing. Always refer to the manufacturer ignition timing data for the correct procedure.

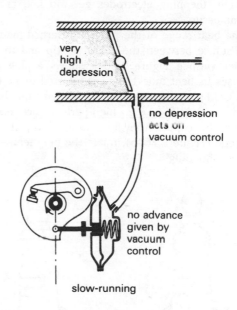

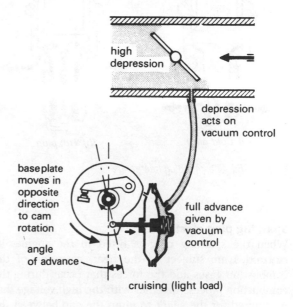

Figure 2.263 A vacuum advance system

2.28.9 Sparking plugs

The sparking plug consists of a steel body, which retains a ceramic insulated centre. The centre electrode connects with the HT lead, and is generally made of a nickel alloy. One or more earth electrodes are welded to the body, the earth electrode is adjusted to produce a sparking plug gap suitable for the engine.

Most plugs have a 14 mm diameter thread, but 10 mm and 18 mm are occasionally used. The length of thread, termed the 'reach', is governed by the distance through the cylinder head to the combustion chamber.

To function successfully, the plug must operate at the correct temperature. Too low a temperature allows oil and carbon to form on the insulator. The fouling of the insulator causes the electrical charge to short to earth and leads to misfiring. When plug temperature is too high, the plug electrodes get too hot, and pre-ignition occurs.

The heat range of the plug is governed mainly by the distance between the electrode tip and the heat transfer washer. Figure 2.264a shows a plug which disperses its heat quickly and is referred to as a 'cold plug'. Cold plugs are suitable for an engine that has hot cylinder conditions, e.g. high-performance engines. Moving the copper transfer washer away from the electrode (Figure 2.264b), raises the plug temperature to give a 'hot plug'.

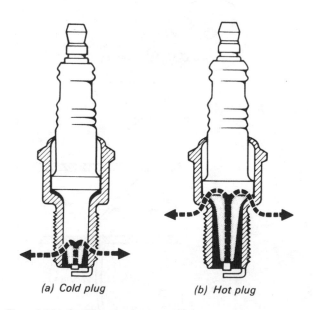

(a) Cold plug   *(b) Hot plug*

Figure 2.264 Sparking plug heat range

Sparking plug electrodes

When the sparking plug is fitted in the engine, its electrodes are subject to the heat, corrosion of the combustion gases and the forces that occur during the combustion process together with the high voltage that is required for the spark to jump the gap between the two electrodes. Conventional sparking plug electrodes

have been made of a nickel alloy, however, due to the higher combustion pressures and voltages, copper-core electrodes have replaced the nickel alloy. Copper-core electrodes also improve the thermal conductivity of the sparking plug, reducing the heat at the tip of the electrode. The shape of the electrode will affect the voltage required to discharge the spark at its tip. A thin electrode tip allows the spark to be discharged easily while a round electrode makes it very difficult to discharge the spark. Although a thin tip allows the spark to be discharged very easily, the thin tip will shorten the service life of the plug as the gap increases faster as the electrodes wear. A larger sparking plug gap causes misfiring and associated problems.

With vehicle manufacturers increasing the time and mileage between service intervals, copper-cored electrodes will erode before the sparking plugs are due to be replaced. Modern engines can be fitted with platinum tipped sparking plugs which considerably decrease the erosion of electrodes. If the tip of the electrode has a platinum tip, the width of the electrode tip is considerably reduced, improving the performance of the sparking plug.

Interference

Whenever an electric spark occurs, waves of electrical energy are radiated which can cause interference with domestic television receivers, electronic systems and car radios. To limit this interference, the law stipulates that some effective form of 'suppression' must be used.

The ignition system is the main source of interference, so resistors are fitted to the ignition HT circuit. These generally have a resistance value between 5000 and 25,000 ohms, which can be incorporated in:

1 HT leads or distributor cap
2 a carbon brush, fitted between rotor and centre distributor terminal
3 a fixed resistance, which is inserted in the HT lead.

Note: With the introduction of electronically controlled systems throughout the vehicle, all sources of interference must be suppressed to ensure that these systems operate correctly.

Centre electrode polarity

When a metal is heated it emits electrons, which possess a negative charge of electricity. The hottest part of a sparking plug is the centre electrode, so if this is arranged to be of negative polarity, the electron flow due to the heat will be in the same direction as the charge given by the ignition coil. A centre electrode having negative polarity gives a more effective spark for a given coil output.

The sparking plug centre electrode polarity is controlled by the connection of the coil windings in relation to the battery polarity. In order to obtain a 'negative spark' the LT connections on the coil are marked '+' and '−'.

2.28.10 Contact breaker setting

Dwell angle

In the past the method of setting the contact breaker gap was to rotate the distributor cam until the rubbing surface of the points was against the full lift position of the cam. The gap between the points was then measured with a feeler gauge and adjusted as per specifications. The method was often inaccurate because it was impossible to take into account the position the cam occupied when the engine was running.

Any wear to the driving shaft bearings gave an incorrect gap which led to incorrect timing of the spark and often caused poor ignition performance at high engine speeds because of the comparatively short time that current was flowing in the primary circuit. Furthermore, operation of most contact sets causes a transfer of metal from one contact to the other and this results in a 'pip' building up on one contact and a 'hole' forming in the other. This would defeat the feeler gauge method unless the 'pip' was ground away.

Electrical automotive test equipment generally incorporates a meter that measures the 'dwell angle'. This is used as an alternative to the feeler gauge method.

Applied to ignition units, 'dwell' is the period that the contacts are closed during a cam movement, equal to the angle between the cam lobes. The dwell is therefore the period when current flows through the primary winding and charges the ignition coil.

The dwell period is checked with the engine cranking or running which allows any wear in the distributor to be checked.

Figure 2.265 shows a diagram of a cam suitable for a four-cylinder engine. In this case the closed period or dwell angle is 60°. This is typical for a four-lobe cam, whereas a cam used with a six-cylinder engine generally has a dwell angle of 35°; both cases give a tolerance of about ±2°.

Some manufacturers state the setting as 'percentage dwell'. This indicates as a percentage the period that the contacts are closed or:

$$\text{Dwell (\%)} = \frac{\text{Dwell angle (closed)}}{\text{Angle between camlobes}} \times 100$$

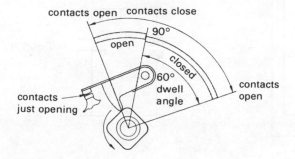

Figure 2.265 Dwell angle

The percentage dwell for the cam in Figure 2.265 is:

$$= \frac{60}{90} \times 100 = 67\%$$

Double contact breakers

Consideration of the dwell angles of units fitted to four- and six-cylinder engines show that dwell angle is reduced as the number of cylinders increases. If a single contact breaker were used on an eight-cylinder engine, then the short dwell period would seriously affect the coil's performance at high engine speeds. To overcome this problem, a double (or two sets) of contact breakers is often used (Figure 2.266).

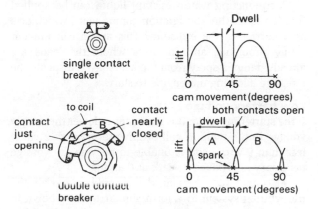

Figure 2.266 A double contact breaker

Contact set A is connected in parallel with set B so the circuit is only interrupted when both contacts are open simultaneously. As soon as contact A opens to give a spark at the plug, the other contact closes to re-establish the primary circuit.

2.28.11 Ballast resistor

The maximum output from a normal coil decreases as the engine speed is increased, so to give a more constant output, a ballast resistor is sometimes fitted in the primary circuit. This should not be confused with the resistor fitted to improve cold-starting.

At low engine speeds the relatively large current flow in the LT circuit causes the resistor to get hot, which causes the resistance of the resistor to increase and so limit the current flow. When engine speed is high the resistor runs cooler, reducing its resistance.

2.28.12 Starting problems

Starting difficulties with modern engines are rare and when they arise the trouble can often be blamed on inadequate servicing. Whenever certain models are prone to a particular fault then attention is focused on possible causes and this generally leads to either a modification or a recommendation of a suitable repair or remedy. Two examples of problems are dampness and low battery voltage.

Dampness

This can be caused by under-bonnet condensation, climatic conditions or any means that allows water to come into contact with high-tension ignition leads. Moisture on these leads causes the HT current to short-circuit to earth. This external 'leakage' of electric current prevents a spark occurring at the plug. In the past the manner in which this trouble was avoided was to protect the equipment by preventing moisture from coming into contact with the HT system. If this precaution was not followed, it meant that the distributor cap, with leads attached, had to be removed to dry out.

A conducting water-resistant liquid can be applied from an aerosol to the ignition components, which acts as a barrier to the moisture. This action can prevent future problems, and in cases where the leads are already damp, a spray from the aerosol will disperse the moisture allowing the engine to start.

Low battery voltage

If the starter motor load is sufficient to lower the supply voltage to the ignition coil positive terminal to a value less than 9 V, the coil is unable to provide the voltage necessary to produce a spark at the plug.

Manufacturers recognized this problem and altered the ignition system to a form similar to that shown in Figure 2.267. This shows that the normal 12 V coil has been replaced by a 7.5 V coil and a ballast resistance inserted in series in the primary circuit. When the engine is running, the resistor drops the voltage from 12 V to 7.5 V. During the starting phase the starter switch bypasses the resistor and applies 'full' battery voltage to the ignition coils, thereby increasing the coil output.

2.28.13 Electronic ignition

Although the conventional ignition system gave good service, the demands of lower emissions, an increase in fuel economy and reliability demanded that improvements were made to the ignition system. Modification or elimination of the contact breaker was the main alteration because the traditional mechanical contact breaker system has the following disadvantages:

1 Ignition timing varies from specification. The timing alters owing to contact breaker:
    a) Wear at the heel, cam and spindle and erosion of contact faces,
    b) Contact bounce and inability of the heel to follow the cam at high speed.
2 Dwell angle variation due to change in engine speed or wear at contacts.
3 Servicing requirements are frequent.
4 It cannot effectively control a current greater than about 3 amps through the primary circuit.

Electronic ignition systems

The function of a conventional contact breaker is to:

1 trigger the system when the spark is required.
2 interrupt the primary current flow to induce a high voltage in the secondary circuit.

Breakerless ignition systems (sometimes called 'transistorized' ignition systems) use solid-state electronic devices to perform the two contact breaker duties. Normally they work in conjunction with a low-inductance ignition coil.

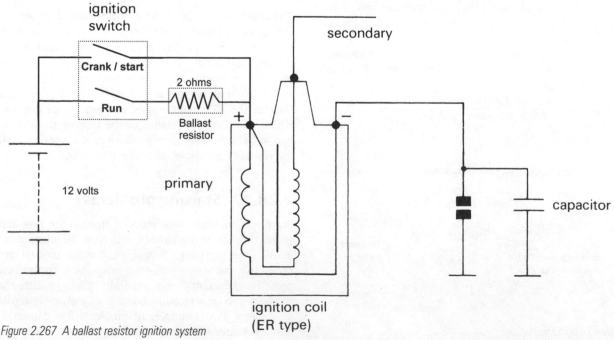

Figure 2.267 A ballast resistor ignition system

The simplified layout of an electronic system (Figure 2.268) shows its similarity to a conventional contact breaker ignition system. The distributor assembly incorporates a typical type of automatic advance mechanism (mechanical and vacuum) and HT distributor. The contact breaker is replaced by a transistorized switch (within the control module) to 'trigger the spark'.

Limitations of conventional coil systems

The conventional ignition coil primary winding has a large number of turns. During operation of this coil, interruption of the primary circuit mutually induces an EMF in the secondary, and self-induces in the primary winding, an EMF of polarity similar to that which existed before the circuit was broken.

Self-inductance slows down the rate of build-up and collapse of the magnetic field and this is one reason why the performance of the standard ignition coil falls as engine speed increases. The problem becomes acute on engines that demand a large number of sparks per second, e.g. a multi-cylinder two-stroke engine or an eight-cylinder unit.

Low-inductance coil

A low-inductance (low resistance) ignition coil has a smaller number of turns on the primary winding so as to reduce self-inductance. This gives a sharp interruption when the circuit is broken, but the lower primary resistance means that the current flow in the primary circuit is much greater. Normally it is about three times as great, so the life of the contact breakers is much shorter.

In addition to good high-speed performance the low-inductance coil also gives a good energy release during the spark period, so these advantages make this type of coil popular. Increased use of this coil type is accompanied by the need for a circuit breaker which does not have the disadvantages associated with the conventional contact breaker arrangement.

2.28.14 Trigger systems

Figure 2.268 shows the main layout of an electronic ignition system. The distributor unit is similar to a conventional unit with the exception that the contact breaker is replaced by a sensor called a pulse generator. This device generates an electrical pulse to signal to the 'control module' when a spark at the plug is required. When the trigger produces a pulse, the control module breaks the primary circuit, which causes the ignition coil to produce the HT voltage.

The three main types of pulse generator are:

- inductive
- hall
- optical.

The inductive pulse generator

Figure 2.269 shows one type of 'inductive' pulse generator, located in a distributor suitable for a four-cylinder engine. It consists of a permanent magnet, coil winding and iron rotor, which acts as a reluctor. The number of teeth on the rotor is equal to the number of engine cylinders. Two leads connect this unit to the control module.

A magnetic flux field surrounds the permanent magnet. When the reluctor rotates, the tooth of the reluctor passes the permanent magnet and the air gap

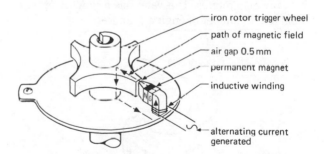

Figure 2.269 An inductive pulse generator

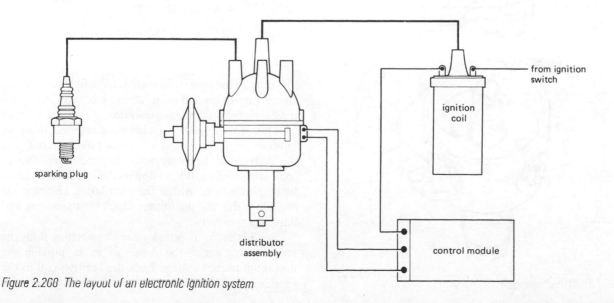

Figure 2.268 The layout of an electronic ignition system

decreases. The reluctor rotates further and the air gap increases. The movement of the reluctor changes the magnetic flux and induces an EMF in the coil. Since this EMF varies between 0.5 V and 100 V (the output depending on the speed of the reluctor), the voltage variation together with the frequency provides a sensing signal.

Note: The inductive pulse generator is also used in conjunction with many other electronic systems to monitor the speed of rotating components, e.g. wheel speed sensors on an ABS.

The size of the air gap between the reluctor and the magnet on some systems is critical; the air gap should not need to be altered during normal servicing of the vehicle.

The Hall generator

Figure 2.270 shows a distributor unit fitted with a Hall generator; it gets this name because the system is based on the 'Hall effect'.

The unit consists of a permanent magnet, vane and semi-conductor chip (Hall IC), which is supplied with a voltage. A three-core cable connects the Hall generator with the control module, Hall IC supply voltage, Hall-output signal and earth.

The Hall IC is located adjacent to the magnet. The vane is connected to the distributor shaft, which passes between the Hall IC and magnet. When the shaft rotates the vane also rotates. The vane has a number of gaps equal to the number of engine cylinders.

When the vane passes between the magnet and Hall IC, the vanes divert the magnetic flux from the magnet away from the Hall IC. The change in magnetic flux causes the Hall IC to switch the sensor on and off. A signal voltage is passed to the control module. The control module is therefore able to detect the engine speed and position from the Hall IC-generated signal. The signal for the spark occurs the instant the vane leaves the air gap.

Note: With the ignition switched on, the Hall generator produces a signal, which will trigger a spark, even when the engine is being turned over by hand. Extreme care should be exercised when handling this system owing to the risk of receiving an electric shock.

The optical pulse generator

Figure 2.271 shows a conventional distributor unit with an optical trigger. The optical system consists of a shutter (chopper), which is connected to the distributor shaft cam. Either side of the shutter is a light-emitting diode (LED) and a phototransistor (a semiconductor switch that is sensitive to light intensity).

When the distributor rotates, the shutter passes between the LED and the phototransistor and the projected beam of light is interrupted. The on and off signal voltage that is produced by this action is passed to the control module and used to determine the engine speed and position.

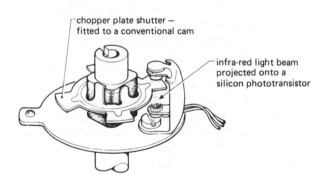

Figure 2.271 An optical trigger system

2.28.15 Control modules

The duty of the control module is to switch the primary circuit current on and off in accordance with the signal it receives from the pulse generator.

The control module (sometimes referred to as an ignition amplifier or igniter) can be fitted externally to the distributor, however with the miniaturisation of solid-state devices, it has allowed the control module to be accommodated within the distributor. Locating the module within the distributor simplifies the wiring and improves reliability.

In addition to its primary circuit switching duty, the module also varies the dwell so as to provide the maximum output voltage from the ignition coil to the sparking plugs. At low engine speeds the dwell angle is

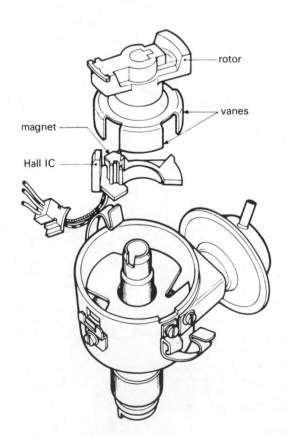

Figure 2.270 Hall generator

small and at high engine speeds, larger. Systems having this feature are often referred to as 'constant energy' ignition systems.

It is also common for control modules to feature primary circuit current limiting devices. Current limiting devices allow the initial current flow through the ignition primary circuit to be high, therefore the ignition coil can charge quickly. When the current through the primary circuit has reached a high level (coil fully charged) the control module limits the current until the end of the dwell period. With this provision it is not necessary to fit a ballast resistor in the primary circuit to limit the current flow.

The inductive storage system uses a primary circuit layout, similar to a conventional contact breaker ignition system (Kettering-type) except that a robust power transistor ('Darlington transistor') in the control module is used to make and break the primary circuit, i.e. the transistor performs the task previously carried out by the contact breaker.

The principle of a transistor

The principle of a transistor is shown in Figure 2.272.

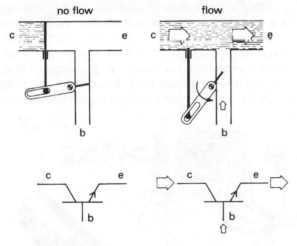

Figure 2.272 Principle of a transistor and a water valve

Using the water analogy, it will be seen that water flow in a large pipe, c to e, can be controlled by water pressure in the small pipe b. At times when the pressure of water in the small pipe is insufficient to open the small valve, the large valve will remain closed and the main flow will be interrupted. When the pressure in pipe b is sufficient to open the small valve, water will flow from c to e.

In a similar way (Figure 2.272), a transistor will not allow current flow between c and e unless a small voltage is applied to b. When a small current is applied at terminal b, the transistor allows current to flow between c and e.

Note: Transistors are switched by various methods. Refer to the *Fundamentals of Automotive Electronics* for further information on transistors and electronic circuits.

The switching feature of a transistor is of great value as a transistor enables a large current to be controlled (switched on and off) by a very small current. In this application it is used as an alternative to a relay, but whereas a relay is comparatively large and consists of mechanical moving parts, a transistor is very small and is a solid-state device.

Primary current switching

A simplified layout of the electronic ignition circuit is shown in Figure 2.273. The power transistor is connected, by terminals c and e, in the primary circuit between the ignition coil winding and earth. Terminal b is connected to the trigger section of the electronic circuit.

The transistor is switched 'on' when a voltage is applied to the base (b) which is signalled by the trigger. When this occurs, the primary circuit is closed and the ignition coil is able to build up its magnetic flux. When the control module identifies from the trigger pulse that a spark is required, the small current to the transistor base is interrupted and the ignition coil primary circuit is switched off.

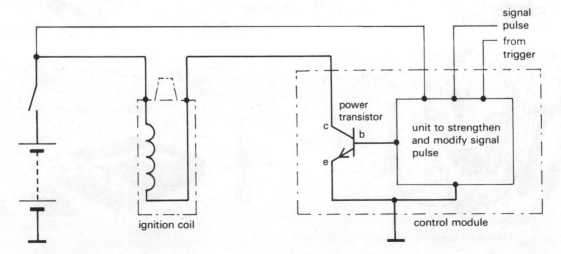

Figure 2.273 A breakerless ignition circuit

2.28.16 Computer-controlled ignition systems

Due to the demands of lower emissions levels, more power and an increase in fuel economy, breakerless ignition systems have replaced the conventional contact breaker ignition systems. With the development of vehicle electronic technology, the ignition module has been incorporated within a computer-controlled system. These systems have been developed to provide even greater control of the ignition system throughout all engine operating conditions.

Computer-controlled ignition systems eliminate the requirement for mechanical centrifugal and vacuum advance arrangements. The timing of the spark is still controlled in relation to the trigger signal (breakerless ignition systems), however, the ignition advance is set in accordance with the data stored in the pre-programmed memory of the computer.

A number of sensors are positioned around the engine to monitor operating conditions such as engine temperature, load speed and detonation. Signal information is passed from these sensors to the computer, and after the computer has compared these values with data stored in the memory, it is able to determine the optimum ignition timing for most engine operating conditions.

The ignition timing can be finely controlled during engine warm-up periods due to the additional temperature sensor information. By advancing the timing when the engine is cold, the mixture has longer to burn and therefore emission levels during this period can be significantly reduced.

A number of these computer-controlled systems also monitor engine detonation with the use of a knock sensor (Figure 2.274). The knock sensor is situated near to the combustion chamber, either in the cylinder block or in the cylinder head. The sensor contains a crystal, that when subjected to the vibrations caused by combustion knock, creates a small electrical signal which is passed to the control module. The computer retards the ignition timing by small increments until the combustion knock disappears. The computer can then slowly advance the ignition timing until the sensor detects combustion knock again. Using ignition timing control, the computer-control system can provide the optimum ignition timing under all engine operating conditions.

With computer-controlled ignition systems the engine speed and position sensor can be located on the crankshaft (Figure 2.274), replacing the distributor and associated drive mechanisms. The ignition timing is not affected by component wear, therefore the timing should remain accurate for the duration of the engine's life.

The distributor fitted to an engine with a computer-controlled ignition system only needs to fulfil its main duty, namely to distribute the HT 'spark' to the respective cylinders (Figure 2.274). The ignition timing, advance and retard is carried out by the computer being supplied various signals from sensors. The computer-controlled ignition system could therefore eliminate the

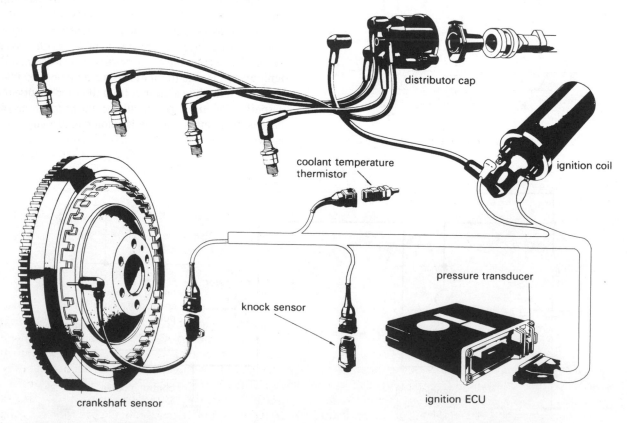

distributor cap

ignition coil

coolant temperature thermistor

pressure transducer

knock sensor

crankshaft sensor

ignition ECU

Figure 2.274 A programmed ignition system

need for a distributor, the 'spark' being supplied directly from the ignition coil. Distributorless ignition systems are used for this purpose.

The distributorless ignition system

A distributor can be eliminated by connecting the pairs of sparking plugs of 'companion' cylinders in the manner shown in Figure 2.275. The ignition system is often referred to as a 'wasted spark' type of ignition system. In a four-cylinder engine, the cylinder pairs are 1 and 4, and 2 and 3. A separate ignition coil is required for each pair of sparking plugs. Note that each end of the secondary coil is connected to a sparking plug and the primary circuit has no internal coil connection to the secondary circuit.

When pistons 1 and 4 reach TDC, one of those cylinders is completing the compression stroke (cylinder contains a highly compressed air/fuel mixture) and the other companion cylinder is completing the exhaust stroke (cylinder under low pressure). The primary circuit is interrupted in the normal manner and the secondary HT voltage produces

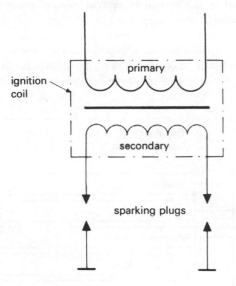

Figure 2.275 A distributorless ignition system

a spark at *both* sparking plugs simultaneously. Since only one cylinder is primed for ignition the companion cylinder spark will not perform any useful function other than completing the secondary circuit.

Note: Cylinder pressure affects the voltage required to jump the sparking plug gap. A cylinder under high pressure requires very high voltage but a cylinder under relatively low pressure requires a lower voltage. The voltage required in the low-pressure cylinder is similar to the voltage required to cross the rotor to distributor gap of a conventional ignition system.

When the crankshaft rotates through 360°, the engine cycles for cylinders 1 and 4 are now reversed although both pistons are approaching TDC (again cylinder 1 is now completing the exhaust stroke, while 4 is completing the compression stroke).

2.28.17 Introduction to engine management systems

Emission legislation has also forced manufacturers to use precisely controlled fuel systems. These have evolved into computer-controlled fuel injection systems. Computer-controlled ignition and fuel systems use similar sensor signal information, e.g. engine coolant temperature and an engine speed sensor.

Rather than have several sensors monitoring the same component on the engine, the sensor information is shared between the ignition system and the fuel systems. The ignition and fuel control systems have been integrated into one computer (ECU) referred to as an engine management system. The integration of the two systems provides precise control of the ignition timing, which operates in conjunction with the fuel system. Co-operation between the two systems provides the optimum ignition timing together with the correct mixture over the entire operating range of the engine, thus giving the lowest emissions.

Note: For further information on engine management systems refer to the following section and also to Hilliers Fundamentals Book 2 as well as *Fundamentals of Automotive Electronics*.

2.29	ENGINE MANAGEMENT

2.29.1 The requirement for an engine management system

The modern vehicle is subject to stringent emissions legislation determined by governments around the world, together with the driver expectations of higher performance and lower fuel consumption. To meet these requirements vehicle manufacturers have had to continually develop the design of the engine

components such as the inlet and exhaust systems to obtain near-perfect combustion of the air/fuel mixture.

To allow near-perfect combustion to take place, the ignition spark has to occur at precisely the right moment in the engine cycle, with sufficient energy to ignite the correct quantity of air/fuel mixture for the engine operating conditions and driver demands. Another part of the legislation dictates that the ignition and fuel systems should maintain sufficiently low emissions over the life of the vehicle and provide a diagnostic system in case a fault occurs with the system.

Previously electronically controlled systems had been used to provide control of either the ignition system or the fuel delivery system. Developments in vehicle technology produced an electronic ignition system that increased the electrical energy over the conventional contact ignition system, and provided a low maintenance ignition system. The electronic ignition system was succeeded by a 'maintenance-free' computer-controlled ignition system, which provided a system that continually adjusted the ignition timing to suit the engine conditions.

At the end of the 1980s, the requirement for cleaner emissions meant that the carburettor fuel system needed to be replaced by an electronically controlled fuel system. Although some vehicle manufacturers produced systems that provided electronic carburettor control, the more demanding emission legislation required precise control of the fuelling system. Electronic petrol injection provides precise fuel delivery and therefore cleaner emissions, usually with an increase in engine power and lower fuel consumption.

To monitor the engine's operating conditions these electronically controlled ignition and fuel systems used very similar sensor information, although each system was completely independent. Therefore, the ignition ECU used a programme stored in its memory to control the ignition timing, and the fuel injection ECU used a programme stored in its memory to control the timing of the injection point and the quantity of fuel delivered. Although the ignition system adapted itself slightly with changes in engine performance (i.e. with the use of knock sensors) the fuel injection system maintained a fixed fuel delivery based on its own sensor information.

Integrating these two control systems into one engine management system and therefore one ECU allows the sharing of information provided by all of the sensors. Such integration also allows the ignition and fuel injection programmes to interact with each other and therefore provide the optimum control signals for both ignition and fuel throughout all engine operating conditions. The requirement for lower emissions has led to the fitment of the exhaust catalyst, which reduces emissions to an even lower level. To enable the catalyst to function efficiently, the content of the exhaust gas entering the catalyst has to be precisely controlled. The engine management system has to therefore control the ignition and fuelling systems accurately, to control the content of the exhaust gases entering the catalyst. The system also provides accurate control of engine idle speed.

Figure 2.276 shows typical sensor input signal information necessary for the ECU to calculate the correct output signals used to control the various actuators, the ignition, injectors and idle speed control.

Emission regulations are becoming increasingly strict, so the engine management system has to monitor

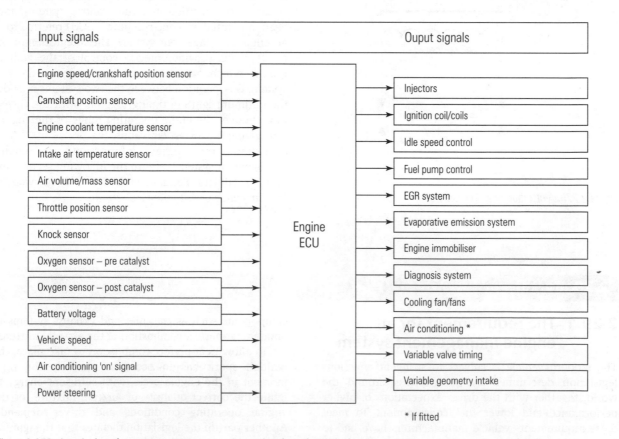

Figure 2.276 A typical engine management system, input signals and output signals

and control additional engine components as well as those that have a direct effect on emission levels. The demand on the modern engine is to also provide excellent fuel economy together with good engine power output. The engine management system can also adapt itself to the changing conditions of the engine components, thereby providing a low level of emission throughout the vehicle's life.

Integrated into the system is a self-diagnostic facility that constantly monitors the sensor and actuator signals. If a fault is detected, the system registers it and usually signals to the driver.

Note: Although the engine management system can be classed as a completely integrated ignition and fuel system, they are described separately in this section to help simplify the examination.

2.29.2 Ignition system

The engine management system controls the ignition coil primary winding by making and breaking the primary circuit, i.e. in a similar manner to that of the contact breaker ignition system.

The engine management system may also use the ignition system in conjunction with the idle speed control to provide a stable engine idle speed by altering the ignition timing to suit.

Modern engine management systems generally use distributorless-type ignition systems, either using the wasted spark principle (as detailed in section 2.28.16 of this book) or with the use of a 'direct ignition system' (DIS). Direct ignition systems use one ignition coil per cylinder. The DIS-type ignition coils are normally fitted directly to the top of the sparking plug (Figure 2.277), therefore no secondary HT leads are required.

An ignition coil primary circuit is required for each ignition coil, which is controlled by the ECU. The switching of the ignition coil primary circuit is carried out using an ignition amplifier, similar to that used with

an electronic breakerless ignition system. The ignition amplifier may be either integrated into the engine management ECU, or situated externally to the ECU as a separate assembly. Many are integrated within the body of the ignition coil.

If the amplifier is a separate unit, the ECU supplies the amplifier with a low-voltage switching signal, which the amplifier uses to control the ignition coil primary circuit in the normal manner to provide the HT spark. Each ignition coil produces one spark for each engine cycle, i.e. one spark for two crankshaft revolutions. The ignition coils are similar to those previously detailed in section 2.28 of this book.

The ECU provides an ignition control timing signal to each ignition coil, which is dependant on the firing order of the engine. For a four-cylinder engine the firing order is typically 1-3-4-2 and therefore the spark for each cylinder ignition coil will occur in that order.

To enable the engine management ECU to control the DIS, the ECU requires additional information other than that provided by a crankshaft position sensor, i.e. engine speed and crankshaft position. The crankshaft rotates twice per engine cycle, therefore cylinder 1 piston could be on one of two strokes (compression or exhaust) when the piston is at TDC. The ECU therefore requires further information on the engine cycle, i.e. when cylinder 1 is nearing TDC completing the *compression stroke*. The camshaft only rotates once per engine cycle, therefore the engine cycle can be determined from the camshaft position. A sensor, often referred to as the 'cylinder identification sensor', is located adjacent to the camshaft. The sensor provides the ECU with engine cycle information so that each ignition coil primary circuit can be controlled at the correct time in the engine's cycle.

2.29.3 Fuel systems

Modern engine management systems use a fuel injection system, which is very similar in operation to the electronic petrol injection system previously detailed in this book. To provide precise control of the fuel delivery, timing and quantity, an engine management system requires additional information on the engine operating conditions, so the following sensors are used to provide the information.

Air sensing

The intake volume of air drawn into the engine is either measured by monitoring the inlet manifold pressure, using a MAP sensor, or by monitoring the mass airflow with a hot wire (Figure 2.278) or hot film air mass sensor. The MAP and hot wire air mass sensor are described in the electronic petrol injection section of this book. The hot film air mass sensor operates using a very similar principle to that of the hot wire, the hot wire being replaced with a hot film resistor made of platinum.

Figure 2.277 An ignition coil connected to a sparking plug

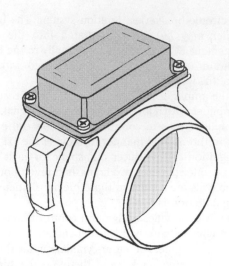

Figure 2.278 The hot wire air mass sensor

Throttle position

The throttle position switch used previously with the fuel injection system to monitor throttle position has been replaced with a throttle position sensor (Figure 2.279). The throttle position sensor incorporates a potentiometer. The wiper of the potentiometer is connected to the throttle butterfly spindle, so that as the throttle is moved from closed through to wide-open, the signal voltage from the sensor changes. The signal voltage is passed to the ECU and used to determine the exact position of the throttle and the rate at which the throttle is being opened or closed. The ECU determines when the throttle is in the idle position through the signal voltage, which is typically low, when the throttle is closed.

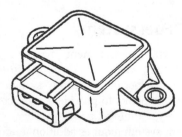

Figure 2.279 Throttle position sensor

Crankshaft and camshaft position

Engine speed and crankshaft position information is supplied from a sensor which is usually situated at the front or rear of the crankshaft. Note that distributor-located engine speed sensors are generally being replaced with crankshaft-located sensors, as worn distributor drives and associated components can affect the accuracy of the engine speed signal.

A camshaft position sensor, or cylinder identification sensor is used to determine the engine cycle position. The information is used to provide individual cylinder ignition and injection control. Many engine management systems use an inductive type of sensor that is located near the camshaft; when the camshaft rotates a single signal is passed to the ECU to indicate a reference point in the engine cycle. Some system manufacturers may use a Hall effect-type sensor.

Temperature

A sensor is used to monitor the temperature of the engine coolant (Figure 2.280). The ECU provides a rich mixture when the engine is cold which gradually weakens as the temperature of the engine increases. The ECU will also slightly increase the engine idle speed when the engine is cold. The engine management ECU usually controls the operation of the electric cooling fans. When the engine temperature has reached a predetermined temperature, sensed by the coolant temperature sensor, the ECU provides a control signal to the appropriate a relay which supplies power to the cooling fans.

An additional temperature sensor is used to monitor the intake air temperature. The air temperature sensor is usually incorporated within the airflow or air mass sensor, however, if the volume of air is monitored with a MAP sensor, the air temperature sensor is normally fitted as a separate sensor in the air induction pipe near to the air filter casing.

Figure 2.280 Engine coolant temperature sensor and intake air temperature sensor

Combustion knock

Engine combustion knock is monitored with a knock sensor, fitted to the cylinder block or cylinder head. Four-cylinder engines are typically fitted with only one knock sensor, mounted centrally between the cylinders of the engine block. Engines of five cylinders or more are typically fitted with additional sensors. The vibration created by combustion knock causes the knock sensor to generate an electrical signal, which is passed to the ECU. Combustion knock can lead to severe engine damage; the sensor must be able to recognize engine knock during all engine operating conditions especially at high engine speed and high loads. If the ECU detects combustion knock, the ignition timing is retarded until no further knock is detected; the timing is then advanced, providing the optimum ignition timing for the engine. The ECU constantly alters the ignition timing while the engine is running.

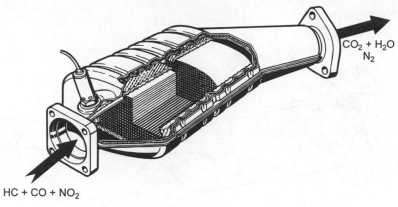

CO₂ + H₂O
N₂

HC + CO + NO₂

Figure 2.281 Internal construction of a catalytic converter indicating exhaust gas conversion

Catalytic converters and exygen sensors

To meet the required emission legislation, a catalytic converter is fitted to the exhaust system. The catalyst reduces the harmful gasses CO, HC and NO_x, which are produced by combustion. During the conversion process, these harmful gases are converted to H_2O, CO_2 and N_2, which are all harmless. To enable the catalyst to do this it is necessary to supply the catalytic converter with the correct concentration of exhaust gases. The correct concentration of exhaust gas occurs when the engine's air/fuel mixture is chemically correct, at an air fuel ratio of 14.7:1. The catalyst will not function correctly if supplied with either too weak or too rich a mixture.

Note: Providing an excessively rich or weak mixture to the catalytic converter reduces the efficiency of the catalyst. If the incorrect mixture is passed through the catalyst for a long period, permanent poisoning of the material that coats the catalyst substrate or failure (melting) of the substrate will occur.

To ensure that the air/fuel mixture is chemically correct, an oxygen (O_2) sensor (Figure 2.282) is fitted in the exhaust upstream of the catalyst, between the exhaust manifold and the catalyst. Monitoring the oxygen content in the exhaust gases indicates if the mixture is correct, too rich or too weak. The ECU senses the oxygen content in the exhaust gas by monitoring the electrical signal produced by the oxygen sensor.

The ECU responds to the oxygen sensor signal by altering the quantity of fuel injected (injection duration) to maintain the chemically correct air/fuel ratio of 14.7:1. To enable the engine to start, be driven from cold and produce power when accelerating, the engine must operate on a rich mixture. During these periods of enrichment the ECU does not respond to the oxygen sensor signal and thus is referred to as 'open-loop control'. At all other times the ECU constantly alters the fuelling to provide the correct air/fuel ratio of 14.7:1, referred to as 'closed-loop control'. During such times when the driver requires engine power, a rich mixture is required, only then does the ECU exit the closed loop control to provide a rich mixture for the

short period while the vehicle is accelerating. The ECU then returns to closed-loop control allowing the engine to operate with a chemically correct air/fuel ratio.

Oxygen sensors will not operate correctly until the sensor is at the correct operating temperature. Sensors start to function at approximately 350°C, but for the sensor to react rapidly to changes in mixture strength the temperature of the sensor needs to be approximately 600°C. Note that for short periods of time the sensor may reach temperatures of 900°C (i.e. during acceleration), however if this temperature is maintained or exceeded for too long, damage to the sensor will soon occur. The operating temperature of the sensor is affected by the location in the exhaust; too close to the exhaust manifold can lead to overheating, too far from the exhaust manifold and the sensor may not reach its correct operating temperature.

Many oxygen sensors are provided with a heating element that ensures a very short sensor warm-up time, therefore the ECU can operate using closed-loop fuel control sooner after starting the engine. On modern systems the operation of the heater circuit is usually controlled by the ECU.

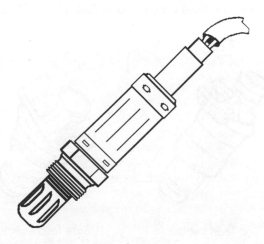

Figure 2.282 An oxygen (O_2) sensor

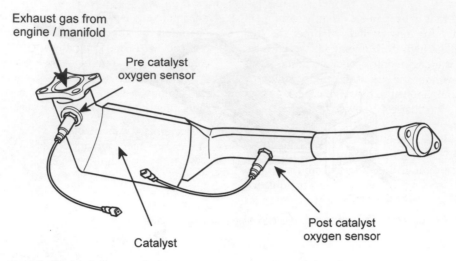

Figure 2.283 Location of pre- and post-oxygen sensors

A second oxygen sensor (Figure 2.283), located downstream of the catalytic converter, is now fitted to engine management systems. The second sensor provides confirmation to the ECU that the catalyst is functioning correctly. The ECU monitors the electrical signal from the sensor and compares the signal with the electrical signal from the oxygen sensor upstream to the catalyst. If the catalyst is functioning correctly and converting the harmful gases to harmless ones, the electrical signals from the oxygen sensors will vary from each other. If the signals are the same the ECU can identify that the catalyst is not functioning.

Injectors and injector control

The electromagnetic injectors are similar to those used with fuel injection systems. The injector is supplied with pressurized fuel which passes through the injector and is prevented from exiting at the bottom by a needle valve. When the injector is operated by the ECU the needle valve lifts from its seat and fuel is injected into the inlet manifold.

Some injectors are supplied with fuel from the inside. The side-feed injector is inserted into the fuel rail and continually immersed in fuel, which aids good starting and improves the driving response.

The injector solenoid is supplied directly from the battery via a relay, the earth circuit for the injector is controlled by the ECU. When the ECU completes the earth circuit, the injector circuit is completed and the injector valve opens and fuel is delivered into the inlet manifold. The time during which the injector is open dictates the quantity of fuel delivered to the cylinder and is referred to as the 'injection duration'. The ECU calculates the injection duration for the engine operating conditions from information provided by the sensors.

The spray pattern of the injector is dictated by the design of the engine and inlet manifold. The action of the needle valve atomizes the fuel as it leaves the injector nozzle. Many modern engines are of a multi-valve design and the shape and pattern of the fuel sprayed into the inlet manifold ensures that the fuel is mixed thoroughly in the airstream. Care is taken to prevent the injected fuel from contacting the cold inlet manifold walls.

Previous electronic petrol injection systems operated all of the injectors at the same time (simultaneously), the injectors being opened twice per engine cycle. Many engine management systems now operate the fuel injectors sequentially. Each injector earth circuit is controlled individually by the ECU and is operated once per engine cycle, normally just before the inlet valve opens for the corresponding cylinder. The total quantity of fuel is delivered for one engine cycle during one injector-opening period. The ECU uses the information provided by the cylinder recognition sensor to inject fuel into the inlet manifold at the correct time in the engine cycle, i.e. the ECU operates the injectors in the engine firing order, for a four-cylinder engine 1-3-4-2.

Idle speed and maximum engine speed

The ECU maintains the engine idle speed at a given value, the 'target' idle speed. The ECU identifies when the engine is at idle from the information supplied by the throttle position sensor. Fuel consumption at idle speed is determined by the engine's efficiency at low

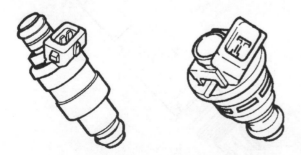

Top feed injector   Side feed injector

Figure 2.284 Types of fuel injector – top and side feed

speed. A vehicle that is used in an urban environment will be stationary for long periods of time; the fuel consumption will be high if the engine idle speed is set high. Therefore the engine idle speed should be set as low as possible without the risk of the engine stalling if additional loads are applied to the engine, such as high load electrical ancillaries, power steering, air-conditioning etc.

The engine idle speed is controlled by the engine management ECU using an idle speed control valve (Figure 2.285), although the ECU will also alter the engine speed by varying the ignition timing or adjusting the air/fuel ratio to compensate for minor irregularities in speed, maintaining a very smooth idle speed. The idle control valve is used to either regulate the bypass of air around the throttle butterfly or as a throttle motor controlling the position of the throttle butterfly. The ECU constantly alters the control signal to the motor or valve to maintain a constant idle speed.

All engine management systems limit the maximum engine speed permissible, which prevents engine damage due to over-revving. The ECU monitors the engine speed with an engine speed sensor. When

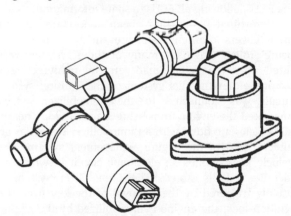

Figure 2.285 Types of idle speed control valve: stepper motor and solenoid

maximum engine speed is reached the ECU prevents the operation of the injectors until engine speed has reduced to a safe limit, then reinstates the injection control, thereby limiting engine speed. The injection system is used to control the engine speed rather than the ignition system, to prevent unburned fuel from damaging the catalyst.

Other emission controls

The engine management system also controls the fuel vapour (hydrocarbons) produced by the fuel stored in the fuel tank. This is often referred to as an 'evaporative emission system' (Figure 2.286). The fuel vapour is collected in a charcoal-filled canister and under certain engine operating conditions (i.e. cruise conditions) the ECU operates an electromagnetic solenoid valve which allows the fuel vapour to be drawn out of the charcoal canister and into the engine by the inlet manifold depression. The ECU monitors the change in mixture strength using the oxygen sensor signal and alters the volume of fuel injected accordingly to maintain the correct air/fuel ratio.

During certain engine operation, high levels of oxides of nitrogen (NO_x) are formed. Oxygen and nitrogen combine when the combustion temperatures are high. If the combustion temperature is reduced, the NO_x levels emitted from the engine can also be reduced. By recirculating a small proportion of the exhaust gas into the induction system, the combustion temperature can be reduced together with the NO_x level. If this exhaust gas recirculation (EGR) were to be constantly used under all engine operating conditions, the engine would be unstable at idle speed with a reduction in engine power output at higher engine speeds. The ECU controls the operation of the EGR valve and limits the EGR operation to prevent such effects at idle speed and high engine speeds. An EGR system is now fitted to many modern engines to reduce the combustion temperature. Alternatively some engines use variable valve timing to control the level of NO_x. Variable valve

1 Line from fuel tank to activated-charcoal canister, **2** Activated-charcoal canister, **3** Fresh air, **4** Canister-purge valve, **5** Line to intake manifold, **6** Throttle assembly with throttle valve. Δp Difference between manifold pressure p_s and ambient barometric pressure p_u.

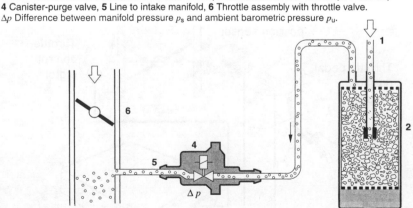

Figure 2.286 The charcoal canister evaporative (EVAP) emission system

timing allows some of the exhaust gases to enter the induction system when the valve timing is advanced during the inlet and exhaust valve overlap periods.

Other controls and sensors

The ECU may additionally control the valve timing and variable induction systems which assist in providing lower emissions together with improved engine power output.

To provide the ECU with total control of the engine's operation some systems utilize an electronic throttle (Figure 2.287), often referred to as 'drive by wire'. Previous carburettor, electronic fuel injection and engine management fuel systems used an accelerator cable which allowed the driver to mechanically open and close the throttle butterfly. Opening and closing the throttle butterfly controls engine power output from the engine. An electronic throttle control system eliminates the accelerator cable.

The ECU controls the position of the throttle butterfly from information received from an accelerator pedal position sensor together with additional information supplied from other system sensors. The engine management system ECU can therefore control the throttle butterfly opening and closing to provide the lowest emission levels together with the lowest fuel consumption possible. The accelerator pedal position is monitored by a sensor which is fitted to the accelerator pedal linkage. The sensor, similar in operation to a throttle butterfly position sensor, usually contains two potentiometers within one sensor and therefore the sensor produces two signal voltages. The use of two potentiometers in one sensor allows the ECU to detect a sensor fault and therefore provides a high level of safety in the event of a sensor failure.

The ECU controls the position of the throttle butterfly with a throttle control motor connected to the throttle spindle; as the motor rotates the throttle butterfly changes position. A throttle butterfly position sensor monitors the position of the throttle butterfly. The throttle butterfly position sensor also has two potentiometers, which again provide a high level of

safety and diagnosis. If a fault does occur in the electronic throttle control system the ECU uses a limited operating strategy that limits the engine speed and power. The engine management ECU controls the idle speed via the throttle control motor, therefore an idle speed control valve is no longer required. The engine ECU can reduce engine power by closing the throttle during circumstances in which limited power is required (i.e. traction control operation) and also operate the throttle during circumstances which require more engine power (i.e. cruise control).

Most modern engine management systems share information with other electronic control systems, e.g. automatic transmission, anti-lock brake system (ABS), air-conditioning, etc. Sharing sensor information between these electronic systems eliminates the duplication of sensors monitoring the same component, so, for instance an engine management system and an automatic transmission system both require information on throttle position. Older electronic systems shared information by monitoring the signal voltages from sensors. Modern systems use a 'multiplex communication system' to pass the information between the ECUs, allowing all ECUs to share information.

Unfortunately, it has been necessary to fit immobilizers to an engine to prevent the vehicle from being stolen. Originally many of these systems were fitted after the vehicle had left the manufacturer's factory, either the fuel system or the ignition system circuit was connected to the immobilizer, which prevented the engine from being started. Today nearly all vehicles are fitted with an immobilizer system as an integral part of the engine management system. The vehicle key contains an electronic circuit in which an identity code is stored. The immobilizer system is usually triggered by the removal of the key from the ignition lock; the engine is immobilized by the engine management ECU, preventing ignition and fuel systems from operating. Inserting the correctly coded key into the ignition lock reinstates the correct operation of the engine management system. If additional keys are required for the vehicle, each new key has to be

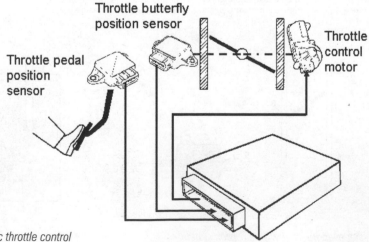

Figure 2.287 An electronic throttle control

registered with the immobilizer ECU before the engine can be started.

The engine management system also incorporates a self-diagnostic element. The diagnostic system monitors the functionality of the engine sensors together with the control systems. If the ECU detects a fault within the engine management system, it will operate, if possible, with a limited operating strategy (LOS). The LOS ensures that the vehicle can still be driven, although with limited engine power output while maintaining the lowest emission levels possible. The system is also designed to ensure that the ECU can provide the best possible fuel and ignition control to protect the catalyst against failure.

If a fault is detected by the ECU, a warning lamp is illuminated within the instrument panel to inform the driver that a fault has been detected with the system. The ECU will also store a fault code in the ECU memory which refers to the fault detected. Fault code 14, for instance, indicates an engine coolant temperature sensor fault. The technician interrogates the ECU with a diagnostic tool often referred to as a 'fault code reader', which is used to extract the fault code from the ECU memory. The diagnostic tool is connected to the vehicle via a diagnostic socket (Figure 2.288). The fault code retrieved indicates the electrical circuit in which the ECU detected the fault. The technician tests the circuit indicated with appropriate test equipment and repairs the fault as necessary. After the repairs have been successfully carried out the technician should erase the fault code from the ECU memory. Note that the diagnostic tool can often be used to provide additional information to aid diagnosis with engine management system faults.

2.29.4 Direct injection

The fuel injection systems previously described in this section are referred to as 'indirect' injection systems. The injectors are situated in the inlet manifold and spray fuel onto the back of the inlet valve before it opens. The fuel atomizes and the fuel is drawn into the cylinder with the fresh charge of air when the inlet valve opens.

A direct injection system (Figure 2.289) injects fuel directly into the cylinder combustion chamber during either the induction stroke or during the compression stroke, depending on the load applied to the engine. Direct injection fuel systems can greatly reduce emissions and fuel consumption when compared to in-direct injection systems. Manufacturers suggest during urban driving, a 25% improvement in fuel consumption can be achieved with the use of a direct injection system. The direct injection system allows ultra-lean burn air/fuel ratios to be used, as lean as 40:1 during some engine operating conditions without misfire occurring. The intake manifold and combustion chamber is designed to promote air turbulence and swirl within the cylinder when the fuel is injected.

Direct electronic petrol injection systems are similar to the indirect injection systems previously described in this section, although the injector is located within the cylinder, normally near to the location of the inlet valve. The injection timing and the fuel spray pattern changes depending on engine speed and load. The spray pattern can be changed by the pressure within the cylinder during injection, and also by varying the fuel pressure.

The fuel is passed from the fuel tank to the high-pressure pump by an electrically driven pre-supply

Figure 2.288 Diagnostic scan tool

MED 7 Motronic system for direct fuel injection on spark-ignition (SI) engines

1 Air-mass meter
  with temperature sensor,
2 Throttle valve (ETC),
3 Intake-manifold
  pressure sensor,
4 High-pressure pump,

5 Pressure-control valve,
6 Fuel distributor/Fuel rail,
7 Ignition coil,
8 Lambda oxygen sensor
  (LSU),
9 NO$_X$ catalytic converter

10 Lambda oxygen sensor
  (LSF),
11 Fuel-supply module
  including
  presupply pump,
12 Fuel injector,

13 Pressure sensor,
14 EGR valve,
15 ECU.

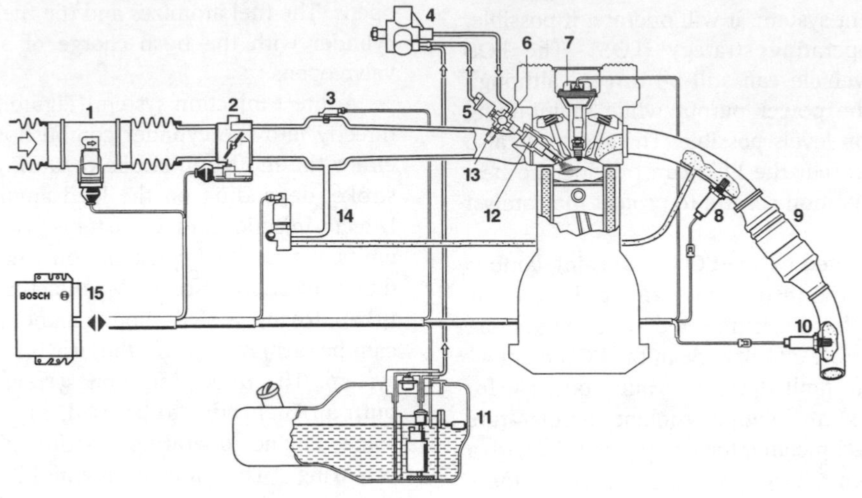

Figure 2.289 Overview of a direct injection system

pump, which is located in the fuel tank. The pre-supply pump supplies the fuel at a pressure of approximately 3.5 bar. A pressure regulator is an integral part of the pre-supply pump; excess fuel pressure is returned directly to the fuel tank.

The high-pressure fuel pump is driven by the engine, normally by the engine camshaft at half crankshaft speed. The high-pressure fuel pump increases the fuel pressure to between 80 bar and 130 bar. The fuel pressure is monitored by the ECU using a fuel rail pressure sensor. The ECU controls the fuel pressure with a solenoid-operated control valve on the high-pressure pump. Closing the solenoid valve increases fuel pressure, opening the solenoid valve reduces the pressure. By constantly altering the control signal to the high-pressure pump solenoid valve during engine operation, the output pressure of the fuel pump is maintained at the correct value. The ECU controls the fuel pressure to suit engine operating conditions.

The fuel is passed from the high-pressure pump to the fuel rail which acts as an accumulator; the pulsations caused through the pump operation and the opening of the injectors is dampened by the fuel rail. A fuel pressure regulator and a fuel rail pressure sensor are also fitted to the fuel rail. The injectors are supplied with fuel from the rail, which is used to secure the injectors by clamping them between the fuel rail and cylinder head.

The injector opening period (injection duration) and the timing of the injection of fuel in relation to the engine position is controlled by the ECU. Compared to indirect injection, injectors fitted to a direct injection system require a higher electrical current to initially

open the injectors, overcoming the higher fuel pressure acting on the injector valve. The higher electrical current levels may require an external electronic control unit in addition to the engine management ECU to provide the additional current. The ECU determines the injection duration and the timing of the injector opening, based on sensor signal information. The direct injection fuel system ECU is fitted with many of the components previously detailed for an indirect fuel injection system. The timing of the injection is dependant on the engine load conditions.

2.29.5 The operation of direct injection at different engine speeds

Idle speed and low engine loads

At low engine speeds the injection timing is retarded, so fuel is injected into the cylinder at the end of the compression stroke when the piston is nearing TDC (inlet valve closed). The fuel is injected into the air within the cylinder which is highly compressed, and the swirl of the compressed air concentrates the fuel around the sparking plug. The compressed air resists the flow of the injected fuel and breaks the fuel spray into finely atomized particles. The atomized fuel cannot penetrate the remaining compressed air within the combustion chamber and therefore an air/fuel ratio of between 14 and 15:1 exists *surrounding the sparking plug*. The remainder of the cylinder consists of an insulating layer of air and exhaust gas which protects the air/fuel mixture from contacting the cold combustion chamber surfaces, thus increasing the thermal efficiency of the engine. The layer of air/fuel mixture and the layer of surrounding air within the combustion chamber are referred to as a 'stratified charge'. The overall air/fuel ratio of the cylinder is between 30:1 and 40:1; the stratified charge allows the engine to operate on very lean mixtures which results in low fuel consumption.

Engine torque is proportional to the volume of fuel delivered by the injector; the volume of air will have little effect on the torque produced by the engine and therefore the throttle butterfly can be fully opened during these stratified charge operating conditions. Direct injection fuel systems use a 'drive by wire' or electronic throttle which is controlled by the ECU. With the engine operating with such lean mixtures it is possible to use a high volume of exhaust gas recirculation (EGR) to limit combustion temperature, thus reducing the formation of oxides of nitrogen during combustion. The lean mixtures also reduce the level of carbon dioxide (CO_2) emissions, which although not harmful to humans, contribute to global warming.

Medium to high engine loads

With an increase in engine load, the injection timing is advanced. Fuel is injected into the cylinder during the induction stroke (inlet valve open). The cylinder is filled with an evenly mixed (homogeneous) air/fuel charge at a ratio of 14.7:1. The richer mixture ensures maximum power. The engine torque is now controlled by the volume of air inducted into the cylinder. The throttle opening controls the volume of air and is in turn controlled by the position of the accelerator pedal.

Transition between low and high load conditions

The engine therefore operates at idle speed and under low load conditions with a stratified charge (fuel injected during compression stroke) where the volume of fuel and the injection timing controls the engine torque. During high engine load, the engine operates with a homogeneous charge (fuel injected during the induction stroke) and the engine torque is controlled by the throttle angle. The transition period between the two types of fuelling, is controlled by the ECU. The throttle is wide open during idle and low load conditions; to ensure a smooth transition, the throttle is closed by the ECU before the ECU changes to the homogeneous operation. The closing of the throttle reduces the pressure in the inlet manifold (vacuum) which enrichens the mixture. Simultaneously, the ignition timing is retarded to reduce the torque from the engine and ensure a smooth transition between the two operations. When the transition from high engine load to idle/low engine load occurs, the procedure is reversed.

2.30   VEHICLE EMISSIONS

2.30.1 Emission legislation

Environmental considerations have forced many countries to introduce regulations to limit the pollution caused by motor vehicles. It is claimed that emissions from motor vehicles damage human health, plant life and the environment. This problem is particularly severe in areas where the geographic and climatic conditions create an atmospheric envelope which traps the pollutants.

Countries of the world that first introduced stringent emission controls were Australia, Japan, Sweden and the USA, in particular the state of California. In recent years, as these countries lowered the maximum allowable emission limits, other countries, including those of the EU, introduced their own emission legislation and standards.

Each time new emission standards are introduced, the limits are reduced. Manufacturers have to continually update or modify their vehicles to meet the particular requirements set out for the country in which the vehicle is to be sold.

Table 2.2 indicates the main pollutants and their sources. They arise in the following systems:

Exhaust gas

The exhaust gas can contain unburned fuel (HC), partially burnt fuel (CO), dangerous nitrogen oxides (NO_x) from combustion, and lead (Pb) from petrol additives.

Crankcase

During the engine operation, emissions are passed into the crankcase, including some combustion gases which pass the piston, vaporized lubrication oil (HC) and corrosive acid compounds.

Fuel system including fuel tank

The petrol that is stored in the fuel tank gives off a vapour (HC).

Devices used to 'clean up' vehicle pollutants are costly and their use often results in a lower power output and higher fuel consumption. Consequently, manufacturers often only fit emission control devices that are required to meet the local country regulations.

Many emission controls are now fitted as standard, and some of these are detailed in this book under the appropriate section heading.

Table 2.2 The main pollutants and their sources and effects

Pollutant	Origin	Effects
CO (carbon monoxide)	Incomplete combustion or partially-burnt fuel	Poisonous to human beings when inhaled. CO adheres to haemoglobin in the blood and prevents oxygen being carried to body cells.
HC (hydrocarbons)	Unburnt fuel, vaporized fuel escaping from fuel system	Irritates eyes and nose. Cancer risk. Odour.
C (carbon)	Partially burnt fuel	Smoke – restricts visibility. Can be carcinogenic (cancer causing constituents). Odour.
NO_x (oxides of nitrogen – mainly NO and NO_2)	Very high combustion temperatures cause nitrogen to combine with oxygen	Toxic to humans. NO_x combines with water to form nitrous acid, which causes lung disorders. It combines with other exhaust products to give eye and nose irritants; also affects nervous system. Smog.
Pb (lead)	Added to petrol to raise octane rating	Toxic to humans. A cumulative poison causing a wide range of physical and mental disorders. Causes irreversible damage to children.

2.30.2   EU emission regulations for petrol engines

Before any new vehicles can be sold in an EU country, a number of vehicles must be submitted to the regulating body of a Member State to enable tests to be carried out to confirm that the vehicle type meets current EU standards.

To comply with the emission limits set by the Council of European Communities each vehicle has to complete a test cycle which reflects the vehicle being driven in an urban environment. The vehicle is started from cold and subjected to various speeds, including motorway driving at speeds up to 120 km/h. To monitor the emissions accurately tests are carried out with the vehicle attached to a dynamometer. The tests involve a standardized driving procedure including engine at idle, gear changing and braking to simulate driving conditions in a reasonable size town.

Previous emission regulations limits were determined on the cubic capacity of the engine, however in 1993 the EU introduced EU Stage I emission regulations with which all new vehicles had to comply. In January 1996, the EU imposed stricter emission limits with the introduction of emission standards EU Stage II. In 2000 vehicle manufacturers had to ensure that vehicles met EU Stage III emission standards before they could be sold. In 2005 all new vehicles must comply with EU Stage IV.

The emission regulations so far described cover engine combustion-related emissions. The vehicle is also subject to evaporative emission testing, emissions that are emitted through the vaporization of fuel stored in the fuel tank and contained in the fuel pipes. These tests are carried out in a gas-tight chamber at various ambient temperatures, with the engine stationary and running.

Engines submitted for test must be designed to run on unleaded petrol; this is to reduce and eventually stop the use of lead-based additives in fuel. In addition, the petrol tank filler pipe must be so designed that it prevents the tank from being filled from a petrol pump delivery nozzle having an external diameter of 23.6 mm or greater. This regulation means that nozzles of pumps supplying lead-free petrol have to be smaller than those used with pumps dispensing leaded fuel.

The approach adopted by an engine designer to meet the emission limits depends on the technology available to a manufacturer. The cost of fitting a catalyst and its accompanying fuel mixture control system on small and medium-sized cars, forced many manufacturers to develop lean-burn engines. Tests show that this type of engine gives a good fuel economy and a much lower emission level than conventional engines. It was expected that the lean burn-type engine would meet future emission requirements, but the introduction in 1989 of a more stringent standard based on a new European Extra-urban Driving Cycle (EUDC) has meant that to attain the new limits the lean-burn engine requires the fitment of an exhaust catalyst.

Table 2.3 EU emission regulations

Standard	Year of introduction	CO g/km	HC g/km	NO_x g/km	NO_x + HC g/km
EU Stage I	July 1992	2.72	N/A	N/A	0.97
EU Stage II	January 1996	2.2	N/A	N/A	0.5
EU Stage III	January 2000	2.3	0.2	0.15	N/A
EU Stage IV	January 2005	1.0	0.1	0.08	N/A

The exhaust emission limits detailed so far refer to petrol engine vehicles; however, diesel and dual fuel engine vehicles (i.e. LPG) have to comply with separate EU emission regulations. Diesel engines must meet emission legislation and, as in the case of petrol engines, the limits laid down by the EU are gradually being tightened to ensure a cleaner environment. Diesel vehicle emissions are similar to those of a petrol engine, covering hydrocarbons (HC), carbon monoxide (CO), nitrogen oxides (NO_x), particulate matter and smoke.

All diesel engine passenger cars sold in Europe that used an indirect injection engine (pre-combustion chamber design), were required to meet EU Stage I emissions in 1993. Direct-injection diesel engines are cleaner in operation and therefore produce lower emissions as a result of the injection design. In 1997 all diesel engine cars had to meet Euro Stage II regulations. EU Stage III regulations were implemented in 2000 with EU Stage IV to be met in 2005.

2.30.3 Control of engine emissions

Engine emissions are due to many engine components and systems, from combustion chamber design through to the ignition and fuel system designs. Various design modifications and extra fitments are necessary to control engine emissions. The following provides a summary of the emission gases and the features necessary to prevent the production of excessive emissions:

Carbon monoxide (CO)

Carbon monoxide is formed when the fuel is only partially burnt (incomplete combustion). The combination of a carbon atom from hydrocarbon fuel with an oxygen atom from the inducted air forms CO. It is produced when a cylinder receives either a rich mixture or a poor mixing of fuel and air leading to isolated pockets within the mixture. Carbon monoxide also forms when the mixture is excessively weak, although not in such concentrations as when the mixture is rich. It is therefore a good indicator of a rich mixture, although not of a weak mixture.

Methods of reducing CO emissions are:

1 **Control of mixture strength** supplied by the fuel system, especially under slow-running and cold-starting conditions. Engine management control has improved this under all conditions.
2 **Improved distribution of the fuel.** Multi-point fuel injection has overcome this problem. Distribution was difficult to achieve with a carburettor or single-point injection fuel system.
3 **More precise engine tuning.** Engine management systems ensure that the correct air/fuel mixture is supplied to the engine during all operating conditions, therefore no adjustment is possible for the technician to alter the mixture strength.

4 **Compact combustion chamber.** Modern engine design promotes very compact combustion chambers. Long narrow chambers associated with an over-square engine often gave a high CO content.
5 **Throttle positioner system.** Opening the throttle slightly when the engine is at idle or when decelerating. (This also reduces HC emission.)
6 **Precise ignition timing.** Ensures that the spark occurs at the correct time and remains constant between servicing intervals. Computer-controlled ignition and engine management systems achieve this requirement.

Hydrocarbons (HC)

Hydrocarbons in the exhaust gas are unburnt fuel that has not been burnt due to incomplete combustion. A rich mixture, lack of oxygen or excess fuel, results in high HC, as the excess fuel cannot be burnt within the combustion chamber. Any reduction in combustion efficiency will result in high HC level, i.e. a cylinder misfire caused through an ignition fault or low compression. Excessively weak mixtures will also result in high HC levels, as weaker mixtures will not support complete combustion within the combustion chamber. HCs are also formed when fuel vaporizes and escapes into the atmosphere from the fuel system.

Methods of reducing HC emissions are:

1 **Closed crankcase ventilation systems.** Unburned fuel passing the pistons and entering the crankcase is prevented from escaping to the atmosphere by a positive crankcase ventilation (PCV) system. The unburnt fuel is returned to the induction system.
2 **Sealed fuel systems.** A fuel evaporative emission control (EVAP) system seals the fuel tank, collects the vaporized fuel, passes it through a charcoal-filled canister and delivers it to the induction manifold for combustion in the engine cylinders.
3 **Altering the advance of the ignition.** Retarding the ignition timing when the engine is slow-running or decelerating. Computer-controlled ignition systems accurately control the ignition timing during such conditions, providing the optimum ignition control.
4 **Mixture adjustment during deceleration.** Fuel injection systems provide precise metering of the fuel during deceleration ('decel fuel cut off').
5 **Exhaust gas oxidation.** Many engines cannot meet the emission limits, so a catalytic converter is fitted in the exhaust system.

Carbon dioxide (CO_2)

In theory, if the correct amount of air combines with the correct amount fuel during perfect combustion, the result is carbon dioxide (CO_2), water (H_2O) and nitrogen (N_2). Carbon dioxide is a therefore a product of complete combustion. Although it is not possible for perfect combustion to occur in the real world, the more efficient the combustion process the higher the CO_2 content in the exhaust. It is therefore necessary to provide the correct air/fuel ratio to produce as near perfect combustion as possible. Any fault in the ignition system, fuel system or combustion efficiency will lower the CO_2 content in the exhaust gas.

Carbon dioxide is not harmful to humans and at present not regarded as a pollutant, but CO_2 is harmful to the environment in which we live and contributes to global warming. Therefore, if the combustion process is more efficient and uses less air/fuel the CO_2 level will also reduce.

Oxygen (O_2)

Oxygen is an essential element to the combustion process. During combustion oxygen should combine with the hydrocarbons to form carbon dioxide and water, leaving no oxygen or HCs in the exhaust gas. Although not a harmful emission, the exhaust gas contains a very small percentage of oxygen. A rich mixture will result in no oxygen in the exhaust gas while a weak mixture caused through insufficient fuel (or an air leak in the inlet manifold) will result in a high oxygen content in the exhaust gas.

A reduction in combustion efficiency (i.e. misfire) results in some of the fuel and oxygen not being burnt which will increase the oxygen content in the exhaust. Excess oxygen can combine with additional gases to form other pollutants such as NO_x. If the air/fuel ratio is chemically correct and the combustion process is efficient, oxygen output should be virtually zero.

Oxides of nitrogen (NO_x)

Nitrogen monoxide and nitrogen dioxide are grouped under oxides of nitrogen (NO_x). The atmosphere consists of approximately 78% nitrogen and 21% oxygen. The air drawn into the combustion chamber is heated during the combustion process and under certain conditions oxygen and nitrogen can combine to form harmful NO_x. The formation of NO_x typically begins at combustion temperatures of 1300°C. However, combustion temperatures can exceed 2500°C, at which point formation of NO_x increases substantially.

Methods of reducing NO_x are:

1 **Decrease in flame speed.** Exhaust gas recirculation (EGR) systems direct some exhaust gas back to the induction manifold to slow down the combustion when the engine is under high load. The EGR system reduces the maximum power of the engine.
2 **Combustion chamber alteration.** Chamber shape is changed to increase the flame speed. Used in conjunction with lower compression ratios, these chambers reduce the NO_x content, but normally only at the expense of fuel economy and engine power.
3 **Increase in air/fuel ratio.** The highest flame speed and NO_x content occurs when the mixture is about 12% richer than the chemically correct value. An engine designed to operate on a weak mixture improves the emission problem, but the vehicle driveability suffers unless the ignition timing and air/fuel mixture is set correctly. (Driveability is the manner in which a vehicle responds during acceleration, and the smoothness of engine operation throughout the speed range, especially during the warm-up period.) Some engines, such as direct injection types (stratified charge), are designed to operate on ultra-weak mixtures with air/fuel ratios higher than the operating limit of a conventional engine. The stratified charge engine uses a layer of rich mixture in the region of the sparking plug to ignite the very weak mixture in the main part of the cylinder.

4 **Ignition timing alteration.** Computer-controlled ignition systems can control the ignition timing to prevent an advance in ignition timing for a given time when the throttle is snapped open. A spark control (SC) valve in the vacuum pipe of a conventional ignition system delays the advance of the vacuum-operated distributor mechanism.
5 **Valve timing.** By changing the inlet and exhaust valve timing (overlap period) the combustion temperature can be lowered by inducing exhaust gas into the intake port. The use of variable valve timing can optimize the overlap period during engine operation.
6 **Intake air temperature.** Reducing the intake air temperature can lower the combustion temperature and therefore lower the NO_x content. If the engine is fitted with a turbocharger, the fitting of an intercooler can reduce the NO_x content significantly.
7 **Three-way catalyst.** The fitment of a three-way catalyst (TWC) in the exhaust system reduces the level of NO_x.

Note: 'Catalyst' is the name given to a material that produces a chemical reaction without undergoing any change itself.

Two-way converters change the gas by oxidizing the hydrocarbon and carbon monoxide emissions to form water and carbon dioxide. To meet tighter emission limits, modern catalytic converters have to remove oxygen from the nitrogen oxide compounds; these converters are referred to as three-way catalysts (TWC).

2.30.4 Catalytic converter construction

There are two basic types of converter, monolith and pellet (bead). In the monolith type the large catalyst surface area needed for exposure to the gas is achieved by using a honeycomb construction, whereas the pellet type has a number of aluminium-coated wire baskets to support the catalyst covering.

At present, the precious metals platinum, palladium and rhodium are the most suitable catalyst agents. The actual metal used (or mixture of metals), governs the type of converter. A two-way oxidizing type uses platinum and palladium whereas the three-way oxidizing/reducing converter uses platinum and rhodium. Since each converter contains about 4 grams of precious metal, cheaper converters using base metals such as copper and chromium are being developed. At present these metals are more prone to being 'poisoned' by small quantities of sulphur present in the fuel.

All converters become ineffective if the catalyst comes into contact with lead. Failure to use a lead-free fuel results in lead being deposited on the catalyst surface; this causes the catalyst to be isolated from the harmful exhaust gases.

Monolith type converters

The construction of this 'single block' type of converter is shown in Figure 2.290. In this type the aluminized ceramic or steel honeycomb forms a stable and secure base for the catalytic deposit of precious metals, besides providing a gas exposure area equivalent to several football pitches.

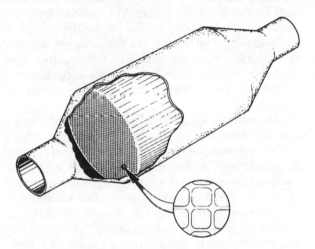

Figure 2.290 A monolith-type catalytic converter

When used with a lean-burn engine, a two-way catalyst uses the excess oxygen exhausted from the engine to react with the hydrocarbons. In the case of a three-way catalyst fitted to a conventional engine, the nitrogen oxide content in exhaust gas acts as the oxidizing agent to promote combustion of carbon monoxide and hydrocarbons to carbon dioxide and water while the nitrogen oxides, being stripped of their oxygen, are reduced to nitrogen.

The three-way catalyst only operates effectively when used with a fuel control system such as a 'closed-loop' electronic engine management system; this ensures that the air/fuel ratio is maintained at the precise stoichiometric point (chemically correct ratio). The engine management system maintains the correct air fuel ratio by monitoring the oxygen content in the exhaust gas with an oxygen sensor. The sensor passes a voltage signal to the ECU, which then alters the fuel accordingly, ensuring the air/fuel ratio is always suitable for the catalyst to operate efficiently.

For a converter to operate efficiently, and to avoid a fire hazard in the area of the converter, the engine must not:

- use leaded fuel
- be slow-run for long periods
- misfire
- operate in a condition that delivers neat fuel to the exhaust system.

To meet emission legislation, it has become necessary for the engine management system to monitor the efficiency of the catalyst, which has meant the fitting of a second oxygen sensor after the catalyst. If the catalyst is operating efficiently, oxygen will be used during the oxidizing process within the catalyst, resulting in a differing signal voltage between the two oxygen sensors. If the two sensor signals differ, it indicates that the catalyst is operating, but if the two sensor signals are similar, the catalyst is clearly not functioning correctly.

2.30.5 Lean-burn engine technology

Lean-burn engines have been designed to operate efficiently on lean mixtures up to an air/fuel ratio of about 22:1. When compared with conventional engines, the lean-burn arrangement gains in fuel economy and has a lower level of emission. For engines of capacity less than two litres the lower emissions levels, the retention of a high compression ratio and the ability of the engine to use low-octane, unleaded fuels, makes the lean-burn design attractive.

Two major sources of unburnt HC in a conventional engine are:

1 crevices in the combustion chamber that trap the unburnt mixture, especially crevices in the regions of the piston ring and head gasket
2 absorption and desorption of HC by the oil film and combustion chamber deposits.

Attention to these factors, together with features that give high turbulence at low loads without sacrificing volumetric efficiency for full-load operation, enables such engine's to operate satisfactorily on lean mixtures. At steady cruising speeds this gives a reduction in the HC emission, and because the combustion temperature is lower, the NO_x emission is also reduced. Lean-burn engines have lower power losses from pumping, heat transfer and dissociation (fuel breakdown at high temperature into its separate chemical elements without being burnt), so these factors contribute to the higher fuel economy.

Most lean-burn engines use a hemispherical or four-valve combustion chamber design and have specially shaped inlet ports, which speed up and direct the incoming mixture to give 'barrel swirl', a gas movement shown in Figure 2.291a.

The tumbling motion of the gas continues until the latter part of the compression stroke. At this stage the main swirl motion is broken up into small swirl patterns as shown in Figure 2.291c. It is this 'micro-turbulence' action, generated just prior to the point of ignition that allows the engine to operate on lean-burn mixtures.

Lead (Pb)

Lead is present in the exhaust when tetramethyl lead and/or tetraethyl lead (TML/TEL) is used as a cheap additive to improve the octane rating of a fuel, i.e. to improve the fuel's resistance to combustion knock. With an octane rating of 98 RON, high compression ratios in the region of 9:1 were used that resulted in a high thermal efficiency, hence good fuel consumption.

To comply with EU and UK regulations the lead additive in fuels has gradually been reduced from 0.84 g/litre in 1972 to 0.15 g/litre in 1989. This has made it difficult for many petrol companies to maintain the 97 RON minimum for the '4 star' grade of fuel with the result that knock-free operation of high-compression engines is not always possible.

In addition to 'leaded' petrol, the introduction of a 'lead-free' fuel, with a target lead content similar to the USA content of 0.005 g/litre, has been introduced for engines having catalytic converters and for drivers who are conscious of the ill effects of lead.

Lead-free fuel, with its lower octane rating (95 RON), may be used on about 60% of engines produced between 1985 and 1988, assuming the engine is tuned to accept this fuel type. Compared with past designs, these engines have a lower compression ratio, a retarded ignition setting and a valve and seat material that allows a low-octane fuel to be used without damage.

By the early 1990s, the EU, in company with many other countries, only allowed the manufacture of engines that were suitable for operation on lead-free fuel. Since January 2000, many countries have banned altogether the sale of leaded fuel, although a small quantity of leaded fuel may still be available for classic cars, racing cars and other vehicles that cannot use unleaded fuels.

In the future it may not be economically viable for fuel companies to produce leaded fuel. Fuel companies have developed 'lead replacement fuels' (LRP) from unleaded fuel by adding potassium-based additives to the fuel during production. LRP fuel, which has an octane rating of 97 RON provides protection against engine valve and valve seat damage, but it can damage the catalyst and oxygen sensor in a similar manner to leaded fuel.

2.30.6 Emission testing

To enable the manufacturer to sell vehicles, they must comply with the emission regulations for the market into which they are to be sold. For example, if a vehicle is to be sold into a country within the EU, that vehicle must comply with the regulations at the time of production, i.e. EU Step IV emission regulations.

In many countries it is mandatory to periodically test the emissions of a vehicle to ensure that it complies with local emission legislation. The emission levels are set by a governing body (in the UK the Department of Environment) which legislates the emission limits. If the vehicle passes the emission test together with additional checks, the vehicle is given a certificate of compliance for a specific time period, usually 12 months.

The emission test is carried out using an exhaust gas analyser. Although gas analysers are used for vehicle testing purposes, a gas analyser is a very useful diagnostic tool in the vehicle workshop. Older gas analysers measured only a single gas, carbon monoxide (CO), and therefore gave only a limited indication of the mixture setting for the engine. Modern gas analysers measure CO, hydrocarbons (HC), oxygen (O_2) and carbon dioxide (CO_2). They are normally referred to as 'four-gas analysers'. Some gas analysers may also measure a fifth factor, oxides of nitrogen (NO_x), although at present, these are not normally part of an emission test.

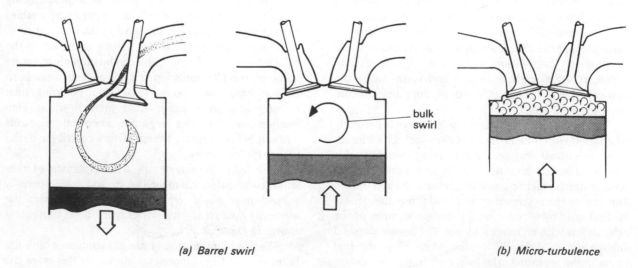

(a) Barrel swirl   *(b) Micro-turbulence*

Figure 2.291 Turbulence in a lean-burn engine

The gas analyser may also be able to calculate the air/fuel ratio mixture of the engine. From the exhaust gas drawn into the analyser, the calculation for the air/fuel ratio is based on the following components: CO, HC, O_2, CO_2. The ideal air/fuel ratio (chemically correct mixture) for a petrol engine is 14.7:1, referred to as 'stoichiometric' or 'lambda 1'. It is also essential that an engine management system maintains this air/fuel ratio to ensure that the catalytic converter functions efficiently.

The gas analyser must be set up correctly to measure the exhaust gas content accurately. The analyser should initially be switched on for a period of time to enable the components within the machine to warm up.

The exhaust gas content is measured by passing the gas through a test cell, which uses infrared radiation. The emitter has to reach a predetermined temperature before the analyser can measure gas content correctly.

When the analyser has warmed up, it will prompt the user to carry out a leak check on the sample hose. The check ensures that there are no leaks in the flexible pipe between the test probe (inserted into the vehicle exhaust tail pipe) and the gas analyser. Normally a pump within the analyser draws in the exhaust gas, but when the leak check is carried out the end of the test probe is blanked off which causes a vacuum to be applied by the analyser. After the gas analyser has warmed up and the leak check is successfully carried out, the analyser is ready to use.

Under engine operating conditions the exhaust gas contains a certain amount of soot, water vapour and other such particles especially if the engine is running poorly. If these unwanted substances were to enter the internal test chamber of the analyser, inaccurate gas analysis would soon occur. The analyser is normally fitted with a water trap, and several filters of various sizes to prevent moisture and dirt particles from entering the test chamber. It is also necessary to ensure that the gas analyser is periodically calibrated to ensure the accuracy of its measurements; this is usually compulsory if the instrument is used to certificate vehicles.

2.31 THE DIESEL FOUR-STROKE CYCLE IN DETAIL

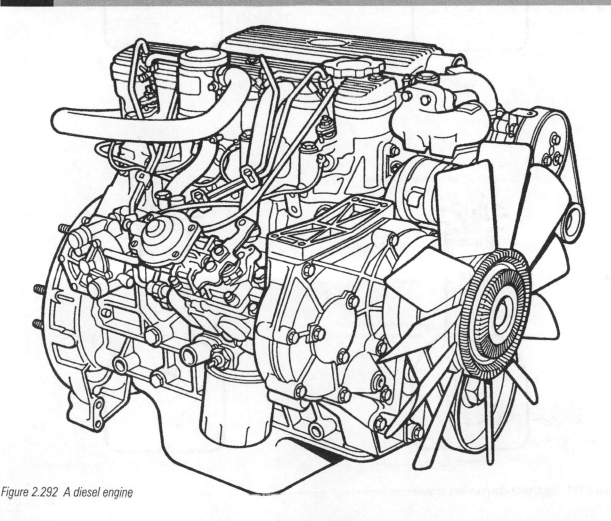

Figure 2.292 A diesel engine

2.31.1 Four-stroke operation

In many ways, the operation of cycles for the diesel (or compression-ignition (CI) engine is very similar to that of the four-stroke petrol engine. Both occupy 720 degrees, or two revolutions of the crankshaft, to complete the four strokes – induction, compression, power and exhaust.

Figure 2.293 illustrates the sequence of operations, and also the main constructional differences between petrol engines (spark ignition, SI) and CI engines, i.e. the elimination of the carburettor or the petrol fuel injection system and the substitution of a fuel injector which is used in place of the sparking plug.

A difference which is not apparent is the compression ratio, which is much higher in the case of CI engines. Engines can have ratios as low as 11:1 or as high as 26:1, whereas petrol engines seldom use a ratio greater than 13:1.

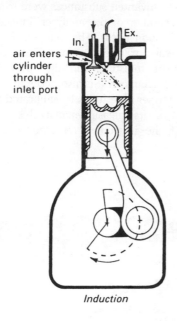

Induction

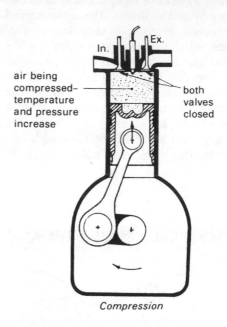

Compression

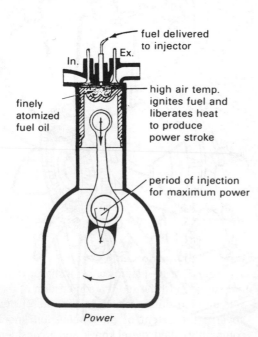

Power

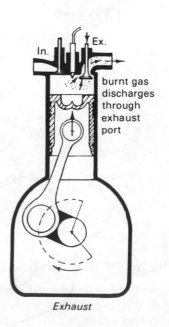

Exhaust

Figure 2.293 The four-stroke cycle – a compression-ignition engine

The CI four-stroke cycle sequence is as follows:

Induction
The descending piston increases the cylinder volume and decreases the pressure within the cylinder. Due to higher pressure of the atmospheric air, air is forced through the open inlet port into the cylinder. The inlet valve closes at the end of the induction stroke.

Compression
Both inlet and exhaust valves are closed and so the ascending piston compresses the air charge and raises the temperature of the air within the cylinder. For a compression ratio of 14:1, the final temperature and pressure will be 650°C and 3.5 MN m^{-2} (500 lbf in^{-2}).

Power
Just before TDC, fuel oil (diesel), having a self-ignition temperature of 400°C, is injected into the cylinder at a high pressure, e.g. 17.2 MN m^{-2} (175 bar), by means of an injector pump. After a short delay, the fuel begins to burn (ignition) within the cylinder and liberates heat, which raises the pressure to 6.2 MN m^{-2} (900 lbf in^{-2}), providing the thrust necessary for the power stroke. The amount of power is controlled by the period of injection, i.e. the quantity of fuel injected.

Exhaust
The piston nears the end of the power and stroke and just before BDC, the exhaust port is opened. The ascending piston pumps out the burnt gas in readiness for the new cycle.

Note: The temperatures and pressures in the cylinder quoted are approximate and are only intended as a guide, since engine design and other factors can alter conditions considerably.

2.32 DIESEL COMBUSTION

2.32.1 Combustion process

Combustion in the chamber of a petrol or spark ignition (SI) engine originates at the sparking plug and progresses throughout the combustion chamber and cylinder. In the case of a compression-ignition (CI) engine, combustion of the fuel is started by the heat of the air in the chamber. As a fuel droplet passes through the air it absorbs heat, and, if the temperature is high enough, the fuel vaporizes and ignites. Wide distribution of the fuel occurs during the heating phase and so combustion will begin at many points in the chamber.

In the case of one type of diesel engine (direct injection), once ignition has taken place, most of the burning will tend to concentrate in zones fairly close to the injector. These zones must be fed with air in order to sweep away the burned gases and supply the oxygen necessary for complete combustion.

Insufficient oxygen in the combustion region leads to black smoke in the exhaust. Since power is governed by the quantity of fuel injected, and this, in turn, is limited by the point at which smoke is emitted, some system must be used to introduce an orderly supply of air to the injected fuel. The airflow is called swirl, a term used in preference to turbulence, since turbulence implies a disorderly movement.

2.32.2 Phases of combustion

Figure 2.94 shows the phases in the combustion process of a CI engine that is operating at full-load. The combustion process of a CI engine can be separated into three phases.

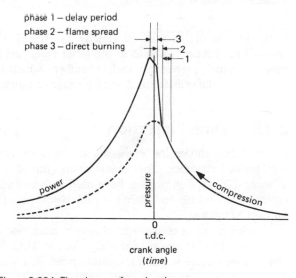

Figure 2.294 The phases of combustion

Phase 1 Ignition delay period
This is the time taken (or angle turned by the crankshaft) between the start of injection and the commencement of the pressure rise. During this important period, the injected fuel particles are being heated by the hot air to the temperature required for the fuel to self-ignite.

Phase 2 Flame spread
The spread of the flame causes a sharp rise in cylinder pressure due to the sudden combustion of the fuel that was injected during phase 1. The rate of pressure rise governs the extent of the combustion knock. This is commonly called 'diesel knock' and is considered to be a disadvantage of the CI engine.

Phase 3 Direct burning

The fuel burns as it enters the chamber, giving a more gradual rise in cylinder pressure. When the engine is operating at less than full load, this phase does not exist.

Consideration of the diagram shows that if the delay period is shortened, the quantity of fuel in the chamber is less so the engine is quieter and smoother.

Design factors which increase swirl, atomization and temperature give a shorter delay period, but perhaps one of the most important factors is the ignition quality of the fuel. Unlike a petrol fuel, diesel fuel must be capable of igniting in a heated air mass without the aid of an electrical spark. The ability of a fuel to ignite, (its 'ignition quality') is expressed as a 'cetane rating'.

Classification is obtained by comparing the fuel with a good fuel, cetane, rated at 100 with poor fuel, alpha-methylnaphthalene, rated as 0. Most of the fuels which are commercially available have a cetane rating of about 50.

2.33 DIESEL ENGINE COMBUSTION CHAMBERS

2.33.1 Types of combustion chamber

There are many good designs of CI combustion chamber, each arranged so as to provide an effective swirl pattern. These designs can be divided broadly into two main classes:

- direct injection
- indirect injection.

In the former, fuel is injected directly into the closed end of the cylinder, whereas in the latter type, fuel is sprayed into a separate small chamber, which is connected to the cylinder by a small passage or throat.

2.33.2 Direct injection

Figure 2.295 shows the essentials of an open type combustion chamber. For many years the direct injection (DI) type shown has been used on heavy and commercial vehicles and since the mid-1980s, popular for car CI engines.

A deep cavity or combustion chamber, machined in the piston, contains most of the air, since at TDC the piston is very close to the flat cylinder head. To obtain the necessary compression ratio, overhead valves are essential. Shallow recesses in the piston crown provide clearance for the valve heads.

Note: Inaccurate setting of the valve timing can allow the valves to strike the piston.

A multi-hole injector allows finely atomized fuel under high pressure (approximately 175 bar) to penetrate the fast-moving air and just enter the cavity of the piston.

Swirl is produced in two planes, vertical and horizontal. The ascending piston causes the air to be directed into the cavity and move in the manner shown in Figure 2.295. As the piston approaches TDC, this motion will speed up because of the squish action of the air between piston and head. Horizontal or rotary swirl is obtained by inclining the inlet port tangentially to the cylinder, or masking the inlet valve. Figure 2.295 shows

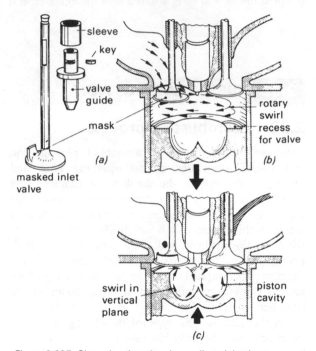

Figure 2.295 CI combustion chamber – direct injection type

the latter arrangement, which is the most popular. Combining both swirl movements gives a vortex airflow in the cavity, and ensures a good supply of oxygen to the combustion region.

2.33.3 Indirect injection

Up until the mid-1980s the indirect injection (IDI) type was commonly used on small CI engines as fitted to light vehicles. Compared with the traditional heavy vehicle DI engine, the IDI ran more smoothly and since the IDI type used lower injection pressures, the engine was more able to operate over a large speed range.

Many IDI combustion chambers have been based on the Ricardo Comet design shown in Figure 2.296. In this arrangement a 'swirl chamber' is connected to the main

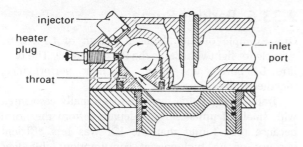

Figure 2.296 CI combustion chamber – indirect injection type

chamber by a throat, which allows it to operate at a higher temperature than the surrounding metal.

Air is pumped through the hot throat into the chamber during the compression stroke, so by the end of this stroke the ante-chamber contains very hot air in a high state of swirl. Fuel injected into this fast moving air mass is quickly atomized into a very fine state. This atomization is very effective even though the fuel is injected in the form of a 'soft' spray by a pintle or single-hole nozzle set at a comparatively low pressure (e.g. 100 bar).

After combustion has been initiated in the swirl chamber, burning fuel, together with the unburnt and partially-burnt fuel, is carried into the piston cavity in the main chamber. When the injection period is increased to produce a higher engine power, most of the fuel that is injected towards the end of the spraying period does not ignite until it mixes with the air in the main chamber. This ensures that during the combustion period the burning can continue for a relatively long time until it finally reaches a stage at which the fuel cannot find sufficient oxygen. Beyond this point black smoke starts to be emitted from the exhaust. The black smoke point dictates the maximum amount of fuel that can be injected without sacrificing economy and also represents the maximum power that can be legally obtained from the engine.

In an IDI engine the combination of hot air and excellent atomization gives a short ignition delay. Compared with the DI type, the intensity of diesel knock is lower, the engine runs more smoothly and the cetane rating of the fuel that is required can be lower with IDI engines.

2.33.4 Preheating system

All CI engines require some special provision for cold-starting. The injection of a larger quantity of fuel, and the greater amount of easily ignitable fractions contained in the injected charge, are generally sufficient to start a cold DI engine although many modern DI engines require a provision for cold-starting to reduce harmful emissions when the engine is initially started.

The greater heat losses of IDI units require these engines to have extra cold-start provisions. Compared with ratios of about 16:1 that are used with DI, IDI

engines use ratios around 22:1, or, in some cases as high as 30:1.

In addition to the cold-starting requirement, a high ratio is also used to raise thermal efficiency, i.e. economy, to that of a DI engine. This feature tends to counteract the greater heat loss due to the larger surface area of an IDI combustion chamber.

When cold-starting a CI engine, one or more of the following are used:

Heater plug
This is a hot bulb, often called a 'glow plug' that is fitted in the combustion chamber (Figure 2.297). The air in the chamber is heated by an electrical heating element for a few seconds prior to starting the cold engine. The time the glow plugs operate is usually dependant on engine temperature; the colder the engine, the longer the glow plugs function. The glow plugs are usually controlled automatically by a timer relay or the electronic control unit (ECU) when the ignition is switched on; the controller usually illuminates a glow plug warning light situated in the instrument panel to warn the driver when the glow plugs are operating. Modern DI engines use a glow plug fitted to each cylinder for this purpose. The glow plugs used on many modern CI engines remain switched on after the engine has started for a few minutes 'post glow' normally with a reduced electrical current to prevent the glow plugs from overheating and burning out. The post glow function provides additional heat in the combustion chamber to improve the combustion process and therefore lower emissions when the engine is started from cold.

Manifold heaters
This is an electrical unit fitted to pre-heat the air as it passes through the inlet manifold to the cylinder.

Pintaux injector
This is a pintle-type injector, which has an auxiliary hole to direct fuel down the throat of the chamber during the cranking period.

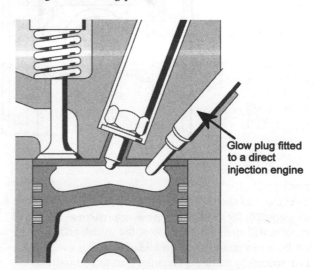

Figure 2.297 Glow plug fitted in a combustion chamber

2.33.5 Modern power units used on light vehicles

The small, modern CI engine, with a fuel consumption up to 40% better than that of a petrol engine of equivalent power, has made the CI engine very attractive for use in cars. This advantage becomes even more attractive when the vehicle is used more than average to fully exploit the saving in fuel cost and offset the higher initial cost of the engine.

The benefit of low fuel consumption, together with the rising demand for this type of engine, has induced car manufacturers to offer a diesel alternative engine for cars across most of their range.

In the past, small CI engines were noisy and unresponsive compared with a comparable spark-ignition engine, but considerable advancements in technology have been made during recent years. Combustion improvements and sound damping have reduced the noise levels, and with the advancement of electronically controlled diesel fuel systems the performance gap has been significantly narrowed.

2.33.6 Perkins Prima

One example of an advanced design of CI engine suitable for light vehicles is the Perkins Prima. The two-litre DI power unit offers excellent performance, together with economy.

Traditionally IDI is the system normally associated with small CI units. Perkins departed from the norm because they found that the IDI was less efficient because of its high-energy consumption; this was caused by the high compression ratio and large pumping losses that resulted from the rapid movement of air between the main chamber and the swirl chamber.

Figure 2.298 shows the layout of the Perkins Prima combustion chamber. The 'bowl-in-piston' combustion cavity, together with an inclined (helically shaped) inlet port to achieve high-speed rotary swirl, gives high power and excellent economy up to a rated engine speed of about 4500 rpm.

Glow plugs are used for cold-starting which operate when the driver turns the ignition key to the ignition position. During the cranking period the injection timing is advanced to give easier combustion, but when the engine fires the injection timing is quickly returned to normal; this reduces noise and gives smoother operation during warm-up.

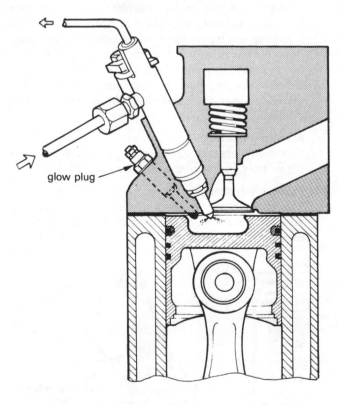

glow plug

Figure 2.298 The Perkins Prima combustion chamber

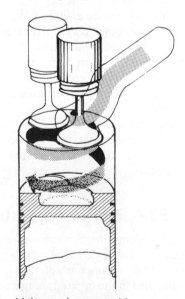

high-speed rotary swirl
produced by inclined inlet port

2.34 MAIN COMPONENTS OF THE DIESEL ENGINE

2.34.1 Diesel engine main components

The higher cylinder pressures of CI engines demand stronger components although, for economic reasons, manufacturers of light CI units often use some engine components, such as cylinder blocks and crankshafts, that are interchangeable with spark-ignition (SI) versions. Although some of these components may seem similar in appearance, different manufacturing processes together with minor structural changes may be used to make the components stronger and more durable for use with the CI engine.

2.34.2 Cylinder block

The cylinder block is normally made from cast iron that has the excellent strength properties required to withstand the forces exerted by the pistons, crankshaft and other reciprocating components.

2.34.3 Piston

Pistons are usually made of aluminium alloy, often with steel inserts in the skirts to control expansion. They are made longer than petrol engine pistons to accommodate the combustion cavity. Three or more piston rings are used and the top ring groove is generally armoured by using an insert to resist wear. The crown of the piston is usually shaped to allow for combustion chamber design and valve operation.

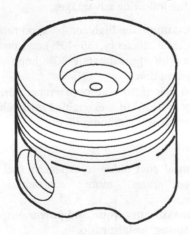

Figure 2.299 A typical diesel engine piston

2.34.4 Crankshaft

The crankshaft used with a CI engine has to be more robust to withstand the higher pressures and shock loads, and fillets are normally rolled to improve fatigue life. Generally the main bearings, situated between each crank throw, are copper–lead and the big-end bearings are either fully copper–lead or copper–lead/tin–aluminium with the heavier duty material fitted to the connecting rod side of the bearing.

2.34.5 Cylinder head

Similar to the SI engine cylinder heads, cylinder heads fitted to a CI engine seal the top of the cylinder and accommodate the inlet and exhaust valves and possibly the camshaft if the engine is of OHC design. Diesel fuel injectors are normally situated in the cylinder head, the injector nozzles inject fuel into the combustion chamber which is an integral part of the cylinder head if the engine is of indirect injection design. The glow plugs used for cold-starting are fitted into the cylinder head, so the tip of each glow plug enters the combustion chamber.

The cylinder head has to withstand the very high compression in the CI engine and therefore has to be very strong. Many CI engine cylinder heads are manufactured from cast iron, cast iron being stronger than aluminium, which is a common material for SI engine cylinder head.

2.34.6 Inlet manifold

The inlet manifolds used with a CI engine serve a similar purpose to those in a petrol engine fitted with a fuel injection system. The purpose of the manifold is to distribute the air to each cylinder inlet port. Air cleaning and induction silencing are still necessary, so these functions, together with manifold heating for starting, speed governing and turbo-charging, require a suitable manifold. Note that many older diesel engines are not fitted with a throttle butterfly at the beginning of the inlet manifold. The volume of fuel delivered during the injection period controls the power and engine speed of the CI engine, therefore a throttle butterfly is not required. Note that many modern electronically controlled diesel engines are fitted with a throttle valve; the valve is used to control emissions during certain engine operating conditions.

It should be noted that although not used extensively, some manufacturers have used variable-length induction to increase the volumetric efficiency of the CI engine and therefore to increase the power produced and help reduce emission levels.

2.34.7 Valve timing

The valve opening and closing periods used for light vehicle CI engines applications are similar to those used on the SI engine, because the breathing requirements are basically the same. Heavy CI engines have a much lower maximum operating speed (e.g. 2000 rpm) because of the mass of the components, so in these the valve periods are smaller; inlet valve angles of 10° before, to 40° after, and exhaust angles of 40° before, to 20° after, are typical on heavy engines.

Modern CI engines are constantly adopting much of the technology that has evolved for SI engines, such as variable valve timing to provide the optimum filling of the cylinder with a fresh charge of air, therefore increasing the volumetric efficiency of the engine.

2.34.8 Valve operating gear

Compression-ignition engines use very similar types of valve operating gears (i.e. camshaft configuration, camshaft drive etc) to SI engines. Although many older types of CI engine use two valves per cylinder (one inlet and one exhaust valve) many modern diesel engine manufacturers are developing multi-valve engines with, for example, two inlet valves and two exhaust valve per cylinder, increasing the volumetric efficiency of the engine.

The camshaft is driven by the crankshaft, using either a chain, gear or timing belt drive (Figure 2.300). The main difference is that the diesel injection pump is usually driven from the camshaft drive, the injection pump, like the camshaft and SI engine ignition distributor, needs to be driven at half engine speed to provide the diesel fuel injection for each cylinder. Many manufacturers use a flexible rubberized timing belt similar in construction to that used in the SI engine.

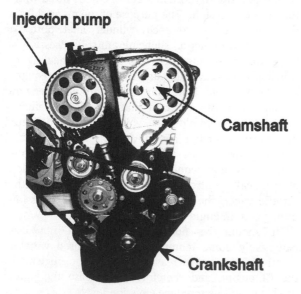

Figure 2.300 Diesel engine valve gear layout (timing belt driven)

Once again, as with many diesel components, the belt is slightly larger and stronger to withstand the additional forces applied during engine operation. If a rubber timing belt is used to provide the drive from the crankshaft to the camshaft it is essential that the timing belt is replaced at the recommended service interval as detailed by the vehicle manufacturer. Due to the high compression ratios used in CI engines, the valves are very close to the piston crowns during engine running; if the belt fails during engine operation valve damage can occur. Many vehicle manufacturers fit additional warning indicators which alert the driver when a critical component such as a timing belt needs to be replaced.

2.34.9 Engine lubrication

High combustion temperatures and elements such as sulphur in the fuel make the CI engine more prone to deposits of carbon, formation of gums around the piston rings, and lacquer deposits on the side of the pistons.

These conditions are minimized by using a 'heavy-duty detergent oil'. Detergent additives in these special oils maintain engine cleanliness, and dispersant additives hold the carbon and soot in suspension in the oil so that the foreign particles harmlessly pass around the system until the oil is next drained.

2.34.10 Advantages and disadvantages of diesel engines

Compared with a petrol engine of the same size, a diesel engine has the following advantages:

1 **Fuel economy** – the high compression ratio gives a good thermal efficiency (35–40%) and provides the operator with approximately 30% improvement in fuel consumption.
2 **Reduced risk of fire** – at room temperature, the low volatility of DERV (diesel engined road vehicle) fuel makes accidental ignition difficult.

The disadvantages are:

1 **High initial cost** – due to expensive fuel injection equipment and more substantial engine construction.
2 **Lower maximum torque and power output.**
3 **Lower power/weight ratio.**
4 **Greater noise in operation.**

2.35 MECHANICAL ASPECTS OF THE DIESEL FUEL SYSTEM

2.35.1 Mechanical systems

Early CI engines used air pressure to deliver the fuel into the cylinder, but modern CI engines use high-pressure fuel delivery pumps; the fuel is delivered via small-bore steel pipes to the injector. The fuel pump system (or jerk pump), which is shown in simplified form in Figure 2.301, is often termed mechanical or solid injection pump, since the ejection of the fuel is brought about by the action of the plunger on a 'solid' column of oil.

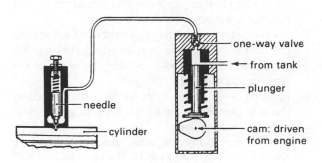

Figure 2.301 Principle of the mechanical system of fuel delivery

The fuel equipment must be capable of accurately metering and delivering the fuel at the correct pressure and at the precise time. When it is said that the volume of fuel injected into the cylinder per cycle is often less than the volume of a small pinhead, and the variation between cylinders must not exceed 2%, it can be appreciated that a high-precision unit is required.

Very close limits and small clearances demand special precautions to prevent dirt from entering the system. For example, the clearance between plunger and barrel is less than 3 μm (0.0001 inch). Clean fuel, regular replacement of filters and close attention to cleanliness during overhaul of equipment are all essential if the apparatus is to perform its exacting task.

The layout of a typical system is shown in Figure 2.302. A low-pressure feed pump or gravity supply ensures that the injection pump receives a continuous flow of clean-filtered fuel. The system incorporates many filters: a fine gauze unit(s) is fitted on the inlet side of the pump, and a felt, cloth or paper filter is inserted between feed pump and injection pump. Injection, in the case of a four-stroke, occurs every other revolution and therefore the injection pump must

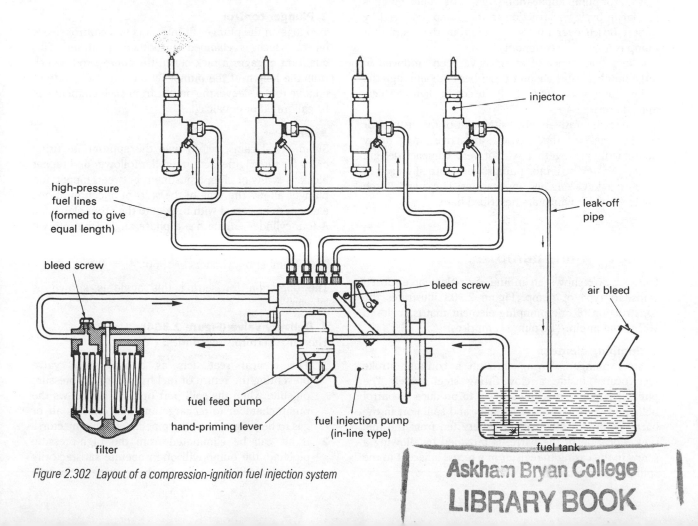

Figure 2.302 Layout of a compression-ignition fuel injection system

be driven from the timing gears or camshaft at half engine speed. At the appropriate time, fuel under high pressure is conveyed to the injector by fuel lines, which should be of equal length to maintain an equal injection delay (the period between the time when a high pressure builds up in the pump and the time when fuel begins to spray from the injector).

Lubrication of the main working parts of the system is usually done by the fuel oil itself. A predetermined leakage past the injector needle is directed to waste or returned to the fuel tank.

The pump will not function correctly if air is present in the system, and therefore venting screws or valves are provided at various points to allow air to be bled out. It is normally necessary to bleed the fuel system after disturbance of supply lines or 'running-out' of fuel. Usually a priming lever allows the feed pump to be operated manually. With the air vent (bleed screw) open, operation of the feed pump forces a column of fuel through the line and allows the air to be driven from the system.

2.35.2 The injection pump

Until recently most CI engines were fitted with either an in-line pump or a distributor pump often referred to as a distributor pump application (DPA). The in-line pump is similar in basic construction to the pump produced by Robert Bosch over fifty years ago, but the distributor pump is now more commonly seen.

Since both types of pump have been produced in large numbers, this chapter describes both although the in-line pump is now rarely used in light vehicle applications.

The comparatively low initial cost of the distributor pump makes this type attractive to many manufacturers, together with it very compact design. Two types of distributor pumps were normally used in light vehicle CI engines applications: Lucas and Bosch pumps, both of which are described here.

2.35.2 In-line pump

Figure 2.302 shows an in-line, four-element enclosed camshaft type of pump. Figure 2.303 illustrates the construction of one pumping element that is enclosed within the pump. The pump comprises:

1 Pumping element

A steel plunger moving through a constant stroke reciprocates inside a close-fitting steel barrel. The plunger is partly machined away to produce a control helix and vertical groove. An inlet and spill port in the barrel communicates with a gallery fed from the fuel tank. Location of the barrel is provided by allowing a screw in the casing to register in a recess adjacent to the spill port in the barrel.

Partial rotation of the plunger varies the output from zero for stopping the engine, to maximum for starting. Between these limits a variable supply of fuel is necessary to meet engine power and speed requirements.

The operation of the pumping element is shown in Figure 2.303. The positions of the element are as follows:

A When the plunger is at BDC, the depression in the pump chamber causes fuel to enter both ports.

B This position, known as the 'point of port closure' (or 'spill cut-off' with this type of pump), is generally regarded as the theoretical point of injection. Both ports have been covered, so the ascending plunger raises the pressure of the fuel to produce injection.

C Injection stops when the edge of the helix uncovers the spill port. Pressure is relieved by fuel passing down the vertical groove, around the waist of the plunger and out of the spill port.

D Rotation of the plunger causes the helix to uncover the spill port either earlier or later, to give less or more fuel respectively.

E Moving the plunger to make the vertical groove coincide with the spill port means that the port will remain open, therefore no fuel will be delivered and the engine will stop.

2 Plunger control

Two lugs on the plunger fit into slots in a control sleeve on to which is clamped a toothed quadrant. This quadrant engages a rack cut in the control rod, which runs the length of the pump. By moving the quadrant relative to the sleeve, the output from each element can be calibrated or equalized.

3 Drive

Symmetrical cams, set to give the appropriate firing order for the engine, act on a roller follower and tappet block. A screw or shim adjustment between tappet and plunger allows the time of the start of injection of one element to be varied with respect to the other elements. A four-cylinder engine has a phase angle (the interval between injections) of:

$$360°/\text{Number of cylinders} = 360°/4 = 90°$$

The operation for setting this angle is known as 'phasing'.

4 Delivery valve (Figure 2.304)
The valve performs two duties:

1 The conical seat acts as a non-return valve preventing the return of fuel from the high-pressure pipeline when the spill port opens. This allows the pump chamber to recharge and also enables air or gas to be purged from the pipeline via the injector.

2 If air can be eliminated from the high-pressure pipeline, the pump will often operate satisfactorily without a delivery valve. On the opening of the spill

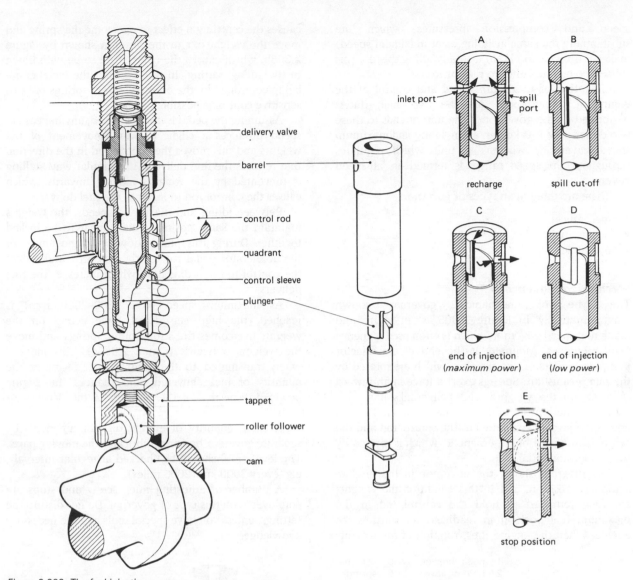

Figure 2.303 The fuel injection pump

port the pressure at the injector will fall rapidly to pump inlet pressure giving a sharp closing of the injector. The fitting of a non-return valve, however, traps pressure in the pipeline while the injector is still open. This pressure can only be relieved by fuel continuing to pass the injector at a diminishing

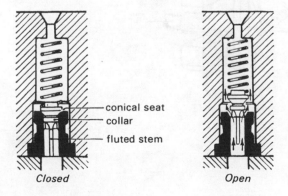

Figure 2.304 Delivery valve

pressure, resulting in the last few droplets of fuel merely 'dribbling' out, causing incomplete combustion, carbon formation, smoky exhaust and high fuel consumption.

The collar below the conical seat acts as a piston and withdraws a small amount of fuel from the high-pressure pipeline as the valve closes, causing the necessary rapid pressure drop to ensure a sharp cut-off of injection.

5 Governor

Higher gas pressures in the cylinder of a CI engine usually demand stronger components than those used in a petrol engine. Strength is normally improved by increasing the component dimensions, but this also increases weight and leads to engine damage if the speed exceeds a given value, which is governed by the components' strength/weight ratio.

A pump with a 'rising output' characteristic (i.e. for a given control rod setting the output increases with speed and compression pressures, which are substantially the same at idling as at maximum speed) makes it difficult to obtain a steady idling speed – this causes the engine either to race or to stall.

Limitation of maximum speed and control of the engine at idling speed are the two main duties performed by the governor. If the unit attends to these two duties only, it is known as an 'idling and maximum speed governor', whereas a unit which regulates throughout the speed range, is termed an 'all-speed governor'.

There are three main types of governor:

- mechanical
- pneumatic
- hydraulic.

Mechanical governors

The type of mechanical governor shown diagrammatically in Figure 2.305 is an idling and maximum speed governor, which is often used on heavy vehicle engines. Mounted at the end of the injector pump, it consists of two weights, which are rotated by the pump camshaft. Springs exert a force in an inward direction on the weights, and bell cranks link each weight to the bottom end of a floating lever. The top end of the lever is connected to the control rod and the centre is mounted on an eccentric, which is rotated by the accelerator pedal.

The diagram shows the governor in the engine-stationary position, and in this condition the weights are fully retracted to hold the control rod in the maximum fuel position in readiness for starting the engine. When the engine fires, rotation of the weights causes the centrifugal effect to overcome the spring and move the weight out to the position shown by Figure 2.305b, which causes the control rod to be withdrawn to the 'idling' setting. In this position the weights are being controlled by the outer (weaker) springs only, so sensitive control is possible.

Assuming the pedal is not depressed, any increase in speed produces a slight outward movement of the weights and this moves the control rod in the direction that reduces the fuel delivery. In a similar way, stalling is prevented by the weights moving inwards, which causes the control rod to increase the fuel delivery.

Between idling and maximum speeds, the weights maintain the same position, and appear to be locked together. During this phase, downward movement of the accelerator pedal rotates the eccentric and moves the control rod in a direction, which increases the fuel delivery.

As maximum speed (e.g. 1800–2000 rpm) is reached, the high centrifugal force acting on the weights overcomes the strong outer springs and move the weights outwards (Figure 2.305c). This motion, when transmitted to the control rod, decreases the quantity of fuel delivered, and reduces the engine power, irrespective of the position of the accelerator pedal.

A small quantity of engine oil, contained in the separate governor housing, lubricates the moving parts. The level of oil should be checked at regular intervals, e.g. every 3000 km (2000 miles).

A number of adjusting nuts, screw and stops are employed with this type of governor. Do not disturb the settings, unless you have special tools and the necessary knowledge.

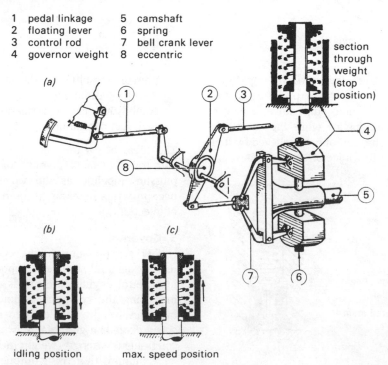

1	pedal linkage	5	camshaft
2	floating lever	6	spring
3	control rod	7	bell crank lever
4	governor weight	8	eccentric

Figure 2.305 Idling and maximum speed mechanical governor

Pneumatic governors

In-line pumps fitted to light CI engines often use the all-speed type of governor. Holding the accelerator pedal in a set position, the governor maintains a constant speed up to the point where the load on the engine is too great.

Figure 2.306 shows the main construction of this type. A spring-loaded diaphragm, connected to the control rod, is mounted to seal a chamber, which is linked by a pipe to a venturi control unit in the inlet manifold. A butterfly valve, fitted in the waist of the venturi, is connected directly to the accelerator pedal.

When the engine is at rest, the diaphragm spring forces the control rod to the maximum fuel or excess fuel position.

Note: Many pumps are fitted with an excess fuel device. This is a manually operated control fitted at the end of the pump that enables extra fuel to be delivered for cold starting. It cannot be operated from the driving position.

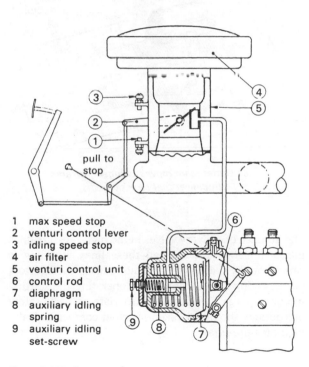

1 max speed stop
2 venturi control lever
3 idling speed stop
4 air filter
5 venturi control unit
6 control rod
7 diaphragm
8 auxiliary idling spring
9 auxiliary idling set-screw

Figure 2.306 A pneumatic governor system

Closing the accelerator pedal after starting produces a depression in the venturi and diaphragm chamber. This causes atmospheric pressure to force the diaphragm and control rod to the idling setting. With the pedal in any set position, an increase in speed increases the venturi depression, which reduces the control rod opening. A decrease in speed will produce the opposite condition.

As the accelerator pedal is depressed, the butterfly valve is opened and the venturi depression is decreased. This causes the spring to open the control rod and increase the engine speed until a balance is reached between the spring thrust and venturi depression.

A stop screw, acting on the lever controlling the butterfly valve, limits the maximum speed. When the valve reaches its stop, any tendency for the engine to increase speed will intensify the venturi depression and reduce the control rod opening.

A 'stop' control on the dashboard enables the driver to override the governor and move the control to the 'no-fuel' position.

Note: Do not start the engine with any part of the governor system disconnected.

Hydraulic governors

This type of governor is used with in-line pumps where smooth, slow idling speeds are demanded (e.g. for coaches) but high cost tends to limit its use. A gear-type oil pump, driven from the end of the pump camshaft supplies oil through various valves to operate a piston linked to the control rod.

2.35.3 Lucas distributor pumps

Figure 2.307a shows a DPA-type pump suitable for a four-cylinder engine. Connected to the engine by a flange and driven by a splined shaft, this unit resembles the distributor used on a petrol engine; fuel lines to the injectors occupy the position of the HT leads.

A single-element, opposed-plunger pumping unit supplies fuel to either a four- or six-cylinder engine. Except for the cam and the number of outlet ports, the other parts are the same for both four- and six-cylinder engines. Operated by a non-rotating cam, the single element provides a correctly phased and balanced output of fuel over a very large speed range.

The pumping unit, shown diagrammatically in Figure 2.307b, consists of two plungers mounted in a rotor, which turns in a fixed hydraulic head. Ports in the head and rotor line up in certain positions to allow either inward or outward flow of oil. Figure 2.307c shows the inlet port open. Pressure from a transfer pump fitted at the end of the main pump, directs fuel oil along the centre of the rotor to force out the plungers. Figure 2.307c shows that the uncovered outlet port will allow the cam to force the plungers together and discharge the fuel to the injector.

Cam ring shape

Dribble is eliminated by using a special cam design to stop fuel delivery sharply (Figure 2.308). At the end of each pumping stroke the roller, which operates the pumping plunger, suddenly moves outwards and drops the pumping pressure.

This retraction arrangement overcomes the need for a delivery valve.

Fuel system

Figure 2.309 shows a typical fuel system. A feed pump supplies fuel via a filter, to a sliding vane transfer pump which directs the oil through a driver-controlled metering valve to the rotor. Transfer pump pressure is

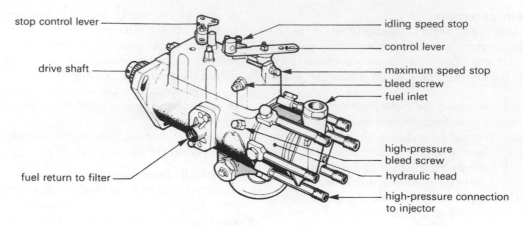

(a) Distributor pump fitted with mechanical governor

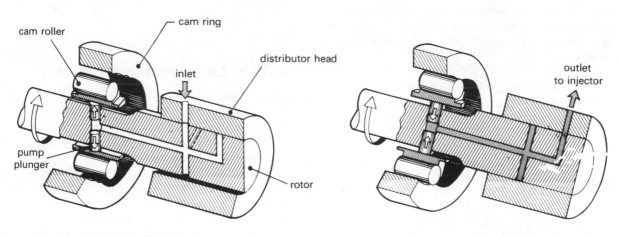

(b) Inlet (fuel forces plungers apart)

(c) Outlet (cam moves plungers inwards to deliver fuel to injectors)

Figure 2.307 The Lucas CAV distributor pump

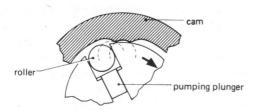

Figure 2.308 cam shape to retract roller

limited by a regulating valve, and oil, which escapes from the pumping element, returns to the filter after lubricating the working parts.

The quantity of fuel delivered to the injector is governed by the position of the metering valve. Figure 2.309 shows a partly opened valve restricting the flow of oil to the rotor. This reduction in oil flow prevents the full outward travel of the plungers, hence the shortened stroke gives reduced fuel and lower engine power.

On fitting a 'new' pump, it is essential to fill the pump completely with clean fuel oil before attempting to start the engine. Various venting screws are provided to bleed air from the system.

The absence of delivery valves in the high-pressure lines makes it necessary to bleed these lines. Bleeding is carried out by slackening the union nuts at the injectors and cranking the engine. Before operating the starting motor to purge the air, the appropriate personal safety precautions should be taken to avoid contact with the high-pressure spray.

Automatic advance mechanisms

An automatic advance mechanism is provided for engines that have a wide speed range. This consists of a spring-loaded piston which rotates the cam ring against the direction of rotation when the transfer pump output pressure increases (Figure 2.310).

Governor

The governor used with a Lucas distributor pump is either a hydraulic or mechanical type.

Hydraulic governor

Control of engine speed is achieved by utilizing the transfer pump and the fuel-metering valve (Figure 2.311).

The driver controls the valve through a spring, so if he depresses the pedal by a given amount, the valve

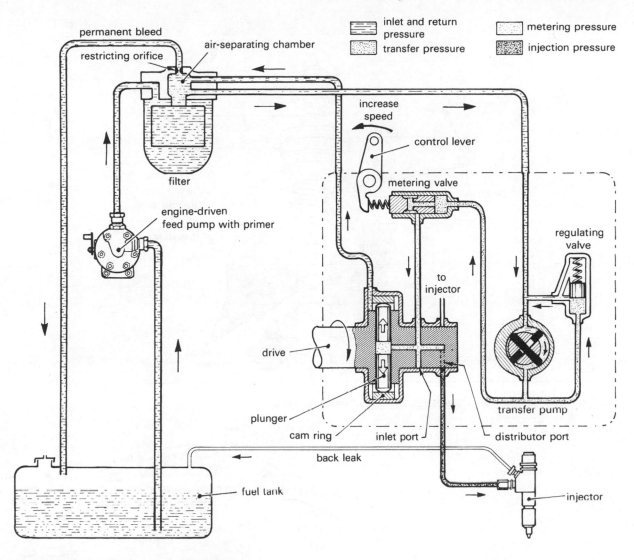

Figure 2.309 Fuel system for a Lucas CAV distributor pump

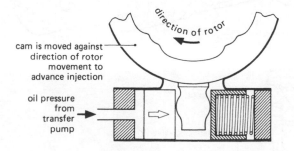

Figure 2.310 An automatic advance mechanism

opens wide and allows the speed to increase. The build-up in engine speed increases the transfer pump pressure. The increase in transfer pump pressure gradually moves the metering valve towards the closed position until a point is reached at which the speed will not increase any more. These events recur throughout the range.

Mechanical governor

This type is recommended when more precise control of engine speed is required. It can be recognized by the longer pump housing which is needed to accommodate the flyweights.

Figure 2.312 shows the constructional details of a simplified layout. Rotation of the input shaft causes the weight (1) to be thrown outwards and move a sleeve (2) against a control arm (3). The pivot on this arm causes the upper part of the arm to move in the opposite direction which pulls on the rod (4) and closes the metering valve (5). All of these movements are resisted by the control spring (6). The tension on the control spring is dictated by the driver's control lever.

When the driver requires an increase in power, movement of the control lever extends the spring. The larger force given by the spring resists flyweight movement until engine speed is sufficient to enable the flyweight to move.

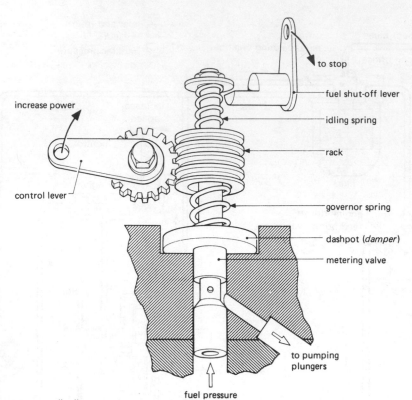

Figure 2.311 Hydraulic governor – distributor pump

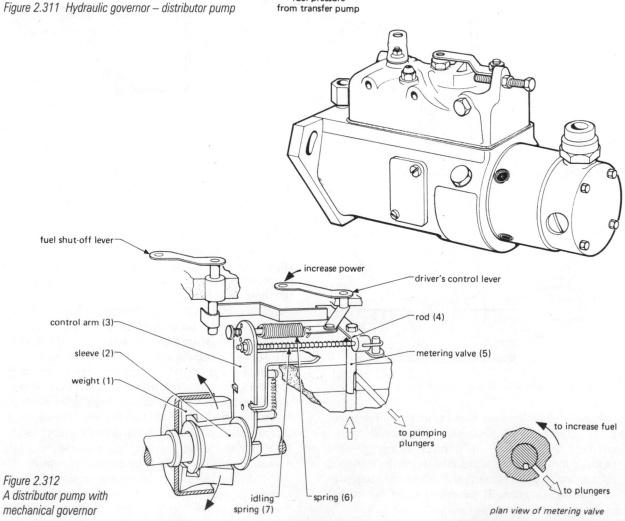

Figure 2.312
A distributor pump with
mechanical governor

Under idling conditions, tension is removed from the main governor spring and a light idling spring (7) is used to resist movement of the flyweights.

At any time the engine can be stopped by a shut-off lever. This overrides the governor and moves the metering valve to the 'no fuel' position.

2.35.4 Bosch distributor pumps

Figure 2.313 shows a VE-type pump fitted in a self-bleeding fuel system layout similar to that used on light vehicles.

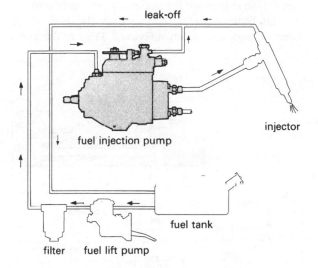

Figure 2.313 A Bosch distributor pump fuel system

As with other rotary pumps, this type has one pumping element and a number of high-pressure outlets, one for each engine cylinder.

In addition to the basic features associated with modern distributor-type rotary pumps, various add-on modules can be fitted to the VE pump. These include:

- A solenoid-operated fuel cut-off to give the driver a key start/stop operation.
- automatic cold-starting module to advance injection.
- A fast-idle facility to give even running during warm-up.
- Torque control for matching the fuel output with the fuel requirement.

The simplified section through the pump (Figure 2.314) shows the layout of the basic sub-systems. These include:

- low-pressure fuel supply
- high-pressure fuel supply and distributor
- fuel shut-off solenoid
- distributor plunger drive
- automatic injection advance unit
- pressure valve
- mechanical governor.

Low-pressure fuel supply

Driven at half crankshaft speed by a drive shaft, a transfer pump having four vanes delivers fuel to the pumping chamber at a pressure set by the regulating valve. This fuel pressure, which rises with engine speed,

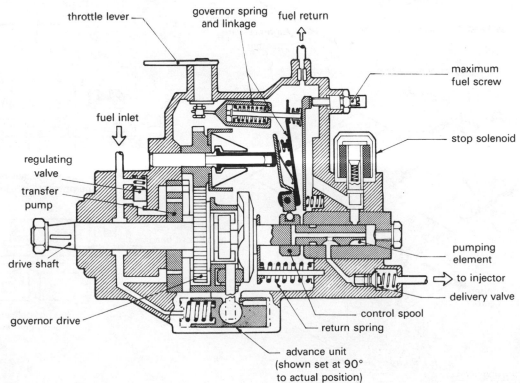

Figure 2.314 The Bosch VE distributor pump (simplified)

is used to operate the automatic advance unit. Also, it gives an overflow through the pump body, which aids cooling and provides the self-bleeding feature. After passing through a small restriction at the top of the pump the surplus fuel is returned to the fuel tank.

High-pressure fuel supply

Figure 2.315 is a simplified view of the pumping chamber with part of the distributor head cut away to show the pump plunger. Besides rotating in the head to give a valve action, the plunger is reciprocated through a constant stroke to produce the high pressure. The axial movement is provided by a cam plate moving over a roller ring. The quantity of high-pressure fuel delivered to the injector via the outlet bore is controlled by the position of the control spool. The control spool varies the effective pumping stroke, the stroke increases as the spool is moved towards the distributor head and therefore increases the quantity of fuel delivered.

In the position shown in Figure 2.315a the rotation of the plunger has caused one of the metering slits to open the inlet passage. At this point all outlet ports are closed. Prior to this, the plunger had moved down the chamber to create a condition for the fuel to enter and fill the high-pressure chamber.

Slight rotation of the plunger closes the inlet port and causes the single distributor slit in the plunger to open one of the outlet ports. While in this position the plunger is moved up the chamber to pressurize the fuel and deliver it through the outlet bore to the injector.

The position of the plunger at the end of the injection period is shown in Figure 2.315b. At this point,

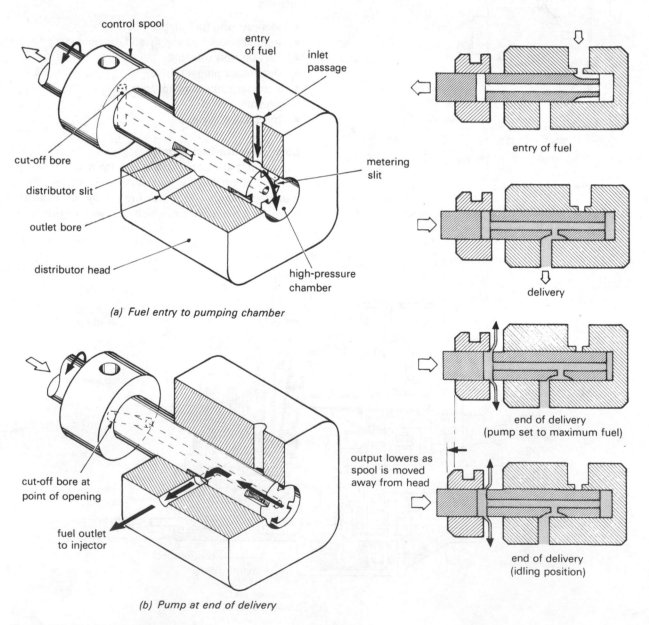

(a) Fuel entry to pumping chamber

(b) Pump at end of delivery

Figure 2.315 Principle of the VE pumping unit

the control spool has already allowed a considerable movement of the plunger before the cut-off bore in the plunger has been uncovered. The exposure of this port instantly drops the pressure and terminates injection.

Further pumping movement of the plunger causes the fuel in the pumping chamber to be returned to the pump cavity. With the spool set in this maximum fuel position, which corresponds to the fuel requirement for starting, a movement of the control spool to an extreme position away from the distributor head reduces the output to a minimum; this is the spool setting for slow running.

Fuel shut-off

The 'no fuel' or 'stop' position is provided by a solenoid-operated valve. The solenoid cuts off the fuel supply to the inlet passage when the ignition key is switched off.

Distributor plunger drive

The plunger must be rotated and reciprocated. Figure 2.316 illustrates how this is achieved.

The distributor pump drive-shaft is rotated at half crankshaft speed (for a four-stroke engine), and this is transmitted via a yoke and cam plate to provide rotary motion to the pump plunger.

Reciprocating motion is provided by the rotation of a cam plate as it moves over four roller followers fixed to a roller ring. In a pump suitable for a four-cylinder engine, four lobes are formed on the cam plate and contact between the plate and rollers is maintained by two strong plunger return springs. A yoke positioned between the drive-shaft and the cam plate allows the plate to move axially while still maintaining a drive.

Pressure valve

A delivery valve having a similar construction to that used on in-line pumps, is fitted in the distributor head at the connection point to the high-pressure fuel lines. The duty of this valve is described in the 'in-line pump' section of this book and its use on this type of pump

overcomes the need to bleed the high-pressure fuel lines.

Automatic injection advance unit

The roller ring assembly is not fixed rigidly to the casing; instead it can be partially rotated through an angle of up to 12° to allow the automatic advance mechanism shown in Figure 2.317 to vary the injection timing.

When the pump is rotated, fuel under pressure from the transfer pump is delivered to the timing advance chamber via the pump cavity. A rise in the pump speed causes the transfer pump pressure and flow to increase. The increase in pressure moves the timing-advance piston against its spring, which in turn, causes the actuating pin to rotate the roller ring in a direction opposite to the direction of rotation of the drive-shaft. The rotation of the roller ring advances the injection timing.

Governor

The VE pump is fitted with either a two-speed or an all-speed governor. The layouts of these types of governor are similar, but differ in the arrangement of the control springs.

Figure 2.318 shows the main construction of a two-speed governor, which controls the engine during the phases of idling and maximum-speed operation. At other times the driver has near-direct control of the quantity of fuel delivered, and hence the power output of the engine.

The centrifugal governor, which consists of a series of flyweights, is driven from the drive shaft through gears having a ratio that steps up the speed. The high-speed flyweight rotation given by this ratio ensures good sensitivity of the governor, especially during the idling phase.

An increase in engine speed, and the associated centrifugal action on the flyweights, produces an

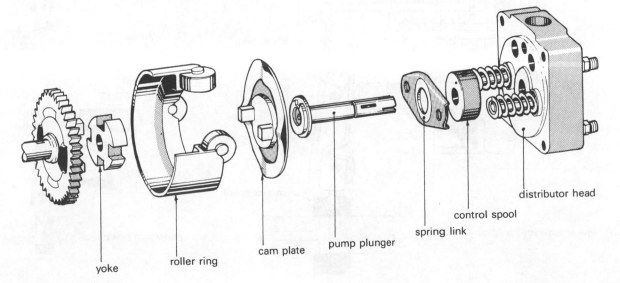

Figure 2.316 Plunger drive

outward force that pushes a sliding sleeve against a control lever system. Movement of this lever, which is connected at its lower end to the control spool on the pumping plunger, can only take place when the sliding sleeve is able to overcome the reaction of the spring that is in use at that time.

Starting

With the accelerator pedal half-depressed and the governor stationary the starting spring pushes the sliding sleeve towards the flyweights and moves the control spool to the 'maximum fuel' position.

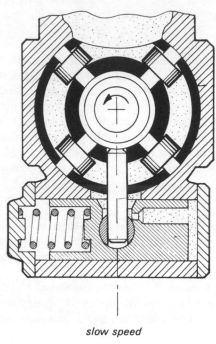

slow speed

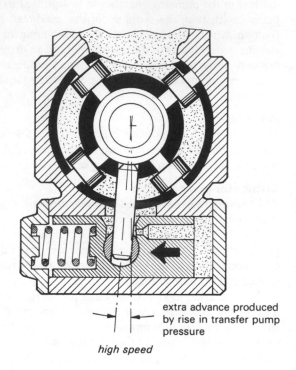

extra advance produced by rise in transfer pump pressure

high speed

Figure 2.317 Principle of the automatic advance

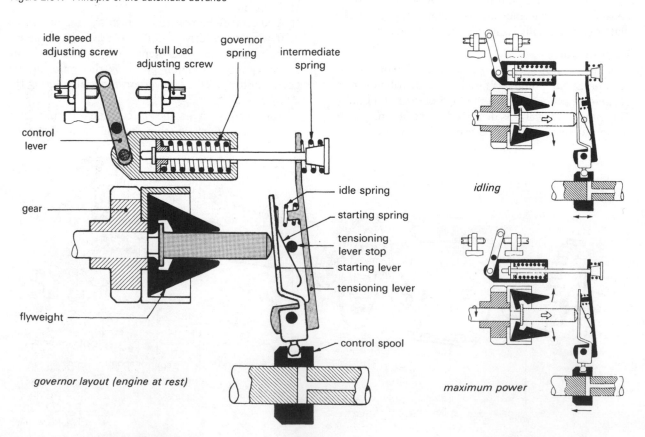

Figure 2.318 Governor – mechanical type

Idling

When the engine starts, the release of the accelerator combined with the outward movement of the flyweights, causes the lever to move the control spool to the minimum fuel position. When the engine is operating in this phase, smooth idling is obtained by the interaction of the flyweights and idling spring.

With the accelerator pedal lever against the adjustable idling stop, any small speed increase causes the flyweights to exert a larger force on the sliding sleeve. This slightly compresses the idling spring and, as a result, the spool control lever moves the spool and reduces the fuel delivery. Any slight drop in engine speed produces the opposite action, so smooth idling under governor control is obtained.

Mid-range operation

Once the idling range has been exceeded the larger governor force puts the idling and starting springs out of action. At this stage the intermediate spring comes into use to extend the idle control range and so smooth the transition from idle to mid-range operation.

The intermediate spring is stronger and provides a flexible link between the driver's pedal and the control spool lever so that when the accelerator pedal is depressed, a slight delay in engine response is introduced.

Beyond this phase any movement of the accelerator produces a direct action on the control spool.

Maximum speed

During mid-range operation, the pre-load of the main governor spring causes the spring assembly to act as a solid block. However, when the engine reaches its predetermined maximum speed, the force given by the flyweights equals the spring pre-load.

Any further speed increase allows the flyweights to move the spool control lever. This reduces the quantity of fuel being delivered and so keeps the engine speed within safe limits.

2.35.5 Injectors

The purpose of the injector (or sprayer) is to break up the fuel to the required degree (atomize) and deliver it to the combustion region in the chamber. This atomization and penetration is achieved by using a high pressure to force the fuel through a small orifice.

Vehicles in this country use a type of injector that incorporates a valve. The closed system is responsive to pump pressure – raising the pressure above a predetermined point allows the valve to open, and stay open until the pressure has dropped to a lower value. The 'snap' opening and closing of the valve give advantages, which make this system popular.

The complete injector, shown in Figure 2.319a, consists of a nozzle and holder, which is clamped to form a gas-tight seal in the cylinder head. A spring, compressed by an adjusting screw to give the correct

breaking (opening) pressure, thrusts the needle on to its conical seat. Fuel flows from the inlet nipple through a drilling to an annular groove about the seat of the needle. A thrust, caused by fuel acting on the conical face X, overcomes the spring and lifts the needle when the pressure exceeds the breaking pressure. The opening of the valve permits discharge of fuel until the pressure drops to the lower limit. Any fuel which flows between the needle and body acts as a lubricant for the needle before being carried away by a leak-off pipe.

Nozzle types

There are three main types of nozzle:

- single-hole
- multi-hole
- pintle.

Single-hole (Figure 2.319b)

A single orifice, which may be as small as 0.2 mm (0.008 in), is drifted in the nozzle to give a single jet spray. When this nozzle is used with indirect injection systems, a comparatively low injection pressure of 80–100 bar is used.

Multi-hole (Figure 2.319c)

Two or more small orifices, drilled at various angles to suit the combustion chamber, produce a highly

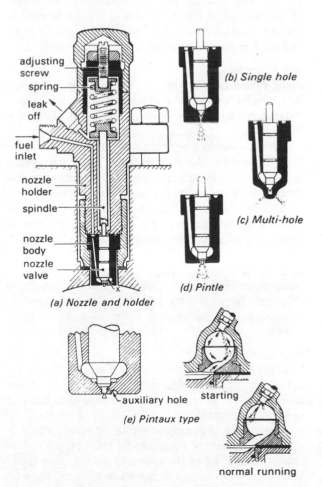

Figure 2.319 The injector

atomized spray form. Many engines with direct injection systems use a four-hole nozzle with a high operating pressure of 150–250 bar. A long-stem version of this type simplifies the accommodation of the injector in the head.

Pintle (Figure 2.319d)

Swirl chambers can accept a soft form of spray, which is the form given by a pintle type of nozzle when set to operate at a low injection pressure of 110–135 bar.

A small cone extension on the end of the needle produces a conical spray pattern and increases the velocity of the fuel as it leaves the injector. This type tends to be self-cleaning.

The elimination of heater plugs on some light indirect injection engines has been made possible by the invention of a special pintle nozzle known as the pintaux (pronounced 'pintawks') type, shown in Figure 2.319e. Starting conditions produce a small needle lift, and so fuel passes through the small auxiliary hole and is directed to the hottest part of the chamber. Under normal running pressures, the full lift of the needle discharges the fuel through the main orifice.

2.35.6 Injector servicing

With the engine at its operating temperature, the colour of the exhaust smoke, if any, acts as a guide to injector operation and is also used to assess the condition of an engine. The general rules relating to smoke colour are:

Black smoke

Black smoke results when all the injected fuel is not being burnt. It means that either the engine is receiving too much fuel or is receiving insufficient air, a rich mixture.

The fuel will not be completely burnt if the injector fails to atomize the fuel correctly or if any engine condition, such as poor compressions or incorrect valve timing, delays the start of combustion.

If the fuel injection timing is advanced, the combustion temperature and pressure is too low to ignite the fuel resulting in retarded ignition of the fuel. Similarly, if the injection timing is retarded, the fuel injected will burn rapidly due to the very high combustion chamber temperature. The ignition flame will ignite some, but not all, of the fuel and therefore incomplete combustion will occur resulting in black smoke.

Blue smoke

Blue smoke on any engine is a sign that lubricating oil is being burnt. Any mechanical condition that allows lubricating oil to enter the combustion chamber will result in blue smoke.

The engine operating condition at which smoke is emitted often acts as a guide to the cause, e.g. a puff of smoke emitted when the engine is started, after it has been allowed to stand idle for a few minutes, suggests that valve guides or valve stem seals are worn. If the

engine is poorly maintained, premature engine wear may occur. Rapid wear to the turbocharger bearings will also affect the bearing seals allowing the lubricating oil to be drawn out by the induced air and burnt by the engine.

White smoke

Incorrect fuel pump timing of the engine produces this colour but it should not be confused with the natural white colour of water vapour (steam) which occurs when a cold engine is started and the steam partially condenses as it passes through the cold exhaust system.

Other signs of injection faults

In addition to the emission of black smoke, faulty injectors cause low power output and intense engine knocking (diesel knock).

A faulty injector can often be traced by listening to the change in engine note which occurs when one injector at a time is cut out by slackening the pipeline union. Before this is attempted, special personal safety precautions must be taken which should include:

1. Diesel fuel should not be handled if it can be avoided. Where fuel is likely to come into contact with hands, gloves or a barrier cream should be used. This prophylactic cream reduces the risk of a skin inflammation disease (dermatitis).
2. Fuel oil under injection pressures can penetrate the skin, so no part of the human body should be exposed to fuel spray from an injector.
3. Eye protection in the form of safety glasses should be used to prevent fuel under pressure (low or high) from entering the eyes.
4. A well-ventilated work area, with special extraction equipment is needed to prevent atomized fuel from being inhaled into the lungs.

General maintenance

Injectors should be regularly cleaned, adjusted and tested. Injector servicing requires special cleaning tools and equipment in order to carry out the following tests:

- **Seat tightness (front leak)** – this ensures that the nozzle valve seat is sound when the pressure is below the opening pressure.
- **Needle wear (back leak)** – this indicates the amount of fuel that is passing from the needle or pressure faces to the leak-off pipe.
- **Pressure setting** – the opening pressure, sometimes called the breaking pressure, must be checked, and if incorrect, reset to the recommended value.
- **Spray pattern** – the spray pattern of the injector, when this is operating under its working pressure, should be observed. A poorly atomized spray of streaky appearance indicates that the nozzle orifice is partially blocked.

When refitting an injector to the engine, a new seat washer should be used and the damping arrangement should be tightened to the correct torque.

2.36 ELECTRONIC DIESEL FUEL SYSTEM

2.36.1 Electronic diesel control

An ever-increasing demand on the compression-ignition engine to develop more power with lower emissions together with an increase in fuel economy has led to the electronic control of the diesel fuel system.

Modern diesel engine vehicles are now subject to strict emission regulations that are imposed by government legislation, in a similar manner to that on petrol engine vehicles.

An electronic diesel control (EDC) system can give the following advantages:

- lower emission
- lower soot emissions
- increased engine output.

Although the Bosch VE pump accurately controls the quantity of fuel delivered by the injectors with the use of the control spool, the governor and the automatic advance unit, external influences (i.e. engine temperature and air density) affect engine performance and also emissions. Precise control of the fuel system can be achieved using EDC.

The EDC electronic control unit (ECU) controls the fuel system via two actuators, a solenoid-operated control spool and a solenoid-operated timing advance unit (Figure 2.320). These two actuators are situated in the distributor pump. The pump uses many of the components fitted to the VE-type distributor pump, including the fuel shut-off valve and the fuel delivery plunger.

The ECU monitors the engine operating conditions from information supplied by sensors and provides the correct control signals to the actuators, providing precise control of the fuel delivered to the injectors. The EDC system uses sensors very similar in operation to those used with petrol fuel injection systems.

An accelerator cable between the throttle pedal and the distributor pump is no longer required to control the fuel volume. The position of the throttle pedal is monitored by the EDC ECU with a throttle position sensor fitted to the throttle pedal linkage. The ECU controls the volume of fuel delivered to the injectors using a solenoid-operated control spool.

The engine speed is monitored by a sensor fitted to the engine crankshaft. The sensor is usually of the inductive type. An additional sensor is fitted to the distributor pump, which monitors the speed and position of the fuel control spool in relation to crankshaft position. The ECU uses the information from theses sensors, together with additional sensor information, to determine the volume of fuel and fuel injection timing.

Distributor injection pump for electronic diesel control

1 Control-collar position sensor, **2** Solenoid actuator for the injected fuel quantity, **3** Electromagnetic shut-off valve, **4** Delivery plunger, **5** Solenoid valve for start-of-injection timing, **6** Control collar.

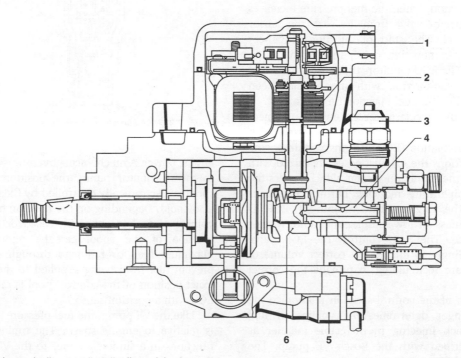

Figure 2.320 An electronically controlled distributor injection pump

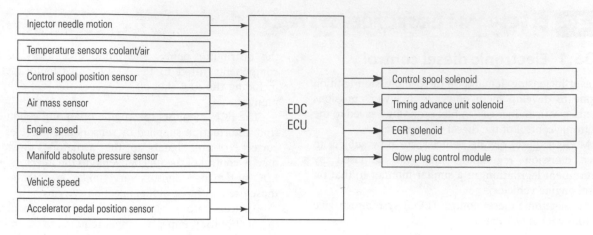

Figure 2.321 Electronic diesel control ECU input signals and output signals

A manifold absolute pressure (MAP) sensor enables the ECU to monitor the volume of air entering the engine. The ECU calculates the air density from the MAP sensor signal in conjunction with the intake air temperature sensor signal. The MAP sensor signal is also used to monitor and control the turbo boost pressure. The ECU controls the turbo boost pressure with a waste gate actuator solenoid.

Two temperature sensors are used: an engine coolant temperature sensor to monitor engine temperature and an intake air temperature sensor. The ECU uses temperature information for fuel volume control. The information is also used to control the length of time the glow plugs operate after starting.

An injector motion sensor is fitted to one of the injectors (Figure 2.322) usually to cylinder 1. At the start of fuel injection, when the fuel pressure increases and lifts the injector valve from the seat, the sensor produces a signal. The start of injection influences engine starting, combustion noise, fuel consumption and emissions. The ECU monitors the sensor signal and determines, in conjunction with the engine speed sensor information, the fuel injection timing control.

To enable the modern diesel engine to meet emission regulations, many engines are fitted with exhaust gas recirculation (EGR). During certain engine operating conditions the exhaust gases are mixed with the fresh air in the induction system, which lowers the combustion temperature reducing harmful emissions produced by the engine. The volume of EGR is measured by a mass airflow sensor, either a hot wire or a hot film type. The ECU controls the EGR valve actuator accordingly to ensure the correct volume of exhaust gases are recirculated to provide the correct emission levels.

The position of the control spool in relation to the distributor plunger determines the volume of fuel delivered to each injector, in the same manner as previously described with the Bosch VE pump. The volume of fuel delivered dictates the engine speed and

Nozzle-and-holder assembly with needle-motion sensor

1 Setting pin, **2** Sensor winding, **3** Pressure pin, **4** Cable, **5** Plug.

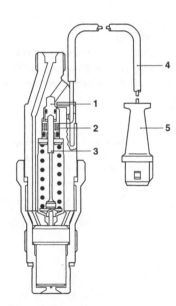

Figure 2.322 An injector with motion sensor

engine power. A mechanical governor is no longer fitted to the distributor pump, the position of the control spool is electronically controlled by the EDC ECU using a solenoid. Depending on the position of the spool, the volume of fuel is either increased or decreased. The position of the spool can be altered to provide maximum fuel for full load through to zero fuel to prevent fuel from being supplied to the injectors. The exact position of the control spool is monitored by the ECU with a position sensor.

Like the VE pump, the fuel pressure inside the pump is relative to engine speed. The timing advance unit functions in a similar manner to the VE pump, except that the fuel pressure applied to the advance unit is controlled by the EDC ECU with the timing advance unit solenoid. Fuel injection timing can either be advanced or retarded by altering the control signal to the solenoid.

The EDC ECU controls the engine idle speed by controlling the volume of fuel delivered. To ensure that the engine idle is as smooth as possible, the ECU will slightly vary the volume of fuel to each cylinder.

The EDC ECU also incorporates a diagnostic function similar in operation to that of a petrol engine management system. If a fault occurs with the system, the ECU will if possible operate a limited operating strategy (LOS). If a sensor circuit fails, the ECU will substitute the value of the sensor circuit, to provide limited emergency operation of the system. If the ECU detects a system fault, it illuminates a warning lamp in the instrument panel to alert the driver that a fault has occurred – the fault will also be recorded in the memory of the ECU in the form of a code. To diagnose a system fault, information can be retrieved from the EDC ECU memory using the appropriate diagnostic test equipment.

Many modern vehicles are protected from unauthorized use by the fitment of an engine immobilizer. Early immobilizer systems prevented the diesel engine from being started by isolating the power supply to the distributor pump stop solenoid, preventing fuel from entering the plunger. Modern electronically controlled diesel fuel systems are immobilized within the ECU. If the ECU receives an incorrect immobilizer code from the driver, it prevents fuel from being supplied to the injectors by isolating the control signals to the distributor pump solenoids.

2.36.2 Electronically controlled common rail diesel fuel systems

Direct injection and inline injection fuel systems have been used in commercial applications of diesel engines for many years. Direct injection is a more efficient method of fuel delivery and develops more power than indirect injection, where the fuel is delivered into a pre-combustion chamber. Direct injection does however have a disadvantage; the combustion noise is greater than with indirect injection, which is undesirable in passenger motor vehicles. Direct injection provides a significant reduction in fuel consumption compared with indirect injection.

In-line fuel pumps have been used on commercial applications including locomotives and ships and are still used today. Injection pressures are significantly higher than those used in distributor pump application diesel fuel systems as described in the previous sections. In-line diesel fuel systems use injection pressures of up to 1350 bar, while distributor pump applications use pressures typically between 300 and 400 bar.

Common rail diesel fuel systems have been widely used in commercial applications for many years. The increase in vehicle electronic technology combined with stricter emission requirements mean vehicle manufacturers have now applied common rail diesel fuel system technology to light commercial and passenger vehicles.

The electronically controlled common rail fuel system provides a high injection pressure that is supplied to the injectors from a common rail assembly. The

Common rail accumulator injection system on a 4-cylinder diesel engine

1 Air-mass meter, **2** ECU, **3** High-pressure pump, **4** High-pressure accumulator (rail), **5** Injectors,
6 Crankshaft-speed sensor, **7** Coolant-temperature sensor, **8** Fuel filter, **9** Accelerator-pedal sensor.

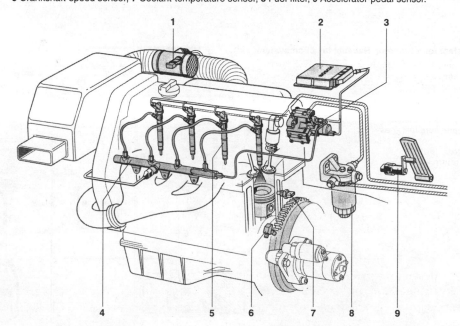

Figure 2.323 A common rail fuel system (Bosch)

pressure at which the fuel is injected into the combustion chamber can be altered to suit the engine operating conditions and cylinder pressure. With the use of electronic control, the injection timing can be accurately controlled to allow the fuel to ignite and burn within the combustion chamber correctly. Conventional diesel fuel systems inject all of the fuel required by the cylinder during one injector opening; with a common rail system and higher fuel pressure, the volume of fuel can be injected into the combustion chamber in stages, a pilot injection, main injection and post injection.

The ECU determines the volume of fuel and the time at which the fuel is injected to provide the required power from the engine.

The electronically controlled common rail diesel fuel system can be divided into two sub-systems, the fuel pressure system and the fuel injection system.

Fuel pressure system

The fuel pressure is produced by means of a low-pressure pump that supplies fuel from the fuel tank via a fuel filter to a high-pressure pump. The ECU controls the operation of the low pressure pump. The pump location and design is very similar to that used in a petrol fuel injection system.

The high-pressure pump, normally driven at half crankshaft speed by the camshaft, generates the high fuel pressure which is stored in the common fuel rail, hence the name 'common rail diesel' (Figure 2.324). The ECU varies the pressure produced by the high-pressure pump up to a maximum pressure of 1350 bar using electrically operated solenoid valves within the pump assembly. The ECU varies the fuel pressure according to engine operating conditions, so the fuel pressure is not directly related to engine speed. The diesel fuel lubricates the internal cams and plungers of the high-pressure pump.

The fuel pressure produced by the high pressure pump is monitored by the ECU using a fuel pressure sensor situated in the common rail, so the fuel is always at the correct pressure to suit the engine operating conditions. The fuel passes from the fuel rail to the injectors in metal fuel pipes. These pipes are approximately equal in length and manufactured without excessively sharp bends which may restrict fuel flow. Note that if any of the fuel pipes are disconnected during service or repair they should be renewed. The pipes are made from steel which deforms to the common rail high pressure pump connections when tightened, ensuring a fuel-tight seal.

The common rail acts as an accumulator or reservoir of fuel in which pressure fluctuations in the high-pressure system due to the pumping action and injection are dampened. The fuel rail is also fitted with a fuel pressure regulator, if the fuel pressure becomes abnormally high, the excess pressure is vented through the pressure-limiting valve to the fuel tank. The fuel pressure-limiting valve on early generation common rail fuel systems was mechanical. With later systems, the ECU controls the fuel rail pressure with an electrically operated solenoid valve. Note that the ECU monitors the fuel pressure in the fuel rail and controls the pressure with a solenoid valve on the side of the high-pressure pump.

Fuel injection system

The ECU controls the injectors in much the same way as in petrol fuel injection. The common rail fuel system uses many of the sensors that provide information for an electronically controlled distributor pump diesel fuel system; these include, engine speed sensor fitted to the crankshaft, camshaft position sensor, accelerator pedal position sensor, MAP sensor, engine coolant and intake air temperature sensor and air mass sensor. These

Fuel system for a Common Rail fuel-injection system

  1 Fuel tank,
  2 Pre-filter,
  3 Presupply pump,
  4 Fuel filter,
  5 Low-pressure fuel lines,
  6 High-pressure pump,
  7 High-pressure fuel lines,
  8 Rail,
  9 Injector,
10 Fuel-return line,
11 ECU.

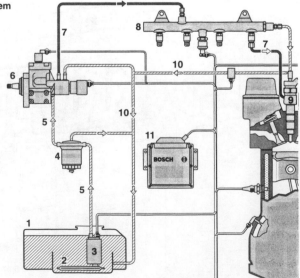

Figure 2.324 Common rail diesel – the fuel system

sensors are used to monitor engine-operating conditions. The accelerator sensor tells the ECU whether the driver wishes to accelerate, decelerate or allow the engine to idle while stationary. The ECU uses the sensor information to calculate the desired fuel pressure, injection volume and duration that produces optimum engine power and torque to meet driver needs.

The fuel pressure within the common rail is constant during injection and therefore the volume of fuel injected is also constant during the injector-opening period. The precise volume of fuel can be delivered during the injector-opening period. The injectors are connected to the fuel rail with short, high-pressure metal fuel pipes.

The EDC ECU determines the injector opening period (injector duration) from sensor information and provides a control signal to the injector accordingly. The high fuel pressure exerts a great force at the injector needle valve, so a very high voltage and current is required to initially open the injector. The injector driver control module provides the necessary high voltage control signal to the injector. The module may

be located within the ECU or in some cases fitted as a separate unit. The ECU uses the engine speed sensor to provide the timing control for each injector, and additional information is required to synchronize each injector with the cylinder cycle. A cylinder recognition sensor monitors the camshaft position, which provides the ECU with the information necessary to control the phasing of the injectors. The injectors are situated in the cylinder head and spray fuel into the swirling air within the combustion chamber, which is normally integrated into the crown of the piston.

If current is switched off to the solenoid circuit, the injector needle valve is closed which prevents pressurized fuel leaving the injector nozzle (Figure 2.325a) The high pressure fuel is applied to the needle valve at the lower section of the injector and also to a control chamber which is located on top of the injector needle valve within the top section of the injector. The force of the solenoid spring and the needle valve spring is higher than the fuel pressure applied and therefore the needle valve remains closed.

The ECU determines the injection period during which the injector opens and injects a volume of fuel

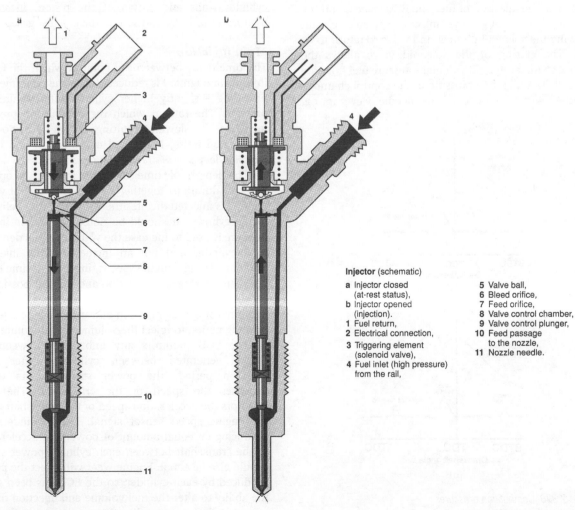

Injector (schematic)

a Injector closed
    (at-rest status),
b Injector opened
    (injection).
1 Fuel return,
2 Electrical connection,
3 Triggering element
    (solenoid valve),
4 Fuel inlet (high pressure)
    from the rail,

5 Valve ball,
6 Bleed orifice,
7 Feed orifice,
8 Valve control chamber,
9 Valve control plunger,
10 Feed passage
    to the nozzle,
11 Nozzle needle.

Figure 2.325 Common rail injector (Bosch)
a Injector closed   b Injector opened

into the combustion chamber. The ECU provides the injector with a control signal that energizes the injector solenoid (Figure 2.325b) The solenoid valve lifts, allowing the fuel pressure to escape from the control chamber into the chamber above. The fuel passing to the chamber returns to the tank via the fuel return system. The initial current required to lift the solenoid is high due to the force of the spring. Once open, a smaller current is required to maintain the solenoid position, and the ECU applies this 'holding current'. An orifice restriction prevents the high-pressure fuel from rapidly re-entering the control chamber, as the control chamber pressure is lower than the fuel pressure applied to the needle valve. Due to the difference in fuel pressure between the control chamber and the fuel pressure at the needle valve, the valve lifts from the seat and fuel is expelled through the injector nozzle into the combustion chamber. The pressure of the injected fuel is equal to the pressure in the fuel rail. The high fuel pressure together with the design of the injector nozzle allows excellent atomization of the fuel injected, which promotes good mixing of the air and fuel within the combustion chamber. Thoroughly mixing the air and fuel reduces the HC and soot emissions.

To end the injection of fuel, the ECU switches off the current flow through the injector solenoid circuit, allowing the solenoid plunger and valve to return to its seat. The closing of the solenoid valve allows the control chamber to refill will high-pressure fuel from the fuel rail. The high fuel pressure in the control chamber, together with the force of the needle valve spring,

exerts a greater force than that of the high fuel pressure at the base of the needle valve; the needle valve returns to its seat and injection ceases.

Pilot injection
Earlier types of diesel fuel system inject all of the fuel during one injector opening period for one cylinder cycle (2.326a). There is a short period between the start of injection and the start of ignition. When the fuel ignites, the cylinder pressure rapidly increases which pushes the piston down the cylinder. The sharp rise in cylinder pressure is heard and referred to as diesel knock.

The common rail fuel system normally injects fuel in two injection stages. These stages are often referred to as pilot injection and main injection (Figure 2.326b). A small volume of fuel is injected before the piston reaches TDC. The small volume of fuel (typically 1–4 mm³) conditions the cylinder before the main volume of fuel is injected. The pilot injection raises the cylinder pressure slightly due to the combustion of the fuel and therefore the heat within the cylinder also rises. If the pilot injection occurs too early in the compression stroke, the fuel will adhere to the cold cylinder walls and crown of the piston, increasing hydrocarbons (HC) and soot in the exhaust gases.

Main injection
The time delay between the point at which the fuel is injected and ignited is reduced due to the pilot injection providing a slightly higher cylinder temperature and pressure. The rate at which the combustion pressure increases is slower resulting in a reduction of combustion noise, lower fuel consumption and lower emission levels.

The length of time that the injector is opened (injector duration) together with the pressure at which the fuel is injected dictates the volume of fuel delivered to the cylinder. It should be noted that a rise in fuel pressure is used to increase the volume of fuel delivered to a cylinder and not an increase in the injection duration. At high engine speeds, insufficient time exists between the stages of injection and it is not possible to provide pilot injection. The ECU combines both pilot and main stages of injection and uses a single injector-opening period to inject the volume of fuel required.

The ECU monitors any imbalance between the torque generated between cylinders. After each injection period, the power stroke occurs which increases the speed of the crankshaft. The ECU monitors the acceleration speed of the crankshaft using the engine speed sensor signal. If all cylinders are producing an equal amount of power, the acceleration of the crankshaft between each cylinder power stroke should also be equal. Engine wear will affect the power produced by each cylinder, so the ECU has been given the ability to alter the fuel volume and injection timing to each cylinder to equalize the power produced at low engine speeds. Unequal power between cylinders is

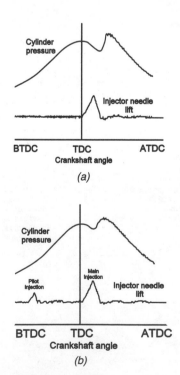

Figure 2.326 Combustion pressures
a without pilot injection
b with pilot injection

very apparent at idle, and the ECU stabilizes engine speed ensuring a smooth engine idle.

The ECU controls the turbo-charger boost pressure. The ECU monitors the inlet manifold pressure using a pressure sensor. If the pressure is too high (overboost) the ECU regulates the pressure with a waste-gate in the exhaust manifold. Some later vehicles are fitted with a variable geometry turbo, in which the ECU alters the geometry inside the exhaust turbine to vary the boost pressure (refer to supercharging).

The ECU controls the exhaust gas recirculation (EGR) that returns some of the exhaust gasses into the induction system to reduce harmful emissions. The ECU monitors the air mass sensor signal situated in the air induction system, which provides an indication of the volume of exhaust gas recirculated. Many induction systems are fitted with a throttle plate in the induction system. The throttle plate used in a petrol engine alters the volume of air entering the engine and therefore alters engine power. The throttle plate used in a diesel engine is used to alter the rate of EGR. During low engine speeds, the angle of the throttle plate is adjusted to provide a depression in the manifold which induces the rate of EGR. At high engine speeds the throttle plate is fully open during high engine load and speed to prevent restriction to the flow of air into the engine. The throttle plate is either operated by a stepper motor or by the modulation of a vacuum switching valve.

2.37 | DIESEL EMISSIONS

2.37.1 Diesel vehicle emission regulations

The exhaust emission limits detailed so far in this book refer to petrol engine vehicles. However, diesel powered vehicles also have to comply with separate EU emission regulations. Diesel engines must meet emission legislation, and like petrol engines, these emission limits laid down by the EU are gradually being tightened to provide a cleaner environment.

Diesel vehicle emissions are similar to those of a petrol engine: hydrocarbons (HC), carbon monoxide (CO), nitrogen oxides (NO_x), smoke and other particulate matter.

All diesel engine passenger cars sold in Europe that used an indirect injection engine (pre-combustion chamber design), were required to meet EU Stage 1 limits in 1993.

Direct injection diesel engines are cleaner in operation and therefore produce lower emissions as a result of their engine and fuel system designs. In 1997 all diesel engine cars had to meet EU Stage II regulations. EU Stage III regulations were implemented in 2000 with EU Stage IV adopted in 2005.

Table 2.4 EU emission regulations for diesel engines

Standard	Type of test	Year of introduction	Engine type	CO g/km	NO_x + HC g/km	Particulates g/km
EU Stage I	Homologation	July 1992	Indirect injection	2.72	0.97	0.14
	First registration	January 1993		3.16	1.13	0.18
EU Stage II	Homologation	July 1996	Indirect injection	1.0	0.7	0.08
	First registration	January 1997	Direct injection	1.0	0.9	0.1
EU Stage III	Homologation and first registration	January 2000	Indirect injection and direct injection	0.64	0.56 (0.5 NO_x limit)	0.05
EU Stage IV	Homologation and first registration	January 2005	Indirect injection and direct injection	0.5	0.3 (0.25 NO_x limit)	0.025

2.38   ROUTINE ENGINE MAINTENANCE

2.38.1   Engine maintenance

Already mentioned in previous sections of chapter 2 are some components that require routine maintenance during the expected life of a vehicle. Vehicle manufacturers carry out vigorous tests throughout the development of a vehicle to determine if and when components either require checking to ensure that they are still fit for service (e.g. brake pad lining thickness) or that a component requires replacing at a specified interval before it wears out and causes breakdown of the vehicle (e.g. engine oil).

Over recent years routine maintenance service intervals have increased. Routine maintenance was once carried out every 3000 miles; the service interval on many modern vehicles is now in excess of 10,000 miles with a major service required at 40,000 miles.

The following section details those components that require inspection or replacement during routine servicing. The following engine items normally require attention during routine maintenance:

- Engine oil and oil filter
- Engine cooling system
- Valve clearances
- Ancillary drive belts
- Timing belt
- Engine (general)
- Exhaust system.

Figure 2.327 Engine oil and filter change

2.38.2   Engine oil and filter

Engine oil should be changed in accordance with the vehicle manufacturer's guidelines. Most manufacturers suggest that the engine oil and filter be changed at every service interval.

Although engine oil is used principally to reduce friction between components during operation, the oil also reduces the corrosion of engine components, transfers heat away from internal components and holds harmful substances in suspension as the oil flows around the engine.

These substances are deposited either in the sump of the engine or collected by the filter as the oil flows through the oil filter element. The oil therefore becomes contaminated and loses some of its lubricating properties between oil changes. The dirty particles that are collected by an oil filter reduce the effectiveness of the filter over a period of time. It is therefore imperative that the oil and oil filter are changed on a regular basis. During the oil and filter change, ensure that any additional lubrication components (e.g. oil cooler, oil cooler hoses, etc.) are in good condition.

The vehicle should be placed on a level surface. Ideally the oil should be changed when the engine is warm, but not so hot that it may burn the technician.

Allow the engine to run for a short period if the engine oil is cold. It may be necessary to raise the vehicle to gain access to the engine sump plug and oil filter. The oil should be drained into a suitable container, large enough to hold the volume of oil contained in the engine sump. Once the oil is drained, if necessary fit a new sealing washer to the sump plug, and replace it.

The oil filter should be renewed in accordance with the maintenance schedule, ensuring that all sealing rings and gaskets are renewed as necessary. The oil filter should be tightened to the correct specification when refitting the new filter, usually three-quarters of a turn after the initial contact with the oil filter housing.

Refill the engine with the specified quantity of oil. Start the engine, checking that the oil warning light extinguishes and that there is no oil leak from the sump plug and oil filter. The oil level should be checked with the engine oil dipstick; add oil to the full mark ensuring that the engine is not overfilled. Damage to the engine can occur if it is overfilled with oil.

It may be necessary to clean any spillages of oil. Ensure that the engine oil filler cap and the engine dipstick are fitted correctly.

Ensure that the waste oil and oil filter are disposed of within your local authority guidelines.

2.38.3 Engine cooling system

The engine cooling system transfers the heat generated by combustion and ensures that the engine is controlled at the correct temperature. Nearly all today's vehicles are of the liquid-cooled type and therefore it is essential that the cooling system is maintained to ensure that the engine does not overheat, or freeze when the vehicle is driven in cold climates.

During routine maintenance of the vehicle the cooling system should be checked for:

Coolant

The coolant level should be set to the maximum level when the engine is cold. If the coolant level is low, the system should be inspected for leaks. It may be necessary to pressure test the cooling system to locate leaks if not immediately apparent. In many cases it may be necessary to tighten a loose hose clip. Ensure caution is taken when removing the pressure cap; the hot coolant under pressure can cause serious injury.

Figure 2.328 Checking the strength of antifreeze in the coolant

Coolant contains additives which prevent corrosion of internal engine components, and antifreeze additives which prevent the coolant from freezing during cold weather. Over a period of time the coolant will lose some of these additive properties through constant topping up of the coolant level and therefore dilution of the additives. The strength of the additives may also change due to chemical reactions that occur during the heating and cooling of the coolant. It may therefore be necessary to replace the coolant during routine maintenance or to check the specific gravity of the antifreeze strength in the coolant with a hydrometer.

Condition of cooling system components

Many of the cooling system components are manufactured from flexible materials such as rubber, including hoses, pressure cap seals, etc. Over time, the constant changes in coolant temperature can affect the material from which these components are made. It is therefore necessary to check all of the flexible rubber hoses and pressure cap seals for swelling and cracking. It is advisable to replace any hoses that display signs of failure.

The radiator is exposed to the airstream as the vehicle moves, and is therefore subject to flying debris either blocking or damaging the fins. The radiator should be check for leaks and damage and repaired or replaced as necessary.

If the cooling system has to be drained, many cooling systems provide either a drain tap or drain plug to allow this to be done easily. Some cooling systems provide air bleed taps which allow trapped air in the cooling system to escape after refilling the system. The removal of the air in the system during refilling prevents air locks occurring which can lead to overheating as they may prevent the coolant from flowing through the cooling system.

2.38.4 Valve clearances

The inlet and exhaust valves require a small clearance to ensure that they return to their fully closed position, providing an airtight seal during the compression and power strokes. The valve clearance allows for expansion of the valve operating gear and therefore the clearance is larger when the engine is cold and smaller when hot. Many manufacturers set the valve clearance tolerances when the engine is cold, but always ensure the clearances are checked as per manufacturer information.

During engine operation, the valves, camshaft and associated operating gear will wear over time; sometimes valve clearances will increase, on other occasions the clearances can decrease. The change in valve clearance can affect the performance of the engine causing higher emissions than normal together with an increase in noise from the valve gear. Although many engines today feature hydraulic tappets, it may still be necessary to check and adjust the valve clearances as part of a maintenance schedule.

The method used to check valve clearances will depend on the valve gear design. Due to the many configurations in use today, it is necessary to follow the procedures in the workshop manual to carry out this

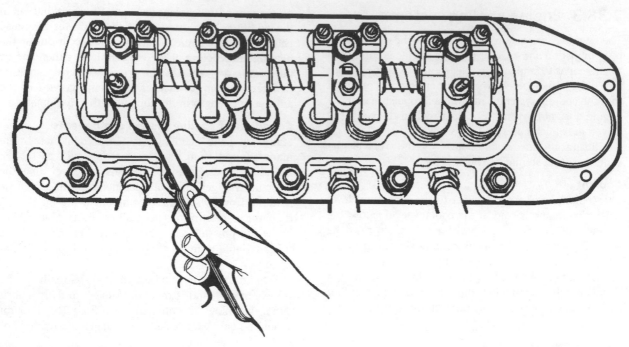

Figure 2.329 Checking valve clearances

operation. The manual will also specify the tolerances and whether the clearances should be adjusted with the engine cold or hot.

2.38.5 Ancillary drive belts

Drive belts are used to drive ancillary components such as the alternator, water pump, hydraulic power steering pump and possibly the air-conditioning compressor. The belt is usually made from rubber, which is reinforced with fibres. When the belt is new, it is tensioned, preventing the belt slipping on the pulleys when additional loads are applied to the ancillary components. The drive belt will gradually stretch and eventually slip when loads are applied to the components.

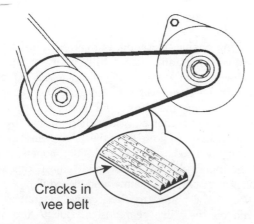

Cracks in
vee belt

Figure 2.330 Ancillary drive belt, vee-belt and multi-vee belt faults

The belt may also suffer from splits and cracking due to constantly rotating around different sizes of pulley. The engine crankshaft may use one, two or more belts to drive the ancillary components fitted. Many vehicles are now fitted with a '*serpentine belt*' that drives many ancillary components from one belt; as the name suggests, the belt winds its way around the component pulleys before returning to the crankshaft pulley.

It is therefore necessary during routine maintenance to ensure that the belt is in good condition, i.e. the belt is free from cracks, excessive wear and is tensioned correctly. Many manufacturers specify a belt tension to be obtained with a special belt tension gauge. The belt tension is normally adjusted by moving one of the components, which pivots, allowing either the tensioning or de-tensioning of the belt. Note that many new vehicles fitted with serpentine-type drive belts are fitted with automatic tensioning jockey wheels. The belt is therefore always at the correct tension.

2.38.6 Timing belt

The timing belt is used to drive the camshaft pulley from the crankshaft pulley. The timing belt, constructed from rubber and reinforced with glass fibres, has a number of teeth, which allow the timing between the crankshaft and the camshaft pulleys to remain constant.

After time, it becomes necessary to replace the timing belt. The belt rubber hardens and eventually cracks and breaks off. This rubber forms the teeth on the belt; if the teeth break off, valve timing can slip. If the belt breaks, the crankshaft rotates and the camshaft remains stationary for a very short period of time. With modern engine design, the valves operate in very close proximity to the piston crowns, and if the valve timing slips there is a strong possibility that the valve may still be partially open when the piston reaches TDC. If this happens the piston crown strikes the head of the open valve, generally causing internal damage to the engine. It is therefore wise to replace the timing belt at the specified service intervals.

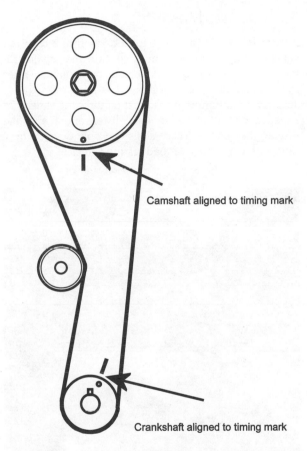

Camshaft aligned to timing mark

Crankshaft aligned to timing mark

Figure 2.331 Timing belt – aligning marks on the cam and crank pulleys

To replace the timing belt it is necessary to initially align the timing belt marks on the crankshaft and camshaft pulleys. The timing belt cover should be removed, which normally entails the removal of the crankshaft front pulley. The timing belt is tensioned by an idler pulley, which applies pressure on the smooth side of the timing belt. To remove the belt, first release the belt tension.

Various substances can affect the rubber and glass fibre materials from which timing belts are made. Premature failure of the timing belt can occur if it is exposed to oil or water. When replacing the belt ensure no leaks exist in the vicinity of the belt. Do not allow the belt to become twisted or kinked as this can break the glass fibre strands within the belt's structure.

Check that the timing marks on both the camshaft and crankshaft remain aligned. Replace the timing belt, remembering that some belts have an arrow printed on them to indicate the direction of rotation with which the belt should be fitted. Re-tension the belt as per manufacturer's specifications and refit the parts removed. Before the timing cover is refitted it is good practice to rotate the engine in the normal direction of rotation through one full cycle (two rotations of the crankshaft). This procedure is commonly used to ensure that the timing belt marks realign correctly before refitting the timing belt cover, etc.

2.38.7 Engine general

A general inspection of the engine should be made during a routine service. This should include checks to ensure that all gaskets and seals are in good condition. Often a faulty part can be seen by the leakage of a fluid e.g. engine oil or engine coolant. The smooth operation of the engine should be checked to see if all of the cylinders are operating efficiently. Often, if a cylinder is operating inefficiently, the engine will run poorly or even misfire. The early diagnosing of an engine fault during the routine servicing of a vehicle can reduce the repair costs later.

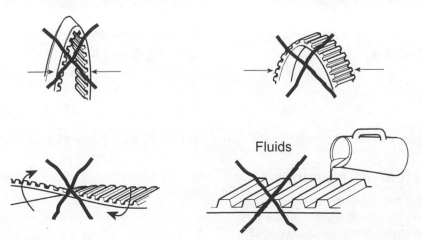

Fluids

Figure 2.332 Timing belt premature failure through twisting, bending, oil and water on belt, etc.

2.38.8 Exhaust system

The exhaust system should be inspected for excessive noise, the security of mountings, and exhaust gas leaks from joints as well as leaks from silencers and pipes. The exhaust system fitted to a vehicle is subject to corrosion, internally and externally. The by-products from combustion (i.e. water vapour and corrosive acids) can prematurely corrode the steel of the exhaust. The exhaust can also suffer damage from being hit by debris as the vehicle moves; it is therefore important that the exhaust is inspected from the underneath of the vehicle, i.e. on a vehicle ramp.

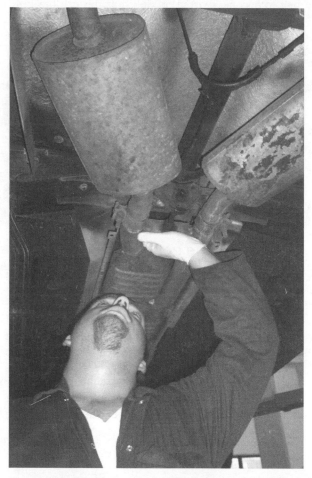

Figure 2.333 Exhaust system – items to check when servicing a vehicle, i.e. mounting, silencer, joints

Many vehicles are now subject to exhaust gas emission testing carried out with an exhaust gas analyser fitted to the tailpipe of the vehicle while the engine is running. The emission test is part of the UK vehicle MOT test. Note that modern vehicles are fitted with a catalytic converter at the front of the exhaust system. The test analyses the exhaust gases to ensure that the engine, fuel system and ignition system are operating correctly and the catalyst is functioning efficiently.

2.38.9 Road test

A thorough road test can be used to confirm a reported vehicle fault, diagnose a fault, confirm the repair of a fault or check the overall vehicle performance after routine maintenance or a repair has been carried out. To carry out a thorough road test requires the skill of an experienced technician to look, listen and feel while driving the vehicle. These skills can only develop over time with experience of road testing vehicles.

Figure 2.334 A road test

ROUTINE MAINTENANCE OF THE PETROL FUEL SYSTEM

2.39.1 Fuel system maintenance

The requirements of the fuel system are to store fuel and supply a volume of fuel to a metering device that then delivers a precise quantity of finely atomized fuel into the inlet manifold, normally using a carburettor or a fuel injection system. The fuel system components that require routine maintenance are:

- fuel tank and supply pipes
- fuel filter
- carburettor/petrol injection system.

2.39.2 Fuel tank and supply pipes

The fuel is stored in the tank, which is normally located at the rear of the vehicle. The filling of the fuel tank requires the removal of the fuel cap. It is good practice during a service to check the fuel tank cap for security and to ensure that the cap seals correctly to prevent further ingress of dust and dirt into the fuel tank.

Legislation requires that all modern vehicles be fitted with sealed fuel systems to prevent the loss of fuel vapour (HC) into the atmosphere. If the cap is not sealing correctly or the correct cap for the vehicle is missing, the fuel cap should be replaced.

The fuel tank and fuel pipes should be checked for security and damage which may require an under-vehicle inspection. Fuel pipes are made from various materials; after a period of time they can deteriorate. Ensure that all fuel pipes are in good condition and securely fixed to the body.

2.39.3 Fuel filter

The fuel tank can contain many impurities such as fine particles of dirt and in some cases water. These impurities generally enter the vehicle fuel system when the fuel tank is refilled at a service station. If allowed to enter the fuel metering system these impurities will, over time, prevent the fuel system from operating correctly by clogging the very fine jets and valves.

The fuel filter is designed to prevent impurities from entering the fuel system. The fuel filter is normally situated between the fuel pump and the fuel metering system, i.e. carburettor or injectors. The filter element is housed in a container which is normally a sealed item. The element is designed to filter the impurities from the fuel and, over a period of time, fuel flow through the element can become restricted. It is therefore necessary to change the fuel filter during scheduled routine maintenance, as specified by the manufacturer.

The filter is normally held in a bracket to prevent the filter assembly from vibrating when the vehicle is moving.

To replace the fuel filter, first disconnect the fuel supply and delivery pipes from the filter housing. Before disconnecting the fuel pipes from the housing, it may be necessary to clean around the fuel pipe connections to prevent dirt from entering the system when the pipes

are disconnected. Note the fuel pipe connections and the direction of fuel flow through the filter.

The fuel filter housing normally indicates with an arrow which direction the fuel flows through the filter. If the fuel pipes are fitted incorrectly fuel flow through the filter may be impaired.

The fuel pipes may contain fuel that is under pressure, so caution is required when the fuel pipes are loosened. A method of depressurizing the fuel system is usually detailed in the vehicle workshop manual. Disconnect the fuel pipes from the fuel filter. Discard the old fuel filter safely; the filter will contain a quantity of highly inflammable fuel and is therefore a fire hazard.

Replace the filter and wherever necessary fit new gaskets and seals to prevent leakage. Ensure that all retaining clips, bolts, etc. are tightened securely. Refit the fuel filter housing into the retaining bracket, checking the security of the filter after refitting. Wipe off any spilt fuel, start the engine and check for fuel leakage from the filter assembly.

2.39.4 Carburettor fuel system

It is necessary to check the operation of a carburettor during the routine servicing of a vehicle to ensure that the correct air/fuel ratio is being supplied to the engine for the engine operating conditions and therefore that the exhaust emissions are correct. To gain access to the carburettor it may be necessary to remove components such as the air filter assembly.

Check the operation of the choke mechanism, manual and automatic versions. A poorly adjusted choke can increase fuel consumption and cause poor performance from the engine. Ensure that when the choke is operated, the linkage moves freely and when the choke is released it returns to the fully off position.

Check the throttle linkage. The linkage should allow the throttle butterfly to return to the idle position when the throttle pedal is released, and when the throttle pedal is fully depressed, the throttle butterfly should be wide open, providing full throttle and maximum power.

Carburettor adjustment

Some of the engine components, ancillary devices, etc. gradually alter over a period of time through normal wear. The carburettor therefore has to be adjusted to compensate for these slight changes.

Carburettor adjustments should be checked to ensure that the engine idle speed and the choke fast idle speed are set correctly. The idle mixture should be set to yield the correct exhaust gas emissions. These adjustments should be carried out in accordance with the manufacturer's workshop manual procedures. Note that many adjusting screws are sealed. It may be necessary to remove these seals to carry out adjustments. Always fit new seals after the adjustments have been carried out. *Before* carburettor adjustments are carried out you should carry out the following:

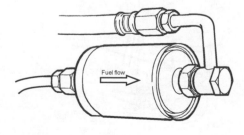

Figure 2.335 Fuel filter replacement

- set the ignition contact beaker gap (if fitted) and the ignition timing
- fit the air filter assembly
- make sure all breather hoses and vacuum pipes are connected
- ensure that the engine is at the correct operating temperature
- switch off additional engine loads
- connect a tachometer to measure engine speed.

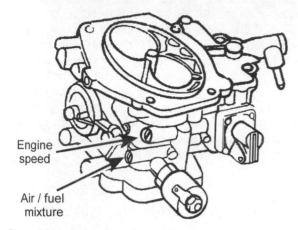

Figure 2.336 Carburettor adjustments

Idle speed

The engine idle speed should be adjusted with the idle speed adjusting screw. The screw usually acts on the throttle linkage, although some idle speed screws alter the air bypassing the throttle butterfly. Set the idle speed using the tachometer.

Idle mixture

To set the idle mixture accurately, it is necessary to use an exhaust gas analyser. Insert the gas analyser sample pipe in the exhaust tailpipe. Run the engine at a high cruise speed for approximately 30 seconds and allow the engine to idle. Check the exhaust gas content and either richen or weaken the mixture with the mixture adjusting screw. Each time an adjustment is carried out, raise the engine speed to a cruise speed before rechecking the idle mixture. The adjustment of the mixture may alter the idle speed, therefore it may be necessary to reset the idle speed too during the mixture adjustments.

Choke fast idle speed

To check the fast idle speed on carburettors fitted with automatic chokes, it may be necessary to carry out certain procedures to persuade the choke to operate.

With manual choke carburettors, allow the engine to idle, slightly depress the accelerator and slowly pull the choke out. The idle speed should be seen to rise. Release the choke after a short period once the maximum fast idle speed has been reached. If the engine speed did not rise to the correct speed, adjust the fast idle adjusting screw/s on the choke or throttle linkage, then retest.

2.39.5 Petrol injection fuel system

The fuel injection system requires only limited maintenance, which includes many similar maintenance tasks to those on the carburettor fuel system.

Check the throttle linkage to ensure that it allows full throttle when the accelerator pedal is fully depressed and that the linkage returns to the closed throttle position.

It may be possible on some fuel injection systems to adjust the idle speed and idle mixture settings. The idle speed adjustment is normally carried out with an air bleed screw, which allows air to bypass the throttle butterfly without altering its angle. The position of the throttle butterfly is monitored by a sensor, so altering the angle of the throttle butterfly can affect the control of the fuel injection system.

It is possible to adjust the idle mixture setting on early fuel injection systems. The procedure is similar to that on carburettor fuel systems. The idle mixture is adjusted by a screw either on the airflow meter (air bleed or electrical), or a separate electrical idle mixture adjuster which is normally situated within the engine compartment (refer to manufacturer's data). It is necessary to check the idle mixture using an exhaust gas analyser using the same process as used to check the exhaust emission on a carburettor fuel system.

Modern petrol engine fuel systems are controlled by the engine management system, which also controls ignition. Engine management systems constantly monitor and control the idle speed and the fuel mixture settings for all engine operating conditions. It is therefore not possible with these types to make any adjustments to the fuel system.

The ECU constantly monitors the system for faults. If a fault is detected within the system the ECU records the relevant fault code in its memory. The ECU may also illuminate a warning lamp on the instrument panel, indicating to the driver that a fault has been detected. The ECU memory can be read using specialized diagnostic test equipment.

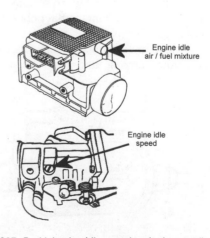

Figure 2.337 Fuel injection idle speed and mixture adjustments

Figure 2.338 Diagnostic test equipment connected to vehicle

2.40 IGNITION SYSTEMS – ROUTINE MAINTENANCE

2.40.1 Ignition system maintenance

Lack of maintenance of ignition systems, especially conventional contact breaker ignition systems, probably causes more breakdowns than any other engine fault. The following points outline some of the important checks that should be periodically carried out:

- sparking plugs
- contact breaker points
- dwell angle
- ignition timing
- electronic ignition systems.

Sparking plugs
During the running of the engine, the sparking plug is constantly producing an arc to ignite the air/fuel mixture. Due to the arcing, eventually the sparking plug electrodes wear and therefore require replacing during the routine servicing of the vehicle. The service interval for the sparking plugs will vary depending on the type of plug fitted to the engine. The vehicle manufacturer will state the service interval of the sparking plugs fitted to the engine.

Care should be taken when disconnecting the sparking plug HT leads to prevent damage to the lead, as these leads are often securely fastened to the top of the plugs. Always ensure that the correct type of sparking plug (i.e. heat range) is fitted to the engine. The appearance

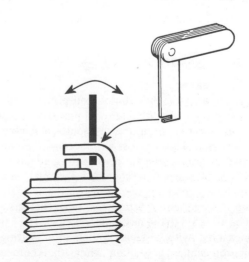

Figure 2.339 Adjusting the plug gap using a gap gauge tool

of the sparking plug electrode may indicate an engine, ignition or fuel system fault, so the appearance of the electrodes and insulators should be noted when the plugs are removed from the cylinder.

Platinum-tipped and copper-core sparking plugs are dealt with below.

Platinum tipped

These type of sparking plugs are generally fitted to most modern engines and require very little maintenance between services. They generally require replacement approximately every 100,000 km. Platinum-tipped sparking plugs should not be cleaned as cleaning may remove the platinum coating at the tip of the electrodes. If the gap requires adjustment check the gap with a plug gap gauge but do not touch the platinum tip. To adjust the sparking plug gap, bend the earth electrode using a plug gap gauge tool. Plug gap settings for platinum-tipped sparking plugs are generally in excess of 1.0 mm.

Copper core/nickel alloy

These should be removed and replaced at the recommended service intervals (e.g. every 10,000–20,000 km). If necessary they can also be cleaned, re-gapped, tested (if equipment is available) and refitted. Carbon can be cleaned off with a small wire brush, however the best results are obtained by sandblasting. If this method is used then all traces of sand must be removed from the plug, especially from the thread. The gap between the centre electrode and the earth electrode is measured with a feeler gauge. Adjustment of the plug gap is by bending the earth electrode with a plug gap gauge tool.

On refitting, the sparking plug should be tightened to the correct torque, as specified by the manufacturer. If a torque setting is unavailable, the following technique can be used as a guideline:

Gasket seat Tighten 'finger-tight' and then rotate the plug one-quarter turn with a plug spanner.

Taper seat Ensure that the seat is clean, tighten 'finger-tight' and then use a plug spanner to rotate the plug one-sixteenth turn.

2.40.2 Contact breaker-type ignition systems

Contact breaker

To provide a spark, the ignition coil primary circuit is switched on and off with a set of contact breaker points which are located within the distributor assembly. The current which passes across the faces of the contacts eventually corrodes the surfaces of the contacts. About every 10,000 km a new contact set should be fitted although some manufacturers suggest replacement at a higher mileage. After fitting the new contacts, they must be adjusted to the recommended gap. The gap can be measured with a feeler gauge after setting the distributor cam in a position where the contacts are fully open. The contact points gap can then be adjusted

by moving the base of the points either nearer or further from the distributor cam.

Use of a dwell-meter gives greater accuracy when setting the contact gap. An increase in the gap reduces the dwell and advances the timing of the spark. **Example:** If the dwell angle is reduced by 5°, then the timing will be advanced by 5°.

Distributor assembly

The following items should be checked within the distributor assembly for wear during routine servicing of a distributor-based ignition system. Note that the HT voltage passes through the distributor cap and rotor arm; the high voltage can cause arcing if a fault exists with any the components. You should check:

- distributor cap for cracks
- distributor HT terminals for security and wear
- rotor arm for cracks
- centrifugal mechanism for wear and seizure
- vacuum advance mechanism for wear, and the unit's diaphragm for leakage.

Excessive moisture or dirt on the secondary components can also cause arcing. It may be necessary during routine servicing to clean the distributor cap and ignition coil to prevent such arcing.

Ignition timing

Replacement of the contact points can alter the ignition timing; it is therefore very important that the ignition timing is checked and adjusted as necessary during routine servicing. Timing marks are normally provided on the crankshaft pulley to enable the ignition timing to be set. An outline procedure is as follows:

1. Ensure that the engine is at the correct operating temperature.
2. Stop the engine to allow a stroboscope (timing light) to be connected to No. 1 plug lead. It may be necessary to disconnect the vacuum advance pipe and plug the end of the hose (refer to manufacturer's data).
3. Restart the engine, set the engine speed to the recommended speed (usually at idle or slightly higher).

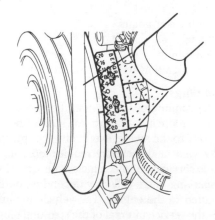

Figure 2.340 Checking of ignition timing

4 Direct the flashing light at the timing mark near to the front pulley. The 'freezing' of the motion enables the position of the timing marks on the pulley to be observed.

5 Check the ignition timing against manufacturer data.

Note: The flashing light also gives the impression that the moving parts of the engine are stationary, so extreme care must be taken to avoid injury.

6 If the ignition timing is incorrect, loosen the distributor clamp and rotate the distributor to obtain the correct ignition timing. Correct timing of the spark is important. If the spark is over-advanced, pinking and perhaps engine damage will result. Retarded timing causes poor power, increased fuel consumption and overheating.

It is also possible to check the operation of the advance mechanisms as engine speed and loads are changed with the engine running. For these procedures refer to manufacturer's data.

2.40.2 Maintenance of electronic systems

Apart from maintenance of common items such as sparking plugs and distributor assemblies, the various electronic control modules require little maintenance and are generally very reliable. Breakerless electronic ignition systems require ignition timing checks to be carried out at specified service intervals due to wear on distributor and associated drive components.

Computer-controlled ignition systems and engine management systems are generally non-serviceable, however the systems can usually be checked for serviceability with specialized test equipment. If the ECU has detected a fault, it may be possible to interrogate ECU for a fault code, applicable to the malfunctioning circuit within the system. Initial checks on external wiring and multi-pin connectors should be carried out, and individual units then tested as recommended. When units are identified as defective, they are replaced.

Warning: Extra care should be exercised when checking or handling electronically controlled ignition systems. These systems generate extremely high voltages; an electrical shock from these systems can cause injury or in some cases can be fatal.

2.41 ROUTINE MAINTENANCE OF THE DIESEL ENGINE

2.41.1 Diesel engine maintenance

Although the diesel engine is mainly used for high mileage vehicles, diesel engine vehicles require routine maintenance at similar service intervals to equivalent petrol engine vehicles.

The following areas normally require attention during routine maintenance:

- diesel fuel system
- diesel engine in general.

2.41.2 Fuel system maintenance

The diesel fuel system has to deliver a precise volume of fuel into the combustion chamber during each four-stroke cycle. The volume of diesel injected controls the power that a diesel engine develops. The components within the system, the injector pump and injectors are manufactured to very fine tolerances; some internal components within the injection pump are machined to tolerances within 1/1000 mm.

If impurities such as dirt or water enter the injection pump, these accurately machined components soon wear prematurely, allowing inaccurate fuel delivery, resulting in high smoke and soot levels from the exhaust.

A diesel fuel filter is used to remove these impurities. The fuel filter is normally situated between the fuel tank and the fuel pump. The diesel fuel filter is similar in construction to the petrol fuel filter although usually larger. During routine maintenance it is necessary to change the fuel filter. Two types of fuel filter are often used:

- element-type
- cartridge-type.

Element-type fuel filter

To change the element-type fuel filter it is necessary to remove the lower body of the fuel filter; the filter element can then be changed. Sediment and water collects in the bottom of the filter housing lower body so it is necessary to thoroughly clean the body of the filter housing before renewing the filter element. When refitting the filter housing, it is of great importance to fit new sealing gaskets/O-rings to the filter housing and retaining bolt. Air bleeding into the system will affect the running of the engine.

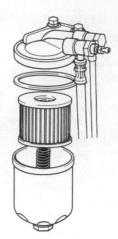

Figure 2.341 An element-type fuel filter

Cartridge-type fuel filter

The fuel filter element is contained within a cartridge, therefore to change the fuel filter the cartridge is unscrewed from the fuel filter housing and replaced with a new cartridge element. If the filter is fitted with an integral sediment filter switch, the switch needs to be changed to the new fuel filter before refitting.

Note: The fuel filter should be disposed of in a safe manner. Although diesel fuel does not produce a highly inflammable vapour, diesel fuel will harm the environment if disposed of improperly.

If the diesel fuel system is disturbed (i.e. a fuel system component is changed) and air enters the fuel system, it is usually necessary to bleed the air from the system before the engine can be restarted. The diesel fuel pump normally compresses the fuel in the system, which allows it to be drawn through the system. When air enters, the fuel pump compresses the air which is very compressible and therefore the fuel cannot be drawn through the system. A priming pump is usually fitted to the fuel system for this purpose. The pump is hand operated until the filter is full of fuel, usually felt through the action of the priming pump.

Water sediment filters

Many diesel fuel systems are fitted with a water sediment filter. Moisture forms within the fuel tank during certain weather conditions, and the diesel fuel carries this moisture in suspension through the fuel system. Water can corrode the internal components of the injection pump, therefore a sediment filter is fitted before the injection pump to collect the water.

The sediment filter is an integral part of the modern cartridge-type fuel filter. If the sediment filter is a separate component from the fuel filter, it should be drained during routine service of the vehicle. The sediment filter is usually fitted with a level indicator; if the sediment filter is full before the vehicle is due for a routine service, a warning light illuminates in the instrument panel to indicate to the driver that the filter requires emptying. A drain tap or plug is fitted at the bottom to allow water to be drained from the filter without removing the filter from the filter housing.

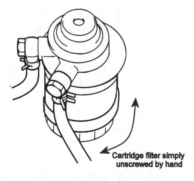

Cartridge filter simply unscrewed by hand

Figure 2.342 A cartridge-type fuel filter with sediment filter

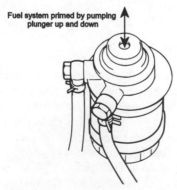

Fuel system primed by pumping plunger up and down

Figure 2.343 A diesel priming pump

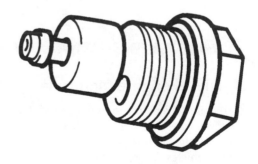

Figure 2.344 A diesel water sediment filter

2.41.3 Diesel engine general

Although a diesel engine generally requires similar maintenance to a petrol engine, the diesel engine is subject to more vibration, so flexible hoses, mounting etc. are all exposed to this vibration as well. A detailed check should be made on all flexible components and replacement carried out as necessary.

A diesel engine is not subject to an exhaust gas emission test as used on a petrol engine, although a diesel engined vehicle is subject to a smoke test during its annual MOT test. It is therefore necessary to check for excessive smoke emissions while road testing the vehicle. Excessive smoke and the colour of the smoke can be used to diagnose engine faults.

2.42 ALTERNATIVE TYPES OF ENGINE AND FUEL

2.42.1 Propulsion units

Internal-combustion engines, both petrol and diesel, use fuel refined from crude oil, a fossil fuel. The global reserves of fossil fuels are gradually declining, therefore scientists are constantly researching and developing engines, which either consume less fossil fuel and are less polluting in operation, or use an entirely different type of power source which is more freely available and also pollution-free.

The motorist has become familiar with the internal-combustion engine over many years; the engine is relatively small, yet powerful. Petrol and diesel fuels used are relatively easy to access from a network of fuel stations and the cost is reasonable which has allowed motoring to become widely available to the world's population.

However, development of alternative fuels and power sources is accelerating so the following sections are included to highlight some of the alternative sources of power and fuel. Some are already available to the motorist, while others are at the stages of being developed or evaluated in a commercial environment.

2.42.2 Electric propulsion

For many years it was felt that electrically propelled cars had great potential, but to date various attempts to offer this type of vehicle have not generated sufficient sales to justify widespread development of this smooth and quiet system.

Before the electric power unit becomes a serious rival to the internal-combustion engine, a low-priced design of battery must be developed, which must be light in weight, cheap and have a large energy storage capacity for its volume. Until this type of battery is commercially available, the conventional lead-acid battery must be relied on to store electrical energy.

The present day electric vehicle has to use a large number of heavy batteries that occupy a lot of space. Operational problems include the limited range of the vehicle and its comparatively low maximum speed. Nevertheless, there are many applications, such as local domestic delivery vehicles, for which an electrically propelled vehicle is ideal for the task it has to perform.

There has been a continuous process of development and research vehicles have been exhibited that, due to improved battery and electric motor design, have been able to achieve acceptable levels of performance. Weight, space and cost, however, still represent major hurdles to the production of such vehicles, along with the need to recharge the batteries at fairly regular intervals. Of course, there is also still a requirement to generate the electricity at a power generating station, which itself results in undesirable pollution.

2.42.3 Gas turbines

The gas turbine is now firmly established in aircraft, marine and industrial applications, but is making less rapid progress in the motor vehicle field. A Rover gas turbine car was first shown in 1950, and in 1952 was demonstrated at speeds of over 240 kilometres per hour (150 mph). We have also seen several experimental gas turbine-engined racing cars, but as yet no such car is on sale to the public.

Figure 2.345 illustrates a very simple model of a gas turbine. A shaft, mounted axially inside a tube, is supported on bearings and has fixed to it two 'fans', one near each end. Rotation of the shaft causes one of the fans to blow air along the tube and this moving air tends to rotate the second fan in the manner of a windmill. The power developed by the second fan would only just be enough to drive the first fan if there were no friction, and clearly the device could not be used to drive any outside mechanism.

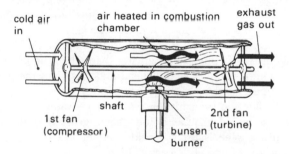

Figure 2.345 An elementary gas turbine

However, by inserting a burner between the two fans, the air passing along the tube can be heated, causing it to expand. The expansion causes the flow of air to increase speed, thus it will pass the second fan at a higher speed than the speed at which it passed the first fan. This enables the second fan to develop more power than is needed to drive the first fan.

Figure 2.346 shows a simple combustion chamber in which the gas is merely heated by the continuous combustion of fuel. In the gas turbine all the energy put

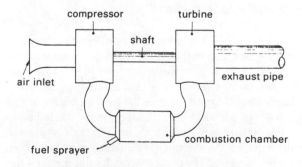

Figure 2.346 Diagram of a simple shaft gas turbine

into the gas by the combustion of fuel is available for driving the turbine, and as there is usually far more than is required merely to drive the compressor, the turbine shaft therefore has an excess of power which can be harnessed in some way. With a jet engine, as used in aircraft, this additional energy is used to provide a thrust by discharging the hot gases through a jet pipe after they have passed the turbine.

The turbine shaft can of course be connected to some kind of mechanism such as the transmission system of a motor vehicle or an electricity generator. In this form the gas turbine would not be very satisfactory for vehicle propulsion, since the torque developed depends upon compressor speed. The torque would be low at low turbine speeds, and a mechanism similar to the clutch and gearbox used with a piston engine would be essential.

A considerable improvement can be achieved by using the arrangement illustrated in Figure 2.347. Here, one turbine is coupled to the compressor while a second turbine is mounted on a separate shaft. The 'power turbine' can be coupled to the driving wheels of a vehicle, and this arrangement allows the vehicle to remain stationary with the power turbine stopped but the compressor turbine running. The torque on the output shaft when the power turbine is stationary and the compressor is running at its maximum speed is about two to three times greater than when the power turbine is running at full speed and this gives the gas turbine something of the characteristics of an automatic variable-ratio transmission system. For example, a car, which would require a four-speed gearbox when a petrol engine is used, would need only a two-speed gearbox if fitted with a gas turbine.

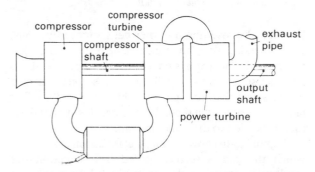

Figure 2.347 A gas turbine with separate compressor and power turbines (two-shaft gas turbine)

Early gas turbine engines were less efficient than piston-type engines, and had relatively high fuel consumption. Several methods have been adopted to improve this. The first is by the use of a heat exchanger, shown in diagrammatic form in Figure 2.348. The object of this device is to put some of the heat normally carried away by the exhaust gas into the air leaving the compressor, thus reducing the amount of fuel which must be burned to provide a given temperature rise. By this means it has been possible to achieve considerable improvements in

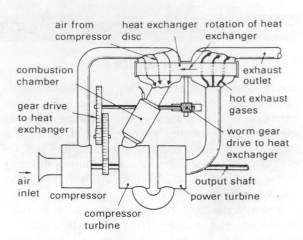

Figure 2.348 A two-shaft gas turbine with heat exchanger

fuel consumption, and some of the most recent gas turbines are claimed to have a fuel consumption comparable with that of a compression-ignition engine.

Several types of heat exchanger have been tried. One type consists of two large discs, about 0.6 m in diameter, of a ceramic material having numerous small transverse passages through them, disposed vertically on each side of the engine and rotated at about 1/2000 the speed of the compressor shaft. Exhaust gases from the power turbine are led through ducts to one half of each disc and in passing through the small passages in the disc give up some of their heat to the discs before being discharged through the exhaust system. As the discs rotate the heated portions are carried into ducts, which direct air from the compressor through the discs before it passes into the combustion chamber, thus heating this air.

A second method by which the efficiency of a gas turbine can be improved is by raising the temperature of the gases entering the turbine. Typically, the temperatures at this point are in the region of 1000–1500°C, which dictates the use of more expensive materials such as special alloys or ceramics.

The maximum gas temperature is limited by restricting the quantity of fuel delivery to the combustion chamber to a value that is below the maximum. This results in an air/fuel ratio that is considerably weaker than the chemically correct mixture.

A gas turbine engine is usually started by driving the compressor shaft with an external power source; usually an electric motor. When the compressor is turning fast enough to blow air into the combustion chamber, the fuel supply is turned on and fuel is sprayed continuously through a sprayer nozzle into the combustion chamber. Combustion is initiated by a sparking plug and once started, combustion will continue as long as fuel continues to be supplied. Varying the rate of fuel delivery regulates power output. Compressor speed ranges from about 15,000 rpm when idling, to a maximum of about 40,000–50,000 rpm or more. The power turbine speed varies from zero to about 35,000–40,000 rpm. For automotive applications, it is therefore necessary to have a speed-reducing gear giving a ratio of the order of about 10 to 1 between the power turbine shaft and the vehicle propeller shaft if a conventional final-drive ratio is to be used.

The main advantages claimed for the gas turbine are:

1 High power output from a given weight.
2 The torque output characteristics permit a notable simplification of the transmission system.
3 Smooth power with very low vibration due to absence of reciprocating parts.
4 No rubbing parts (such as pistons) so that internal friction and wear are almost eliminated.
5 Easy starting.
6 Can use a wide range of fuels and does not require expensive anti-knock additives.
7 Low lubricating oil consumption.
8 No water-cooling system needed.
9 Requires little routine maintenance.

Compared with a conventional engine the main disadvantages are:

1 High fuel consumption during part-load operation.
2 Takes a comparatively long time for the engine to accelerate from idle to normal operating speed.
3 A large space is occupied by the heat exchanger.
4 The characteristic 'whine' from the engine becomes troublesome for the driver on journeys during which speed is sustained.

2.42.4 Wankel engine

As long ago as 1769 James Watt took out a patent for an engine in which steam pressure drove a rotating vane in a circular housing, and there have since been many attempts to produce an internal-combustion engine in which the pressure of gases after combustion acted upon rotating components enclosed in a suitable casing. For a variety of reasons none of these showed any likelihood of challenging the piston engine. However, towards the end of 1959, it became known that a German engineer, Felix Wankel, had devised an engine working on the equivalent of the four-stroke cycle but employing only rotating parts. The German firm of NSU took up development of this engine and early in 1965 they produced a small car with one of these engines for sale to the public. Two years later they announced the production version of a large car having the equivalent of a two-litre engine.

In 1965, Toyo Kogyo (Mazda) of Japan also introduced a car fitted with a rotary engine and the company has remained loyal to this type of engine for use in some of its sports cars.

During recent years, the difficulty of meeting both the emission requirements and fuel economy regulations has caused many manufacturers to turn away from the rotary engine, although Mazda are still continuing to use and develop this type of engine.

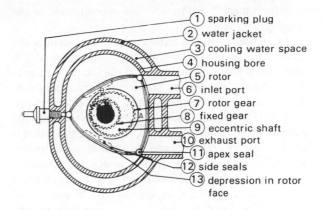

1 sparking plug
2 water jacket
3 cooling water space
4 housing bore
5 rotor
6 inlet port
7 rotor gear
8 fixed gear
9 eccentric shaft
10 exhaust port
11 apex seal
12 side seals
13 depression in rotor face

Figure 2.349 The main working parts of a Wankel engine

Each 'element' or power chamber of this engine consists of three main parts: a housing, a rotor, and a shaft. Figure 2.349 shows a section through one element.

The housing contains a shallow bore (4) of a special shape known as epitrochoidal. (An epitrochoid is the line traced out by a point between the centre and the circumference of a circle as the circle rolls round the outside of another circle twice as large.) Carried on bearings co-axial with the centre of the housing bore is a shaft on which is formed an eccentric (9) over which fits a rotor (5) shaped like an equilateral triangle but with curved sides or flanks. An internal gear (7) concentric with, and fixed to, the rotor engages with a fixed gear (8) secured centrally in the housing and having a hollow centre through which the shaft passes. This fixed gear has two-thirds the number of teeth in the internal gear (7) in the rotor.

The result of this arrangement is that when the shaft is rotated, the rotor is not only carried round eccentrically with it but also rotates in the same direction as the shaft but at one third the speed.

In every position of the rotor its three corners or apices (plural of apex) touch the housing bore so that three compartments or chambers are formed between the housing bore, the flanks of the rotor and the end plates of the housing. These chambers are made gas-tight by special seals at each apex (11) and the sides (12) of the rotor.

For every three revolutions of the shaft, the rotor rotates once. During this time the volume of each chamber passes through two maximum and two minimum values, so that the operations of the four-stroke cycle will be carried out in each of the three chambers. The difference between the maximum and minimum volumes represents the swept volume of each chamber, and the ratio of maximum volume divided by minimum volume is the compression ratio. The minimum volume is what would be called the clearance volume in a piston engine, and the greater part of this is contained in a depression (13) in each rotor flank.

An inlet port (6) and an exhaust port (10) enter the housing at the points indicated in Figure 2.349 and a sparking plug (1) is fitted in the opposite side of the housing.

In Figure 2.349 the letters A, B and C identify the flanks of the rotors, and in the description of the operation which follows we use these letters to refer to the chambers between the housing and the appropriate rotor flank. In the position shown, chamber A is in one of its two minimum volume positions, in this case the equivalent in a piston engine to TDC when the piston is at the end of exhaust and beginning of induction strokes. Chamber B has passed its position of maximum volume and the gas in it is now being compressed ready for ignition. Chamber C is approaching its position of maximum volume and the gas in it is expanding, the equivalent of the expansion or power stroke on a piston engine.

Figure 2.350 shows the events that occur in each chamber as the shaft completes one revolution. The shaft is shown turning anticlockwise and Figure 2.350a shows the position when the shaft has turned through 90° from the position shown in Figure 2.349.

Fresh mixture is being induced into chamber A, which is in communication with the inlet port but cut off from the exhaust port; this is the early part of the induction stroke.

Chamber B is still decreasing in size and is approaching the end of the compression stroke.

Chamber C has just reached its position of maximum volume, equivalent to BDC in a piston engine, when the piston is at the beginning of the exhaust stroke, and this chamber is already open to the exhaust port.

In Figure 2.350b the shaft has turned a further 90° and chamber A has completed about two-thirds of its induction stroke.

Chamber B is in the position of minimum volume corresponding to TDC at the end of the compression stroke of a piston engine. The mixture has been ignited and combustion is taking place.

Chamber C has completed about a third of its exhaust stroke: its volume is decreasing and the burned gases are being forced out of the exhaust port.

Figure 2.350c shows the position after the shaft has turned its third quarter of a revolution. Chamber A has reached its position of maximum volume, corresponding to BDC at the end of the induction stroke of a piston engine, and the inlet port is beginning to close.

Chamber B is increasing in volume at the early part of the power stroke.

Chamber C is just starting the last third of its exhaust stroke.

Finally Figure 2.350d shows the situation at the end of one complete revolution of the shaft. This is similar to the position shown in Figure 2.349 except that the chambers have all moved round one place. During the next revolution of the shaft, chamber A will carry out the same operations as chamber B did on the revolution just described, chamber B will repeat those of chamber C, and chamber C those of chamber A.

During the following revolution of the shaft (the third) chamber A will repeat the operations just described for chamber C, chamber B those of chamber A, and chamber C those of chamber B, and the position will by then have returned to that shown in Figure 2.349.

Thus it is seen that the engine produces one power stroke per revolution of the shaft, and it is therefore equivalent, in this respect, to a single-cylinder two-stroke engine or a two-cylinder four-stroke engine having a cylinder swept volume equal to the swept volume of one chamber.

If two of these 'elements' are used, the firing frequency of a four-cylinder four-stroke engine is obtained. Such an engine is called a 'two-rotor' or 'twin-rotor' engine.

Although air-cooled engines of this type have been built, those at present in production have the housing water-cooled. The rotor is cooled by circulating oil from the lubrication system around its hollow interior, and this necessitates the use of an oil cooler.

The main advantages of this type of engine are:

1 Simplicity. Each 'element' has only two moving parts – the rotor and the eccentric shaft, and because communication between the chambers and the ports is controlled by the rotor, valves and their operating gear are completely eliminated.
2 The absence of reciprocating parts should allow the engine to operate at higher speeds.
3 Since all moving parts have simple rotary motion they are easily balanced and vibration can be eliminated.
4 If peripheral ports are used they are never closed. This leads to improved volumetric efficiency. Values in excess of 100% have been claimed.

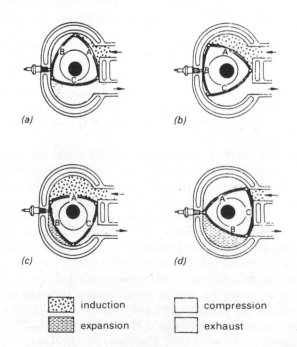

(a)   (b)   (c)   (d)

	induction		compression
	expansion		exhaust

Figure 2.350 Operation of the Wankel engine

5 For a given swept volume the engine is lighter and less bulky than a piston engine. The gain in this direction increases as the number of rotors is increased.

2.42.5 Stirling engine

Introduced in Scotland during the mid-nineteenth century, this type of engine has been considered for vehicle propulsion. The clean exhaust is its main appeal, but as yet it cannot compete with conventional types of engine.

In the past the Stirling engine was called a steam engine because in the early days the pistons were powered by steam heated by an external combustion source. Modern units are far removed from the ideas suggested by the term 'steam engine'. Although combustion still takes place outside the cylinder, the fluid used to drive the pistons is hydrogen, helium or Freon.

Principle of operation

Figure 2.351 shows a simplified, two-cylinder, double-acting engine, which in this case, uses a swash plate to rotate the output shaft. As both sides of the pistons are used, the piston rods are fitted with effective seals to prevent loss of the operating fluid. When a conventional crankshaft is used, the thrust from the piston rod is applied first to a crosshead and then on to a conventional connecting rod and crankshaft.

In the diagram, the fluid above Piston A has been heated and the expanding vapour is driving the piston down the cylinder. Below Piston A the cooler has lowered the vapour temperature and the fluid is contracting. This action is repeated in each cylinder to provide the working power of the engine.

Unlike the normal engine, the Stirling works on a 'closed cycle': this means that the operating fluid does not leave the engine and that the energy given to the fluid conversion process is by means of a heat exchanger supplied from an external heat source.

Combustion within the heater is continuous and in many ways similar to the process used in a gas turbine. Fuel is sprayed at low pressure into a chamber and initially ignited by electrical means. The amount of heat that is then passed across to the operating fluid depends on the quantity of fuel injected, so power output can be easily regulated. At first it would appear that response would be slow, but results from prototype engines show that the time from zero torque to maximum torque is only about 0.1 s.

A prototype engine is shown in Figure 2.352.

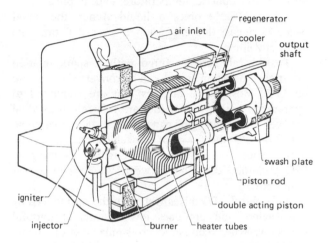

Figure 2.352 A Stirling-type engine

The advantages of the Stirling engine are based mainly on the continuous combustion process.

1 **Low exhaust emission.** Excess air of 20–80% in the air/fuel mixture, together with adequate combustion time and no quench of the flame by 'cold' metal surfaces, gives near-complete combustion. Smoke level is also much lower.

2 **Fuel economy.** The engine accepts a large range of liquid or gaseous fuels. There are no special fuel requirements such as octane or cetane. It is expected that a brake thermal efficiency of about 40% is possible and even under part-load conditions, the efficiency is at least as good as the CI engine.

3 **Low noise level.** A silencer is unnecessary because the noise level is only about 25% of that emitted by a fully-silenced CI engine. No valve mechanism is fitted, so mechanical noise is very low.

These advantages make the engine most attractive, but there is still much development work needed to improve the reliability of new engine components such as fluid seals. When cost and reliability approach the standard of conventional engines, then widespread use of this type of engine could be possible.

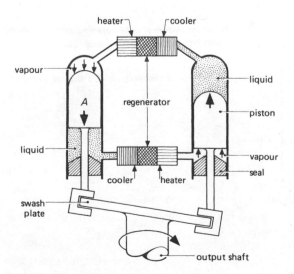

Figure 2.351 Principle of the Stirling engine

2.42.6 Dual fuel vehicles – liquid petroleum gas

Liquid petroleum gas (LPG) is the general name for a mixture of two gases, butane and propane. The gases are either produced from the refining of crude oil or extracted from gas fields in the same way as oil. Natural gas has similar energy properties to LPG, however LPG is easier to store than natural gas and therefore more suitable for automotive use. To transport natural gas in a vehicle, the gas either requires compressing to a very high pressure (160–200 bar), or cooling at a low temperature (minus 160°C), so changing the gas into a liquid. Depending on the conditions at which the LPG is stored, it is either a gas or a liquid. When stored at normal atmospheric temperature and a pressure of 2–20 bar, LPG becomes a liquid. When the liquid becomes a gas, this expansion is over 250 times its original volume.

Possibly all vehicles fitted with a spark ignition internal-combustion engine can be converted to operate on LPG. Most petrol engines that are converted to operate on both types of fuel are referred to as 'dual fuel' vehicles. The engine can either be set to operate on petrol or LPG, the driver of the vehicle changes to the desired fuel type with a switch. Engines operating on LPG generally consume between 20–30% more gas than petrol.

Like petrol, LPG mixes well with the air induced by the engine, and produces lower levels of harmful emissions when compared to similar petrol engine vehicles. Many countries are tempting vehicle owners to purchase new vehicles or convert their existing vehicles to operate on LPG by providing lower taxes on LPG or by offering other incentives. The use of LPG in motor vehicles is limited in some countries and locations due to the fact that not all filling stations store LPG readily as they do petrol or DERV. Conversions to LPG are readily available for fuel-injected engines as well as older carburettor designs.

LPG systems operate by passing gas vapour into the air stream in the inlet manifold, in place of the atomized petrol. In a dual fuel vehicle the engine is normally started on petrol and switched over to LPG once the engine is running. The LPG system utilizes many of the electronic sensors that supply information to a fuel injection ECU.

Figure 2.353 illustrates an LPG fuel system fitted to a petrol engine with a petrol injection system. The gas is stored in a gas cylinder, which is normally situated at the rear of the vehicle. A gas valve allows the tank to be filled at a filling station with the use of a suitable connection. Note that the volume of LPG is limited to 80% of the cylinder's capacity, the remaining space inside the cylinder allows for the expansion of the liquid LPG during transportation. The LPG, which is in a liquid state, flows from the cylinder (LPG tank) to the evaporator pressure regulator. The pressure of the LPG is lowered, which turns the liquid LPG into a gas. The gas passes to the distributor, which is controlled by an LPG ECU. The LPG ECU makes use of the information form the sensors, and then controls the volume of LPG emitted by the distributor.

The illustration shows the gas mixing with the air stream in the inlet manifold while passing through a venturi, similar to the principle used with a carburettor. Other LPG systems may use one injector per cylinder to mix the gas with the air for each cylinder, similar to the fuel injection principle.

The ideal air/fuel ratio (chemically correct mixture) of LPG differs slightly to that for petrol, being 15.5:1 rather than 14.7:1. If the vehicle emissions are tested with a gas analyser, the gas analyser settings should be changed from the petrol to the LPG setting before testing commences, otherwise inaccurate test results will be displayed.

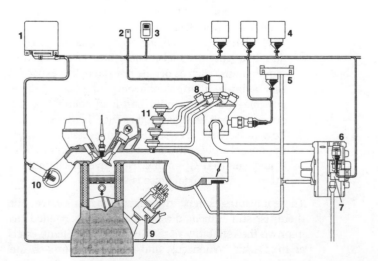

Schematic diagram of an LPG system (injection principle)

1 ECU, 2 Diagnosis plug, 3 Fuel selection switch, 4 Relay, 5 Air-intake pressure sensor, 6 Evaporator-pressure regulator, 7 Flow-interrupt valve, 8 Distributor with step motor, 9 RPM signal, 10 Lambda O_2 sensor, 11 Gas injector nozzle.

Figure 2.353 LPG fuel system fitted to a spark-ignition engine with a petrol injection system

2.42.7 Hybrid vehicles

A hybrid is a vehicle that has two or more power sources to propel it. An example that is often seen is a moped; the petrol engine is one power source and the rider provides the second power source by 'pedal power'. Other vehicles that are classed as hybrid include some trains (diesel and electric) and submarines (nuclear and electric).

The development of hybrid vehicles has also led to the production of hybrid cars. The electric power source, previously outlined in this section, has been used to propel many types of vehicles from local domestic delivery vehicles through to trucks and buses. Although very quiet in operation and producing almost zero emissions, the disadvantages of the electric vehicle is often the heavy weight of batteries required to propel it, and also the very short distance which can be covered before it is necessary to recharge the batteries.

Petrol engine cars are both lightweight and can cover extensive distances before they need to refill the fuel tank. Refilling the fuel tank is very rapid compared with the time taken to recharge batteries. The disadvantages of the petrol engine are high emissions and high fuel consumption when compared to electric power.

A hybrid car combines the low emissions and fuel consumption of an electric vehicle and provides a lightweight vehicle that can travel a long distance. The hybrid vehicle effectively makes use of one or both of the power sources to propel the vehicle. Depending on how the hybrid system is designed, the petrol engine may simply function as a means of driving a generator. The generator then charges the batteries that power the electric motors, which provide power to the vehicle transmission. Alternative designs allow the petrol engine and/or the electric motors to be selected to provide power to the vehicle transmission system.

Research has shown that the average driver of a vehicle uses the maximum power of an engine less than 1% of the overall driving time. Therefore, the size of the petrol engine used in the current range of hybrid cars provides sufficient power to be acceptable to most drivers.

To propel an automotive vehicle, the power source has to initially overcome the friction between the road and tyres, together with the resistance of the vehicle passing through the air. The power source also has to provide power for the accessories that aid the driver, such as lighting, power steering, even air-conditioning. The power consumed to overcome these energy requirements is very small in relation to the maximum power that the average size engine is capable of producing. The remaining engine power is used to provide acceleration – the available power dictates the rate of acceleration.

The petrol engines used in a hybrid car are lightweight and very fuel efficient; they typically produce approximately 70 brake horsepower which is supplemented with an electric motor rated typically at approximately 50 horse power.

A typical hybrid car contains the following components, as shown in Figure 2.354:

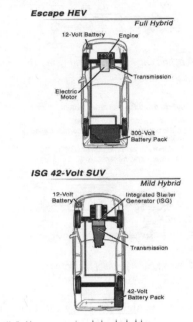

Figure 2.354 Components of the hybrid car

Petrol engine The engine is similar to those fitted to conventional vehicles e.g. four cylinders, four-stroke normally aspirated, etc. However, the capacity of the engine used is usually relatively small.

Electric motor The electric motor is used to propel the car, however with the use of electronic technology, the motor can also function as a generator to recharge the batteries.

Transmission The transmission can be either manual or automatic.

Fuel tank The fuel tank is used to store petrol for the petrol engine.

Batteries The batteries provide the energy source for the electric motor, either recharged by an external power source or recharged by the generator or electric motor when it is functioning as a generator.

The two power sources are combined in one of two forms, either in parallel or in series.

The parallel hybrid connects the petrol engine and the electric motor to the gearbox (Figure 2.356), so both power sources can apply their energy to the gearbox independently or simultaneously.

The series hybrid utilizes the power of the petrol engine and electric motor in a different manner (Figure 2.355). The power of the petrol engine is applied to a generator, which is then used to either charge the batteries or to directly power an electric motor. The electric motor then applies power to the gearbox. Note that on series applications, the petrol engine is never used to directly supply power to the gearbox. The power sources are connected in series, hence the name series hybrid.

Hybrid drive *Series arrangement*
VM *Internal-combustion engine,*
EL *Electric drive (motor or generator-based operation),*
BA *Battery or external power supply,*
LSG *Power shift transmission.*

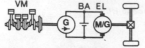

Figure 2.355 A hybrid car – series hybrid-type

Hybrid drive *Parallel arrangement*

VM *Internal-combustion engine,*
EL *Electric drive (motor or generator-based operation),*
BA *Battery or external power supply,*
LSG *Power shift transmission.*

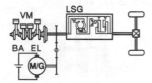

Figure 2.356 A hybrid car – parallel hybrid-type

The hybrid car offers high efficiency yet it also has high performance. It utilizes the power of the electric motor to supplement the energy provided by the petrol engine during situations such as accelerating from a standstill or driving up hills.

While a conventional vehicle is braking, the kinetic energy in the moving vehicle is absorbed or removed by the braking system in the form of the heat generated during braking. However, with a hybrid car, during deceleration the electric motor becomes a generator (electronic control enables the components of the motor to function as a generator). The motor/generator is used during the deceleration period to recharge the batteries. If the hybrid car reduces speed over longer periods, rather than during rapid stops, more of the kinetic energy can be used to recharge the batteries. The use of the electric motor to recharge the batteries also assists with the braking effect of the car, thus reducing wear on the brake components.

The hybrid car can reduce the waste of energy and the production of emissions in many driving situations, e.g. the petrol engine is switched off while the car is stationary. The car generally operates on battery power alone, but when additional power is required for accelerating or if the batteries require charging, the petrol engine starts and supplements the battery power. Battery power alone can accelerate the car to around 42 kilometres per hour (15 mph). Additionally, a separate starter motor is no longer required to start the petrol engine because the hybrid car uses the electric motor to start the engine when the vehicle is moving.

Vehicle manufacturers have also made use of the latest technology in other areas of these hybrid cars, to ensure that the vehicle is as efficient as possible. The design of the car usually provides the best

aerodynamics for the intended purpose of the vehicle (e.g. a family-sized car or a sports car). Materials used throughout the car are as light as possible (e.g. carbon fibre, aluminium) and tyres with the lowest rolling resistance are used to increase efficiency.

The initial cost of a hybrid car is normally higher than that of a conventional petrol engine car, however the emission levels and fuel consumption are lower than petrol engine vehicles. Due to the high efficiency and low emissions, some governments and local authorities encourage the use of hybrid cars with special tax reductions and the waiving of levies and tolls.

2.42.8 Fuel-cell vehicles

The combustion engines already described in this book all use forms of fossil fuel to provide energy, whether the fuel is crude oil (petrol and diesel) or a gas. All these fuels are located underground, recovered from the ground, refined into a useable commodity and then sold to the end user.

The consumption of fossil fuels is very high as they are used throughout the world in a vast array of industries. Once consumed, fossil fuels will eventually disappear, or at least become inaccessible. The conversion of all these fossil fuels into an energy source that is usable for everyday purposes also creates emissions that are usually harmful to humans or to the environment in which we live. Scientists are constantly searching for alternative sources of energy that can be used for automotive applications into and beyond the next few centuries, that will also avoid the harmful by-products of fossil fuel combustion.

Fuel cells appear to be a source of energy that may be an alternative; they could be used to replace many fossil fuel applications.

Basic principles of fuel cells

Fuel cells, certainly those that are being developed for automotive applications, make use of hydrogen and oxygen to produce water. During the process in which hydrogen and oxygen are converted into water, electricity is also created.

Conversion of the gases into water is effectively a chemical change. The hydrogen and oxygen are pressurized and passed into the fuel cell. Within the cell are an anode and a cathode, (effectively a negative and positive electrical terminal) which form the ends of an electrical circuit. In some ways, the fuel cell is therefore similar to each individual cell of a lead–acid battery, which also has an anode and a cathode.

A fuel cell also contains a catalyst, which is a material that naturally causes a reaction or chemical change when other substances come into contact with it. The catalyst in a fuel cell is porous and allows the oxygen and hydrogen to pass through it. However, as the gases pass through, a chemical change takes place.

When the hydrogen is forced into the fuel cell, it passes through the catalyst, which causes a separation of the hydrogen into hydrogen ions and electrons. The electrons then flow via the anode through the electrical circuit back to the cathode. This flow of electrons is an electric current. Although the hydrogen electrons are now providing some useful function, the hydrogen ions remain free within the fuel cell.

When oxygen is forced into the fuel cell and through the catalyst, the oxygen is split into atoms. These oxygen atoms attract the free hydrogen ions (which have a positive charge). In addition, the hydrogen electrons (which have now passed through the electrical circuit to the cathode) also combine with the oxygen atoms and hydrogen ions. The net result of the process within the fuel cell is the production of water, but additionally a flow of electrons is created, which is an electric current.

Each individual fuel cell only produces a small amount of electrical energy, however it is possible to create a stack of fuel cells that together can produce sufficient electrical power to drive an electric motor that would in turn power a motor vehicle.

Although the above information represents a very simplified explanation of fuel cell operation, it is hopefully sufficient for the reader to appreciate that fuel cells provide a clean and relatively efficient means of producing electricity. The main emission from the fuel cell process is water. Oxygen is freely available from the air, but producing the hydrogen represents the major hurdle. At the moment, the production of hydrogen is an expensive process and although fuel cell technology is developing rapidly, the viability of fuel cells will depend on the cost of the hydrogen and its availability.

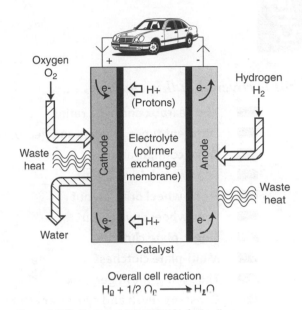

Figure 2.357 Operating principle of a fuel cell

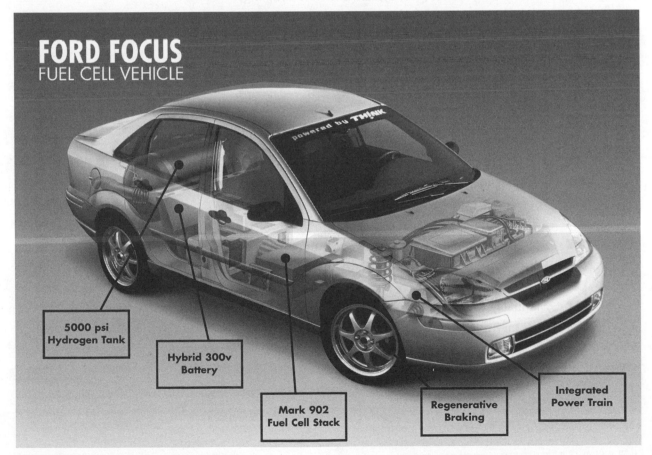

Figure 2.358 Components of a fuel cell vehicle

TRANSMISSION SYSTEMS

what is covered in this chapter . . .

3.1 THE GEARBOX AND GEAR RATIOS

Figure 3.1 A simple manual transmission system

3.1.1 Reason for a gearbox

The internal-combustion engines generally used in motor vehicles typically operate over a relatively limited effective speed range, say 1000–7000 rev/min. Within this speed range an engine will produce a varying level of torque (turning effort), with low engine speeds generally giving low torque levels. When the speed is too low, or if the load is too great, the engine stalls.

If a vehicle were not fitted with a gearbox (i.e. there was a direct connection between the engine and the final reduction gear/differential) the following disadvantages would be apparent:

1 *Poor acceleration from rest*
   Due to the low torque and power at low engine speeds, it would be necessary to apply high engine revolutions and slip the clutch for a considerable period of time to avoid stalling the engine. A road speed of at least 24 km/h (15 mph) would have to be reached before full clutch engagement could take place and, during this time, the driving force at the wheels (tractive effort) would only be slightly greater than the force opposing the motion of the vehicle (tractive resistance). The acceleration is governed by the difference between the tractive effort and tractive resistance; if this difference is small, the acceleration will be poor.

2 *Poor hill-climbing ability*
   When the gradient of a hill increases, it increases the resistance to the vehicle movement. This means that as soon as a hill is approached the engine would slow down and eventually stall. This could be overcome by employing a larger engine with higher torque output, but it would be uneconomic for most vehicles.

3 *Vehicle could not be driven at low speeds*
   When the vehicle speed is decreased, the engine speed would also decrease. Slipping of the clutch

would be necessary to avoid stalling if the vehicle had to be driven at low speeds.

4 *No neutral or reverse*
   The clutch would need to be disengaged all the time the vehicle were stationary. The vehicle could not be manoeuvred as required.

The four items listed above highlight some of the reasons for fitting a gearbox and its importance.

3.1.2 Gear leverage

As a simple means of illustrating leverage, Figure 3.2 shows how human effort could be applied with the aid of a lever to help move a vehicle.

When the human effort is applied to the vehicle without a lever, there isn't sufficient force to move the car up the hill. However, by using the lever, which is pivoted at the bumper, the same amount of force will move the car. Note that the length of the lever above the pivot point is greater than the length below the pivot point. Effectively, the lever provides a multiplication of the force applied by the human. The amount of multiplication will be the same as the ratio of the two lengths of the lever (above and below the pivot point).

Other devices can function in the same way as this simple lever, using many different mechanical arrangements to achieve similar results. Although not always called levers, these other devices are in fact still providing leverage. Figure 3.3a shows another simple form of lever using weights and pulleys. A force applied at the end of the lever (using weight m and the pulleys) lifts a load four times as great (weight M). This shows that a small force can be amplified by using a lever system.

Figure 3.3b shows how two discs or wheels may be used to obtain leverage when they are connected together at their outer edges (circumferences). In this example a mass acting on shaft C will support a larger mass on shaft D. The weight acting on shaft C is half of the weight acting on shaft D, but the disc A is half the diameter of disc B.

Figure 3.2 Human effort needed can be reduced by using a lever

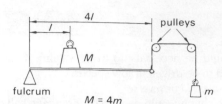

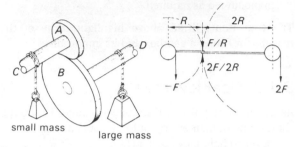

(a) Large mass lifted by a small mass

(b) Torque multiplication

Figure 3.3 Gear leverage

This arrangement may be considered a simple gearbox, with the engine connected to shaft C, and the road wheels connected to shaft D. In this example, the output torque is double the engine torque (ratio of disc B to disc A), and if disc B is made three times the diameter of A, the output torque will be trebled. This appears to produce something for nothing, but speed must be taken into account. It will be seen that as the torque increases, the speed decreases proportionally, and therefore the power produced remains the same (assuming the mechanism is 100% efficient). In Figure 3.3b the speed ratio (movement ratio, also called the gear ratio) which in this case is 2:1, indicates that two revolutions of the input shaft are required to rotate the output shaft by one revolution.

Belts, pulleys and friction drives were used on early designs of motorcar, but when Panhard introduced a sliding gear wheel arrangement, the other systems gradually disappeared.

3.1.3 Determining the correct gear ratios

High maximum vehicle speed, combined with good acceleration and economy over the whole speed range, requires a system of gearing that allows the engine to operate at the speeds at which it develops its best performance. Maximum engine power, torque and economy usually occur at different engine speeds, so this makes the task of matching the gear ratio difficult, especially when variable operating conditions and driver demands have to be taken into account.

The gear ratios chosen need to take into account the engine requirement to suit a given operating condition (Table 3.1).

Table 3.1 Engine requirements

Operating condition	Requirement
Maximum vehicle speed	Maximum engine power
Maximum acceleration	Maximum engine torque
Maximum traction	Maximum engine torque
Maximum economy	Engine at mid-range speed and under light load with a small throttle opening

The type of engine usually installed in a modern light vehicle requires a gearbox that provides a minimum of four forward speeds and a reverse gear. This gives a reasonable performance to suit most driving conditions apart from economy, which normally requires an extra forward gear ratio, that is a fifth gear that is higher than the conventional 'top gear'.

It should be noted that a high gear normally means one that has a ratio with a low numerical value, i.e. a ratio of 1:1 is higher than the ratio of 2:1. The lower the gear, the greater is the reduction between the engine and road wheels; this means that for a given engine speed, the road wheel speed is lower.

Maximum vehicle speed

This is achieved when the highest gear is in use and the throttle is held fully open.

To minimise friction losses, a gear ratio of 1:1 (direct drive) is chosen for 'top gear' wherever possible. Consequently, the setting of 'top gear' is really the choosing of a final drive ratio to suit the diameter of road wheel and engine characteristic. In theory, the overall gearing is calculated so that the maximum speed of the vehicle is achieved when the engine is at a speed that is providing maximum power. In practice, top gear on many vehicles (e.g. fifth gear) is in fact more suited to cruising and economy, with fourth gear producing maximum speed.

Figure 3.4 shows the considerations that have to be made to ensure that a vehicle can attain a high maximum speed. It shows the balance between the engine power required and the engine power available. Data relating to the power available is gathered by performing an engine power curve test (often referred to as the 'brake power curve' of the engine because the test is carried out on an engine brake dynamometer). The data for the available engine power is obtained from a calculation of the power that is required to overcome the tractive resistance of the vehicle when it is moving along a level road.

The tractive resistance (sometimes called total resistance) includes:

1 *Air resistance* – due to movement of the vehicle through the air.
2 *Rolling resistance* – due to friction between the tyre and road. This is largely influenced by the type of road surface and tyre size and type.

3 *Gradient resistance* – increases as the steepness of the incline (hill) acts against the vehicle motion.

Figure 3.4a indicates that the engine power needed to propel a vehicle increases with the speed of the vehicle. Generally, if the speed of the vehicle is doubled, the engine power required is eight times as great. In this example a power of 150 kW is needed to drive the vehicle at 200 km/h.

The power output of the engine fitted to this vehicle is shown in Figure 3.4b. This power curve shows that the engine produces a peak brake power of 150 kW at 5000 rev/min.

If the maximum road speed is to be as high as possible, the gear ratio of this vehicle must be set so that the peak of the 'power available' curve occurs at a road speed of 200 km/h. In this case the overall gear ratio (gearbox ratio × final drive ratio) must ensure that an engine speed of 5000 rev/min drives the vehicle at 200 km/h.

Once the relative positions of the two curves have been decided, it is then possible to examine the general performance with respect to acceleration. The vertical difference between the two curves is the surplus power available for acceleration, so this can be plotted as a separate curve to show the speed at which maximum acceleration is achieved.

Assuming friction is ignored, it must be appreciated that a gearing system neither increases nor decreases power; the power output from the transmission system is similar to the power delivered by the engine, irrespective of the gear ratio.

Therefore, a change in the gear ratio of the vehicle shown by the curves in Figure 3.5 will cause the peak P to move horizontally from the position it occupied in Figure 3.4c. Lowering the ratio (curve A) moves the 'power available' curve to the left and raising the ratio (curve C) moves it to the right. These two conditions are called under-gear and over-gear respectively.

In both conditions the maximum possible speed is reduced, but this is not the prime consideration. When compared with the optimum gearing needed to obtain the ideal maximum speed, the advantages of the two gearing conditions are as follows:

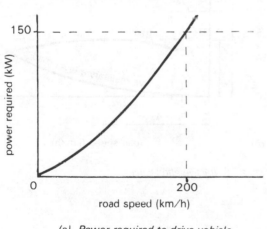

(a) Power required to drive vehicle

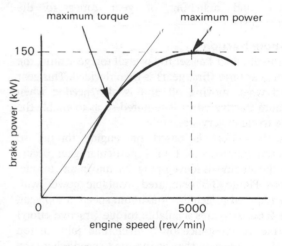

(b) Power available to drive vehicle

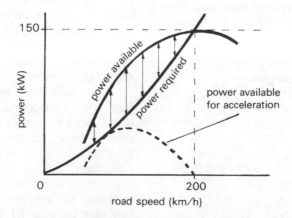

(c) Curve shows balance between power available and power required

Figure 3.4 Power balance

Condition	Advantages
Under-gear	1 More power for acceleration, so the vehicle is more lively. 2 Flexible top gear performance, so less gear changing is necessary when the vehicle encounters higher tractive resistances.
Over-gear	Lower engine speed for a given road speed, so: 1 Better economy. 2 Lower engine noise level. 3 Less engine wear.

The advantages of under-gearing can be used to overcome the disadvantages of over-gearing and vice versa. A comparison of these two conditions shows that under-gearing is more suitable for the average car, so under-gearing to the extent of about 10–20% was quite common at this time. This means that the engine power peak occurs 10–20% before the maximum possible vehicle speed is reached. However, modern vehicles now make use of five or six gears and this enables better selection and matching of gear ratios to the requirements.

Maximum traction

Once the designer has set the overall top gear ratio, the bottom gear ratio (first gear) is then decided. This gear is used when moving off and is also needed when maximum tractive effort is required so as to enable the vehicle to climb very steep hills.

Tractive effort is based on engine torque; so maximum tractive effort in a particular gear occurs when the engine is developing its maximum torque. Whereas Figure 3.5 compared available power with power required to achieve maximum speed in top gear, Figure 3.6a compares available torque (tractive effort) with tractive resistance on a level road (also in top gear). It can be seen that at the road speed where the maximum tractive effort (torque) is available, it is substantially greater than the tractive resistance. The difference between the tractive effort and tractive resistance curves represents the force available for

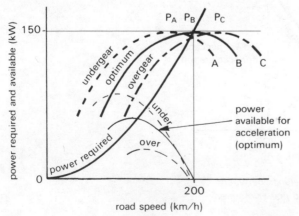

Figure 3.5 Under-gear and over-gear

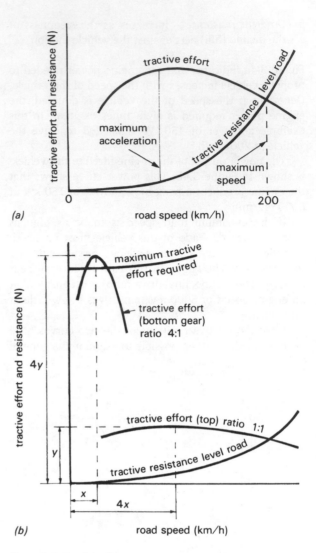

Figure 3.6 Tractive effort curves

acceleration. In this example therefore, although the top gear is selected there is sufficient difference between tractive effort and tractive resistance to enable good acceleration. The selection of top gear in this example illustrates that maximum tractive effort is available at approximately 40% of maximum vehicle speed (approximately 80 Km/h).

Figure 3.6b shows the effect on the tractive effort curve when a lower gear is selected. When a lower gear is selected, it results in a lower road speed for the same engine speed. Therefore, although the engine is producing the same torque, it is occurring at a lower road speed but in addition, the lower gear ratio multiplies or amplifies the available engine torque thus increasing the available tractive effort. In this case a first gear ratio of 4:1 is used, which multiplies the available tractive effort by four and is sufficient to meet the hill-climbing requirement.

In Figure 3.6b the gradual engagement action of the clutch must be used to provide a tractive effort build-up sufficient to move the vehicle on the steep hill, (represented by the upper curves on the graph). Once the clutch is fully engaged, and the engine is operating in the region of maximum torque, a small acceleration is possible, this assumes the engine speed does not drop too low. Although there has been a multiplication of the torque or tractive effort, the tractive effort required to move away and accelerate on the steep hill is much higher than on a level road. There is therefore only a small difference between tractive effort available and tractive effort required, but it is sufficient to enable acceleration.

The bottom gear ratio is calculated by dividing the maximum effort required by the maximum effort available in top gear. If the effort required is four times greater than the effort available in top gear, then the gear ratio should be 4:1.

Intermediate gear(s)

Having set the top and bottom gearbox ratios, the intermediate ratios are then inserted so that they form a geometric progression (GP). This means that all the individual ratios advance by a common ratio. For example, assuming the top and bottom overall ratios (including the final drive ratio) are 4:1 and 16:1 respectively, then the sets of ratios for the three- and four-speed gearbox are:

- three-speed gearbox: 4, 8 and 16 (common ratio between each gear is a multiplication of two).
- four-speed gearbox: 4, 6.35, 10 and 16 (common ratio 1.59)

To obtain optimum speed and acceleration performance, the engine should be operated in the speed range between the limits of maximum torque and maximum power (usually referred to as the power band). The wider this power band, the smaller is the number of ratios required to bridge the gap between top and bottom gears. Many car engines produced during the 1960s to 1980s had a relatively narrow power band range (especially some high performance engines), therefore gearboxes fitted in conjunction with these engines normally had at least four forward ratios, whereas earlier vehicles had only three gears. However, increased performance expectations and the use of smaller engines wherever possible has resulted in the common use of five forward gears for most light cars.

Additionally, since most cars are under-geared, it is now common practice to provide the extra fifth gear, to offset some of the drawbacks associated with the under-gear condition. Often, the fifth gear is an overdrive, that is it has a ratio that allows the output shaft to be driven faster than the speed of the engine.

It is not now uncommon for some vehicles to be fitted with gearboxes having six gears in total (even seven). Vehicle manufacturers are designing engines that develop maximum power together with high torque within a very narrow engine speed range, normally occurring at relatively high engine speeds. The addition of another intermediate gear allows the gear ratios to be closer together, which during acceleration maintains the engine speed within the optimum range to develop the best power and torque from the engine. If a gearbox is fitted with six gears, fifth gear normally has a ratio of 1:1, therefore second, third and fourth gears provide the intermediate gears. Sixth gear is an overdrive and drives the output shaft faster than the input shaft.

There is however a progressive trend towards high torque engines (due to the benefits of modern engine technologies which enable high torque levels to be produced at low engine speeds). In such cases, it would be possible to use fewer gears but customer expectations of performance and smoothness as well as economy and emissions dictate the use of five, six or even seven gears on automatic as well as manual gearboxes.

3.2 DIFFERENT TYPES OF GEARS AND GEARBOXES

3.2.1 Types of gearing

Various types of gearing are used throughout the motor vehicle. The sets of gears used within the gearbox employ one or more of the following:

1 *Spur gears* – teeth parallel to the axis of rotation, used on sliding-mesh gearboxes.
2 *Helical gears* – teeth inclined to the axis of rotation to form a helix.
3 *Double helical gears* – two sets of opposing helical teeth.
4 *Epicyclic or planetary gears* – spur or helical gears rotating about centres which are not stationary.

Manual gearboxes (constant-mesh and synchromesh) generally use helical types of gear.

Automatic gearboxes generally use epicyclic gearing.

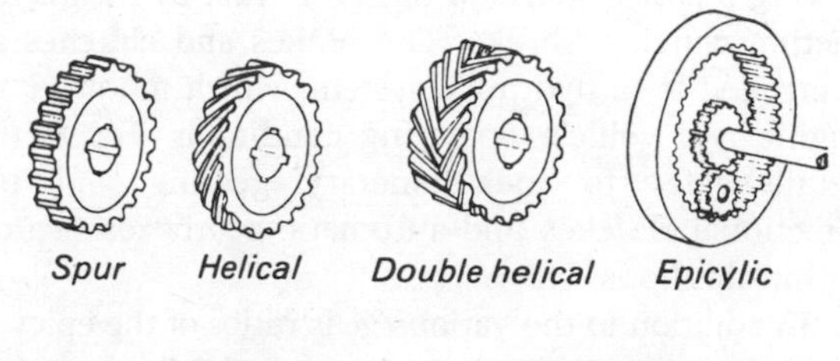

Spur Helical Double helical Epicyclic

Figure 3.7 Types of gearing

3.2.2 Gear material

The gear teeth have to resist severe shock loading, huge forces and be resistant to wear, so a case-hardened steel is used to provide a tough core and a very hard surface.

3.2.3 Manual gearboxes

Gearboxes can be divided into two main groups by the manner in which the gear ratio is selected: 'manual' and 'automatic'. The use of a manual gearbox indicates that the driver of the vehicle has full control of the selection of the available gear ratios. By means of a manual control lever (gear stick), the driver selects an appropriate gear ratio to suit the engine speed and driving conditions.

The number of forward gear ratios or 'speeds' provided by a manual gearbox is normally five, with some four-speed gearboxes still in use and six-speed gearboxes becoming more common. In the past a three- or four-speed gearbox was commonly used, mainly due to cost and manufacturing reasons. A reverse gear is provided with all motor vehicle gearbox applications.

The main types of manual-change gearboxes that have been used in motor vehicles are:

- sliding-mesh
- constant-mesh
- synchromesh.

The synchromesh is the most common type now in use. The synchromesh type of gearbox was a development of the sliding-mesh and constant-mesh types, and it is for this reason that the simple sliding-mesh type can be used to explain the principles of gear selection.

3.2.4 Automatic gearboxes

The term automatic gearbox refers to systems in which the gears are automatically changed by the gearbox itself, instead of being manually selected by the driver, as in the manual gearbox. Once the driver has made the initial selection to determine the direction in which the vehicle is to move and the gear range to be used, all other decisions are made within the gearbox.

In the USA a gearbox is called a transmission, which explains why an automatic gearbox is sometimes called an automatic transmission unit.

Most automatic gearboxes use an epicyclic gear system. The required gear is obtained by holding or driving a part or parts of the gear train by means of a friction clutch or brake. The brakes and clutches are controlled by a hydraulic system, which monitors the engine and vehicle operating conditions. For further details refer to the Planetary gearing and uni-directional clutches and automatic gearboxes sections within this book.

In addition to the various gear ratios of the epicyclic gearbox, most automatic systems require the fitment of a fluid clutch, referred to as a torque converter, between the engine and gearbox. The torque converter replaces the normal friction clutch used with a manual gearbox to provide two functions:

1   The torque converter automatically disengages the engine from the transmission when the engine speed is below about 1000 rev/min.
2   The torque converter provides an infinitely variable torque and speed ratio to bridge the steps between each of the gearbox epicyclic ratios.

The combination of a torque converter with an automatic gearbox forms an automatic transmission system.

3.2.5 Stepped transmission

Stepped transmission effectively describes the way in which most manual and automatic gearboxes make use of steps in the gear ratios.

A comparison of the curves for tractive effort available using a traditional three-speed manual gearbox with an ideal curve is shown in Figure 3.8. This graph indicates why the term stepped transmission is used to describe any system that gives this kind of stepped output in tractive effort.

Gearboxes having only three forward gears need the engine to provide a high power output over a very wide speed range, which means that the tractive effort at many road speeds is far less than ideal. Increasing the number of gear ratios gives a considerable improvement, and although this is increasingly the approach with the use of modern five-, six- or even seven-speed gearboxes, commercial vehicle

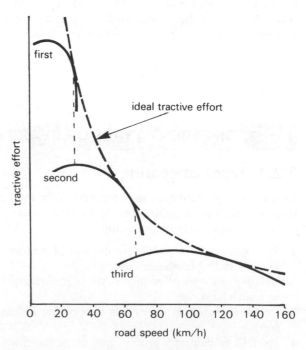

Figure 3.8 Conventional stepped transmission

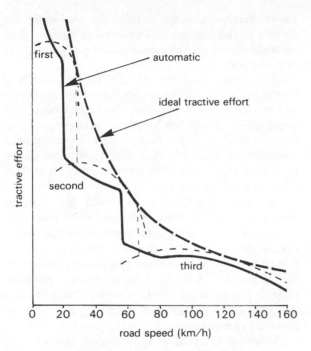

Figure 3.9 Tractive effort with a three-speed automatic gearbox

the ideal tractive effort curve is achieved by using an automatic gearbox with a torque converter. Although the converter is very inefficient at low engine speeds, the effect of the torque converter's infinitely variable ratio between about 2:1 and 1:1 gives a smooth transition, and positive drive, between the stepped ratios of the main automatic gearbox (Figure 3.9).

3.2.6 Other types of gearbox and transmission

Many modern automatic gearboxes retain the traditional mechanical operation of the automatic gear change process but benefit from electronic or computer control, which oversees the gear changes in line with driving conditions and driver demand.

A number of vehicle manufacturers have also fitted different forms of 'continuously variable' transmission systems, which eliminate the steps between the gears.

There is also now a trend to make use of electronic control for manual gearboxes where the selection of the gears remains under control of the driver but the gear change is selected via a switch. The switch may in fact be connected to the gear lever or to buttons or paddles on or around the steering wheel. The electronic systems usually make use of a computer, which in turn regulates or controls a hydraulic system that moves the applicable selector mechanism in the gearbox.

The various transmission systems are dealt with in the relevant sections of this book and the advanced book that follows on from it.

applications may often have ten or more gears. Once the number of ratios is increased to about ten, the combination of the narrow engine speed range needed to 'bridge the gap' between the ratios, and the close approximation of the actual tractive curve to the ideal, allows the engine to operate entirely within its optimum speed range.

Since the number of ratios in a motorcar gearbox is restricted for reasons of weight and cost, an approach to

3.3 DRIVE CONFIGURATION

3.3.1 Drive arrangements

The power produced by the engine is used to propel the vehicle by driving the road wheels, power which is transmitted from the engine via the gearbox and final drive. Most light vehicles have four road wheels, although some three-wheeled vehicles are produced in small numbers. The options therefore exist to transmit the power to one, two or more wheels.

Four-wheeled vehicles traditionally transmit the power to either the rear wheels or the front wheels, therefore there are usually only two driven wheels. However, it is increasingly popular to make use of four-wheel drive systems where the power is delivered to all four wheels. Although four-wheel drive systems have been fitted to off-road vehicles, recreational vehicles and some sports vehicles, it is now also not uncommon for conventional family saloons to employ such systems.

Three-wheeled vehicles generally have a single wheel at the front with the power delivered to the two

rear wheels (usually from a rear-mounted engine). There have, however, been examples of three-wheeled vehicles where the power has been delivered to the single front wheel via a small engine that is mounted on a sub-frame along with the front wheel. The sub-frame then swivels within the vehicle chassis, allowing the engine and wheel assemblies to turn and so steer the vehicle.

The type of drive configuration chosen by the vehicle manufacturer is dependant on a number of factors including the size of vehicle, purpose to which it is to be used, the cost of the vehicle and other factors. Each derivative of the drive configuration used has its advantages and disadvantages; these have to be taken into consideration when the vehicle is being designed.

3.3.2 Rear-wheel drive layout

The traditional layout shown in Figure 3.10 has the engine and gearbox situated with its output shaft set longitudinally. In this arrangement the rear wheels act as the driving wheels and the front wheels swivel to allow it to be steered. In the past rear-wheel drive was a natural choice because of the difficulty of transmitting power to the front wheels, which also had to swivel for steering purposes.

Spacing out the main components using this layout makes each unit accessible, but one drawback is the intrusion of the transmission components into the passenger compartment. These create a large bulge in the region of the gearbox and a raised ridge (the tunnel) down the centre of the car floor for the accommodation of the propeller shaft.

Using the rear wheels to propel the car utilises the load transfer that takes place from the front to rear of the vehicle when the car is climbing a hill or accelerating. Good traction is obtained, but when the wheels lose adhesion (especially when one wheel has less grip than the other) the driving forces provided by the wheels tend to move the rear of the car sideways. The sideways motion causes the car to 'snake' and requires the driver to make considerable movements of the steering wheel if the vehicle is to maintain a straight path.

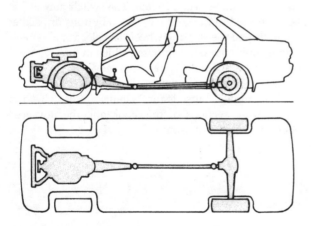

Figure 3.10 Rear-wheel drive

3.3.3 Front-wheel drive layout

The compactness of the layout shown in Figure 3.11 has made it very popular for use with light cars. Originally introduced in mass-produced cars during the 1950s for 'baby' cars such as the Mini, with the developments in car design and manufacture processes, the front-wheel drive design is now used in the majority of small- and medium-sized cars.

The engine and transmission are normally mounted transversely across the front of the vehicle. For space reasons the length of the engine is the limiting factor, but the increased use of V-type engines for larger power units has enabled many of these engines to be placed transversely. Accommodating all the main components under the bonnet in one compartment

allows maximum space within the car while the absence of floor bulges and a tunnel to accommodate the transmission provides more room for the occupants of the vehicle.

Transverse mounting of the engine simplifies transmission, because the output shafts from the engine and gearbox rotate in a similar plane to the wheels. This arrangement avoids the need for a bevel-type final drive; instead a simple final drive reduction gear is required that incorporates a differential. The output from the differential is then transmitted by short drive shafts to the road wheels.

To allow for suspension movement and steering, each drive shaft is fitted with an inner and outer universal joint. Since the outer joint must accommodate the steering action, it is specially designed to ensure that an even speed is obtained as it rotates. This avoids vibration even when the drive is being transmitted through a large angle. These specially designed joints are referred to as 'constant velocity joints' and are covered in greater detail later in this chapter.

Mounting all the main units (engine, gearbox, etc.) in one assembly sometimes makes it difficult to gain access to some components. Often many of the items requiring service access are relatively easily reached, to reduce servicing costs, although access to larger components, such as the clutch, may still require the removal of the engine. With the increase in component reliability, the cost of many major repairs during the life of the vehicle is minimized.

One disadvantage of front-wheel drive is that the driving wheels have less grip on the road during accelerating and hill climbing when the weight of the vehicle is transferred from the front of the vehicle to the rear. Although this characteristic can be partly corrected by placing the engine as far forward as possible, which increases the load on the driving wheels, the car is then liable to become 'nose-heavy'. The effect of this is to make steering the car more arduous and can affect road handling under certain conditions. In cases where the

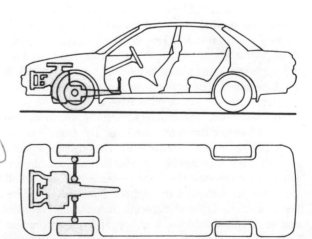

Figure 3.11 Front-wheel drive

driver's steering effort is considered excessive, the car is often fitted with power-assisted steering (PAS). This assists the driver to turn the steering wheel.

Using the front wheels for delivery of power as well as steering allows the driving force to act in the same direction as the wheel is pointing. This feature, together with the fact that the vehicle is being 'dragged' by the front driving wheels, can improve vehicle control, especially in slippery conditions.

3.3.4 Four-wheel drive

The arrangement, shown in Figure 3.12, offers a number of benefits because it distributes the drive to all four wheels. The sharing of the load between the four wheels during acceleration reduces the risk of wheel spin. Also, the positive drive to each wheel during braking minimizes the possibility of wheel lock-up.

A further advantage of this layout is apparent when the vehicle is driven on slippery surfaces such as snow and mud. When on an icy road, or driving cross-country (off-highway) a two-wheel drive vehicle soon becomes difficult to drive or even undrivable because grip is lost on one or both wheels. Note that with a conventional differential system, the loss of grip of one of the driving wheels causes the wheel to spin and because a normal differential always transmits an equal share of the power to both wheels, the small driving force applied to

the non-spinning wheel is insufficient to propel the vehicle (see final drive differential later in this chapter).

Four-wheel drive arrangements are expensive to produce and are therefore usually only fitted to vehicles where maintaining traction in slippery or difficult conditions is important. Vehicles normally fitted with a four-wheel drive system are those used 'off-road' and sports cars with high performance engines where 4WD provides the maximum amount of traction possible without a wheel spinning during acceleration and cornering.

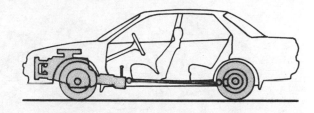

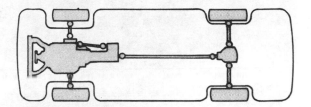

Figure 3.12 Four-wheel drive

3.4   REAR-WHEEL DRIVE LAYOUT

3.4.1 Advantages

Placing the radiator, engine, gearbox and propeller shaft in-line with the length of the vehicle provides a simple construction method for a rear-wheel drive (RWD) vehicle, and produces the following advantages:

- The manufacturing process for, and construction of, components is relatively simple.
- Weight can be evenly distributed throughout the vehicle, resulting in good vehicle stability and handling.
- Accessibility of vehicle components is relatively easy, reducing maintenance costs.
- The effort required to steer the vehicle is small.
- Larger sized engines can be fitted.
- Many of the components are situated in close proximity to the driver (i.e. gearbox) therefore a direct linkage can be fitted which provides more positive control.
- There is the space and freedom to use various suspension arrangements to provide additional comfort for passengers.

Although many small- and medium-sized vehicles use a front-wheel drive arrangement, most large vehicles are still RWD.

3.4.2 Torque reaction

'To every action there is an equal and opposite reaction.'

This statement of Newton's third law of motion means that every component that produces torque will also suffer an equal torque in the opposite direction. For example, when the engine crankshaft exerts a torque in a clockwise direction, the cylinder block will try to rotate in an anti-clockwise direction.

A further example of torque reaction is shown in Figure 3.14a, which represents a tractor with its rear driving wheels locked in a ditch. In this situation the driver must be careful, because torque reaction is likely to lift the front of the tractor rather than turn the rear wheels.

When the law stated above is applied to rear axles, it is understood that an arrangement must be provided to prevent the axle casing turning in the opposite direction to the driving wheels.

Figure 3.13 Rear-wheel drive arrangement

3.4.3 Driving thrust

A torque t applied to the wheel, which may be considered as a lever (Figure 3.14b), produces a tractive effort T_e at the road surface, and an equal and opposite force at the axle shaft. In order to propel the vehicle, the driving thrust must be transferred from the axle casing to the vehicle body or frame.

The maximum tractive effort is limited by the adhesive force P of the tyre on the road. The tractive force depends on the coefficient of friction μ between the tyre and the road and the load W exerted on the wheel.

3.4.4 Transmitting driving thrust to the body and controlling axle torque reaction

When power is applied to the rear wheels in order to move the vehicle, a force or thrust is created that must then be transferred to the vehicle body or frame.

Depending on the drive system design and the suspension design, different arrangements are used to

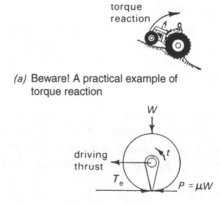

(a) Beware! A practical example of torque reaction

(b) Lever action of a wheel

Figure 3.14 Torque acting on a lever

attach the axle or the final drive assembly to the vehicle. In most cases, the thrust is transferred to the vehicle via these location points, although additional components and linkages may be used to transfer the thrust.

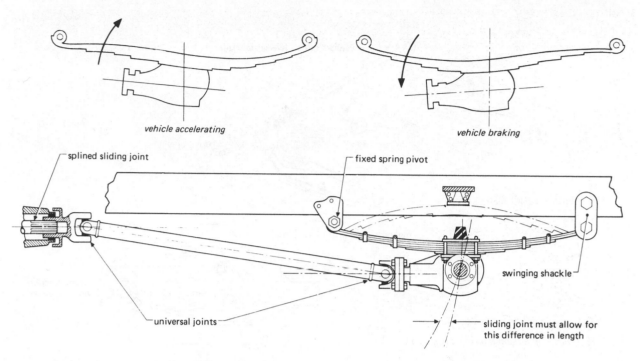

Figure 3.15 Hotchkiss open-type drive (light commercial vehicle)

Additionally, as highlighted previously, when the power or torque is applied via the drive shafts to the driving wheels, a torque reaction will result in the axle casing or final drive assembly trying to rotate in the opposite direction to the rotation of the wheels. The arrangement for locating the axle casing or final drive assembly must therefore also be able to prevent the axle casing or final drive assembly from rotating.

For many years, one of the most popular suspension systems for solid axle, rear-wheel drive vehicles made use of leaf springs. It was possible to directly locate the axle to the springs, which were also utilized as a means of transferring the thrust to the vehicle body, and to resist axle rotation. Such an arrangement is illustrated in Figure 3.15.

Different drive systems and arrangements have, however appeared over the years. Four notable rear-wheel drive systems have been used by various vehicle manufacturers. Although these systems have been modified to suit modern vehicle requirements, many of the principles are still used today.

The drive systems are:

- Hotchkiss open-type
- Four-link (semi-Hotchkiss)
- Torque-tube
- de Dion.

The arrangements indicate the components used to resist the various forces associated with the propulsion of a vehicle. Knowledge of the forces should assist with the diagnosis of many of the 'knock, clonk and vibration' faults associated with drive systems.

3.4.5 Hotchkiss open-type drive

The Hotchkiss drive arrangement shown in Figure 3.15 has been used on many commercial vehicle applications. Two rear leaf springs, longitudinally mounted, are connected to the frame by a 'fixed' pivot at the front. The rear spring mounting point, swinging shackle, allows the length of the spring to alter during spring deflection as the vehicle travels over bumps.

At each end of the exposed ('open-type') propeller shaft is fitted a universal joint, with provision made for alteration in shaft length, which occurs when the springs are deflected.

Torque reaction is resisted by clamping the axle to the springs by means of U-bolts. When the vehicle accelerates, the springs deflect up at the front and down at the rear, and vice-versa during braking. This deflection movement helps to damp driving shocks and improve transmission flexibility. Because the axle continually moves up and down, there is an obvious need for universal joints on the prop shaft.

Driving thrust is transferred from the axle casing to the spring, and then transmitted through the front section of the springs to the vehicle frame. If the U-bolts become loose, the spring centre bolt (axle location bolt) takes the full driving thrust, the high shearing force soon fractures the bolt.

3.4.6 Four-link drive system

Car manufacturers have used the four-link system in conjunction with helical springs and a live rear axle. The

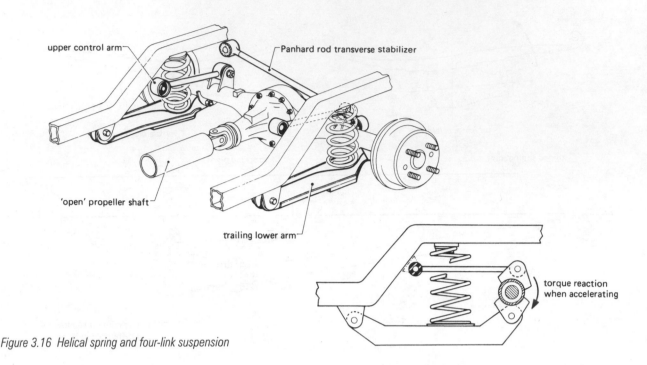

Figure 3.16 Helical spring and four-link suspension

helical springs support the weight of the vehicle but they cannot transmit the driving and braking thrust torque reaction, or give lateral support to the rear axle. Therefore, additional components must be fitted to transmit the driving forces from the axle to the vehicle body.

In the layout shown in Figure 3.16 the rear axle is positioned by upper and lower trailing suspension arms; these arms transmit driving thrust and prevent rotation of the axle casing.

A transverse stabiliser called a panhard rod connects the rear axle to the vehicle body and therefore controls sideways movement between the axle and the body. Rubber mountings at each connection point reduce transmission noise, eliminate the need for lubrication at the fixing points and also provide slight flexibility to allow for drive movement and geometric variations during spring deflection.

Initially it may appear that the helical spring gives a reduction in the unsprung weight, but when the weight

of the additional arms and rods etc. needed for this drive arrangement is considered, the unsprung weight difference is very small. However, the accurate positioning of the axle in this system together with the use of helical springs is an advantage.

3.4.7 Torque-tube drive

Whereas the Hotchkiss drive uses stiff springs to resist torque reaction and driving thrust, the torque-tube (or enclosed) drive relieves the springs of all duties other than functioning as suspension springs. This means that a softer ride can be achieved by using either 'softer' springs or another form of spring, e.g. helical.

Figure 3.17 shows a layout using laminated springs, which are connected to the frame by a swinging shackle at each end. Bolted rigidly to the axle casing is a tubular member which extends to the rear of the gearbox or gearbox cross-member. Bracing rods, connected between the axle casing and the torque tube, strengthen the construction at the rear of the tube and the front of the tube is attached to the gearbox or cross-member by a ball and socket joint. Mounted in the centre of the ball joint is a universal joint to allow for angular deflections of the drive. A small-diameter propeller shaft is fitted inside the torque tube and splined to the final-drive pinion.

In this arrangement the torque reaction of the axle and the driving thrust are taken by the torque tube. When the forward thrust from the ball is taken on the rear housing of the gearbox, an arrangement must be provided to transfer this force through the gearbox mountings to the body or frame.

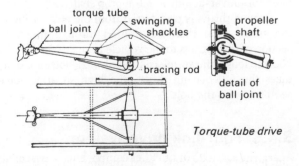

Figure 3.17 Torque-tube drive

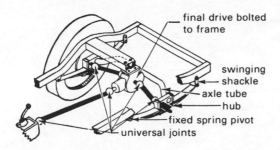

Figure 3.18 de Dion tube drive

Helical or torsion bar springs may be used as alternatives to laminated springs, and in these cases, side movement of the axle must be controlled by fitting some form of transverse stabiliser, e.g. a Panhard rod, between the frame and the axle.

3.4.8 de Dion drive

The de Dion axle is often regarded as an intermediate stage between the normal live or solid axle and independent suspension. Many of the advantages of the latter are achieved in this layout, but since the rear wheels are still linked by an axle tube, the system cannot be classed as fully independent.

Figure 3.18 shows a basic drive arrangement. Laminated leaf springs are connected to the frame by a 'fixed' pivot at the front and a swinging shackle at the rear. Each spring carries a hub mounting to support the

stub axle shaft to which the wheels are mounted. Each hub mounting is then rigidly connected to a transversely located tubular axle beam, which means that the two wheels are not fully independent of each other with regard to suspension movements.

Bolted to a cross-member of the body or frame is the final-drive unit, and from this the power is taken through two universally-jointed drive shafts to the wheels. The main propeller shaft is fitted with a universal joint at each end to allow for flexing of the frame.

The torque reaction of the final-drive casing is taken by the body or frame and the driving thrust is resisted by the springs.

The major advantage of this layout is the reduction in unsprung weight. This ensures wheel spin is reduced by allowing the light driving wheels to follow the contour of the road surface closely.

Wheel spin can also be caused by the tendency of a live or rigid axle to rotate around the pinion shaft when a high propeller shaft torque is exerted. In effect, if the propeller shaft and pinion shaft are rotating clockwise, the axle will try to rotate anti-clockwise which would cause one wheel to try and lift from the ground; if not actually lifting it would certainly reduce the grip on that one wheel. With the de Dion system, the final drive assembly is attached to the vehicle frame or body, which restricts the tendency for the final drive to rotate, but also the wheels are not rigidly connected to the final drive. The torque reaction therefore does not cause one wheel to lift.

Other rear-wheel drive arrangements are discussed in the independent rear suspension section in this book.

3.5.1 Advantages

Concentrating the engine and transmission system in one unit and placing the assembly at the front of the vehicle to give front-wheel drive (FWD), produces the following advantages:

- Compact vehicle construction.
- A flat floor within the passenger compartment – no propeller shaft tunnel or gearbox bulge.
- Good traction because the majority of weight is placed above the driving wheels.
- The engine can be mounted transversely, which reduces the length of the bonnet and increases the size of the passenger compartment.
- Good steering stability – the driving thrust of the wheels is aimed in the direction that the vehicle is intended to follow. FWD vehicles rarely suffer from the oversteer characteristics.

Although FWD vehicles need more complicated drive shafts, the many advantages outweigh the

disadvantages. The FWD layout is very suitable for small- to medium-sized cars and even some large cars now make use of FWD.

3.5.2 Transverse engine layout

Figure 3.19 shows a typical FWD layout. The transversely mounted engine is fitted to a gearbox unit, which is referred to as a 'transaxle'. The unit gets its name from the two words transmission (a term used in America for gearbox) and axle.

Note that in the past with rear-wheel drive vehicles, the general term 'rear axle' often applied to the whole assembly, including the various final drive gearing assemblies and axle casing. Today, the various drive arrangements make it necessary to restrict the use of the term 'rear axle' to the casing or the member that performs the axle duty. Other components or assemblies inside the axle casing would be identified separately.

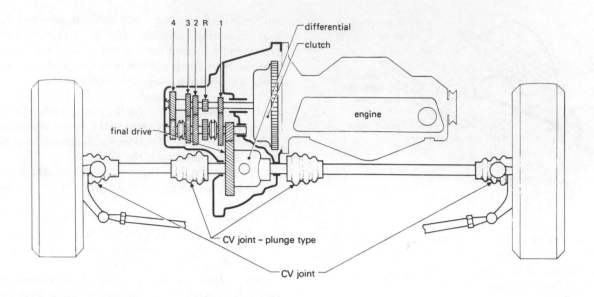

Figure 3.19 Front-wheel drive layout

The same rule therefore also applies to front axles.

In Figure 3.19, a four-speed gearbox forms part of an assembly along with the engine. Within this four-speed gearbox the power is transmitted along two shafts: an input shaft splined to the clutch and a mainshaft, which is connected to the final drive pinion.

In this example, for the final drive gearing assembly, the engine position allows the use of normal helical gears but if the engine were mounted longitudinally a bevel gear final drive would be necessary. Power from the final drive assembly is transmitted through the differential to the two drive shafts. Speed variation due to drive shaft angularity is prevented by using constant velocity universal joints at each end; the inboard joint at each side being of the plunge type (see also the section dealing with universal joints later in this chapter).

During acceleration, or when the engine is used as a brake, the torque reaction is transmitted through the drive shafts, which tends to make the engine rotate about the crankshaft (this is a similar problem to the torque reactions created on a rear axle). To prevent the movement of the engine and transaxle caused by the torque reactions, suitably spaced engine mountings and stabiliser bars are fitted.

Due to the configuration of the engine and the transaxle (i.e. the transaxle is normally located at one end of the engine and is therefore closer to one side of the vehicle than the other) the drive shafts are normally unequal in length. Because of this there is a tendency for the torque to be greater on one side than the other. This torque difference can lead to 'torque steer' during acceleration, which can be noticeable on vehicles with high performance engines and is more exaggerated when higher levels of torque are applied. The driver of the vehicle feels the car pulling to one side during rapid acceleration. Vehicle manufacturers normally reduce the amount of torque steer by using a split drive shaft

fitted to the longer shaft, or by altering the front suspension steering geometry.

Driving thrust and braking torque are taken by the suspension components, with various suspension configurations used to control these reactions. The weight of the vehicle body is usually supported by a helical spring, which is often fitted to a suspension strut as illustrated in Figure 3.20.

The wheel hub assembly, to which the drive shaft is connected, is fitted to the lower end of the suspension strut. To prevent the strut moving laterally, a track control arm is fitted between the strut and the vehicle body or frame. Depending on the design of the arm, a tie bar may also be fitted between the track control arm and the body; this prevents the strut assembly moving longitudinally.

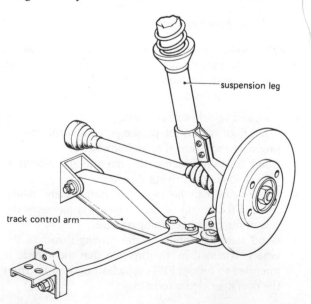

Figure 3.20 Front-wheel drive suspension layout

3.6 FOUR-WHEEL DRIVE LAYOUT

3.6.1 Advantages

There is an obvious disadvantage to two-wheel drive systems and it applies to both front- and rear-wheel drive. If one of the wheels loses traction on a slippery surface the vehicle can lose drive entirely. Although various additional systems are used, such as limited slip differential systems, the end result is that at most only two wheels are transferring the power to the road surface. For general driving on normal road surfaces, two-wheel drive is sufficient, but when the surface is slippery or the vehicle is being driven on rough or muddy ground, there is an obvious advantage to having all the wheels transmitting the power. The problems of two-wheel drive are exaggerated when high torque and power is provided by the engine. Under these conditions there is greater risk of losing traction under acceleration.

Four-wheel drive (4WD) vehicles transmit the power through all four wheels and therefore if one of the front wheels loses traction, drive is transmitted through the rear wheels, or vice versa. Further details on the operation of four-wheel drive are given under four-wheel drive systems later in this chapter.

Four-wheel drive vehicles offer the following advantages:

- The power is distributed between all four wheels and therefore wheel spin is less likely than with a two-wheel drive vehicle.
- The weight of the vehicle is distributed over the driving wheels and therefore driving all four wheels provides greater stability than a two-wheel drive vehicle.

The driving forces applied to a four-wheel drive vehicle are similar to those of both the front-wheel drive and rear-wheel drive layouts. Therefore similar components are used to resist the movements due to torque.

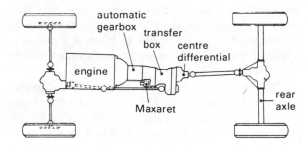

Figure 3.21 Four-wheel drive arrangement using a mechanical centre differential

3.7 SINGLE-PLATE CLUTCHES

3.7.1 The necessity for a clutch

A clutch provides a means of disconnecting the power produced by the engine from the manual gearbox. A clutch also provides a means of progressively connecting the power to the gearbox and transmission system.

When an internal-combustion engine operates at low speed, (typically below 1000 rev/min) it does not produce enough power to propel the vehicle. The engine must therefore be rotating at a speed that produces sufficient power before the drive is transmitted to the wheels.

The use of a dog clutch (Figure 3.22a) would be impractical since the connection of an engine rotating at high speed to a stationary transmission shaft would jolt the vehicle as the clutch engaged and soon damage the transmission.

The clutch used must therefore allow the drive between the engine and the transmission to be taken up smoothly so that the vehicle can gradually move away from the stationary position.

Once the vehicle is moving, it will be necessary to change gear, so a disengagement of the engine from the transmission is required. This is also part of the clutch's function.

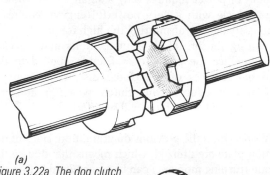

(a)
Figure 3.22a The dog clutch

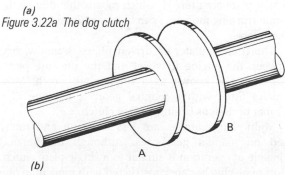

(b)
Figure 3.22b The friction clutch

The clutch therefore provides for: (i) the smooth up-take of drive (ii) disengagement of the drive to allow the vehicle to be stationary and to allow changing of gears. Note that the clutch must also be able to transmit the maximum torque from the engine through to the transmission without slip occurring. These duties can be performed by various mechanisms. The friction system is considered to be one of the most effective and efficient, but hydraulic and electric systems are also employed on motor vehicles.

3.7.2 The friction clutch

The two discs shown in Figure 3.22b demonstrate the operation of a friction clutch. If discs A and B are connected to engine and transmission respectively, then when the discs are held apart, no drive will be transmitted from disc A to disc B. When A is moved to contact B, the friction between the surfaces will allow a drive to be transmitted.

The level of force that pushes the discs together governs the amount of drive (torque) that is transferred between the two discs. Therefore, if the level of force is gradually increased, the amount of torque that can be transmitted will increase proportionally. Gradual engagement of the friction clutch allows the vehicle to move smoothly from stationary.

When the drive is fully engaged, both discs must rotate at the same speed, so the clutch designer must ensure that there is enough pressure and friction to ensure this condition. The amount of pressure and friction required will depend on the size and power output of the engine and the weight of the vehicle. A small vehicle fitted with an engine developing a limited amount of power requires only a small clutch, while a large vehicle with a very powerful engine requires a clutch capable of transmitting the high torque.

During the life of the clutch, faults may develop which reduce the pressure or friction applied to the frictional surfaces of the clutch disc. If pressure or friction are reduced, the clutch will slip and the performance of the vehicle will be affected.

The clutch shown in Figure 3.23 is a construction developed from the previous diagram. Both sides of the friction plate are utilized, which means that double the torque (turning moment) can be transmitted before slip takes place.

The friction plate, or driven plate, is sandwiched between the engine flywheel and the pressure plate. This design is known as a single-plate clutch. Most vehicles fitted with a manual gearbox use one of a number of designs of single-plate clutch.

Multi-plate clutches are less common and rarely used on manual gearboxes. Although the general principle of operation is similar to a single-plate clutch, multi-plate clutches are constructed with more than one friction or driven plate; these clutches are dealt with in section 3.8.

3.7.3 Single-plate clutch arrangements

The single-plate clutch is relatively simple, smooth in operation and has the advantage of producing a quick engagement and disengagement.

Figure 3.23 shows a simple clutch assembly. This type of single-plate clutch is now seldom used, but the diagram provides a simple view of the basic principles.

The driven or friction plate (1) is splined to the gearbox primary shaft (2). Riveted to the driven plate is a pair of friction linings (3) made of a suitable resin material, which have a satisfactory coefficient of friction and other useful properties, such as low wear rate.

The pressure plate (4) is located by a number of studs (5) fixed to the flywheel. The pressure plate is forced towards the flywheel (6) by means of springs (7) so the driven plate is sandwiched between the flywheel and pressure plate. Pressure from the springs causes the pressure plate, driven plate and flywheel to be clamped together.

Note that one of two types of spring may be used to provide the clamping force:

1 *Coil spring* – (Figure 3.23) although multi-coil spring clutches were used for all vehicles in the past, this type of clutch spring may now only be found on heavy commercial vehicles.
2 *Diaphragm spring* – universally used for motor cars and light commercial vehicles. Diaphragm spring clutches are dealt with in section 3.7.5.

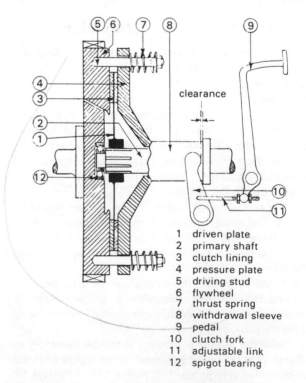

1 driven plate
2 primary shaft
3 clutch lining
4 pressure plate
5 driving stud
6 flywheel
7 thrust spring
8 withdrawal sleeve
9 pedal
10 clutch fork
11 adjustable link
12 spigot bearing

Figure 3.23 Construction of a simple single-plate clutch

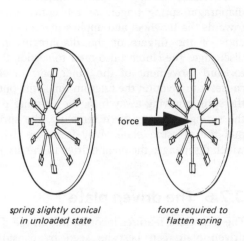

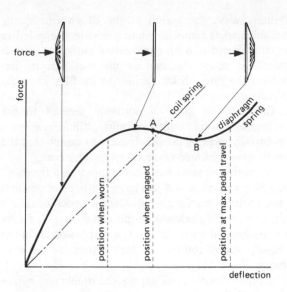

Figure 3.24 Characteristics of the diaphragm spring

A withdrawal sleeve (8) allows the clutch pedal (9) to act on the clutch forks (10). When the pedal is depressed, the pressure plate is withdrawn from the flywheel.

An adjustable link (11) is set to provide a small clearance between the clutch fork and the withdrawal sleeve to ensure that the full force of the springs is applied to the driven plate.

At the centre of the flywheel is fitted a spigot bearing (12), which locates and supports the front end of the gearbox primary shaft. The bearing allows for the difference in rotational speed between the flywheel and the primary shaft when the clutch is not fully engaged. The bearing used can take the form of a ball race or plain bush. A ball race is normally sealed with a metal cover to prevent the lubricant escaping on to the clutch plate linings. If a plain bearing is used, the bearing is generally manufactured from phosphor bronze, and made porous so that the bush can be impregnated with graphite to make it self-lubricating.

3.7.4 Single-plate clutch operation

When the driver depresses the pedal, the clutch forks push the pressure plate away from the flywheel to release the pressure from the driven plate. The driven plate is no longer clamped between the flywheel and pressure plate and can therefore rotate at a different speed to that of the flywheel. The drive between the engine and the transmission is now disengaged.

On releasing the clutch pedal, the spring thrust forces the pressure plate towards the flywheel and sandwiches the driven plate between the two surfaces. The driver of the vehicle must gradually release the pedal, or the full force of the springs will suddenly be applied to the driven plate, causing the vehicle to jolt.

When the clutch pedal is fully released, the drive can take two paths from the flywheel to the gearbox primary shaft. The drive can be transferred directly from flywheel face to driven plate, or alternatively can be taken via the studs and pressure plate to the rear face of the driven plate.

During the engagement of the clutch, the force transmitted to the driven plate must be applied gradually. Any jerky movement between the friction surfaces can give a pronounced judder through the transmission system. The flywheel/pressure plate connection must limit the slip–grip action caused by friction at that point. If the clutch in Figure 3.23 suffers a jerky engagement, a judder will be evident when the vehicle is moving off from rest, i.e. when the pressure plate moves towards the flywheel and driving torque is attempting to resist this axial movement.

3.7.5 Diaphragm spring (DS) clutch

The diaphragm spring clutch is lightweight and very compact. It has few working parts and a spring that is particularly suited to light vehicle applications.

Diaphragm spring action
The force needed on the pressure plate is provided by a diaphragm spring. This is a circular, slightly conical, tempered steel disc with radial slits cut from its centre to give flexibility.

Whereas a coil spring gives a force that progressively increases with deflection, a diaphragm spring exerts a force that varies in a more complex way as its shape is altered. Initially, the force gradually increases like the coil spring but after the diaphragm spring has reached its 'flat' position, the force decreases and then increases once again (Figure 3.24).

In many ways the action of the diaphragm spring resembles what happens when pressure is applied to the convex end of a tin can – when sufficient force is applied to move the end of the can past its flat position the end 'clicks' rapidly to its fully inwardly dished state.

The pressure plate is normally secured to the flywheel by a number of fixing bolts, although there are also usually locating dowels (studs) to ensure that the clutch cover is located correctly on the flywheel.

When the pressure plate is mounted on a flywheel, the spring is compressed just beyond the point where it is flat (point A on the graph). Over a period of time a reduction in the thickness of the clutch friction facing (due by general wear) causes the diaphragm spring to 'release', which causes the spring pressure force to increase.

Compared with a coil spring, the diaphragm spring offers the following advantages:

- It is compact and lightweight.
- It is suitable for high engine speeds. Coil springs bow outwards owing to centrifugal action and this lowers the spring force; it can also cause vibration owing to imbalance.
- A lower pedal force is required to release the clamping pressure applied to the clutch driven plate. Less unwanted friction since fewer parts are needed to operate the clutch. Also the force-deflection curve suits the application.
- The clamping force on friction facings does not decrease as the friction facings wear.

Pressure plate construction

Figure 3.25 shows the construction of a diaphragm spring clutch. This particular design uses only five main working parts: cover, diaphragm spring, fulcrum rings, pressure plate and driving straps.

Turnover tabs on the cover hold the fulcrum rings, which act as a pivot for the diaphragm spring. Note that as the cover bolts are tightened, the pressure plate pushes the diaphragm spring away from the flywheel and deflects the spring to a near-flat shape. In this position the reaction of the spring on the pressure plate provides the clamping force on the driven plate.

A single-plate clutch has two driving surfaces: the flywheel and the pressure plate (both of which act on the driven or friction plate). In the clutch shown in Figure 3.25, a strap drive is used to transfer the drive from the cover to the pressure plate. Three flexible steel straps working in tension allow the pressure plate to move smoothly towards, and away from, the flywheel, but prevent rotational movement relative to the cover.

Disengagement of the clutch compresses the spring and as the graph in Figure 3.24 shows, the pedal force required by the driver is less in the disengaged position (B) than that required during the commencement of the pedal travel. The forces required to operate the

diaphragm spring clutch are opposite to those with coil spring-type clutch.

A release bearing (which is attached to either the diaphragm spring fingers or the clutch fork), moves towards the flywheel and applies pressure to the inner ends of the fingers of the diaphragm spring; this disengages the clutch (also refer to section 3.7.9). The forward movement of the inner part of the spring causes it to pivot on the fulcrum rings, the outer part of the spring moving away from the pressure plate. With the spring clamping force removed, the spring straps pull the pressure plate away from the driven plate, which disengages the engine drive to the driven plate.

3.7.6 The driven plate

The important features incorporated in the design of a driven plate can best be seen by considering the disadvantages of using a plain steel plate with a lining riveted to each side. These may be listed as:

- Buckling of the driven plate due to heat.
- Drag, due to the plate rubbing against the flywheel whenever the clutch is disengaged.
- Very small movement of the clutch pedal between the engaged and disengaged positions, with very little control between these points.

To overcome these problems, the driven plate is normally slotted, or set in such a manner as to produce a 'flexing' action. This is generally known as crimping, and Figure 3.26 shows one form. Each segment is dished slightly, so that the linings tend to spring apart as the clutch is disengaged, preventing clutch drag.

If the clutch is in the driving position (engaged) and the pedal is depressed, the driven plate will tend to jump away from the flywheel to give a 'clean' disengagement of the drive. While in this position, the friction linings will be held apart and air will flow between the linings to dissipate heat built up in the driven plate. During engagement, axial compression of the driven plate spreads the engagement over a greater range of pedal travel and therefore makes it easier for the driver to make a smooth engagement of the drive.

The friction surface of the clutch driven plate is lined with a long lasting, hard wearing material that is also able to withstand the heat generated when the clutch is intentionally slipping (during engagement and disengagement). In the past, asbestos fibres were used as a friction material. These fibres were moulded together with resins to provide a material that had good thermal and friction qualities. Asbestos has been implicated in illnesses such as lung cancer, therefore alternative materials have had to be developed to replace the asbestos. Materials including man-made fibres such as Kevlar® together with steel and minerals are now used to provide a lining material that is comparable to asbestos. The lining is usually riveted to the crimped steel driven plate.

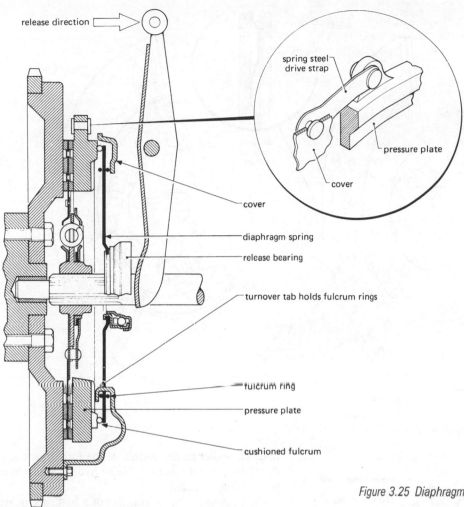

release direction

spring steel
drive strap

pressure plate

cover

cover

diaphragm spring

release bearing

turnover tab holds fulcrum rings

fulcrum ring

pressure plate

cushioned fulcrum

Figure 3.25 Diaphragm-type clutch

Figure 3.26 shows two types of driven plate: a plate with a rigid hub and another fitted with a spring hub. The rigid hub is simply riveted to the driven plate. This rigid hub arrangement is occasionally used, but in most cases the hub is mounted independently of the main driven plate.

Mounting the hub independently is usually made possible by fitting a series of springs together with a special friction damper fitted between the plate and the hub. With the use of this energy-absorbing hub, it is possible to absorb the torsional shocks due to clutch engagement or the more troublesome engine vibrations that can cause transmission noise and rattle.

3.7.7 Multi-coil spring clutch

This type of clutch spring had been used for many years, but the popularity of the diaphragm spring type has meant that multi-coil spring clutches are now only used on heavy vehicles.

Pressure plate construction

A series of coil springs are positioned between the pressed steel cover and the cast iron pressure plate

(Figure 3.27). Spring steel straps are used to transmit the drive from the cover to the pressure plate. Four release levers (pivoting on fulcrum pins supported in adjustable eye bolts), connect the release lever plate to the small struts placed between the lever and the pressure plate. These struts improve the efficiency of the release mechanism and, in conjunction with the steel driving straps, allow the pressure plate to move smoothly when taking up the drive, avoiding the jerky action which would cause clutch judder. The release bearing can be either a graphite block or ball race type.

3.7.8 Balancing

The clutch assembly (clutch-driven plate and pressure plate) is fixed to the flywheel and therefore rotates at the speed of the engine. It is therefore necessary for the manufacturer to balance the clutch components to prevent engine vibration. The clutch cover is fitted to the flywheel with the use of retaining bolts. Since it is necessary to allow a clearance for the cover retaining bolts, a means must be provided to keep the clutch concentric with the flywheel, so dowels are fitted for this purpose.

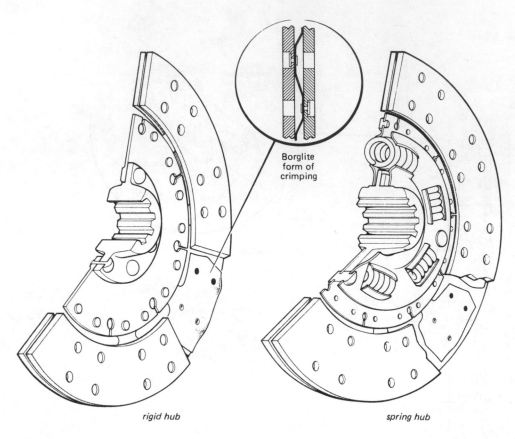

Borglite
form of
crimping

rigid hub   spring hub

Figure 3.26 Driven/friction plate construction

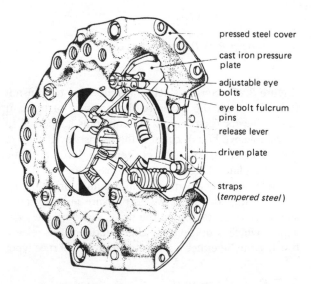

pressed steel cover

cast iron pressure
plate

adjustable eye
bolts

eye bolt fulcrum
pins

release lever

driven plate

straps
(tempered steel)

Figure 3.27 Multi-coil spring clutch

3.7.9 Clutch release bearing and pedal linkage

Release bearing

The purpose of the release bearing is to transmit the force applied by the driver (via the clutch pedal and clutch fork) from the clutch fork to the rotating diaphragm spring. The fork is pivoted at the bell housing, either in the middle of the fork or at the end, depending on whether a cable or hydraulic mechanism is used (Figure 3.28).

The release bearing consists of a ball race bearing, which contacts the diaphragm spring fingers. This race is sealed with metal end covers to retain its lubricant. In many cases the release bearing is connected to the clutch fork by a plastic holder which allows the bearing to centralize itself with the centre of the diaphragm spring and provide a smooth clutch operation.

When the clutch is engaged (i.e. drive is transmitted between the engine and transmission) a small clearance should exist between the release bearing and the diaphragm. This clearance (normally measured at the clutch pedal pad) is referred to as the free-pedal movement. The movement is necessary for two reasons:

1   It keeps the release bearing clear of the rotating spring (preventing premature wear of the clutch release bearing).
2   It ensures that the full pressure of the spring acts on the pressure plate whenever the clutch is engaged. During the life of the clutch, the driven plate friction lining wears, causing the clearance between the release bearing and the spring to decrease. Therefore, unless a periodic adjustment is made of the clearance, the clearance will disappear, the spring pressure on the pressure plate will decrease and the clutch will slip.

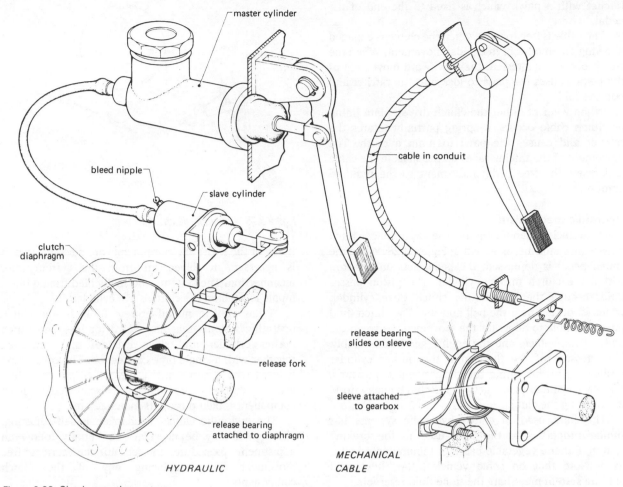

Figure 3.28 Clutch operating systems

Pedal linkage

The clutch pedal is fitted remotely from the clutch release mechanism. A linkage is therefore required to allow the clutch pedal to operate the clutch release mechanism. The clutch pedal linkage is generally either a mechanical cable or a hydraulic system.

To reduce engine vibrations through the body of the vehicle, the engine and gearbox assembly are fitted with rubber mounts, which allow the assembly to move slightly. The movement of the engine should have no effect on the operation of the clutch release mechanism. If the clutch mechanism were rigid and the clutch pedal was partly depressed, movement of the engine could adversely affect the smooth operation of the clutch, and 'judder' would result.

Figure 3.28, overleaf, shows the two systems that are commonly used.

Mechanical mechanism

The mechanical system uses a cable to link the pedal to the clutch release mechanism. A manual cable adjustment may be provided, allowing the correct free pedal movement to be maintained.

If there is no clearance, the release bearing will be in constant contact with the clutch diaphragm. The release bearing will wear prematurely and clutch slip will result.

Note: This effect can also be produced if the driver rests his foot on the pedal when the clutch is engaged.

If the clearance is too great, the pedal will reach the end of its travel before the clutch is fully disengaged. The clutch will therefore not completely release and the clutch plate will 'drag', making gear engagement difficult.

Automatic clutch adjustment

During vehicle operation the type of mechanical linkage shown in Figure 3.28 causes the free pedal movement to alter as the cable stretches or the clutch lining wears. Periodic adjustment of the cable must be made to avoid clutch drag or clutch slip, which results when the free pedal movement is incorrect. To help reduce maintenance costs, manufacturers provide an automatic cable adjuster similar to that shown in Figure 3.29.

The type shown uses a conventional cable arrangement from the clutch release bearing through to the point where the cable normally connects to the clutch pedal. At this point the cable is attached to a ratchet assembly; the action of the pedal engages the ratchet with a pawl, which is fixed to the end of the pedal.

The cable is free to move when the clutch is engaged allowing an amount of free pedal movement. When the clutch pedal is depressed, the downward movement of the pedal causes the pawl to lock into the ratchet and pull the cable.

When wear of either the clutch driven plate lining or clutch cable occurs, a spring partially rotates the ratchet and causes the pawl to jump a tooth. The movement of the ratchet takes up the slack in the cable and resets the free pedal movement to the required amount.

Hydraulic mechanism

Many vehicle manufacturers use hydraulic clutch release mechanisms, as shown in Figure 3.28. When the clutch pedal is depressed, the pedal acts on a piston within the clutch master cylinder. The piston passes fluid through the pipe to the clutch slave cylinder, which is located near the bell housing. The clutch fluid pipe is flexible to allow for the movement between the body of the vehicle and the engine/gearbox assembly. The pressure of the fluid from the master cylinder pushes the piston within the slave cylinder outwards. The slave cylinder piston acts on the clutch release fork, disengaging the clutch.

The fluid used in clutch hydraulic systems has similar properties to the fluid used in the braking system. Either a vegetable-based or mineral-based oil is used. Note that on some vehicles, the clutch and braking system may share the same fluid reservoir.

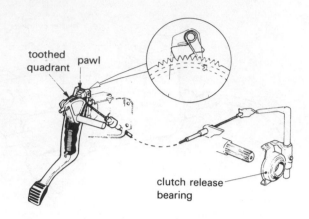

Figure 3.29 Automatic clutch adjustment

If any of the hydraulic components are disconnected, it is necessary to bleed air from the system after reconnection. The system is normally bled from a bleed nipple located on the clutch slave cylinder.

A few vehicle manufacturers fit hydraulic clutch operating systems that are sealed for life. The clutch master cylinder and slave cylinder are connected together with a single pipe connection. The connection is fitted with a non-return valve, which prevents fluid loss if either component is disconnected. Each component is bled during its manufacture.

The hydraulic clutch mechanism is self-adjusting, although it may be necessary to initially follow an adjustment procedure to set up the correct free movement when replacing any of the clutch components.

3.8   MULTI-PLATE CLUTCHES

3.8.1 Transmitting high torque outputs

The torque that can be transmitted by a plate-type clutch depends on four factors; these are shown in the following formula which is used to calculate the torque capacity:

$t = sp\mu r$

where:

t = torque transmitted (Nm)
s = number of friction contacts
p = total spring thrust (N)
μ = coefficient of friction
r = mean radius (m)

The important points to remember are that if the coefficient of friction is fixed (i.e. the material on the driven plate is already selected and not changed) the influences on how much torque can be transmitted are:

- the size of the clutch (its radius)
- the pressure applied by the pressure plate
- the area of contact for the driven plate(s) or friction area.

There are applications where the friction area or the radius of the clutch is restricted (motor cycles are a good example). In these cases the number of plates has to be increased to provide increased friction area, which ensures that the maximum torque can be transmitted without slip. A clutch having more than one driven plate is called a multi-plate clutch.

Although this type of clutch was widely used on cars up to about 1930, the numerous advantages of the single-plate clutch, especially its ability to disengage the drive completely and quickly (its resistance to drag) has meant that a multi-plate unit is now rarely used as the clutch between the engine and the manual gearbox on mass-produced cars.

However, a common application of the multi-plate clutch is in motor vehicles with an automatic gearbox. Automatic gearboxes require a number of clutches to transmit the drive through the various gear elements of an epicyclic gear train. Since the clutch diameter in this application is limited, multi-plate clutches are commonly used.

Figure 3.30 shows the main constructional details of a multi-plate clutch similar to the type used as a main engine to gearbox clutch on early motorcars.

Bolted to the flywheel is a cover. Outer plates engage with the cover by means of external splines. These outer plates, which may be plain steel or fitted with cork or friction material inserts, act on inner plates, which are splined to the inner hub. Thrust springs force the plates together to provide the clamping force.

To disengage the clutch, the end plate is withdrawn to compress the springs, the clamping force is removed from the clutch plates and the drive is disengaged.

It is difficult to ensure that all the plates disengage when the clutch is operated. To overcome the problem, the plates are either slightly dished or fitted with small springs between the outer plates which push the plates apart as the clutch is operated.

The multi-plate clutch may be either of a 'wet' or 'dry' type. A wet-type clutch is saturated with a fluid, normally oil. The advantage of using a wet-type clutch is that it reduces the fierce engagement by allowing the oil to flow around the clutch housing. Some applications actually allowed engine oil to pass through to the clutch housing.

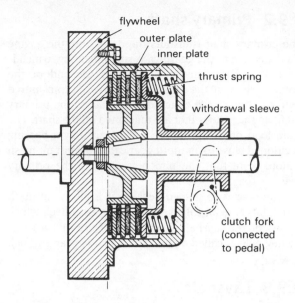

Figure 3.30 A simple multi-plate clutch

The multi-plate clutch employed in automatic gearboxes is generally of the wet type. The clutch is operated by a piston, which is controlled by hydraulic pressure. The clutch plate friction surfaces are normally faced with sintered bronze (manufactured by partially fusing powdered bronze), or compressed paper. The porous surface traps the oil, to give long life and smooth operation.

The use of multi-plate clutches within an automatic gearbox is detailed in the automatic gearbox section of this chapter.

3.9 THE SLIDING-MESH GEARBOX

3.9.1 Basis of the modern manual gearbox

Although today, the sliding-mesh gearbox is rarely used, the basic principle of its operation still underlies the working of most modern types of gearbox. The technician should therefore have an understanding of these basic operating principles before studying further manual gearbox applications.

The basic layout of a four-speed and reverse gearbox is shown in Figure 3.31. The various spur-type gears are mounted on three shafts (alternative shaft terminology in brackets):

- primary shaft (input or first motion shaft)
- layshaft (countershaft)
- mainshaft (third motion shaft or output shaft).

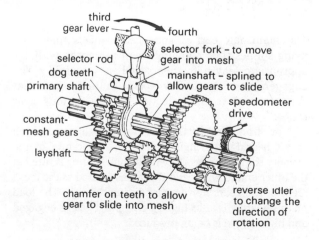

Figure 3.31 Four-speed and reverse sliding-mesh gearbox

3.9.2 Primary shaft

The primary shaft transmits the drive from the engine via the clutch to the gearbox. A spigot bearing, which is located in the crankshaft, supports the end of the primary shaft at the engine. The drive is transmitted from the hub of the clutch-driven plate to the primary shaft via the splines that are machined on the shaft. The main load on the primary shaft is taken by a bearing positioned close to an input gear called a constant mesh pinion. Note that the pinion is fixed to the primary shaft.

The gear is so named because it is always in mesh with a larger gear, called a constant mesh wheel, which is part of the layshaft gear cluster. Note that a small driving gear is called a pinion and a large gear a wheel.

3.9.3 Layshaft

The layshaft, which is normally fixed to the gearbox so that it cannot rotate, supports the driving pinions (of various sizes) of the layshaft gear cluster. The gear cluster rotates around the layshaft.

Bearings are placed on the layshaft and the gear cluster rotates on these bearings. The type of bearing depends on the loads; for a comparatively light load, a phosphor-bronze plain bush is suitable, but heavy-duty applications call for a more efficient bearing such as a caged needle roller.

As well as allowing the gear cluster to rotate freely, there are considerable loads applied to the gears and the bearings when the meshed teeth of the gears are forced apart during rotation of the gears. The bearings must therefore be capable of resisting these loads. Suitable bearings will also help reduce the noise that can be produced when the meshed teeth are forced apart.

In most cases the end float of the layshaft gear assembly, and in consequence the alignment of the gears, is controlled by flat thrust washers situated between the gear cluster and the gearbox casing.

3.9.4 Mainshaft

The mainshaft carries spur gear wheels that slide along splines thus allowing them to engage with the appropriate layshaft gears when required. The engagement of the gear wheels with the layshaft gear cluster provides the selection of the various gear ratios.

The 'front' end of the mainshaft is supported by a spigot bearing, which is situated in the centre of the primary shaft. A heavy-duty radial ball bearing is fitted at the other end to withstand the forces created as the mesh teeth of the gears move apart during rotation. The load on this bearing is at its highest when first gear is engaged and high torque is being produced.

3.9.5 Gear selector

A gear lever transfers the movement initiated by the driver to the appropriate gear via a selector rod and a selector fork.

The selector is a fork, mounted on a rod, which fits into a groove in the gear wheel. The function of the fork is to slide the gear wheel along the mainshaft so that the gear can engage and disengage with the matching gear pinion mounted on the layshaft.

To enable a four-speed gearbox to operate, three selector forks are required. Each of these forks is usually operated with three separate selector rods. The rods are normally situated at the top of the gearbox.

Normally one fork controls the selection of first and second gears, and the second fork controls the selection of third and top gears. Reverse has a separate fork; the reverse fork is normally longer than the other two as the reverse gear is positioned lower within the gearbox.

3.9.6 Gear wheel positions when different gears are selected

(Refer to Figure 3.32 opposite.)

Neutral
Whilst the neutral gear is selected, all the mainshaft gear wheels are positioned so they do not align with any of the layshaft gears and can therefore rotate freely. The primary shaft drives the layshaft gear, but the mainshaft will not be driven whilst all the gear wheels are in the neutral position.

First gear
The first-speed gear wheel (A) on the mainshaft is slid backwards to engage with pinion B on the layshaft gear. All other gears are positioned in neutral.

The drive will pass from the primary shaft to the layshaft gear cluster, and because the first speed gear wheel is now aligned with the gear cluster (engagement of first gear), rotation of the gear cluster will cause the mainshaft to also rotate.

In this gear, the reduction in speed that occurs as the drive passes through the constant-mesh gears E and F, is reduced further by the first-speed gears A and B.

The gear ratio in this example is calculated by:

$$\text{Ratio} = \frac{\text{Number of teeth on driven wheel}}{\text{Number of teeth on driving wheel}}$$

Since two sets of gears are used in a gearbox to provide first gear, then:

$$\text{Ratio} = \frac{\text{Driven}}{\text{Driver}} \times \frac{\text{Driven}}{\text{Driver}}$$

Note: To determine the overall gear ratio, the two ratios are multiplied together.

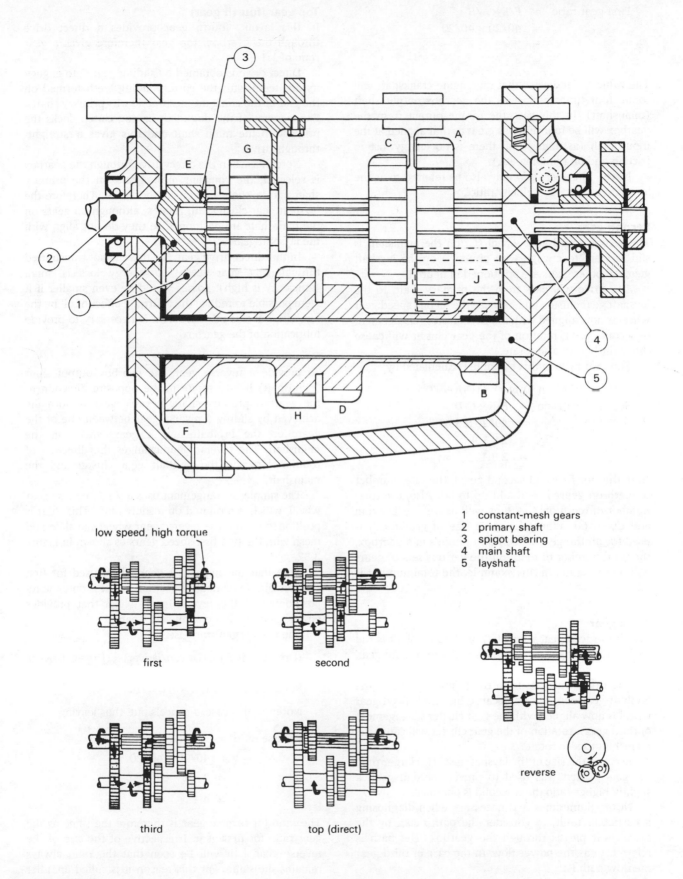

1   constant-mesh gears
2   primary shaft
3   spigot bearing
4   main shaft
5   layshaft

low speed, high torque

first

second

third

top (direct)

reverse

Figure 3.32 Gear positions (sliding mesh). Four-speed and reverse sliding mesh gearbox

First gear ratio $= F/E \times A/B$
$= 40/20 \times 40/20$
$= 2 \times 2$
$= 4:1$

The value 4:1 indicates that the engine crankshaft will rotate four times as fast as the gearbox output shaft (mainshaft). In this case the torque output from the gearbox will be four times as great as that applied at the input shaft (assuming that there is no energy lost to friction and oil pumping etc.).

Note: The gear ratio may also be referred to as the 'movement ratio' or 'velocity ratio'.

Second gear

The second-speed gear wheel (C) on the mainshaft is slid forward to engage with pinion D on the layshaft gear. All other gears are positioned in neutral.

The drive will pass from the primary shaft, to the layshaft gear cluster, and because the second speed gear wheel is now aligned with the gear cluster (engagement of second gear), rotation of the gear cluster will cause the mainshaft to also rotate.

The gear ratio in this example is calculated by:

Ratio $=$ (Driven/Driver) $\times$ (Driven/Driver)
Second gear ratio $= F/E \times C/D$
$= 40/20 \times 35/25$
$= 2 \times 1.4$
$= 2.8:1$

Note that for first and second gears, the total number of teeth on gears F + E add up to 60. Also, the total number of teeth on A + B as well as on C + D again add up to 60. When the same size of gear tooth is used for all the gear wheels and pinions in a gearbox, the total number of teeth on the various sets of gears will be the same. In this example, the total number is 60.

Third gear

The third-speed gear wheel (G) on the mainshaft is slid backwards to engage with pinion H on the layshaft gear. All other gears are positioned in neutral.

The drive will pass from the primary shaft, to the layshaft gear cluster, and because the third speed gear wheel is now aligned with the gear cluster (engagement of third gear), rotation of the gear cluster will cause the mainshaft to also rotate.

Because the size of the layshaft gear H is larger than the gear D that was used to provide second gear, a slightly higher ratio tha n second is obtained.

Note: Sometimes it is necessary when diagnosing a particular fault, to consider the path taken by the drive as it passes through the gearbox. The path is referred to as the power flow. In the case of third gear the flow path is:

Primary shaft $\rightarrow$ gears E, F, H, and G $\rightarrow$ and mainshaft

Top gear (fourth gear)

In this layout, fourth gear provides a direct drive through the gearbox; top gear therefore gives a gear ratio of 1:1.

Direct drive is obtained by sliding gear G to engage its dog-teeth with the corresponding teeth formed on the end of the constant mesh pinion E (primary shaft). Engagement of the dog-teeth or dog clutch, locks the primary to the main shaft and this gives a 'straight-through' drive.

Note that when the direct drive through the gearbox is selected, the constant mesh gears on the primary shaft and layshaft are constantly driven. Therefore the layshaft gear cluster still rotates, although all gears on the mainshaft are positioned so they do not align with the layshaft gears.

In this direct drive gear, the drive is not transmitted through any gear teeth, so energy loss is small (efficiency is high). Losses would be even smaller if it were possible to reduce the churning effect of oil by the layshaft, but this oil movement is necessary to provide lubrication of the gearbox.

Reverse gear

To provide a reverse gear, the gearbox output shaft (mainshaft) has to rotate in the opposite direction to the gearbox primary shaft. Reverse gear is normally achieved by sliding a reverse gear between one of the gears on the layshaft and a gear wheel on the mainshaft. The reverse gear changes the direction of rotation between the layshaft gear cluster and the mainshaft.

The simplest arrangement uses a single reverse gear wheel, which is mounted on a short shaft. This shaft is positioned so that the reverse gear wheel can slide and mesh with the two first-speed gears as shown in Figure 3.32.

Note that the mainshaft gear wheel used for first gear remains in its neutral position and it is only the re-positioning of the reverse gear wheel that provides engagement of all the applicable gears.

The reverse gear ratio is:

(Driven/Driver) $\times$ (Driven/Driver) $\times$ (Driven/Driver)

Reverse ratio $= F/E \times J/B \times A/J$

Note: In this case, J cancels out, thus leaving:

Reverse ratio $= F/E \times A/B$
$= 40/20 \times 40/20$
$= 2 \times 2$
$= 4:1$

The ratio for reverse gear is therefore the same as the gear ratio for first gear. Irrespective of the size of the reverse gear J, it will be seen that the ratio always remains the same. For this reason it is called an 'idler gear'. It changes the drive's direction of rotation, but does not alter the ratio.

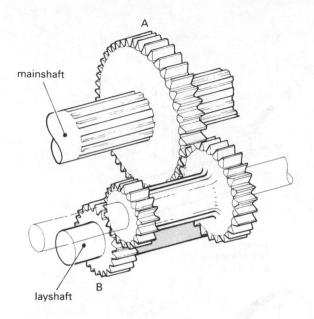

Figure 3.33 Compound reverse gear

With the idler arrangement, some drivers slip the clutch to maintain a slow reversing speed. However, slipping the clutch will inevitably cause excessive clutch friction lining wear.

A different design of reverse gear can in fact provide a lower ratio, which will allow slower speeds to be achieved with less slipping of the clutch.

A lower reverse gear ratio is achieved by using the arrangement shown in Figure 3.33. Instead of the single idler, the compound reverse gear has two gear pinions, which are joined together forming a small cluster of gears.

When reverse gear is selected, the reverse gear cluster is then positioned so that the two gear pinions align and mesh simultaneously with the appropriate layshaft and mainshaft gears. Because the two reverse gear pinions have different numbers of teeth, it provides an additional gear ratio reduction.

3.9.7 Gear changing

The gears indicated previously are selected with the vehicle stationary. When the vehicle is moving, the gearbox is driven by the power of the engine through the primary shaft, through the layshaft and on to the mainshaft/output shaft. In top gear the power passes direct from the primary shaft to the mainshaft/output shaft.

While changing gear when the engine is running and the vehicle is moving, when one gear is moved to engage with another gear, if the peripheral (outside) speeds of the gears does not match it is likely that a grating noise will result.

To avoid this, drivers of vehicles fitted with a sliding-mesh type gearbox perform an operation referred to as double declutching during gear changing.

The technique used by the driver is as follows. On changing up (e.g. from first to second) the clutch-driven plate, primary shaft and layshaft gear cluster must be slowed down. This is achieved by initially disengaging the clutch and moving the gear lever to neutral. The clutch is then re-engaged and the driver closes the throttle whilst neutral is selected. The engine slows down at a faster rate than that of the layshaft assembly, so a braking action on the layshaft assembly is obtained. The clutch can then be disengaged again and second gear selected, thus allowing the clutch to be re-engaged and allow second gear to transmit the power.

The opposite is required for changing down (e.g. from fourth to third) when the speed of the layshaft cluster must be speeded up. To achieve this, the engine is reconnected to the gearbox (clutch engaged) while the lever is in neutral, and the accelerator pedal is quickly depressed to increase the engine speed. When the layshaft assembly has reached the required higher speed, the accelerator is released. The clutch pedal is depressed, and the gear lever moved to the lower gear. Finally, as the clutch is being released, the engine must be accelerated sufficiently to match the engine speed to the road speed and ensure a smooth engagement of drive without a jolt.

The tooth of each gear is chamfered on the engagement side to allow for an easier entry between the layshaft gear and the sliding gear. However, if the driver makes a mistake and fails to match the speed of the gears during gear changes, as well as the loud noise created by the gear teeth rubbing against each other, burring of the teeth will occur and in some cases the teeth will chip or break off.

3.9.8 Selector mechanism

A selector fork of the type shown in Figure 3.34 is used to slide a gear wheel along the mainshaft to find the appropriate gear. It is mounted on its own rod and links the driver's gear stick to the sliding gear wheel.

Three selector forks are needed for a four-speed and reverse gearbox. The gear stick can be a direct-acting lever (situated on the gearbox) or it can be mounted remotely from the gearbox. If mounted remotely, a gear selector mechanism is required to allow the movement of the gear lever to be transferred to the gearbox.

Every gearbox selector must be fitted with the following:

- *A selector detent* – this holds the gears and selectors in the required position, preventing unintentional gear engagement or disengagement due to vibration.
- *An interlock mechanism* – this prevents the engagement of two gears simultaneously. If two gears were to be selected simultaneously, the gearbox would lock up and shaft rotation would be impossible due to the two different ratios.

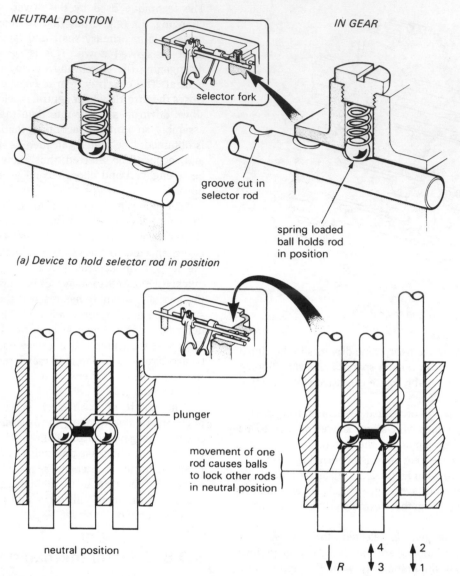

NEUTRAL POSITION

IN GEAR

selector fork

groove cut in
selector rod

spring loaded
ball holds rod
in position

(a) Device to hold selector rod in position

plunger

movement of one
rod causes balls
to lock other rods
in neutral position

neutral position

R   4   2
     3   1

(b) Ball and plunger type of interlocking mechanism prevents two gears engaging at the same time

Figure 3.34 Selector mechanism

Note: Severe damage will occur if the interlock mechanism is omitted during a gearbox overhaul.

Selector detent

Figure 3.34a shows a typical arrangement suitable for a layout having the selector fork locked to the selector rod. The device consists of a steel ball that is pressed by a spring into a groove that is located in the rod.

Into the rod are ground three grooves; these correspond to the rod positions for neutral (centre groove) and for the two gears served by the selector. Retention of the rod is governed by the strength of the spring. It must be set sufficiently tightly to prevent the gear from jumping out of mesh, but not so much so that it makes gear changing difficult.

Each selector rod has a separate spring-loaded detent.

Interlock mechanism

Every gearbox must have some form of this device fitted to prevent two gears (e.g. second and top) engaging simultaneously. The mechanism is fitted in addition to the selector detent. Although the interlock device takes a number of different forms, the arrangement shown in Figure 3.34b is one of the most common.

The mechanism consists of a plunger and two balls. Note that the diameter of each ball is greater than the spaces between the rods.

When one of the outside selector rods is moved to select a gear, the full diameter of the rod presses its adjacent ball into the groove ground in the centre rod. The action of the ball retains the centre rod in the neutral position, but it also pushes the plunger (situated in the centre selector rod) against the second ball thus locking the other selector rod in its neutral position.

When the gear selector is in the neutral position, the movement of the centre selector rod carries the plunger with it. The full shaft diameter of the selector rod pushes both steel balls into the grooves machined in the outer rods, locking the two outer rods in the neutral position.

The technician should note that it is impossible to dismantle the selector mechanism until the gearbox selector rods are positioned in neutral.

It should also be noted that when dismantling a gearbox for repair, it is advisable to ascertain the type of interlock mechanism used on the particular gearbox and its components. If the components were to remain in the selectors during cleaning, it is easy for either a ball or the plunger to drop out of the selector. If the missing ball or plunger were not noticed when the gearbox was reassembled, there is a high risk of gearbox seizure when the vehicle is moving.

3.9.9 Lubrication

A sliding-mesh gearbox uses heavy-type gear oil as a lubricant. If this type of gearbox were in use today, then oil similar to that used in a rear axle, such as extreme pressure (EP) type gear oil, would be suitable. This assumes that precautions had been taken by the manufacturer to avoid corrosive attack by this oil on non-ferrous materials such as phosphor bronze.

The gearbox oil level is set at layshaft height. The constant rotation of the layshaft gears carries the lubricant around the gears in a pump-like manner. This simple method of lubrication ensures that all meshing teeth have an adequate supply of oil. Splash lubrication, set up by the churning action on the oil of the layshaft gears, is the method used to lubricate the other gearbox parts.

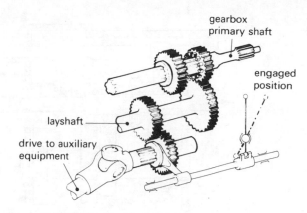

Figure 3.35 Power take-off arrangements

Some form of oil sealing arrangement is necessary to the primary and output shafts extending from the front and rear of the gearbox casing. These seals prevent loss of oil and possible contamination of the clutch plate friction facings.

3.9.10 Power take-off arrangements

As well as the mechanism used for driving a vehicle along a road, an additional power supply is often required to operate various external items of auxiliary equipment.

The application of the power take-off unit depends on the use of the vehicle. Many specialised off-road vehicles (i.e. agricultural vehicles) are fitted with a power take-off unit. The portable power source is used for driving winches, saws, drifts, pumps, etc.

Figure 3.35 shows a typical power take-off arrangement. The power take-off in this example is driven from the gearbox layshaft. The extra take-off gear, which is mounted on a flange on the side of the gearbox, is slid in to mesh with one of the sliding-mesh gears of the layshaft by a separate selector lever.

3.10   CONSTANT-MESH AND SYNCHROMESH GEARBOXES

3.10.1 Evolution from the sliding-mesh system

Although the sliding-mesh gearbox dealt with in the previous section is now rarely used, many of the design features and principles used within modern gearbox systems have evolved from it. It is therefore an advantage to understand the basic principles of the sliding-mesh gearbox before studying constant-mesh and synchromesh systems.

3.10.2 Disadvantages of the sliding-mesh gearbox

Although the mechanical efficiency of the sliding-mesh gearbox is high, the sliding-mesh design has two disadvantages:

1   Gear noise due to the spur-type gear. The straight cut parallel teeth can create a 'chatter' effect as the teeth mesh and move apart.

2   The difficulty of obtaining a smooth, quiet and quick change of gear without the application of great skill, technique and judgement by the driver (the double declutching process).

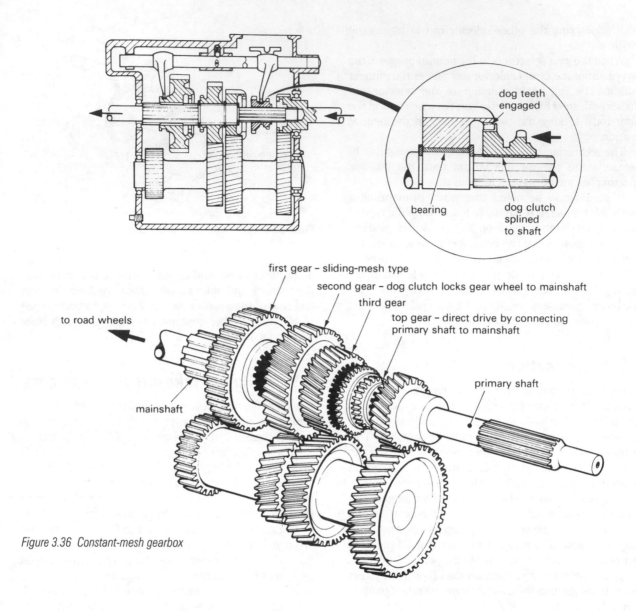

Figure 3.36 Constant-mesh gearbox

Gearbox designs introduced over the past few decades have endeavoured to overcome these disadvantages of the sliding-mesh gearbox. The initial development came with the introduction of the constant-mesh-type gearbox.

3.10.3 Constant-mesh gearboxes

The general layout of a constant-mesh is very similar to that of a sliding-mesh gearbox. A primary shaft, layshaft and mainshaft (output shaft) remain the key components of the constant-mesh gearbox, along with the gear clusters and gear wheels. However, the main differences are the types of gear teeth or gear wheels used and the methods used to engage the gears. Figure 3.36 shows the main details of a constant-mesh gearbox system.

One important feature of this type of gearbox is the use of the stronger helical gears (or double helical gears

in some cases), which lead to quieter operation. Because of the angle or helix arrangement of the teeth, there is always one part of the tooth on a gear that is in contact with a tooth on the other gear, this reduces the chattering effect that is common on the spur-type, straight-cut teeth.

Each pair of connecting gears (a layshaft cluster gear and a mainshaft gear) remain in constant mesh i.e. the mainshaft gear wheels do not move out of engagement with the layshaft cluster gears as is the case with the sliding-mesh system. However, the mainshaft gears are not locked to the mainshaft, the gears are therefore free to rotate around the mainshaft. The selection and de-selection of each forward gear is, however, achieved by a mechanism that locks and unlocks the respective mainshaft gear to the mainshaft. The locking mechanism used is a form of dog clutch (refer to section 3.7.1).

The mainshaft gear wheels are mounted on the shaft and are free to rotate on bearings, usually bushes or needle rollers. The correct positioning of the gear wheels on the mainshaft is achieved with the use of thrust washers.

When a gear is selected, the dog clutch, which is splined to the mainshaft, is slid along the mainshaft by the selector fork so that it engages with the dog teeth formed on the gear. This therefore has the effect of locking the gear wheel to the mainshaft.

There will still be noise if the dog teeth are not rotating at the same speed when the engagement is made, and so double declutching may still be necessary, but damage caused by a 'bad' change will be limited to the teeth on the dog clutch.

3.10.4 Synchromesh (constant load type)

Compared with the sliding-mesh gearbox, the constant-mesh systems provided a number of improvements, especially in the reduction of gear noise. However, a certain amount of skill was still required by the driver to produce a quick, quiet gear change.

The skill of gear changing was in the technique of double declutching. The purpose of carrying out this operation as previously described in section 3.9.7 was to equalize the speeds of the two sets of gears on sliding-mesh gearboxes before engaging the gear or equalizing the speeds of the dog teeth on constant-mesh gearboxes. To allow for an easier gear change, a device was required to synchronize the speeds mechanically. The device used to overcome the problem, is referred to as the synchromesh system.

Gearboxes were initially fitted with the synchromesh units controlling only third and top gears. Figure 3.37 shows the main details of the unit used for selection of third and top gear. Fundamentally the synchromesh-type gearbox is laid out in the same configuration as a constant-mesh gearbox, with the exception that a cone clutch system is fitted. The cone clutch is created by forming a male cone on the side of the mainshaft gear wheel; a female cone is formed on the side of the dog clutch assembly.

When the dog clutch is moved towards the gear wheel during gear selection, the male and female friction cones are then forced to make contact.

The dog clutch is made of two components: the inner component (or hub) and the outer component (or sleeve). The hub, which contains the female cone, has an internal spline that engages on the mainshaft thus allowing the hub to move along the mainshaft. The hub has a second spline, which is located on the outer surface. This spline engages with a spline on the inner surface of the sleeve thus allowing the sleeve to move on the hub.

Note that the spline on the sleeve is the same pitch as the dog teeth on the gear wheel, which means that if the sleeve is moved so that it connects to the gear wheel, the drive passes from the gear wheel to the dog clutch assembly and then to the mainshaft. A selector fork, which is connected to the gear lever, locates on the sleeve and therefore gear lever movement will move the position of the sleeve.

A series of spring-loaded balls is carried in radial holes within the hub, and these push outwards into a

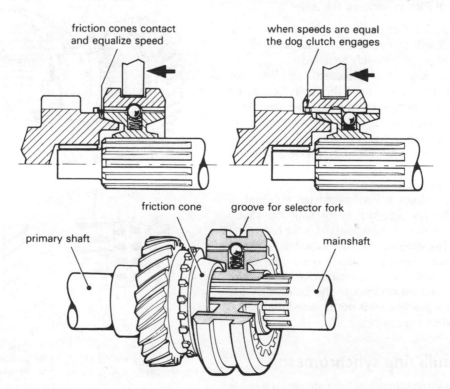

friction cones contact and equalize speed

when speeds are equal the dog clutch engages

friction cone

groove for selector fork

primary shaft

mainshaft

Figure 3.37 Principle of the synchromesh gearbox

groove machined on the inner face of the sleeve. The spring pressure acting on the balls creates a resistance against movement of the sleeve across the hub. Therefore, the driver must apply additional pressure on the gear lever to overcome the resistance.

Operation

The initial movement of the selector moves the dog clutch (sleeve and hub) towards the gear wheel; the male and female friction cones are therefore brought into contact. At this point, the friction between the two cones will cause the speed of the gear wheel to become closer to, or even match, the speed of the hub and mainshaft. Additional pressure on the gear lever then allows the sleeve to override the resistance created by the spring-loaded balls, which allows the spline on the sleeve to engage on the gear wheel dog teeth.

The initial movement of the gear lever therefore allows the friction cones to synchronize the speeds of the gear wheel and dog clutch/mainshaft. Once the speeds are synchronized, additional pressure on the gear lever allows the dog clutch to engage on the gear wheel, thus fully selecting the desired gear.

If the gear change is too quick, there will not be enough time for synchronization and the gear engagement will be noisy. The time taken for the speed of the teeth to synchronize is governed by the frictional force that exists between the cone faces. This force is controlled by the:

- total spring strength
- depth of groove in the sleeve
- angle of the cone
- coefficient of friction between the cones.

If any mechanical defect reduces any of these factors, synchronization will take longer, and the noise of the dog teeth meshing will probably be heard.

This delay factor has presented problems for lubrication manufacturers, since the high-viscosity oil required for gear operation takes a considerable time to disperse from the face of the cone. The solution to this problem was to use lower viscosity oil (similar to medium engine oil – SAE 30) and provide a series of grooves on the cone face to cut through the oil film and disperse the lubricant.

Up to recent times it was considered essential to drain and refill the gearbox every 8000 km (5000 miles), to remove the particles worn from the cones and gear teeth. With extended service schedules now in operation, this mileage has been increased considerably, and some manufacturers have recommended that no changes of the gearbox oil are necessary or the gearbox oil is not renewed during the life of the gearbox.

3.10.5 Baulk ring synchromesh

The baulk ring system, which is used almost exclusively in the manufacture of modern gearboxes, is a development of the previously described constant load system. To overcome the main disadvantage of the constant-mesh system (i.e. noise or crashing of the gears during engagement due to a quick gear change by the driver) a baulk ring or synchro ring is added in the synchromesh system.

Two main features are incorporated in the baulk ring system:

1 The friction cone pressure, or load, is proportional to the speed of change.
2 An interception device prevents positive gear engagement until the speed of the two gears is equal.

Gearbox manufacturers use various constructions to produce these features, and Figure 3.38 shows one system that is in common use.

Operation

Three spring-loaded shifting plates (also referred to as detent plates), push out from the hub into a groove in the sleeve. The ends of the shifting plates fit into slots that are located in the edge of the baulk ring. The baulk ring also has a friction cone which functions in a similar manner to the friction cones described in the previous section.

The slots in the baulk ring are slightly wider than the shifting plate to allow for a small amount of rotation of the cone. This clearance between each side

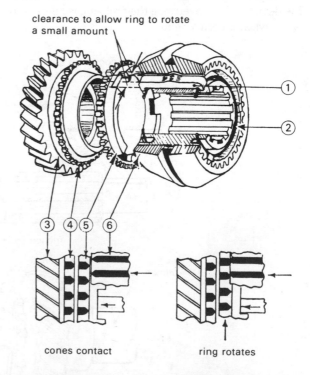

clearance to allow ring to rotate
a small amount

cones contact   ring rotates

1   shifting plate   4   gear dog teeth
2   circlip spring   5   baulking cone and ring
3   gear   6   sleeve

Figure 3.38 Baulk ring synchromesh unit

of the shifting plate and the slot is in fact equal to half the pitch of the splines on the sleeve. The clearance is a design feature, which is explained later in this section.

The baulk ring, which is made of phosphor bronze, has specially chamfered teeth on the outside; the pitch of the teeth is the same as that of the spline of the sleeve, and also the same as the pitch of the dog teeth on the gear wheel. Therefore, when the sleeve moves towards the gear wheel, the spline on the sleeve should slide over the teeth on the baulk ring before the spline can engage on the gear wheel dog teeth. The baulk ring must therefore be turning at a similar speed to the gear wheel and the teeth should be almost in alignment, before the sleeve can engage the gear wheel and transfer the drive to the mainshaft.

Movement of the selector fork, initiated by moving the gear lever, moves the sleeve and shifting plates towards the gear wheel. The shifting plates push the friction cone on the baulk ring into light frictional contact with the gear friction cone, which in turn results in the rotating speeds of the baulk ring and gear wheel tending to synchronize.

Assuming that the gear wheel and baulk ring speeds become identical (which also means that the sleeve and mainshaft speed is the same as the gear wheel speed), the sleeve could then slide over the baulk ring and engage on the gear wheel dog teeth. If, however, the speeds are not synchronized, the baulk ring (which is partially in contact with the gear wheel friction cone) will be trying to rotate at a different speed to the sleeve and hub assembly. However the edges of the slots on the baulk ring will contact the shifting plates, which will then force the baulk ring to rotate at the same speed as the sleeve and hub assembly.

Importantly, when the edges of the baulk ring slots are forced against the shifting plates, the teeth on the baulk ring are completely out of alignment with the spline on the sleeve; this prevents the sleeve from sliding across the baulk ring under such conditions. Gear selection will be 'baulked' i.e. gear selection is not possible.

Because the gear has not been engaged, the driver will apply extra pressure on the gear lever, which will tend to move the sleeve closer towards the gear wheel, which means that the shifting plates will apply greater pressure on the baulk ring. As the friction between the baulk ring and gear wheel friction cones increases, the gear wheel will increase speed to synchronize with the baulk ring and sleeve.

When the speeds of all the components are synchronized, the slots in the baulk ring are not forced against the shifting plates, in fact the baulk ring can now float slightly due to the slots being larger than the shifting plates. This means that the teeth on the baulk ring will more closely align with the spline on the sleeve. Even if there is slight misalignment of the teeth and spline, the chamfer on the baulk ring teeth allows the spline to progressively slide over the teeth and eventually full alignment is achieved. This also then allows the sleeve to fully engage on the gear wheel dog teeth thus achieving gear selection. The power now passes from the gear wheel, through the sleeve and hub assembly to the mainshaft.

With this system, the gear is engaged quickly, without any engagement noise. If the gear does not engage when the gear lever is first moved, additional pressure causes additional pressure to be applied to the baulk ring thus ensuring that the speeds are more quickly synchronized. The whole system results in quicker and quieter gear changes.

3.11 REAR-, FRONT- AND FOUR-WHEEL DRIVE GEARBOXES

3.11.1 Rear-wheel drive gearboxes

Four-speed and reverse

Figure 3.39 shows, by means of an exploded view, the gear layout of a four-speed and reverse gearbox suitable for a rear-wheel drive car. This gearbox uses a baulk ring type synchromesh on all forward speeds. To simplify the construction, a simple sliding-mesh arrangement is used for reverse.

The type of baulk ring shown in Figure 3.39 is slightly different in construction to that shown in Figure 3.38 but the basic principle is the same.

The type of unit shown in Figure 3.39 uses spring-loaded balls located in the hub to act against a small recess on the inner surface of the sleeve. When the sleeve is positioned so that no gear is selected, the pressure of the balls prevents the sleeve from moving along the hub until the driver applies pressure to the gear change mechanism.

The sleeve has the slots (unlike the baulk ring shown in the previous example) and the baulk ring has three protrusions or 'tangs' that fit into the slots. The tangs and slots have the same function as the slots and shifting plates described on the previous example.

The reverse gear idler wheel engages onto the teeth on the outer face of the sleeve used to select first and second gears. When reverse gear is selected, the idler engages a gear on the layshaft cluster and passes the power through to the first/second gear sleeve, which in turn drives the mainshaft (but in the reverse direction).

Uncaged needle rollers are used in this layout to support the layshaft gear cluster. This bearing

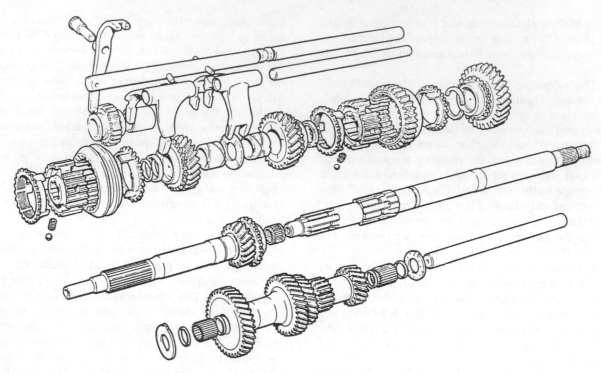

Figure 3.39 Gear layout – four-speed and reverse

arrangement is now common because in addition to having low friction, the extra rigidity of a needle roller compared with a plain bush gives a more precise gear mesh. As a consequence, the noise is reduced when the gearbox is under load. This construction makes it more difficult to reassemble the box, but with the aid of a dummy layshaft of length equal to the gear cluster, the task is made easier.

Every gearbox must have some provision to prevent the escape of oil. For flange joining, either the fitment of a paper-based sealing joint or, on metal-to-metal faces, the application of a sealing compound, is used.

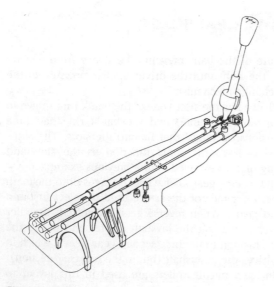

Figure 3.40 Remote control lever

Fitting lip-type seals normally prevents leakage along the shafts and through the bearings. These seals are positioned on the clutch side of the primary shaft bearing and at the universal joint end of the gearbox extension housing.

a Speedometer drive
The speedometer is driven by means of a skew gear from the main shaft. A steel worm, mounted on the mainshaft and located in the gearbox extension housing generally drives a plastic moulded pinion that is connected to either a flexible cable or an electrical transducer.

b Gear change mechanism
The driver's seating position often means that the gearbox selectors are situated well forward of the driver's body. In the past a long 'floppy' lever was used, but modern vehicles use the rigidity of a short lever and a remote control mechanism, which enables the driver to select the gears with greater precision.

Some form of 'blocker' arrangement is fitted to the gearbox to prevent the accidental engagement of reverse gear when the vehicle is moving forward. The simplest form is a spring-loaded detent; the driver must overcome the resistance to movement created by the spring pressure before the lever can be moved to the reverse position. To overcome this spring the driver either has to lift the gear lever, depress a collar or exert extra pressure.

Five-speed and reverse
The improved fuel consumption achieved by using a fifth 'overdrive' gear, has made the five-speed gearbox a

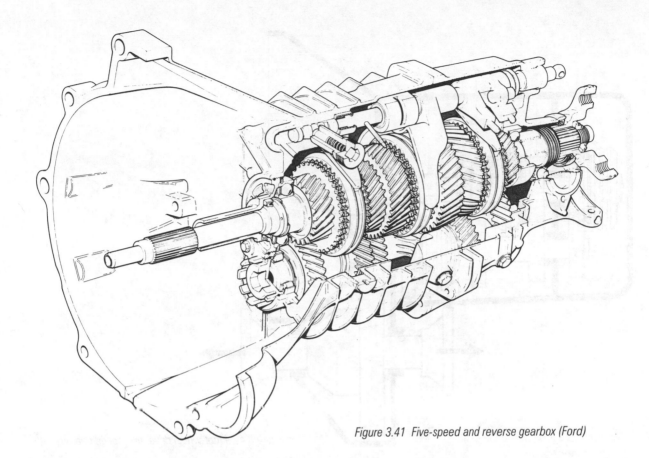

Figure 3.41 Five-speed and reverse gearbox (Ford)

common feature of the modern car. The term overdrive means that the propeller shaft turns faster than the engine, so in a five-speed gearbox the fourth gear is the normal 'top' or direct-drive gear.

Figure 3.41 shows a heavy-duty, five-speed gearbox in which all gears, including reverse, are synchromesh. Helical gears are used throughout and each gear on the mainshaft is supported on needle rollers; this reduces noise and improves efficiency. The gearbox casing, which is ribbed to avoid distortion under load, is a lightweight aluminium-alloy die-casting.

Computer-controlled manufacturing processes have made it possible to produce gears with great accuracy. This allows running tolerances to be reduced, which in turn leads to quieter operation. These developments allow the use of oils of low viscosity, and by expending less energy to rotate the layshaft, the gearbox efficiency is improved. In the gearbox shown, very thin oil similar to that used in automatic transmissions is recommended.

In common with many other five-speed gearboxes, the fifth-speed gears of the gearbox shown are situated at the rear of the gearbox.

Five-speed gearboxes sometimes use a gear lever pattern of movement (gate pattern) whereby fifth and reverse are in the same plane, e.g. fifth and reverse are obtained by forward and backward movement of the lever. In these cases a positive 'gate lock' is often used. To engage reverse on many gearboxes, the driver has to lift a collar on the gear lever.

3.11.2 Front-wheel drive gearboxes

A transversely mounted engine and transmission assembly is the common arrangement for a front-wheel drive car. This compact transaxle configuration normally requires the gearbox input and output shafts to be at the same end, so a two-shaft layout is used. Since a simple (single-reduction) system of gearing is used instead of a compound (double-reduction) system, a layshaft is not needed.

Figure 3.42 shows the layout of a five-speed and reverse gearbox. In this design each shaft is supported by a ball race at the non-driving end; at the other end the radial load is much heavier, so a roller race is fitted. Axial thrust on each shaft is taken by a radial-type ball bearing, which locates the shaft, maintains alignment and takes the thrust of the helical gears.

The spigot bearing, which is normally used to locate the front of the mainshaft on a rear-wheel drive gearbox with a layshaft, is unnecessary with the two-shaft layout, and this allows for a more rigid gear assembly and a quieter gearbox. A further improvement can be made when needle rollers are used to support the gears on the shafts.

Speedometer drive

The speedometer is normally driven by a skew gear mounted adjacent to the final drive assembly. This drive point is more accessible than the output shaft of the rear-wheel drive gearbox.

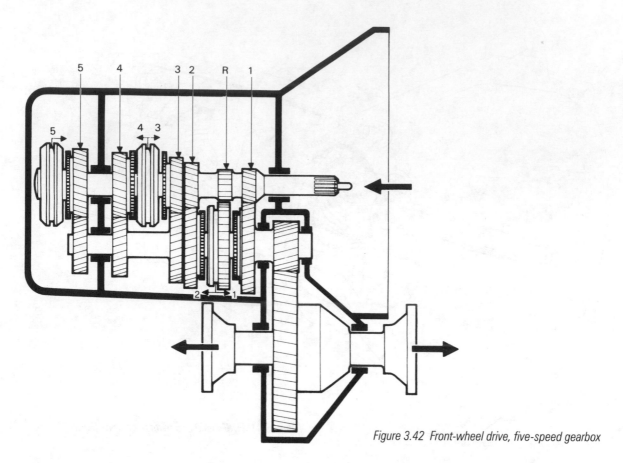

Figure 3.42 Front-wheel drive, five-speed gearbox

In the past, most speedometers were connected to the skew gear by a cable, however, in many modern vehicles the traditional mechanical speedometer has been replaced with an electronic speedometer. An electrical signal is therefore required, which is usually produced by a transducer. The transducer or signal generator may be located in the gearbox and driven from the output shaft or the final drive assembly. It is, however, increasingly common for vehicles to be fitted with electronic controlled anti-lock brake systems (ABS) which rely on speed signals from the road wheels. In these cases it is possible to obtain a speed signal from the ABS.

Gear change mechanism
Some form of remote control mechanism is essential, because a long lever is far too flexible. The linkage used must be capable of transmitting two distinct motions: longitudinal movement of the gear lever as it is moved from, say, first to second, and transverse or sideways movement, as needed for the selection of another pair of gears.

Figure 3.43 shows the principle of two systems in common use: a single rod linkage and a twin cable arrangement.

Any movement of the engine, due to torque reaction, is accommodated by using either a universal joint or relying on the inherent flexibility of the cable.

3.11.3 Four-wheel drive gearboxes

A four-wheel drive vehicle requires the gearbox to distribute the drive between the front and rear wheels. Many of these vehicles are relatively large, which allows the engine and gearbox to be mounted 'in-line' with the vehicle body (similar to many rear-wheel drive vehicles). The gearbox is typically fitted with five speeds and uses the same layout and components detailed for the rear-wheel drive gearboxes already discussed.

However, because the drive must be passed to all four wheels, a transfer-box is fitted to the end of the gearbox output shaft, which splits the drive to the front and rear axles by means of propellar shafts.

Many of today's smaller four-wheel drive vehicles use a gearbox that has been adapted from a version previously used for two-wheel drive purposes. The additional drive to either the front wheels or the rear wheels is provided by means of a transfer-box fitted to the output shaft of the gearbox.

In fact modern four-wheel drive vehicles may be fitted with an automatic gearbox and the vehicle can also be based on a front-wheel drive layout. In most cases, gearboxes are adaptations of front- or rear-wheel drive systems.

Further details are given in the four-wheel drive section of this book.

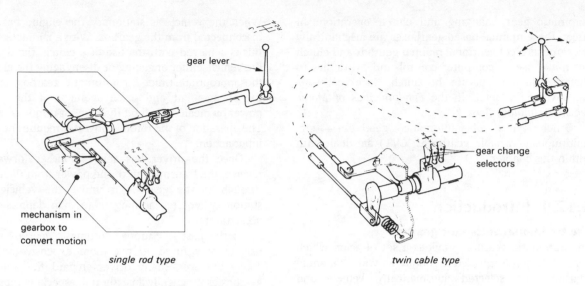

Figure 3.43 Gear change mechanisms for front-wheel drive gearboxes

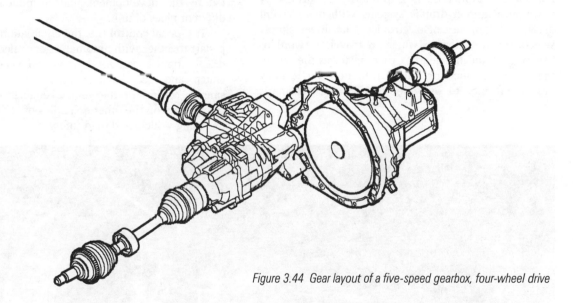

Figure 3.44 Gear layout of a five-speed gearbox, four-wheel drive

3.12   AUTOMATIC GEARBOX (GEAR SYSTEM AND FLUID COUPLING)

Note 1

The traditional automatic gearbox makes use of two very distinct mechanical systems:

1 a configuration of gears referred to as planetary or epicyclic gears.
2 a means of connecting engine power to the gearbox using a fluid coupling (either a torque converter or fluid flywheel).

Before providing in-depth details of how automatic gearboxes function, it is necessary to understand the operation of planetary gear systems and the fluid couplings. Sections 3.12.2 and 3.12.3 deal with these topics. Read these prior to the full explanation of the automatic gearbox.

Note 2

The automatic gearboxes covered within this section are traditional types of automatic unit that have developed over many years; they have come to employ a very different arrangement of gears and systems compared with a manual gearbox. There is, however, a more recent development where manual-type gearboxes are controlled using a computer or ECU (electronic control unit), which in turn controls a hydraulic actuation system.

Although these manual-type gearboxes are intended to provide the driver with the ability to change gear using switches (often using paddles located behind the steering wheel), there is usually a built-in facility that allows the computer to provide automatic gear changing and clutch operation. In effect, these manual-based gearboxes are mechanically the same as a conventional manual gearbox and clutch but make use of computer control and hydraulics to change gear and operate the clutch. Such gearboxes are covered in detail in the *Fundamentals of Motor Vehicle Technology Book 2*.

Other types of automatic gearboxes (e.g. continuously variable gearboxes, CVT) are dealt with within this chapter.

3.12.1 Introduction

The traditional automatic gearbox

The automatic gearbox provides a set of gears which instead of being selected manually as with a 'manual gearbox', are selected automatically. Vehicle and engine speeds, driving loads and driving style all influence the process of selecting the appropriate gear, but the selection process is primarily performed by mechanical and hydraulic systems with more recent designs making use of electronics. The driver simply selects the direction in which to travel (forward or backwards) and the gearbox then performs the rest of the selection functions. The driver, however, usually has the facility to override most of the automatic process.

When the vehicle is stationary the engine has to be disconnected from the gearbox. With a manual gearbox this is achieved with the use of a clutch, the driver of the vehicle either engaging or disengaging the clutch at the appropriate time. An automatic gearbox achieves the engagement and disengagement of the engines power by means of a fluid flywheel or torque converter. The operation of the torque converter requires no driver input action.

Once the driver has selected either forward or reverse, the transmission of the power from the engine through to the gearbox to move the vehicle from stationary requires nothing more than depressing the accelerator.

In the past in Europe, automatic gearboxes were usually only fitted to the more expensive vehicles. Today however, many drivers regard the automatic gearbox as practically an essential, especially those who spend a considerable amount of time driving as part of their occupation. The popularity of automatic cars has led to the development and introduction of many different types of unit.

Two-pedal control (i.e. the elimination of the clutch pedal) together with automatic gear selection, reduces driver fatigue because it overcomes the need for tedious clutch and gear change operations. Consequently, simpler control of the vehicle enables the driver to concentrate on the other essentials of vehicle handling, including vehicle and road safety.

Figure 3.45 Exploded view of ZF 6 speed automatic gearbox used fitted to some Jaguar models

Some early designs of automatic gearbox were criticised because they robbed the driver of the gear selection control. Modern units have overcome this drawback by allowing drivers to override the gearbox when they wish to take full command, making the automatic gearbox perform like a manual gearbox when desired.

Other disadvantages were a loss in engine power and an increase in fuel consumption due to torque converter slip. These drawbacks have been overcome with the fitting of a 'lockup clutch' fitted to the torque converter together with developments in electronic control.

The incorporation of electronic gearbox control has enabled the gearbox to be operated in a mode to match the driver's technique and performance requirement, (e.g. sports mode and economy mode). Advanced electronics has enabled the automatic gearbox ECU (electronic control unit) to communicate with other ECUs fitted to the vehicle, for example the engine management ECU. The ECUs share information, which provides even greater gear selection control allowing a very smooth operation. Some systems can assess the driver's intentions by monitoring the pattern in which the vehicle is being driven and selecting an appropriate driving mode.

Up until the mid 1970s, Borg Warner was a dominant name in automatic gearbox manufacture, especially for European vehicles. Borg Warner manufactured a range of units to suit engine sizes typically between 1.5 and 5 litres.

In the USA, because automatic gearboxes have been standard on most vehicles for many years, vehicle manufacturers themselves have also produced their own gearboxes. For virtually all markets, most vehicle manufacturers produce a gearbox either 'in house' or specifically made under licence by one of a number of specialist manufacturers.

3.12.2 Planetary gearing

A conventional gearing system has gears that are mounted on shafts in fixed positions; the gears then rotate around those shafts. Planetary gearing (also called epicyclic gearing), is a system in which one or more of the gear elements rotates around another gear. The manner in which they rotate can be compared to that of the planets revolving around the Sun in the solar system, hence the name planetary gears. The planetary gear system utilises the movement of some of its gears, together with their mounting shafts, to produce the required direction of rotation and gear ratio.

A planetary system can be arranged in many ways and since this type of gearing offers a number of specific advantages over conventional gearing, it is used in several different automotive applications, the most common being the automatic gearbox.

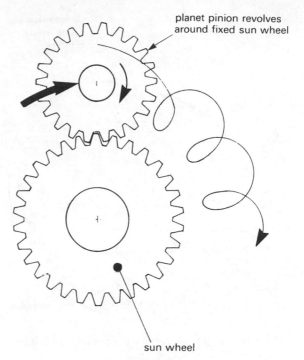

Figure 3.46 Epicyclic gear action – planet revolving around fixed sun wheel

The dictionary states that 'an epicycle is a small circle rolling on the circumference of a greater circle'. Therefore when a gearing system uses a small pinion to roll around the outside of a larger gear, the term epicyclic is appropriate. Figure 3.46 shows an epicyclic gear action; the motion of the pinion rotating around the larger, fixed gear is similar to that of the Earth rotating around the Sun. This similarity is used to obtain the names of the gears; planet for the pinion and sun for the gear wheel.

It should be noted that when a planet gear revolves around a fixed sun wheel, the number of revolutions it makes might be more than what initially appears to be logical. For example, if the planet and sun are fitted with 20 and 40 teeth respectively, the planet will rotate three times as it travels around one circumference of the sun wheel.

Another form of planetary gearing, which is shown in Figure 3.47, meshes a planet pinion with an internally toothed ring gear (often called an annulus). When the annulus is fixed, rotation of the planet causes it to 'walk around' inside the annulus. Note that when compared to the previous example of the planet and sun gears, it takes many more revolutions of the planet to travel around one circumference of the annulus.

Simple epicyclic gear trains

With the use of the epicyclic gearing components (sun wheel, planet pinion and annulus) a compact gearing arrangement can be formed.

The most common epicyclic gear arrangement, sometimes called a 'Simpson gear', uses a sun and

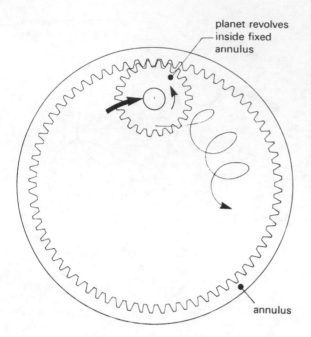

Figure 3.47 *Epicyclic gear action – planet revolving inside fixed annulus*

annulus with two or more planet pinions positioned as shown in Figure 3.48. This arrangement is also commonly referred to as an epicyclic gear train.

In this arrangement the input shaft is connected to the sun gear and the output shaft is connected to the planet gears via a planet carrier plate. An external contracting friction brake surrounds the circumference of the annulus, which is used to hold the annulus stationary when necessary. The friction brake is normally referred to as a brake band.

Whenever the brake is released (right-hand illustration Figure 3.48), the natural resistance to movement of the output shaft (planet carrier) will cause the planets to act as idler gears. As a result, the

forward-moving sun wheel will cause the annulus to be driven in the opposite direction. No drive will be transmitted through the gear train to the output shaft.

When a positive drive through the gear train is required, the friction brake is applied to hold the annulus stationary (left-hand illustration Figure 3.48). In this state, the rotation of the sun wheel drives the planet pinions, which will cause them to 'walk around' the inside of the annulus. The planet carrier and output shaft rotate in the same direction as the input shaft, but at a much slower speed. The speed at which the output shaft is driven will depend on the ratio between the gears.

Note that an epicyclic gear train unit will not transmit a drive unless one member of the unit is held stationary or is also driven at a fixed speed. This action is produced with either the use of a friction brake band or a multi-plate clutch.

Gear leverage

The use of a gear as a lever has already been considered in section 3.1.2. Figure 3.49 shows the action of a planet pinion as a lever. When the annulus is held stationary by a brake band, and the sun wheel is moved through a small angle *A*, the 'planet lever' pivots about a tooth (fulcrum) on the annulus. This action causes the centre of the lever to prise forward the planet carrier and rotate it about its axis to the extent of angle *B*. The movement of the planet carrier rotates the output shaft.

A comparison of the movement of the input shaft and output shaft, as shown by the angles *A* and *B*, indicates that a gear train of this size provides a reduction between the input shaft and output shaft in a ratio of about 3:1.

Gear ratio

The number of teeth on the sun wheel and annulus of a simple epicyclic gear train determines the gear ratio. This is given by:

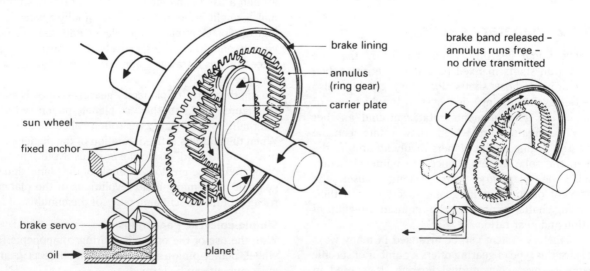

Figure 3.48 *A simple epicyclic gear train*

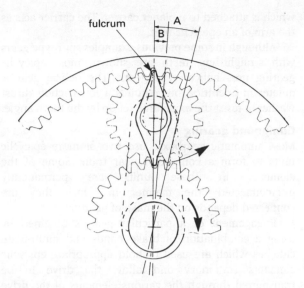

Figure 3.49 A lever action of planetary pinion

$$\text{Ratio} = \frac{A + S}{S}$$

A = number of teeth on annulus

S = number of teeth on sun wheel

Example:

If $A = 100$ and $S = 20$, the gear ratio is 6:1.

Brake action

When an epicyclic gear train is used in any form of gearbox, the friction brake action overcomes many of the disadvantages associated with gear engagement in a conventional gearbox. The action of the brake is both quick and quiet in its operation and during engagement the initial slipping action prevents a sudden jolt of the vehicle.

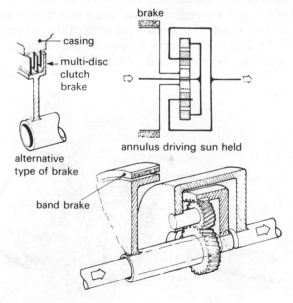

Figure 3.50 Brake applied to sun wheel

Although this feature could be used in a transmission system to perform the function of the main clutch (as used on a manual gearbox), inevitable rapid wear of the brake band friction surface would take place. It is therefore necessary to retain a more substantial mechanism to function as a main clutch thus allowing the brake band to be applied at a rate that provides a smooth operation together with a good friction material life. Figure 3.50 shows the principle of both multi-plate/disc clutches and brake band clutches when applied to the sun wheel.

With the use of a brake band mechanism and multi-plate clutches to achieve gear changes on a planetary system, it is not necessary to disconnect the power from the engine during gear changes (which is the main function of a conventional clutch on a manual gearbox).

There therefore remains only the requirement to smoothly deliver the power to the gearbox when the vehicle is moving away from the stationary position. A fluid coupling or clutch can be used to satisfactorily meet this requirement, so this type of clutch is fitted in most cases in conjunction with an automatic gearbox.

Brake applied to sun wheel

There are many occasions when an epicyclic gear train is required to provide a comparatively high gear ratio. The high ratio can be achieved by connecting the gear elements in the manner shown in Figure 3.50 (also in Figure 3.51, illustration 1.2:1 forward). In this case the brake is applied to the sun wheel, and the input shaft is connected in such a way that it drives the annulus gear. Either a brake band or a multi-disc clutch can be used to hold the sun wheel stationary.

By applying the same principle of the lever in the previous gear leverage example, the point of contact between the planet pinion and sun wheel makes the planet the lever and sun wheel the fulcrum.

The ratio achieved by this arrangement is:

$$\text{Ratio} = \frac{A + S}{S}$$

Using the same number of teeth as in the previous gear ratio example, $A = 100$ and $S = 20$, the ratio of this drive arrangement is 1.2:1.

The gear ratio obtained is very close to direct drive (1:1); so this gear configuration has many uses.

Simple epicyclic drive arrangement

The term 'simple' in this context means that the gearing system is based on one epicyclic unit comprising a sun, planet set and annulus.

Another type of commonly used epicyclic drive arrangement is a 'compound' gear train; the term is used to describe one epicyclic unit driving another.

Figure 3.51 shows how different gear ratios together with forward and reverse gears can be obtained from a simple epicyclic unit. These are achieved by altering either the brake position or the input drive point.

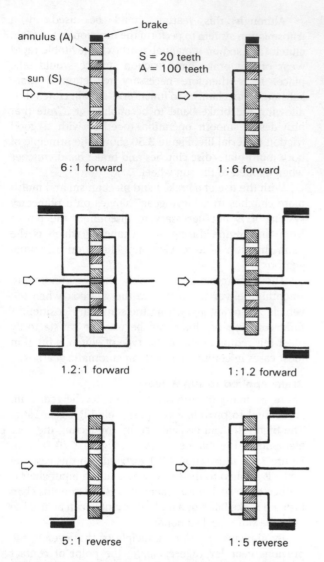

Figure 3.51 Various methods of connecting a simple epicyclic gear train

By using a number of clutches and brakes with this simple unit, various interconnections can be made to achieve a gearbox speed range such as first, second, direct drive, reverse and neutral.

In applications other than a transmission gearbox, the appropriate arrangement is selected from the layouts shown in Figure 3.51. A neutral position is not needed when a fixed ratio is required, so in this case the 'braked' element is often an integral part of the housing.

Construction

To simplify the previous epicyclic diagrams only one planet pinion has been shown. The arrangement of only one planet pinion is impracticable because a single pinion would give an unbalanced thrust on the sun and annulus members, as they are forced apart under load. Fitting three equally spaced planet pinions overcomes this balance of thrust. Figure 3.52 shows an exploded view of a simple epicyclic gear unit. Each planet pinion is supported by a ball race that is fixed to a short shaft,

which is attached to a planet carrier. The carrier acts as the arm of an epicyclic unit.

Although in some previous examples spur-type gears with straight cut teeth are shown, most epicyclic gearing uses helical type gears. The helical gear is quieter in operation but requires a low-friction thrust washer to resist the axial force set up by the tooth angle.

Compound gearing

Most automatic gearboxes use two or more epicyclic units to form a compound gear train. Some of the elements in these units are permanently interconnected; the manner in which they are connected depends on the make of gearbox.

Engagement of a particular gear is obtained by using a combination of brake bands and multi-plate clutches which are used to hold appropriate epicyclic elements stationary and allow the drive to be transmitted through the various elements of the drive train.

Figure 3.53 shows a compound gear train that uses two clutches and two brakes to provide three forward gear ratios and a reverse gear. The configuration of this unit is used to illustrate the basic principle of operation of a compound epicyclic gear train in Table 3.2.

Unidirectional clutches/free-wheel units

The unidirectional clutch is also referred to as a free-wheel or one-way clutch. Its action is similar to that used on a bicycle – it transmits drive in one direction only.

Application of free-wheel units

Used in a manual transmission application, the free-wheel unit was often fitted as a separate unit behind the gearbox. When used in this application it enables the vehicle to be free-wheeled or coasted when the road conditions are favourable for its use. Although the free-wheel unit slightly improved fuel consumption, the distinct disadvantage of the unit was the increase in brake lining wear because even when the throttle was fully closed, the engine was no longer able to offer any braking effect. The device also enabled the driver to make a gear change on a manual gearbox without operating the main clutch. Once the vehicle was in motion, release of the accelerator caused the one-way clutch to disconnect the road wheels from the gearbox;

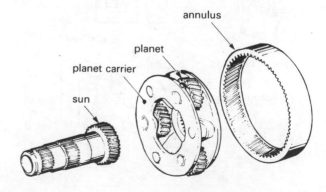

Figure 3.52 Simple epicyclic gear train

Table 3.2 Action of a compound gearing system (see Figure 3.53).

Gear	Clutch and brake engagement	Operation
First	C_1 and B_1	When vehicle is stationary, drive to A_1 causes the idler action of P_1 to drive S_1 in the opposite direction. This motion applied to S_2 allows the idler action of P_2 to drive A_1 forward at a slow speed. Even when the output shaft starts to move, the relative motion of the gear members remains the same.
Second	C_1 and B_2	Drive to At causes the planet carrier PC_1 to be driven around the faced sun S_1 at a speed slightly faster than in first gear. Rear unit is inoperative.
Third	C_1 and C_2	Driving both S_1 and A_1 causes the complete unit to revolve as one; this gives a direct drive. Rear unit is inoperative.
Reverse	C_2 and B_1	Driving S_2 and holding PC_2 in the rear unit causes P_2 to act as a reverse idler. Front unit is inoperative.

this removed the driving load from the gears and so allowed easy movement of the gear change lever.

At times when the driver did not require the free-wheel feature, the unit was locked by a gear to give a fixed-wheel condition. This was necessary to obtain reverse, so provision was made to lock the unit automatically when reverse gear was selected.

Modern applications

Today the unidirectional clutch is used widely throughout a vehicle. In particular in the torque converter, automatic gearbox and overdrive units. The unit limits the movement of a particular member to rotate in one direction only. In these examples, the unidirectional clutch provides a simple means for either driving or holding one part of an epicyclic gear train so that it can only rotate in one direction.

Types of unidirectional clutch

The two main types of unidirectional clutch are:

- Roller-type
- Sprag-type

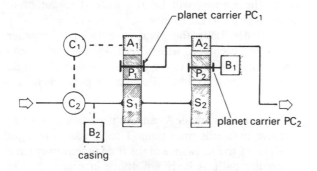

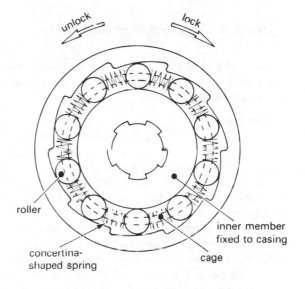

Figure 3.54 Roller-type unidirectional clutch

Roller-type

This type uses a number of parallel rollers, which are sandwiched between the inner member and the inclined cam faces of a cylindrical outer member (Figure 3.54). The type shown uses a series of concertina-shaped strip springs to wedge the rollers between the two faces.

The unidirectional clutch application shown in Figure 3.54 is a torque converter (dealt with in section 3.12.4). The hub of the unidirectional clutch is mounted on the casing so as to control the direction of movement of the converter stator.

The inner member is rigidly secured to a component casing. An anticlockwise movement of the outer member releases the rollers from the inclined cam faces of the outer member, and the outer member rotates freely.

If the direction of the outer track is reversed, the rollers are forced between the inner member and the outer inclined cam faces of the outer member. The rollers are wedged and prevent any slip taking place

Figure 3.53 Compound epicyclic gear train ZF planetary pinion

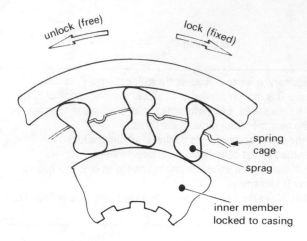

Figure 3.55 Sprag type unidirectional clutch

between the members. In this case the clutch will be fixed when the outer track is turned clockwise, and free when moved anticlockwise.

Sprag-type

The main features of this design are shown in Figure 3.55. A number of inclined wedges called sprags are held in a spring cage and positioned between inner and outer cylindrical tracks. The spring is designed to twist the sprags in the 'wedge direction' and keep them in contact with both the tracks.

When the inner member is rigidly secured to a component casing, an anticlockwise movement of the outer track releases the wedge action of the sprags and as a result allows the outer track to move freely.

Reversing the direction of motion of the outer track, the friction between the sprag and the track greatly increases the wedge action and prevents any slip taking place between the members. In this case the clutch will be fixed when the outer track is turned clockwise, and free when moved anticlockwise.

On a schematic drawing illustrating power flow, the operating direction can be indicated by using the same symbols used on electrical wiring diagrams to represent direction of current flow.

Unidirectional clutch faults

The two operating states of a unidirectional clutch are free and fixed, so the two main faults are 'free when it should be fixed' and vice versa, i.e. slip and seizure respectively.

A broken spring is a common cause of slip, and a fractured roller or sprag causes seizure because the unit wedges in both directions.

To rectify these faults it is necessary to replace the complete free-wheel unit.

3.12.3 Fluid clutch or fluid flywheel

This arrangement was originally intended for marine use, and was invented by Dr Fottinger in 1905. It was not until 20 years later that a British engineer (H. Sinclair) introduced the fluid drive on a motor vehicle. With this type of drive, the transmission is connected to the engine by hydraulic means, forming a fluid coupling. This type of coupling, or clutch system, provides an effective damper to the torsional vibrations set up by the engine, as well as a smooth take-up to move the vehicle from rest. The development of the fluid clutch has led to the torque converter, which as the name suggests is a device that amplifies the torque of the engine.

The fluid clutch assembly often forms part of the engine flywheel and is therefore sometimes referred to as a fluid flywheel.

Principle of the fluid-coupling flywheel

To help understand the principle of operation of the fluid coupling, consider the following steps.

Figure 3.56a shows a 'grapefruit' member, which is filled with a fluid. When the unit is rotated, the fluid is thrown tangentially outwards and upwards.

If a plate is held over the member (Figure 3.56b), the fluid will strike the plate and tend to rotate it in the same direction. The force and torque acting on the plate will depend on the speed of rotation – the greater the speed, the greater will be the force, because more energy is given to the fluid.

In Figure 3.57a the plate is replaced by another 'grapefruit' member, which receives the drive and diverts the fluid back to the driving member. The fluid 'circuit' can be traced by following the path taken by a particle of fluid.

1   Rotation of member A causes the particle of fluid to move outwards from point 1 to 2. This is brought about by the resistance of the fluid to movement in a circular path. A body will move in a straight line unless acted upon by a force.
    Note: if you consider a plan view of A, you will see that the straight-line path will take the particle of fluid to the outside. The further the particle moves from the centre, the faster it will have to travel; consequently, energy will be extracted from the engine.

2   The shape and outward motion will force the particle upwards and cause the tangential flow to strike the vanes of member B, the force of impact

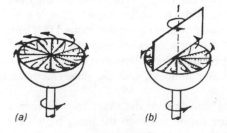

(a)   (b)

Figure 3.56 Principle of the fluid flywheel

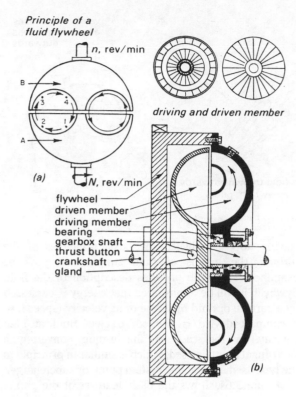

Principle of a fluid flywheel

driving and driven member

flywheel
driven member
driving member
bearing
gearbox shaft
thrust button
crankshaft
gland

Figure 3.57 The fluid flywheel

being governed by the speed difference of the two members. At position 3, the energy possessed by the particle is less than at 2, since the force of impact also causes energy to be given up in the form of heat. This means that the energy remaining in the particle is less than that given to it by the engine, and therefore the output speed will be lower than the input.

3 The fluid following the particle will push it, against its natural tendency, to point 4. During this movement, the linear speed of the particle is decreased and energy is given up to drive the output shaft. If the speed of both members is the same, the outward force at point 4 will be equal to that at point 1, and no circulation will take place. Since the operation depends on fluid passing from one member to the other, it is fortunate that the driven member B rotates more slowly.

4 As the particle moves from 4 to 1, the engine will have to supply extra energy to speed up the fluid. This is necessary because the fluid is rotating more slowly than the driving member and is acting as a brake on the engine.

Note: A fluid torque converter uses an additional member to overcome the braking effect.

Figure 3.57b shows the main constructional details of a fluid coupling. An oil similar to light engine oil is introduced to the level of the filler plug, which leaves an air space for expansion. To allow for the difference of speed between the driven and driving members, a bearing is fitted between the two members, and a guide

ring is sometimes incorporated to provide a smooth flow path for the fluid.

When the engine is running, the oil circulates in the direction shown. The speed of the oil is fast when the driven member is stationary, but as the two members approach the same speed, the speed of the oil slows down. During 'overrun' conditions (the driven member driving the driving member), the direction of oil flow in the axial plane is reversed, and a drive from the output shaft to the crankshaft provides engine braking.

Apart from a periodical check on the oil level, the coupling needs very little attention. If a fault arises, it is normally either:

(a) Over-heating, due to excessive slip, which may be caused by low oil level.
(b) Noise, due to bearing wear, which allows the faces of the members to touch.

3.12.4 Hydraulic torque converter

The converter component fulfils one of the most important tasks in a modern automatic transmission system, and in its simplest form it provides an infinitely variable ratio up to approximately 2:1. It is also responsible for similar duties to those performed by the fluid flywheel. More sophisticated types of converter are capable of providing greater torque ratios.

Principle of operation

Before considering the operation of the converter, an appreciation of the following experiments may be of help in understanding the principles involved.

Anyone who has used a hosepipe will realise that the water leaves the nozzle at a considerable speed. A moving fluid possesses energy and this means that it is capable of doing work.

Directing a flow of fluid on to a plate causes the fluid direction to change; the extent of change in direction governs the force that acts on the plate (Figure 3.58). Adjusting the tap can vary the speed of the fluid, thus the force that the fluid exerts on the plate is altered. A low fluid speed contains very little energy and therefore only exerts a small force on the plate.

Altering the angle at which the fluid strikes the plate, can also change the force exerted on the plate. If

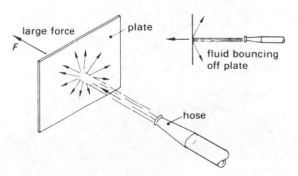

large force
F
plate
fluid bouncing off plate
hose

Figure 3.58 Fluid exerting a force on a plate

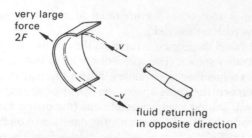

Figure 3.59 Effect of a curved plate

the angle of the plate is moved in such a manner, the plate will travel with the fluid.

Note: When the plate travels with the fluid, the speed of the fluid relative to the plate decreases, therefore the force exerted by the fluid on the plate will be less. The extremes are when the plate is not able to move, the force exerted by the liquid will be at its highest. If however the plate is moving at the same speed as the water, the force will be zero.

Figure 3.59 shows a curved plate. In this case the fluid strikes the plate with a velocity v and the curved surface redirects the fluid back at a velocity $-v$ towards its source. Roughly double the force is obtained with this curved plate arrangement, since the plate not only stops the fluid, but the fluid is sent back at the same speed.

Mounting a series of these curved plates on to a shaft (Figure 3.60) forms a simple turbine. Each plate, which is now called a vane, extracts the energy from the moving fluid to produce a turning action on the shaft. Consideration of the previous experiments will show:

1. Low fluid velocity produces a small turning movement or torque.
2. High torque occurs when the fluid velocity is high and the shaft speed low.
3. A gradual decrease in torque occurs as the shaft speed increases.

Note: Although a liquid has been used to demonstrate the principle of the vane in the previous experiments, the experiment can be conducted with air or any fluid. The arrangements considered can be applied to gas turbines, turbochargers or hydraulic converters since the basic principle is similar.

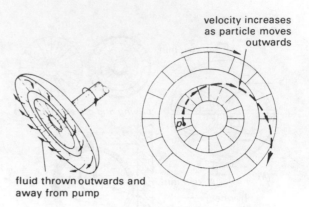

fluid thrown outwards and away from pump

Figure 3.61 Pump action

Having now established the basic principles of the turbine, the means of fluid supply will now be examined. From the previous description of the fluid flywheel, it will be appreciated that energy is possessed by a particle of fluid by virtue of its velocity (speed), so a compact device is needed to eject fluid at high velocity. In the case of the torque converter, a centrifugal pump is used, which is similar in principle to the type used in a cooling system pump or supercharger.

Figure 3.61 shows the basic features of the pump. Rotation of the pump member causes the particle of fluid P to move in the path shown. Initially the movement is towards the outside of the member. Note that the greater the distance the particle of fluid has to travel in one revolution, the more the velocity of that particle increases. Work has to be done by the engine to achieve this increase in the particle's energy.

Encasing the pump within a container causes the fluid to move away from the pump as shown in Figure 3.62. Examining the diagram shows the fluid moving around the circumference, and it is the speed in this direction that governs the driving force that is being delivered by the pump. The resemblance between the flow given by the pump and the nozzle shown in Figure 3.60 should now be apparent. The effect of engine speed on the pump's performance will be easy to understand; low engine speed will give a small flow (low velocity) of fluid, consequently each particle of fluid will possess only a small amount of energy.

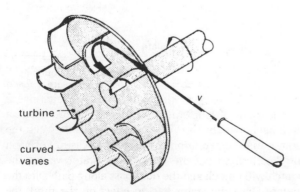

Figure 3.60 Energy extracted from fluid to give turning moment

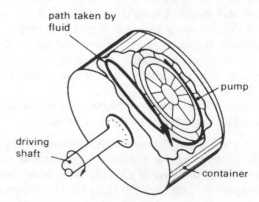

Figure 3.62 Container fitted to pump

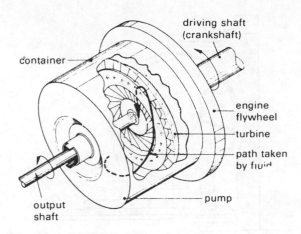

Figure 3.63 *Fluid path from pump to turbine*

The pump is placed adjacent to a turbine (Figure 3.63). The pump driven by the engine imparts energy to the particle of fluid as it moves towards the outside. The turbine extracts the energy created by the pump by moving the fluid inwards towards the shaft, thus causing the fluid to slow down.

Placing the pump adjacent to the turbine shows how the drive from the engine is achieved.

To summarise this stage:

Pump: Connected to the engine, speeds up the particle of fluid and imparts energy.
Turbine: Connected to the gearbox, slows down the particle of fluid and extracts energy.

The arrangement in Figure 3.63 is similar to a fluid flywheel and in this form the torque output is always less than the torque input.

However, applying the earlier analogy of the hosepipe would indicate that when the pump is turning faster than the turbine, the force of impact of the fluid striking the turbine vanes should give a torque increase. This would be true if the fluid did not have to return to

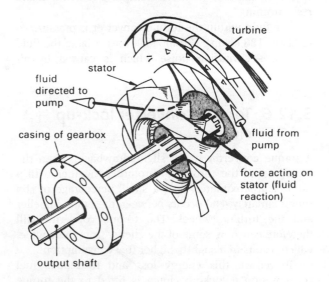

Figure 3.64 *Action of stator*

the pump, but since this fluid has to recirculate, the speed of the fluid compared to the speed of the pump vane must be considered.

To give a high impact force on the output member (driven turbine), the pump must be turning at a higher speed than the turbine, but when the fluid is returned to the pump it is travelling slower than the pump vane. In this condition the vane will strike the slower moving fluid particle and this will give a force, which is acting against the motion of the pump, i.e. the fluid will tend to act as a brake on the pump.

The greater the speed difference between pump and turbine, the greater will be the impact force on the turbine, but this will also result in a larger braking action on the pump.

To obtain a torque multiplication, this braking action must be eliminated, which is achieved by fitting a separate member called a stator (stationary member) between the turbine and the pump. Mounted on an extension of the gearbox casing, the stator consists of a number of vanes that are shaped as shown in Figure 3.64. Fluid returning to the pump is redirected such that it now enters the pump at a suitable speed and direction. If the path of the oil returning to the pump is considered, the system can be shown diagrammatically as in Figure 3.65.

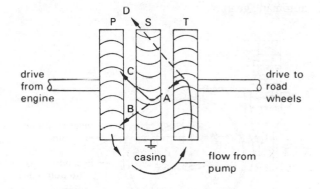

Figure 3.65 *Turbine operation*

Fluid from the pump acts on the turbine T, but if the turbine is turning slower than the oil, the oil will be deflected in the path marked A. The stator acts as a reaction member and redirects the fluid from path B to path C, a suitable direction for the pump to receive the fluid.

When the turbine speed increases, the fluid taking path A will gradually change until it is taking path D. Fluid attempting to flow along path D will now be obstructed by the stator vanes. The disturbance caused by the obstruction of the stator vanes would give a considerable drop in efficiency. To limit this drawback, a unidirectional clutch (free-wheel) is fitted between the stator and the extension of the gearbox casing. As soon as the fluid strikes the back of the stator vanes, the clutch will unlock and the fluid pass along path D to the pump. Once the stator has no effect on the fluid, the unit will act similarly to a fluid coupling.

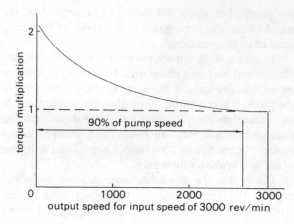

Figure 3.66 Torque output variation

Figure 3.66 shows the torque output in relation to turbine speed for a given speed of the pump. It will be seen that the output torque is approximately equal to input torque when the turbine speed is about 90% of the pump speed.

Three-element torque converter

Figure 3.67 shows the arrangement of a three-element, single-stage converter, which is quite common and is used in conjunction with many different types of automatic gearbox.

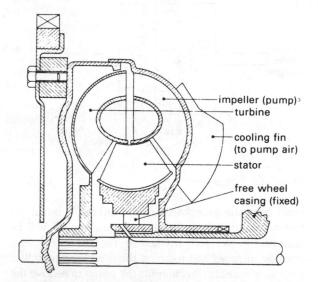

Figure 3.67 Three-element, single-stage torque converter

Multi-stage converter

When greater torque multiplication is required a multi-stage converter is often used. This type uses a series of turbines and stators and Figure 3.68 shows its main features.

When the converter is placed under conditions of low pump and low turbine speeds, the fluid will follow the path shown in Figure 3.69. The energy in the fluid is gradually extracted as it passes through each turbine and stator stage.

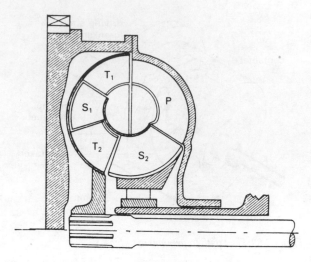

Figure 3.68 Layout of a multi-stage torque converter

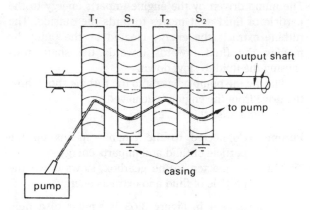

Figure 3.69 Principle of a multi-stage torque converter

3.12.5 Torque converter fluid

The automatic gearbox supplies the fluid for the torque converter. The fluid is generally a low-viscosity mineral oil, which contains additives to improve lubrication and resist frothing.

The fluid within the torque converter is pressurized to about 138 kN m⁻² (20 lbf/in²), pressurizing the fluid minimizes cavitation noise which is caused by air circulating in the converter.

3.12.6 Torque converter lock-up clutch

A torque converter has a slight drawback; when the impeller and the turbine are rotating together with a ratio of approximately 1:1, a small percentage of slip (approximately 4%) occurs between the pump impeller and the turbine wheel. The torque converter will therefore consume some of the energy from the engine, which results in a slightly higher fuel consumption.

To reduce this energy loss and to reduce fuel consumption a lock-up clutch is fitted to the torque converter. During cruise conditions, the lock-up clutch is engaged which connects the impellor to the turbine; the impellor is therefore locked to the turbine, which prevents torque converter slip occurring.

The clutch used is similar to that of the single plate clutch employed with a manual gearbox. The clutch is splined to the hub of the turbine, the frictional surface of the clutch acting on the impellor casing.

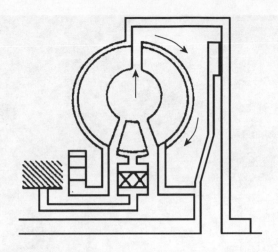

Figure 3.71 Lock-up clutch – engaged

Note: The lock-up clutch will normally only operate when the automatic gearbox is in top gear (direct drive) or overdrive.

The hydraulic circuit for the lock-up clutch is normally controlled by a hydraulic governor, or by the electronic control unit (ECU) on electronically controlled gearboxes. The volume of fluid is returned to the transmission sump via a hydraulic control valve.

The fluid pressure behind the clutch plate increases, forcing the clutch plate to contact the impeller casing. The impeller casing and turbine are locked together with the use of the clutch plate, preventing slip between the impeller and the turbine (Figure 3.71).

When the speed of the vehicle reduces or the engine load is increased, the control valve supplies fluid (under pressure) between the clutch plate and the impeller casing, which equalizes the pressure on both sides of the clutch. The frictional surface of the clutch is forced away from the impeller casing, disengaging the lock-up clutch, allowing the torque converter to function normally.

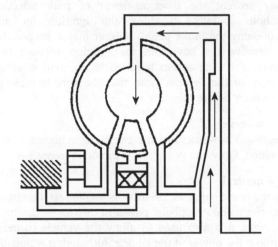

Figure 3.70 Lock-up clutch – disengaged

Operation

When the lock-up clutch is disengaged (Figure 3.70), the fluid, which is under pressure within the torque converter, flows on either side of the clutch. Equal pressure on each side of the clutch plate disengages the clutch, allowing normal operation of the torque converter.

When the vehicle reaches a predetermined speed and engine load (usually cruise conditions), the automatic gearbox hydraulic circuit provides a path, which allows the fluid to exhaust from between the clutch plate and the impeller casing

3.13 AUTOMATIC GEARBOX (OPERATION)

Note: To simplify illustrations and descriptions, much of the following information refers to a typical automatic gearbox with three forward ratios). References are, however, made to gearboxes with more than three speeds. Also note that this chapter relates primarily to gearboxes that are not electronically controlled; such systems are covered in section 3.14.

3.13.1 Automatic gear selection

An automatic gearbox provides a number of gear ratios to allow the effective use of engine power. The power

from the engine is transmitted to the automatic gearbox by the use of fluid coupling, which in the case of most modern vehicles is a torque converter (refer to 3.12.4). However, other than selecting the direction of travel, the driver does not need to manually select gears. Nor, because of the use of a fluid coupling, is the driver required to operate a clutch.

The driver selects the direction of travel, (forward or reverse), using the selector lever. Reverse gear consists of only one gear ratio, but when forward drive is selected, four or five gear ratios are usually provided (three speed automatic gearboxes remained in popular use until the mid 1990s). However, with high engine

Figure 3.72 The gear selector

performance, fuel economy and emissions in mind, modern automatic gearboxes generally incorporate five gear ratios, with six-speed automatic gearboxes now becoming more common. The highest gear is often referred to as an overdrive.

Normally, when moving forward 'drive' is selected (indicated by the letter 'D' on the selector). D provides the fully-automatic mode; the gearbox automatically selects the appropriate gear for the driving conditions. The driver simply controls the vehicle using only the accelerator and the brake pedals. Mechanical and hydraulic systems work together to select and engage the gears, but modern automatic gearboxes have the additional advantage of a computer to provide electronic control.

3.13.2 Selector features

The gear selector, which is normally either floor-mounted between the front seats or attached to the steering column, is marked with a series of letters and numbers.

For safety reasons, the selector mechanism incorporates an inhibitor switch which prevents the operation of the starter motor in any position other than P and N (park and neutral).

Most gear selectors, for a gearbox with three forward ratios, provide the following selection options:

P R N D 2 1

Gearboxes with four gear ratios usually add the number 3, and for five-speed gearboxes there would be numbers 3 and 4.

These letters and numbers indicate the following on a three-speed gearbox:

P – park

A parking pawl, mounted to the gearbox casing, is engaged with a gear connected to the gearbox output shaft. This provides a powerful lock that positively prevents the movement of the gearbox output shaft and transmission.

Many modern vehicles are fitted with an electronically-controlled transmission system, which may prevent the disengagement of park selection without initially switching the ignition on and depressing the brake pedal. Neither may it be possible to remove the key from the ignition without first selecting P. The action required is normally a safety feature of the vehicle. Note that the vehicle must be stationary before selecting P.

R – reverse

Rearward movement of the vehicle is achieved in this position. Only one gear ratio is provided in reverse.

N – neutral

As the name suggests, no drive is applied so the engine can run without applying power to the transmission.

Neutral is also used to allow the vehicle to move without the power of the engine. Although it is possible to tow the vehicle in neutral, the distance travelled should be kept to a minimum. Damage can occur owing to the lack of lubrication within the gearbox if the vehicle is towed more than the specified distance or at a high speed.

D – drive

Drive is the 'normal automatic mode' which permits the automatic transmission to select the full range of forward gears automatically. The automatic selection is based on the operating conditions and driving style.

2 – second gear

This does not allow any gear higher than second to be engaged. It allows automatic changes from: first gear to second gear, and also second to first, normally with engine braking in second gear.

1 – first gear

Position 1 (or 'low') provides selection of the lowest gear ratio (first gear) only. When 1 is selected, there will usually be no free-wheeling action, which therefore makes it suitable for engine braking. No automatic up-changes (up-shifts) occur while the selector is in this position. It should be noted that some automatic gearboxes might allow downshifts when '1' is selected when the vehicle is moving in a higher gear. Once first gear has been engaged, no up shifts are then permitted.

Note: If the transmission is fitted with additional gear ratios i.e. fourth gear, the gear selector will usually provide a position for the other gear ratios to be selected manually, except the highest or top gear. The driver will still have to select D to allow top gear to be engaged.

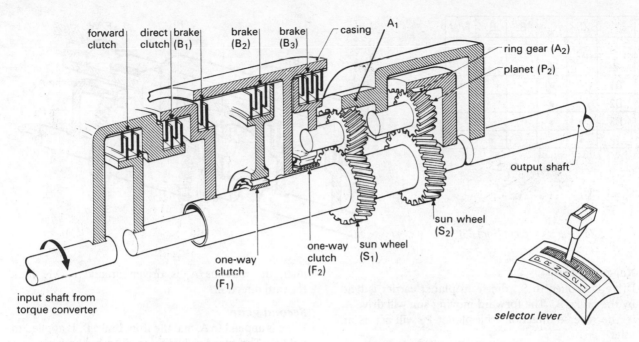

forward clutch · direct clutch (B₁) · brake (B₁) · brake (B₂) · brake (B₃) · casing · A₁ · ring gear (A₂) · planet (P₂) · output shaft · sun wheel (S₂) · one-way clutch (F₂) · sun wheel (S₁) · one-way clutch (F₁) · input shaft from torque converter · selector lever

Figure 3.73 Gear train layout and table showing gear ratios and clutch/brake selection.

Although not common, if the vehicle is fitted with an 'overdrive' gear, an additional switch may be fitted to the gear selector lever. When the selector is in D and the overdrive switch is on, the automatic gearbox selects overdrive when vehicle conditions allow. Note that electronically-controlled gearboxes may use the overdrive indicator light as a warning light to indicate a failure within the system. Refer to manufacturers details for further information.

3.13.3 Mechanical gear train

Although there are a number of different gear train layouts used on automatic gearboxes, the following examples are representative of the basic principle. In both examples, there are two interconnected, epicyclic gear trains, which form a compound system.

Example 1 A simple three-speed gearbox

Figure 3.73 shows how it is possible to use a multi-plate clutch mechanism to provide a braking action on the various elements of the gear train. Merits of this design include a smoother gear change and elimination of periodic adjustment of the brake bands.

The automatic gearbox shown provides one reverse and three forward gear ratios. The basic layout of the epicyclic gear train is similar to that employed by many manufacturers.

The table indicates which clutches and brakes are applied to select the various gear ratios.

Example; When D2 is selected (gear lever in position D and second gear engaged), the forward clutch is applied, giving a gear ratio of 1.452: 1.

Gear	Fwd clutch	Direct clutch	F_1	F_2	B_1	B_2	B_3	Ratio
1	•						•	2.452 Lock up
2	•					•		1.452 Lock up
D1	•			•				2.452
D2	•		•					1.452
D3	•	•						1.000
R		•					•	2.212

Note that gears 1 and 2 listed on the table are when the driver has selected either 1 or 2 on the gear lever (engine-braking is provided when either position 1 or 2 is selected). D1, D2 and D3 on the table are applicable when the driver has selected D and the gearbox is then making automatic changes through first, second and third gears (no engine braking with this selection).

First gear
Drive is applied to A_2, and the front planet carrier is held either by the freewheel F_2 (position D, gear 1 engaged) or the brake B_3 (position 1, gear 1 engaged).

Forward motion of A_2 drives both S_1 and S_2 in the opposite direction; this causes P_1 to act as an idler and drive A_1 in a forward direction.

Second gear
Drive is applied to A_2. The sun S_2 is held by either the freewheel F_1 (position D, gear 2 engaged) or the brake B_1 (position 2, gear 2 engaged).

Forward motion of A_2 'walks' the planet P_2 around the fixed sun S_2; this action causes the planet carrier and output shaft to move as given by the ratio $(A + S)/A$.

Third gear
Drive is applied to A_2 and S_2. Direct drive is obtained because both gear members rotate at the same speed.

	C_1	C_2	B_1	B_2	F/W
1		●		●	
2		●	●		
D1		●			●
D2		●		●	
D3	●	●			
R	●			●	

Figure 3.74 Gear train layout (Ford C3)

Reverse gear

Drive is applied to S_1, the front planet carrier is held by the brake B_3. The forward moving sun will drive A_1 in the reverse direction; the planet P_1 will act as an idler.

Example 2 Alternative three-speed layout

The gear train layout shown in Figure 3.74 was used by Ford on their C3 Bordeaux generation gearboxes and is similar to that used by other American manufacturers, (e.g. the Chrysler 'Torque Hite'). Although of an older design compared with current gearboxes, it illustrates an alternative method of selecting gears on a three-speed system.

A five-position selector, marked P R N D 2 1, controls the action of two clutches, two brake bands and a freewheel.

First gear

Drive is applied to A, and the rear planet carrier is held by either the freewheel (position D, gear 1 engaged) or the rear brake B_2 (position 1, gear 1 engaged).

The resistance to movement of the output shaft, which is connected to the front planet carrier, causes the front planet to drive the two suns (S_1 and S_2) in the opposite direction. With the rear planet acting as an

idler, the annulus A_2 is driven around slowly in a forward direction.

Second gear

Drive is applied to A_1 and the front brake B_1 is applied to hold S_1. The speed reduction is given by the front gear set, the ratio being $(A + S)/A$.

Third gear

Drive is applied to A_1 and S_1. This causes both A_1 and S_1 to rotate at the same speed; direct drive is obtained.

Reverse gear

Drive is applied to S_2 and a brake holds the rear planet carrier. Reverse is obtained by the rear gear set, the planet P_2 acting as an idler.

Overdrive gear set

A four-speed automatic gearbox having an overdrive as the highest gear ratio can be achieved by adding an additional gear set to the rear of a normal three-speed epicyclic train.

In the overdrive layout shown in Figure 3.75, fourth gear is obtained by holding sun S_3 with a brake; the drive is applied to the planet carrier PC_3.

Driving the planet carrier around the fixed sun causes A_3 to rotate at an overdrive speed as given by the ratio $A/(A + S)$.

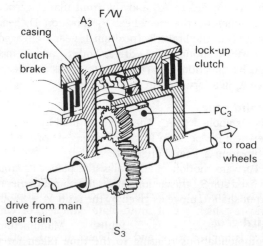

Figure 3.75 An overdrive gear set (ZF)

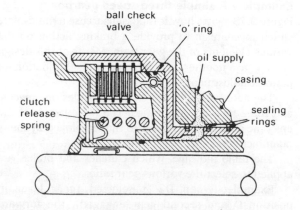

Figure 3.76 A multi-plate clutch

In other gear positions the overdrive gear set is put out of action by either the lock-up clutch or the freewheel, the former being used for reverse and also for gear positions designed to give engine-braking.

3.13.4 Multi-plate clutch actuation

Note: A number of brake bands and multi-plate clutches are used in an automatic gearbox. The various clutches and brake bands are used to hold part of the gear train stationary, enabling the various gear ratios to be selected. With modern automatic gearboxes, multi-plate clutches are normally used instead of brake bands. The use of clutches makes the gearbox more compact and lighter; it also overcomes the need for adjustments that must be carried out periodically to compensate for friction lining wear.

Oil pressure, produced by an oil pump which is driven at engine speed from the torque converter drive, is distributed by various control valves to the appropriate clutch and brake pistons when actuation of these parts is required.

The automatic gearbox is normally fitted with several wet-type multi-plate clutches, which are used to hold the appropriate parts of the epicyclic gear train stationary and so obtain the gear ratios. Most of these clutches operate on the same principle.

Figure 3.76 shows a typical construction. Two sets of steel plates, inner and outer, are connected alternately by protruding tabs to the hub and drum respectively. Bonded to the faces of the inner plates is a friction material having either a hard or comparatively soft texture. The hard facing is made of a cellulose compound, or synthetic fibre, bonded together with a phenol resin to obtain a suitable friction value. The soft facing, which is based on paper, is more porous and elastic. Paper-based facings normally give a smoother and quieter take-up when operated over a wide temperature and pressure range.

When the clutch is to be engaged, oil under pressure is supplied through a drilling in either the casing or the shaft, to the clutch-operating cylinder (Figure 3.77). Oil pressure is prevented from leaking by fitting a number of synthetic rubber O-rings and square-section, cast-iron seals to the piston and other moving parts.

The torque transmitted by a given multi-plate clutch depends on friction value and operating pressure, so a fault with either one of these will cause the clutch to slip.

Drag between the plates when the clutch is disengaged is an energy drain, so provision is made to separate the plates. A large clutch release spring returns the operating piston, and in some cases the steel outer plates are slightly dished to aid the separation.

Immediately after the clutch has been disengaged, the centrifugal action of the residual oil in the operating chamber would apply the piston and cause slight drag.

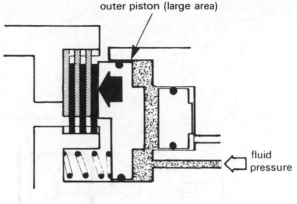

high thrust on clutch

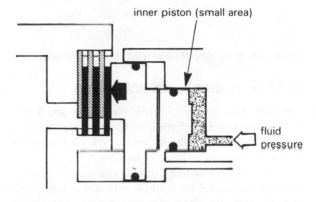

low thrust on clutch

Figure 3.77 Clutch operation with two pistons

Fitting a check valve to the assembly releases the pressure, preventing clutch drag.

When oil pressure is applied to the clutch, the check valve is held closed. Releasing the pressure from the clutch piston allows the ball to move outwards, owing to the centrifugal effect, and opens the release hole. The clutch is quickly disengaged.

Two pistons may be used to operate the clutch, one with a small surface area and the other with a large surface area. This construction, which is shown in Figure 3.77, allows the thrust on the plates to be varied to suit the conditions; this achieves a smoother operation.

Clutch slip

This fault produces similar symptoms to those given by slip of a main clutch in a manual transmission. If the fault is allowed to persist, the accelerated wear of the friction facing, together with the effects of the high temperature caused by the slip, can only be remedied by renewing the clutch or brake unit.

Slip of the clutches can be diagnosed when a stall test is carried out. A test using each gear position may indicate which set of multi-plate clutches, or which brake band, is faulty. Manufacturer's recommendations relating to the time taken for the test must be observed.

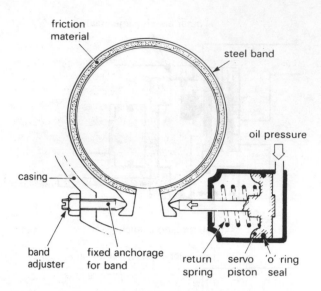

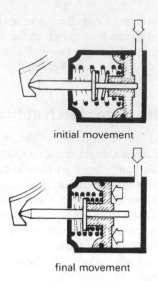

Figure 3.78 Brake band actuation by a single-acting servo

Figure 3.79 A delay servo

3.13.5 Brake band actuation

Normally two or more brake bands are fitted in a gearbox to prevent rotation of the gear members. An external contracting, single-band type brake is used and Figure 3.78 shows its basic construction.

The band is anchored at one end to the casing to resist the rotational force and is actuated by a hydraulic servo at the free end. Maximum braking torque is achieved by siting the anchor in such a position that the rotational force of the drum produces a self-wrapping action.

The spring steel brake band is internally lined with a hard friction material; the lining material is bonded to the brake band. When the brake is applied this material makes contact with a steel drum connected to a part of the gear train.

An adjuster is provided at the brake band anchor; this allows the correct clearance to be set during gearbox assembly or to compensate for wear during the service life of the unit. The screw for this adjuster is often carried through the gearbox casing to allow maintenance without dismantling the gearbox. Adjustment of the band normally involves releasing the lock nut and tightening the screw to a given clearance or torque setting.

Various types of servo actuator are used to suit the gearbox. The commonest types are:

* single-acting
* delay
* double-acting.

Single-acting servos

The basic type of servo shown in Figure 3.78 consists of a single hydraulic piston fitted in a cylinder that is fixed to the gearbox casing. Fluid leakage past the piston is prevented by a synthetic rubber O-ring and a spring is fitted in the chamber to return the piston when the fluid pressure is released.

The force exerted by a servo must be sufficient to prevent slip of the drum, so bands controlling gears having a high torque output are fitted with a servo cylinder which has either a large area or a high operating pressure.

Delay servos

When the vehicle is in motion, a sudden engagement of the brake can cause a jolt or harsh gear change. A well-designed system incorporates devices to limit this action, one of which is the delay servo shown in Figure 3.79.

The delay feature is achieved by using a second (inner) spring and a piston rod, which can slide through the piston, instead of being rigidly attached as in the basic type.

When fluid pressure is applied, the initial piston movement compresses the inner spring. Once this has taken place, positive contact between the piston and rod is made and the full force is applied to the brake in the normal way.

The cushioning action of the inner spring gives a gradual application of the brake. It also dampens the vibration produced by the band during the initial stage of brake band engagement.

Double-acting servos

With this type of servo, fluid can be directed to one or both sides of the piston. In Figure 3.80a fluid under pressure supplied at A will act on the small surface area part of the piston and apply the servo in the normal way.

When an equal fluid pressure is applied to A and B (Figure 3.80b), the piston moves in the 'release' direction. The servo releases due to the unequal thrust produced on the piston by the fluid pressure acting on the side of larger area.

A double servo can be used to provide a smooth change between second and third gears, in this case application of the brake servo engages second gear. When a certain speed is reached, a change to third is

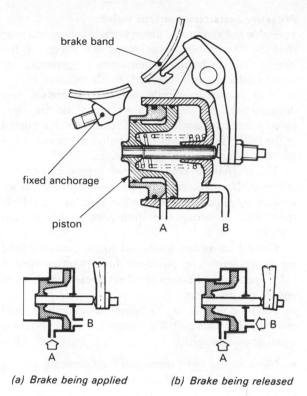

(a) Brake being applied   (b) Brake being released

Figure 3.80 A double-acting servo

made by directing fluid from a single line to the appropriate clutch and also to the 'release' side of the brake servo. Besides reducing the number of hydraulic lines, this arrangement gives a quick down-change because as soon as the fluid is released from one side of the servo, the second gear immediately comes into operation.

The majority of automatic gear changes are made while the drive is being transmitted through the gearbox. If a brake or clutch were released before the next gear units were partly engaged, the engine would suddenly speed up due to clutch (or brake band) slip. This condition, called flare-up, is prevented by overlapping the engagement of the new gear with the disengagement of the old gear.

If the period of overlap is too great, then a harsh gear change condition, sometimes called 'tie-up', results. Tie up occurs because the two 'gears' oppose each other, i.e. each gear attempts to drive the output shaft at a speed dictated by its ratio, with the result that the gearbox partially locks up.

Brake slip

As with clutch slip (refer to 3.13.4), this fault produces similar symptoms to those given by slip of a main clutch in manual transmission.

Again, as is the case with slip of the gearbox clutches, a stall test can be carried out. A test using each gear position may indicate which set of multi-plate clutches or which brake band is faulty. Manufacturer's recommendations relating to the time taken for the test must be observed.

3.13.6 Hydraulic control of actuators

The clutches and brake bands of most automatic gearboxes are operated (actuated) by hydraulic means. An oil pump, driven at engine speed by the torque converter casing, generates the fluid pressure. A gear-type pump is typically used, similar to that used in an engine application. The pressure produced should be sufficiently high to lock the clutch plates or brake drum, but not so high as to waste energy. Distribution of fluid to the clutches and brakes is by means of a control valve, called a manual valve, linked to the driver's selector lever.

Although many valves are used in automatic gearboxes, the basic principle of operation of each valve is the same. The valves are contained within a chest, which is situated at the lowest point of the gearbox. In the following paragraphs, construction and operation of some of the valves is considered.

Regulator valves (relief valves)

The main purpose of this type of valve is to limit the hydraulic line pressure to a pre-determined maximum pressure. The three main types, shown in Figure 3.81, are as follows:

Ball and piston-type relief valve

Ball and piston-type valves are similar to the oil pressure relief valve used on engines. When the pressure acting on the valve produces a thrust greater than the force exerted by the spring, the valve lifts and so prevents any further increase in pressure. Operation is based on the relationship:

Thrust = Pressure × Area

Spool-type relief valve

Simple spool valves are similar to the plunger-type except that they are waisted (reduced in area at the centre) to control the fluid flow. For the spool valve shown in Figure 3.81, the areas of A and B are the same, so the pressure in the waist region will exert an equal thrust upwards and downwards; as a result the pressure in this region will not affect the movement of the valve.

When pressure is sufficient to lift the valve, a port is uncovered. Fluid then flows to the waisted part of the

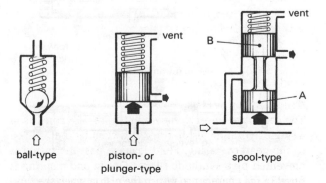

Figure 3.81 Types of regulator valve

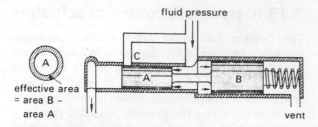

Figure 3.82 A simple pressure regulator valve

valve from where it is either returned to the reservoir or passed to a line that acts on another part of the system.

Differential spool valves

These have two spool plungers of different diameter similar to the type shown in Figure 3.82. As fluid pressure begins to build up, the spool moves to the right; this is because the effective area B exposed to the fluid is larger than A. The actual movement of the spool is controlled by the spring strength. The spring is situated in a chamber that is vented to avoid a pressure build-up behind the valve. When the pressure reaches a set value dictated by the spring, the spool uncovers the port C; this spills out the fluid and prevents any further rise of pressure.

Control valves

The purpose of this type of valve is to direct the fluid to a hydraulic line that either activates or controls the appropriate clutch and/or brake.

Manual control valve

The manual valve situated in the valve chest, is linked by a rod or cable to the gear selector lever. The position of the manual valve is therefore dictated by the gear position set by the driver.

Figure 3.83 shows a very simple manual valve used to control forward and reverse movement of a vehicle. In this case, operation of the lever moves the valve and uncovers the port that supplies either the forward or reverse gear actuators. Positive location of the valve is obtained by a selector ball detent arrangement.

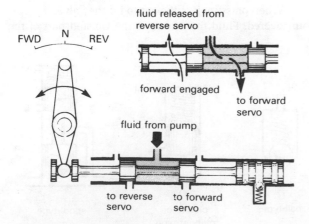

Figure 3.83 A simple, manual control valve to control forward or reverse gear selection

Pressure sensitive control valves

To enable the gearbox to automatically control the gear changes, the system must sense the speed of the vehicle. The hydraulic system uses a 'governor' for sensing vehicle speed (detailed later in this section).

Note that electronically-controlled gearboxes may dispense with the mechanical governor and rely on a speed signal from a wheel speed sensor which is passed to the ECU. The ECU will then control the operation of the hydraulic valves and gear changes.

The mechanical-type governor is mounted on the output shaft, and therefore rotates with it. The governor generates a fluid pressure that increases as the vehicle speed rises. Governor operation is covered in section 3.13.7.

Control valves are connected to the governor fluid circuit and sense its pressure. At the appropriate time, a valve operates and directs the fluid through the lines to engage the new gear.

Figure 3.84a shows a spool valve with a fluid connection at each end. If the areas of faces A and B are equal, the valve will:

- Move to the right when the fluid pressure at C is greater than at D and vice versa.
- Remain in a central position when pressure at C equals pressure at D.

Any pressure given by the fluid at E will have no effect on the movement of the valve because the thrust tending to move the valve to the right will be balanced by an equal and opposite thrust acting on the other face. In many ways this is similar to the action of the two springs.

Making the surface area of one spool larger, as shown in Figure 3.84b, will cause the pressure acting on the larger area to give a greater thrust on the valve than that given by the same pressure at C.

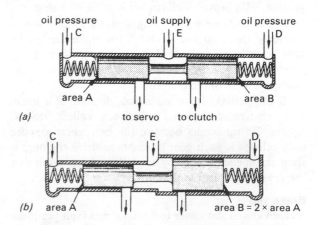

Figure 3.84 A spool valve controlling flow to either the servo or the clutch

3.13.7 The main hydraulic system

The hydraulic system described in this section does not represent a specific hydraulic system used in any

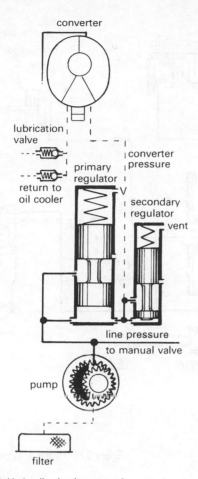

Figure 3.85 Hydraulic circuit – stage 1

particular make of gearbox. The system illustrates the basic principles of automatic control using a much-simplified system, to allow the student to understand the construction and operation of an automatic gearbox hydraulic system (non-electronic control-type).

The hydraulic system is considered in a series of stages.

Stage 1
Figure 3.85 shows the layout of a simple fluid supply system used to operate a clutch and torque converter.

Pump
Normally an internal–external gear pump is used (refer to the engine section within this book for further information on oil pump operation). The oil pump is driven at engine speed by tangs formed on the torque converter casing. The fluid is drawn from the reservoir (located in the lower section of the gearbox) and passed to the pump through a very fine screen-type filter so as to remove any small dirt particles.

Note: Many automatic gearboxes have only one oil pump, which is situated at the front input shaft. It is therefore not possible to tow start the engine because the engine and pump will be stationary. Hydraulic pressure will not be generated in the system to activate any clutch and brake so neutral gear will result.

Primary regulator
The primary regulator uses a spool valve, which controls the 'line pressure' that is applied to the manual valve. In the system shown the line pressure always remains constant.

Note: This arrangement is unsuitable for a modern gearbox because the high pressure required to prevent slip under conditions of high torque, will give harsh gear changes when the engine is driven under light loads.

Fluid released from the valve is passed back to the inlet side of the pump instead of discharging into the reservoir. This action saves energy that would be used if the fluid had to again be drawn through the fine-mesh filter screen.

Secondary regulator
Line pressure is too great for the converter, so the secondary regulator acts as a pressure reducer. A portion of the fluid returning from the converter passes either to an oil cooler, or to a line that provides low-pressure lubrication of the gearbox.

Manual valve
Under the control of the driver this valve distributes the fluid to the various valves, clutches and brakes. When the manual valve is in the position shown in Figure 3.86, hydraulic fluid is delivered to the front clutch at line pressure.

Sequence of clutch and brake application
The order in which the clutch and brake actuators are applied to operate the various gears depends on the type of gear train used. The layout used here has a drive range as shown in Table 3.3.

The table indicates that the three forward gears in the 'drive' (D) range all use the front clutch. The particular gear i.e. second or third gear, in the D range is determined by the actuation, or non-actuation, of the rear clutch and brake band.

The use of the front clutch in this manner is common to many three-speed gearboxes. It should be noted that wear on the forward clutch is minimal because, unlike the rear clutch, the application of the forward clutch is only carried out when the vehicle is stationary.

Table 3.3 Clutch and brake band operation

Gear	Front clutch	Rear clutch	Brake band
D1	●		
D2	●		●
D3	●	●	●

Speed and load sensing
Gear changes must be made when a pre-determined road speed is reached, so some form of sensor is necessary to 'inform' the gearbox when it is necessary to change gear. The engine load also determines the gear change. When the engine is lightly loaded, the gear

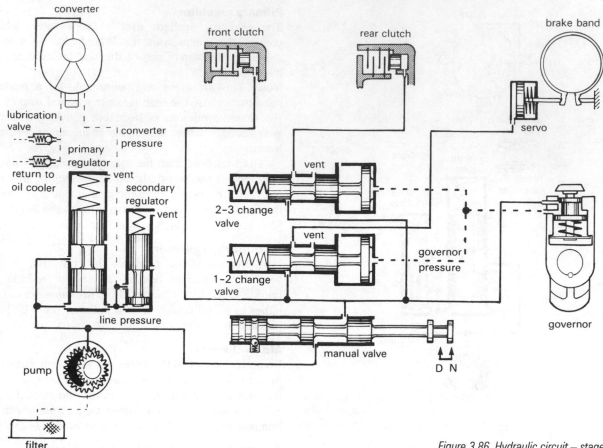

Figure 3.86 Hydraulic circuit – stage 2

change can occur earlier; however, if the engine is under a high load (i.e. accelerating) the gear change needs to occur later.

Speed sensing

Automatic gearboxes use one of the following to determine the speed of the output shaft:

- a mechanical governor
- a hydraulic governor
- an electronic speed sensor.

The speed sensor must work in conjunction with a shift valve (also known as a change valve). The duty of this valve is to direct the fluid to the clutches and servos and thus change the gear when a suitable road speed is reached.

Mechanical governors

The mechanical type of governor is driven from the gearbox output shaft and uses a centrifugal system, which consists of two flyweights. When the shaft and governor rotate, the weights are thrown out against the resistance of a spring as the speed of the gearbox output shaft increases. The movement of the flyweights act on a hydraulic spool valve that directly controls the gear changes.

Very few gearboxes now use this system of speed sensing.

Hydraulic governor

The hydraulic governor was a development from the mechanical type of governor. It uses a spool valve, sensitive to a centrifugal effect given by its rotation, to generate a fluid pressure that increases with speed.

Electronic speed sensor

An indication of the road speed is required for many electronic systems used on modern vehicles (i.e. speedometer, engine management system). The vehicle speed information is provided by some form of speed sensor fitted to the output shaft of the gearbox or to the road wheels. Signals from the sensor are passed to an ECU for processing; the data can then be used for particular electronic systems such as the gearbox control.

Stage 2

Comparing Figure 3.86 with Figure 3.85, the former has the addition of two change valves (shift valves) and a hydraulic-type governor.

Shift valves

Two shift valves are shown in Figure 3.86. One valve controls the up and down changes between first and second gear (1–2 change valve) and the other the changes between second and third gear (2–3 change valve).

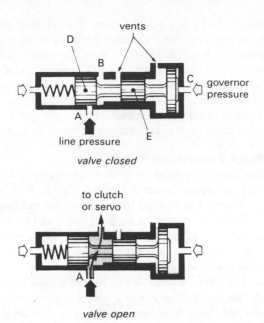

Figure 3.87 A gear change shift valve (change valve)

A simplified change or shift valve is shown in Figure 3.87. Line pressure from the manual valve is applied at A, the line supplying the appropriate clutch or servo is connected at port B. The valve is kept closed by the spring acting on the valve. Movement of the valve is produced by the pressure of the fluid from the governor (governor pressure) at port C.

When the governor pressure is sufficient to overcome the spring, the shift valve moves, connecting port A with port B. Line pressure is applied to the applicable servo or clutch to produce the change of gear.

It should be noted that by fitting a stronger spring to the 2–3 shift valve (or making the valve smaller in area)

it is made to open at a much higher governor pressure than the 1–2 valve.

The diameter of plunger D is larger than plunger E. This feature is effective after the valve has opened and its use prevents a gear 'hunting action'. This action is a severe vibration of the vehicle caused by the shift valve oscillating between the open and closed positions. Once the valve starts to open, the extra thrust on piston D adds to the thrust given by governor pressure; as a result of this added thrust the valve is opened fully. The use of this arrangement makes the up-changes occur at higher road speeds than the down-changes.

Hydraulic governor

The hydraulic governor valve is a form of regulator valve. The duty of the valve is to alter the fluid pressure in the governor line in proportion with the road speed, i.e. as the vehicle speed increases, the fluid pressure rises. The pressure passing out from the governor valve (governor pressure) is applied to the ends of the shift valves. When the governor pressure is high enough, it causes the shift valves to operate and allows the next gear to be selected.

Note: In the examples shown there are two shift valves (for gear change 1–2 and for gear change 2–3). If the spring in the 2–3 change valve is stronger than the spring in the 1–2 change valve, then a higher governor pressure will be required to move the 2–3 change valve. In effect, to change from first to second gear requires a lower governor pressure acting on the appropriate shift valve, but a higher pressure is required to change from second to third gear.

The principle of operation of a hydraulic governor is shown in Figure 3.88. Connected to the gearbox output shaft is a governor assembly. The assembly contains a

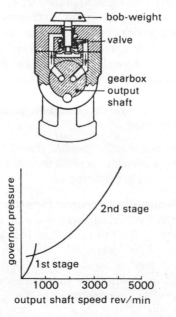

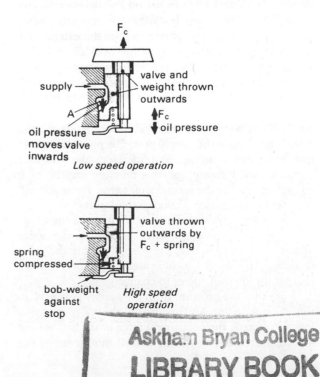

Figure 3.88 Governor operation

valve body with a bob-weight fitted into the centre of the valve; this allows the bob-weight to slide in and out within the valve body. When the speed of the output shaft increases, the bob-weight is progressively forced outwards by centrifugal force. Because of the spring located between the base of the bob-weight and the valve body, the valve body will tend to move outwards with the bob-weight.

A supply port allows hydraulic pressure (generated by the pump and passed via the manual valve) to enter the valve chamber. A second port allows pressure from the valve chamber to pass down the outlet line to the shift valves; the pressure in this line is referred to as the governor pressure.

When the valve body is fully inwards (output shaft not rotating, therefore no centrifugal force), the top edge of the valve blocks the supply port, therefore there is no pressure in the valve chamber and no pressure passing to the outlet (no governor pressure). When the valve moves outwards due to centrifugal force (output shaft rotating due to vehicle movement), the top edge of the valve slightly uncovers the supply port; this applies pressure in the valve chamber and outlet port (governor pressure). Note, however, that because the supply port is only partially uncovered, this small hole or orifice represents a restriction, which allows only a low pressure in the valve chamber (similar in principle to squeezing the middle of a rubber hose to reduce the pressure of the water after the restriction).

Because there is a low pressure in the valve chamber, this means that the pressure passing from the chamber to the shift valves is also low (low governor pressure). The low pressure may not be sufficient to move the shift valves, so there will not be a change of gear.

If however the vehicle speed (and therefore the output shaft rotational speed) increases, this causes a greater centrifugal force to act on the bob-weight and valve body. The valve body moves outwards again which uncovers the supply port to a greater extent. This allows a higher pressure to pass into the valve chamber and out to the shift valves. This increased pressure (high governor pressure) may be sufficient to operate the shift valve that causes a change from first to second gear.

Additional output shaft speed will cause a further outwards movement of the valve which leads to a further opening of the supply port. The pressure passing into the valve chamber, and therefore the governor pressure, will increase and this pressure may be high enough to operate the second shift valve. The result will then be a change from second to third gear.

So, as the vehicle and output shaft speeds increase, the increased centrifugal force acting on the valve allows an increase in fluid pressure to exist in the valve chamber. This results in increased governor pressures and causes the shift valves to change gear.

Note that the pressure from the supply port acts on the valve at point A. This causes the valve to move inwards against the centrifugal force of the bob-weight and against the spring. The inward movement of the valve closes the supply port thus cutting off any pressure to the valve chamber and preventing governor pressure from increasing. It is therefore only the increase in output shaft speed and centrifugal force on the bob-weight and valve that will cause the valve to move outwards and re-open the supply port. It is thus an interaction of spring pressure and the speed-related centrifugal force that controls the governor pressure.

Stage 2 operation
The automatic selection of three gears can be achieved with the layout shown in Figure 3.86.

When 'D' is selected by the driver, the manual valve supplies line pressure to the front clutch and with the aid of a freewheel, first gear (D1) is obtained. Line pressure is also applied to the other valves in the system, but these valves remain inactive at this pressure.

However, as soon as the vehicle moves, rotation of the output shaft produces a governor pressure and this acts on both shift valves. When a pre-determined vehicle speed is reached, the governor pressure has increased to a level that overcomes the spring force in the 1–2 change valve. The valve moves to the left (in the illustration) and this in turn allows line pressure to pass through the change valve to the brake band servo thus causing second gear to be engaged (D2).

A further increase in road speed causes the governor pressure to rise until it reaches a point where it overcomes the stronger spring in the 2–3 change valve. At this speed the opening of the 2–3 change valve causes line pressure to act on the rear clutch and engage third gear (D3).

Load sensing
Although the governor can cause gears to change at pre-determined road speeds, the road speed at which the up and down gear changes occur should ideally vary with the load of the engine, i.e. the speed at which the changes occur increases with position and movement of the accelerator pedal.

This feature mimics the technique used by a driver on a manual gearbox: light throttle pressure, early changes; heavy throttle pressure, delayed changes.

Various methods are used to sense the driver's driving style or load, most automatics use one of the following:

- a manually operated throttle valve
- a vacuum-operated throttle valve
- an electronic control.

Manually operated throttle valve
The function of this valve is to produce, in a separate line, a fluid pressure that increases as the accelerator pedal is depressed. The 'throttle controlled fluid pressure' is applied to the opposite end of the shift valves to which the governor pressure acts. In effect, the throttle pressure opposes the governor pressure. The result of the opposing pressures is that shift valve movement depends on the governor pressure and the

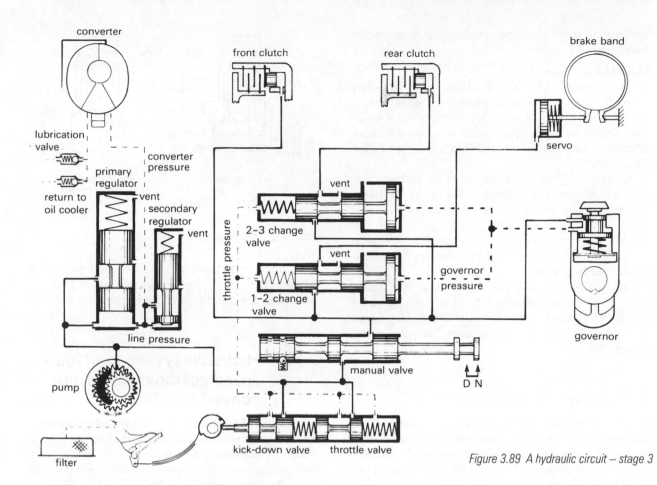

Figure 3.89 A hydraulic circuit – stage 3

throttle controlled pressure; gear changes will therefore still be dependent on vehicle speed but also throttle position or movement.

The manual throttle valve is operated by a cable which connects a lever on the side of the gearbox to some part of the throttle linkage; as the throttle is opened the cable is pulled. The action rotates a cam in the gearbox and compresses a spring that acts on the throttle valve.

The Stage 3 layout (Figure 3.89) shows how a simple throttle valve is positioned in the fluid system to control flow and pressure in the throttle line (the dotted line leading from the throttle valve).

With the throttle closed, line pressure (from the pump) cannot pass the spool of the throttle valve. However, if the throttle is opened by a given amount, the spring on the cam side pushes the valve to the right. The port that connects with the line pressure is partially uncovered, and allows a limited amount of line pressure fluid to pass through the throttle valve which results in a pressure existing in the throttle line. This throttle line pressure is passed to the ends of the shift valves thus providing an opposing force to the governor pressure.

A connection between the throttle line and the chamber at the end of the throttle valve causes pressure to be felt 'behind' the throttle valve. As throttle line pressure builds up, the valve moves slightly to the left, this reduces the flow from the main line until a balance is reached.

Further depressing the accelerator repeats this sequence; the only difference being that the increased spring thrust in the throttle valve resulting from the new position of the cam, requires a greater pressure in the throttle line to 'balance' the valve. So the more the throttle is depressed, the greater the pressure in the throttle line, and the greater the pressure acting on the shift valves.

As well as acting in conjunction with the governor pressure to control gear change speeds, the throttle line pressure can also be applied to the end of the main regulator valve. This results in a variation of regulated line pressure to suit the load on the engine (different line pressure will result in different gear change speeds).

Vacuum-operated throttle valve

Inlet manifold depression gives a good indication of the engine load, so some automatics have a throttle valve operation that is controlled from a vacuum chamber situated on the side of the gearbox. The action of the vacuum chamber on the throttle valve is very similar to that of the mechanically operated throttle valve.

Electronic control

The engine load can be sensed by an engine load sensor (from either manifold pressure or air flow) or a throttle position sensor; the sensor signal is then passed to an ECU. After processing the signal, the ECU controls the position of an electric solenoid which moves the appropriate shift valve, therefore causing a change of gear to occur.

Kick-down valves

During driving, there are occasions, such as when overtaking, when a driver requires quick acceleration. On such occasions it is necessary to change to a lower gear. On an automatic gearbox this is achieved by fully depressing the accelerator pedal to a position called 'kick-down'.

In a basic system, a movement of the pedal to this position operates a kick-down valve in the hydraulic system (see Figure 3.89). The operation of the kick-down valve causes a sudden drop in pressure in the throttle line. Up to a certain road speed in each gear position, this drop in pressure produces an immediate down-change of gear.

In Figure 3.89, the kick-down valve is situated between the throttle valve and the cam. When the pedal is fully depressed the cam moves the kick-down valve to the right so as to cause a pressure increase in the throttle line.

3.13.8 Additional features

An automatic gearbox has a number of features in addition to the basic system previously described. These are fitted to make gear changes smoother and the vehicle more economical, and to give the driver more control over the gearbox.

Such extra parts include the following:

Modulator valve

This type of valve is fitted to reduce the pressure in a part of a given line to suit some special operating condition, for example fitted in the throttle line supply to the regulator valve. In this case it modulates (makes less sudden) the rise in throttle pressure that acts on the regulator.

Accumulator

The purpose of a hydraulic accumulator (sometimes called a damper) as applied to an automatic gearbox, is to reduce the rate at which a clutch or brake is actuated. It cushions the shock by delaying the full application of the fluid pressure.

Figure 3.90 shows an accumulator consisting of a spring-loaded piston in a chamber that is connected in the fluid line between the change valve and clutch (or brake servo). When the change valve is opened, the time taken for the fluid to compress the accumulator spring ensures that the pressure rise in the line is gradual and that the application of the clutch or brake is progressive (which results in a smoother gear change).

Torque converter lock-up

In the interests of economy, most automatic gearboxes are fitted with a torque converter lock-up clutch within the torque converter (refer to section 3.12.6). To operate the clutch, a torque converter clutch lock-up

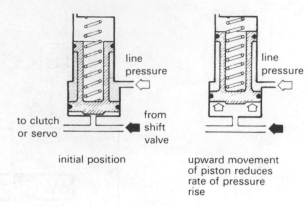

Figure 3.90 Accumulator action

valve is required. The valve provides fluid pressure to the converter clutch when top gear is selected and the road speed is sufficient for the converter slip to be by-passed.

3.13.9 Hydraulic system for a four-speed gearbox with torque converter lock-up

Development of the basic three-speed gearbox

Developments in automatic gearboxes have resulted in gearboxes with four, five, six and even seven gears. However, these later gearbox developments are generally adaptations of the original three-speed designs, with additional epicyclic gear trains or overdrive units, which form more complex compound gear trains.

In addition, the modern generation of automatic gearboxes make use of electronic control to replace or supplement some of the hydraulic valves and controls of the older designs. Within this book therefore, the basic understanding of the three-speed designs is sufficient to provide a general understanding of automatic gearbox operation.

The following information provides a basic outline of the hydraulic system for a four-speed gearbox and section 3.14 does provide an initial introduction to electronic control of gearboxes. However, more detail of the electronic control systems and further studies of 4–6-speed gearboxes can be found in *Fundamentals of Motor Vehicle Technology – Book 2*.

Four-speed hydraulic system

Figure 3.91 shows a hydraulic valve block arrangement for a particular type of ZF transmission unit. This design has three forward speeds, an overdrive fourth gear and a lock-up converter clutch, as well as providing neutral and reverse gears. Figure 3.92 (on page 318) shows the hydraulic circuit along with identification of the valves and components connected to the circuit.

Reference should be made to previous sections in this chapter relating to torque converter lock-up clutches (section 3.12.6) and overdrive units (section 3.13.3).

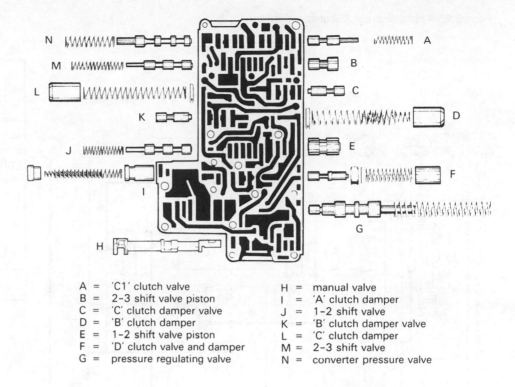

Figure 3.91 A hydraulic valve block ZF four-speed gearbox

A	=	'C1' clutch valve	H =	manual valve
B	=	2–3 shift valve piston	I =	'A' clutch damper
C	=	'C' clutch damper valve	J =	1–2 shift valve
D	=	'B' clutch damper	K =	'B' clutch damper valve
E	=	1–2 shift valve piston	L =	'C' clutch damper
F	=	'D' clutch valve and damper	M =	2–3 shift valve
G	=	pressure regulating valve	N =	converter pressure valve

3.13.10 Automatic transmission fluid

The fluid used in an automatic gearbox must be capable of performing many functions. It serves to operate the torque converter, actuate the clutches and brakes through hydraulic pressure, lubricate the various gears and bearing surfaces and act as a coolant to the internal components of an automatic gearbox.

Each of these duties demands special properties, so it is essential that the fluid used contains additives, which will satisfy the recommended specification.
In traffic conditions a torque converter gets very hot, and although an oil cooler is now common, the high temperature reached by the fluid must neither cause excessive oxidation nor vary the viscosity adversely to make the gear changes harsh or noisy.

Additives, to resist wear of the rubbing surfaces and foaming of the fluid, are also essential because a long period between fluid changes is demanded, with some gearboxes now being sealed for life (i.e. no fluid changes).

Another important consideration is the need to use a fluid that gives a stable friction value. A fluid of the incorrect type can cause the clutch and brake unit to engage either too quickly or too slowly.

Automatic gearboxes traditionally used a fluid made to the General Motors specification DEXRON® II. There are, however, several different specifications of DEXRON® II and also DEXRON® III (including synthetic-based oils), therefore always refer to manufacturer's literature before adding to, or replacing gearbox oil. It should be noted that the fluid used must be of a specification to suit the design of the box. Gearbox problems will occur if the wrong type of gearbox fluid is used.

Older gearboxes often used an ATF (automatic transmission fluid) to the Ford standard F.

Fluid level

A dipstick is normally employed to indicate the correct volume of oil in the gearbox. The dipstick is usually accessible from the engine compartment. Alternatively the gearbox oil is checked by using a plug fitted to the sump of the gearbox casing. Refer to manufacturer's literature before checking the level of the gearbox oil.

If a dipstick is used, the dipstick is marked to show the correct level when the fluid is hot. Note that the volume of oil will vary depending on its temperature. Many of today's automatic gearboxes require the level to be set at an exact temperature, which requires the use of specialised tools connected to the vehicle diagnostic system.

The automatic gearbox oil level is normally checked with the engine running at idle speed. Since the reservoir level varies with the position of the selector, it is essential to set the lever as recommended by the manufacturer.

Note that a number of faults may arise if the level is set either higher or lower than recommended.

Figure 3.92 A hydraulic circuit ZF four-speed gearbox

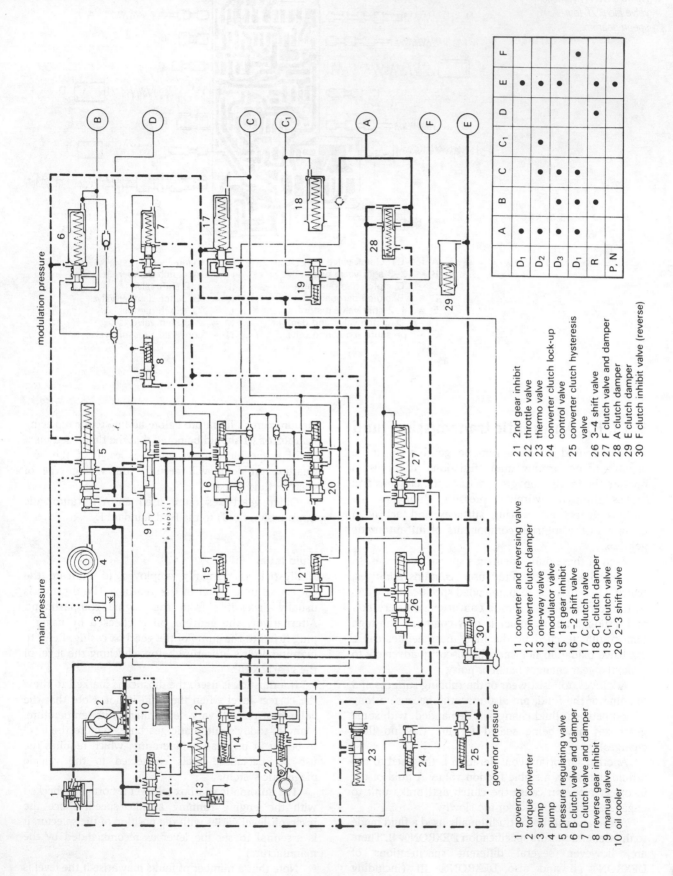

	A	B	C	C_1	D	E	F
D_1	●					●	
D_2	●		●	●		●	
D_3	●		●			●	
D_1		●	●				●
R					●	●	
P, N						●	

1 governor
2 torque converter
3 sump
4 pump
5 pressure regulating valve
6 B clutch valve and damper
7 D clutch valve and damper
8 reverse gear inhibit
9 manual valve
10 oil cooler

11 converter and reversing valve
12 converter clutch damper
13 one-way valve
14 modulator valve
15 1st gear inhibit
16 1-2 shift valve
17 C clutch valve
18 C_1 clutch damper
19 C_1 clutch valve
20 2-3 shift valve

21 2nd gear inhibit
22 throttle valve
23 thermo valve
24 converter clutch lock-up
   control valve
25 converter clutch hysteresis
   valve
26 3-4 shift valve
27 F clutch valve and damper
28 A clutch damper
29 E clutch damper
30 F clutch inhibit valve (reverse)

modulation pressure

main pressure

governor pressure

3.14.1 Improved operation and other benefits of electronic control

Today, most automatic gearboxes fitted to motor vehicles are electronically controlled. Although these gearboxes are controlled by an ECU together with sensors and actuators, the principle of operation of the gearbox is essentially similar to that of a mechanically controlled automatic gearbox using epicyclic gearing, clutch sets, brake bands, etc.

Sharing information and communication of ECUs

Electronic control of the gearbox has many advantages over the mechanical/hydraulic control that has previously been used. By controlling the operation of the gearbox electronically, the optimum gear can be selected to suit the road and engine operating conditions.

The automatic gearbox ECU usually communicates with, (or may even be integrated within) the engine management ECU. Many of the sensors used by the engine management system can also be used by the automatic gearbox ECU.

Combining the engine and automatic gearbox ECUs into a single, integrated control unit allows rapid interaction between the two electronic control systems. However, even where two separate ECUs are used, communication is very rapid due to the advances in electronic communication.

The communication between the two systems provides the smoothest control of both the engine and gearbox. The engine ECU can control the engine's torque (or power) to suit the gearbox operation, which allows the smooth operation of the gearbox.

Control of engine torque is achieved in a number of ways, with electronic throttle control being the most recent and effective development. The use of electronic throttle control 'drive by wire' combined with changes in engine fuelling and ignition timing enables rapid changes to engine torque to be achieved.

If the gearbox ECU indicates to the engine management ECU that there is a gear change taking place, it is then possible to momentarily alter the throttle position, ignition timing or fuel delivery to achieve a brief change in the engine torque. This then ensures that gear changes are very smooth, and the driver of the vehicle may not notice that the gearbox has changed gear even during acceleration and deceleration.

It is of course also possible for the engine management ECU to influence the gear change operation. As an example, if the driver has placed the engine under full load to overtake another vehicle, and then quickly releases the throttle, the engine management ECU can indicate this reduced engine load to the gearbox ECU. The gearbox ECU can then immediately cause a change-up of gears.

This information exchange between ECUs enables a more rapid initiation of gear changes than would be possible with mechanical-type systems.

It is now common for an electronically-controlled gearbox to have a minimum of four speeds, with five speeds being common, and six speeds becoming more popular. The highest gear (top gear) may still be an overdrive gear, which would be used in conjunction with a torque converter lock-up clutch to achieve good economy.

Emission control

As well as providing a more responsive and smoother gear change, electronic control of the gearbox helps to improve emissions from the vehicle. This is especially true when the gearbox ECU communicates with the engine management ECU.

Overall emission levels from the engine can increase when incorrect gears are selected and when throttle control is not matched to the selected gear for the driving conditions e.g. climbing a steep hill slowly in top gear with a fully open throttle.

By ensuring that gear changes and gear selection are matched to the driving conditions and driving style, it is possible to reduce emissions levels over a wide range of driving conditions. Legislation relating to emissions control is increasingly placing pressure on vehicle manufacturers to reduce emissions under all driving conditions, and electronic control of the gearbox can assist in meeting these demands.

3.14.2 Operation of the electronically controlled automatic gearbox

Sensors and actuators

Electronically controlled systems generally make use of various sensors, which provide information to the computer (ECU). The computer then uses the information to calculate what actions to take. In the case of the automatic gearbox, the actions taken are primarily related to when a gear change should take place. The actions are carried out by actuators, which on an automatic gearbox are usually solenoid-controlled valves. The ECU therefore creates a control signal that is passed to an electrical solenoid, which in turn moves the change valves in the valve body thus causing the desired gear change.

An example of the sensors and actuators used for a modern automatic gearbox are indicated in the schematic electrical circuit shown in Figure 3.93.

Various items of information can be provided by sensors, and some of these are listed in the following paragraphs:

Speed, load and temperature sensing

Engine speed

Engine speed is monitored by a sensor, which is usually fitted to the engine crankshaft. The sensor is a standard feature for the engine management system and is usually referred to as a 'crankshaft speed/position sensor'.

Vehicle speed

On older mechanical gearboxes, the governor fitted to the gearbox output shaft controlled the hydraulic pressure applied to the change valves etc. As vehicle speed increased the pressure applied to the change valves increased proportionally with vehicle speed. An electronically controlled automatic gearbox monitors vehicle speed using a vehicle speed sensor.

Although in many cases the sensor may be fitted to the output shaft of the gearbox, if the vehicle is fitted with an anti-lock braking system (ABS), the vehicle speed signal is passed from the ABS wheel speed sensor via the ABS ECU to the gearbox ECU. The gearbox ECU uses the vehicle speed signal as a primary item of information along with the engine speed and load signals to determine when gear changes should occur.

Additional speed sensors

The gearbox may also be fitted with additional speed sensors to monitor the speeds of the gearbox input shaft and intermediate shafts. Speed sensor information is used by the ECU to monitor the engagement of the different gear ratios so that the ECU can alter the engine torque to ensure a smooth gear change.

Note: Like most speed sensors used, many of these sensors are of the inductive or magnetic type and therefore pass an AC voltage signal dependant on shaft speed to the ECU.

An inhibitor switch, usually fitted to the selector linkage, allows the operation of the starter motor only while the selector lever is in the P or N positions.

Vehicle driving load

Previously, with mechanically controlled automatic gearboxes, engine load was assessed by the use of a throttle cable connected to the throttle linkage. When the throttle cable moved, it affected the position of the throttle valve in the valve body. With an electronically controlled gearbox, engine load is monitored with a throttle position sensor in conjunction with the air volume or load sensor. These sensors are a standard part of the engine management system (the hot wire air mass sensor or a manifold absolute pressure (MAP) sensor).

Oil temperature sensor

The temperature of the gearbox oil affects its viscosity and therefore the rate at which the fluid flows in the hydraulic circuits, and the rate at which the fluid enters and exits the pistons of the clutches and brake

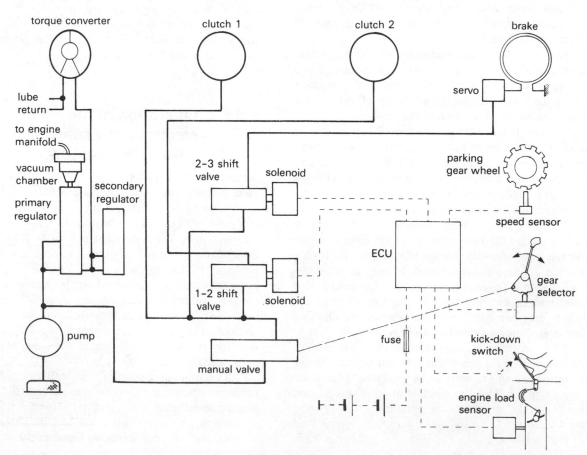

Figure 3.93 Schematic layout of a typical ECU-controlled automatic gearbox electrical system

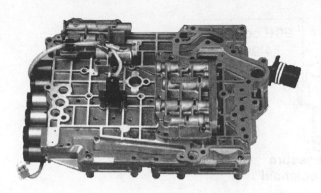

Figure 3.94 Solenoid valves fitted to valve body

bands. This will in turn influence the speed at which the clutches and brake bands are engaged or disengaged. The temperature of the gearbox fluid is monitored with an oil temperature sensor. The sensor is usually fitted near the valve body within the gearbox thus ensuring an accurate measurement of fluid temperature. The ECU alters the delay period between the gear changes ensuring smooth changes at different oil temperatures.

Basic operation

The ECU controls the operation of the gearbox (gear selection) using actuators, which are electrically operated solenoids. The solenoids are used to control the position of the hydraulic change valves and where fitted, the torque converter lock-up clutch. The solenoids are therefore directly located on the valve body (Figure 3.94).

The ECU energises or de-energizes the appropriate solenoid when a change of gear is required. When the ECU energizes the appropriate solenoid, this causes line pressure to be applied to the change valve. The line pressure alters the position of the change valve in the valve body, which then allows hydraulic pressure to be applied to the relevant piston of the clutch or brake band. When the solenoid is disengaged, the fluid in the main line (line pressure) is allowed to flow back through the solenoid valve to an exhaust or drain port in this valve. The fluid and pressure are therefore exhausted back through the solenoid valve to the reservoir in the gearbox sump. Energized and de-energized positions (on and off) of the solenoid and valve are shown in Figure 3.95.

The torque converter lock-up solenoid is energized dependant on gear selection (fourth gear in this example), engine load and road speed. Accumulators are used in conjunction with the change valves to provide a smooth engagement of the clutches.

Line pressure

Regulating valves are used to maintain line pressure at the desired value. The regulating valves can either be controlled mechanically (as previously detailed for older systems) or electronically.

If the line pressure is controlled electronically a single, primary, regulating valve is used, its position being controlled with a line pressure control solenoid (Figure 3.96). The position of the electrical solenoid has to be constantly altered to provide the correct line pressure to suit gearbox operating conditions.

The line pressure solenoid is controlled from information received from the various engine and gearbox sensors. The ECU changes the line pressure by varying the electrical control signal applied to the solenoid, ensuring that the gear changes are at the correct vehicle and engine speeds and providing a smooth operation.

Reduced number of hydraulic valves

Figure 3.97 shows a modern 6-speed electronically controlled automatic gearbox. Compared to the conventional automatic gearbox, the number of hydraulic valves is considerably reduced. This is because the various tasks previously performed by hydraulic valves and other components such as the governor, are now undertaken by the ECU with the use of solenoids.

Kick-down

The kick-down, which was previously achieved using a throttle cable or mechanical linkage connected to a kick-down valve, is now controlled electronically. The throttle position is either monitored with the use of a throttle position sensor or a kick-down switch connected to the throttle linkage. If the ECU detects that full throttle has been applied, the ECU selects a lower gear (assuming that conditions permit) thus allowing the driver to accelerate quickly. Once the maximum permissible engine speed has been reached or the throttle position is changed in the lower gear, the ECU then re-selects a higher gear.

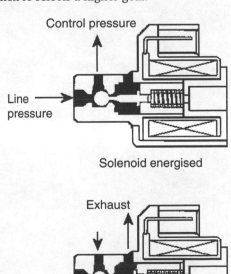

Figure 3.95 A solenoid valve – energized and de-energized

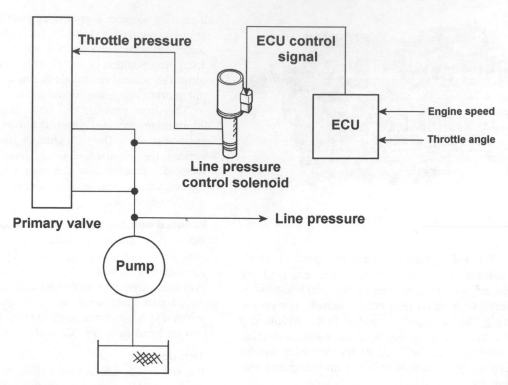

Figure 3.96 Line pressure control solenoid

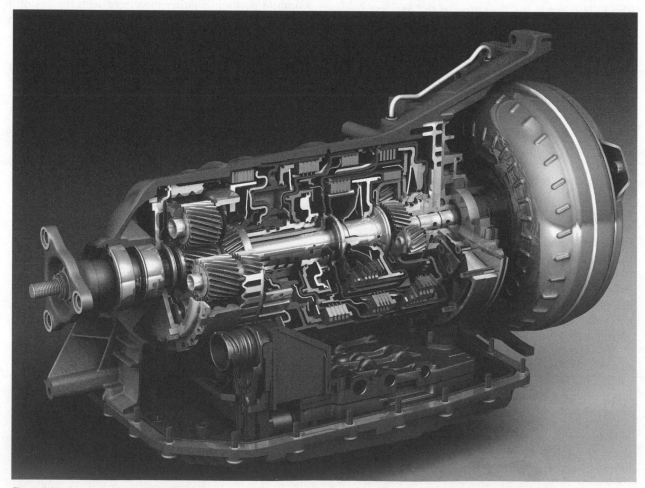

Figure 3.97 An electronically controlled gearbox

Gear selection

The driver selects the direction of drive with the gear selector lever inside the vehicle. The selector lever is connected to the automatic gearbox by a cable.

Park

When P is selected the parking pawl (as used on older designs) is still used to prevent the movement of the vehicle by locking the gearbox output shaft to the gearbox casing.

Initial gear selection

When the driver selects a forward or reverse gear, the selector position switch, either located on the side of the gearbox or within the selector lever assembly, passes a signal to the gearbox ECU; the signal indicates the selected gear. The ECU then operates the appropriate electrical solenoids to allow the gearbox to operate.

Safety

To prevent the selector being accidentally moved from the P position to a gear selection position, many vehicle manufacturers are fitting a P lock solenoid. If the driver wishes to move the selector lever from P into another gear, he must first switch the ignition on and apply the footbrake. Applying the footbrake causes a solenoid (located within the selector mechanism) to energise, which allows the movement of the selector from the P position through to R and other selector positions.

Smooth selection process

When the driver selects a forward gear with the selector lever (e.g. 1 or D) the ECU selects first gear. During the engagement of first gear, the vehicle will normally 'lurch' forward as the gearbox applies the forward drive to the transmission. Modern automatic gearboxes may initially select a high gear (i.e. third gear) when D is selected, limiting the torque applied to the transmission, thus reducing the lurching feeling felt by the driver as the drive is engaged. Once the high gear is engaged, the ECU selects first gear enabling the vehicle to be driven from the stationary position in the normal manner.

Mode selection

Electronically controlled gearboxes are sometimes fitted with an 'economy' or 'sport' mode selector switch. The interaction of the gearbox ECU and the engine ECU allows the reconfiguration of engine performance in conjunction with changes in the gear shift pattern.

Note: On some vehicles, the sport mode selector may only affect the engine or gearbox operation, and not necessarily both systems.

If the driver selects economy mode, the gearbox changes into a higher gear at a lower engine speed and engine performance is limited, which together provide lower fuel consumption.

If sport mode is selected, the gearbox changes gear at a higher engine speed and engine performance is increased by changes in fuelling and ignition. The increase in performance also increases the fuel consumption; the driver therefore has the option as to which mode to select to suit personal preference and driving conditions.

The automatic gearbox ECU may also provide the driver with a selectable 'snow' mode setting; the mode helps to reduce wheel spin if slippery conditions are encountered. When the snow mode is selected, the ECU selects a higher gear (i.e. second gear) as the vehicle is pulling away from stationary, thus reducing the torque applied at the driven wheels. The engine ECU also reduces the engine power, which assists in reducing the possibility of wheel spin on slippery surfaces.

Adaptive operation and artificial intelligence

Development in electronic technology have allowed some automatic gearbox systems to become 'artificially intelligent' and adapt to different conditions. In reality, 'adaptive' and 'artificial intelligence' are rather different processes or functions but the result is that the gearbox system either adapts to a certain driving style, driving conditions, or it pre-judges the requirements for gear changes ahead of driver input.

The ECU constantly monitors input signals from the engine and gearbox sensors and, from these signals the ECU can interpret the manner in which the vehicle is being driven. The ECU adjusts the output control signals to automatically provide the driver with the performance or economy with which they wish to drive.

The ECU may also be able to detect when the vehicle is travelling uphill or downhill from a combination of sensor signals. If, for example, the vehicle is travelling uphill it may be appropriate to select a lower gear to improve the engine's ability to maintain speed. The gearbox system may therefore change to a lower gear before the driver applies more throttle.

Manual gear selection

Although an automatic gearbox automatically selects the appropriate gear when D is selected, it is normally possible for the driver to select a gear manually using the selector lever. Selecting 1, 2 or 3 (on a four-speed gearbox) allows manual selection of those gears, normally with the addition of engine braking in the very low gear ratios.

Sequential gearbox

Many modern automatic gearboxes allow the driver to select the gears manually, in a sequential order i.e. the gears are selected, 1 to 2, 2 to 3, 3 to 4, etc, from the selector lever, as shown in Figure 3.98.

The sequential selection is made by selecting the manual gear option with the selector lever. In a similar manner to a manual gearbox, the driver selects first gear with the lever, and when required selects second gear and so on through to the highest gear.

When a lower gear is required, the driver operates the lever in the reverse direction thus enabling selection of lower gears in the same sequential manner.

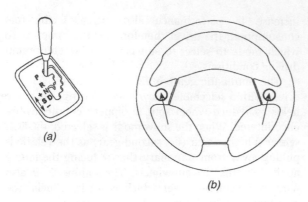

(a)

(b)

Figure 3.98 Gear selection
a Sequential
b On steering wheel

Note that to prevent engine and transmission damage, the ECU will not allow gear changes if the driver selects a lower gear when the vehicle speed is too high.

The gear selection signals are passed to the ECU which then provides the appropriate solenoid control signal to select the required gear. The gear selected is usually displayed on the instrument panel.

The vehicle may also be fitted with additional gear selection controls, situated on the steering wheel. The driver may opt to use the steering wheel controls, allowing her hands to remain on the steering wheel during gear changes. Two buttons or selector controls are provided; one each for up-shifts and down-shifts.

Note that manual gearboxes may also be adapted to allow sequential change control. Some manual gearbox systems, although they have conventional manual gear arrangements and gear change selectors, also have a hydraulic system to move the selectors. An ECU controls the hydraulic system, so many sensors can be used to

assist in controlling the gear changes. The clutch (which once again is conventional in operation) is also actuated by the hydraulic system, which in turn is controlled by the ECU, and can be employed even for pulling away from rest.

The driver can select gear changes using either a gear selector lever or buttons and paddles located on the steering wheel.

Because an ECU is controlling the actuation of the gear change and clutch mechanisms, it is also possible to select a fully automatic gear change process even though the gearbox and clutch are essentially manual type. Some vehicles (including some Ferrari models) use the same manual gearbox fitted with either manual selection and clutch operation or electro-hydraulic selection and actuation.

Fail safe

As is the case with most modern electronically controlled vehicle systems, in the event of a fault within the automatic gearbox, the ECU will operate (where applicable and possible), with a limited operating strategy (LOS). The ECU will also illuminate the gearbox diagnostic warning light located on the instrument panel to signal to the driver that a fault has occurred.

If it is not possible for the gearbox ECU to change gears it will normally select an intermediate gear, (i.e. third gear and reverse), enabling the vehicle to be driven at a moderate speed to the workshop for repair.

The gearbox ECU normally records a fault code relevant to the fault detected. When the technician diagnoses the automatic gearbox fault the ECU is interrogated with diagnostic test equipment, which extracts the fault code from the ECU memory. The technician then follows the appropriate repair procedure in the workshop manual to repair the fault.

3.15   CONTINUOUSLY VARIABLE TRANSMISSION (CVT)

3.15.1 Introduction

The continuously variable transmission (CVT) unit was originally developed as the Van Doorne system, and used on small DAF cars from 1955. The system remained in use for a number of years and after acquisition by Volvo, DAF-based Volvo vehicles still used the system.

In 1987, Ford and Fiat introduced a CVT-type gearbox system which retained many of the same principles as the Van Doorne system, but with some fundamental changes in the construction and design. Many other vehicle manufacturers have since developed gearboxes that operate on a similar CVT principle.

Both manual and automatic gearboxes demand stepped gear ratios by providing a specific number of selectable gears. The gear trains in manual and automatic gearboxes consist of either a conventional

gear cluster or epicyclic gear sets which are combined with clutches and brake bands.

The CVT gearbox has an infinite number of gear ratios within its operating range (the range is effectively the maximum and minimum ratios). With CVT systems, it is therefore possible to provide the exact ratio required for any given driving condition. Additionally, it is possible to select a specific engine speed and have the gear ratio alter from a low ratio to a higher ratio and back again as the vehicle speed changes.

CVT can therefore allow engine speed to be maintained within a specific rpm range (e.g. at its most efficient) reducing exhaust emissions, and also providing the lowest fuel consumption. Although the modern CVT system is ideally suited to front-wheel drive cars up to 1.6 litres, it is expected that

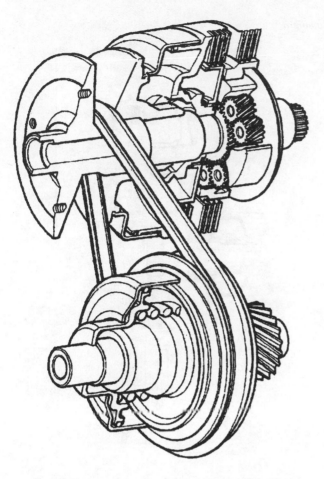

Figure 3.99 Components of a continuously variable transmission unit (CVT)

developments may allow greater torque and power outputs to be transmitted by a CVT-type gearbox.

It is generally claimed that a CVT is more economical than a conventional automatic gearbox.

Basic layout

Unlike a conventional automatic gearbox that uses a torque converter to transmit power from the engine to the gearbox input shaft, CVT uses a torsion damper, which is bolted to the engine flywheel. The torsion damper drives at engine speed the CVT input shaft, which is connected to the epicyclic planet gear carrier.

The Ford/Fiat CTX (continuously variable transaxle) uses the same belt-drive principle as the Van Doorne unit, but instead of using two rubber drive belts in tension, the Ford CTX employs a single steel belt that works in compression (the transmission of power is achieved by the belt pushing the output pulley rather than pulling).

3.15.2 Operation

Two sets of multi-plate clutches control the epicyclic gear train to give forward and reverse motion. One clutch connects the sun wheel and planet carrier

together to give forward drive, the other locks the annulus to the gearbox casing to provide reverse. These clutches are immersed in oil and are designed to slip at low speed. This feature allows the transmission to operate without a plate clutch or fluid coupling, and also enables the car to 'creep' when manoeuvring.

Figure 3.100 shows how the system is built around an enclosed vee belt, which runs between two adjustable cone-shaped pulleys. The thrust belt consists of a large number of vee-shaped steel elements retained on two steel bands. When the belt is driving, each steel element transmits thrust by pushing against its forward neighbour.

The primary pulley is connected to the engine via a single-stage epicyclic gear train having compound planets, and the secondary pulley is connected through a pair of reduction gears to the final drive. One half of the primary pulley is fixed, the other half is connected directly to a hydraulic servo, and is moved closer or farther away from the fixed half when a change in gear ratio is required (this effectively alters the width of the pulley).

By altering the width of the pulley, the effective diameter at which the belt sits in the pulley can be gradually changed while drive is being transmitted.

Belt tension is maintained by varying the diameter of the secondary pulley in conjunction with the changes in the primary pulley; as the primary pulley gets wider, the secondary gets narrower. This is achieved by using a strong spring to push the two halves of the secondary pulley together. The two moving halves of the primary and secondary pulleys are diagonally opposite each other, to prevent the misalignment of the steel belt during changes in ratio.

When a low ratio is required (i.e. moving from a stationary position) the two halves of the primary pulley are set wide apart giving a small diameter pulley, the secondary pulley halves are therefore set close together giving a large diameter pulley. The steel belt is positioned within the vee of the two pulleys.

As vehicle speed increases, the two halves of the primary pulley slowly become closer together giving a larger diameter; simultaneously the two halves of the secondary pulley become further apart providing a smaller pulley which gives a higher gear ratio. An overdrive ratio (greater than 1:1) is normally provided when the highest gear ratio is obtained, the secondary pulley rotating approximately 2.5 times as fast as the primary pulley.

The two pulleys are constantly lubricated by an oil jet, located in the side of the transmission casing.

The hydraulic system and driver controls are similar to a conventional automatic transmission. When the driving mode is selected, hydraulic pressure from an engine-driven pump acts on the appropriate clutch actuator. With the vehicle in motion, ratio changes are brought about by the action of the hydraulic valve unit; this varies the pressure that is applied to the pulley servo in accordance with the signals it receives from the

gear ratio diagram

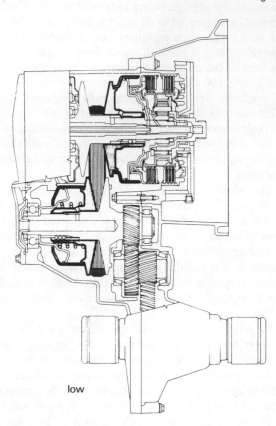

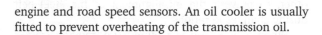

low   high

Figure 3.100 The Ford CTX unit

engine and road speed sensors. An oil cooler is usually fitted to prevent overheating of the transmission oil.

Gear selection

The gear selector is very similar to that of a conventional automatic gearbox. The gear selector for the CVT is normally marked: P R N D L. The selector lever is linked to the transmission with a flexible steel cable which acts on a manual control valve within the valve body in the transmission.

P – park

The mechanism acts directly on the secondary pulley, locking the secondary pulley to the transmission casing and preventing the front wheel from moving.

R – reverse

The reverse clutch is applied preventing the annulus from rotating, allowing the planet carrier to drive the planet gears. The sun gear is driven in the opposite direction. The sun gear is connected to the primary pulley and therefore the vehicle will move in reverse. When reverse is selected, the pulleys maintain a low gear ratio at all vehicle speeds.

N – neutral

Both sets of clutches are inactive and therefore drive is not transmitted through the gear train.

D – drive

The forward clutch is applied, the gear assembly rotates as one unit. Drive is transmitted directly to the primary pulley. The gear ratio is controlled by the driver using the throttle pedal.

L – low

Selecting L provides the driver with a different gear ratio to engine speed, ideally suited to mountainous driving and towing conditions. L provides additional engine braking during deceleration. The transmission can still select a high gear ratio to provide maximum vehicle speed. The transmission allows switching between L and D when the vehicle is being driven.

When the vehicle is accelerated or decelerated, the behaviour of the engine and gearbox may initially seem strange to drivers who normally use conventional systems. Since the CVT system selects the ideal ratio to suit the conditions, the engine does not have to be accelerated through each gear before the vehicle reaches its operating speed.

It should also be noted that vehicles fitted with a CVT should only be towed with the driven wheels raised clear of the ground as damage will occur if the transmission is rotated by the driven wheels.

3.16 OVERDRIVE SYSTEMS

3.16.1 Introduction

The term 'overdrive' in the context of a vehicle transmission system means when the overall gearbox input to output ratio is greater than 1:1. The gearbox output shaft then rotates faster than the input shaft (which is driven by the engine). An overdrive gear is normally used when the vehicle is cruising. Overdrive gives an improved fuel consumption, reduced engine wear and less engine noise due to the reduction in the speed of the engine in relation to vehicle speed.

Today most overdrive arrangements are an integral part of the gearbox. The most common use of an overdrive arrangement is the addition of a fifth gear in a manual gearbox. Many automatic gearboxes are also fitted with an overdrive, usually referred to as fourth or fifth gear in such applications.

However, the above information relates to an overdrive gear ratio, created by using additional gears or arranging the gears so that the top gear ratio is an overdrive ratio. In these cases, the overdrive ratio is part of the gearbox assembly.

In the past many four-speed gearboxes had a separate overdrive unit fitted as an optional extra, usually mounted in place of the gearbox extension housing. The commonest type used was made by Laycock, developed from the de Normanville unit. This is the type of unit considered here.

3.16.2 Separate overdrive units

The Laycock-type overdrive was fitted in the past to many three- and four-speed gearboxes. If the overdrive unit was only allowed to function when the main gearbox was in top gear (normally a 1:1 ratio), it provided just one additional gear. The additional gear created by the overdrive unit was effectively a fifth gear (on a four-speed gearbox) and provided an overdrive ratio. On some gearboxes the overdrive would work on third and fourth gears too, thus providing two additional ratios.

Construction and operation

A simple epicyclic gear set is used in this type of overdrive, which gives either a direct-drive or an overdrive gear. To achieve this gear selection process, the epicyclic gear set is controlled in a similar way to the epicyclic gear sets on an automatic gearbox i.e. by holding one element of the epicyclic gearing (planet gear, sun gear etc.). A simple electro-hydraulic actuation system is used.

The electrical system, controlled by the driver using a selector switch, activates a hydraulic system to move a cone-type clutch forwards and backwards, to either hold or drive a sun gear.

The layout of the gear set is shown in Figure 3.101. Drive is applied to the planet carrier and the sun wheel, which is mounted on a bearing on the input shaft. The sun gear can be connected by a friction cone-type clutch to either the annulus or the casing.

Direct drive

Spring pressure pushes the cone clutch to the right, which connects the sun wheel to the annulus and locks the complete gear assembly together.

Drive from the engine is transmitted through the freewheel unit, the cone clutch and epicyclic gear unit to accommodate overrun and reverse conditions. The freewheel unit will not transmit a drive when the vehicle is driven in the reverse direction.

Overdrive

Oil, under pressure from a pump driven by the input shaft, acts on pistons that force the cone clutch against the casing of the overdrive assembly to prevent the sun wheel from rotating.

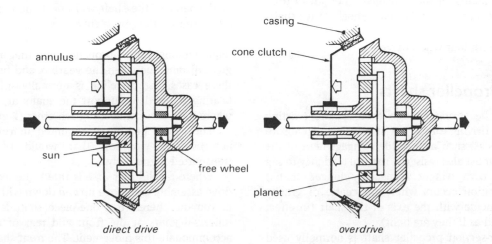

Figure 3.101 An overdrive gear train set

The input shaft will rotate, causing the planet gears to rotate around the fixed sun gear. This motion drives the annulus at a slightly faster speed than the input shaft, to give the overdrive ratio. The overdrive is engaged without using the main clutch, the engagement of the overdrive unit is therefore quick and smooth.

The operation of the overdrive is not permitted in either the low gears (typically first and second gears) or in reverse. The torque developed by the lower gear(s) is too great for the overdrive unit, so an external inhibitor switch is fitted to the gear selector mechanism to disengage the overdrive during reverse and low gear operation.

3.17 PROPELLER SHAFTS AND DRIVE SHAFTS

3.17.1 Introduction

Propeller shaft
The term 'propeller shaft' is often referred to as being inherited from either the aircraft or boat industry. In an automobile application, the shaft which transmits the power from the gearbox output shaft to final drive unit (located in the rear axle) is still referred to as a propeller shaft (sometimes also referred to as a carden shaft or prop-shaft).

Although historically, the term propeller shaft applied to rear-wheel drive vehicles, on some types of four-wheel drive vehicles (where the engine gearbox layout is the same as for rear-wheel drive), a propeller shaft may transmit power from the gearbox to the front final drive unit as well as the rear final drive unit.

The propeller shaft is normally tubular in section and of one- or two-piece construction. A two-piece shaft is supported at the mid-point by a rubber-mounted bearing.

If a one-piece shaft is used (especially for long shafts), there is a greater tendency for the shaft to 'whip' or bend in the middle. A two-piece shaft provides two short shafts that are less likely to whip during rotation.

Drive shafts
Short drive shafts are used in both front- and rear-wheel drive arrangements for the transmission of power from the final drive assembly to the road wheels. Drive shafts are therefore used on front- and rear-wheel drive layouts and with four-wheel drive.

3.17.2 Propeller shafts

Shafts must be strong enough to resist the twisting action of the driving torque but also resilient to absorb torsional shocks, such as a sudden engagement of the clutch. They must also resist the natural tendency to sag under their own weight (especially longer shafts) because vibration occurs when the centre of gravity does not coincide with the axis of the shaft (in effect shafts respond as if they are bent).

A tubular-section propeller shaft is normally used because it has the following benefits:

- light in weight
- high resistance to misalignment (especially sag)
- good torsional strength (a tubular shaft is only slightly weaker than a solid shaft of similar diameter)
- low resistance (low inertia) to changes in angular speed which arise when a Hooke-type coupling is used to drive the shaft.

A propeller shaft rotates at high speed. In fact, assuming that the gearbox has a 1:1 top gear ratio then the propeller shaft will be rotating at the same speed as the engine, which could be in excess of 7000 rpm when the vehicle is travelling near its maximum speed. The shaft must therefore be made accurately balanced as well as including any design features. During the manufacture of the shaft, small patches are spot-welded onto the 'light parts' of the tube; these patches act as balance weights to correct any imbalances.

Even when the static alignment of a shaft is perfect, the weight of the shaft makes it bow at the centre. When this is excessive, rotation of the shaft causes the bow to increase owing to the centrifugal effect. This deformation, or whip of the shaft, sets up a vibration that becomes severe as it approaches the 'whirling' speed. The critical speed at which this condition occurs depends on two vital dimensions: the mean diameter of the tube and the length of the shaft. Changes in length or diameter of the shaft will affect the exact speed at which the whirling problem arises.

Many rear-wheel and four-wheel drive vehicles require a longitudinal propeller shaft that has to span a great distance between the gearbox and final drive. In these cases, the driveline is normally split. A centre bearing is fitted to support the shafts at, or close to, where the shafts connect to each other (Figure 3.102).

The centre bearing is mounted in rubber, which absorbs any vibration that would otherwise be transmitted to the body.

Where a solid rear axle is fitted, the axle and final drive assembly will move up and down with suspension movement, therefore a one-piece shaft is fitted with universal joints at the front and rear of the shaft to accommodate this movement. The front shaft universal joint also accommodates any body flex as well as

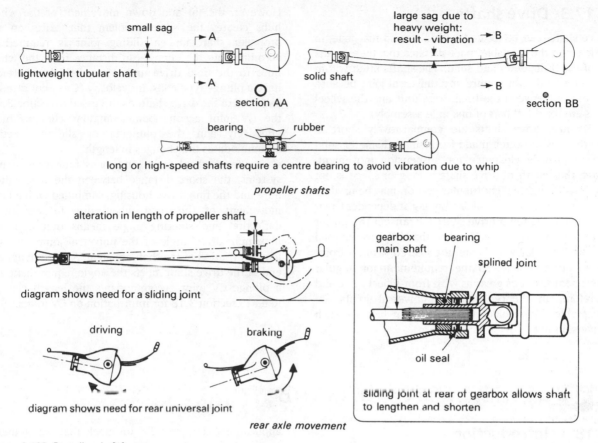

Figure 3.102 Propeller shaft features

gearbox/engine assembly movement (due to the assembly being fitted on rubber mounts).

The simple Hooke-type universal joint (refer to section 3.18) is less effective when the angles through which the joint has to operate become larger. With a two-piece shaft, because the rear shaft is much shorter than a single long shaft, a given axle movement will result in a greater angle of operation for the universal joint. Therefore a two-piece shaft is usually fitted with additional rubber couplings or constant velocity (CV) joints to accommodate the larger angles of operation.

When the axle moves up and down, or twists up and down at an angle, due to torque reaction on the axle, the distance between the final drive and the gearbox alters slightly. To accommodate this change in distance, the front of the propeller shaft is normally fitted to the gearbox output shaft by a sliding-joint arrangement. Transferring the power from the gearbox shaft to the propeller shaft is usually achieved with a spline, and by allowing the propeller shaft spline to slide on the gearbox spline, this allows for changes in distance (Figure 3.102).

Composite propeller shafts

The composite propeller shaft shown in Figure 3.103 is a modern alternative to the divided (two-piece) arrangement. The tubular shaft is made of epoxy resin, which is strengthened with glass and carbon fibres and

bonded to a steel spigot for connection to the universal joints.

Compared with a conventional two-piece steel shaft arrangement, the advantages of the composite shaft are:
- a weight reduction by about 50%
- high internal shock absorption
- good noise-vibration harshness (NVH) performance
- exceptional corrosion resistance.

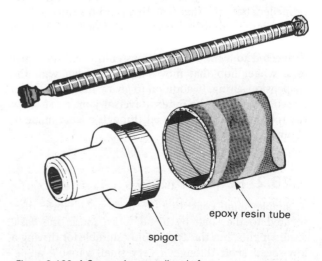

Figure 3.103 A composite propeller shaft

3.17.3 Drive shafts

Drive shafts can be located within a solid rear axle, in which case the available space dictates that these shafts be of small diameter and solid. The shafts fitted within a solid axle do not require any universal joint because the angles between the final drive unit and the wheel hubs are fixed (all part of one axle assembly).

Because drive shafts are comparatively short in length, they are often made from small diameter solid rod to provide clearance for suspension movement. When the length of drive shaft is long or space is not restricted, a lightweight tubular section may be used.

Rear-wheel drive vehicles having independent rear suspension require a drive shaft to transmit the power from the final assembly (fixed to the body) to the road wheels. The rear wheels are not steered (as in a front-wheel drive vehicle) so the requirement for angular movement is not as great as with front-wheel drive and therefore, in theory, standard universal joints are acceptable. Many older vehicles did in fact use such universal joints.

However, the up and down movement of the wheel hubs creates the same problem that exists on the propeller shaft i.e., a sliding joint is required to accommodate the changes in distance from the wheel hubs to the final drive unit. Many vehicles therefore have a plunge-type constant velocity (CV) joint fitted at each end of the drive shaft. As discussed in section 3.18, the CV joint accommodates angular changes more effectively and the plunging or sliding function accommodates the changes in length.

For front-wheel drive (and many four-wheel drive) systems, the short distance between the road wheel hubs and the final drive housing, combined with a large movement of the road wheel due to suspension deflection and steering angle means that both the maximum drive angle of the universal joints and the length variation of the shaft are great. A CV joint at each end of the drive shaft meets the angle requirement and a plunge CV joint accommodates the length change. Refer to section 3.18 for information on CV joints.

3.18 UNIVERSAL AND CONSTANT VELOCITY

3.18.1 Introduction

A universal joint (UJ), sometimes called a carden joint, allows the drive to be transmitted through a variable angle.

The need for a UJ is shown in Figure 3.102. The illustration indicates a rear-wheel drive layout with the gearbox mounted on the frame and the rear axle bolted to the road springs.

Road shocks will deflect the springs to the position shown. The angle of the propeller shaft relative to the gearbox and final drive will therefore constantly alter as the vehicle's suspension springs move up and down. Unless a universal joint is fitted to each end of the propeller shaft, the shaft will bend and fracture.

A similar problem occurs on front-wheel drive vehicles. In this case, one end of the driveshaft is connected to a fixed transaxle assembly and the other to a wheel hub that moves up and down with the suspension spring. In addition to giving flexibility in this direction (plane), the outer universal joint must allow the road wheels to be steered through a large angle of about 25°.

3.18.2 Requirements

A simple joint consisting of a flexible fabric disc, secured to the shaft by metal forks, meets the basic requirements, but this type is only suitable for driving a low-speed shaft through a very small variable angle. This type of joint is still used for some engineering

applications, but it fails to meet the requirements expected of a modern universal joint, which are:

- *Strength* – high torque must be transmitted with the minimum energy loss due to friction.
- *Compactness* – space is limited so the joint must be small yet robust.
- *Large drive angle* – modern road springs allow large wheel deflections so the joint must be able to accommodate the large drive angle given by this movement.
- *Shaft balance* – severe vibration occurs if the shaft runs out-of-true, so the joint must maintain good alignment.
- *Operating speed* – the joint must operate efficiently at high speed under conditions of high torque and variable drive angle. This requirement is combined with the need for the joint to have a long life and need minimum maintenance.

3.18.3 Basic types of universal joint

Cross-type joint

The cross-type universal joint is widely used on prop shafts fitted to rear-wheel drive vehicles. It is often called a Hooke-type coupling because it was developed from the joint claimed to have been invented by Robert Hooke in the seventeenth century.

The joints shown in Figure 3.104 are a basic Hooke-type joint and a development known as the cross-type joint. These joints have two yokes set at 90° to each

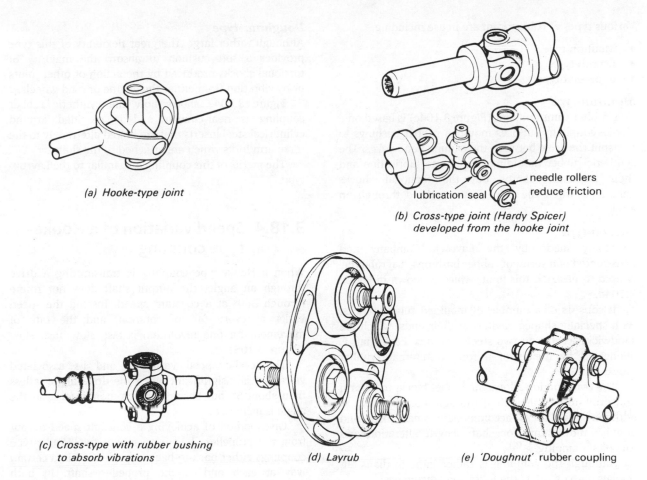

(a) Hooke-type joint

needle rollers
reduce friction

lubrication seal

*(b) Cross-type joint (Hardy Spicer)
developed from the hooke joint*

*(c) Cross-type with rubber bushing
to absorb vibrations*

(d) Layrub

(e) 'Doughnut' rubber coupling

Figure 3.104 Types of universal joint

other; the yokes are joined to each other by a cross-shaped trunnion block. Contact between the yoke and the trunnion is made by needle roller bearings, which are held in a hardened steel cup retained in each arm of the yoke. Alignment of the trunnion is achieved by making the bottom of the cup contact the end of the block.

Lubrication of the bearings is provided using a special, viscous oil, similar to that used in a final drive. This is contained in a reservoir formed by drifting out the centre of the trunnion arms. The oil is introduced by pre-filling the small reservoir which should then be sufficient for the life of the joint. Note that on older vehicles and in some other engineering applications, the oil is introduced via a lubrication nipple, and this normally involves adding oil on an occasional basis (in line with manufacturers recommendations). An oil seal, retained on each arm of the block presses against the cup and prevents escape of the lubricant.

The cups are retained in the yoke either with circlips or by staking. Peening over the edge of the yokes to stake the cups makes replacement of worn parts in the joint more difficult. If the joint becomes worn it is normal practice to replace the complete shaft assembly unless specialized equipment is available to replace the joint.

The merits of this type of joint are:

- compactness
- high mechanical efficiency
- ability to drive through a large occasional 'bump' angle (maximum about 25°)
- accurate centring of shaft, hence the joint is suitable for high-speed operation.

Lubrication failure, especially in cases where a 'lubrication' nipple in the trunnion block is missed when the vehicle is serviced, causes the needle rollers to indent or damage the bearing surfaces. This type of wear gives a slight angular movement; this allows the slackness in the joint to produce a noise, often described as a 'clonk', during the change-over from drive to over-run and vice versa. Failure to rectify this fault accelerates the rate of wear of the joint, which soon leads to misalignment and severe vibration.

Rubber joints

One disadvantage of the cross-type joint is its lack of flexibility in relation to the absorption of torsional shocks and drive-line vibrations, especially when a comparatively rigid transmission system is used. A smoother and less harsh drive can be obtained by using one or more rubber joints in the transmission driveline.

Various types of rubber joint are in use including:

- Moulton-type
- Layrub-type
- doughnut-type.

Moulton-type

This rubber trunnion joint (Figure 3.104c) is based on a Hooke coupling, but uses moulded rubber bushings to transmit the drive between the trunnion and yokes. The synthetic rubber mouldings require no lubrication and their resilience damps out the torsional shocks generated when the drive is transmitted through an angle.

Layrub-type

Originally made by the Laycock Company and constructed of a series of rubber bushings, 'Layrub-type' is used to describe this joint, which is shown in Figure 3.104d.

It consists of a number of moulded rubber blocks, with specially shaped cavities at their ends, which are sandwiched between two steel pressings. Each shaft is connected by means of a fork to alternate rubber blocks.

The construction allows the rubber blocks to deform and drive to be transmitted through a small angle. In addition, the blocks accommodate small axial and angular movements for shaft length alteration and torsional damping.

Although the coupling is rather large in diameter, the layrub-type offers the following advantages:

- no lubrication required
- it is capable of driving through bump angles up to about 15°
- it allows for axial movement, hence no splining of the shaft is necessary
- its flexibility damps shocks and insulates the vehicle from transmission noise.

Doughnut-type

Although rather large, the great flexibility of this type provides a soft cushion to absorb the majority of torsional shocks produced by the action of other joints or by vibration from either the engine or road wheels.

Figure 3.104e shows how the synthetic rubber coupling is near-circular and is moulded around cylindrical steel inserts that are bolted alternately to the three-arm forks which are attached to the shafts.

The merits of this coupling are similar to the Layrub-type.

3.18.4 Speed variation of a Hooke-type coupling

When a Hooke-type coupling is transmitting a drive through an angle, the output shaft does not rotate through 360° at a constant speed. Instead the speed varies at every 90° of rotation, and the rate of movement for one revolution is fast, slow, fast, slow (Figure 3.105).

This cyclic speed variation, and its associated vibration, is insignificant when the drive angle is less than about 5°, but becomes much more intense as the angle is increased.

One method of achieving a constant speed output from the propeller shaft is to mount two Hooke-type couplings either back-to-back or positioned in a certain way at each end of the propeller shaft. In both configurations the relative positions of each coupling must be arranged so that the speed change of one coupling is counteracted by the other. The 'phasing' of Hooke-type couplings, as applied to two separate driveline layouts, is shown in Figure 3.106.

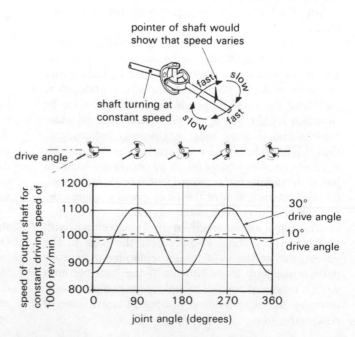

Figure 3.105 Speed variation with Hooke-type joints

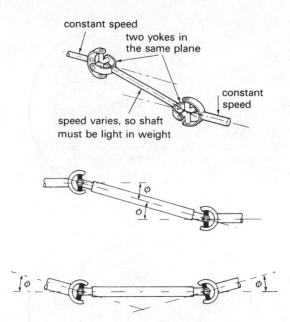

Figure 3.106 Phasing of Hooke-type couplings

This diagram shows that to restore a constant speed, two conditions must be satisfied:

1 Yokes at each end of the propeller shaft must be positioned in the same plane.
2 The drive angle of each coupling must be the same.

3.18.5 Constant-velocity joints

A constant-velocity (CV) universal joint is a type that provides an output shaft speed equal to that of the input in all shaft positions within the working range of the joint.

These joints are commonly used in drivelines because of their smooth operation. They were originally introduced for situations where the drive angle was large, such as at the wheel end of a front-wheel drive vehicle when the steering is set in the full-lock position.

Geometry of a typical CV joint can be appreciated if the action of a Hooke-type coupling is considered. The speed variation of a Hooke-type joint is caused by the alteration in leverage between the yokes and trunnion block. When the coupling is viewed from the side and the input shaft is rotated through 90°, the trunnion block is seen to oscillate back and forth from the vertical through an angle equal to the shaft drive angle.

A 'constant angular velocity' condition occurs with this joint when the trunnion block is at the mid-point of its rocking movement. If this condition could be maintained a constant-velocity universal joint would be obtained, i.e. constant-velocity conditions are achieved when the connecting device between the driving and driven yokes is positioned in a plane that bisects the angle of drive.

The various CV joints in use have a construction which is based on either the twin Hooke-type coupling arrangement or on the 'angle bisect' principle.

Constant-velocity joints in common use are:

- Tracta
- Rzeppa
- Weiss
- Tripode.

Tracta CV joints

The need for CV joints was discovered in 1926 when the first FWD vehicle was made in France by Fenaille and Gregoire – the Tracta (traction-avant) car. When the second car was made, the drive line incorporated CV joints, and the type used on that car is now known as a Tracta joint. Figure 3.107 shows the main details.

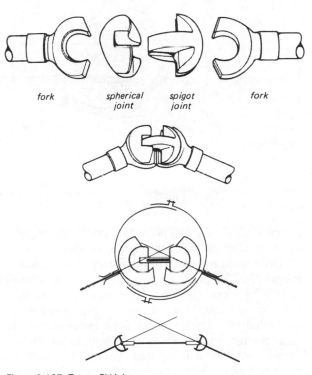

Figure 3.107 Tracta CV joint

Reference to the line sketch shows that the operating principle is similar to two Hooke-type joints: the angles are always kept constant and the yokes are set in the same place.

The joint is capable of transmitting a drive through a maximum angle of about 40° and its strong construction makes it suitable for agricultural and military vehicles, but the friction of the sliding surfaces makes it rather inefficient.

Rzeppa-type CV joints

This joint was patented by A. H. Rzeppa (pronounced Zeppa) in America in 1935. A development of this type of joint is widely used today; it is referred to as a Birfield joint.

Figure 3.108 shows the construction of a Birfield joint and the line sketch shows its principle of operation.

Constant velocity is achieved if the device (steel balls in this case) connecting the drive shaft to the

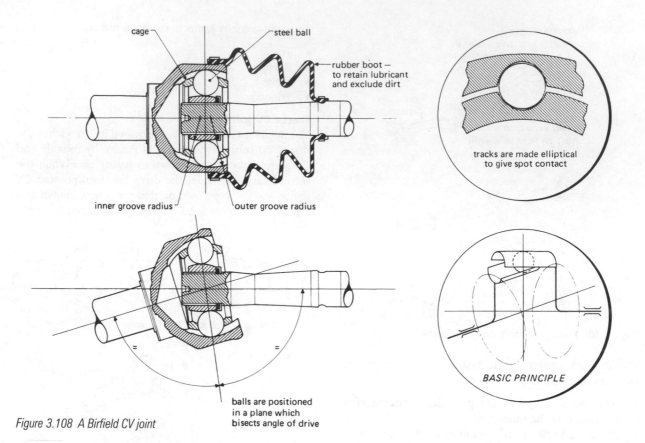

Figure 3.108 A Birfield CV joint

driven shaft rotates in a plane that bisects the angle of drive. The Birfield joint achieves this condition.

Drive from the inner to outer race is by means of longitudinal, elliptical grooves, which hold a series of steel balls (normally six) in the bisecting plane by a cage. In the original Rzeppa joint the cage position was controlled by a small plunger fitted between the two shaft centres, but noise was a problem. In the Birfield design the plunger is omitted. Instead, the balls are made to take up their correct positions by offsetting the centres of the radii for inner and outer grooves.

A Birfield joint has a maximum angle of about 45°, but this angle is far too large for continuous operation because of the heat generated. The joint is lubricated by grease, the appropriate quantity being packed in the joint 'for life'. A synthetic rubber boot seals the CV unit and prevents the ingress of dirt, etc.

Weiss-type CV joints

This type was patented in America in 1923 by Weiss and later developed by Bendix. Figure 3.109 shows a simplified drawing of this type.

The two forks have grooves cut in their sides to form tracks for the steel balls. There are four tracks, so four balls are used to transmit rotary motion and a fifth ball placed at the centre of the forks locates the two forks and resists the inward force. The driving balls work in compression, so two balls take the forward drive and the other two operate when reverse drive is applied. The complete joint is contained in a housing filled with grease. Maximum angularity is about 35°.

Constant velocity is achieved in a manner similar to the Rzeppa joint – the balls always take up a position in a plane that bisects the angle of drive.

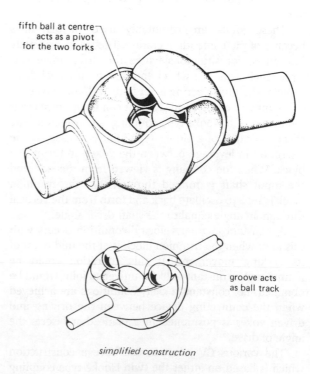

Figure 3.109 A Weiss CV joint

Tripode-type CV joint

This compact joint has been developed over recent years and, because of its ability to operate efficiently at high speed, it is widely used by vehicle manufacturers.

Besides providing good resistance to high-speed centrifugal effects, the construction of this joint, combined with the reduced working clearances achieved by modern production techniques, produces a transmission drive line with good noise-vibration harshness (NVH) performance.

In the construction shown in Figure 3.110 the three-armed support (tripod) carrying the spherically shaped rollers is fixed to the outer housing. On both sides of each driving fork, which also has three arms, grooves are cut to form a bearing track for the rollers.

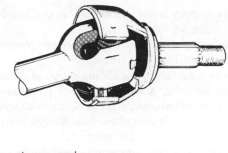

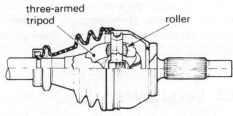

Figure 3.110 A Tripode CV joint

Drive through the joint is produced by the force exerted by the side of the driving fork on the rollers. This force is transmitted to the tripod and joint housing.

Alteration of the drive angle causes the roller to move backwards and forwards along the grooved track as the joint rotates through one revolution. A small clearance is given between the roller and track to permit this movement.

Homokinetic motion (constant velocity) is achieved with a Tripode joint because of the path taken by the rollers with respect to the contact point on the track.

This type of fixed joint accepts an occasional drive angle up to about 45°.

3.18.6 Plunge joints

The up and down suspension movement causes an alteration in the length required of many drive shafts. A special CV joint, called a plunge joint must therefore be used to allow for this alteration in drive shaft length.

The alternative is to use splines to allow the joint to slide back and forth along the shaft, but lubrication often causes a problem here.

Two plunge joints that are commonly used by vehicle manufacturers have been developed from the fixed Birfield and Tripode CV joints.

Birfield plunge joint

Development work on the original Rzeppa joint by Löbro in Germany in the late 1950s produced the type known in this country as the Birfield CV joint. In 1960 the Löbro company redesigned this fixed-type joint and produced it in a plunge form to satisfy the needs of front-wheel drive vehicles that were starting to become popular at that time.

The constructional features of this joint are shown in Figure 3.111. In this type, the grooves that act as the tracks for the balls are straight instead of curved as in the fixed version. This allows the drive shaft length to vary up to about 50 mm.

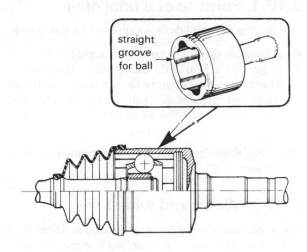

Figure 3.111 A Birfield plunge joint

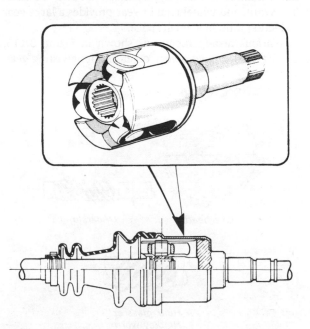

Figure 3.112 Tripode plunge joint

When the shaft angle is increased, the rolling action of the balls in the inner and outer grooves positions the cage in the bisecting plane to give a CV drive.

The maximum drive angle of 22° is considerably less than for the fixed type. For the application of front-wheel drive vehicles, the plunge joint is positioned at the transaxle end of the drive shaft.

Tripode plunge joint

Comparing the Tripode plunge joint in Figure 3.112 with the fixed Tripode shows that the basic construction is similar. The main visible difference is that the plunge joint has roller tracks that are straight instead of curved.

The type shown permits a maximum plunge of 55 mm and a drive angle up to 25°. It should be noted that with all types of plunge CV joints, the working angle should be less than 10°.

Later types of Tripode-type plunge joints normally use needle roller bearings to reduce the friction between the contact surfaces. These improve the NVH performance and allow the joint to operate efficiently at high speed.

3.19 FINAL DRIVE GEARS

3.19.1 Purpose of a final drive

The purpose of a final drive, as applied to a rear axle, is:

- to transmit the drive through an angle of 90°
- to provide a gear ratio that reduces the speed at which the gearbox output shaft rotates, which then allows the use of a direct drive (top gear) through the gearbox. In the case of many cars, this requires a final drive ratio of approximately 4:1.

These functions can be performed by either bevel or worm gears.

3.19.2 Worm and wheel

The worm and wheel drive is rarely used as a final drive on light vehicles due to its cost, but it is used on some applications of heavy vehicles. The worm and wheel drive is included in this section because this type of gear has a number of other applications on motor vehicles. The worm and wheel type of gear provides a large gear reduction ratio in a small space.

Various arrangements, as shown in Figure 3.113, can be used to give a very quiet and long-lasting gear,

but its efficiency is not as good as that of a bevel (about 94 % against 98 %).

The worm may be mounted above (overhead) or below (under-slung) the wheel.

Friction caused by the sliding action of the worm is reduced by using a worm wheel of phosphor-bronze and a worm of case-hardened steel, but even with these materials, the unit gets rather hot. A large, well-cooled sump is used to reduce oxidation of the oil. Oxidation of the oil occurs at high temperature and causes the oil to thicken. To improve the boundary lubrication, a vegetable-based oil is sometimes used as an alternative to straight gear oil.

3.19.3 Bevel gears

The geometry of a bevel gear layout may be seen in Figure 3.114.

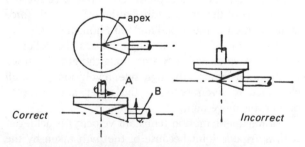

Figure 3.114 *Friction cones representing a bevel gear drive*

The drawing indicates two friction cones:

A – the 'crown wheel'.
B – the 'pinion'.

To avoid slipping and wear, the apex of the pinion must coincide with the centre line of the crown wheel.

If the pinion is incorrectly positioned, it will be seen that the peripheral speeds of the crown wheel and pinion will not be equal. Mounting the gear in the correct position shows that the angle of the bevel is governed by the gear ratio.

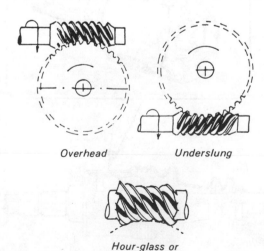

Overhead   *Underslung*

Hour-glass or Hindley worm

Figure 3.113 *A worm drive*

There are three types of bevel gears in general use and these are described below:

Straight bevel

Figure 3.115 illustrates the main features of the bevel type of gear. Tapered teeth, generated from the centre, are machined on the case-hardened steel gears, the gears are then ground together to form a 'matched pair'.

The direction of rotation of the axle shaft is determined by the position of the crown wheel relative to the pinion.

The gears are aligned correctly using distance pieces, shims or screwed rings. These forms of adjusters enable the correct mesh and backlash to be set. When the clearance between the teeth (backlash) is too small, expansion due to heat and wear and damage caused by lack of lubrication will result, whereas excessive clearance produces slackness and noise.

Each manufacturer recommends a suitable backlash; this is normally in the region of 0.15 mm (0.006 in) for cars and 0.25 mm (0.01 in) for heavy vehicles.

Spiral bevel

Although a straight bevel is relatively inexpensive to produce and mechanically efficient, one disadvantage was its excessive noise which was unacceptable to the occupants of the vehicle. The noise was caused by the meshing of the gears. The noise is reduced when a helical form of tooth is employed. It is impossible to generate a helix tooth on a tapered pinion, so the type of gear used is known as a spiral bevel.

The construction of the spiral bevel gear is shown in Figure 3.116. A number of teeth, generated from the centre of the crown wheel, form (in the case of the pinion) a left-handed spiral. This direction causes a large outward thrust on the drive and a smaller inward thrust on the over-run; therefore pinion-bearing wear increases the backlash rather than causing seizure of the gear.

The teeth on the crown wheel are inclined to the teeth on the pinion, therefore when the pinion is driving the pressure exerted on each tooth is much higher. The high-viscosity gear oil, which was satisfactory for the straight bevel type, gives poor results when used in

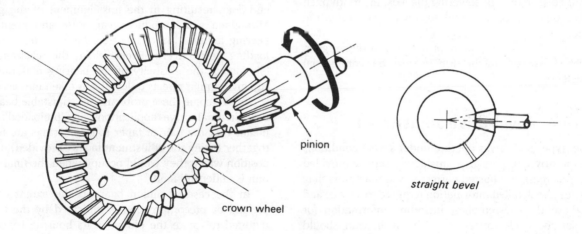

Figure 3.115 A straight bevel gear

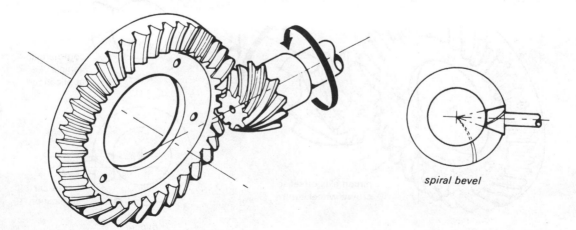

Figure 3.116 A spiral bevel gear

spiral bevel units. The oil film breaks down under high loads, which results in rapid wear and scoring of the teeth.

Special oils to lubricate the surface after rupture of the oil film were developed and these are known as extreme pressure (EP) lubricants. They contain various additives such as sulphur, chlorine and phosphorus compounds. These compounds react chemically at high temperatures with the surface of the tooth to form a compound of low frictional resistance. The compounds also include fatty acids to improve boundary lubrication at low temperature.

Hypoid bevel

The hypoid type of gear shown in Figure 3.117, is widely used on modern vehicles. The pinion axis is offset to the centre line of the crown wheel. The centre line of the pinion can be placed either above or below the centre. In the case of cars, the centre line is always placed below the crown wheel to provide a low propeller shaft together with a reduction in the tunnel height. Pinion offset varies, but an offset equal to one-fifth of the crown wheel diameter is commonly used.

It will be seen that, by lowering the axis, the tooth pitch of the pinion increases, and so, for a given ratio, the pinion diameter can be larger (30% for a normal offset pinion). The larger pinion provides a stronger gear, which is an advantage for its use on commercial vehicles.

3.19.4 Bevel-drive adjustment

Bevel-type final drives operate under severe conditions but the drives usually give satisfactory service provided the gear mesh is adjusted correctly. Manufacturers may provide the detailed information required to service and overhaul these assemblies, including information for special tools, clearances, etc. The technician should always refer to such information before attempting such tasks.

The following general points should be a guide:

- Noise from the final drive is usually caused by either bearing defects or incorrect meshing (the latter may be caused by bearing wear). Generally, a noise such as a 'whine' occurs when the gear is too deep in mesh, and 'noise' on the over-run is caused by insufficient depth of mesh.
- Whenever a final-drive noise develops, the cause of the problem should be determined as soon as possible. Misaligned gears will quickly 'mate' to the new position (wear to each others characteristics).
- The mating of the gears may make it impossible to obtain a quiet operation even when the adjustment is corrected. If repair is delayed the final drive will probably require a new crown wheel and pinion as well as new bearings.

Preloading of bearings

Adjustable taper roller bearings are commonly used in a final drive assembly to support both the crown wheel and pinion.

If each bearing were set to give a small clearance between the rollers and tracks, each gear would have end-float, resulting in the misalignment of the gears. Misaligned gears produce gear noise and premature bearing failure, due to incorrect meshing and uneven loading respectively. Even when the clearance is eliminated, the elasticity of the bearing material will still give similar effects unless this is taken into account.

To overcome these problems, all adjustable bearings used in final drive applications are 'preloaded'. This means that the pair of taper roller bearings are forced together (using the adjustment facility provided), to the position which they would occupy when the final drive unit is under full load.

In the case of pinion bearings the extent of this preload or precompression is indicated by the torque required to rotate the pinion in its housing (once the preload is set). As an example a specification may state that:

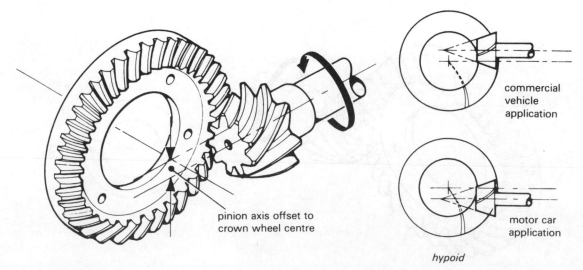

pinion axis offset to crown wheel centre

commercial vehicle application

motor car application

hypoid

Figure 3.117 Hypoid bevel

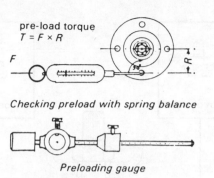

Checking preload with spring balance

Preloading gauge

Figure 3.118 Measurement of preload

'A torque of 1.36 N m (12 lbf in) is required to rotate the pinion'.

The recommended preload (indicated in the workshop literature) normally states the conditions under which it should be measured, e.g. with the bearings dry and the oil seal removed.

Figure 3.118 shows two ways of checking the preload of a pinion.

Pinion adjustment

The method adjusting the pinion bearing preload depends on the type of spacer used to hold the bearings apart. Figure 3.119 shows the two main arrangements: a rigid spacer and a collapsible spacer.

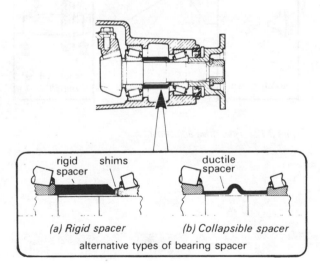

Figure 3.119 Pinion bearing adjustment

A bearing arrangement controlled by a rigid spacer (or solid spacer) has a series of variable sized shims to control the static load on the bearings (Figure 3.119a). With this type of adjustment, the pinion must be fully tightened before the preload is measured. If the preload is found to be incorrect when rechecking the adjustment, then shims have to be either added or removed to provide the correct preload.

Note: The rigid spacer simplifies the task of replacing the pinion oil seal, because the bearing preload is not altered by seal replacement provided the pinion nut is fully tightened to the correct torque setting.

Figure 3.119b shows a collapsible spacer. In addition to retaining the bearings at the correct preload specification, this ductile steel spacer collapses when placed under pressure from the pinion nut. Therefore the collapsible spacer allows the preload to be set in one operation.

With the pinion, bearings and oil seal assembled in the correct position, the nut is tightened sufficiently to give the recommended preload. When the preload is correct, the nut is locked in position. A ductile material has very little elasticity, so if the bearing preload is too high a new collapsible spacer is required. The time required to set the pinion preload is less than for the rigid type of spacer.

Note: Great care must be taken with final drive units having a collapsible spacer when a new pinion seal has to be replaced to cure a pinion oil leak. Prior to unlocking the pinion nut, the precise position of the nut relative to the pinion must be noted. Unless this precaution is taken during the dismantling procedure, the crown wheel will have to be removed so that the pinion bearings can be preloaded.

The pinion position relative to the crown wheel must be set accurately in order to position the apex point of the pinion correctly. Noise, in the form of a 'whine', and possible breakage of the gear teeth is likely to occur if this is incorrectly set. A special 'dummy pinion' jig is normally used to carry out this operation, although in the past the initial position of the pinion was set by aligning it with the edge of the crown wheel teeth.

Crown wheel adjustment

After setting the pinion correctly, the crown wheel is fitted to the assembly. When doing this it is important to fit the correct bearing cap, because the caps are machined in place and are therefore not interchangeable.

Backlash

Backlash between the teeth of the crown wheel and pinion is adjusted at this stage by moving the crown wheel either towards or away from the pinion. Before taking the final measurement of backlash with a dial test indicator (DTI) gauge, it is wise to check that the crown wheel run-out is within the limits recommended.

Meshing

Meshing of the gear is carried out by applying a smear of marking compound to the driving side of a few crown wheel teeth and then turning the pinion in the direction of rotation (DOR) while applying a resistance to the crown wheel.

The marking obtained indicates the mesh of the gears with respect to pinion position and backlash.

Figure 3.120 shows the 'correct' marking and the changes in markings when the position of the pinion is changed. It should be noted that the correct marking shows only a limited contact between the teeth under light load test conditions. When full load is applied to

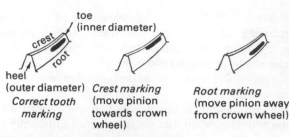

Figure 3.120 Crown wheel tooth marking

the gear, the contact area between the two teeth covers the complete crown wheel tooth.

Crown wheel preload

Housing rigidity and accurate gear alignment are essential with a hypoid gear if the low noise level possible with this type is to be achieved. To do this, end float in the crown wheel bearings must be eliminated by preloading the bearings.

Various methods are used to measure the preload; it is necessary to use the method as indicated in the workshop literature to carry out this adjustment.

The most common method is to measure the spread (outward deflection) of the bearing caps when the adjusters are screwed together. For example, a preload cap spread of 0.1 mm (0.004 in) means that after preloading the side bearings, the distance between the bearing caps has increased by 0.1 mm.

If shims are used to control the backlash, the preload is achieved by increasing the shim thickness on each side of the crown wheel (the shims are added after the backlash has been set). Axles having this type of construction need a special tool to 'spread the caps' before the crown wheel assembly is removed or refitted into the axle casing.

A visual summary of the main adjustments is shown in Figure 3.121.

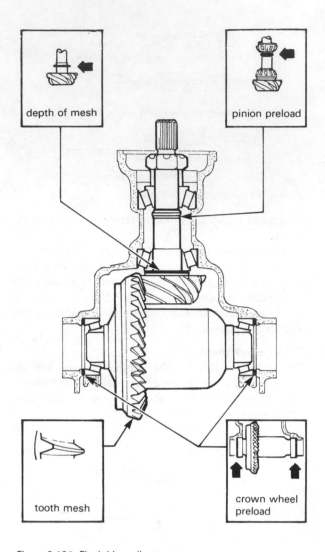

Figure 3.121 Final drive adjustments

3.20 THE DIFFERENTIAL

3.20.1 Purpose of a differential

If both driving wheels were connected to a common driving shaft, which would cause the two wheels to rotate at exactly the same speed at all times, two effects would soon show up:

1 difficulty in turning corners
2 rapid tyre wear

Figure 3.122 shows that when a vehicle is travelling straight ahead the driving wheels rotate an equal number of times over a given distance (same rotational speed).

However, when the vehicle is cornering, the outer wheel must travel a greater distance and so must rotate faster. If the wheels are connected to a common driving shaft and cannot rotate at different speeds they will try to keep travelling in a straight line. If the vehicle does in fact turn, the tyres will have to 'scrub' over the road surface to negotiate the turn.

This problem could be minimised by allowing one wheel to drive the vehicle and the other wheel to run free, but the unbalanced driving thrust and unequal cornering speeds make this arrangement unpopular.

The prime solution to the problem came in 1827 when Péqueur of France invented the 'differential'. This mechanism allows the wheels to rotate at different speeds, but still maintains a drive to both wheels.

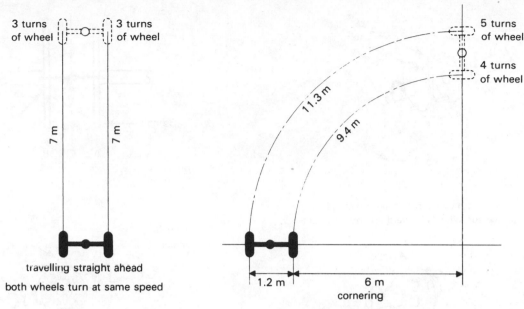

Figure 3.122 The need for a differential

3.20.2 Principle of operation

Consider the axle shown in Figure 3.123a. A disc is fitted to the shaft, which is connected to the wheel. Each disc is interconnected with a lever. When a driving force is applied at the centre of the lever, each disc will receive an equal share of the driving force i.e. half the driving force.

The movement of the discs will depend on the resistances opposing the motion of the shafts i.e. the resistance at each wheel.

If the resistance at each wheel is the same, the driving force will be distributed evenly between the two wheels and the vehicle is driven straight ahead.

If a larger resistance acts on disc B, the lever will tilt, and push disc A forward a greater amount; this condition is shown in plan view in Figure 3.123b. The illustration indicates:

Increase in distance moved by A
     = Decrease in distance moved by B

Increase in speed of A
     = Decrease in speed of B
Therefore: A + B = 2C

In Figure 3.123c the disc system is replaced by bevel gears. The discs are referred to as sun wheels and the levers are referred to as planet gears. The drive is applied to the cross-pin and pushes the planet gears forward to exert an equal torque on each sun wheel irrespective of speed.

When the vehicle is driven straight ahead, the whole unit rotates at the same speed. When the vehicle turns a corner, the inner wheel slows down and causes the planets to rotate on their own axis to speed up the outer wheel.

The complete differential is shown in Figure 3.123d. This arrangement shows a crown wheel bolted to a differential cage. The cage supports the sun wheels on plain bearings, the drive is transmitted from the crown wheel to the sun gears via the cross-pin and the planet gears.

Low-performance cars only require two planet gears, but it is necessary to fit four planet gears on high-performance and heavier vehicles to reduce tooth pressures.

Lubrication of the differential assembly is provided by the final drive oil, which can splash through holes in the differential cage.

3.20.3 Differential lock

The driving force using a conventional differential is transmitted through the driven wheel with the lowest resistance. Therefore if one driving wheel loses traction (on a two-wheel drive vehicle), the wheel will spin but it will also receive the driving force. This results in the vehicle being immobilised. On these occasions the differential action is undesirable, so, on vehicles designed to operate over low grip surfaces, a differential locking arrangement is often fitted.

The differential action can be prevented by locking together any two individual units of a differential; Figure 3.124 shows one arrangement. Splined to a differential sun wheel (axle shaft) is a sliding dog clutch member, which engages with dog teeth formed on the cage of the differential. The clutch is engaged by means of a fork which can be moved by a lever fitted on the outside of the axle casing.

In the engaged position, the sun wheel (and consequently the axle shaft and rear wheel connected to

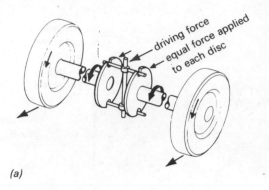

(a)

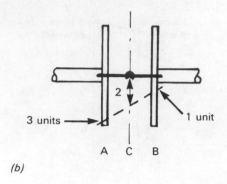

(b)

when vehicle is moving in a straight path, planet
gears move sun wheels forward an equal amount

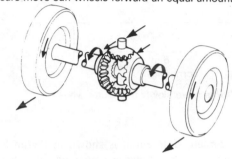

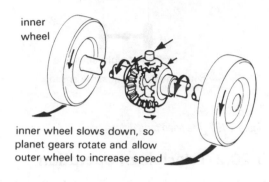

inner wheel slows down, so
planet gears rotate and allow
outer wheel to increase speed

(c)

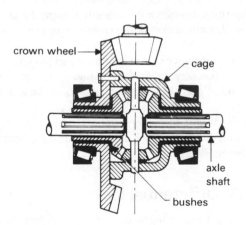

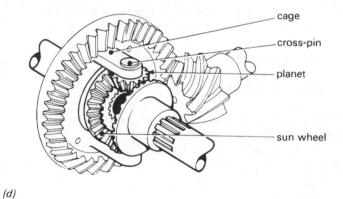

(d)

Figure 3.123 The action of a differential

this sun gear) are made to turn at the same speed as the
cage. Locking one sun gear to the cage in this way
ensures that the other sun gear rotates at the same
speed.

3.20.4 Limited-slip differential

Although a high mechanical efficiency is desirable for
the majority of mechanical components, it is a
disadvantage in the case of differential action i.e. too
much differential action allows a slipping wheel to
receive the driving force. In addition to the reduced
traction over slippery surfaces, a 'low friction'

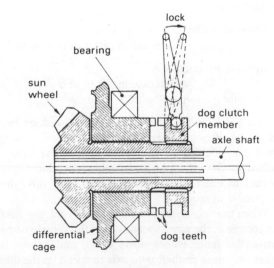

Figure 3.124 Differential lock

differential fitted to a high-powered vehicle limits acceleration and causes excessive tyre wear. If one wheel slips during acceleration, all of the power is applied to that wheel.

Observation of such a vehicle during acceleration shows that torque reaction of the engine tends to lift the left-hand driving wheel off the ground and when this is accompanied by an uneven road surface, excessive wheelspin becomes apparent. To restrict these drawbacks, the differential action is opposed by artificially increasing the friction between the sun wheel and the differential cage. Arrangements having this feature are referred to as 'limited slip differentials' (LSD).

There are two basic types of differential, which give this, or a similar action. These are:

- mechanical limited-slip differential
- visco-differential.

Mechanical limited-slip differential

Figure 3.125 shows the layout of one type of differential, which is bolted to the crown wheel.

A multi-disc clutch pack fitted behind each sun wheel has the inner and outer plates splined to the sun and cage respectively. Since bevel gears are used, an axial thrust will be developed which is proportional to the torque applied by the crown wheel to the differential. Under low torque conditions, the differential functions in the normal manner, but if the torque is increased, the clutch pack becomes loaded by the axial thrust and this will resist any attempt at a different rotational speed between the sun gear and the cage (Figure 3.126).

To increase the load on the clutch pack even further, many designs incorporate:

- A Belleville disc-spring washer between the cage and the clutch discs of each pack to provide an initial load on the discs.
- Angled cam faces between the cage and the cross-pins. Driving thrust exerted by the cage on the pin causes the pin to force the planets against the side gear ring. When four planets are used, two separate pins, flexibly linked at the centre and having opposite cam faces, cause two planets to act on one clutch pack and the other two to exert force in the opposite direction.

Note: The technician should remember the action of the limited-slip differential when working on a vehicle.

Figure 3.125 *Final drive assembly with limited-slip differential*

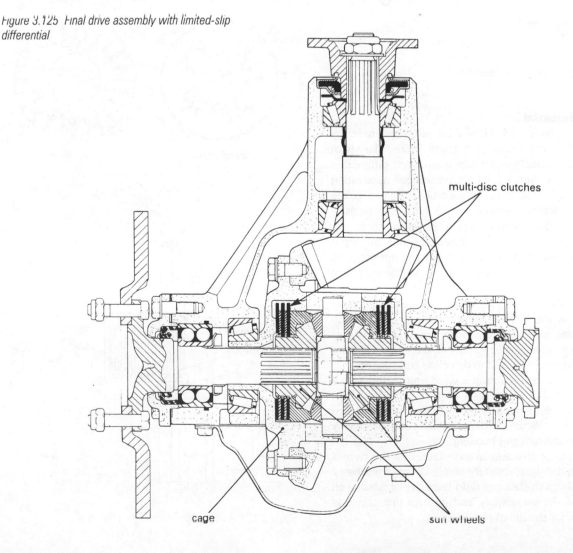

multi-disc clutches

cage

sun wheels

With only one driving wheel lifted off the ground, the drive will still be transmitted to the wheel that remains on the ground, which enables the vehicle to be driven.

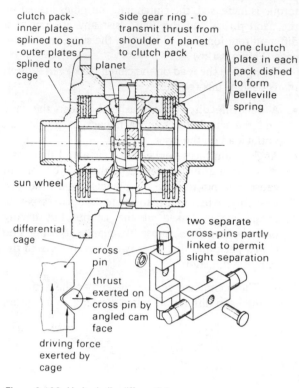

Figure 3.126 *Limited-slip differential*

Visco-differential

Viscous couplings have been used more and more by vehicle manufacturers since the late 1960s. The visco-differential assembly combines a standard differential with a viscous coupling. This transmission application uses the coupling as a viscous control device to regulate the speed difference between the two driving wheels.

Whereas the locking action on a mechanically operated, limited-slip differential depends on input torque, the viscous type depends on the difference in speed between the driving wheels. Very little resistance is offered when the speed difference between the driving wheels is small, but the resistance progressively builds up as the difference increases. Compared with the mechanical limited-slip differential, it is claimed that this type gives lower tyre wear, easier steering and lower stress levels applied to driveline components.

The basic construction of a visco unit is similar to a multi-plate clutch. It consists of a housing and hub, between which is sandwiched a series of perforated metal plates (Figure 3.127), which are alternately attached to the hub and housing.

The housing also acts as a container for the viscous silicone fluid. A heat-resistant seal, made of fluorinated rubber, isolates the silicone fluid from the lubricating oil in the final drive assembly and ensures that the fluid will suffice for the life of the coupling.

The operating principle of the viscous coupling is based on the fact that the shear force (drive) given by the fluid on a plate depends on the shear rate (speed difference). By using a high-viscosity fluid, the coupling can be designed to output a comparatively high torque, which progressively builds up as the shear rate is increased.

The relationship between torque and shear rate is affected by a number of factors such as fluid viscosity, the gap between plates and plate perforation. By varying these design factors, the coupling can be 'tuned' to suit the application.

Prolonged slipping of the coupling generates heat and this causes the fluid to expand and take up some of the space occupied by the air. Where spacers are not used to hold the plates apart, the combination of the increase in air pressure due to fluid expansion, and the reduction in fluid pressure in the gaps, causes the plates to be pushed together. These actions cause metal-to-metal contact and at this point (the hump point) the coupling temporarily departs from its viscous mode operation. As it passes through this phase the torque output rises considerably; in some designs it can be six times as great.

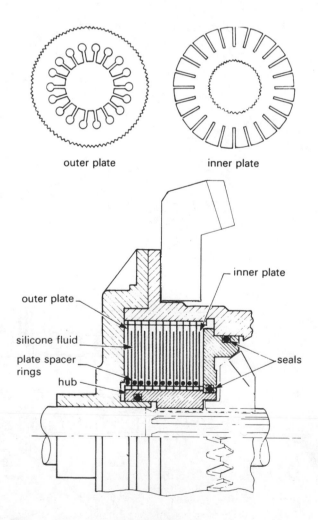

Figure 3.127 *A visco-differential unit*

Viscous couplings can be used to control front, rear and centre differentials (centre differentials are used on some four-wheel drive vehicles). Each application has different requirements in view of its position, speed of operation and the type of vehicle to which it is fitted. For example, a viscous control unit at the rear of a powerful car requires some form of overload protection, so the 'hump' is used to fill this need. On the other hand, a viscous coupling used for a front-wheel drive car should have no 'hump', because a unit with this characteristic would adversely affect steering.

The viscous control unit can be installed and connected within a differential in two ways:

- shaft-to-shaft
- shaft-to-cage.

Shaft-to-shaft viscous coupling

Figure 3.128 shows a differential having a viscous control unit connected between the two axle shafts. The hub holding the inner plates joined to one shaft, and the housing with its outer plates connected to the other shaft. Space is made available for the unit at the centre of the crown wheel by moving the differential to one side.

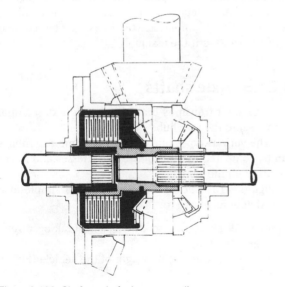

Figure 3.128 Shaft-to-shaft viscous coupling

When the car is moving without wheel slip (i.e. in a straight line) the visco control unit is out of action.

At times when a high difference in speed exists between the axle shafts, such as when one driving wheel loses adhesion or when wheelspin occurs during acceleration, the resistance offered by the unit ensures that the driving torque transmitted to each wheel is maintained.

Shaft-to-cage viscous coupling

The cheaper arrangement shown in Figure 3.129 has the housing of the viscous control unit integral with the differential cage and the hub connected to one axle shaft.

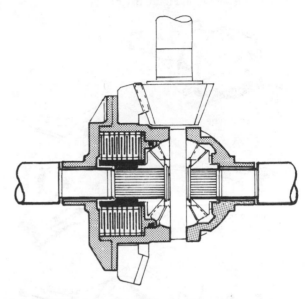

Figure 3.129 Shaft-to-cage viscous coupling

The speed difference between the cage and axle shaft is half the difference of the road wheels, so compared with the shaft-to-shaft type, the shaft-to-cage unit must have a torque characteristic about three times greater to achieve the same locking effect.

The viscous coupling unit has been used for many years to limit the slip within a final drive differential. It is also commonly used in four-wheel drive vehicle applications. The viscous coupling is used in conjunction with a central differential to control the drive transmitted to the front and rear axles.

Note: Further information on four-wheel drive operation is provided in the four-wheel drive sections 3.6. And 3.22 within this chapter.

3.21 REAR AXLE CONSTRUCTION

3.21.1 Dead and live axles

Although most modern vehicles make use of independent rear suspension, some vehicles may still be fitted with a solid axle. Solid axles are often referred to as being either 'dead' or 'live', and there are fundamental differences between the two types.

A dead axle only has to support the weight of the vehicle. A live axle has to support the weight of the vehicle and contain a gear and shaft mechanism to drive the road wheels. Such axles are normally used in commercial vehicle applications.

3.21.2 Axle casing construction

The type of axle casing dictates the method that must be used to remove the final drive assembly. Axle casings are normally of either the banjo or carrier type.

Note: In the past a type known as a split, or trumpet casing was occasionally used. The three types of casing are shown in Figure 3.130.

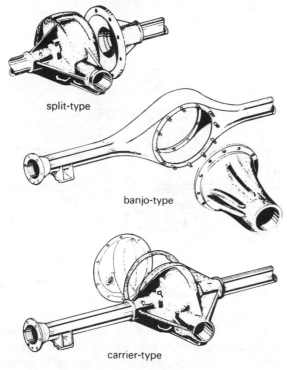

Figure 3.130 Types of rear axle casing

Banjo axle

The tubular axle section is built up of steel pressings, which are welded together and suitably strengthened to resist the bending load. The centre of the casing, combined with the axle tube on one side, resembles a banjo, hence its name.

The final drive assembly, which is mounted in a detachable malleable iron housing, is fitted in the centre of the axle and secured by a ring of bolts to the axle casing. When the final drive assembly is in position, the axle shafts are slid in from the road wheel end of the casing.

On some banjo axles a domed plate is bolted to the rear face of the casing. Removal of this plate allows the final drive gears to be inspected and, in cases where the axle shaft is secured to the differential, the access point enables the axle shaft to be unlocked from the sun gear (side gear).

A lubricant level plug, set at a height about one third up the crown wheel, is screwed into the domed cover or

the final drive housing. The correct level is normally set just below the axle tubes, so lubrication of the hub bearings is from the splash caused by rotation of the crown wheel.

Note: Overfilling of the axle casing should be avoided, excessive oil can swamp the axle shaft oil seals and cause oil to enter the brakes which are fitted at either end of the axle casing.

When in operation the final drive assembly becomes hot and the rotation of the gears produces pressure, so some form of air vent is provided to release the pressure in the axle casing, which prevents oil being forced past the oil seals.

Carrier axle

The carrier type of axle casing is more rigid than the banjo type casing and is often used to support a hypoid gear final drive unit. The carrier type of axle is therefore fitted to vehicles carrying heavy loads, such as commercial vehicles.

The final drive assembly is mounted directly in a rigid, malleable cast iron carrier, into which the axle tubes are pressed and welded. Extra rigidity is obtained by using reinforcing ribs that extend from the pinion nose to the main carrier casting. Access to the final drive gear is by means of a domed plate at the rear of the casing.

Note that if repair of the final drive assembly is necessary, the use of specialized tools may be required to remove and refit the assembly.

3.21.3 Axle shafts

The axle shaft transmits the drive from the differential sun wheel to the rear hub.

The various types of axle shaft and hub assemblies can be compared by considering the stresses and forces imparted on the shaft.

Figure 3.131 shows a line sketch of a simple axle shaft that is subjected to:

- torsional stress due to driving and braking torque (Figure 3.131a)
- shear stress due to the weight of the vehicle (Figure 3.131b)
- bending stress due to the weight of the vehicle (Figure 3.131c)
- tensile and compressive stress due to cornering forces.

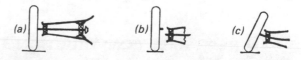

Figure 3.131 The effect of load on a simple axle shaft

The manner in which the axle shafts are supported can be categorised into three main groups. The type used will depend on the stresses to which the shaft is subjected during the vehicle's use. Support may be:

- semi-floating
- three-quarter floating
- fully-floating.

Semi-floating

Figure 3.132a shows a typical mounting of an axle shaft suitable for light cars. A single bearing at the hub end is fitted between the axle shaft and the axle casing, so the shaft will have to resist all the stresses previously mentioned. To reduce the risk of fracture at the hub end, the shaft diameter is increased (a fracture of the shaft at the hub end would allow the wheel to fall off). Any increase must be gradual, since a sudden change in cross-sectional area would produce a stress-raiser and increase the risk of failure due to fatigue. (Fatigue may be defined as breakage due to continual alteration of the stress in the material.)

Although the final-drive oil level is considerably lower than the axle shaft, the large amount of 'splash' causes the lubricant to work along the shaft. To prevent the oil entering the brake unit, a sealing arrangement is used which normally consists of an oil seal fitted at the hub end of the shaft. The lip of the seal is positioned towards the final drive.

Fully-floating

A fully-floating axle shaft is generally fitted on vehicles where torque and axle loads are great. The fully-floating axle shaft is fitted to many four-wheel drive vehicles and commercial vehicles that are subjected to high stresses and loads.

The construction shown in Figure 3.132c consists of an independently mounted hub, which rotates on two bearings widely spaced on the axle casing. This

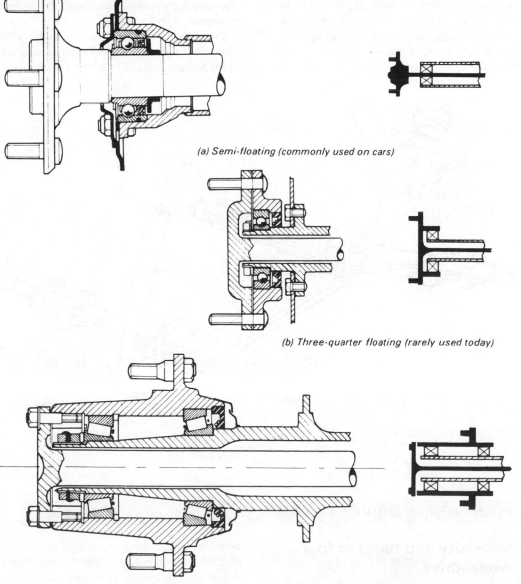

(a) Semi-floating (commonly used on cars)

(b) Three-quarter floating (rarely used today)

(c) Fully floating (commonly used on heavy vehicles)

Figure 3.132 Rear hub construction

arrangement relieves the shaft of all stresses except torsional, so the construction is very strong. Studs connecting the shaft to the hub transmit the drive.

Note: It may be possible to withdraw the shaft from the axle without jacking up the vehicle by removing the nuts on these studs.

Three-quarter floating

Having defined the semi- and the fully-floating shaft arrangements, any alternative between the two may be regarded as a three-quarter floating shaft.

Figure 3.132b shows a construction which has a single bearing mounted between the hub and the casing. The main shear stress on the shaft is eliminated but all other stresses still have to be resisted. This type of arrangement is typically used on light commercial vehicles.

Axle shaft material

A tough, hard material must be used to withstand the various stresses, resist spline wear and provide good resistance to fatigue. A medium carbon-alloy steel containing such elements as nickel, chromium and molybdenum is the usual choice.

3.21.4 Front live axle

Many four-wheel drive vehicles are fitted with a live front axle (Figure 3.133). The axle is similar in construction to the rear axle previously described, incorporating the final drive gears and the differential gears. The axle shafts pass from the differential to the wheel hubs.

To allow the vehicle to be steered, it is necessary for the front wheels to swivel, therefore the drive also needs to be transmitted through the steered angle. A universal joint is fitted to each end of the axle shaft, which allows the drive to be transmitted through the steered angle. The universal joints used are a form of constant velocity joint. The CV joints are housed within a ball that forms the end of the axle casing. The ball supports the hub assembly with the use of swivel pins at the top and bottom. The swivel pins allow the hub assembly to move from side to side horizontally (allowing for steering movement), but prevent vertical movement.

Four-wheel drive vehicles fitted with a live axle are generally fitted with fully-floating shafts, which allow for high stress loads to be exerted on the axle.

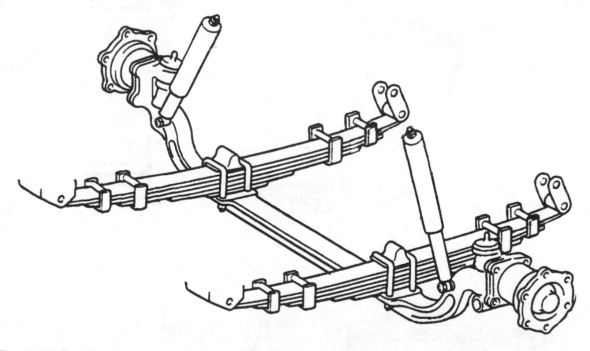

Figure 3.133 Front live axle construction

3.22 FOUR-WHEEL DRIVE SYSTEMS

3.22.1 Necessity and types of four-wheel drive

Compared with traditional front- or rear-wheel drive vehicles, a four-wheel drive vehicle can transmit drive to all four wheels unlike most light cars and commercial vehicles. Four-wheel drive vehicles are often referred to as 4 × 4 ('four by four') vehicles.

There are two main traction difficulties with a two-wheel drive (4 × 2) vehicle. These are:

1 Loss of traction during cross-country operation.
2 Loss of adhesion during acceleration.

The intended use of the vehicle governs the type of 4 × 4 drive system that is fitted by the manufacturer.

Vehicles that are to be driven both 'on-road' and 'off- road' (i.e. vehicles in the 'Land-Rover' category) are designed to work efficiently both on and off the highway. Older types of these vehicles provided two-wheel drive for use on 'hard' surfaces (i.e. normal road conditions). The driver would select four-wheel drive, to provide traction for cross-country work where the vehicle is likely to encounter muddy surfaces that could lead to a complete loss of traction from the two driving wheels. Such selectable four-wheel drive is often referred to as a 'part-time' four-wheel drive system.

Modern on- and off-road vehicles are usually fitted with a 'full-time' or permanent four-wheel drive system. The four-wheel drive system is permanently engaged and is therefore used during all terrains encountered. Modern high-performance cars that are built for highway and loose gravel road conditions also use a permanent four-wheel drive system. The total weight of the vehicle is spread over all of the driving wheels, which increases the tractive effort that can be applied to the car; as a result a high rate of acceleration can be achieved. Providing permanent four-wheel drive also improves the handling and gives extra safety. A full-time four-wheel drive system cannot be disengaged to allow two-wheel drive only.

Each vehicle manufacturer uses a slightly different operating system, however the principle of operation is the same.

Cross-country operation

The limitation of a conventional two-wheel drive vehicle is soon appreciated when it encounters the rough terrain and the muddy conditions, normally associated with cross-country. In these slippery conditions the driving wheels at the rear of the vehicle soon lose their adhesion between the tyre and the surface on which the tyre is placed (the muddy surface). Consequently the traction available is insufficient to provide drive. The conventional differential adds to these difficulties since if the adhesion of one of the driving wheels is lost, the drive to the other wheel is generally too low to propel the vehicle. Although a differential locking device (or limited-slip differential) reduces the chance of this, there are still many occasions when both driving wheels are rendered ineffective. It is to overcome this situation that four-wheel drive is provided – when either front or rear axles lose traction the other axle maintains a drive to move the vehicle out of the difficulty.

Hard surface operation

Tractive and braking efforts are limited by the adhesive force at the road wheels; this force is calculated from:

$$\text{Adhesive force} = \text{Coefficient of friction} \times \text{Load on wheel}$$

Considering this expression, it can be seen that the total weight of the vehicle must be fully utilised if the maximum adhesive force is to be obtained.

When only two driving wheels are provided, the loss of 'weight' on the non-driving wheels proportionally reduces the adhesive force; as a result the maximum tractive effort that can be safely applied to the vehicle is limited.

Beyond the point where the tractive effort equals the adhesive force, the driving wheel spins. This spinning not only limits the rate of acceleration, but can also lead to loss of control of the vehicle with dangerous results. This effect also relates to braking; skidding occurs beyond the point where the braking force equals the adhesive force.

By spreading the driving (and braking) forces over all of the wheels, greater safety is achieved. In addition to providing this force distribution, using a device for sensing the approach of wheelspin or slip and then adjusting the effort accordingly, leads to even greater safety.

Cars of this type are not designed for 'serious' off-road use, but they do give the all-weather driver an added sense of security when driving in icy or wet conditions.

One of the first people to appreciate the importance of 'all-wheel drive' was Harry Ferguson, the inventor of the lightweight tractor. It was in 1954 when he took out a patent, the 'Ferguson Formula' (FF), and this was used on the Jensen car in the early 1960s (see section 3.22.4).

3.22.2 Part-time four-wheel drive

Figure 3.134 shows a typical layout for a four-wheel drive vehicle. Drive is transmitted from the engine through a conventional gearbox, either manual or automatic.

Mounted behind the main gearbox is a transfer gearbox. This unit divides the output drive from the gearbox between the front and rear axles via the propeller shafts. The transfer box for off-road vehicles normally incorporates an extra set of gears that provides either a high ratio, which is used for normal road conditions, or a very low ratio which can be used for extreme conditions such as steep gradients requiring very low speeds with high torque.

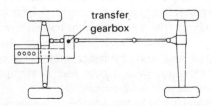

Figure 3.134 A part-time four-wheel drive system

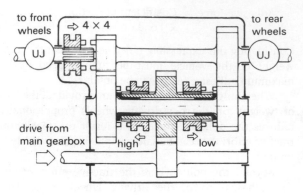

Figure 3.135 Transfer box
The transfer box contains a sliding dog clutch, which can be moved to engage drive between to the front wheels (giving 4WD). Additionally, the transfer box shown has the option to select a high or low ratio to suit different driving conditions. Note that the selection of 4WD and high or low ratios are carried out manually by the driver, but only when the vehicle is stationary.

The driver uses the main gearbox gear lever to select the appropriate gear in the normal manner. A part-time four-wheel drive system enables the driver to select either two-wheel drive or four-wheel drive. The transfer box is generally fitted with two control levers; one lever for selecting either two-wheel drive or four-wheel drive and the other to give either a 'high' or 'low' gear ratio.

Drive to the front wheels is transmitted via a final drive, differential and drive shafts. Steering movement of the front wheels is achieved by fitting extra universal joints at the wheel end of the drive shafts and, in order to overcome vibration, a CV joint is generally used.

A simple part-time four-wheel drive arrangement should not be operated with four-wheel drive selected on a hard surface (e.g. a tarmac road) because of the risk of transmission 'wind-up'. When a vehicle using this arrangement turns a corner the mean speed of the front wheels is higher than that of the rear wheels, so the speed difference causes the propeller shafts to deflect, winding up the transmission, a similar effect to that of winding up an elastic band. After a period of time the wind up of the transmission can increase the tyre wear because the tyres attempt to release the wound up energy stored in the transmission. In extreme cases this wind up of the transmission will cause stress damage to the transmission components.

Part-time four-wheel drive vehicles are sometimes fitted with locking hubs; these units are fitted to the front axle hub and allow the transmission to be engaged or disengaged from the front wheels. If the front wheels are not being driven and the hubs remain engaged, the rotation of the front wheels drives the axle driveshafts, differential and front propeller shaft. This consumes energy, resulting in a higher fuel consumption and additional wear of components.

With locking hubs fitted to the front axle hubs, their disengagement allows each front wheel to rotate

without driving the transmission components. Each of the front hubs is fitted with a dog clutch or sliding sleeve, when disengaged the drive cannot be transmitted in either direction. When the hubs are engaged drive is reinstated to the front wheels when four-wheel drive is selected. These locking hubs are usually manually operated and therefore require engagement before the vehicle is driven on slippery surfaces, but some are automatically operated when the driver selects four-wheel drive.

3.22.3 Full-time four-wheel drive

To enable a four-wheel drive system to be used on hard surfaces, a third differential is required. The third differential is normally incorporated in the transfer box assembly, often referred to as the 'centre' differential (Figure 3.136). Four-wheel drive vehicles fitted with a third differential are referred to as having 'full-time four-wheel drive, or 'permanent four-wheel drive'. If a centre differential is fitted to a vehicle designed for cross-country work, it is necessary to lock the centre differential when slippery conditions are encountered. Without this centre differential lock, if one wheel loses adhesion the vehicle would be immobilised by the operation of the centre differential.

If a conventional differential is used, the differential is locked using a dog clutch. If the traction is lost at either the front or rear wheels, the differential lock is engaged. The locking mechanism is either operated by the driver with a lever or is electronically controlled by an electrical solenoid.

It is now common for full-time drive systems to use a viscous coupling type of differential (Figure 3.137). In a similar manner to the action of a viscous coupling used in a limited-slip differential (described in section 3.20.4) the viscous coupling allows some difference in

Figure 3.136 Full-time four-wheel drive system

speed between front and rear propeller shafts, but if there is a substantial difference in speed (such as when the wheels on one axle lose their grip or traction), the coupling will effectively lock, thus maintaining power to those wheels that have maintained traction. Also refer to section 3.22.5.

The transfer box fitted to an off-road vehicle is usually equipped with high and low ratio gears. These additional ratios are achieved by the use of conventional helical gears or an epicyclic gear train. Engagement of each ratio is achieved with a dog clutch. An increasing number of four-wheel drive vehicles are fitted with an automatic gearbox, together with additional electronic controls. Such vehicles can be fitted with high and low ratios that are obtained through the use of an epicyclic gear set, the high and low ratios being changed by an electric motor controlled by the transmission ECU.

3.22.4 Ferguson Formula (FF)

Figure 3.138 shows a typical FF layout as applied to a Jensen car. A transfer box, containing the sensing mechanism, is adjacent to a centre (third) differential, and propeller shafts transmit the drive to front and rear axles. A Maxaret unit prevents the possibility of all wheels locking during braking. Driven by the transmission it senses the mean deceleration of front and rear road wheels and just before the wheel locks the hydraulic pressure to the brake is relieved.

The basis of the Ferguson control system is a master differential and two, one-way, multi-disc clutches. The unit divides the torque in the ratio of 37% to the front wheels and 63% to the rear wheels, besides allowing for a speed variation between front and rear wheels.

The differential is a simple epicyclic gear train, which has the input shaft driving the planet carrier, the

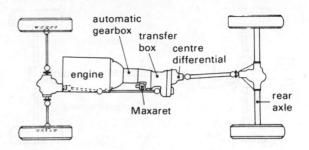

Figure 3.138 Ferguson Formula transmission layout (Jensen)

annulus and sun being connected to rear and front wheels, respectively. Application of a force to the centre of the planet gives equal force at the annulus and at the sun. Since the force at the annulus is acting over a larger radius, the torque is greater, so this member is connected to the rear wheels.

The use of a differential allows a speed variation to take place between the front wheels and the rear wheels. In this arrangement the difference in speed between the output shaft and the planet carrier causes the planet to rotate around the slower-moving gear, a motion which speeds up the other member.

The extent of this speed variation is limited by the control unit and in this particular design the front wheels are only permitted to over-run the rear ones by 16.5%, whereas the rear wheels can only over-run to the extent of 5.5%. Once this limit is reached a multi-disc clutch locks the planet carrier (input shaft) to the sun wheel (front output shaft), so the centre differential is put out of action. This action can occur during acceleration or when the vehicle is braking.

3.22.5 Four-wheel drive using a viscous coupling

Unless some form of control is used to limit the action of a central differential, the loss of adhesion at any one wheel will cause the vehicle to become immobile. Previously this was achieved on the conventional differential by the use of a dog clutch fitted to the centre differential lock. If a central differential is not fitted, driveline components will be stressed because of transmission wind-up.

A compromise is achieved by using a viscous coupling. This can be arranged in one of two ways: it can be used either as a control unit to limit the speed difference between front and rear wheels or as a viscous transmission to connect the front drive system to the rear when conditions demand it.

Four-wheel system derived from the standard rear-wheel drive

The parallel axis of the engine makes it necessary to use a transfer gearbox; this is positioned behind the main gearbox (Figure 3.139). If this layout is used, an

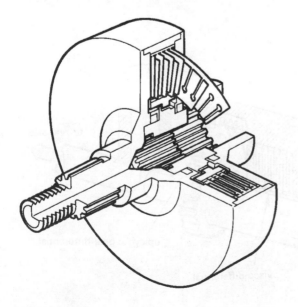

Figure 3.137 Centre differential fitted with a viscous coupling

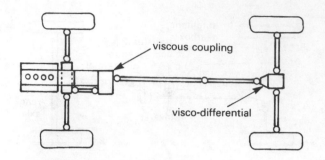

Figure 3.139 A 4 × 4 layout – a longitudinal engine (viewed from the underside)

epicyclic gear set is used as a central differential and a viscous coupling to control the speed difference between the front and rear wheels (Figure 3.140).

The input shaft to the differential is connected to the planet carrier and the front- and rear-wheel output shafts are linked to the sun wheel and annulus respectively. This gives a torque split between the front and rear axles of 34:66, which is a typical proportion for this type of car.

At the front, a standard differential is fitted, the drive is transmitted to the front wheels with the use of drive shafts fitted with CV joints.

Note: Compared with a rear-wheel drive vehicle, the front axle steering geometry must be modified to take into account the different driving conditions i.e the front wheels are applying a driving force instead of being pushed by the vehicle movement.

The rear axle is driven in the normal manner; this includes a two-piece propeller shaft and a visco-differential.

On the four-wheel drive system shown (Figure 3.140), the power take-off to the offset output shaft, which connects with the front axle shaft, is by means of

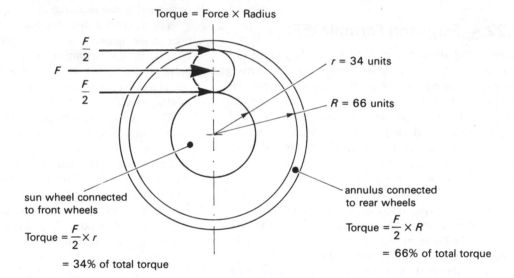

Torque = Force × Radius

r = 34 units

R = 66 units

sun wheel connected to front wheels

annulus connected to rear wheels

Torque = $\dfrac{F}{2} \times r$

= 34% of total torque

Torque = $\dfrac{F}{2} \times R$

= 66% of total torque

epicyclic differential to divide front/rear torque in the proportion 34/66

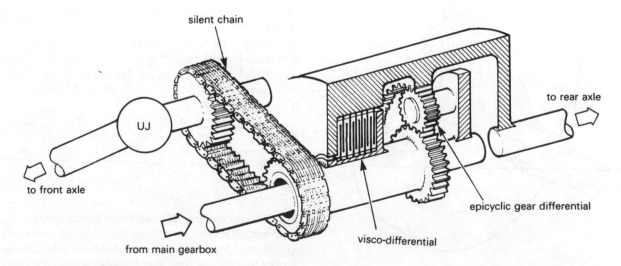

Figure 3.140 One type of transfer box system, as used by Ford

a silent chain. The viscous coupling is a shaft-to-shaft design (refer to section 3.20.4 for further information on viscous couplings). Connected 'between the axles' in this manner the coupling senses the speed differences between the axles, allowing a difference in torque twice that of the value transmitted by the coupling.

Control of drive by the coupling to the front and rear wheels varies with the operating conditions. At times when the mean speed of front and rear wheels is nearly equal, the coupling is ineffective, but as the speed difference increases, the coupling resistance, and associated locking, rise progressively.

Complete loss of adhesion at any wheel causes a large slip in the coupling; as a result the coupling exerts a high locking torque on the gears so as to maintain a drive to the wheels that are attempting to spin. Extended use of the coupling under maximum slip conditions would soon cause it to overheat, so to give it protection, the coupling is designed to go into the 'hump mode' (refer to section 3.20.4).

Four-wheel system derived from the front-wheel drive

The basic arrangement of the front wheel drive drive layout is comparatively easy to adapt to a 4 × 4 system because the relatively complex part of the assembly, namely the front drive layout and steering geometry, has already been developed.

Front-wheel drive cars normally use a transaxle, the drive for four-wheel drive purposes is taken from this transaxle unit, through a central differential to the rear wheels (Figure 3.141).

The torque distribution proportion varies with the make of car, but most front-wheel drive vehicles are small or medium in size. It depends on the weight distribution, in particular the location of the engine, and the characteristics that are desired. The front/rear proportion varies from about 56:44 to 35:65.

Most central differentials use an epicyclic gear set. This is controlled by a viscous coupling mounted in one of two ways:

- Shaft-to-shaft between take-offs to front and rear axles
- Between the input drive and take-off to either the front or rear axle.

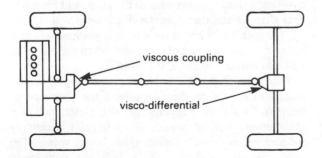

Figure 3.141 A 4 × 4 transverse engine

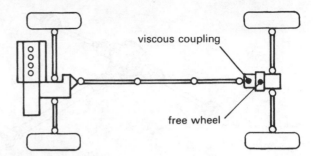

Figure 3.142 A 4 × 4 viscous transmission

Variable four-wheel drive

The variable 4 × 4 system achieves the benefits of four-wheel drive, but without the drawbacks of a permanently connected arrangement.

The viscous transmission layout shown in Figure 3.142 uses a propeller shaft and viscous coupling to interconnect the two axles. A central differential is unnecessary, but a freewheel is fitted in the rear axle final drive gear.

During normal operation, when the axle speeds are nearly equal, the coupling ensures that the rear wheels are only driven to a very limited extent, i.e. the vehicle behaves like a normal front-wheel drive car. But when the front wheels lose their adhesion, the difference in speed causes the coupling to make use of the rear wheels for propulsion.

The freewheel ensures that no drive is transmitted from the rear axle to the engine during overrun, so this feature makes the arrangement suitable for use with anti-lock brake systems. A freewheel locking device, operated by an electro-pneumatic system when reverse gear is selected, makes four-wheel drive available for reversing.

Another adaptation of a vehicle utilising a viscous coupling is shown in Figure 3.144. The transaxle (manual or automatic) provides the drive to an intermediate drive unit. The drive is transmitted to the front wheels through a differential. The intermediate drive unit transmits drive to the rear wheels via the propeller shaft.

A slightly higher final drive gear ratio is used to drive the rear wheels; under most conditions the power is transmitted through the front wheels as in a front wheel drive vehicle.

During vehicle over-run conditions, the rear wheels drive the propeller shaft at a slightly higher speed than that at which the intermediate drive unit drives the propeller shaft. A speed difference therefore exists between the front propeller shaft and the rear propeller shaft. A viscous coupling is located in the centre coupling of the propeller shaft that allows the two shafts to rotate at slightly different speeds. The viscous coupling offers little resistance to the speed difference of the two propeller shafts and therefore the drive is biased towards the front wheels, making this effectively a frontwheel drive vehicle.

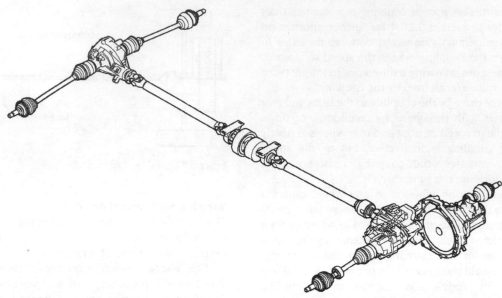

Figure 3.143 4 × 4 Land Rover Freelander

When the vehicle encounters slippery conditions and the front wheels lose traction, a large difference in speed exists between the front and rear propshafts. The large difference in speed between the two shafts causes the fluid (normally a silicon 'jelly') inside the viscous coupling to become agitated by the action of the discs.

The fluid within the viscous coupling is heated rapidly, changing the viscosity of the fluid into a jelly and expanding at the same time. The discs are forced closer together reducing slippage between the two shafts. When the speed difference between the two shafts is extreme, the viscous coupling will lock the two shafts together and drive is transmitted to the rear wheels.

When the conditions change and traction to the front road wheels is regained the shaft speeds are similar, allowing the fluid to cool and slip to occur between the two sets of plates in the viscous coupling, thus disconnecting drive from the back wheels.

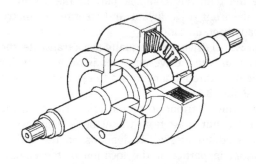

Figure 3.144 A 4 × 4 viscous coupling

3.23 CLUTCH ROUTINE MAINTENANCE

3.23.1 General maintenance

The clutch assembly and release mechanism requires little maintenance during the life of the clutch but there is the possibility of minor adjustments on some systems.

The life of the clutch depends on the use of the vehicle; the more frequently the clutch is used and the greater the power applied to the clutch when purposely being slipped, the greater the wear on the clutch components.

An example can be given of two similar vehicles driven under different conditions that will indicate the possible life of the clutch. A vehicle that is driven in an urban environment requires the frequent engagement and disengagement of the clutch each time it starts and stops, and during each gear change. Clutch wear will therefore be high. A vehicle driven on the motorway, yet covering a much greater overall distance, will have few gear changes and therefore the clutch wear will be low.

The manner in which the clutch is engaged will also affect its wear. Slipping of the clutch when pulling away will also reduce the life of the clutch.

The wear on the clutch driven plate linings, pressure plate and release mechanism affects the clutch pedal freeplay. Too little freeplay and the clutch will slip (promoting further wear), the freeplay normally reduces as the clutch driven plate lining wears. Too much freeplay and the clutch will not completely disengage creating difficult and stiff gear changes.

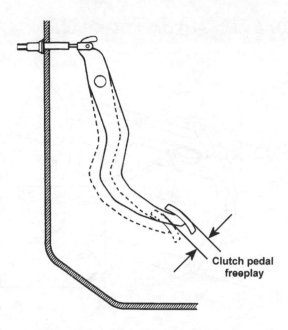

Figure 3.145 Clutch pedal freeplay and adjustment

Many clutch release mechanisms are self-adjusting so little or no maintenance is required. These types of mechanism are generally fitted with a self-adjusting cable mechanism that allows the length of the cable to alter as the clutch wears. For a hydraulic clutch release mechanism, the position of the hydraulic slave cylinder changes as the clutch wears.

Maintenance-free clutches allow a reduction in labour time during routine maintenance and therefore a reduction in cost to the vehicle owner.

Clutches without a self-adjustment mechanism require the clutch pedal freeplay to be checked and adjusted (if required) during maintenance.

3.23.2 Clutch pedal adjustments

The clutch pedal mechanism may allow the height of the pedal to be adjusted when it is fully released. To check this height, measure the distance from the floor (this may require the carpet and insulation to be moved) of the vehicle to the surface of the clutch pedal pad. The clutch pedal stop screw normally provides adjustment of the pedal height.

The pedal freeplay is usually checked by pushing the clutch pedal down using hand pressure and feeling the resistance of the pedal. Two differing levels of resistance should be felt, a slight resistance felt as the free play is taken up, and then as the release mechanism begins to act on the pressure plate, the resistance is felt to increase. The distance between the light pressure and the firm pressure required to depress the pedal is the freeplay, which should be as specified by the manufacturer. Generally this freeplay measurement is approximately 15–30 mm.

Adjustment of the pedal freeplay is provided by either adjusting the length of the outer cable (cable-operated clutches) or adjusting the length of either the master cylinder or slave cylinder push rods (hydraulically operated clutches).

3.23.3 Clutch maintenance

If the clutch is operated hydraulically, the level of clutch hydraulic fluid within the reservoir requires checking and topping up during routine maintenance.

If the level reduces slightly between maintenance schedules, the cause is probably the self-adjustment of the clutch release mechanism. If the level has reduced significantly, a possible leak exists in the hydraulic system and further investigation is required into the loss of fluid.

Always ensure that the reservoir is filled to the full mark, normally indicated on the side of the reservoir. The clutch reservoir is normally a separate component from the brake fluid reservoir, however because the same type of fluid is used for the clutch and brake hydraulic systems, the reservoir can be shared in some vehicles.

It is not normally possible to lubricate the clutch release mechanism components due to the inaccessibility of the linkage, therefore the mechanism is lubricated while the clutch is assembled during vehicle production or repair.

Routine maintenance should conclude with a road test, which should include checking the operation of the clutch. The clutch should be checked for the following faults: slip, drag, judder and fierceness of operation.

Figure 3.146 Topping up the reservoir to the full mark

3.24 ROUTINE MAINTENANCE OF MANUAL AND AUTOMATIC GEARBOX

3.24.1 General checks

The gearbox normally requires little maintenance except the checking of the oil level, checking for oil leaks (i.e. from the input and output shafts) and checking the selection of gears during a road test.

Before checking the oil level, ensure that the vehicle is placed on a level surface; a vehicle lift is ideal as this normally allows access to the underside of the vehicle to check for leaks.

Note: The gearbox oil and surrounding components i.e. exhaust, may be very hot; care should be taken to avoid personal injury during procedures to change and check the oil level.

3.24.2 Manual gearbox

The oil in a gearbox provides lubrication for the gears and bearings, it is therefore subject to high pressure as the oil is forced out between the gears when they rotate. The gears rotate at a very high speed when the vehicle is driven and therefore the oil also acts as a coolant, removing heat from the gears and bearings.

Some vehicle manufacturers recommend that the gearbox oil is changed during certain maintenance schedules, other manufacturers indicate that only checking and topping up of the oil level is necessary during routine maintenance.

The oil level is usually checked by removing a filler plug situated on the side of the gearbox; the height of the plug on the side of the gearbox casing determines the volume of oil contained within the gearbox. To drain the oil from the gearbox, a drain plug is normally fitted at the bottom of the gearbox casing.

The correct grade of oil should be used to refill or top up the gearbox; the incorrect grade of oil can lead to the premature failure of the gears, bearings and selector hubs or difficulty in selecting gears during driving.

3.24.3 Automatic gearboxes

The oil in an automatic gearbox performs several functions like in a manual gearbox; the oil lubricates the epicyclic gear trains and bearings. An automatic gearbox includes multi-plate, wet-type clutches and brake bands, which require to be immersed in oil to prevent premature wear.

The gearbox oil also acts as a hydraulic operating fluid, providing hydraulic pressure for the valves, pistons within the gearbox and torque converter . A great amount of heat is generated within an automatic gearbox and therefore the oil acts as a coolant to dissipate heat from the internal components of the gearbox. An oil cooler is usually fitted to the lubrication system of an automatic gearbox to aid this cooling.

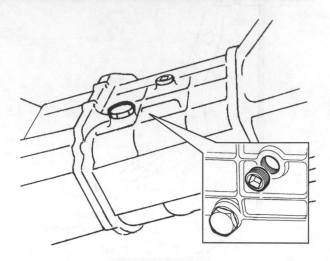

Figure 3.147 Manual gearbox level check and filler plug

Most manufacturers recommend the automatic gearbox oil be changed periodically as it deteriorates over a period of time and loses some of its lubricating properties. Wearing of the clutches and brake bands will also contaminate the oil with abrasive materials from those components.

A drain plug is normally provided in the sump of the gearbox, although some gearboxes require the removal of the sump to drain the gearbox oil. Automatic gearboxes are fitted with a fine filter located within the gearbox, which is usually part of the oil pick-up situated in the sump of the gearbox. The oil filter requires the removal of the gearbox sump so the changing of the oil is a necessity during this operation.

Checking of the automatic gearbox oil level should be carried out with the gearbox at normal operating temperature and with the engine running. Note that the volume of oil required to fill the gearbox to the full mark will change as the oil temperature changes.

Many manufacturers specify that before the oil level is checked the oil should be at a specified temperature. If necessary allow the engine to run for a period of time or alternatively the vehicle should be driven for a short distance to allow the oil to reach a suitable temperature.

The torque converter is only full of oil when the engine is running so the gearbox oil level should be checked with the engine running. The level of the gearbox is usually checked with a dipstick, which is sufficiently long to reach from the engine compartment into the gearbox, allowing the gearbox oil level to be checked without having to raise the vehicle from the floor. The dipstick is normally marked 'automatic gearbox' (or similar) to avoid confusion with the engine oil dipstick. Alternatively the level plug may be incorporated within the sump plug. Details of checking

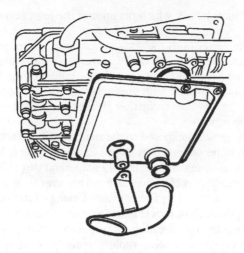

Figure 3.148 Automatic gearbox oil filter

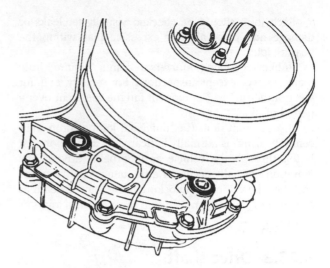

Figure 3.149 Four-wheel drive gearbox and transfer box

the level are detailed in the vehicle's workshop manual.

Before checking the oil level, select all gears with the use of the selector lever and return the lever to the Park position. Always fill the gearbox oil level to the full mark.

Many transaxles, front-wheel drive gearboxes incorporating the final drive differential, are filled with two different types of oil. The main automatic gearbox is filled with automatic transmission oil, while the differential is filled with final drive grade oil. The two oils are prevented from mixing by the fitting of a seal to the output shaft of the automatic gearbox.

3.24.4 Four-wheel drive gearboxes

If the gearbox is part of a four-wheel drive transmission, the transfer box which distributes the drive between the front and rear axles, is normally filled separately to the main gearbox. The transfer box may have a separate oil level filler plug and therefore requires checking independently of the main gearbox.

The transfer box may also use a different grade of oil to the main gearbox. It is therefore essential to check the grade of oil required, before adding new oil to the gearbox and transfer box.

3.25 ROUTINE MAINTENANCE OF PROP SHAFT AND DRIVE SHAFT

3.25.1 General maintenance requirement

When the vehicle is driven, each universal joint moves through an angle as the drive shaft or prop shaft rotates. It is therefore necessary to provide and maintain a small quantity of lubricant within the joint to prevent premature wear or seizure. Older vehicles, and some modern commercial vehicles, may be fitted with lubrication nipples for the joints; the manufacturer's information should therefore be checked.

Most modern light vehicles have universal joints that are sealed for life, and unless the protective gaiters and covers are damaged there should be no need to add lubricant.

3.25.2 Prop shaft

Cross-type joints, (i.e. Hooke-type joints) are widely used for prop shaft universal joints. The constant

variation in angle as the shaft rotates necessitates the need for joint bearings to be filled with a suitable lubricant, to reduce the level of friction. Insufficient lubricant will increase the wear of these joints and cause excessive vibration and noise.

The universal joints are either fitted with a nipple to refill the bearing with grease during routine maintenance or sealed during manufacture and therefore lubricated for the life of the bearing. Grease is added to the joint with the use of a grease gun. The gun connects with the nipple and when operated, the grease is forced from the gun into the joint.

If the joint is fitted with a nipple, ensure that the correct grade of grease is added to the bearing; different types of joint require various grades of grease so refer to manufacture specification. The prop shaft is often fitted with a sliding joint, which allows the prop shaft to alter in length as the vehicle is being driven. These sliding joints are lubricated with grease; once again the joint may be fitted with a grease nipple or sealed for life.

Each joint should be checked visually for leaks or damage and physically for excessive play within the bearing joint.

Rubber coupling universal joints require little maintenance, except inspections for security and for wear of the rubber. Component fatigue can occur over a period of time.

A prop shaft fault (i.e. universal joint or prop shaft centre bearing) is normally indicated by a vibration that is felt through the vehicle as it is being driven. The vibration normally occurs at a frequency relative to the speed of the vehicle. A knocking noise may be heard as the power is initially transmitted through worn joints or bearings.

3.25.3 Drive shaft

Drive shaft joints are of the constant velocity type and allow for the movement of the suspension, and when fitted to front-wheel drive vehicles, allow for the wheels to be steered.

Constant velocity joints require lubrication with grease, typically a molybdenum-based grease. The grease is prevented from escaping from the joint with a rubber bellows-type gaiter (sometimes referred to as a 'drive shaft boot'), which fits around the joint and drive shaft.

The gaiter both prevents grease from escaping and also prevents the ingress of water and dirt from the road, which would cause premature failure of the joint. The joint is packed with grease before the fitting of the gaiter and requires no further grease to be added during routine servicing.

The gaiter is exposed to the road conditions and can therefore be damaged by debris as the vehicle is being driven, allowing the grease to escape and dirt to enter the joint. The rubber can also perish over a period of time, encouraged by the constant flexing of the rubber during drive shaft movement. Once the grease has been expelled by the rotation of the shaft, the constant velocity joint will wear rapidly, leading to premature failure and breakage of the drive shaft joint. It is therefore important that each of the constant velocity rubber gaiters are inspected for damage, leakage and security during routine maintenance.

If the constant velocity joint becomes worn, a rapid knocking noise is normally heard when the vehicle is driven, especially when the joint transmits the drive through a large angle, i.e. when the steering is turned to the full-lock position.

3.26　CLUTCH FAULT DIAGNOSIS

3.26.1 Clutch release mechanism

The release mechanism components are usually made from metal; but the points of contacts between them are generally separated by bushes, typically nylon or plastic. These bushes help to reduce noise and the friction between the components when the clutch is operated.

With repeated use of the clutch, the lubrication of the release mechanism linkage slowly reduces, increasing the friction between the components. The increase in friction is normally felt through the clutch pedal as an increase in effort required by the driver to depress the clutch pedal and engage the clutch.

A cable-operated clutch can be used as an example of the increased friction of the clutch release mechanism. With a cable-operated clutch, the inner cable and outer cables are separated by a nylon sleeve, which acts as a lubricant between the two cables. If the sleeve becomes worn, the friction between the two cables increases and the effort required to depress the clutch pedal rises. A partially worn nylon sleeve can also give a 'notchy' feel as the pedal is depressed.

3.26.2 Clutch assembly

Due to the loads and forces exerted on the clutch by the engine and transmission during engagement and disengagement, various faults can occur within the clutch assembly (driven plate, clutch pressure plate and release mechanism).

There are four main clutch faults:

1 slip
2 drag or spin
3 judder
4 fierceness.

Slip symptoms
- During acceleration, the engine speed increases without giving a corresponding increase in vehicle speed.
- Smell of burning driven plate lining material.
- In very bad cases the vehicle will not drive up steep hills.

Possible causes
Any defect that allows insufficient pressure being applied to the clutch plate friction surfaces.

Such defects include:

- Insufficient free pedal movement.
- Worn clutch driven plate facings.
- Partial seizure of pedal linkage (including slave cylinder) or fouling of the pedal so as to prevent the linkage returning to the fully engaged position.

- Oil-contaminated facings. (**Note:** The source of oil leakage *must* be identified; usual indication of crankshaft rear oil seal of gearbox input shaft oil seal failure.)
- Defective pressure plate, i.e. broken spring(s) or partially seized mechanism.

Spin or drag symptoms

Spin is generally associated with a design fault of the driven plate and drag is due to a defect that could develop during the clutch life. Since the symptoms are very similar, both faults are often grouped together.

- Difficulty in engaging first gear or reverse gear from neutral; a 'grating' noise is normally heard while selecting reverse gear.
- Vehicle jolts when changing gear with the vehicle in motion.
- In very bad cases, the vehicle will continue to move even when the clutch pedal is fully depressed.

Possible causes

Any defect that prevents the clean separation of the driven plate from both driving surfaces. Such defects include:

- Excessive free pedal movement caused by the need for adjustment. Lack of fluid within the hydraulic operating system, or air in the fluid.
- Fouling or wear of the linkage such that the pedal cannot be fully depressed.
- Oil-contaminated facings causing one face to stick to a driving surface.
- Defective driven plate, buckled plate or seizure on splines. The driven plate can seize on the gearbox input shaft splines if the vehicle is not used for a period of time.
- Misalignment of friction faces.
- Partially-seized, or collapsed, spigot bearing.

Judder symptoms

A severe, low-frequency vibration, which normally occurs when the clutch is released, while the vehicle is moving from stationary.

Possible causes

Any defect that prevents the smooth engagement of the clutch. Such defects include:

- Jerky pedal operation: sticking cable or slip/grip movement of a pivot.
- Excessive engine movement during the take-up of the drive. Note that a defective engine mounting can cause this fault. Wear in the drive line or suspension points can also be the cause.
- Oil-contaminated facings such that the slip/grip take-up action is amplified.
- A defective pressure plate. Often this is due to high friction in regions where the plate should move smoothly through the cover.
- Misalignment of friction faces.
- Defective driven plate: broken springs in the hub or a partially sheared plate.
- Defective diaphragm spring causing an imbalance in the clamping force of the pressure plate.

Fierceness symptoms

A sudden engagement of the clutch, felt as a jolt through the vehicle even though the clutch pedal is released gradually.

Possible causes

Any defect that allows the clutch take-up to be faster than the movement of the pedal. Such defects include:

- Partial seizure of the pedal linkage or contamination of fluid in the hydraulic operating system. These defects produce an erratic movement of the pressure plate.
- An oil-contaminated driven plate.
- Misalignment of the friction faces.

Clutch bearing noise symptoms

When the engine is running and the clutch pedal is depressed, a bearing noise is heard. The bearing noise disappears when the clutch pedal is released.

Possible causes

- Clutch release bearing noise. Over a period of time, the release bearing wears, producing a noise as pressure is applied to the bearing during clutch disengagement. Incorrect clutch freeplay adjustment will promote bearing wear.
- Worn spigot-bearing noise. This is usually heard as a whining noise. The spigot bearing is situated in the end of the crankshaft and supports the gearbox primary shaft when the clutch is disengaged.

3.27 MANUAL GEARBOX FAULT DIAGNOSIS

3.27.1 General diagnosis

The gearbox transmits the power produced by the engine to the driven wheels via various gear ratios. Each gear ratio and its components are therefore subject to the extreme forces. These components occasionally become faulty over a period of time.

The faults can range from difficulty in gear selection or engagement (either when the vehicle is stationary or moving) through to various noises caused by rotational of components and meshing of gears.

On most vehicles, there is little that can be carried out by way of adjustment; however, some vehicles do have a form of adjustment for the selector linkage.

It is sometimes necessary to align the gear linkage fitted to the vehicle to that of the gearbox; this is normally only necessary when the gearbox has been removed or the gear linkage has been replaced.

To diagnose a gearbox fault accurately, the conditions during which the fault occurs should be taken into account. A road test, if possible, can be used to recreate the fault and should include driving the vehicle in all gears and at various vehicle and engine speeds, as well as varying the engine load. If the fault can be tracked to a single component within the gearbox, the repair time can be reduced, although while dismantling the gearbox it is usual to inspect other components within the gearbox for wear.

Example

If possible identify whether a fault or noise occurs when a particular gear is selected. If a ticking noise is only apparent when second gear is selected, the fault probably exists with either second gear or its corresponding gear on the lay-gear cluster.

The vehicle should be road tested after the repairs to ensure that the repairs have been carried out correctly.

Table 3.4 highlights some typical gearbox faults and their possible causes.

3.27.2 Common faults and their causes

Table 3.4 Manual gearbox fault table

Fault	Cause
1 Gear whine	a Lack of oil
	b Gear-tooth wear
	c Bearing wear
	d Shaft misalignment
2 'Knocking' or 'ticking'	a Chipped gear tooth
	b Foreign matter wedged between gear teeth
	c Defective bearing
3 Jumping out of gear	a Defective selector detent (e.g. broken spring)
	b Shaft misalignment due to worn bearings
	c Worn gear teeth
4 Gear fails to select	a Incorrect adjustment between gear stick and selector
	b Defective selector

3.28   AUTOMATIC GEARBOX FAULT DIAGNOSIS

3.28.1 General diagnosis

Due to the complexity of an automatic transmission, most manufacturers provide literature which contains suitable test procedures for the diagnosis of a wide range of faults. The manufacturer's fault diagnosis literature should be consulted if a fault, other than the simple ones listed here, is evident.

Before following any automatic gearbox test procedures, the oil level and the condition of the oil should be checked. The oil level should be checked under the manufacturer's stated conditions e.g. vehicle parked on a level surface with the gearbox at the correct operating temperature and engine running.

The condition of the oil should be noted; if the oil is dirty or contains particles of clutch or brake band friction material it indicates a possible failure of the clutches or brake bands and associated hydraulic components.

3.28.2 Common faults and their causes

Regular servicing of the gearbox should avoid many of the problems listed. If a fault is still apparent then a symptom chart can be used to identify the cause of a fault in the areas shown in Table 3.5.

Table 3.5 Automatic gearbox fault table

Area	Cause	Fault
Fluid	Low level	Starvation of the pump prevents the hydraulic system from operating correctly; faults range from non-engagement of gears to erratic operation.
	High level	Governor strikes oil surface, so change speeds are affected.
	Poor quality	Rough gear changes. If oil is contaminated with grit particles, then a valve may stick; the resulting fault is related to the part of the system controlled by the valve.
Selector lever	Incorrect adjustment	Some gears, particularly those at the end of the travel, will not select. (Lever should be adjusted when it is at mid-point of selector range.)
Throttle cable	Incorrect adjustment	Road speed at which changes take place will be either too high or too low.
Starter inhibitor	Incorrect adjustment	Starter will be active in positions other than P and N.

If the oil is at the correct level and is clean (normally a bright reddish colour) and the particular fault is not identified from Table 3.5, a test programme similar to the one detailed below should be carried out (always follow manufacturers' guidelines).

Test sequence

1 *Road test* – follow the procedure suggested by the manufacturer.
2 *Stall test* – a stall test checks the torque converter for stator slip, and the brake bands and clutches for slip. The stall test must not be carried out for an excessive period of time to avoid overheating the gearbox oil and components. Additional information on the procedure of a stall test is detailed below.
3 *Pressure test* – pressure take-off points are provided so that a pressure gauge can be used to check the pressure in the lines under given conditions.

3.28.3 Stall test

The unidirectional clutch (freewheel) is the main mechanical component which can produce the faulty operation of the torque converter. A fault with the freewheel can give rise to a:

- *Slipping stator* – causes the fluid to enter the pump at the incorrect angle; therefore full torque multiplication cannot be obtained. This fault is detected by a stall test.
- *Seized stator* – fluid striking the back of the stator vanes cannot make the stator freewheel at the appropriate time so the fluid acts as a severe brake on the engine and produces overheating of the converter.

A stall test indicates if slip is occurring at the converter freewheel or in the gearbox. A general outline of the method is as follows:

1 Check that the engine is warm and that it is in good condition. Low engine power will give a false result.

2 Connect a tachometer to the engine.
3 Chock the wheels and apply the handbrake and footbrake.
4 Run the engine, select L (or position recommended by the manufacturer), fully depress the throttle and note the maximum engine speed, which should be about 1800 rev/min.

Typical result	*Probable cause*
Below 1000 rev/min	Converter free-wheel slip
About 1200 rev/min	Engine not giving full power
Above 2000 rev/min	Gearbox clutch or band slip

Warning: During this test the engine's power is absorbed by the fluid within the torque converter, which causes a rapid temperature rise. The duration of the stall test should not exceed 10 seconds.

Some adjustments to the automatic gearbox can be carried out, although these are usually limited to the brake bands, starter inhibitor switch and the gear selection cable. Note that these adjustments are also normally carried out after replacing any of the components.

3.28.4 Electronic control diagnosis

Modern automatic gearboxes are controlled by an electronic control unit (ECU). A diagnostic system within the ECU monitors the automatic gearbox system. If a fault is detected with the system, the ECU will record the fault code and an applicable fault code will be stored in the ECU memory.

The driver of the vehicle is informed that a gearbox fault exists by the illumination of the gearbox warning light. To access the fault code information in the ECU memory, it is normally necessary to connect diagnostic test equipment to the vehicle. The test equipment reads the information stored in the ECU memory, which then indicates the area in which the gearbox fault exists. The workshop manual relevant to the vehicle will indicate the diagnostic procedure for the particular fault code.

STEERING AND SUSPENSION SYSTEMS

Chapter 4

what is covered in this chapter . . .

- Directional control and steering systems
- Camber, castor and swivel-axis inclination
- Steering system components
- Power assisted steering
- Rear-wheel and four-wheel steering
- Steering systems and wheel alignment – routine maintenance
- Suspension
- The requirements of a spring
- Types and characteristics of metal springs
- Rubber suspension
- Gas and air suspension
- Suspension dampers
- Rigid axle suspension
- Independent front suspension (IFS)
- Independent rear suspension (IRS)
- Wheels
- Tyres
- Wheel balance
- Steering and suspension maintenance and diagnosis

4.1 DIRECTIONAL CONTROL AND STEERING SYSTEMS

4.1.1 Steering and suspension affecting directional control and stability

Modern vehicles are often driven at high speeds and this highlights the need for precise steering. Steering systems therefore require routine inspection or maintenance and where necessary accurate fault diagnosis and rectification. Steering fault diagnosis and rectification are often ignored in the repair industry, because of a lack of understanding of steering geometry and diagnostic processes. However, faults with the steering are inevitably dangerous to the driver, passengers and other road users. Also, steering faults can cause additional expense to the vehicle owner due to increased tyre wear and fuel consumption, as well as wear or breakage of steering and suspension components. It is therefore essential that the technician has a thorough understanding of steering systems.

It is also important to note that the suspension system has a great influence on the way the vehicle steers. To a large extent, suspension and steering systems interact whilst the vehicle is moving, and therefore a full understanding of suspension systems and steering systems is necessary to enable a technician to diagnose steering faults.

Although the steering system must provide an essential means of giving a driver directional control, it must also contribute to the stability of the vehicle in the straight-ahead position as well as when cornering. The suspension system is primarily tasked with providing comfort but it also greatly influences vehicle stability and handling as well as affecting how well or precisely the vehicle steers.

4.1.2 Basic principles of a steering system

The steering mechanism must enable the driver to:

- maintain the straight-ahead motion of the vehicle without undue effort, even when bumps are encountered at high speeds
- change the path or direction of the vehicle with the minimum amount of driver effort.

Swinging-beam system

Simple steering geometry is illustrated in Figure 4.1.

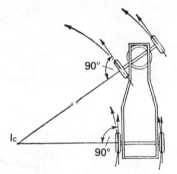

Figure 4.1 Swinging-beam system

A swinging axle beam, mounted on a turntable (or pivot) on the vehicle frame, turns the wheels and allows the vehicle to move around an imaginary centre I_c. It can be seen in the position shown, that all wheels are at right angles to the radial lines drawn from I_c, and each wheel forms a tangent to the curved path that the wheel is actually taking. The natural tendency of a wheel is to travel in a straight line, so a curved path will cause greater tyre wear. Tyre wear can be kept to a minimum if the wheels are accurately aligned.

Ackermann layout

Many of the disadvantages of the swinging-beam system were overcome in 1817 when a Munich carriage builder named Lankensperger first introduced the fixed-beam, double-pivot system. In 1818, his agent in England, Rudolph Ackermann, took out a patent on the steering system (known as the Ackermann layout), which is still widely used by vehicle manufacturers.

Figure 4.2 illustrates the basic principle of the Ackermann layout, which allows for different steering angles at each wheel during a turn. The inner wheel, during a turn, should ideally turn in at a greater angle than the outer wheel (angles A and B); this is because the inner wheel has a tighter turning path to follow than the outer wheel. Using the Ackermann layout allows the inner and outer wheels to follow different paths during a turn, paths that are closer to their ideal paths.

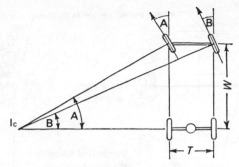

Figure 4.2 Diagram showing why the inner wheel must be moved through a larger angle

Note that if the track width T were to increase or decrease, this would affect the angles for the wheels during turns. The same would apply if the wheelbase length W were increased or decreased. The relationship or ratio between T and W therefore determines the front wheel angles.

The main details of the layout are shown in Figure 4.3. Each wheel hub is mounted on a stub axle, which swivels on either kingpins or ball joints to give the steering action.

Linkage connecting the two stub axles together comprises of a track rod and two track arms, which are fixed to the stub axles. The Ackermann layout is obtained by positioning the track rod joints on an imaginary line that is drawn from the swivel joints (or kingpin) to the centre line of the vehicle. This means that when a track rod is fitted to the rear of the swivel centres, the track rod is narrower than the distance between swivel centres, and the track arms effectively taper in towards the rear of the vehicle. Alternatively the track rod can be located forward of the wheel centres; if the kingpin and track rod joint are positioned on the imaginary lines from the centre of the vehicle, the track rod will be wider and the track arms will taper outwards.

Figure 4.4 shows the steering angles when the track rod length is equal to the swivel centre distance; both wheels move through the same angle during turns. Shortening the track rod length and insetting the track arms to give an Ackermann layout, causes the wheel angles to differ during turns.

The Ackermann action can be seen if during a right-hand turn, the track rod is moved a given distance to the left. The left-hand track arm approaches its effective crank angle (rod and arm at 90°), which gives the track arm a small angular movement (23°). Whereas on the right-hand side the track arm moves away from the effective crank angle and increases the arm and wheel angle (30°). The difference in the angle between the two road wheels increases as the wheels are turned.

It should be noted that the essential feature of the system is the position of the track arm connection to the track rod in relation to the steering swivel axis, and not the shape of the track arms.

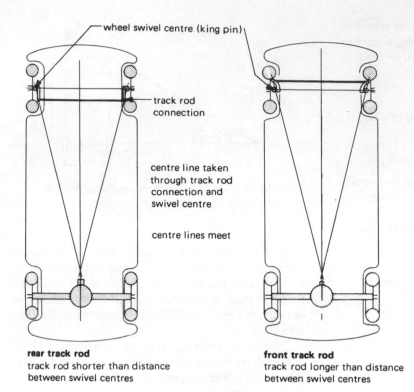

rear track rod
track rod shorter than distance
between swivel centres

front track rod
track rod longer than distance
between swivel centres

Figure 4.3　Ackermann steering system

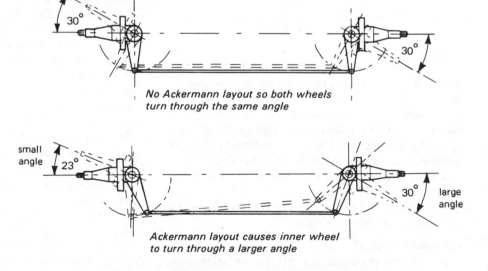

*No Ackermann layout so both wheels
turn through the same angle*

*Figure 4.4　Effect of the
Ackermann layout*

*Ackermann layout causes inner wheel
to turn through a larger angle*

However, any distortion of the arms due to vehicle impact will cause misalignment and incorrect wheel angles. The alignment of the track arms can be checked by placing the wheels on turntables and checking the amount that the wheels move out-of-parallel when one wheel is steered through a given angle – this test is often referred to as 'toe-out on turns'.

4.1.3　Oversteer and understeer

Slip angle

Steering geometry has thus far been based on a vehicle using 'hard' tyres. Low profile tyres together with lower pressure, which are used on modern vehicles, take a different path when subjected to a side force. Figure 4.5 shows a plan view of a wheel travelling in the direction A.

If a side force acts on the wheel, tyre deflection will cause the wheel to take the path B, although the wheel is still pointing in the original direction. The angle between the path that the wheel is actually taking (B) and the intended path (A), is termed the slip angle.

Note: The term slip angle is misleading since no slip is actually taking place. 'Creep angle' might be a better term, but 'slip angle' is in common use.

The slip angle caused by the deflection of the sidewall of a given tyre is proportional to the side force acting on the tyre. This statement is true up to the point

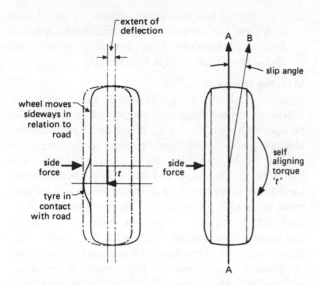

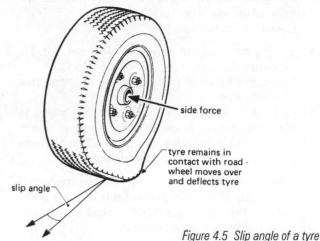

Figure 4.5 Slip angle of a tyre

where adhesion or grip is eventually lost and the tyre starts to slide sideways. During the non-slip phase the following applies:

$$\text{Cornering power (N/degree)} = \frac{\text{Side force (newtons)}}{\text{Slip angle (degrees)}}$$

The cornering power (CP) of a tyre is governed by:

- Inflation pressure – an increase raises the CP.
- Tyre construction – a radial-ply tyre has a higher CP than a cross-ply tyre.
- Tyre size – a low-profile tyre has a smaller wall so a higher CP is achieved.
- Camber (tilt) of wheel – tilting the wheel away from the side force increases the CP.
- Load on the wheel – if the load is varied from the normal, then CP will decrease.

Note: For further details about tyre construction refer to the tyre section in this book.

Tyre slip angles affect the steering characteristics of a vehicle by causing either oversteer or understeer. A side force applied to a wheel, caused by wind, road camber or cornering forces, produces a slip angle at each tyre.

Self-aligning torque

When a side force acts on a tyre, the wall deflects to give a slip angle. Observing a wheel that is rotating in this condition (Figure 4.5), shows that side deflection of the tyre is greater at the point where the tyre leaves the road as it rotates This effect produces a self-aligning torque (*t*), which attempts to turn the wheel to align itself with the actual direction that the wheel is taking.

The effect of this torque is felt by a driver of a vehicle that is travelling along a highly cambered road – the steering will 'pull' to one side.

Oversteer

When the rear slip angles are greater than those at the front (Figure 4.6), the vehicle will turn more sharply than normal – a condition called oversteer. To correct this condition, the driver has to straighten up the

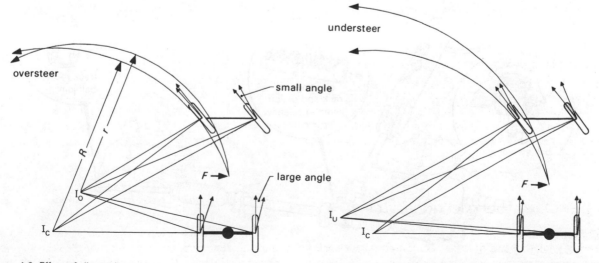

Figure 4.6 Effect of slip angles

steering wheel (effectively reducing the angle of cornering by turning the front wheels towards the direction of the rear wheel oversteer).

Oversteer can be caused by:

- Moving the centre of gravity towards the rear, i.e. increasing the load at the rear of the vehicle.
- Lower tyre inflation pressure at the rear than that recommended.
- Large load transference from inner rear wheel to outer rear wheel when cornering, such as occurs with excessive cornering speeds or sudden attempts at cornering (sudden direction change).

Oversteer can be dangerous for the inexperienced driver, because of difficulty in correcting the slide of the rear wheels. Vehicle designs therefore tend to avoid any oversteer tendencies wherever possible.

Understeer

Understeer is the opposite of oversteer. Understeer is produced when the front slip angles are greater than the rear. This tends to cause the front of the vehicle to move away from the side force and causes the vehicle to take a path of larger radius than intended. A reasonable degree of understeer is desirable, but if it becomes excessive, steering becomes difficult.

4.1.4 Steering mechanism

The mechanism used to link the steering wheel to the road wheels depends on the type of suspension system. Two types of steering mechanism have been widely used:

1　Rack-and-pinion steering, is now almost universally used for modern cars (illustrated in Figure 4.7)

2　The steering box mechanism, which is mainly used with light commercial vehicles and trucks, but was fitted to the majority of cars until the advent of rack and pinion (illustrated in Figure 4.8).

Steering for a car

Figure 4.7 shows a typical layout for a motorcar. Independent front suspension is normal for this type of vehicle, so a split track rod, made up of two or three separate pieces, is necessary to avoid a change in the steering geometry when one or both wheels strike a bump in the road. A rack-and-pinion type steering mechanism takes the place of the centre link of a three-piece track rod, which also eliminates the need for a drag link. These features allow a comparatively direct and positive action when compared with a steering box, making this type of mechanism attractive for a motorcar.

Steering movement of the wheels is normally provided by widely spaced ball swivel joints situated at the outer connection points of the suspension arms.

Steering for a light truck

Figure 4.8 shows a typical layout for a light commercial vehicle, fitted with a dead or solid axle having non-independent suspension.

The steering wheel column is fitted at the lower end to the steering gearbox which is connected by a drop arm. A ball joint on the bottom end of the drop arm connects to a drag link, which pushes and pulls a steering arm mounted on a stub axle. Phosphor-bronze bushes in the stub axle provide for steering movement of the road wheels around a kingpin, which is retained in the axle beam.

If the vehicle is right-hand drive (as shown), the steering box controls the right-hand (off-side) wheel and the steering movement of the other wheel is by means of the track rod linkage.

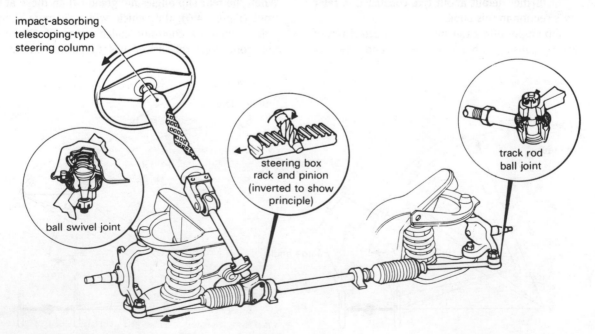

impact-absorbing telescoping-type steering column

ball swivel joint

steering box rack and pinion (inverted to show principle)

track rod ball joint

Figure 4.7 Steering layout, for a car with rack and pinion steering

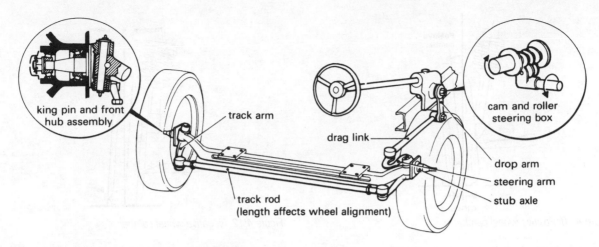

Figure 4.8 Steering layout for a light commercial vehicle

4.2   CAMBER, CASTOR AND SWIVEL-AXIS INCLINATION

4.2.1 Centre-point steering

Figure 4.9 shows a vertical wheel and kingpin arrangement; this has the following disadvantages:

- A large 'splaying-out' effect of the wheel – the wheels are pushed along by the force F, which is opposed by the resistance R. These two forces produce a couple or turning force ($F \times x$), which becomes very large when the front brakes are applied.
- Heavy steering owing to the distance between kingpin and centre line of the wheel. The wheel has to be moved in an arc around the pin, the radius being x.
- The large bending stress exerted on the stub axle and kingpin.

To overcome these disadvantages, the wheel and kingpin are so arranged that the 'offset' distance x is reduced. When the offset is eliminated, i.e. when the centre line of the wheel meets the centre line of the

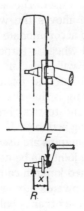

Figure 4.9 Layout showing the need for centre-point steering

kingpin at the road surface, the condition is termed centre-point steering.

Centre-point steering can be obtained by:
- Camber. This is achieved by setting the stub axle at an angle which allows the wheel centre line to meet the kingpin centre line.
- Swivel-axis inclination i.e. the kingpin swivel axis is inclined so that the centre line of the kingpin meets the centre line of the wheel.
- Wheels that are dished towards the middle of the vehicle so that the wheel centre line is more in line with the kingpin centre line.

Centre-point steering appears to be ideal, but the 'spread' effect of the tyre causes the wheel to 'scrub' as the wheel rotates on the road surface and give 'heavy steering' and increased tyre wear.

4.2.2 Camber

When the front wheel is viewed from the front, if the stub axle is made so that it tilts the wheel, the angle formed between the vertical and the wheel centre line is termed the camber angle. When the wheel tilts outwards at the top it is referred to as 'positive camber', or a wheel tilting inwards at the top is referred to as 'negative camber'. The angle at which the wheel tilts from the vertical is measured in degrees.

Positive camber

If the wheel is given positive camber (Figure 4.10), the bending stress exerted on the stub axle and the 'splaying out' are reduced.

However, the wheel angle (lean out) caused by having positive camber will result in different rolling radii where the tyre contacts the road. This results in a

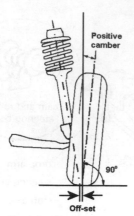

Figure 4.10 Positive wheel camber

cone effect, which causes tyre wear on the outer edge of the tyre and a splaying-out action. Positive camber also reduces the offset (dimension *x* in Figure 4.9), which results in lighter steering.

One other implication of building in camber angle relates to the cone effect. If a cone-shaped object is laid on a flat surface and then made to roll, the cone will roll round in a circle. Therefore, the cone effect created by having a positive camber angle will result in each wheel trying to roll round in a circle or steer the car. The fact that the two front wheels will try to steer outward in opposite directions means that their steering forces are cancelled out.

However, their attempts to turn outwards will cause some tyre scrub and wear. It is possible to slightly reduce the effect by setting each wheel so that it is toeing-in slightly when the steering is in the straight ahead position (both wheels toeing-in slightly will again result in the forces being cancelled).

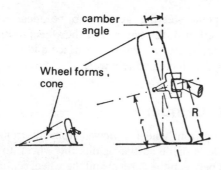

Figure 4.11 Positive wheel camber, creating tyre deflection

Negative camber

A negative camber reduces the camber angle when the vehicle is cornering and the vehicle tilts. A negative camber therefore provides an improvement in vehicle handling whilst the vehicle is cornering.

However, negative camber also increases the offset and therefore produces heavier steering. Note that negative camber will also increase tyre wear as the camber angle increases.

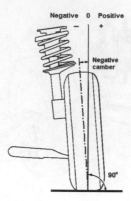

Figure 4.12 Negative wheel camber

Applying equal camber angles to both wheels on the same axle will balance the settings, however if the camber angles between the wheels are unequal, the vehicle will pull to the side of greater camber.

Note: Other factors, such as unequal tyre pressures, will also make the vehicle pull to one side while driving.

Some independent suspension systems vary the camber angle as the spring deflects. The change in camber angle during this deflection can be from positive to negative.

Since camber increases tyre wear, the camber angle seldom exceeds 2°. Many cars today adopt a negative camber, which improves handling but produces heavier steering action. The fitment of power assisted steering reduces the effects of heavier steering.

4.2.3 Kingpin inclination (KPI) or swivel-axis inclination (SAI)

Tilting the kingpin outwards at the bottom produces an angle between the kingpin centre line and the vertical, which is referred to as kingpin inclination (KPI). Modern vehicles are fitted with independent suspension systems and are therefore not fitted with a kingpin; when used with this set-up the angle is referred to as the swivel-axis inclination (SAI) shown in Figure 4.13.

Most layouts require SAI of between 5° and 10°, to obtain the required offset. The larger angles are used when the designer moves the wheel away from the swivel ball joints to accommodate brakes, bearings, etc.

When the road wheel is turned while steering the vehicle, the wheel will move in the plane A–A. This action will tend to lift the front of the vehicle; the reaction to this lifting is that the weight of the vehicle acting down will tend to straighten the wheels again. This is a self-centring action.

When vertical kingpins are used, a simple yoke-and-pin-type of steering joint can be used at each end of the track rod. An inclined kingpin causes the joint to move in the plane B–B, upwards at one end of the track rod and downwards at the other. A ball joint is necessary at each end of the rod to allow for this motion.

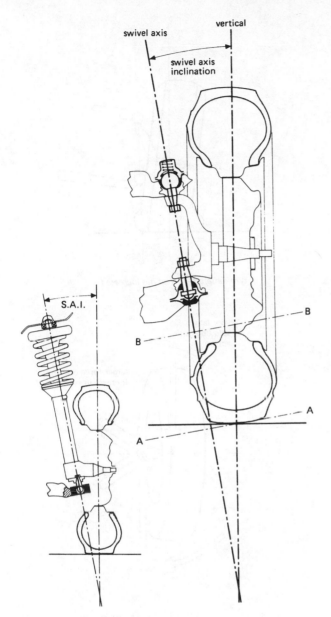

Figure 4.13 Swivel axis inclination

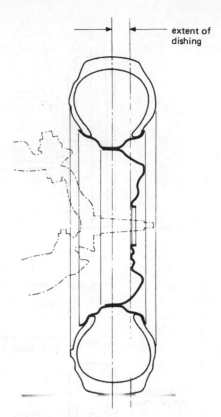

Figure 4.14 A dished wheel

4.2.4 Dished wheels

By slightly dishing the wheel (Figure 4.14) the offset is reduced i.e. the centre line of the wheel is closer to the centre line of the kingpin or swivel point centre line. This will then reduce the need for large amounts of camber and SAI. The light pressed-steel wheel must not be excessively dished or the strength of the wheel will be reduced.

4.2.5 Negative offset (negative scrub radius)

In the past, a positive offset was used. This was obtained by making the centre line of the wheel meet the swivel axis at a point just below the road. The offset

distance (for each wheel) measured at the road surface between the two centre lines should be equal to ensure that the inward or outward 'pull' of one wheel balances the 'pull' of the other wheel.

Note that when one front tyre deflates, the positive offset on that side will increase. The increase will cause the vehicle to pull violently to the side of the deflated tyre and will make it difficult for the driver to maintain control of the vehicle, especially if the brake is applied (Figure 4.15).

However, when the geometry has negative offset, stability is improved. It is obtained by increasing the inclination of the swivel axis further than in the past in order to give an intersection point well above the road surface.

Another advantage in the use of negative offset geometry is its effect when the front brakes are unbalanced owing to poor adhesion of one wheel or failure of one front brake. Even under these adverse conditions the vehicle can still be brought to rest in a straight line.

With the negative offset geometry, the effect of tyre deflation is to reduce the offset. Although the deflated tyre increases the rolling resistance, the shorter offset reduces the leverage of the deflated tyre thus reducing the tendency to change the direction of the vehicle.

For example, if the right-hand front brake fails (Figure 4.16), the geometry causes the braking action of the left-hand wheel to steer the wheels to the right to counteract the loss of brake drag on the right-hand side

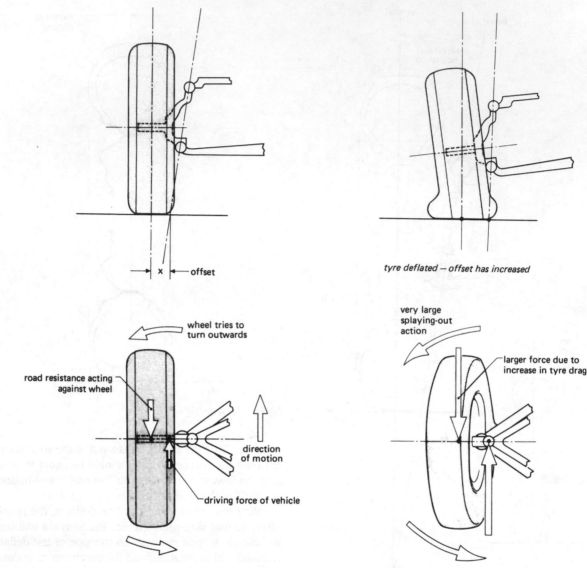

Figure 4.15 Positive offset

of the vehicle. This inbuilt action relieves the driver of a difficult control problem. It also makes the negative offset layout particularly suited to a diagonally connected, split-line braking system.

4.2.6 Castor

Wheel castor is applied to the geometry to enable the driver to 'feel' the straight-ahead position. To overcome the 'self-centring' or castoring action, (which tends to keep the wheels pointing straight ahead), a force must be exerted on the steering wheel. From this introduction it will be seen that too much castor produces heavy steering but too little would cause wander (driver has no feel of straight ahead).

The action of castor angle may be understood by examining the action of a simple trolley castor such as those found on supermarket trolleys (Figure 4.17a).

When a force is exerted on the trolley, it moves in the direction of the force. The effect of this force on the castor is shown in the diagram. The force *F* acting at the pivot and the resistance acting at the wheel produce a couple which rotates the castor to a position where the wheel is following the line of thrust.

On a motor vehicle the pivot centre line is normally made to strike the road in front of the centre of contact of the wheel. In this case the wheel will follow the path taken by the pivot centre line, which will always be in front of the vehicle.

Castor can be obtained by mounting a vertical kingpin in front of the wheel (Figure 4.17b) or by inclining the kingpin forward at the bottom (Figure 4.17c) to give castor angle. The latter is simpler, and most manufacturers use this arrangement.

The angle is generally between 2° and 5°; but once again, reference must be made to the manufacturer's

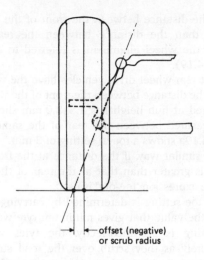

offset (negative)
or scrub radius

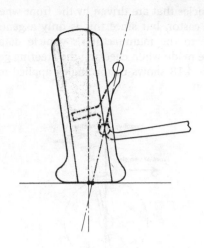

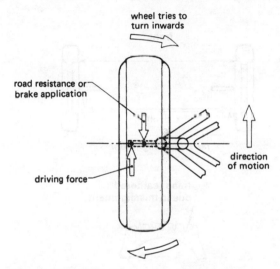

wheel tries to
turn inwards

road resistance or
brake application

direction
of motion

driving force

Figure 4.16 Negative offset

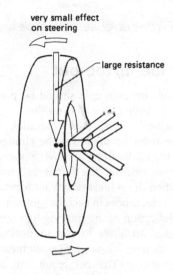

very small effect
on steering

large resistance

recommendation for castor angle and tolerance (normally ±0.5%° for all steering angles).

The inclining of the swivel axis or the tilting of the kingpin can be arranged by using one of the following methods:

- Upper independent suspension members can be mounted slightly to the rear of the lower members.
- The axle beam of a light truck can be tilted by
  a) fitting wedges between axle and spring,
  b) mounting the axle towards the front of a laminated spring,
  c) inclining the laminated spring

Figure 4.17 shows the pivot centre line making contact with the road in front of the centre line of the wheel; this is referred to as positive castor. This geometry is common for a rear-wheel drive vehicle, but is unsuitable for front-wheel drive and four-wheel drive vehicles because the conditions shown in Figure 4.17 are reversed i.e. power is being applied to the front or castor wheels. The wheels are therefore not being pulled by the

vehicle but are in fact trying to pull the vehicle and should ideally have negative castor so that the wheel is in front of the pivot.

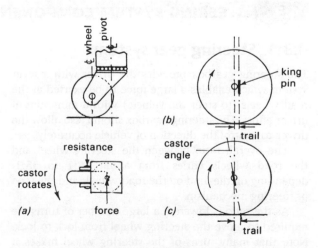

℄ wheel

pivot

king
pin

(b)

castor
angle

trail

resistance

castor
rotates

force

(a)

(c)

trail

Figure 4.17 a, b, c Wheel castor – the principle

Most vehicles that are driven by the front wheels have negative castor, but since this is only a general rule, reference to the manufacturer's vehicle data should always be made when checking the steering geometry.

Figure 4.18 shows castor angles applied to vehicle suspension.

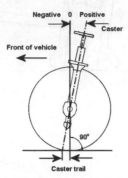

Figure 4.18 Wheel castor applied to vehicle suspension

4.2.7 Toe-in/toe-out

Both wheels on each axle should be parallel when the vehicle is travelling in a straight line.

To achieve this basic parallel condition, an allowance must be made for the change in alignment between the stationary and moving positions. On a rear-wheel drive vehicle, the forces exerted on the front wheels when the vehicle is moving forwards take up the very small clearances in each ball joint and also produce a slight deflection of the steering linkages. Additionally, any flexible bushings in the mountings for steering components may allow small movements and changes in the geometry. The net result can cause the road wheels to splay out. On a front-wheel drive vehicle forces created by the driving wheels can in fact cause the wheels to splay in.

When the distance between the front of the wheels is smaller than the distance between the rear of the wheels, the wheel alignment is referred to as 'toe-in' (Figure 4.19).

Most rear-wheel drive vehicles have the wheels set so that the distance between the front of the wheel rims (measured at hub height) is 1.5–3.0 mm shorter than that measured between the rear of the same wheels. Figure 4.19a shows a toe-in setting of 3 mm.

In a similar way, if the distance at the front of the wheels is greater than that at the rear of the wheels, then the expression 'toe-out' is used.

The toe setting is determined by carrying out tests to find the value that gives minimum tyre wear. If the toe setting is set incorrectly, the tyres will wear prematurely as they scrub over the road surface. An incorrect toe setting produces a feathering affect on the tread of the tyre, as shown in Figure 4.19b.

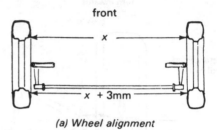

(a) Wheel alignment

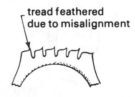

(b) Section through tyre tread

Figure 4.19a and b Toe-in and toe-out conditions

4.3 STEERING SYSTEM COMPONENTS

4.3.1 Steering gear systems

The steering gearbox provides the driver with a lever system which enables a large force to be exerted at the road wheels (to steer the vehicle) with a minimum of driver effort. The steering gearbox should also allow the driver to control the direction of vehicle accurately.

The overall ratio between the steering wheel and the road wheels varies from about 18:1 to 35:1, depending on the load on the road wheels and the type of steering mechanism.

As the ratio is lowered, a large number of turns are required to move the steering wheel from lock to lock. Note that many turns of the steering wheel makes it difficult to change vehicle direction rapidly.

By varying the efficiency of the steering mechanism, the motion is transmitted back to the driver through the steering mechanism, enabling the driver to receive an amount of 'feel' from the road wheels. But such feel should not subject the driver to major road shocks.

Types of steering gear

Over the years a number of different types of steering gearbox have been used. These include:

Steering box

Often used with large vans, trucks and buses, although the steering box was the most common system on light cars through to the 1960s. Various types of steering box have been used, which include:

- worm and sector
- screw and nut
- recirculating ball
- cam and peg
- worm and roller

Rack-and-pinion
Most modern light vehicles are fitted with a rack-and-pinion steering mechanism.

4.3.2 Steering boxes

Worm and sector
This type has been developed from a worm and wheel, which was one of the earliest designs of box.

A case-hardened steel worm and sector are located by bearings in a malleable iron, or light alloy casing. Figure 4.20 shows the worm connected to the inner column and the sector forming a part of the rocker shaft.

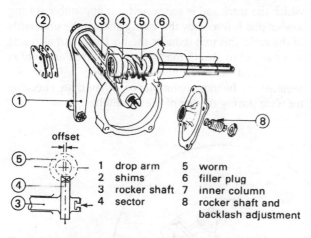

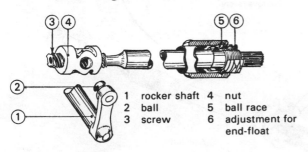

1	drop arm	5	worm
2	shims	6	filler plug
3	rocker shaft	7	inner column
4	sector	8	rocker shaft and backlash adjustment

Figure 4.20 A worm and sector steering box

Screw and nut (Figure 4.21)

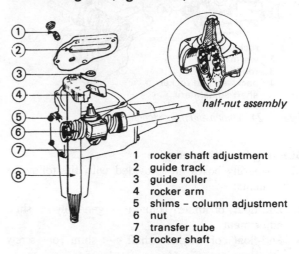

1	rocker shaft	4	nut
2	ball	5	ball race
3	screw	6	adjustment for end-float

Figure 4.21 A screw and nut steering box

A phosphor-bronze or steel nut is screwed onto a multi-start Acme thread formed on the inner column. Rotation of the nut is prevented by a ball fitted in the rocker arm. Axial thrust of the column is taken by a single ball-race fitted at the top end, and the nut sliding

in the housing supports the lower end. The end float of the inner column is adjusted by the nut at the top end.

Recirculating ball (Figure 4.22)

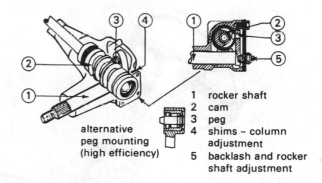

half-nut assembly

1	rocker shaft adjustment
2	guide track
3	guide roller
4	rocker arm
5	shims – column adjustment
6	nut
7	transfer tube
8	rocker shaft

Figure 4.22 A recirculating ball (half-nut) steering box

A higher efficiency (90% as opposed to 50% for the standard worm and nut) is achieved by using a nut with steel balls acting as 'threads'. The type shown in Figure 4.22 uses a half-nut with a transfer tube which feeds the balls back to the nut. A peg on the nut is located in the rocker arm.

Cam and peg (Figure 4.23)

1	rocker shaft
2	cam
3	peg
4	shims – column adjustment
5	backlash and rocker shaft adjustment

Figure 4.23 A cam and peg steering box

A tapered peg in the rocker arm engages with a special cam formed on the inner column. The end-float of the column is controlled by shims, and an adjusting screw on the side cover governs the backlash and end-float of the rocker shaft.

A modified form known as the high efficiency cam and peg gear uses a peg, which is allowed to rotate in bearings in the rocker arm.

Worm and roller (Figure 4.24)
A roller follower fitted to the rocker shaft engages with an hourglass worm. The small offset of the roller to the worm enables an adjusting screw to control backlash and end-float of the rocker shaft.

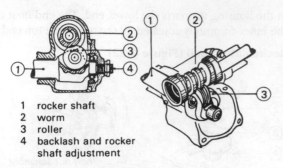

1 rocker shaft
2 worm
3 roller
4 backlash and rocker
   shaft adjustment

Figure 4.24 A worm and roller steering box

Steering box maintenance

Most steering boxes are provided with the following adjustments:

- End-float of inner column – generally a shim adjustment.
- End-float of rocker shaft – shim or screw adjustments.
- Backlash between gears – gears can be moved closer together.

The greatest wear takes place in the straight-ahead position of the box, so the gear is normally made with a larger backlash in the lock positions. This reduces the risk of seizure at full lock when the box is adjusted to compensate for wear. It is essential to reduce end-float and backlash to a minimum, but tight spots must be avoided.

Steering box lubrication is provided by filling the steering box with normal gear oil to the level of the filler plug.

4.3.3 Rack-and-pinion

The rack-and-pinion steering box is today the most common type of steering mechanism fitted on the modern motorcar.

The rack-and-pinion mechanism is used with independent front suspension where the rack acts as the centre section of a three-piece track rod. The steering column is normally connected to the pinion by one or two universal joints, to enable convenient mounting of the rack-and-pinion assembly.

The pinion meshes with the rack and, as the steering wheel is turned, the rack moves either to the left or to the right. Each end of the rack has a ball connection, to which the track rod is connected. An adjustable sprung loaded pad is forced by the spring against the underside of the rack; this pad reduces the backlash and also acts as a damper to absorb road shocks. The rack and pinion is lubricated when the unit is assembled and normally requires no further maintenance other than checking for wear during the life of the assembly.

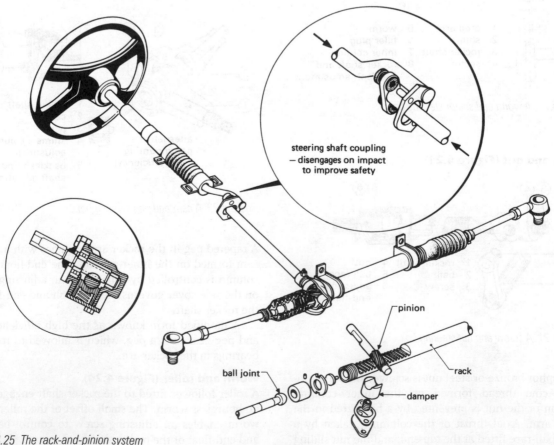

steering shaft coupling
– disengages on impact
to improve safety

pinion

rack

ball joint

damper

Figure 4.25 The rack-and-pinion system

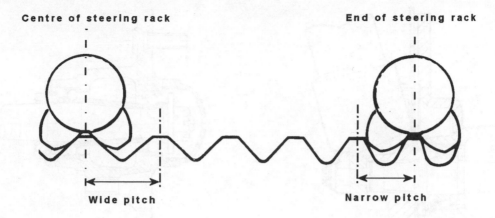

Figure 4.26 A variable ratio rack (note the different pitch for the teeth at the end and the centre of the rack)

Variable ratio rack-and-pinion

One problem with standard rack-and-pinion steering is that the greater the steering angle applied (e.g. full steering lock), the heavier the steering. Some vehicles are therefore fitted with a rack-and-pinion system that has a variable steering ratio. In effect, the gear ratio or leverage ratio changes as the steering is turned.

To achieve variable ratio, the pitch of the teeth on the pinion are uniform, but the pitch of the teeth on the rack gradually decrease towards each end of the rack i.e. the distance between the teeth is less meaning that there are more teeth for a given length of rack.

Therefore, turning the steering wheel through a given angle e.g. 25° around the straight ahead position causes the rack to move a large distance (either left or right). But when the steering is closer to full lock, turning the steering wheel through the same 25° angle results in the rack moving a smaller distance.

When the steering is nearer to full lock, the leverage is effectively increased (due to the change in gear ratio), which reduces the effort required to turn the steering wheel.

4.3.4 Steering joints

The various steering levers and rods are connected by ball joints, which allow universal movement of steering and suspension.

Older types of ball joint were fitted with a grease nipple; this type of joint requires lubrication during routine vehicle servicing.

Modern ball joints similar to the one in Figure 4.27 are self-lubricating. Fitted on either side of the plated steel ball is a split moulded bearing which is compounded with a specially developed metallic lubricant. This type of ball joint is sealed for the life of the component. The boot fitted between the ball pin and the body prevents the ingress of dirt into the joint, which would promote premature wear of the ball and ball seat.

4.3.5 Front hubs

Front hub construction depends on whether the hub has to accommodate the driveshaft assembly and the hub bearings. A driving hub is used for a front-wheel drive vehicle or four-wheel drive vehicle. A non-driving hub is used for a rear-wheel drive vehicle when a stub axle is used to locate the hub and bearing.

Non-driving hub

Figure 4.28 shows a typical bearing arrangement for a non-driving hub. Two adjustable taper roller bearings, spaced as widely apart as possible, are fitted between the stub axle and the malleable iron or steel cast hub.

The hubs are lubricated by packing each bearing, and half the cavity between the bearings, with grease of a type to suit the brake system.

Whereas a lime–soap grease of medium consistency is suitable for a shoe brake, a grease base having a high melting point, such as lithium or bentone, is essential for hubs used with disc brakes. A lip-type synthetic rubber seal prevents the escape of grease.

This type of hub is adjusted by tightening the hub nut until all clearance is eliminated and then slackening the nut off by one 'flat'. To achieve a more accurate setting, some manufacturers recommend that the adjusting nut is tightened to a specified torque before slackening the nut a pre-set amount. This method should not be confused with pre-loading. A hub bearing has to withstand heat from the brakes, so it needs a running clearance; this grade of fit is quite different to that obtained after a bearing has been pre-loaded.

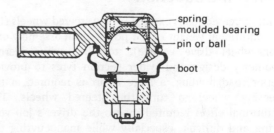

Figure 4.27 A steering joint (self-adjusting)

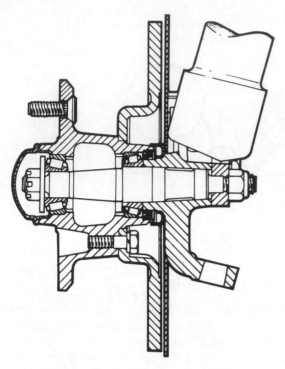

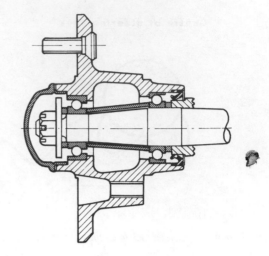

Figure 4.29 Front hub with ball bearings

Figure 4.28 Front hub with taper roller bearing

An alternative bearing arrangement is shown in Figure 4.29. This uses two angular contact type ball-races which are held apart by a rigid spacer. There is no intended adjustment on this type and therefore the hub nut must be tightened fully to the correct torque loading.

Note: For further information on bearing types refer to the bearing section within this book.

Driving hub

A typical hub arrangement used for a front-wheel drive car is shown in Figure 4.30. The stub axle housing contains two bearings and these support both the wheel hub and driving shaft (typically part of the constant velocity joint). The type of bearing used depends on the load carried by the road wheel; either a pair of ball-races or pair of taper roller bearings is used.

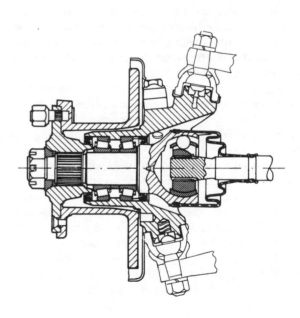

Figure 4.30 Front hub (front-wheel drive arrangement)

4.4 POWER ASSISTED STEERING

4.4.1 Introduction

With increased loads exerted on the steered wheels (i.e. the additional weight of the power train assembly of a front-wheel drive vehicle), together with steering geometry design and wider section tyres to provide better road holding, a large effort is required at the steering wheel to turn the steered wheels. The additional effort required makes the driver's job very tiring and difficult, especially while manoeuvring the vehicle at low speed.

Improvements, such as an increase in the mechanical efficiency of the steering system or lower steering box ratios help to reduce driver fatigue. However, there is a limit to how low the ratio can be because a very low ratio results in a large number of turns of the steering wheel to turn a corner or to turn from lock to lock. To overcome the problems of heavy steering and also provide a reasonably responsive steering ratio, many vehicles are now fitted with power assistance to the steering system.

The power assistance arrangement should obey certain requirements:

- It must be 'fail-safe'. If the power assistance system fails, the driver must still be able to retain effective control.
- The degree of assistance should be proportional to the effort applied by the driver, and the driver must be able to retain the 'feel' of the wheels.

On light vehicles, hydraulic power or electric power is used to assist the driver to steer the vehicle.

4.4.2 Hydraulic system

Hydraulically operated, power assisted systems are based on either a constant pressure or constant flow layout. The former employs a hydraulic accumulator to store the pressure, whereas the latter has fluid flowing around the system continuously until assistance is required. Most modern hydraulic steering systems use the constant flow system.

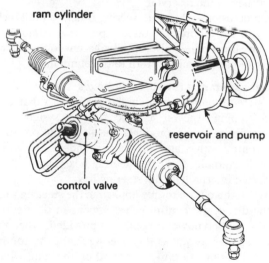

Figure 4.31 shows the essential components required to operate a constant flow system with a rack-and-pinion steering mechanism. In addition to the normal steering components, the system requires a:

- hydraulic pump
- control valve
- ram cylinder.

The hydraulic pump (the pump illustrated is integral with the fluid reservoir), supplies oil to a control valve situated in the housing that supports the pinion shaft. When the steering is in the straight-ahead position (Figure 4.32) the control valve is in the neutral position, the fluid is passed through the control valve and returns to the pump/reservoir.

Note that the pressure applied to the cylinder each side of the piston within the steering rack is equal, therefore the piston will not move or be biased in either direction, and therefore no power assistance is provided.

Movement from the steering column shaft operates the spool control valve via a torsion bar.

Note: The torsion bar acts as a pressure-sensing valve, when the steering wheel is turned slightly the torsion bar detects steering wheel movement.

When the control valve moves, this closes one port in the control valve and directs hydraulic fluid to one side of the piston (which is attached to the steering rack). A large pressure differential exists between the two power cylinders (either side of the piston) and therefore the piston moves in the direction of the cylinder with the lowest pressure, thus providing power assistance to the driver as the steering wheel is turned.

Hydraulic pump

The hydraulic pump is normally driven by a vee belt from the engine crankshaft. The pump is usually either an eccentric rotor type or an eccentric vane type of pump.

The reservoir of fluid that supplies fluid to the pump may be either remote or an integral part of the pump assembly. The hydraulic fluid used is a low-viscosity

Figure 4.31 A power-assisted steering system

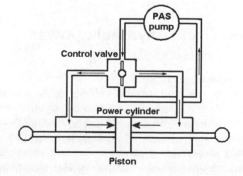
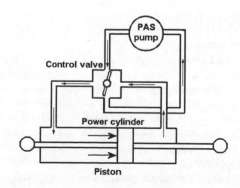

Figure 4.32 Power-assisted steering layout; driving straight ahead and during turns

mineral oil, similar to the type used in an automatic gearbox.

The pump produces pressure as it rotates and forces the fluid to the spool control valve. The maximum pressure that the pump can produce is proportional to engine speed, as the engine speed increases; the maximum pump pressure also increases (7 MN m^{-2} or 1000 lbf in^{-2}). A pressure relief valve is located in the pump; excess pressure is returned to the inlet side of the pump.

Many hydraulic pumps maintain a constant pressure, regardless of engine speed, with the use of a pressure relief valve.

Modern pumps may also feature an additional valve that reduces pump pressure when a predetermined pump speed (engine speed) is reached. At low engine speeds i.e. while the vehicle is manoeuvred at a low speed during parking, the power assistance for the steering is high. Above certain engine speeds (typically 2000 rpm) the level of power assistance is reduced, giving the driver more 'feel' through the steering at high motorway speeds. The excess pressure is returned to the inlet side of the pump.

When the steering is turned, the hydraulic power steering system uses a small proportion of the engine power to drive the power steering hydraulic pump. Many engines are fitted with a component that provides a slightly higher engine idle speed while the power steering is operated.

The 'idle up' device prevents the engine from stalling when the engine speed is low. Engines fitted with a carburettor or simple fuel injection systems normally use a vacuum valve switch, which is fitted in the high-pressure pipe from the pump to the spool control valve. When the pressure is high (steering held on full lock), the vacuum switch opens and allows a small volume of air to bypass the throttle body thus slightly increasing the engine idle speed.

Most engine management systems use a power steering pressure switch, which is fitted to the high-pressure pipe. The switch monitors the pressure and when high pressure exists in the hydraulic high-pressure pipe, the switch passes a signal to the ECU. The ECU increases the idle speed by altering the control signal to the idle air control valve.

Control valve

Figure 4.33 shows a simplified view of a rotary-type spool valve controlled by a torsion bar that is interposed between the steering shaft and the pinion of the steering box. The spool valve is a shaft with six flutes and this is encased by a sleeve, which has six internal axial grooves. Radial ports in the sleeve and shaft pass the oil from the supply to the lines connected to the ram chambers.

A series of splines between the shaft and sleeve limit the twist of the torsion bar to about 7° in each direction; below this angle the torque applied by the driver to the

steering box pinion is transmitted by the torsion bar. This fail-safe feature provides a mechanical drive from the steering shaft to the pinion in the event of a failure of the power system.

The amount of twist of the torsion bar, and the movement of the spool valve, are proportional to the effort applied by the driver. Initial power assistance is obtained at about 0.5° deflection of the bar and this power rises progressively as the bar moves to about 4°, the point of maximum assistance.

With the valve positioned in the 'no-power' position as shown in Figure 4.33, all the ports are open, so oil is allowed to pass through the valve and return to the reservoir.

When the steering wheel is turned against a resistance at the road wheel, the torsion bar is deflected; this allows the spool to rotate relative to the sleeve, cutting off the oil flow both to the reservoir and one side of the ram. At the same time the other side of the ram is subjected to oil pressure, which builds up sufficiently to move the road wheel and return the torsion bar to the no-torque position. During this stage the oil displaced from the unpressurized side of the ram is returned to the reservoir.

On occasions when the steering is held on full lock, the hydraulic oil pressure builds up to its maximum. At this pressure a relief valve, fitted adjacent to the pump, opens and allows oil to return to the pump inlet.

Power assistance for steering boxes

The system operates in a similar manner to that of a rack-and-pinion power assisted steering system. The engine driven pump produces the hydraulic pressure. The control valve and the ram cylinders are either located externally from the steering box (Figure 4.34) or located internally in the steering box.

When there is no torque applied to the steering shaft by the driver, the control valve remains in the neutral position and no power assistance is provided. When the driver applies torque to the steering shaft, the control valve allows pressure to be exerted on the ram, which provides assistance to the steering. When the driver turns the steering wheel in the opposite direction, the control valve applies hydraulic pressure to the opposite side of the piston.

4.4.3 Electro-hydraulic power assisted steering

For a vehicle such as a sports car, with the engine located at the rear of the vehicle, it is not always feasible for the hydraulic pump to be engine driven. In such cases the hydraulic pump can be electrically driven to provide the hydraulic oil pressure required to give the required power assistance.

The electric motor, which drives the hydraulic pump, is typically located at the front of the vehicle near to the steering rack. The movement of the steering

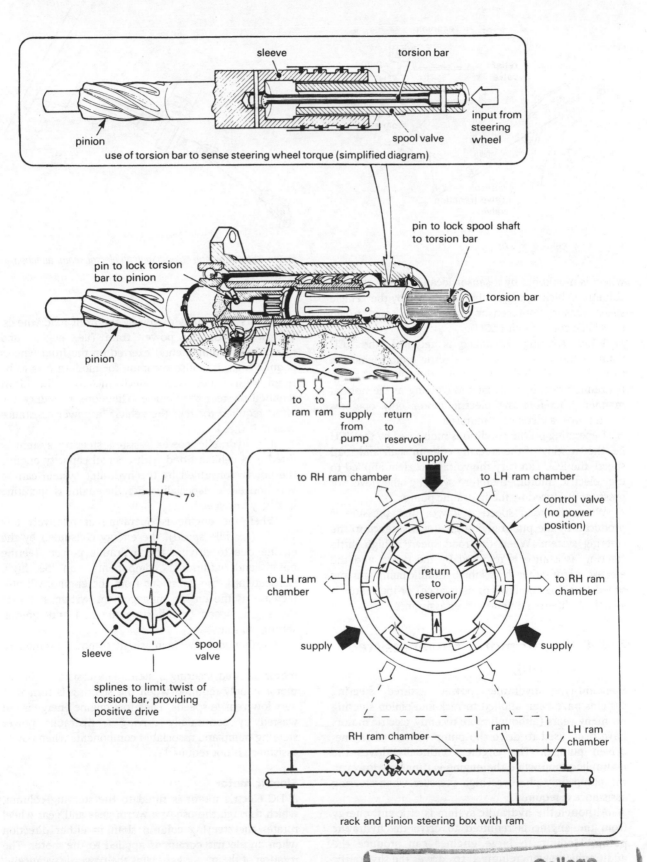

sleeve

torsion bar

input from
steering
wheel

pinion

spool valve

use of torsion bar to sense steering wheel torque (simplified diagram)

pin to lock spool shaft
to torsion bar

pin to lock torsion
bar to pinion

torsion bar

pinion

to   to
ram ram   supply   return
from   to
pump   reservoir

7°

supply

to RH ram chamber

to LH ram chamber

control valve
(no power
position)

to LH ram
chamber

return
to
reservoir

to RH ram
chamber

sleeve

spool
valve

supply

supply

splines to limit twist of
torsion bar, providing
positive drive

RH ram chamber

ram

LH ram
chamber

rack and pinion steering box with ram

Figure 4.33 A spool control valve

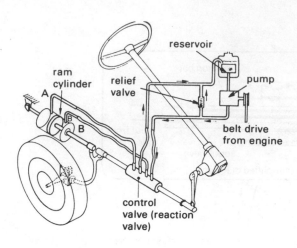

Figure 4.34 Steering box PAS layout

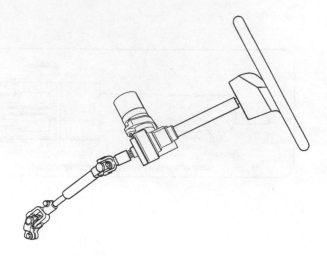

Figure 4.35 A steering column with an electric motor attached

wheel is monitored by a sensor located on the steering column; vehicle speed is also monitored by the vehicle speed sensor. Both sensor signals are passed to an electronic control unit (ECU).

When steering assistance is required, the ECU controls the operation of the electric motor, which in turn drives the hydraulic pump thus providing the hydraulic pressure to assist the steering in the normal manner. Therefore the electric motor only operates when power assistance is required.

Depending on the conditions monitored by the ECU i.e. the twisting of the steering column shaft and road speed, the ECU can vary the voltage/current applied to the electric motor, therefore varying the level of pressure produced by the hydraulic pump.

When the road speed is low, a high pressure is produced by the pump giving greater assistance to the steering system. When the road speed is high, little steering assistance is required by the driver and the electric motor either drives the hydraulic pump at a low speed (limiting the level of assistance) or the motor is switched off, providing no power assistance.

4.4.4 Electric motor power assisted steering

Standard-type hydraulic power assisted steering systems have been applied to rack-and-pinion steering for many years (although more recently, electric motors have been used to drive the pump instead of engine-driven pumps). The engine continually drives the hydraulic pump while the engine is running. However, the pump only produces high pressure when steering assistance is required.

Although the hydraulic system is efficient, energy from the engine is required to drive the hydraulic pump. Medium to large engines can produce the additional power required to drive the hydraulic pump without a noticeable effect in the reduction of engine power.

Small cars are usually driven by the front road wheels. The weight of the power train (i.e. engine and transmission components) exerted on the front wheels is quite high. It is also common for modern cars to be fitted with wider tyres which increases the effort required to steer the vehicle. Therefore, to reduce the effort required to steer the vehicle, a power assistance system is fitted.

If a hydraulic power assisted steering system is fitted to a vehicle fitted with a small capacity engine, the power consumed by the hydraulic system can be very noticeable, especially when the engine is operating at a very low speed.

When the engine is operating at relatively low speeds (i.e. idle speed), the energy consumed by the engine due to driving the hydraulic power steering pump and additional components can be high. Consequently, the emissions from the engine will also increase as the engine management system stabilises the engine speed by adjusting the fuel and ignition settings to suit.

It is therefore now increasingly common for modern vehicles with small engines to be fitted with an electric motor assisted steering system. The assistance of the motor is only required when the steering is turned at very low vehicle speeds. Therefore engine energy is not wasted by continually driving a hydraulic power steering pump and associated components when power assistance is not required.

Electric motor

A DC electric motor is fitted to the steering column, which through the use of a worm gear and gear wheel rotates the steering column shaft in either direction when an electric current is applied to the motor. The rotation of the motor generates the power assistance.

The ECU regulates when the current is applied to the motor.

Steering column torque sensor

A torque sensor monitors the twisting of the steering column by the driver and the direction in which the shaft is being turned. The torque sensor passes an electrical signal to the ECU which indicates the direction of rotation of the steering column. The torque sensor fitted to the steering column is similar to that used for the control valve within a hydraulic power steering system. If the steering column is in a neutral position (steering wheel not being turned) the sensor does not produce an electrical signal.

The sensor is located on the steering column shaft. Two sensors are normally used which enables a high level of safety in the event of a component failure.

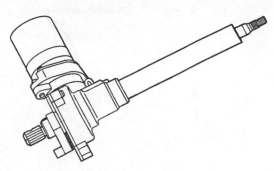

Figure 4.37 Electric power steering motor

Electronic control unit (ECU)

The ECU processes the information received from the torque sensor together with additional signals i.e. vehicle speed and engine speed. The ECU calculates the correct control signal to operate the electric motor thus providing an appropriate level of power assistance to the driver for the conditions. When the road speed is low a high level of steering power assistance is provided. As the engine speed and road speed increase the level of power assistance is decreased.

The ECU constantly monitors the power steering system for system failures. If a failure is detected with the signal input, the electric motor or within the ECU, the instrument warning light illuminates and if possible a fault code is stored in the memory of the ECU. The ECU will normally switch the power steering system off and the steering then operates as normal without any assistance. The driver will instantly notice the illumination of the warning light and the loss of power steering.

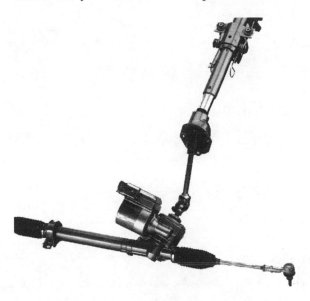

Figure 4.36 A steering rack with electric motor attached

4.5   REAR-WHEEL AND FOUR-WHEEL STEERING

4.5.1 Rear-wheel steering (provided by altering suspension geometry)

It has been known for many years that the front-to-rear wheel alignment plays a significant part with respect to directional stability of a vehicle. This is clearly displayed when a car has worn suspension bushes; often the lack of vehicle stability makes it dangerous to drive at any speed, even in a straight line.

Incorrect rear axle or rear-wheel alignment

It is not just the front steering and suspension geometry that influences the direction of travel of a vehicle. Imagine a solid rear axle that is not aligned correctly with the vehicle body (Figure 4.38). When the driver wants the vehicle to drive straight ahead, the driver will turn the steering wheel so that the front wheels are pointing straight ahead. However, if the rear wheels are angled slightly to one side, the rear of the vehicle will turn. The driver therefore needs to compensate by turning the front wheels in the same direction to prevent the vehicle form turning in a circle.

Although the vehicle will now travel in a straight line, the body will in fact be angled or 'crabbing'. This situation is not uncommon when a vehicle has been poorly repaired after an accident. If the rear axle or rear suspension assembly has been incorrectly fitted, crabbing can result.

Although the example in Figure 4.38 highlights the problem of an incorrectly aligned rear axle, a similar problem would occur on an independent rear suspension system if the suspension links and other components were incorrectly adjusted, or the suspension bushes and joints were worn. Even if only one of the rear wheels were slightly out of alignment

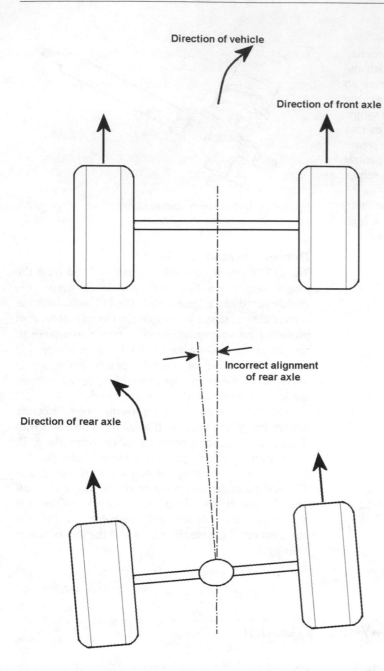

Figure 4.38 Incorrect rear axle alignment
affecting the direction of travel

and therefore angled slightly in or out, this would steer the rear of the vehicle.

Although incorrect rear-wheel alignment is an unwanted situation, the principle of using the rear wheels to assist in steering the vehicle can in fact offer many advantages. Modern vehicles do in fact have rear suspension designs that allow the rear-wheel alignment to alter slightly under certain driving conditions thus assisting in steering the vehicle, or aiding stability.

Overcoming unwanted steering characteristics

Up to the mid-1950s the majority of cars suffered from oversteer i.e. rear of the vehicle had a tendency to steer towards the outside of a turn. A contributory cause to this dangerous condition was rear spring deflection initiated by body roll, which caused the rear axle to alter its alignment. Improved axle location systems

helped to reduce the problem, but there is an inherent tendency to oversteer with the older designs of axle and suspension systems. The obvious dangers associated with an oversteer characteristic are now well known, so to improve stability most modern cars are designed to understeer, especially when they are driven at high speed.

One step towards an understeer characteristic can be achieved by using the natural transfer of the vehicle's weight during cornering to 'steer' the rear wheels. This action is produced either by misaligning the rear axle or, in the case of a car fitted with independent rear suspension, by utilizing a change in geometry of the rear suspension system.

The change in suspension geometry can be achieved through the use of special elastic bushes, which deform when a force is applied in a certain direction. It is therefore imperative that all suspension bushes are aligned correctly when fitting them to the suspension components.

Figure 4.39 shows an independent rear suspension layout. The front and rear bushes fitted to the rear lower suspension arms remain firm when load is applied in one direction. However, when load is applied in another plane, the bushes deform. The deformation of these bushes alters the wheel alignment of each wheel by a pre-determined angle. Note that the lower arm pivots around the ball joints, which are fitted to the lower control arm and the axle.

When the vehicle corners to the left, the forces applied to each wheel deform the bushes as shown in Figure 4.40 at points A and B. Toe-in is applied to the right rear wheel while toe-out is applied to the left rear wheel. The reverse occurs when the vehicle corners in the opposite direction.

The forces imparted by the cornering of the vehicle dictate the amount of rear wheel geometry change. By altering the wheel alignment to each wheel, a small degree of 'self steering' is applied to the rear wheels, which provides additional stability to the vehicle during cornering.

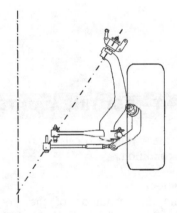

Figure 4.39 Rear suspension geometry

The design of suspension and the deformation of the bushes can also provide changes in camber during cornering and apply toe-in to both rear wheels during straight-line braking which gives additional stability.

4.5.2 Four-wheel steering systems

Although improved safety with respect to stability is associated with understeer, this condition increases the steering effort that must be applied by the driver. Also, since the way in which a vehicle handles can change with road speed, the response to a steering movement, both in time of response and direction, is difficult to predict.

These difficulties can be overcome by using four-wheel steering (4WS). Car manufacturers such as Honda, Mazda and Toyota, have fitted 4WS on some models.

Advantages of 4WS

Compared with a conventional two-wheel steer system, it is claimed that 4WS offers the following advantages:

- superior cornering stability
- improved steering responsiveness and precision
- high-speed straight-line stability
- a notable improvement in rapid lane-changing manoeuvres
- a smaller turning radius and tight-space manoeuvrability at low speed.

Relative wheel angles

The direction that the rear wheels steer relative to the front wheels depends on the operating conditions.

Low vehicle speed

During low-speed manoeuvring, the rear wheels are made to turn in the opposite direction to the front wheels; this simplifies the positioning of the car in

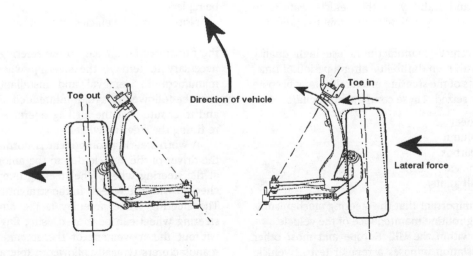

Figure 4.40 Rear suspension geometry changes during cornering

situations such as when parking in a confined space (Figure 4.41). Since the rear wheels are made to follow the path on the road taken by the front wheels, the rear of a 4WS car does not 'cut in' in the normal way, so the risk of hitting an obstacle is greatly reduced.

High vehicle speed

At high speed, when steering adjustments are generally small, the front wheels and rear wheels turn in the same direction. This action causes the car to move in a crab-like manner rather than move in a curved path; this arrangement is beneficial at times when the car has to change lanes on a high-speed road. The elimination of the centrifugal effect and, in consequence the reduction of body roll and cornering force on the tyre, improves the stability of the car and makes it easier, and safer, to control.

Wheel angle control

The two basic systems used for 4WS vary in the manner in which the rear wheel steered angles are controlled. Honda cars use mechanical rear steering, whereas the Mazda arrangement has a rear 'gearbox' that is both power assisted and electronically controlled.

Both systems use a conventional power assisted rack-and-pinion steering mechanism for the front

steering gearbox. The mechanism also provides a take-off connection to control the rear steering gearbox via a centre, or transfer shaft. Two or more universal joints on the shaft are provided to allow for small drive angle variations.

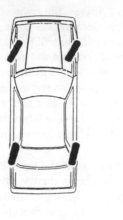

same direction   opposite direction

Figure 4.41 4WS wheel angles (angles shown are exaggerated)

4.6   STEERING SYSTEMS AND WHEEL ALIGNMENT – ROUTINE MAINTENANCE

4.6.1 Steering mechanisms – maintenance

The steering mechanism must be maintained to a very high level throughout the life of the vehicle. The steering should always be precise, without excessive play or stiffness, and either of these defects will affect the handling and stability of the vehicle. Failure to maintain the steering will without doubt render the vehicle dangerous to drive.

Although vehicle manufacturers use high quality components with high durability, after a period of time, the components of the steering mechanism may become either worn or seized. These components include:

- steering wheel
- steering column
- steering gearbox
- steering linkage
- steering ball joints.

It is therefore important that the steering mechanism is checked during routine maintenance of the vehicle.

Note that within the UK, Europe and most other countries, legislation imposes a regular test of vehicle condition. The UK MOT is an annual check which,

amongst other things, deals with steering and suspension condition.

Steering wheel

The security and condition of the steering wheel material should be checked, if the steering wheel becomes worn or damaged, the steering wheel should be replaced.

Note: Many vehicles are now fitted with a supplementary restraint system (SRS) which include the fitment of an air bag to the steering wheel. If it is necessary to remove the steering wheel, the correct manufacturer's removal and installation procedures must be followed to avoid unintended air bag inflation and to ensure that the air bag operates correctly after re-fitting the steering wheel.

A worn steering component is normally noticed by the driver of the vehicle due to the amount of freeplay at the steering wheel. The steering freeplay should be checked with the wheels in the straight-ahead position. The steering wheel freeplay is the amount that the steering wheel can be moved using fingertip pressure, without the movement of the steered wheels. Most manufacturers typically allowed a tolerance, which on older steering system designs could be as much as

25 mm (1 inch). If the steering wheel freeplay is excessive, it indicates a worn component within the steering mechanism or worn bushes.

To check for worn steering components, it is normally necessary for a second person to move the steering wheel to the right and to the left by approximately 30° from the straight-ahead position while the steering mechanism is inspected for wear by a technician. Any component that shows signs of wear should be replaced.

These checks should include steering mechanism components that are located inside the vehicle and also those which are accessed from the underside of the vehicle. Placing the vehicle on a vehicle ramp may aid the technician with the steering checks. The following components should be checked:

Steering column

The steering column connects the steering wheel to the steering gearbox. To allow the steering wheel to be offset from the steering gearbox, universal joints are normally fitted to the column. Each universal joint should be checked for wear.

The steering column top mount also contains some type of bush or bearing, this should also be checked for excessive play or wear.

Steering gearbox

The steering gearbox should be checked for wear. Wear to this component is normally indicated by the steering column shaft turning, while the output shaft (track rod ends or drop arm) remain stationary.

To prevent the ingress of dirt into the rack-and-pinion, the steering rack is fitted with steering rack gaiters to the track rod ends. These steering rack gaiters should be checked for damage, splitting etc, and replaced as necessary.

The steering mechanism should also be checked for physical damage and fluid leaks. The steering gearbox should be checked for fluid leaks, many manually operated steering gearboxes (i.e. rack-and-pinion) are lubricated with grease, added during the assembly of the component. The unit is normally sealed for the life of the assembly.

Other types of steering gearbox are filled with a lubricating oil, normally gear oil. The oil level in these types of steering boxes requires checking and topping up if necessary, during routine maintenance.

Steering ball joints

The steering linkage and ball joints should be checked for wear during routine maintenance. The ball joints should be checked by moving the steering wheel backwards and forwards while a second technician inspects the ball joints for wear.

Ball joints are protected from the ingress of dirt and water with the use of rubber dust covers, it is necessary to ensure these dust covers are in good condition.

Note that many older types of steering mechanisms are fitted with ball joints and idler linkages which are

lubricated with grease. This grease tends to deteriorate over a period of time. It may be possible to add fresh grease to the components during routine maintenance by the use of grease nipples, which are fitted to the applicable steering components.

4.6.2 Hydraulic power assisted steering – maintenance

Steering power assistance is usually provided with the aid of a hydraulic system, which is pressurized with fluid. If the fluid level in the PAS system falls to a low level, the hydraulic system will be unable to produce the assistance required, causing the steering to become very heavy and noisy.

If the fluid level falls to a very low level, damage can occur to the hydraulic pump. The PAS system oil reservoir level should therefore be checked during routine servicing to ensure that the oil level is at the maximum level when the oil is at the correct operating temperature (usually stated in the workshop manual).

The PAS hydraulic system should also be checked for leaks; a leak is typically indicated by a low reservoir oil level. Check for oil leaks from the hydraulic pump, hydraulic pipes, and steering gearbox. To check for oil leaks while the system is under high pressure, the steering can be held on full lock for a short period of time (no longer than 10 seconds). Note that due to the very high pressures that exist in the PAS hydraulic system, a very small leak will lose a large quantity of fluid.

The fluid in the hydraulic system constantly flows through the pump and steering gearbox; a component fault within the system may contaminate the fluid which is usually indicated by the discolouring of the hydraulic fluid.

4.6.3 Wheel alignment – maintenance

Although the alignment and geometry settings of the wheels are set during the production, the settings can alter during the life of the vehicle. The constant movement of the suspension bushes will eventually promote wear, resulting in wheel misalignment.

It is common for a vehicle to be driven over uneven road surfaces, driving over objects such as kerbstones during parking and other obstacles. These forces acting on the suspension components may eventually alter the alignment of one wheel and also the relationship between the alignment of all four wheels. The misalignment of the wheels is normally highlighted by the abnormal wearing of the tyres and deterioration in the quality of steering, handling and stability.

Note: Refer to the wheel and tyre section within this chapter for details and illustrations of tyre wear.

The driver of the vehicle may also notice an abnormality in the handling or stability of the vehicle. If the vehicle has been repaired due to accident damage, the wheel alignment should be checked and adjusted before the vehicle is returned to the customer.

Front-wheel alignment

The suspension components are generally very strong and withstand many of the driving forces. The most susceptible part of the wheel geometry to alter through general driving is the front wheel toe setting. Sharp shocks to the steering linkage can bend the steering linkage and track rods, altering the distance between the front road wheels.

The toe setting of the front wheels can be easily checked with the use of alignment equipment often referred to as 'tracking gauges'. These gauges are fitted to the rim of each front wheel while the wheels are in the straight-ahead position. In the past a 'trammel' gauge was employed to measure the front wheel toe setting, but either optical or electronic tracking gauges now provide a more accurate method of setting the wheel alignment.

Prior to checking the wheel toe-in/toe-out measurements, certain preliminaries should be undertaken, these include:

- Check the tyres are of the correct size and set at the correct inflation pressure.
- Check wheel bearing play.
- Check front suspension components for wear and damage.
- Position the wheels in the straight-ahead position.
- Roll the vehicle backwards then forwards to 'settle the steering'.
- Check the run-out (buckle) of the wheel; the maximum run-out should be positioned so that it does not affect the alignment measurement. Note that many modern alignment check systems include a process to account for wheel run-out.

Excessive play or suspension component faults will affect the front wheel toe setting. It is therefore essential that these checks are carried out before any alignment checks are carried out.

The wheel toe specification is often given as a measurement in millimetres (or in fractions of an inch). The measurement is therefore dependant on the size of the wheel rims fitted to the vehicle. An alternative specification that is independent of the wheel size expresses the toe setting as an angle (in minutes and seconds), e.g. with the steering set straight ahead, the wheels should toe-out so that each wheel makes an angle of 7′ 30″ with the longitudinal axis of the car.

The toe setting is adjusted by altering the length of the steering mechanism track rods. Equal adjustment of the two outer rods is necessary. Carrying out adjustments to only one side steering rod will have two effects: first it will alter the position of the steering wheel with the result that the horizontal spokes will be misaligned, and second the steering locks (turning lock) will be unequal.

Note that most rack-and-pinion steering mechanisms are fitted with right-hand screw-threaded track rods, although on a few vehicles left- and right-handed screw threads on the track rod are used to alter the length of the rod for correction of the alignment.

Incorrect toe-in or toe-out can be recognized by the wafer edge of rubber which remains on the side of the tyre tread pattern after the tyre has been scraped over the road surface. An examination of the manner in which the tread is feathering gives an indication of the fault; a wafer of rubber on the inside of the tread suggests that the wheels are toed-in and vice versa. The feathering of the tread may be more pronounced on one tyre than the other.

The combination of road camber and the action of the tyre's self-righting torque can cause both front

Figure 4.42 Checking front wheel toe-in/toe-out

wheels to turn towards the near-side of the road. This movement affects the steering geometry and explains why a manufacturer may recommend a toe setting that appears to contradict the basic theory.

Interaction between the various wheel geometry settings of a modern vehicle makes it difficult to pinpoint the cause of a fault from a given symptom i.e. tyre wear or the abnormal handling of the vehicle. After carrying out the preliminaries, a front-end check covering all aspects of the suspension geometry is advised, including checking the camber, castor and SAI. Before checking the alignment of each wheel it is necessary to carry out additional vehicle checks as well as those detailed when carrying out the toe setting checks. These should include:

- checking the body to ground clearance (the ride height)
- ensuring the correct loads/weight settings are applied to the vehicle.

Many of the wheel alignment angles are fixed and offer little or no adjustment; if an angle is not within the specification detailed by the manufacturer, it may indicate a defect with a suspension component such as a bent wishbone, suspension strut or ball joint. Rectification is then only possible through the replacement of the component.

Four-wheel alignment

The handling, stability and steerability of a modern vehicle is dependant on the wheel alignment of all four wheels. The alignment of each wheel will have an effect on the alignment of the remaining wheels.

The four-wheel alignment checks include the checking of the camber, castor and SAI at each road wheel, together with the toe setting of each road wheel. To prevent excessive tyre wear and limit the rolling resistance of the vehicle, each wheel must rotate along the same line when the vehicle is being driven in a straight line, often referred to as the 'thrust line'. The thrust line is set perpendicular to the rear axle of the vehicle.

Previous methods of checking the wheel alignment with either optical gauges or simple electronic gauges provided measurement of only the wheels on the same axle, normally the front. With modern test equipment, the technician can check the alignment of all four wheels on a vehicle during one test procedure, often referred to as 'four-wheel alignment'.

The electronic four-wheel alignment test equipment can accurately check the alignment of each wheel including, castor, camber and S.A.I. as well as the toe setting for each wheel. The test equipment also checks the relationship between each of the axles, ensuring that all of the wheels align with each other.

There are many types of four-wheel alignment test equipment available from different equipment manufacturers; the method of using the equipment will vary depending on the type used. Always refer to test equipment instructions for correct use.

Four-wheel alignment equipment often consists of a main control consul or control panel with a VDU. There are also four wheel heads or sensors. When each of the wheel sensors is attached to a wheel, the sensors are then connected to each other using a cable or some form of wireless connection. The sensors are then connected to the main control consul.

It is necessary to place the front wheels onto a turntable to enable them to be turned through a pre-determined angle during the tests. This enables castor and SAI measurements to be established. Note that some turntables have the angles marked on the plate assembly thus enabling some measurements to be established directly from the turntable.

The technician will have to carry out a number of processes (such as turning the steering wheel) to enable

Figure 4.43 Four-wheel alignment check

the sensors to detect the angles and geometry measurements.

Standard vehicle specifications are normally provided by the vehicle manufacturer for a vehicle in good condition and without any modifications, including standard fitment wheels.

Before a four-wheel alignment test is carried out, each of the preliminary checks should be carried out to the front and rear wheels of the vehicle, as detailed with the two-wheel alignment checks. It is also important to ensure that the vehicle is parked on a level surface; if the surface is not level, the test results will be inaccurate. Many workshops carrying out frequent wheel alignment checks have a vehicle ramp/lift that is level and used for the specific purpose of wheel alignment checks. If a vehicle lift is used, after the checks have been carried out it is then possible to make suspension adjustments and then recheck the vehicle measurements without the need to move the vehicle.

Many vehicle manufacturers provide adjustable steering and suspension components to enable the vehicle to be set to the required alignment specifications.

4.6.4 Road testing

After the checks and adjustments have been carried out, ideally the vehicle should be driven to check its handling and stability. Although some vehicles display certain handling characteristics that are inherent in that particular type of vehicle, the vehicle should be checked for the following conditions while it is being driven along a flat road:

- **Driving the vehicle in a straight line.** The steering wheel should be in the straight-ahead (neutral) position. The vehicle should neither pull to the left or to the right.
- **Turning** (while the vehicle is moving). The steering wheel should turn easily without having to use excessive effort. The steering wheel should return to the straight-ahead position when released after turning (self-centre).
- **Braking**. The vehicle should not pull to either side while braking in a straight line. The vehicle should also be checked for abnormal noises while it is being driven and manoeuvring; examples of this include suspension components contacting the vehicle body.

4.7 SUSPENSION

4.7.1 Introduction

The suspension system is fitted between the frame (or body) of the vehicle and the road wheels. The suspension provides the following:

- The suspension system absorbs the bumps and shocks from the road surface to allow the passengers to travel in comfort, provide vehicle stability and vehicle handling. The suspension will try to maintain contact between the road wheels/ tyres and the road surface under all surface and driving conditions.
- The suspension system transmits the engines power (which has been applied to the road wheels) to the body/chassis and therefore also transmits the braking forces from the road wheels to the body.
- The suspension maintains the road wheels in the correct geometry during driving and cornering.

The suspension assembly is made up of the following components:

Road spring

The road springs are used to absorb the bumps and shocks transmitted from the road surface and prevent them from reaching the body of the vehicle. The springs are made from different types of material, each having different characteristics. The weight of the vehicle's body is supported by the road springs.

Dampers

When the vehicle strikes a bump in the road the spring deflects and oscillates. The damper reduces the oscillations of the spring thus improving the ride comfort and the road holding of the vehicle. Dampers are sometimes referred to as 'shock absorbers' although this is probably an incorrect description of the function of the damper. It is the spring and whole suspension system that absorbs the shocks created by the road surface.

Suspension linkage

The suspension linkage connects the vehicle body to the wheel and allows for movement between the body and the wheels.

The suspension layout of a vehicle uses many components. There are generally two types of suspension system in use; the rigid axle suspension system and the independent suspension system, which allows each wheel to move independently of the other wheel on the same axle line. There are some systems, however, that do not use a rigid axle but are not fully independent due to the use of connecting beams between the wheels that effectively prevent fully independent operation.

Rigid axle suspension

The right and left wheels are interconnected by a solid, single beam axle. The layout of the suspension is relatively simple and very strong in construction which makes it suitable for large vehicles i.e. goods vehicles and buses. Many older cars were fitted with rigid front and rear axles, with the rear axle being used to house the final drive assembly and drive shafts for driving the rear wheels.

Figure 4.44 shows a relatively modern design for a rigid axle suspension system using coil or helical springs. These systems are often fitted to light commercial vehicles but are now rarely used on passenger cars.

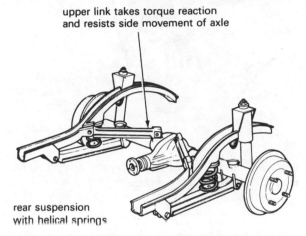

upper link takes torque reaction and resists side movement of axle

rear suspension with helical springs

Figure 4.44 Rigid rear axle on a rear-wheel drive vehicle with coil/helical springs

Figure 4.45 shows a medium-sized commercial vehicle with rigid front and rear axles, both fitted with leaf-type springs.

Independent suspension

With this system right and left wheels are not directly connected together and can therefore move independently of each other. Each road wheel can maintain the optimum wheel geometry and road surface contact over uneven road surfaces and this provides additional passenger comfort and superior road holding compared to a rigid rear axle.

The vehicle's body is supported by the road springs and is referred to as the sprung weight; the wheels and axles are not supported by the springs and therefore referred to as the unsprung weight.

Sprung and unsprung weight

If the sprung weight of the vehicle is high, the passengers will ride in comfort when the vehicle travels over rough surfaces. However, if the unsprung weight of the vehicle is high, the suspension system works harder to control the movement of the unsprung weight, so the body of the vehicle will shake more as the vehicle travels over rough road surfaces.

The type of suspension system used and the manner in which the suspension is set up (soft or stiff springs) affects the comfort of the vehicle's passengers and the stability of the vehicle while driving. The vehicle

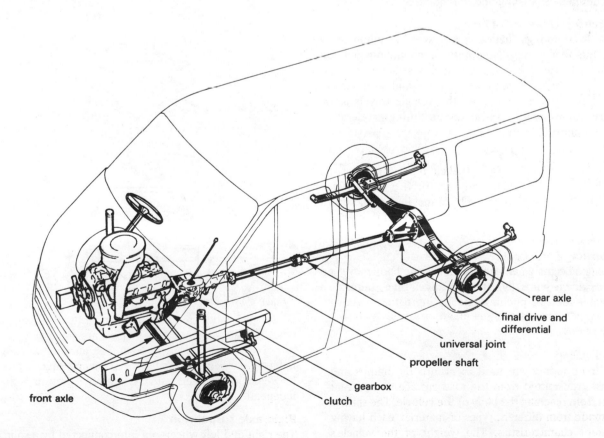

front axle

clutch

gearbox

propeller shaft

universal joint

final drive and differential

rear axle

Figure 4.45 A vehicle with rigid front and rear axles, fitted with leaf-type springs

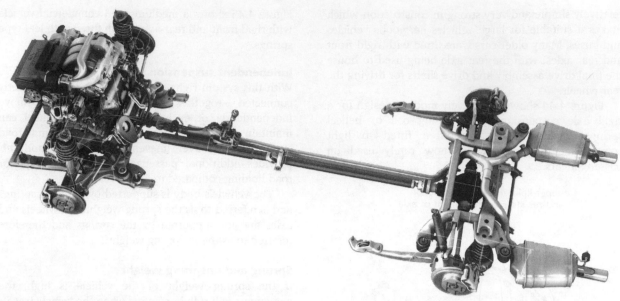

Figure 4.46 A vehicle with independent front and rear suspension

manufacturer must therefore take into account its purpose of use when selecting the type of suspension to be used.

The movement of the body (sprung weight) in relation to the wheels (unsprung weight) changes as the vehicle travels along bumpy roads and corners. The forces exerted on the sprung weight of the vehicle can be defined as pitching and rolling.

Pitching (Figure 4.47)
The front springs (helical-type) extend simultaneously as the rear springs compress, a continuous motion results in the body of the vehicle oscillating up and down at the front and back in a fore-and-aft direction. Pitching often occurs when the vehicle travels along very bumpy roads. It also occurs during acceleration and braking.

Rolling (Figure 4.48)
The left-hand side springs (helical-type) expand as the right-hand side springs compress (or vice versa) which results in the body of the vehicle moving up and down from side to side in relation to the centre of the vehicle. Body roll occurs as the vehicle corners.

Bounce
Bounce occurs when each corner of the body moves up and down virtually at the same time (almost a combination of pitching and rolling acting together).

Bouncing can be caused by the vehicle driving along a road with an undulating surface.

Yaw
Yaw is the turning movement of the body around the centre point of the vehicle. Yaw occurs as the vehicle corners; if the cornering speed is too high, the transfer of weight can cause the vehicle to spin.

Figure 4.47 Pitching

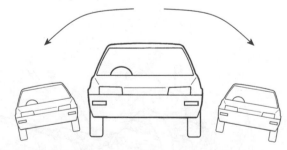

Figure 4.48 Rolling

4.8 THE REQUIREMENTS OF A SPRING

4.8.1 Purpose of a spring

Mounting the axle directly to the frame of a vehicle would subject the occupants and general vehicle components to severe shocks. This can be seen in Figure 4.49a, which shows the upward movement of the frame when the wheel strikes a bump.

In this case the vertical acceleration would cause considerable discomfort to the passengers, and most probably the reluctance of the vehicle frame to move upwards quickly (inertia) would buckle the wheel. A similar effect can be felt when riding a bicycle over a bump.

Additionally, when travelling at speed, it is likely that the wheels will lose contact with the ground. When the bump has forced the vehicle in the upwards direction, the wheel/vehicle may continue to move upwards due to momentum, even though the surface falls away again. When the surface consists of repeated bumps and undulations, the wheel may be out of contact with the road for a high percentage of time. Loss of contact with the road means the wheel/tyre assembly will not provide good grip for cornering, braking and accelerating.

A spring fitted between the wheel and the frame allows the wheel to move up and down without causing similar movement of the frame (Figure 4.49b). The spring absorbs road shocks and allows the wheel to follow the irregular contour of the road surface. For this purpose the wheel assembly should be as light as possible (light unsprung weight).

Note that road shocks can be further reduced by fitting a 'spring' to the wheel; this is achieved by use of a pneumatic tyre.

The suspension system, which includes the springs, components, linkages, tyres etc., therefore provides a means of isolating the road shocks from the vehicle body/chassis. The main benefits are improved driver/passenger comfort and improved grip between the tyre and road throughout the various driving conditions.

In addition, there is an inevitable reduction in noise and flexing of the vehicle structure, which in turn reduces the wear on vehicle fixings and fixtures that can be caused by constant flexing of the vehicle.

The mechanism fitted between the wheel and the frame is termed the suspension system, the main items being the spring and damper.

Types of spring

Various forms of springing can be used. These are:

- steel – laminated, helical and torsion bar
- rubber – hydrolastic
- pneumatic – hydro-pneumatic, air.

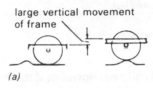
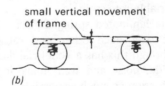

Figure 4.49 Effect of fitting a spring

4.9 TYPES AND CHARACTERISTICS OF METAL SPRINGS

4.9.1 Laminated or leaf springs

Laminated or leaf springs provide a low cost and simple method of connecting a spring to an axle. This therefore makes such springs very popular for rigid axles and they have been widely used with many light commercial vehicles as well as heavy trucks.

The main details of a semi-elliptic spring are shown in Figure 4.50. The main leaf, which is rolled at each end to form an eye, has a number of leaves clamped to it. To ensure a constant stress throughout the spring the leaves are graduated in length. Rebound clips transmit the load to some of the lower leaves during the return motion of the spring, and eliminate the need for fitting a large number of leaves above the main plate.

Rubber bushes, fitted in each eye, allow for movement of the spring, and act as noise insulators. Alteration in spring length (during deflection of the spring) is accommodated by a swinging shackle.

The stiffness or 'spring rate', (the force required to deflect the leaf spring) is governed by:

- the length of the spring – shorter spring, higher rate
- the width the leaf – wider spring, higher rate
- the thickness of the leaf – thicker leaf, higher rate
- the number of leaves – greater number, higher rate.

To obtain a 'soft' ride, a low-rate spring is required; the low-rate spring will deflect a larger amount under a given load. Normal springs have a constant rate, and give a deflection which is proportional to the load

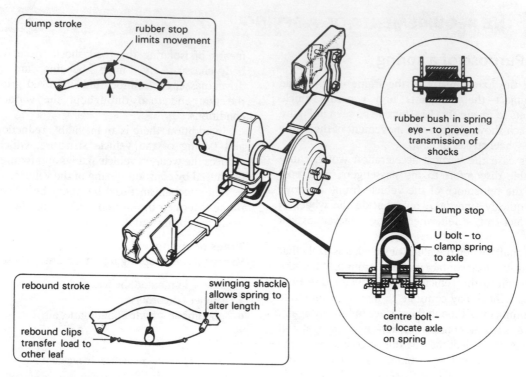

Figure 4.50 Laminated or leaf spring

applied (Hooke's Law). However, if the lower leaves are set to a reverse camber, a stiffening-up of the spring will occur as deflection increases: this is called a progressive spring or variable-rate spring.

When the laminated spring deflects, the plates or leaves slide over each other and cause inter-plate friction. Although this has a beneficial damping effect, the 'hard' ride, noise and wear make it necessary to reduce this friction as much as possible.

Older designs of spring had to be sprayed with penetrating oil, but on newer designs, special features are incorporated to eliminate the need for periodic attention. These are:

- synthetic rubber buttons fitted at the ends of the leaves
- inter-leaf plates of low friction material
- reducing the number of leaves (as the number is reduced, the width must be increased).

To gain the full advantage of the last remedy many springs in use today have only one leaf. Overstressing at the centre of the spring is avoided by using a tapered leaf, wide at the centre and thin at the ends.

4.9.2 Helical springs

Helical springs are often used in conjunction with front or rear independent suspension (Figure 4.51) and therefore the helical spring is the most commonly used on modern light vehicles.

Coil and torsion bar springs (refer to section 4.9.3) are superior to leaf springs as regards energy storage

(energy stored in a given weight of spring). However, whereas the leaf spring fulfils many duties, the other types of spring (helical and torsion bar) require additional suspension members (e.g. struts) which add to the basic weight and complexity.

The helical spring is made from a wire of special spring-steel formed into the shape of a coil. The rate of the spring is governed by the length and diameter of the wire. The length of the spring is controlled by its diameter and the number of active coils.

Helical springs are commonly used to support the rigid or dead axle fitted at the rear of a front-wheel drive car. Figure 4.52 shows a typical layout in which the spring acts directly on to the axle.

Axle location at the top and bottom is provided by the top mounting of the damper (shock absorber) and the trailing arm. As well as providing fore-and-aft stiffness, the lower arm, in conjunction with the damper tube, absorbs the braking torque.

Lateral or side movement of the axle is resisted by a steel rod, commonly referred to as a Panhard rod. The rod has a rubber bush at each end where it is bolted to the axle and body.

On high-performance cars, a rear stabilizer or roll bar is often fitted; the bar connects to each side of the axle as well as to the body. When one side of the axle is forced to move an excessive amount due to body roll, the stabilizer bar (which is effectively a torsion spring) prevents the body from rolling too much. The stabilizer bar does allow the body to rise or fall against the suspension but it ensures that the roll is controlled when the car is cornering.

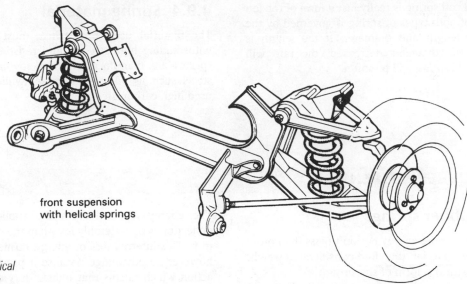

front suspension
with helical springs

*Figure 4.51 A helical
suspension spring*

A different arrangement is illustrated in Figure 4.53. The dampers and springs for each side are combined in a single assembly. Trailing arms are again used for fore-and-aft axle location, but the rear axle beam acts as a torsion bar to resist the twisting force applied when the left and right suspension move up and down in opposite directions.

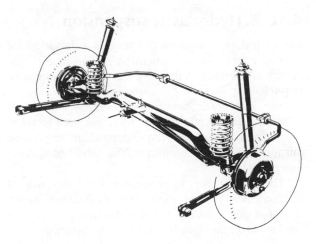

Figure 4.52 Rear suspension for a dead axle using helical/coil springs

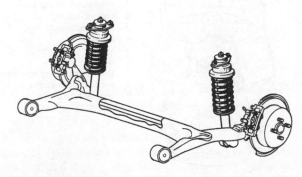

Figure 4.53 A beam rear axle where the beam functions as a torsion bar

When the vehicle corners, the weight of the vehicle body is transferred to the outside of the corner, and the inside corner of the vehicle becomes lighter. The increase in body weight compresses the outer spring while the inner spring expands as the weight reduces. The weight transfer causes the rear axle beam to twist. The torsion bar axle beam opposes those twisting forces applied, which helps to maintain the body at a constant height, in a similar way to the function of a stabilizer bar.

4.9.3 Torsion bar

A torsion bar spring is a straight bar, circular or square in section, anchored to the vehicle body /chassis frame at one end, and at its other end connected to a suspension arm or lever.

Figure 4.54 shows a torsion bar suspension system used on a car. The torsion bar has serrations or splines at each end which connect the bar to the body with the levers. An adjustment is provided at the frame end to 'level' the suspension.

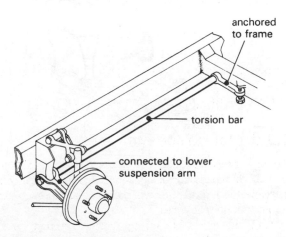

anchored
to frame

torsion bar

connected to lower
suspension arm

Figure 4.54 Torsion bar springing

Since a helical coil spring is really just a form of torsion bar, the rate of both types of spring is governed by the same factors, length and diameter. If the length is increased or the diameter decreased, the rate will decrease, i.e. the spring will be softer.

4.9.4 Spring material

The material used for springs must be capable of withstanding high stresses and resisting fatigue. Most springs are manufactured from low-percentage alloy steels such as silico-manganese, while early designs used high-carbon steel.

4.10   RUBBER SUSPENSION

4.10.1 Rubber springs

Rubber can store more energy per unit mass than other types of spring material, therefore considerable weight can be saved with this form of suspension.

Rubber springs, loaded in compression or shear, can be used to act as the main suspension spring, or fitted in conjunction with metal springs to modify the suspension characteristics. Many suspension arrangements employ a large rubber 'bump stop' to stiffen the suspension spring at maximum deflection.

Figure 4.55 is a simplified drawing of a rubber suspension system, which is similar to the type used on a popular small car. The rubber spring is positioned between the vehicle frame and the top link of the suspension system. By connecting the spring to a point near the link pivot, deflection of the spring can be reduced to a minimum, without reducing the total wheel movement.

The rubber spring design gives a rising-rate characteristic, i.e. it is 'soft' for small wheel deflections but becomes 'harder' as the spring deflects further with greater wheel movements.

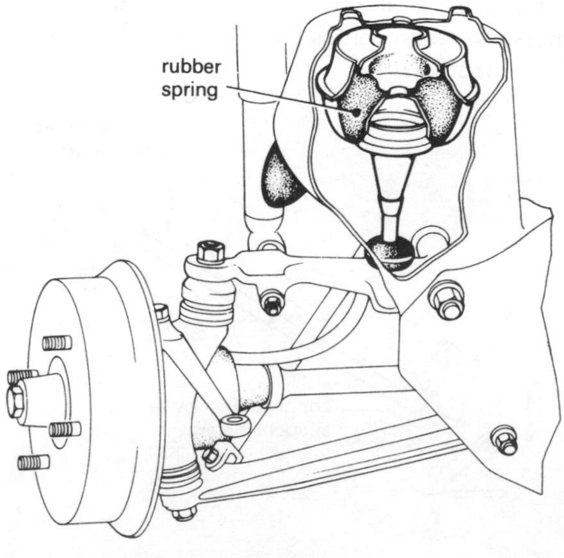

The energy released from the rubber spring after deflection is considerably less than the energy imparted to it. This internal loss of energy, termed hysteresis, as however an advantage because it provides a damping action which means that lighter duty dampers can be used.

Rubber suspension systems typically have a tendency to 'settle down' during the initial period of the life of the car. This means that suspension geometry may alter slightly as the new car is used and allowances must therefore be made in the design of such systems.

4.10.2 Hydrolastic suspension

The hydrolastic suspension system is a development of the rubber type suspension arrangement; the system is intended to improve the vehicle's resistance to pitch.

The hydrolastic layout on a vehicle consists of rubber displacer units (Figure 4.56) mounted between the vehicle frame and the independent suspension linkage (which is controlling the wheel deflection movement).

These units are inter-connected by the use of hydraulic fluid pipes. A pipe is used to link the vehicle's left-hand side units together and another pipe to do a similar job on the right-hand side of the vehicle.

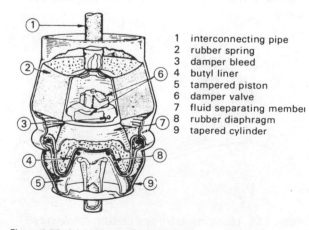

1   interconnecting pipe
2   rubber spring
3   damper bleed
4   butyl liner
5   tampered piston
6   damper valve
7   fluid separating member
8   rubber diaphragm
9   tapered cylinder

Figure 4.55 Rubber spring suspension

Figure 4.56 A hydrolastic displacer unit

The hydrolastic system is pressurized with a liquid (water + alcohol + anti-corrosive agent) after any air has been extracted from the system.

Each displacer unit comprises a rubber spring, a metal separating member holding two rubber damper valves, a rubber diaphragm attached to the suspension linkage holding the wheel, and a metal body which is secured to the frame of the vehicle.

Road irregularities normally cause the vehicle to pitch, roll and bounce, so the operation of the system under these conditions is examined below.

Pitch

A sudden upward movement of the front wheel causes the diaphragm to displace the fluid through the damper. This action will in turn force fluid along the pipe to the rear unit where it will move the diaphragm and raise the rear of the car to the level of the front (Figure 4.57).

When the front wheel descends, the fluid is returned and the vehicle settles back to its normal riding position. During this sequence the fluid has to pass the damper valve in each unit, so restriction to fluid flow at the valves and in the pipeline damps out any pitch oscillation tendency.

Roll

When a vehicle is cornering, centrifugal action causes the body of the vehicle to tilt or roll outwards; this action is apparent when 'soft' conventional springs are used.

The hydrolastic system is 'soft' when a single wheel is moved, but if, as when cornering, the two outside suspension units are loaded as the weight of the vehicle

shifts to the outside of the corner, a stiffening of the system occurs.

Under this type of loading, fluid is not displaced from one unit to the other. Instead the increased fluid pressure deflects the rubber springs and these provide a marked resistance to the roll of the body.

Bounce

This condition causes the four wheels to deflect at the same time, so all the hydrolastic units will perform similarly to the outer units when they were reacting to roll.

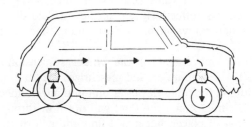

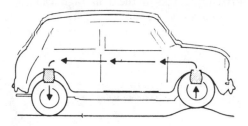

Figure 4.57 Action of hydrolastic units

4.11   GAS AND AIR SUSPENSION

4.11.1 Hydro-pneumatic suspension

This system differs from the normal metal/spring suspension in a number of ways. One main difference is that the suspension unit is supported by a mass of gas and the mass remains constant irrespective of the load carried by the wheel.

However, gas pressure increases progressively as its volume is reduced i.e. when a wheel moves up it compresses the gas into a smaller volume in much the same way as air is compressed when a hand or foot pump is operated (especially if the outlet of the pump is blocked). Additionally, as the gas is progressively compressed, greater effort is required to compress it even more. This feature is desirable and means that the suspension stiffens as the load on the wheel increases. Figure 4.58 shows the basic principle of a hydro-pneumatic system. Liquid contained in the lower chamber of a container is used to transmit the force

from the suspension piston to nitrogen gas, which is stored in the upper chamber of the container. The upper and lower chambers are separated by a diaphragm or separator which keeps the fluid and gas separate but transfers the force from the fluid (which cannot be significantly compressed) to the gas (which can be compressed).

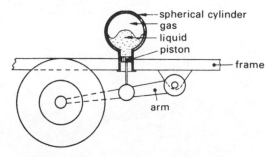

Figure 4.58 A hydro-pneumatic suspension system

4.11.2 Hydragas suspension

This system has been developed from the hydrolastic type of suspension, the main difference being that the rubber spring is replaced by a pneumatic spring.

Figure 4.59 shows the layout of one of the four hydragas units fitted to a vehicle. The units are interconnected in pairs by a fluid pipeline, which links the front unit with the rear unit on the same side of the vehicle. This line allows the liquid fluid pressure in the two units to equalize thus reducing the fore and aft pitching motion, which is most noticeable on short-wheelbase cars.

The hydragas unit consists of three main parts; nitrogen gas (effectively the spring), a fluid displacer and a damper valve block (with bump and rebound valves).

Bump movement of the wheel suspension arm deflects the diaphragm and pressurizes the fluid. If the pressure in the other displacer unit and interconnecting pipe is similar, then the fluid will not flow through to the other displacer, but it will flow through the bump valve in the damper valve block into the chamber. The pressurized fluid acts on the diaphragm causing the gas to be compressed. Compressing the gas creates a resistance to the suspension arm movement, and this resistance progressively increases the more the gas is compressed. On rebound, the fluid flows in the opposite direction through the rebound valve in the damper valve block. Energy which causes the spring to oscillate is absorbed as the fluid is passed through the damper.

The action of the interconnecting fluid lines in relation to pitch, roll and bounce is similar to that of the hydrolastic system.

Citroën system

One particular hydragas suspension system was fitted to many Citroën models, a version of which is shown in Figure 4.60. This pneumatic spring system has a hydraulic control which not only allows the driver to adjust the ground clearance of the body of the vehicle but also maintains this set clearance irrespective of the load carried.

Each wheel is mounted on a suspension arm which is supported by a pneumatic spring. The springs (gas) are interconnected transversely (side-to-side). Between the suspension arms, at the front and rear, are anti-roll bars, which are linked to height correctors by means of control rods.

An engine-driven pump supplies oil under pressure to a hydraulic accumulator and this is connected to the height control or levelling valves.

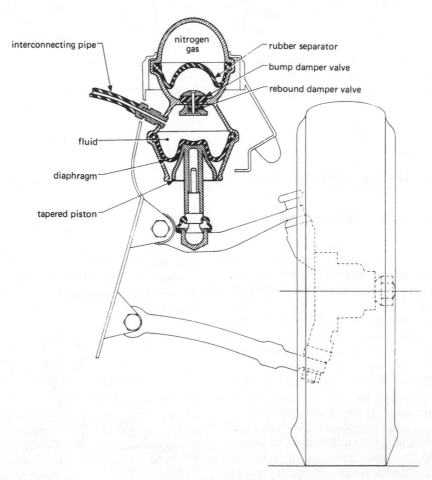

Figure 4.59 Hydragas suspension

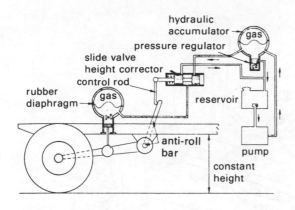

Figure 4.60 Layout of a hydropneumatic suspension system

As the vehicle is loaded, the downward movement of the vehicle structure causes rotation of the anti-roll bar. This moves the slide valve and uncovers the supply port to allow oil to flow from the accumulator to the suspension cylinders. When the vehicle reaches a predetermined height, which can be varied by a selector inside the car, the anti-roll bar and control rod move the slide valve back to the 'neutral' position. A decrease in load gives a similar sequence of events, except that valve movement causes the oil in the suspension cylinder to be discharged back to the reservoir.

A delay device (or dashpot) is incorporated in the height corrector valve to prevent rapid oil flow past the valve when the wheel contacts a bump or dip in the road. Without this dashpot, sudden movements of the wheel would mean that the valve is continually working and this would give an unsatisfactory operation.

Damping is provided by restricting the oil flow from the spherical chamber to the cylinder in which the piston slides. The restriction is created using small holes, which are closed by disc-type valves. This arrangement allows the oil to flow to and from the cylinder and sphere in a manner similar to other hydraulic dampers.

In the Citroën application, the hydraulic pressure was also used for power assistance in steering, power braking and gear changing. One model employed a braking system with independent front and rear brake circuits, interconnected with the hydraulic suspension system. This arrangement proportioned the effort applied at each brake depending on the load carried by the wheel.

4.11.3 Air suspension

Air suspension systems are generally fitted to luxury or four-wheel drive vehicles when it is necessary to alter the body height from the ground. The air suspension also provides a self-levelling facility; if a heavy weight is placed in the luggage compartment, the air suspension system compensates and maintains the vehicle body height at the correct level.

Air suspension uses a chamber of air that replaces the ordinary helical road spring. Each suspension strut is fitted with an air chamber. The air, which is under pressure, is contained within the air spring by a flexible diaphragm.

The height of the vehicle can be altered by increasing or decreasing the air pressure within the suspension strut. Increasing the air pressure within the air chamber increases the distance between the suspension and the body and therefore increases the vehicle height. Decreasing the air pressure lowers the vehicle height.

Varying the pressure in the suspension struts can also maintain the vehicle body at a set level, providing self-levelling suspension. An electronically controlled actuator controls the air entering or exiting the suspension strut air chamber.

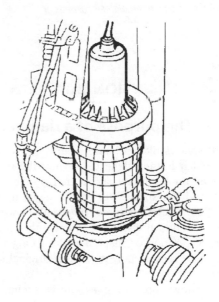

Figure 4.61 Air suspension strut

Air compressor
Air pressure is provided by an electrically driven or engine-driven air compressor pump. An accumulator acts as a reservoir of stored compressed air. Each suspension strut is connected individually to the compressed air reservoir.

Height sensor
The ride height at the front and rear of the vehicle is monitored with the use of suspension height sensors.

Electronic control
An electronic control unit (ECU) controls the operation of the system. The driver of the vehicle selects the suspension height setting for the vehicle with a switch. The ECU controls the vehicle height setting by either adding or reducing air pressure to the appropriate suspension strut via solenoid valves.

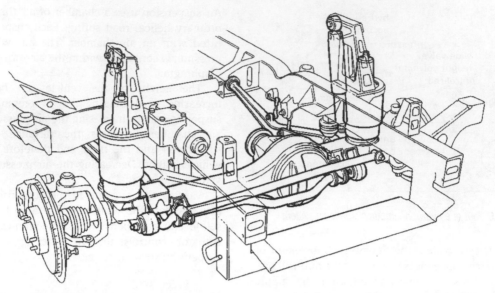

Figure 4.62 A vehicle fitted with air suspension

4.12   SUSPENSION DAMPERS

4.12.1   The purpose of a damper

When a wheel strikes a bump, energy is given to the spring, which is then deflected. When the wheel has passed over the bump, the stored energy in the spring is released and the spring will try to regain its original shape. This is referred to as 'rebound'. However, the rebound action of the spring will carry the spring past the normal position or shape and the spring will then oscillate until it eventually regains its original shape or position.

The spring's oscillating action is similar to the movement of a pendulum; a freely suspended pendulum will oscillate for a considerable time after being struck. Anything made from a springy type of material such as rubber or spring steel will respond in the same way. Even a ball when it is bounced continues to bounce due to the stored energy being released from the compressed air and rubber material. Each time the ball bounces, some of the energy is lost until eventually all the energy is dissipated. However, it is possible to reduce the number of times that the ball bounces by placing a hand over the ball and thus reducing the height that the ball bounces each time. In effect, the hand has absorbed the energy and dampened the bouncing and rebound action.

In order to give a comfortable ride in a motor vehicle, a device must be fitted to absorb the energy stored in the spring and so reduce the number of oscillations occurring between the initial bump and the return of the spring to its rest position. This is the duty performed by the damper (often misleadingly called a 'shock absorber').

Early designs of damper utilized the friction between two sets of plates, one set attached to the vehicle frame, the other set to the axle. This type of friction damper converts the 'spring' energy into heat.

Hydraulic dampers

Hydraulic dampers are the main type in use today. They dissipate the energy by pumping oil through small orifices which provide a resistance to the flow of the oil. The resistance of the hydraulic damper, due to the oil flowing through the orifices, increases as the speed of spring deflection increases, whereas the friction damper gives a constant resistance. The resistance to spring movement can apply either to the rebound stroke only (single-acting), or to both the bump and rebound strokes (double-acting). Hydraulic dampers can also offer a differential action, i.e. resisting both strokes but exerting a greater resisting action on the rebound.

The two main types of hydraulic damper are the lever-type and the telescopic direct-acting-type.

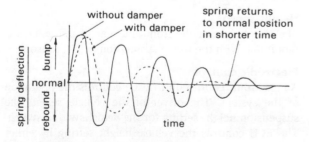

Figure 4.63 Spring oscillation curves

4.12.2 Lever-type dampers

Figure 4.64 shows a diagrammatic view of a lever-type damper, which is mounted to the vehicle frame and connected by a lever and link to the axle. The horizontal cylinder contains two pistons which are fitted with recuperator and pressure valves. A thin, mineral-based damper oil is introduced to the level of the bottom of the filler plug.

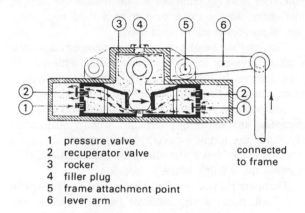

1 pressure valve
2 recuperator valve
3 rocker
4 filler plug
5 frame attachment point
6 lever arm

connected
to frame

Figure 4.64 A lever-type damper

Bump movement of the axle operates the damper pistons and displaces oil from one chamber to the other. The oil, which is now under pressure, opens the pressure valve thus allowing the oil to flow through an orifice that then provides the resistance. The oil then passes through the open recuperator valve to break down the depression created in the other chamber. Rebound of the spring produces a similar action in the opposite direction.

Actual dampers differ from Figure 4.63 in various ways – the valve construction and position are different, and in some designs the cylinders are mounted vertically.

4.12.3 Telescopic direct-acting-type dampers

As the name suggests, this type of damper is directly connected between the body and the suspension member that moves with the road wheel.

It is made either as a separate, bolt-on unit or as an integral part of a suspension system. Direct-acting dampers are made in two basic forms: single-tube and twin-tube.

Single-tube dampers (Figure 4.65)
The operating cylinder is a single tube attached to an eye or stem for connection to the moving part of the suspension. The tube is closed at the bottom end by a cap. A piston slides within the tube, the piston being fitted with two-way reed valves which cover a series of holes through which oil can pass. The piston is attached

to a rod that passes through a guide retained in the top of the tube.

The rod is attached to the car body, and rubber bushes at the attachment points isolate road shocks and allow for slight angular movement of the damper body. A rubber seal, held in place by fluid pressure, is positioned adjacent to the guide to prevent the escape of fluid. An abutment plate fitted to the piston, limits the stroke and provides a flat surface for contact with the top seal when the damper is fully extended. A tubular shield, attached to the rod member, is fitted to protect the rod from dirt and stone damage.

A chamber at the base of the damper, sealed by a free piston, contains a quantity of inert gas. When the damper is completely filled with thin-type mineral oil, this gas is in compressed state.

On the bump stroke the inner movement of the piston displaces oil from the bottom to the top chamber. The energy needed to pump the oil through the drillings and deflect the piston valves provides the damping action. By varying the size of the 'bump' and 'rebound' orifices, the resistance of each stroke can be altered to suit the requirement.

For a given downward movement of the piston, the volume available in the upper chamber for the oil is not as great as the volume required by the oil, so when this action occurs the free piston is forced to move slightly downwards and compresses the gas thus providing increased damping.

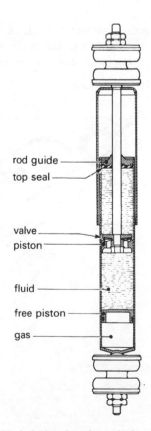

rod guide

top seal

valve

piston

fluid

free piston

gas

Figure 4.65 A single-tube telescopic damper

The single-tube construction has a number of merits: it can displace a large quantity of fluid without fluid aeration or noise and be consistent in service even when installed at a large angle to the main suspension movement. Denting of the single working tube by stones must be avoided, so this is a good reason for placing the damper at the centre of the helical suspension spring.

The potential energy stored in a deflected suspension spring is converted into heat by a damper. With this design good heat dissipation from the damper to the air flow is achieved.

On MacPherson suspension systems (see section 4.14.2), a single-tube, gas-pressurized damper is used as a main suspension 'leg'. In this application a more robust rod guide is fitted to enable it to act as a top bearing to accommodate steering movement.

Twin-tube damper (Figure 4.66)

An extra tube is used on this type to form both a reservoir for the fluid and an overflow region to accommodate fluid resulting from rod displacement and expansion.

The base valve at the bottom of the working chamber has three duties to perform. It controls:

1 the outward flow of fluid into the reservoir during the 'bump' movement
2 the fluid return on the 'rebound' stroke
3 the bleed leakage for reducing the damper's resistance during slow-speed suspension movements.

The life of a direct-acting damper depends on its fluid-sealing ability, so great attention is paid to the design of bearing and seal. The hard chrome-surfaced piston rod works in a sintered iron guide bush or bearing, which is lubricated by a small amount of fluid forced through the bearing on each stroke. A multi-lipped rubber seal placed on the outside of the bush prevents fluid leaking out of the reservoir.

Baffles in the reservoir prevent violent movement of the fluid which would otherwise cause aeration (because air will compress and reduce the damping effect). Any fluid in an aerated state that is allowed to enter the working chamber would render the damper ineffective, so for extra protection a fluid containing special anti-foam additives is used.

The long stroke of a direct-acting damper allows the working pressure to be much lower than with a lever-type damper. In view of this, the direct-acting type is more reliable, and is also cheaper to manufacture.

Although the best performance is achieved when the dampers are mounted vertically, many suspension layouts in use today, especially those used to support a live rear axle, have the dampers set 'diagonally' to improve the stability of the suspension.

Dampers do not offer any resistance to slow-speed body roll, because the inherent bleed feature in the damper allows this movement to take place. High-speed roll is resisted, but manufacturers generally fit a transverse stabilizer, often called an anti-roll bar, to control the roll motion.

Although sophisticated equipment is available for oscillating the dampers to test their operation, a simple test can be carried out by pressing down with your hand on the corner of the car. By noting the number of oscillations made by the spring before the body comes to rest, the effectiveness of the dampers can be ascertained.

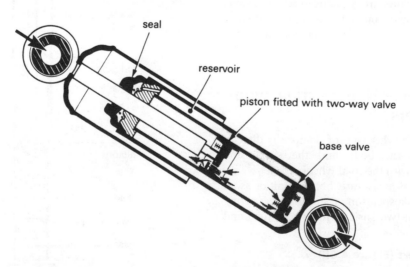

Figure 4.66 Twin tube telescopic damper

4.13 RIGID AXLE SUSPENSION

4.13.1 Advantages and disadvantages of a rigid axle

Note: Also refer to sections 4.9.1, 4.9.2 and 4.9.3 for additional information.

The rigid axle, or beam axle, is simple in construction; a beam links the right-hand wheel with the left-hand wheel. The rigid axle has the following advantages:

- The construction of the axle is simple and therefore the number of components used is few.
- Maintenance of the axle is simple.
- The construction of the axle is very strong; the rigid axle is fitted to goods vehicles and large passenger vehicles.
- Wheels change their alignment when the axle moves up and down, tyre wear is therefore reduced.

Although there are many advantages, the rigid axle also has some disadvantages when compared to independent suspension designs:

- The unsprung weight of the rigid axle is high, providing reduced comfort.
- The movement of one wheel will also influence the movement to the other wheel fitted to the axle.

4.13.2 General construction and applications of a rigid axle

Although popular on older vehicles, rigid front axles are not commonly used on modern light vehicles such as passenger cars. However, some light commercial vehicles and heavier vehicles do still use rigid front axles.

Rigid rear axles are still used on a number of applications, especially for heavier vehicles and light commercial vehicles. For rear-wheel drive vehicles fitted with a rigid rear axle, the rear axle casing often houses the final drive, differential and drive shafts.

Springs and axle location

The rigid axle fitted with leaf springs is normally fitted to light and heavy goods vehicles and large passenger vehicles. The leaf springs often used with rigid axles also act as the suspension linkage by connecting the wheels to the body of the vehicle. Additional suspension linkages are often not fitted when leaf springs are used.

Many four-wheel drive vehicles use a rigid front axle and a rigid rear axle. The leading and trailing arms offer an improved ride quality to the parallel leaf spring because the road springs support only the weight of the body and are not directly locating the axle. The axle-to-body movement is controlled by the use of either leading or trailing arms. Coil springs are used instead of

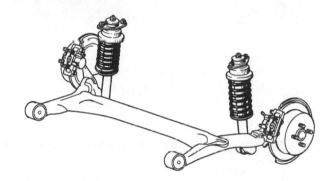

Figure 4.68 Adaption of a rigid rear axle used on a front-wheel drive vehicle

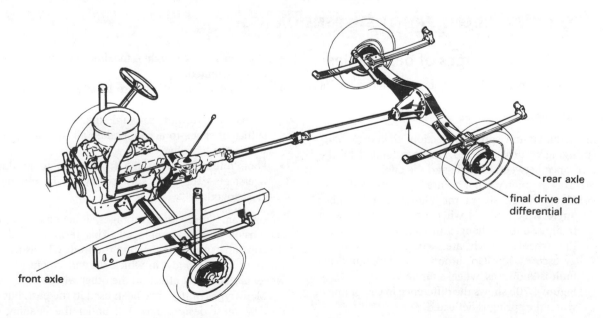

rear axle

final drive and differential

front axle

Figure 4.67 A vehicle with front and rear rigid axles and leaf springs

leaf springs, which by their compression provide a more uniform spring force. The axle is prevented from moving laterally by the fitment of a lateral control rod, occasionally referred to as a Panhard rod.

Note that adaptations of the rigid rear axle are fitted to many front-wheel drive vehicles. Figure 4.69 shows a typical modern rigid torsion bar-type rear axle which has trailing arms locating the axle and coil springs.

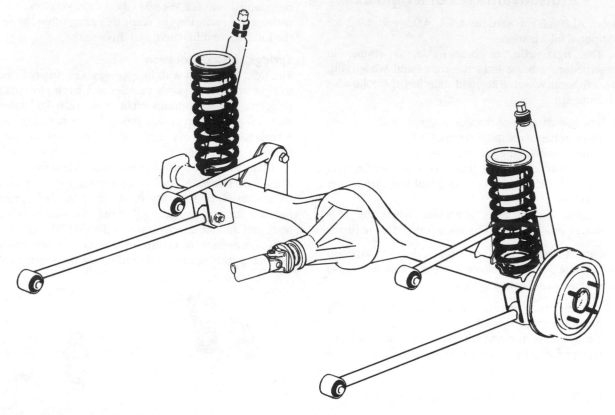

Figure 4.69 Rear axle using coil springs and with leading arm for axle location

4.14   INDEPENDENT FRONT SUSPENSION (IFS)

4.14.1 Disadvantages of beam axles

In order to appreciate the advantages of independent suspension, the disadvantages of a beam axle should be examined. These are:

- Small maximum spring deflection, therefore 'hard' springing-vertical axle movement is limited by the clearance between the axle and the engine.
- Steering geometry is not accurately controlled.
  - (a) Figure 4.70a shows the alteration to camber angle which occurs when one wheel strikes a bump. Sudden changes in camber angle cause the wheels, which are acting as a form of gyroscope, to 'flap' around the kingpin. This fault is known as 'wheel shimmy'.
  - (b) Figure 4.70b shows the difference in castor angle when the spring is deflected.

- High un-sprung weight – maximum wheel adhesion is not obtained.
- The engine normally has to be situated behind the rigid axle to provide clearance. Ideally, the engine should be further forward than this to create sufficient space to accommodate all the passengers within the wheelbase.
- Poor 'roll stiffness' at the front tends to produce oversteer – the front springs have to be mounted close together.

To overcome these disadvantages, independent front suspension (IFS) is employed. This term is used to describe any system connecting the front wheels to the frame or vehicle body, in which the movement of one wheel has no direct effect on the other wheel.

Many types of IFS have been used in the past, but in the UK, most designs now fall under the heading of transverse link system.

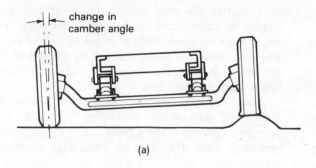

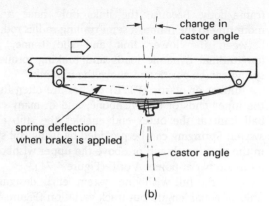

Figure 4.70 Steering geometry alterations

4.14.2 Transverse link IFS

Wishbone and double-link/radlus rod types

The main details of the wishbone system are shown in Figure 4.71. Two links, often parallel in the normal ride position, are made in a wishbone shape to provide fore-and-aft stiffness and resist braking torque. Each wishbone has three bearings or pivot points, two inner bearings connecting the wishbone to the frame and an outer ball joint attaching the wishbone to the stub axle.

Because the lower wishbone pivot points on the link-type system are normally set parallel to the road, the front of the car 'dives' towards the ground when the

brakes are applied. This problem can be minimized by using anti-dive geometry. This is achieved by placing the rear pivot point of the lower wishbone higher than the front pivot.

When the front brakes are applied, the action of the braking torque on the inclined wishbone generates a vertical force that counterbalances the extra load transferred from the rear wheels to the front wheels.

In principle, the double-link system (Figure 4.72) is similar to the wishbone type, but it is simpler in the construction of the wishbones. Two links, mounted in the normal manner, connect the stub axle carrier to the

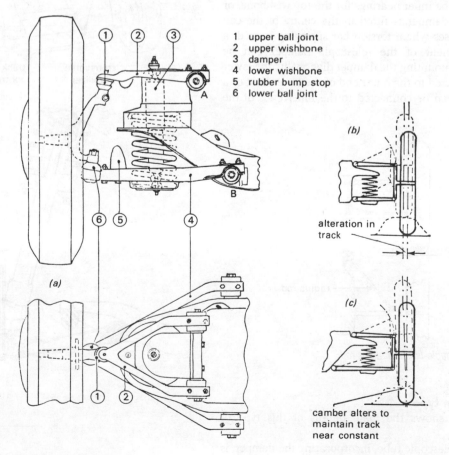

1 upper ball joint
2 upper wishbone
3 damper
4 lower wishbone
5 rubber bump stop
6 lower ball joint

Figure 4.71 Transverse link system; wishbone type

frame/body. Because the links only have a single mounting to the frame, a semi-trailing radius rod, fitted between the lower link and the frame, resists longitudinal dynamic loads and braking torque. The spring can be positioned above the top link.

Rubber or plastic (PTFE) bushes are often fitted at the inner ends of the wishbone, and in many cases a ball joint at the outer end enables the stub axle to swivel. Springing can be provided by using coil springs in the position shown or above the upper wishbone, or a torsion bar at points A or B (Figure 4.71).

As with the full wishbone system, early designs used links of equal length, but track variation (Figure 4.71b) caused considerable tyre wear, although the camber remains unchanged. Track variation can be reduced by using wishbones and links of unequal length, the longer length wishbone being placed at the bottom (Figure 4.71c). The camber then becomes negative on the bump stroke which improves handling during cornering, although there is a small increase in tyre wear.

A constant castor angle is achieved with this design by mounting the top wishbone slightly behind the lower one.

To obtain the maximum wishbone length without restricting engine space, the wishbone axis is sometimes inclined towards the rear.

Either a piston-type damper is mounted to incorporate the inner bearings for the top wishbone, or a telescopic damper is fitted in the centre of the coil spring. In cases where torsion bar springing is used, a large movement of the telescopic damper can be achieved by mounting the damper diagonally; the lower end is connected to the outer end of the lower link, or a torsion bar can be connected to the inner ends of the lower link.

connected to the stub axle at the lower end. Track control is maintained by a single transverse link, attached to the lower body or frame by rubber bushes and then connected to the stub axle by a ball joint. The coil spring is located between the fixed and floating suspension strut members.

Note that the castor, camber and swivel-axis inclination are set in production, although some suspension set-ups allow adjustment of the suspension geometry with the use of adjustable suspension components.

The swivel-axis inclination is the angle formed between the vertical, and the line taken from the centre of the strut thrust bearing to the centre of the ball joint (which connects the strut to the track control arm). For tyre clearance purposes the strut is set to a smaller angle than the swivel axis inclination.

Setting the top of the strut towards the vehicle centre allows the manufacturer to obtain the advantages of a negative offset (negative scrub radius) for the steering.

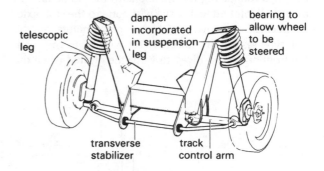

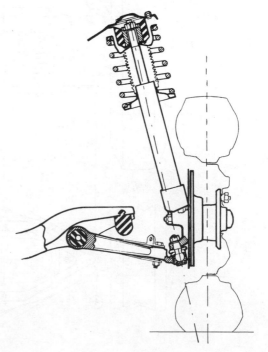

Figure 4.73 The MacPherson strut

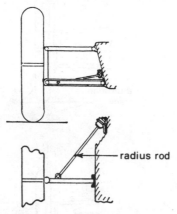

Figure 4.72 Double-link and radius rod

MacPherson type

Figure 4.73 shows the main details of this type of suspension.

A long telescopic tube, incorporating the damper, is pivoted at the top end on the body, and rigidly

Swinging arm

Two leading or trailing arms of equal length (i.e. longitudinally mounted links) are connected between the frame and the stub axle carrier. The spring can be mounted above the top arm, or a torsion bar may be connected to the arm at the frame location point.

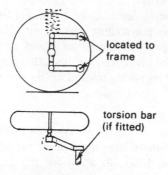

Figure 4.74 A swinging arm

Track-rod linkages

The one-piece track rod used with beam axle layouts is unsuitable for the majority of IFS systems because wheel alignment would be altered if one wheel were deflected up or down. The stub axle carrier in many IFS systems moves in an arc, so as to eliminate misalignment; the track rod connection must move in a similar arc. This condition can be met by using a three-piece track rod similar to the types shown in Figure 4.75.

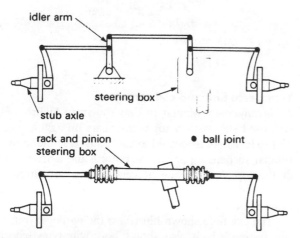

Figure 4.75 Track-rod linkage for IFS

Adjustment of the rack-and-pinion system is provided on both outer track rods. When resetting wheel alignment it is necessary to adjust each rod an equal amount.

Unequal adjustment of the track rods results in:

- incorrect spoke position of the steering wheel
- one steering lock being greater than the other.

Stabilizer bars

A stabilizer bar, often referred to as an anti-roll bar, is normally fitted to independent suspensions to help reduce body roll as the vehicle corners. When a vehicle corners the weight of the vehicle moves laterally from the inside of the corner to the outside of the corner. The transfer of weight causes the springs to deflect, the inner spring expands while the outer spring compresses, causing body roll. The stabilizer bar connects both front suspension lower links together, which also provides the required fore-and-aft stiffness.

If the suspension lower arms are interconnected by the stabilizer bar, when the left and right suspension goes up and down together by equal amounts the stabilizer bar is free of torsion. When the vehicle corners, the outer spring compresses while the inner wheel expands causing the ends of the stabilizer bar to twist in opposite directions. The torsion in the bar resists the twisting effect from the body roll, which then helps reduce the body roll.

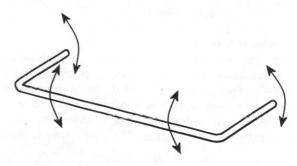

Figure 4.76 A stabilizer bar

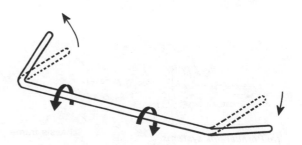

Figure 4.77 The stabilizer bar effect

4.15.1 Advantages of independent rear suspension

Many of the advantages of IFS apply to IRS, but the most important item is the reduction of unsprung weight. The final-drive unit and brakes are the heaviest items, so if 'inboard' brakes are fitted to a frame/body-mounted final drive, as much as a 50% reduction in unsprung weight can be achieved. Many of today's vehicles are of the front-wheel drive layout. Although the suspension systems described in this section feature a final drive, many of these IRS systems also apply to front-wheel drive vehicles, using a stub axle on which to mount the wheel hub.

The similarity between IRS and the de Dion drive (section 3.4.8) often makes it difficult to draw a dividing line, but a division can be made if the definition of independent suspension is remembered, i.e. any system that connects the wheels to the frame or vehicle body, in which the movement of one wheel has no direct effect on the other wheel.

4.15.2 Types of independent rear suspension

Parallel link system

Two wishbone-shaped links, mounted transversely, connect the wheels to a backbone-type frame (Figure 4.78a). Springing is provided by longitudinally-mounted torsion bars which connect with the lower wishbone. Alternatively, modern vehicles fitted with wishbones use coil springs. The coil spring is fitted

between the wishbone and the vehicle body. The drive is transmitted from the final drive through 'wide-angle' universal joints, which form part of the drive shafts.

Swinging arm

An alternative method of mounting the wheels is provided by the trailing arm system shown in Figure 4.78b. A spring, mounted as shown, or a torsion bar, acting at the pivot, may be used. One popular light car used a rubber spring instead of the normal metal type shown.

Swinging half-axles

This system consists of two axle tubes which are jointed to the final-drive housing to allow the wheel to rise or fall (Figure 4.79). To allow for the change in drive angle, universal joints are fitted at the centre of each axle joint.

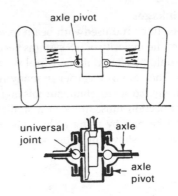

Figure 4.79 Swinging half-axles

Transverse link and coil springs

An arrangement similar to that shown in Figure 4.80 was used successfully for many years on Jaguar cars. The road wheel is located in the transverse plane by a tubular suspension link at the bottom and a drive shaft at the top. Non-plunge universal joints are fitted at each end of the drive shaft to allow for shaft movement.

The example shown illustrates the earlier layout of the system which also shows how wire-type wheels were attached to the drive shafts. Fitting conventional steel or alloy wheels requires a different end fitting to the drive shaft.

Longitudinal stiffness and driving thrust duties are performed by longitudinally mounted radius arms, which connect the wheel end of the link to the body.

Torque reaction caused by driving the wheels and torque from the inboard disc brakes are both taken by the final-drive housing. This housing is bolted to a sub-frame on to which the rear suspension is assembled.

Because the two 'links' are of different length, a variation occurs in the rear wheel camber angle when

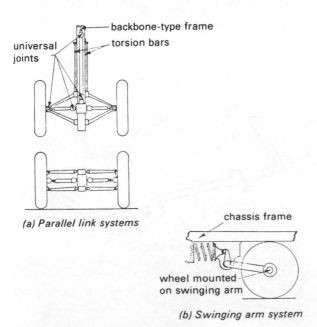

(a) Parallel link systems

(b) Swinging arm system

Figure 4.78 Independent rear suspension (IRS)

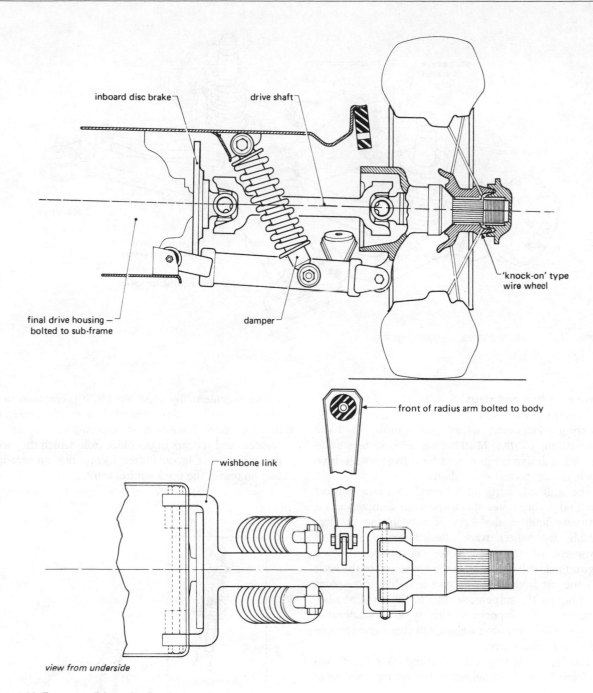

inboard disc brake

drive shaft

'knock-on' type
wire wheel

final drive housing —
bolted to sub-frame

damper

front of radius arm bolted to body

wishbone link

view from underside

Figure 4.80 Transverse links and coil springs

the springs are deflected. Camber angle is adjusted by shims fitted between the brake disc and the universal joint flange.

Semi-trailing arm and coil spring system

This system supports the rear hub by a wishbone-shaped suspension arm mounted diagonally onto a sub-frame that may also carry the final-drive housing. By arranging the suspension arm in this way, the wheel is supported both laterally and longitudinally (Figure 4.81).

Driving torque reaction is transferred from the final-drive housing to the sub-frame and, as in other similar arrangements, the construction prevents the tendency of the right-hand rear wheel to lift during hard acceleration. Braking torque and driving thrust are taken by the suspension arms.

Rubber is extensively used at the suspension arm pivots and for mounting the springs and sub-frame to the body. This gives flexibility, reduces the transmission of vibration and noise, and overcomes the need for lubrication. To allow for alteration of wheel alignment (toe-in), one mounting of each suspension arm is fitted with either eccentric adjusters or shims. The suspension may also provide changes in camber as the suspension moves during cornering and when passing over bumps.

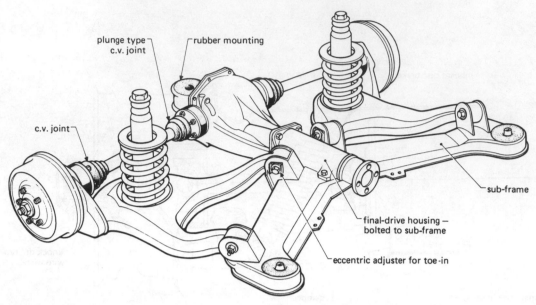

Figure 4.81 *Semi-trailing arm and coil spring system*

Transverse link and strut

The layouts shown in Figure 4.82 for independently mounting each rear wheel are similar in basic construction to the MacPherson IFS system. The suspension design is often used for a front-wheel drive vehicle having no rear drive shafts.

The stub axle is rigidly attached to a long vertical strut that incorporates the suspension damper, and a transverse link, in the form of a wishbone or arm, controls the wheel track. Resistance to rearward movement of the road wheel is provided by a longitudinal tie bar; this links the lower end of the strut with the car body so as to give a stable, three-point mounting for the suspension. Due to the small number of suspension components, this type of suspension provides a low unsprung weight, offering a comfortable ride for the passengers.

The helical spring can be fitted in one of two positions; it can be mounted either on the transverse wishbone or around the strut in true MacPherson style.

On some systems a spring having coils of differing radii is fitted to improve comfort by providing a variable rate. When this progressive-type spring is being compressed, the larger diameter end-coils close up. This action shortens the effective working length of the spring and stiffens the suspension.

As with many other IRS systems, the camber angle changes as the wheel is deflected. This feature is utilized to alter the tyre's cornering adhesion. With careful design, excellent handling characteristics of the car can be achieved.

Since rubber is used at all mounting points, slight deflection of the suspension layout causes a change in wheel alignment. To allow for this, it is common to set the rear wheels so that they toe-in a small amount. On non-adjustable layouts it is important to replace all washers and spacers in the place from which they were removed. Other layouts often incorporate an eccentric bolt on one of the track control arms.

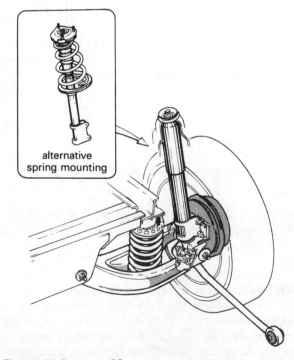

Figure 4.82 *Strut-type IRS*

4.16 WHEELS

4.16.1 Requirements and types of wheels

A wheel must be light, to help to reduce unsprung weight. The lighter the wheel and unsprung weight, the better it will enable the tyre to follow the contour of the road. A wheel must also be strong to resist the many forces acting on it as a result of normal use; but abnormal use also needs to be allowed for in the wheel design.

For mass produced vehicles, the wheel must be cheap to produce, easy to clean and simple to remove.

All of these conditions are met by the detachable-disc type of pressed-steel wheel which is normally bolted to the hub. As an alternative the disc may be permanently connected to the hub with a detachable rim. In either case spherically seated nuts ensure a rigid mounting. To reduce the risk of the wheel accidentally coming off, some goods vehicles are fitted with left-hand threads on the left side and right-hand threads on the right side of the vehicle. Note that a left-handed thread is generally indicated by an 'L' stamped on the nut and in the centre of the stud.

Cars fitted with pressed-steel wheels often have their appearance improved by the fitting of plastic covers, often referred to as 'hub caps'.

The wire or spoke-type wheel, which was common up to about 1935 and remained on sports cars until the 1970s, is now rarely used by vehicle manufacturers. Wire wheels use tangential spokes to transmit driving and braking forces; inner and outer sets of spokes are connected to the hub shell as wide apart as possible to provide lateral stiffness to the wheel. A centre-lock or knock-on mounting is used whereby the drive is taken via serrations or splines, and the shell is located between two cones, one formed on the hub and the other on a single large nut screwed onto the hub to retain the wheel. Left-hand threads on the offside hubs and right-hand threads on the nearside hubs are generally used to prevent the nut working loose. This quick-change type of wheel is strong and light, and ensures good circulation of air to the braking system, but it is difficult to clean.

During recent years, the lightness of the wire wheel and the ease of cleaning of the pressed steel wheel have been combined in a wheel made of light alloy. Although possibly more costly, the appeal of attractive styles of aluminium and magnesium alloy wheels has made this type of wheel very popular. A light alloy wheel is cast to shape (or forged in some cases) and then machined to give the final finish.

The three main types of car wheel are shown in Figure 4.83.

4.16.2 Types of rim

Well-base rims
Figure 4.84 shows the main details of this type of construction. During the fitment of the tyre, the 'well' (or drop centre) enables the tyre to be pressed into this recess, so that the opposite side (adjacent to the valve) may be levered over the rim flange. The air pressure in the tyre causes the bead to ride up the slight taper (5°) and 'lock' the tyre to the rim. Rim diameter is stated on the tyre. For example, a tyre marked '145 × 12' is fitted to a 12 inch diameter rim; the 145 refers to the nominal sectional width of the tyre in millimetres.

Flat-base three-piece rims
The stiff, heavy-bead tyres used on heavy vehicles require a detachable-flange type of rim. A split lock ring, like a large circlip, holds the flange in position. When the flange is pushed towards the tyre, the lock ring may be removed.

Semi-drop centre rims
This two-piece rim is a compromise between the well-base and the flat-base rim, and is suitable for light trucks. A split, detachable flange simplifies removal and

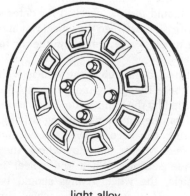

light alloy

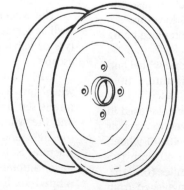

pressed steel disc

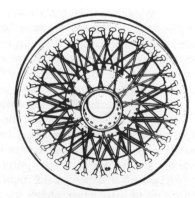

wire

Figure 4.83 Types of car wheel

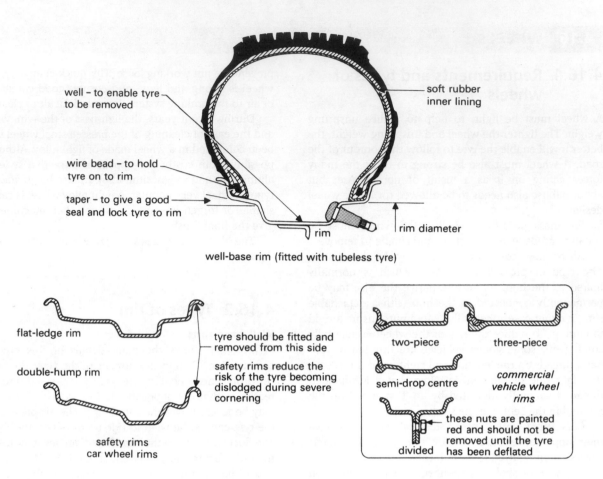

Figure 4.84 Types of wheel rim

the slight taper enables the tyre to 'lock' to the rim. The small well must be used when the tyre is being removed.

Flat-based divided type

Mainly used on military vehicles, this type of rim is made in two sections and bolted together by a ring of nuts, adjacent to the rim. On no account must you remove these nuts when changing a wheel.

Space-saver wheels

A spare wheel has to be carried on a vehicle in case one of the tyres develops a puncture. Various locations are used to carry this wheel, the most common place being the luggage space at the rear of the car.

To reduce the space taken up by the spare wheel and increase luggage capacity, some manufacturers fit a special small-diameter, thin spare wheel.

This 'space-saver' type wheel should only be used in an emergency to allow the car to be driven to a repair location. Sometimes this type is called a 40–40 wheel; the car should not be driven faster than 40 mph (65 km/h) over a distance greater than 40 miles (65 km). Often these space-saver wheels are distinguished from the standard wheel rim fitted to the vehicle by bright coloured markings on their rims.

4.16.3 Wheel maintenance

Wheel rims are subject to damage during driving, especially when the vehicle is being parked i.e. kerb stones. It is therefore necessary to check the edges of the wheel rim for damage, especially alloy wheels, which are made from a very soft material. A defect on the wheel rim can cut into the tyre sidewall, which could cause the tyre to blow out at high speed. A wheel that has struck an object at high speed may become buckled, which may cause steering vibration.

The wheel rims should also be checked for defects such as corrosion; corrosion between the wheel rim and tyre or valve of the tubeless tyre, can allow the air to escape.

Wheel rims are fitted to the hub of the vehicle with wheel nut fixings. These fixings should be set to the torque settings specified by the manufacturer; too loose and the wheel nuts can become loose during driving, too tight and the studs can become overstressed and fracture. Note that steel wheels and alloy wheels may have different torque settings. When the wheel is refitted to the vehicle, the wheel fixings should be tightened evenly to avoid distortion of the wheel rim and extra care should be taken with alloy wheels.

4.17 TYRES

4.17.1 The pneumatic tyre

Early tyres certainly strengthened the wheel, but did little to improve the comfort. It was not until R. W. Thomson in 1845 invented the pneumatic tyre that high-frequency vibration could be reduced. This idea was developed by J. B. Dunlop in 1888 for use on bicycles and was quickly applied to motor vehicles. An air bag or inner tube was contained in a cover so that the vehicle was 'floated' on a cushion of air. Most modern tyres no longer use a separate tube. The tyre forms a seal with the wheel rim and therefore is able to function as the container for the compressed air avoiding the need for a separate tube.

The modern tyre, besides improving comfort, increases adhesion between road and wheel to give satisfactory grip for braking and steering in various driving conditions. The pneumatic tyre also provides a limited form of suspension as sharp road shocks are absorbed by the cushion of air within the tyre.

4.17.2 Tyre construction

Tyres have to be constructed to perform several tasks. They must:

- support the weight of the vehicle
- provide good adhesion with the road surface to provide sufficient grip (friction) to allow for driving and braking, including acceleration, braking and steering
- have sufficient strength to resist tyre damage which may be caused through road surface irregularities.

Figure 4.85 and 4.86 show the constructional details of two types of tyre. The older type of diagonal-ply or cross-ply tyre (Figure 4.85) is seldom used on modern cars. In general, the radial-ply construction is used for passenger vehicles and many lighter commercial vehicles.

Components of the tyre

The tyre is made up of the following components:

Casing

The casing must resist the expansion of the tube, especially when the tube is subjected to road shocks. Fracture of the casing causes the tube to blow out, i.e. burst the tyre; thus the strength of the tyre is governed by the construction of the casing. It is usually made up of four or six layers of fabric; each layer consists of a series of rubberized cords laid side-by-side to form a sheet. A strong casing is produced by placing a number of sheets or plies together. The number of plies and the relative angle between the cord and the tyre bead governs the tyre characteristics. In the past cotton was the main cord material, but modern tyres use man-made fibres such as rayon and nylon. These materials are much stronger and offer greater resistance to the heat built up by the flexing of the tyre. Heavy vehicles and some cars require an even stronger material, so steel cords are needed in these cases.

Bead

The bead consists of a number of hoops of steel wire, which are responsible for retaining the tyre on the rim. The casing is wrapped around the bead wire and moulded into shape.

Tread

The tread is in direct contact with the road surface and therefore has to transmit the acceleration, braking and steering forces. The tread is bonded to the soft rubber which encloses the casing. The material used is natural or synthetic rubber, which is compounded with chemicals such as carbon-black to produce a hard, abrasion-resisting substance. The compound of the tread material must be hard-wearing yet sufficiently soft to provide grip. The tread pattern must be designed to reduce friction between the road surface and the

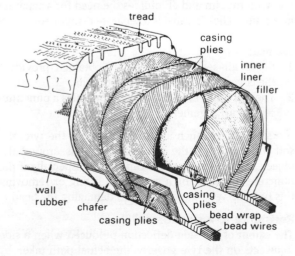

Figure 4.85 Tyre construction – diagonal-ply/cross-ply

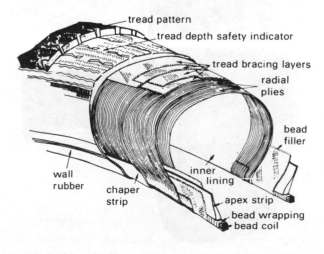

Figure 4.86 Tyre construction – radial

tread material, therefore improving fuel economy. The research and development departments of tyre manufacturers have to design treads to suit many driving conditions.

Various tread patterns are used to wipe water and grease off the road, so that the teeth, formed by the zigzag circumferential grooves, can 'bite' into the surface. An excellent grip, especially on soft surfaces, can be obtained by transversely slotting the tyre to form bold tread bars, but when used on hard roads this type is rather noisy and generally causes the 'heel and toe' form of tread wear.

The tread pattern should be selected to suit the operating conditions.

- **Normal touring** requires a tread which gives quiet operation and provides effective adhesion under wet, dry and greasy conditions.
- **High-speed operation** places emphasis on the heat generated, the noise level and the resistance of the tyre to aquaplane. This is a condition where a water layer completely separates the tyre from the road and totally destroys adhesion.

Cross-country tyres have to bite into mud, snow and loose surfaces, so heavy tread bars are needed. Extensive use of this type of tyre on hard highways causes noise and transmission component wear.

Many vehicles are today fitted with uni-directional tyres that improve grip and water dispersion. The tread of the tyre is designed so that when the tyre is rotated in one direction (the vehicle's forward direction), the water is dispersed by the rotation of the wheel and drains from between the tyre tread very quickly. The tyre has to be fitted in the correct rotational direction to the forward movement of the vehicle. Note that if the tyre is fitted incorrectly, water is sucked into the tyre tread as the wheel rotates,

increasing the possibility of the tyre aquaplaning. The correct direction is show by an arrow on the sidewall of the tyre, indicating the forward direction of the vehicle.

Sidewall

The sidewall of the tyre is constructed from layers of rubber, which protect the carcass from damage yet allow for flexibility when the tyre is subject to forces during driving, such as cornering. The details of the tyre are imprinted on the sidewall, including the tyre manufacturers name, the size and the type of construction.

Breaker

A breaker is fitted to diagonal-ply tyres. It is a layer of fabric which reinforces the bond between the tread and the casing of the tyre. The type of breaker fitted to a radial-ply tyre is referred to as the belt. The belt forms a hoop around the circumference of the tyre to stabilize the tread and resist the enlargement of the tyre on inflation, since the radial cords do not offer the same resistance to tyre enlargement as the cross-ply cords. Textile materials used for these breakers give what is sometimes called a 'belted' type, whereas steel cord breakers give a 'braced' tread type.

Tubed tyres

For a pneumatic tyre to function it is necessary to maintain a specified pressure of air between the wheel rim and the tyre. The tubed tyre uses a rubber inner tube, similar to that used on a bicycle. The valve fitted to the inner tube protrudes through a hole in the wheel rim, the valve being used to inflate or deflate the tyre. The disadvantage of the tubed tyre is that, if the inner tube becomes punctured, the tyre deflates very quickly. The tubed tyre is, however, not now commonly used on passenger cars.

Tubeless tyres

Tubeless tyres are now used on nearly all cars. The inside of the casing and outer surface of the bead is lined with a soft rubber. This rubber forms an air-tight seal with the rim and eliminates the need for a separate inner tube. The air valve is a separate component which fits directly to the wheel rim. Two main advantages are claimed:

1 Better air sealing qualities are obtained providing the cover is correctly sealed to the rim.
2 The soft inner liner of the cover provides a puncture-sealing arrangement.

If a sharp object such as a nail punctures the tyre, the soft inner liner of the tubeless tyre seals around the object, slowing down the escape of air, especially if the puncture occurs at high speed. On fitting or removing this type, be very careful to avoid damaging the bead.

Resistance to a side force

The extent of the side deflection produced when a side force acts on the tyre governs the actual path taken by the wheel (see section 4.1). This side deflection

Figure 4.87 Uni-directional tyres

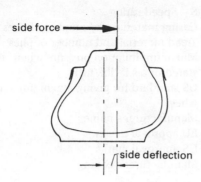

side force

side deflection

Figure 4.88 Resistance to side forces

(Figure 4.88) is increased when the inflation pressure is low but is controlled to a very large extent by the construction of the tyre.

Diagonal-ply

Figure 4.85 shows a tyre with the carcass composed of several layers of casing plies. The cords forming one ply run at an angle of about 100° to the cords of the adjoining ply, and each cord of the ply forms an angle of approximately 40° to the bead. This type is also called cross-ply and has been in use for many years.

Radial-ply

Arranging the cords in a manner such that they form an angle of 90° to the bead (i.e. the cords are radially disposed to the wheel) gives a construction which is called radial-ply (Figure 4.87). This type has the great advantage that it offers a large resistance to side deflection and its effect on the vehicle handling is very noticeable. A vehicle fitted with the old type cross-ply tyres often suffers from side drift when it corners and gives the impression to the driver that the tyres are sliding on the road; radial-ply considerably reduce this effect. Radial-ply tyres can be identified by the word 'Radial' which is moulded on the wall of the tyre. Prior to the general introduction of this method the means of identification was to note the type letters and refer to the manufacturer's catalogue.

Note: Radial-ply and cross-ply tyres should be selected and fitted with great care and under no circumstances must radial-ply be fitted to the front axle when cross-ply are used on the rear wheels. Mixing in this configuration is illegal, because of the over-steering problem, so care is needed to identify the tyres correctly.

Diagonal-ply and radial-ply advantages

Diagonal-ply:
- lighter steering at low speed
- not so critical with respect to steering geometry
- smoother ride at low speed
- cheaper at time of fitting

Radial-ply:
- about 80% longer life
- lower rolling resistance, so fuel consumption is improved

- side deflection is reduced so the vehicle corners without drift
- full width of tread is held on the road when the car is cornering, so grip is improved, especially on wet roads.

Tyre profile

The 'section height' to 'section width' of early tyres was approximately equal and this aspect ratio was therefore called 100%. As increased demands were made for improved vehicle stability, the cornering power of tyres was raised by reducing the aspect ratio. Today low-profile tyres having ratios of about 80% and ultra-low-profile types of 70% are in common use. Many performance cars are fitted with tyres having ratios of 50% or less. These 'wide oval' tyres, and other similarly shaped tyres, can be identified by relating the dimensional markings on the tyre to the manufacturer's handbook.

Valves

Figure 4.89 shows the main details of the Schrader one-way valve used in conjunction with a tubeless tyre.

The core is threaded into the stem until the tapered hard rubber section forms a seal with the stem. Spring pressure forces the centre-wire and rubber-filled cup on to its seat to prevent an outward flow of air. A dust cap acts as an additional air seal and prevents entry of dirt.

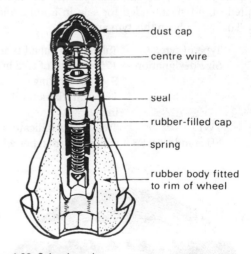

dust cap

centre wire

seal

rubber-filled cap

spring

rubber body fitted to rim of wheel

Figure 4.89 Schrader valve

Inflation pressure

Inflation pressure is governed by the load carried by a given tyre. The vehicle manufacturer specifies the correct tyre pressure according to the weight the vehicle is intended to carry. Tyre pressure may affect the handling of the vehicle and tyre wear characteristics. Large-section tyres use a lower pressure for a given load, and so greater comfort is achieved, but the resistance to rolling is increased.

The pressure recommended by the manufacturer is usually applicable to a cold tyre, i.e. it is the pressure before the tyre is used, and takes into account the average pressure rise (28 kN m^{-2} or 4 lbf/in^2) which is caused by the temperature increase during use. Recommended pressure is normally suitable for sustained speeds up to 130 km/h (80 mph), but a higher pressure is advised if speeds or loads are increased.

Under-inflation or overloading leads to rapid wear on each side of the tread and internal damage to the casing, whereas over-inflation wears the centre of the tread (refer to tyre wear illustrations).

With the advance in electronic and automotive technology, some vehicles are fitted with a tyre pressure monitoring system. The tyre pressure can either be sensed by the monitoring of the wheel speeds or a tyre pressure sensor system is used. A sensor is fitted to each tyre valve and a signal passed to the electronic control unit (ECU), which is located within the vehicle. If the ECU detects low tyre pressure, a warning lamp is illuminated in the instrument panel to inform the driver of a possible tyre deflation or puncture.

Tyre markings

Local statutory regulations based on EC recommendations specify the classification markings that must be shown on the sidewall of a modern tyre. If the tyre is to be sold in different markets throughout the world additional data may have to be included.

Figure 4.90 shows an example of the markings required on a tyre intended for sale in Europe and the USA. The symbols on this tyre are:

1	Type of tyre:	Tubeless or tubed type
2	Size designation:	175 – width of tyre in mm
		S – speed rating
		14 – rim diameter in inches
3	TWI	Tread wear indicators
4 & 5	EU standards: 88 – maximum load per wheel	

Figure 4.90 Tyre sidewall markings

5	S – Speed rating
6	Casing material and number of plies
7	Tread material and number of plies
8	Maximum inflation pressure when cold, stated in p.s.i. (lbf/in^2)
9	US standard for giving maximum load per wheel
10	Manufacturer's name
11, 12	EU approval marks
13	US approval marks
14	Manufacturer's coding.

Speed rating

Tyres are marked to show the maximum recommended speed. The speed marking, indicated by the letters S, H and V to represent 'Speed', 'High speed' and 'Very high speed' respectively, is incorporated in the size marking 165 SR 13. For example, this is a radial tyre of size 165 × 13 and reference to the manufacturer's manual shows that the speed marking 'S' represents a maximum speed of 180 km/h (113 mph). The alternatives for this size of radial tyre are:

Size	Speed limit
165 HR 13	210 km/h (130 mph)
165 VR 13	over 210 km/h

The tyre manufacturer should be consulted if a tyre is required for a vehicle, which is to be subjected to either a high maximum speed or a high consistent speed.

Ply rating

This is an indication of the strength of a tyre and nowadays does not represent the number of layers that form the casing.

Ply rating combined with tyre size are two factors which determine the legal maximum load (plated load) that can be carried by each axle of a commercial vehicle.

Tread wear

The tread of a modern tyre has a pattern which changes when the tread has worn down to a given limit. This safety feature allows an observer to determine the danger limit quickly without having to use a tyre tread depth gauge.

Run-flat tyres

Tyres are constantly being developed by tyre manufacturers for various vehicles and different applications. One of those developments is the 'run-flat tyre'. As the name suggests, in the event of a puncture in which the tyre fully deflates, it is possible to drive the vehicle for approximately 40-50 miles, at a reduced speed of 40–50 mph to have the tyre repaired or replaced. These are similar figures to those quoted for a space-saving tyre.

The sidewall of a conventional tyre collapses when the tyre deflates and if driven, the sidewalls of the tyre flex, becoming excessively hot and the tyre overheats. The overheating of the tyre eventually leads to the disintegration of the tyre itself. The construction of the run-flat tyre permits further driving; the sidewalls support the weight of the vehicle when deflated, and with the use of special rubber compounds the sidewalls remain firm resulting in a tyre which can run with little or no air pressure inside.

4.17.3 Tyre wear

Wheels and tyres transmit the acceleration, braking and steering forces between the suspension and the road surface. It is essential that during routine servicing wheel rims and tyres are maintained correctly, including an inspection for damage and wear. An incorrectly maintained tyre will cause premature tyre wear and poor vehicle stability and handling. An excessively worn tyre is illegal to use and should therefore be replaced immediately.

Many tyre problems are caused through incorrect inflation pressures, typically under-inflation, overloading and exceeding the tyre speed limits.

One other major cause of premature or incorrect tyre wear is incorrect steering and suspension geometry.

Each tyre, including the spare tyre, should be checked for the following faults:

* inflation
* wear
* damage

Inflation

Tyres should be inflated to the correct pressure; different pressures are normally specified depending on the load carried by the vehicle; normally higher loads or speeds require a higher pressure. The pressures may differ between the front and the rear of the vehicle. The tyre pressures should normally be checked with the tyre cold. A low pressure indicates that the tyre may be leaking due to a nail in the tread, leaking sidewall or a valve fault.

Wear

During ordinary use tyres will wear. The rate at which the tyres wear will depend on the manner in which the vehicle is driven and the wear characteristics of the vehicle and tyre. Refer to the tyre tread illustrations in this section showing wear patterns.

If the tyre has worn in an abnormal manner, the steering, suspension and braking components should be checked for a mechanical fault, including wear and damage. If the components are correct, a wheel alignment check should be carried out to identify the cause of the tyre wear.

The tyre tread depth should be checked with a tread depth gauge. If the tyre tread is below the legal limit, the tyre should be replaced.

Tread wear indicators are moulded into the tread of the tyre. These provide a quick visual indication on the tread depth and whether the tyre has worn below the legal tread limit.

Damage

Each tyre should be inspected for damage to the tread and also the sidewall. The inspection of the tread should include checks for nails etc. and cuts which often occur when the tyre runs over sharp objects such as glass. If any part of the tyre carcass is exposed (i.e. cords) the tyre should be replaced immediately.

Interchanging tyres

Front tyres generally wear faster than those fitted to the rear of the vehicle. The forces exerted on the tyres during steering and cornering tend to scrub the front tyres at a faster rate, together with the increased weight of the engine and transmission components. Some tyre or vehicle manufacturers recommend interchanging the tyres between the front and rear axles during maintenance schedules. The manufacturer's guidance should be followed.

Some manufacturers of radial-ply tyres recommend that the front tyres are not moved to the rear because of the different wear pattern of front and rear tyres. Note that if the vehicle is fitted with uni-directional tyres, these tyres must be fitted with the arrows in the forward rotational direction of the vehicle.

Legal requirements

Legislation exists to prevent the use of a vehicle which is fitted with defective tyres. The current regulations for vehicles with a gross weight not exceeding 3500 kg (cars and light commercial vehicles) include:

* the use of unsuitable tyres for the vehicle
* under-inflation
* breaks in the fabric in excess of 2.5 cm (1 inch) or 10% of the section width
* lumps or bulges
* exposure of cords
* the mixing of different tyre construction on the same axle
* tread depth less than minimum requirement. Reference should be made to the latest legislations and regulations but the following represents an example of recent UK regulations: 'Minimum tread depth of at least 1.6 mm across the central ¾ breadth of tread and around the entire circumference of the tyre.

The preceding list of faults is intended to outline the requirements and it is recommended that the current regulations be read to acquire an accurate understanding of the legal requirements.

Diagnosis of tyre wear

Abnormal or incorrect tyre wear is usually caused by either incorrect steering and suspension geometry or incorrect tyre pressures.

Other causes can be brake imbalance, incorrect type of tyre for the vehicle, or incorrect use for the tyre.

Tyres that are wearing in the expected manner, but at a more rapid pace than expected may have been subjected to regular hard acceleration and breaking, or the vehicle may have carried excessive loads on a regular basis.

Figure 4.91 shows the main types of abnormal wear and the cause(s) of each.

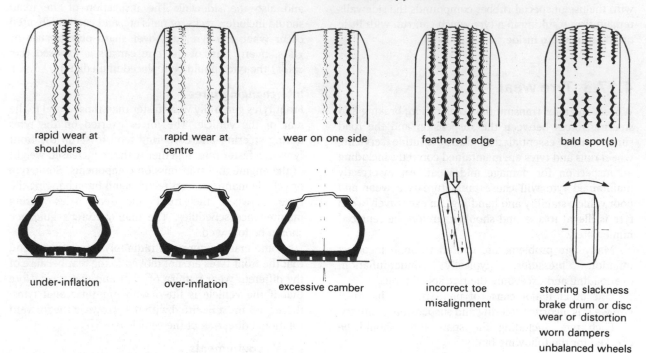

Figure 4.91 Abnormal tyre wear

rapid wear at shoulders

rapid wear at centre

wear on one side

feathered edge

bald spot(s)

under-inflation

over-inflation

excessive camber

incorrect toe misalignment

steering slackness brake drum or disc wear or distortion worn dampers unbalanced wheels

4.18 WHEEL BALANCE

4.18.1 Static balance

Static balance of a wheel and tyre assembly simply refers to whether there is a 'heavy spot' on the assembly. This is apparent when the wheel is mounted on a horizontal shaft with low-friction bearings (Figure 4.92a). If the wheel and tyre assembly does have a heavy spot, when it is allowed to rotate freely and then come to rest, it will always comes to rest in one position. The heavy spot will inevitably be at the bottom of the wheel, directly below the wheel axis (this can be demonstrated using a bicycle wheel, which will usually stop with the tyre valve at the bottom).

A wheel used in this static, out-of-balance condition will lead to the unbalanced centrifugal force tending to lift the wheel off the road periodically (Figure 4.92b), and produce conditions known as 'wheel hop' or 'shimmy', and uneven tyre wear.

4.18.2 Dynamic balance

Dynamic balance is less obvious, especially on narrow wheel and tyre assemblies. If the inner edge of a wheel had a heavy spot (assume at the top of a stationary

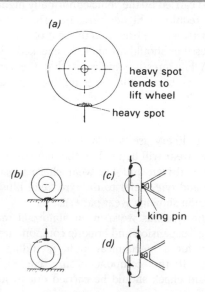

(a)

heavy spot tends to lift wheel

heavy spot

(b) *(c)*

king pin

(d)

Figure 4.92 a, b, c, d Unbalanced wheels

wheel), a good static balance can be achieved by adding the appropriate opposing weight to the outer edge of the wheel (at the bottom). Adding the weight in such a way at the bottom so that it opposes the heavy spot at the top will provide static balance, but because the weight was added to the outer edge and in fact the heavy spot was on the inner edge, the wheel will now be dynamically out of balance.

As an exaggerated example, imagine a wheel and tyre assembly that is exceptionally wide (e.g. 1 metre). If the inner edge of the tyre had a heavy spot (at the top when the wheel is stationary), the inner edge would be out of balance and would tend to hop as the wheel was rotated. Adding an equivalent weight on the outer edge at the bottom, would create static balance. However, the weight that has been added will now represent a heavy spot on the outer edge of the tyre, and this weight would also tend to cause hop as the wheel rotates.

In fact, when the wheel rotates, the heavy spot on the outer edge will try and force the wheel to bend in towards the vehicle. The heavy spot on the inner edge will try and force the wheel to bend out away from the vehicle. But because the heavy spots are on opposite sides, the result will be a wheel that tries to wobble.

Figure 4.92c shows a wheel in good static balance, but when this wheel is rotated, the centrifugal forces acting on each 'heavy spot' does not balance, since the forces are not acting through the same line. In this diagram the wheel axis tends to rotate around the kingpin in a clockwise direction, whereas the opposite applies to Figure 4.92d. Serious dynamic imbalance causes the wheel to 'flap' around the kingpin, a condition known as wheel shimmy.

4.18.3 Wheel-balancing equipment

Wheel-balancing equipment enables the technician to identify unbalanced forces and heavy spots in both static and dynamic situations. The equipment also enables the technician to determine the position and extent of the additional weight that should be added to the wheel rim to balance the wheel. The weights are either clipped onto the wheel rim (steel wheels) or stuck to the inside of the wheel rim (alloy wheels).

The less expensive types of equipment allow for static imbalance to be measured and corrected but more expensive units will enable dynamic as well as static problems to be detected and corrected.

Two types of wheel balancers are available: 'off-the car' balancers and 'on-car' balancers. Generally, an 'off-car' balancer is used; the wheel concerned is removed

from the vehicle and balanced independently from the vehicle. The wheel is then refitted to the vehicle.

An on-car balancer balances the wheel while it is still attached to the vehicle, and therefore the wheel is balanced together with the hub and brake disc/drum. On-car balancers were more commonly used in the past when there was perhaps greater potential for out-of-balance components on the wheel hub and brake assemblies. Although the on-car balancing is in theory more accurate, a high degree of skill is required to balance the wheel while fitted to the vehicle.

Figure 4.93 An off-car wheel balancer

4.19 STEERING AND SUSPENSION MAINTENANCE AND DIAGNOSIS

4.19.1 Component wear

The suspension system is constantly moving up and down, absorbing the road shocks and thus providing a comfortable ride for the vehicle's occupants. The suspension also has to resist the forces imparted during acceleration and braking. The degree of suspension movement is subject to the road and the manner in which the vehicle is driven.

The suspension movement on a vehicle travelling along a smooth road will be small when compared to a vehicle travelling over a very bumpy road; the forces exerted on the suspension system will also be higher. The type of suspension system fitted to a vehicle is designed for the conditions that are probably encountered by that vehicle, i.e. a small car is expected to drive on relatively flat roads and therefore a relatively light suspension is fitted, while a four-wheel drive vehicle is expected to encounter off-road conditions and therefore a very strong suspension is fitted.

Eventually the suspension bushes, ball joints, springs and shock absorbers, etc. will become worn. Note that if a vehicle is driven in an environment to which it isn't suited, the suspension will normally become worn prematurely.

The driver of the vehicle may initially notice worn suspension bushes etc. by a knocking noise caused by two metallic components contacting each other when travelling over bumpy road surfaces. Alternatively, the driver of the vehicle may notice a change in the vehicle's handling or steering.

It is therefore essential that the suspension of the vehicle be thoroughly checked during routine maintenance. The checks should include these components:

- steering/suspension linkages
- steering/suspension ball joints
- steering/suspension bushes
- springs
- dampers.

The manner in which they should be checked will depend on the suspension design. Always refer to the applicable information for the correct procedures to check the suspension. The suspension should also be checked for physical damage and corrosion.

Many older types of suspension were fitted with lubrication points (i.e. grease nipples) although on modern vehicles, these components are typically sealed for the life of the component and therefore require no additional lubrication.

Suspension fixings should be checked for tightness and security. If checking the tightness of the suspension securing fixings, always tighten the fixings to the torque settings specified by the vehicle manufacturer.

The operation of the dampers can be checked by simply bouncing the vehicle up and down at the front and then repeating this action at the rear of the vehicle. The road spring oscillation should be quickly dampened by the correct operation of the dampers. The vehicle should bounce a maximum of two, possibly three times. If the vehicle bounces more, it indicates that the dampers are possibly weak. It is also important to check for fluid leaks from hydraulic dampers.

Suspension springs can sag over a period of time and with use. The ride height of the vehicle should therefore be checked to ensure that the springs are maintaining the vehicle at the correct height and that there is not a broken or weak spring. The vehicle should be parked on level ground and checked for equal height; a tilt to one side or a tilt to the front or rear of the vehicle indicates a possible spring/suspension fault, although always check initially for heavy weights placed inside the vehicle or incorrect tyre sizes and pressures.

4.19.2 Geometry

The geometry of the suspension and steering may fall outside of the specified values due to general wear of bushes, bearings and joints. Additionally, damage to any of the components due to accidents or due to the car being driven over severe bumps and holes can also result in incorrect geometry.

Although incorrect tyre wear or poor steering and handling may be indicators of incorrect geometry, regular checks on the geometry are advisable.

4.19.3 Diagnosis

In reality, apart from accidental damage, suspension and steering systems do not give rise to many faults on modern vehicles, therefore diagnosis relates to detecting noises and performing geometry checks when steering and handling are not as expected.

Most of the maintenance and checks identified in section 4.19.2 provide diagnostic guidance on suspension systems, but reference should be made to section 4.2 for information on steering geometry and applicable checks.

Diagnosis of steering and suspension faults can be supported by examining tyre wear. Section 4.17.3 deals with tyre wear problems.

Chapter 5

BRAKING SYSTEMS

what is covered in this chapter . . .

- Braking principles
- Brake operating systems
- Drum brakes
- Disc brakes
- Hydraulic brake operating systems
- Power assistance
- Anti-lock braking systems
- Brake routine maintenance

5.1 BRAKING PRINCIPLES

5.1.1 Purpose of a brake

When a vehicle is accelerated, energy supplied by the engine causes its speed to increase. Some of this energy is instantly used up in overcoming frictional and tractive resistances, but a large amount remains stored in the vehicle. This energy of motion is called 'kinetic energy'.

The existence of kinetic energy is seen when a vehicle is moving and neutral gear is then selected. The vehicle does not immediately come to rest. Instead the vehicle travels for a considerable distance before it becomes stationary.

In this case the stored energy is slowly being converted and used to move the vehicle against the resistances that oppose its motion. Reliance on these natural resistances to slow down a vehicle would not be safe and would cause many problems, so an additional resistance (applied by the driver) called a 'brake' is needed to convert the energy at a faster rate. The purpose of a brake is to:

'Convert kinetic energy to heat energy'.

The speed of the energy conversion controls the rate of retardation of a vehicle, that is the vehicle's rate of deceleration.

Heat generation at the brake is obtained by rubbing a fixed pad or shoe against a rotating object driven by the motion of the vehicle. In the early days this was achieved by pressing a wooden block against the steel tyre of a road wheel (Figure 5.1).

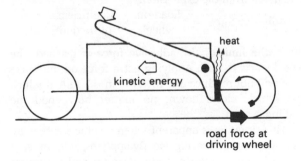

Figure 5.1 The principle of a brake

Apart from its crude operation, the retardation provided by this single brake was limited both by the friction between the tyre and road and by the fact that the braking action was only applied to one wheel.

Fitting brakes to the other wheels increases the stopping power, so when a braking system was introduced that utilised the full 'weight' of the vehicle by fitting a brake to each of the four wheels, a far more efficient system was obtained.

A large step forward was taken when the drum brake was introduced. This uses a rotating drum (fixed to the wheel) on to which a brake shoe (fixed to the vehicle body/suspension) is pressed. The brake shoe was a natural development and an early type is shown in Figure 5.2.

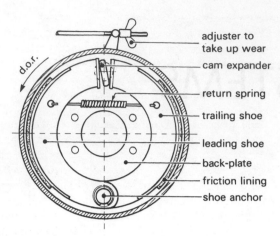

Figure 5.2 A cam-operated brake shoe

5.1.2 Stopping distance and tyre adhesion

It is the strength of the force pressing the shoe against the drum that governs the resistance to the rotation of a road wheel. During braking, the road surface drives the wheel around. The limit of this driving force is reached when the resistance of the brake equals the maximum frictional force that is produced between the tyre and road. The latter is called the 'adhesive force' and can be calculated from the expression:

$$\text{Adhesive force} = \frac{\text{Load on}}{\text{wheel}} \times \frac{\text{Coefficient}}{\text{of friction}}$$

When the limit of the adhesive force is reached, the wheel starts to skid. Applying extra force on the brake shoe will not produce any increase in the rate at which the vehicle slows down, no matter how good the braking system.

This situation is apparent when a vehicle is braking on a slippery surface, e.g. ice. By applying light pressure to the brake, the wheel soon locks up and very poor braking results. The example serves to show that the main factor that controls the minimum stopping distance is the adhesion between the tyre and road.

Road adhesion is affected by:

- type of road surface
- condition of surface, e.g. wet, dry, icy, greasy
- design and construction of the tyre, including the tread, composition of the tread material and depth of tread.

It is sometimes thought that the shortest stopping distance is achieved when the wheel is locked, producing a skid. Experiments indicate that the force required to 'un-lock' a wheel is greater than the force required to keep it locked as the wheel skids over the surface.

It should be noted that a wheel that is held on the verge of skidding not only provides the shortest braking distance, but also allows the driver to maintain

directional control of the vehicle during braking. Although many drivers can brake in an emergency without locking the wheels, many vehicles are now fitted with an anti-lock braking system (ABS); the system prevents the brakes locking in such circumstances no matter how much pressure the driver of the vehicle applies to the brakes.

5.1.3 Main types of brakes

Figure 5.3 shows the two main types of friction brake which are in common use by vehicle manufacturers. They are the:

- drum brake
- disc brake.

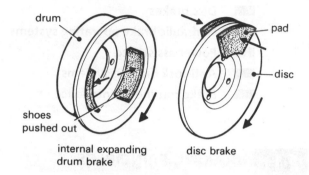

Figure 5.3 Types of brake – drum and disc

Both brake types use a fixed (non-rotating) shoe or pad which rubs against a moving part. Both are described in detail in this chapter.

The friction between the rubbing surfaces (i.e. brake shoe to brake drum or brake pad to brake disc) is increased by attaching a friction material to the fixed brake component, i.e. brake shoe or pad. It should be noted that the friction material used in the past had a high asbestos content, but the health dangers associated with the dust from this material have forced manufacturers to replace it with a safe asbestos-free material.

Note: Although you are now less likely to encounter any vehicles that still have their original asbestos-lined brakes, great care must be exercised to ensure that dust from this material is not inhaled during inspection or replacement. Manufacturers' instructions should be adhered to before attempting to dismantle a brake assembly.

5.1.4 Introduction to drum brakes

The 'internal expanding' type of brake uses two shoes which are attached to a back-plate. The back-plate is fixed to a stub axle or axle tube.

Each shoe is a T-section; a friction lining is riveted or bonded to the outer face of the shoe. At one end of the shoe is fitted a device for expanding the shoe when the brake pedal is depressed. In a simple brake, such as that shown in Figure 5.2, a cam is used as a shoe expander. Although this type of operation has been used in the past, modern drum brakes use hydraulically operated pistons for this purpose.

All shoe-type brakes must have some arrangement to prevent the shoes from turning with the rotating drum when the brakes are applied. The shoes are prevented from rotating by a shoe anchor, which must be rigidly attached to the back-plate. The anchor takes the form of a large pin. The end of the shoe is located on the pin, which also allows the shoe to pivot.

A simple spring and clip arrangement is generally used to retain the brake shoes against the back-plate, another set of springs return the shoes to the 'off' position when the brake is released.

The inner cylindrical surface of the cast iron drum is ground to give a smooth surface on which the brake linings can rub. The drum is generally retained to the hub flange securely by the wheel nuts, although the drum can initially be held in place by small countersunk screws. Wherever possible the drums should be exposed to the airflow so that a good flow of air over the drum is able to dissipate the heat. This helps to prevent loss of brake efficiency that occurs when the assembly becomes very hot during braking.

Some form of adjuster is provided to each brake to take up any increased clearance between the shoe and the drum due to wear of the friction facing. Because a large leverage is needed between the brake pedal and shoe, a large movement of the shoe would mean that the brake pedal would strike the floor before the brake is fully applied. This condition is avoided by either manually adjusting the brakes periodically, or having an automatic adjuster that continually sets the shoes so that they are always positioned very close to the drum.

Advantage of drum brakes

Drum brakes have been used on motor vehicles for many years. Although it was the low manufacturing costs and general evolution of the design that ensured the long success of the drum brake, some advantages of the design are still beneficial and they are still used on many modern vehicles.

One particular feature is referred to as the 'self-servo action', which is the result of the rotating drum helping a brake shoe to exert greater force onto the drum. In effect, when the drum is rotating, it almost pulls a brake shoe into the drum thus producing better braking force.

In one type of drum brake, the design produces a self-servo action on one of the shoes and not the other. However, when the drum is rotating in the opposite direction the self-servo action switches to the other brake shoe. This means that when the vehicle is travelling backwards, the self-servo action assists the braking forces thus ensuring that there is good braking in both forward and reverse directions of the vehicle.

Self-servo action is explained in greater detail in section 5.3.2.

Disadvantage of drum brakes

A disadvantage with drum brakes is 'fade'. Brake fade is a condition where the brake performance reduces drastically when brake components, especially the friction linings, reach a given temperature. When this condition occurs, the driver has to apply a much larger effort, and in extreme cases it becomes almost impossible to bring the vehicle to rest. The problem arises when a drum brake is continually operated for long periods, typically as a vehicle descends a long steep hill or makes repeated stops from high speeds.

The friction between the lining and drum, and the effect of this friction on the application of the shoes, govern the maximum braking torque that a drum brake

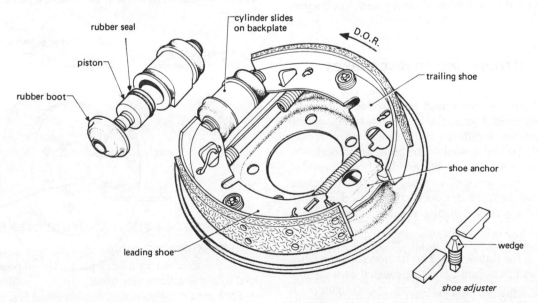

Figure 5.4 Brake drum components

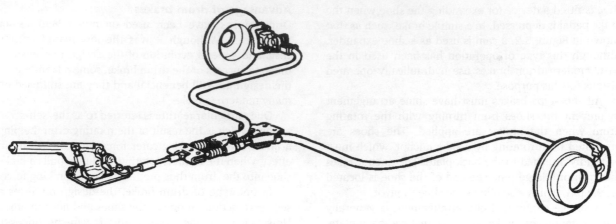

Figure 5.5 Parking brake linkage

can produce. Although modern friction materials have good anti-fade qualities, there remains the chance of fade with a drum brake during periods of long and extreme braking.

Parking brake (drum type)

When drum brakes are fitted on the rear of the vehicle, the rear drums are also normally used to provide the parking brake. When the footbrake is applied, the brakes shoes are normally forced onto the drum friction surface through the use of a hydraulic circuit. However a separate mechanical system is normally used to provide the parking brake actuation.

Although parking brakes have been fitted to the front brakes on a few vehicles in the past, it is more complex due to the need to allow movement of the wheels for steering purposes. Therefore the parking brake is normally fitted to the rear brakes.

In a few circumstances a brake drum is fitted to the prop-shaft, which locks the transmission when the parking brake is applied. This type of parking brake is used on some four-wheel drive and commercial vehicles.

5.1.5 Introduction to disc brakes

Due to the fact that high temperatures can result in brake fade, some means must be provided to dissipate the heat generated while the brakes are being applied. Heat dissipation is difficult in the case of a drum brake because the heated regions of the brake are shrouded by metal. The development of the disc brake provided vehicle manufacturers with a brake design that, because of the exposure to the air flow, dissipated the heat much more easily, greatly reducing the likelihood of brake fade.

The disc brake consists of an exposed disc, which is attached to the hub flange. Two friction pads sandwich the disc, and these brake pads are pressed onto the disc as the disc rotates giving a braking action (Figure 5.6). The brake pad clamping action is produced by hydraulic

pistons working in cylinders formed within a caliper assembly. The caliper is secured to a fixed part of the axle or hub carrier/suspension.

When hydraulic pressure is applied to the two cylinders (contained within the fixed caliper), the pistons move outwards from the caliper, which forces the brake pad friction lining into contact with the rotating brake disc. The sandwiching action of the pads on the disc creates the retarding action due to friction. The heat generated from the energy is conducted to the disc.

A large part of the disc is exposed to the air stream therefore heat is easily transferred to the air, with the result that the brake can be used continuously for long periods before serious fade occurs. Since the friction pads move at a right angle to the disc, any drop in the friction value does not affect the force applied to the pad. The disc brake is therefore not so sensitive to heat.

Note that no assistance is obtained from the rotating disc to aid the driver during the application of a disc brake (no self-servo action). To achieve a given braking

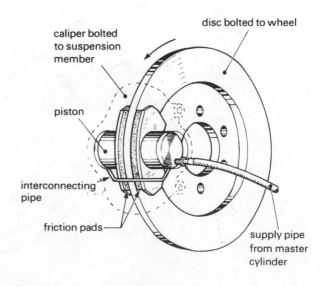

Figure 5.6 Brake disc components

force between the brake pad and the disc when the brakes are applied, the disc type brake requires a greater pedal pressure than that required for a drum brake. When disc brakes are fitted to motor vehicles, some form of power assistance is therefore required to enable the driver to apply sufficient pressure to stop the vehicle without too much pedal effort. Power assistance or servo systems are discussed later in this chapter.

The adjustment required to take up pad lining wear is automatic on disc brakes, so minimum attention is required, although the level of the brake fluid requires checking periodically.

An advantage of the disc brake is the relative ease with which the brake pad lining and disc wear can be inspected. Also, assuming that corrosion is not present, the pads can be easily renewed.

5.2 BRAKE OPERATING SYSTEMS

Until the mid-1930s most braking systems were mechanically operated using rods and cables (similar to brakes on a bicycle). Today most foot brake systems are operated hydraulically, although the handbrake is still usually operated by mechanical linkages. The mechanically operated braking system is considered here for the purpose of appreciating the features offered by modern systems.

5.2.1 Mechanically operated system

A mechanically operated system uses a series of push rods or cables together with levers to push the brake linings against the friction surface. Figure 5.7a shows the layout of a simple mechanical system.

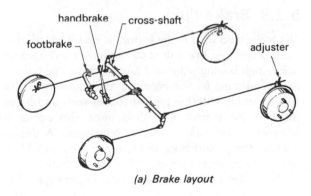

(a) Brake layout

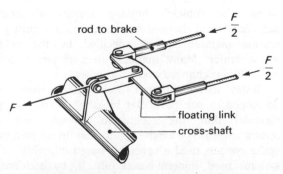

(b) Brake compensator to balance two brakes

Figure 5.7 Mechanical brake layout

Four adjustable rods or cables link the brake shoe-operating levers to a transversely mounted 'cross-shaft'. The footbrake and handbrake controls are connected to the cross-shaft by links having elongated holes to allow independent operation of each control.

In this system each brake receives its share of the brake pedal force only when the mechanism is correctly balanced, i.e. set up so that each shoe contacts the drum simultaneously. If one brake has a much smaller shoe-drum clearance than the others, all the driver's force will be directed to that brake; as a result the unbalanced braking action will cause the vehicle to 'pull' violently to the side on which this brake is situated.

Compensation devices are fitted in the layout to overcome this problem and Figure 5.7b shows a simple arrangement for balancing two brakes.

A fully compensated brake system ensures that each brake is applied at the same time and that each one receives its share of the braking effort. To achieve this condition, the mechanical system shown would require three compensators:

1 front (to balance the front brakes)
2 rear (for the rear brakes)
3 centre (to equalise front and rear sets).

The large force on the brake shoe is achieved by using a compound lever system. The larger the leverage, the smaller is the force needed on the brake pedal, but if a very large leverage is provided, the brake will require frequent adjustment to counteract wear of the brake linings.

Mechanically operated handbrake

To comply with legislation, a vehicle must have a handbrake (parking brake) to hold the car stationary when the vehicle is left unattended. The handbrake also functions as an emergency brake should there be any major failure with the main braking system.

Legal requirements insist that hydraulically operated brake systems must be fitted with a mechanical handbrake that acts on at least two wheels.

Normally a rod or cable is used to link the handbrake with a mechanical lever-type shoe expander fitted to the rear brakes. The system is usually operated via a flexible cable which allows for body and suspension movement.

The handbrake mechanism is usually operated by a hand lever; the lever is held in the 'on' position by a ratchet and pawl mechanism. When the handbrake is disengaged, the pawl is released from the ratchet allowing the brakes to be released. Figure 5.8 shows a mechanically operated handbrake.

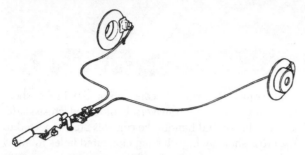

Figure 5.8 Mechanical handbrake system

5.2.2 Hydraulically operated systems

A hydraulic system has a much higher efficiency than a mechanical system and is fully compensated, i.e. brake pressure is balanced to all the brake wheel cylinders. The hydraulic system also allows the brake pressure to be transmitted, with the use of flexible pipes, to the wheel cylinders during suspension and steering movement.

Figure 5.9 shows the main components of a hydraulic braking system. The basic layout consists of a 'master cylinder', which is connected by small-bore tubing (Bundy tubing) to the wheel cylinders which are situated at each wheel. A special hydraulic fluid, known as brake fluid, completely fills all pipelines and working wheel cylinders. A reserve volume of fluid is held in a 'reservoir', placed adjacent to the master cylinder.

Hydraulic brake operation
When the footbrake is depressed, the pedal acts on a piston within the master cylinder which pumps fluid through the brake pipelines to the wheel cylinders. As fluid enters the wheel cylinders, the pistons move outwards to bring the shoe or pad friction linings into contact with the drum or disc. After all movement has been taken up, the force on the master cylinder piston pressurizes the fluid in the system and applies a force at each brake. Note that when this stage is reached, the greater the force applied to the brake pedal, the higher the pressure produced in the hydraulic system.

The pressure of the fluid in each wheel cylinder produces a force that acts on the piston, which is applied to the brake. Because fluid may be regarded as incompressible, and the pressure is the same throughout the system, the pressure exerted on any part of the system is proportional to the surface area exposed to the fluid (i.e. the size of the pistons). In view

of this fundamental law, the force applied to the pistons can be varied to suit the application.

If air is present in the hydraulic system, it causes the brake pedal to lose its 'solid' feel, i.e. the pedal becomes 'springy' or 'spongy' because air is compressed. Air in the hydraulic system can be dangerous because the required fluid pressure cannot always be built up before the master cylinder piston reaches the end of its travel, i.e. brake pedal travel is excessive during braking.

Although the compressibility of air does not prevent the build-up in fluid pressure, its elastic nature makes it necessary to remove the air after any part of the system has been disconnected. The removal of air is referred to as 'bleeding' and valves (commonly referred to as bleed nipples) are fitted at each wheel cylinder to allow the air to be bled from the system.

Although the single-line system shown provides efficient braking it does have one major disadvantage. If a fluid leak occurs in any part of the system due to a component failure, then complete brake failure will result. If this were to occur, the handbrake would need to be used as an emergency brake. Although the handbrake only acts on two wheels, it can be used to bring the vehicle safely to rest in the case of such an emergency.

For safety reasons, modern vehicles use a dual-line or split system. The dual-line layout ensures that at least two brakes can be operated by the foot brake in the event of a leak in one of the two systems.

5.2.3 Brake fluid

The brake fluid used in the hydraulic circuit has to have many properties. Brake fluid should have a low freezing point, high boiling point and low viscosity. The type of fluid used must be non-corrosive and therefore has to be compatible with the type of rubber seals and hoses fitted in the system. The fluid must also act as a lubricant to the brake hydraulic components. Additives improve the performance of the brake fluid, providing additional anti-corrosive and lubrication qualities.

Brake fluids absorb moisture (it is hygroscopic), but different brake fluids absorb moisture at a different rate. It is therefore important that the brake fluid contained within the vehicle's braking system is checked periodically and changed regularly, normally during the routine maintenance as specified by the vehicle manufacturer. Many manufacturers recommend the brake fluid is changed every two years.

Today many different brake fluids have been developed to suit particular braking systems, so it is essential that the technician always uses the recommended type for the application. In the past most brake systems used a vegetable-based oil, while other systems used mineral-based oils. If, by accident, a mineral oil is used to top up a common system filled with vegetable-based oil, damage to the rubber seals, including the wheel cylinder seals, occurs in a very short period of time. It is therefore imperative that the correct specification of brake fluid is used when adding new fluid to a braking hydraulic circuit.

Note: Further brake fluid information can be found in the hydraulic operating system section contained within this book.

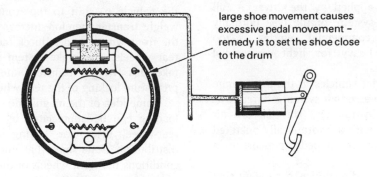

brake requiring adjustment

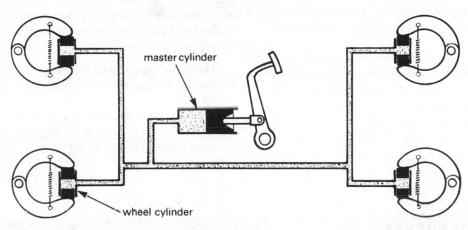

hydraulic brake layout

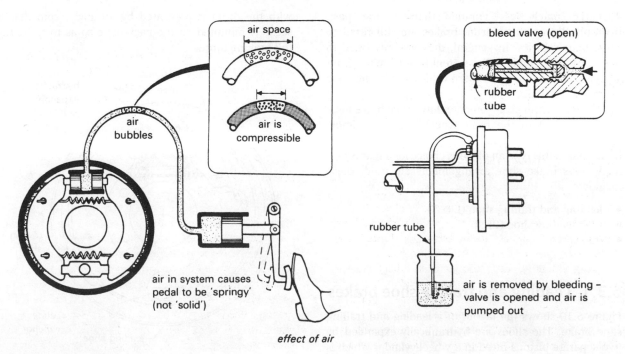

effect of air

Figure 5.9 Hydraulic brake operation

5.2.4 Pneumatic operating systems

Today both low- and high-pressure air brake systems are used primarily on medium and heavy commercial vehicles but most light commercial vehicles only utilise air to boost the effort applied by the driver. A full compressed-air braking system, of the type normally associated with heavy commercial vehicles, is too expensive, bulky and heavy for light commercial vehicles or passenger cars.

Some light commercial vehicles in the three-tonne category use a part compressed-air system referred to as air/hydraulic (air-over-hydraulic). This is an air arrangement, combined with a hydraulically operated system to reduce the maximum pedal pressure to a comfortable level.

The widespread use of disc brakes has meant that most cars are now fitted with a vacuum servo as standard equipment. The vacuum servo uses inlet manifold depression ('vacuum'), generated by an engine-driven pump, to assist the driver in applying the foot brake.

Alternatively, some motor vehicles, typically large four-wheel drive vehicles, use a pressurized fluid system to produce the power assistance required to provide the additional brake force needed by the driver.

5.2.5 Front/rear brake apportionment

When a vehicle decelerates, an inertia force acting at the centre of gravity of the vehicle causes the weight of the vehicle to shift to the front of the vehicle. The weight transfer therefore increases the load exerted on the front wheels and reduces the load exerted on the rear wheels. The brake system design engineer must take this 'weight transfer' into account to prevent premature locking of the rear wheels during braking.

Some idea of the magnitude of the change in wheel loading can be appreciated by considering a typical rear-wheel drive car having a 50:50 static load distribution. Tests show that under maximum braking conditions the front wheels of the car carry about 75% of the total weight. To achieve good braking with this particular car, the front brakes are designed to provide about 60% of the retarding force. This 60/40 apportionment is chosen for safety reasons because it ensures that under maximum braking the front wheels do not 'lock' before the rear.

The 60/40 ratio can be achieved by using:
- discs at front and low capacity drum brakes at the rear
- larger area wheel cylinders at the front
- larger diameter drums at the front
- more effective brakes at the front.

5.3   DRUM BRAKES

Although much less popular than in the past, hydraulically operated drum brakes are still fitted to some light vehicles. In general, they are only fitted to the rear wheels while a disc system is fitted to the front wheels. Note that many modern vehicles no longer have drum brakes at all.

The disc/drum arrangement allows more brake force too be applied to the front wheels, also the simple application of a mechanical handbrake to the rear drum brake makes this type an obvious choice for a rear brake.

Various brake shoe arrangements are used; these include:

- leading and trailing shoe (L & T)
- twin leading shoe (2LS)
- duo-servo.

5.3.1 Leading and trailing shoe brakes

Figure 5.10 shows the layout of a leading and trailing shoe brake. The shoes are hydraulically expanded by two separate pistons fitted in a wheel cylinder which is fixed rigidly to the back-plate. Rotation of the shoes

with the drum is prevented by an anchor pin that is securely mounted on the back-plate so as to resist the full braking torque.

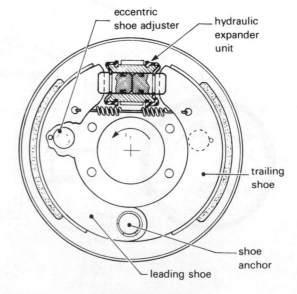

Figure 5.10 Leading and trailing shoe brake

A strong spring is fitted to return the shoes when the brake pedal is released; this in turn forces the brake fluid to return to the cylinders. By mounting this spring on the back-plate side of the shoes, the shoes are pulled against high spots of the back-plate. These high spots are formed on the back-plate to provide a bearing surface for the brake shoe.

A snail cam or eccentric, mounted behind each shoe, was traditionally provided for manual adjustment of the shoes. These cams can be partially rotated with the aid of a shoe adjustment tool without removing the drum. The adjuster cams are positioned so that each shoe is set as close to the drum as possible without causing excessive binding (rubbing).

When the brake drums are not rotating, if pressure is applied to the brake pedal, hydraulic pressure forces both shoes outwards and after the clearance has been taken up, an equal force is applied by each shoe to the drum.

This equal force does not apply when the vehicle is moving and the drums are rotating. The drag of a moving drum on the friction linings causes one shoe to be applied harder and the other shoe to be pushed towards the off position (see section 5.3.2). As a result, the braking torque produced by the shoes is in the ratio 4:1.

Leading shoe

The shoe that carries out the most work is called the 'leading shoe'. The leading shoe can be identified by the fact that the leading shoe is the first shoe after the hydraulic expander (viewed when the wheel rotates in the forward direction).

Trailing shoe

Conversely, the other brake shoe is called the 'trailing shoe'. Since the work done by the leading shoe is much greater, the rate of lining wear of this shoe is higher than that on the trailing shoe. This means that unless a thicker lining is used on the leading shoe, this shoe reaches its wear limit before the trailing shoe.

On the layout shown, the unequal wear pattern can be taken up by the floating pistons in the wheel cylinder. If this were not so, some provision would be needed to allow the brake shoes to be adjusted so that they can be centralized with the drum.

5.3.2 Self-servo action

The effect of drum rotation on a brake shoe can be demonstrated by the arrangement shown in Figure 5.11. Applying an equal force to the free end of the two levers, and rotating the drum in the direction shown, causes the frictional force on lever A to increase. If lever A is regarded as being the leading brake shoe, the friction acting on the brake shoe is increased.

The opposite effect is produced on lever B, therefore this lever, which represents the trailing shoe, is not pressed so hard against the drum.

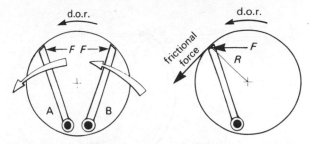

Figure 5.11 Self-servo action

Reversing the direction of the drum changes the action and this converts the leading shoe into a trailing shoe, which is beneficial when the vehicle is travelling backwards.

This condition, whereby a leading shoe is effectively self-applied to the drum, is referred to as a 'self-servo' action. Figure 5.12 shows the three factors that vary the amount of self-servo that acts on a leading shoe. The three factors are:

1. *Position of shoe tip* – self-servo is increased as the leading edge of the friction lining is moved towards the hydraulic expander.
2. *Coefficient of friction (μ) of the lining* – an increase in the friction value gives a larger self-servo action.
3. *Position of the shoe anchor* – moving the anchor towards the centre of the drum increases the self-servo action.

Effects of self-servo

To obtain a leading and trailing shoe brake that has a high braking power (large drum drag for a given application force) a large self-servo action is required. The idea is to use the energy from drum rotation to minimize the effort applied by the shoe expander (hydraulic pistons).

Negative servo action on the trailing shoe, however, must be minimized in order to obtain a powerful brake. Often this is achieved by placing the friction lining of the trailing shoe nearer to the expander than in the case of the leading shoe.

Attention to this feature must be given when reassembling a brake, because if the shoes are reversed a fierce braking action and possible 'grab' (lock-up) will result.

A number of problems arise when a large self-servo action is relied on to give a powerful leading and trailing shoe brake. Since self-servo action relies on friction, any reduction in the friction value seriously affects brake performance. Normally the reduction in the frictional value of the brake lining occurs when the brake reaches a critical temperature; as a result serious brake fade occurs.

Another drawback of a brake that uses a high self-servo action is the variation in braking power that occurs when the force applied to the shoe is varied. Ideally the ratio, 'drum drag/applied force' should be constant because this gives a progressive braking action.

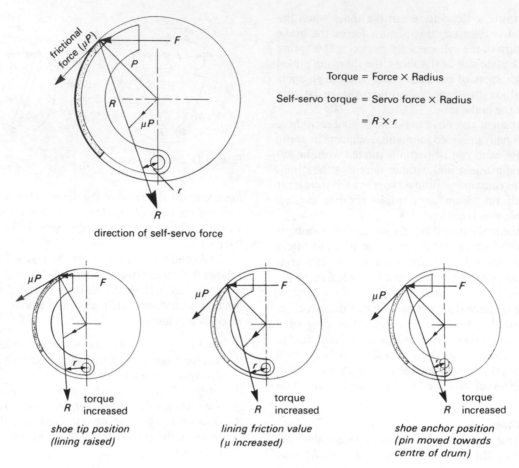

Torque = Force × Radius

Self-servo torque = Servo force × Radius

= $R \times r$

Figure 5.12 Factors affecting self-servo torque

Floating shoes

Figure 5.13 shows a leading and trailing shoe brake
fitted with a wedge-type adjuster. In this design the
brake shoes butt against an adjuster unit that acts as a
fixed anchor for the shoes. Both shoes are free to float

up and down on the anchor. The floating arrangement
allows for shoe centralization and also reduces the
tendency of the brake to grab during application.

When this type of brake is applied, the two shoes are
pushed outwards to contact the drum. Rotation of the

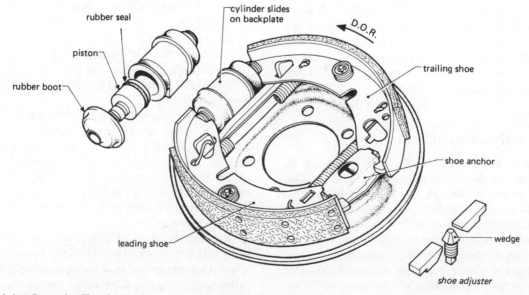

Figure 5.13 Leading and trailing shoe brake

drum forces the leading shoe directly against the anchor; the reaction of the trailing shoe is taken through the expander to the leading shoe.

Note the position of the brake linings on the shoes for this design. This asymmetrical layout means that care is needed to ensure that the linings are refitted in their correct positions after replacement. It is also important to check that the assembled back-plates have not been interchanged with their shoes from left to right and vice versa.

Handbrake operation is by a lever and strut mechanism.

5.3.3 Twin leading shoe brakes

Before the universal adoption of the disc for front brakes, the twin leading shoe (2LS) drum brake was commonly used. Each shoe has its own expander (wheel cylinder), which is positioned so that both shoes are subject to a self-servo action (Figure 5.14).

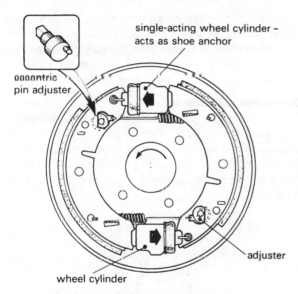

Figure 5.14 *Twin leading shoe brakes*

An interlinking pipe behind the back-plate provides an equal hydraulic pressure to each single-acting cylinder. The cylinder housing also acts as a shoe anchor for the floating end of the shoes, so the cylinders must be rigidly fixed to the back-plate.

Compared with a leading and trailing shoe brake, the 2LS type has the following advantages:

- *Even lining wear* – because both shoes do an equal amount of work, a longer life is achieved, the brake runs cooler and the need for adjustment is less frequent.
- *Equal self-servo* – there are two effective shoes so a more powerful, stable brake is obtained.
- *Greater resistance to fade* – less reliance is placed on one shoe to do the major share of the braking, so the self-servo action on this shoe can be reduced. This

results in a more progressive brake and, as a result, it is less sensitive to heat.

One disadvantage of the 2LS type shows up during reversing. Unless a special double-acting linkage is provided, both shoes become trailing shoes. To allow for this problem, and for provision of the handbrake, most manufacturers retained the leading and trailing drum for the rear brakes.

5.3.4 Duo-servo brakes

This system is often called a self-energizing brake. It is a very powerful brake, but its effectiveness falls tremendously if the friction value decreases.

Figure 5.15 shows a modern, hydraulically operated duo-servo brake. The operating principle is based on the use of drum energy to considerably boost the force applied by the driver.

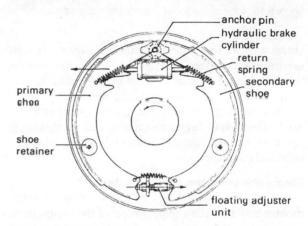

Figure 5.15 *Duo-servo brakes*

When the leading shoe is pushed out into contact with the forward-moving drum, frictional force causes it to rotate partially with the drum. The shoe movement produced by this self-wrapping action is transmitted through a floating adjuster to the trailing shoe, which brings the trailing shoe into contact with the drum. With the trailing shoe against the anchor pin and the shoe-to-drum clearance having been taken up, the force applied by the expander is supplemented by the self-energizing action of both shoes.

To minimize the delay before self-energization assistance comes into action, the trailing shoe is held on the anchor pin by a stronger return spring; this means that the expander only moves the leading shoe. In this case only, the leading shoe is called the 'primary shoe'. The shoe gets this name because the shoe is made to contact the drum before the other (secondary) shoe.

5.3.5 Automatic adjusters

Various methods are used to provide some form of automatic adjuster to set the shoes the correct distance from the drum. Adjustment of front disc brakes is

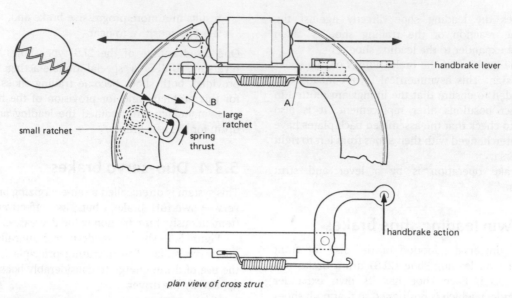

plan view of cross strut

Figure 5.16 Automatic adjuster – footbrake operated

automatic, so to maintain brake efficiency between servicing and reduce servicing costs (longer periods between service intervals), most rear drum brakes are fitted with automatic (or self-) adjusters.

Two main types of self-adjuster mechanism are used. One type functions when the footbrake is operated, the other type of adjuster functions when the handbrake is operated.

Footbrake-operated shoe adjuster

Figure 5.16 shows one of the many adjuster mechanisms that use the operation of the footbrake to take up wear. This type uses a cross-strut, retained to one shoe by a spring, and two ratchets mounted on the other shoe. A spring acting on the small ratchet pushes the fine saw-like teeth towards the large ratchet, which has a slot to receive the cross-strut. When the brake is set up correctly, a small clearance exists at B.

When the shoe-to-drum clearance is small, brake operation allows the ratchets to move with the shoe, but when the outward movement of the shoes exceeds the clearance at B, the strut holds back the large ratchet and causes it to jump a tooth. Consequently, when the brake is released the return movement of the shoe is less than before, adjusting the brake shoe clearance.

The handbrake operates in the normal manner. A cranked lever acts directly on one shoe and the reaction on the pivot pushes the strut against the locked ratchet to expand the other shoe.

Handbrake-operated shoe adjuster

This system utilises the movement of the handbrake to take up lining wear; Figure 5.17 shows one such arrangement. In this case the shoes are held apart by a threaded strut to give the correct shoe-to-drum clearance, and this strut is expanded by a ratchet-toothed wheel. The ratchet is moved by a pawl connected to the handbrake lever.

When friction lining wear takes place, the movement of the handbrake lever gradually increases. When this movement exceeds a given limit, the pawl jumps a tooth on the ratchet. The movement lengthens the threaded strut and sets the brake shoe lining closer to the drum.

Duo-servo adjustment

Duo-servo type brakes often utilize the self-wrapping movement to control the length of the floating adjuster. Some ratchet and pawl arrangements use the forward motion of the car to provide the adjustment, whereas others may operate when the vehicle is in reverse.

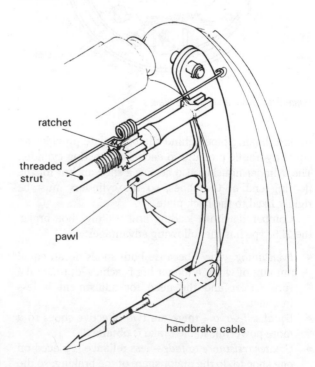

Figure 5.17 Handbrake-operated automatic adjuster

5.3.6 Wheel cylinders

Depending on the design of the shoe-type brake, different types of wheel cylinders are used to expand the shoes onto the drums. Single-acting-type wheel cylinders are used in a twin leading shoe brake, two wheel cylinders are therefore required per brake.

A double-acting-type wheel cylinder is required for a leading and trailing shoe brake, therefore only a single wheel cylinder is required per brake. These types of cylinder are shown in Figure 5.18.

Wheel cylinders are fitted with a bleed valve at the highest part of the cylinder, to bleed air from the system or to allow the fluid to be changed.

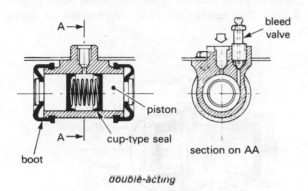

double-acting

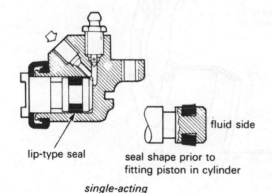

single-acting

Figure 5.18 Types of hydraulic wheel cylinder

5.3.7 Brake drum removal

Over a period of time, the constant operation of the brake shoes wears a groove in the brake drum and as a result it is often found that the removal of the brake drum is difficult. As the brake drum and shoe wear, the self-adjusting mechanism maintains the brake shoe at a minimal clearance to the brake drum. The brake shoes are therefore situated within the groove in the brake drum. To allow the removal of the drum, a hole is often provided in the back-plate, in the region of the automatic adjuster, which allows the adjuster mechanism to be slackened off. The excessive brake shoe clearance then allows the easy removal of the brake drum.

5.3.8 Brake shoe friction material

In the past asbestos fibres were commonly used as the brake lining friction material. These were either woven or moulded and then bonded with a resin to give a friction facing in the required form. Asbestos combines strength with good thermal and friction qualities, and is relatively cheap to produce.

However, it was found that breathing in asbestos dust increases the risk of lung cancer and may cause other problems.

Brake manufacturers have developed asbestos-free materials which are now used to overcome these health issues. It should be noted that all new vehicles use asbestos-free materials for brake and clutch friction linings and although these materials are typically more expensive than asbestos, they provide a comparable performance.

The materials used vary with the vehicle manufacturer, some companies using materials as diverse as Kevlar® fibre and a combination of steel and mineral fibres.

5.3.9 Bonded friction linings

Until a few years ago, friction linings were secured to the brake shoe by the means of brass, copper or aluminium rivets. The modern arrangement is to use a specially cured adhesive to stick the facing on to the brake shoe. As well as giving greater strength and a more accurate profile, this method of attachment also improves heat flow and eliminates scoring of the drum-rubbing surface by the grit-embedded rivets.

Although bonding allows more wear to take place, before the shoe or pad is changed, it is recommended that as a general rule the facing should be changed when it has worn down to one-third of its original thickness. Many manufacturers provide a specification for the minimum thickness of the brake shoe lining.

5.4 DISC BRAKES

5.4.1 Advantages of disc brakes

Disc brakes are now favoured by all car manufacturers, because the disc-type brake offers a number of advantages:

● The disc friction surface on which heat is generated is directly exposed to the air, which is not the case for drum brakes. Easier dissipation of the heat provides a greater resistance to fade.
 High temperature reduces the coefficient of friction of the brake lining, a fact clearly demonstrated when a vehicle fitted with drum brakes descends a long, steep hill; the pedal pressure at the end of the descent needs to be much greater than at the start.
● Independence of self-servo effect; the non-assisted brake may require more effort but its action is progressive, i.e. the brake gives a braking torque proportional to the applied force.
● The brake is not so sensitive to friction changes.
● Self-adjusting linings or pads are used which are usually easily replaced.
● Pedal travel does not increase as the disc heats up (for drum brakes, heating a drum causes expansion, which increases pedal travel).

With the increase in car performance and the need to improve brake efficiency, cars are now generally fitted with disc brakes to the rear as well as the front wheels, although some vehicles may still have drums for the rear brakes.

5.4.2 Two-cylinder caliper

The construction of a light-duty disc brake is shown in Figure 5.20. A split caliper assembly, rigidly attached to the stub axle carrier, houses the hydraulic cylinders. Each cylinder is fitted with a piston. Two opposed pistons act directly on the friction pads (brake pads), one piston on each side of the disc.

A rubber seal, situated in a groove within the cylinder, prevents fluid leakage between the cylinder and piston. Note that the rubber seal also retracts the piston and pad after the application of the brake (Figure 5.20b). This feature not only compensates for lining

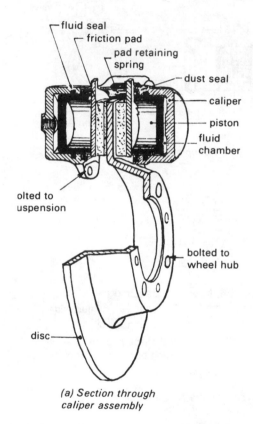

(a) Section through caliper assembly

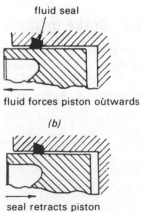

(b)

Figure 5.19 A disc brake and caliper

Figure 5.20 A two-cylinder caliper disc brake

wear but also keeps each pad very close to the disc. A gaiter (dust shield), is fitted between the caliper and the piston, the seal preventing the ingress of dirt and water etc. from damaging or corroding the piston and cylinder.

Internal drillings link the two fluid chambers. When the brakes are applied, equal pressure is applied to both pistons. A bleed screw, often referred to as a bleed nipple, is fitted to each caliper for the purpose of removing the air from the hydraulic circuit or changing the brake fluid.

5.4.3 Four-cylinder caliper

When larger brake pads are fitted a greater brake force will be required to force the brake pads against the brake disc, so a four-cylinder caliper unit may be fitted.

Note: The four-cylinder caliper is often fitted on high performance cars and heavy vehicles such as four-wheel drive off-road vehicles.

The four-cylinder caliper also provides more safety when used in conjunction with a tandem master cylinder. One opposing pair of cylinders in the caliper is connected to the primary master cylinder piston and the other pair of cylinders to the secondary. In the event of a line failure (fluid leak), one pair of cylinders will still work.

5.4.4 Single-cylinder caliper

The limited road wheel-to-disc clearance on vehicles with a steering geometry based on the negative offset principle (negative scrub radius) is often insufficient to accommodate a caliper having two opposed pistons. In these cases a single-cylinder caliper similar to Figure 5.21 may be is used.

The piston housing is keyed to the pad housing, which is bolted to the wheel suspension member. Hydraulic pressure moves the piston in one direction and the piston housing in the opposite direction.

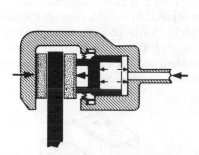

disc is sandwiched by the action of the piston
and the reaction of the cylinder

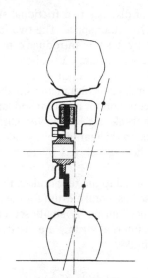

diagram shows that negative offset layout
needs a compact caliper

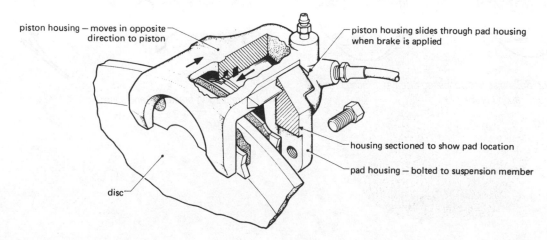

piston housing – moves in opposite direction to piston

piston housing slides through pad housing when brake is applied

housing sectioned to show pad location

pad housing – bolted to suspension member

disc

Figure 5.21 A single-cylinder caliper

5.4.5 Brake discs

The brake disc is generally manufactured from grey cast iron, although some high performance vehicles can have ceramic-based or carbon fibre-based discs. The disc is bolted to the wheel hub; therefore the disc rotates at the same speed as the road wheel. The brake disc friction surface is exposed to the atmosphere; so the air flow around the disc as the vehicle moves cools the disc. The brake disc is either of a solid or ventilated type.

Solid discs

The solid disc has two frictional surfaces; the heat generated by the application of the brakes is radiated by the disc friction surface. The build-up of heat within the centre of the disc material can become very great during heavy and prolonged braking and lead to the overheating of the disc, brake fade and warping of the brake disc.

Ventilated discs

The ventilated type of disc has two frictional surfaces, which are separated by an air space. The two frictional surfaces being joined by fins that introduce cool air into the centre of the disc as it rotates. Ventilated discs can radiate the high temperatures that are generated during braking, preventing brake fade and increasing the life of the brake pads. It is common for medium and large cars to be fitted with front brake disc of the ventilated type. If brake discs are fitted to the rear wheels, solid discs are often fitted, as the heat generated by rear brakes is considerably less.

If brake discs are fitted to the rear brakes, the centre of the disc is often used as a brake drum for the purpose of the handbrake mechanism. A small set of brake shoes, fitted to the internal drum, are used only to provide the parking brake.

5.4.6 Brake pads

The brake pad is fitted with a friction lining; the lining is forced against the disc by the caliper when the brakes are applied. The friction lining material has to be hardwearing yet heat resistant. The friction material used is similar to that used for brake shoe lining. All brake pad friction material is asbestos-free for the health reasons already detailed in the brake shoe section of this book.

One problem with the asbestos-free materials is the increased heat flow from the rubbing surface to the brake fluid. Even with the use of disc brakes, the heat generated by the constant application of the brakes can raise the temperature of the brake fluid to dangerous levels. In some cases boiling of the brake fluid can occur.

Vehicle tests are carried out in mountainous terrain, so that materials can be selected that limit the maximum fluid temperature to 175°C. Since this is close to the 210°C boiling temperature of normal brake fluid, various means, such as under-lays, are used to act as a heat barrier between the disc pad and the piston caliper.

Asbestos-free brake pads are comparatively rigid, so slots are formed in the lining to improve flexibility for bedding. The friction coefficient of these new materials is higher than that of asbestos materials – an average of 0.43 compared to the 0.3 used in the past. Sometimes this high friction results in brake squeal, which is caused by vibration between the pad and piston. To overcome this problem the back of the pad is coated with either rubber or a copper compound.

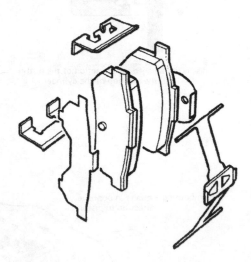

Figure 5.23 A brake pad and shim

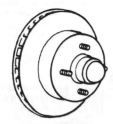

Figure 5.22 Solid disc and ventilated disc types incorporating internal drum parking brake

5.5 HYDRAULIC BRAKE OPERATING SYSTEMS

5.5.1 Benefits of hydraulic systems

Hydraulically operated braking systems are generally used with light vehicles. These systems offer the following advantages:

- They are fully compensated – the brake pressure from the master cylinder is passed to each brake evenly.
- They offer high efficiency
- They allow for suspension and steering movement – suitable for vehicles having independent suspension and allows for movement of the steering wheels.
- Distribution of the brake pressure from the master cylinder can be changed – the force exerted on a piston is governed by the piston surface area, i.e. the larger the piston surface area, the greater the thrust exerted.

For example, if the manufacturer requires a greater thrust on the trailing shoe of a drum brake, a larger piston can be used.

5.5.2 Layout of system

Refer to sections 5.3 and 5.4 for information on drum and disc brake hydraulic pistons and cylinders.

Figure 5.24a shows a simple, single-line hydraulic layout used to operate a drum and disc brake system.

Each wheel cylinder (disc brake and drum brake) is supplied with brake fluid from a master cylinder, the pressure of which is controlled by the driver via the footbrake. A volume of brake fluid is held in a reservoir, which is usually an integral part of the master cylinder.

Regulations demand that a separate mechanical parking brake must be provided on at least two wheels.

(a) Layout of system

(b) Master cylinder

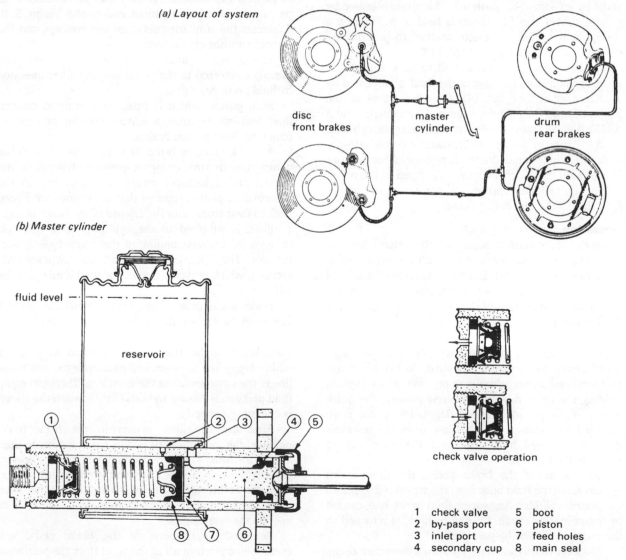

disc front brakes	master cylinder
	drum rear brakes

fluid level

reservoir

check valve operation

1	check valve	5	boot
2	by-pass port	6	piston
3	inlet port	7	feed holes
4	secondary cup	8	main seal

Figure 5.24 A hydraulic brake system

The parking brake could also enable the driver to stop the vehicle in the event of failure of the hydraulic system. In the system shown, the parking brake, or handbrake, acts on the two rear wheels (not shown).

5.5.3 Master cylinder

Two types of brake master cylinder have been widely used by vehicle manufacturers; the single-cylinder and the dual-cylinder (tandem) design, these types of master cylinders are used for single-line and dual-line system layouts respectively.

5.5.4 Single-cylinder type

Figure 5.24b shows the layout of a single-cylinder type master cylinder.

Construction

The master cylinder piston (6) is linked to the brake pedal by an adjustable push rod. The piston is sealed by a main rubber cup (8), which is held in position by a spring, and seated on a thin washer to prevent the rubber cup entering the feed holes (7).

An inlet port (3) allows fluid to pass around the waist of the piston. Leakage of the fluid is prevented by a secondary rubber cup (4). Outward travel of the piston beyond the cylinder is limited by a circlip, and a rubber boot (5) prevents dirt from entering the cylinder.

A 0.7 mm by-pass port (2), counter-bored half-way with a drill of 3 mm diameter, is positioned just in front of the main cup. A check valve (1), fitted at the outlet end of the cylinder, ensures the non-return of aerated fluid during the bleeding process.

Operation

When the brake pedal is depressed, the piston forces the fluid into the brake pipeline until all the brake lining clearance (shoe or pad), has been taken up. Additional thrust on the pedal then pressurizes the hydraulic system and forces each of the brake linings against the friction surface.

If the clearance is too great (i.e. if the brake shoes require adjustment) the piston will reach the end of its travel before the brakes are applied. To overcome this problem, the driver should pump the pedal rapidly, holding the pedal down after a few pumps. The quick return of the piston creates a depression in the main chamber and causes fluid to flow from the reservoir through the feed holes and over the main cup to recharge the cylinder.

On release of the brake pedal, the shoe return springs force the fluid back from the wheel cylinder into the master cylinder. Any excess fluid in the line, caused by 'pumping' or expansion due to heat, is returned to the reservoir via the by-pass port.

Blockage of this small port prevents the return of the fluid and leads to 'binding' brakes, so to ensure that the main cup does not obstruct the port when the brake is off, a small amount of 'free pedal' movement is given.

If a fluid leak were to occur (i.e. due to a wheel cylinder failure or a fractured pipe) in the hydraulic circuit operated by a single-cylinder type of master cylinder, the result would be a complete failure of the footbrake system.

5.5.5 Tandem (dual-) cylinder type
Construction

To avoid complete failure of a hydraulic system, a tandem-type master cylinder is used. Two independent brake circuits are controlled through the use of one brake master cylinder. A hydraulic failure in one of the brake pipelines results in a loss of only one circuit or two of the brakes. Effective footbrake control is retained and safety is improved.

Operation

In general the tandem cylinder may be considered as two single cylinders mounted end-to-end. Figure 5.25 illustrates the similarity between this concept and the actual hydraulic circuit layout.

The master cylinder contains two pistons, one directly connected to the pedal and the other operated by fluid pressure.

Each piston, which is fitted with seals to prevent fluid leakage, controls a separate brake pipeline to either the front or rear brakes.

A check valve is fitted at each of the two outlet points. One return spring is positioned between the pistons and a stronger return spring, acting on the independent piston, ensures that the pistons are forced back to their stops after the release of the brake pedal.

Fluid is supplied to the cylinders by a reservoir through inlet ports, similar to the single-type master cylinder. The reservoir is divided into two separate sections, which prevents the loss of fluid if one pipeline fails.

Under normal conditions, the movement of piston 1 causes an increase in the fluid pressure in the chamber controlled by piston 1. Pressure from this chamber is transmitted to the front brake line and to piston 2 which, being free to move, will pressurize the rear brake line to the same extent as the front line. Therefore equal fluid pressure is passed to both circuits when the circuit is operating correctly.

Assuming a failure occurs in the front brake pipeline, the movement of piston 1 will discharge fluid at the fracture. The loss of fluid will allow the two pistons to make contact, the two pistons acting as one. Although at this stage some of the pedal travel has been used, the remainder of the movement is available to operate the rear brakes.

Repeated applications of the brake pedal will eventually discharge all of the fluid from the section of the reservoir which supplies the faulty pipeline section.

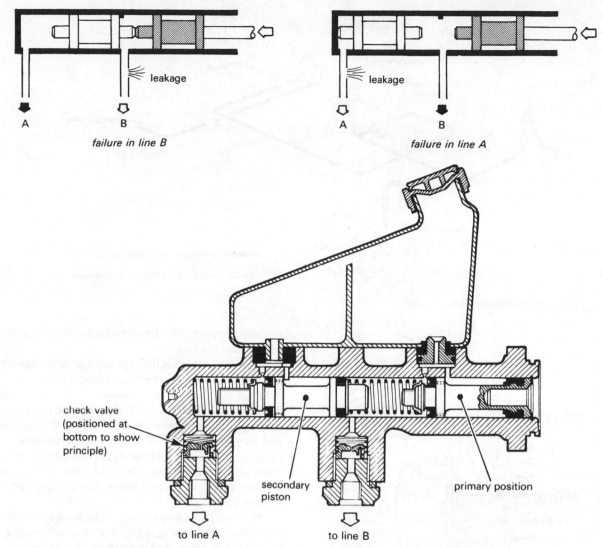

Figure 5.25 Tandem master cylinder

Failure in the rear line causes the initial pressure to move piston 2 to the limit of its travel. Once this point is reached the front brake can be operated successfully. An additional rubber seal fitted to piston 2 prevents fluid from leaking from the serviceable section of the hydraulic circuit into the fractured line.

Hydraulic circuit configurations

Although this description of the tandem cylinder has referred to the two lines as being front and rear, it must be pointed out that other configurations exist.

One common arrangement used is a 'split-line, diagonally linked' hydraulic system. This configuration connects the brakes diagonally into two separate circuits i.e. left-hand front to right-hand rear and vice versa (Figure 5.26).

The diagonally linked layout, together with negative offset (negative scrub radius) steering geometry, improves the safety by overcoming the problems of front–rear systems i.e. reducing the braking force exerted on the lightly loaded rear wheels which may

result in the spinning of the vehicle due to the rear wheels locking.

A more expensive brake system configuration uses the four-cylinder type calipers on each front disc. Independent brake pipelines from the tandem cylinder supply each pair of caliper cylinders. Failure of one pipeline ensures that the other pipeline keeps both front disc brakes and one rear brake in operation.

5.5.6 The pressure regulating valve

When a vehicle decelerates, the inertia forces acting at the centre of gravity cause the load on the front wheels to increase and that on the rear wheels to decrease.

The pressure-regulating valve (Figure 5.27) is fitted in the rear brake line. The valve is designed to reduce the risk of the rear wheels locking during heavy braking by limiting the brake fluid pressure acting on the rear brakes.

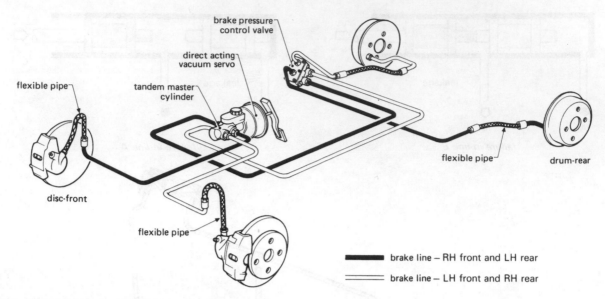

Figure 5.26 Split line diagonally linked system

━━━━ brake line – RH front and LH rear

═══ brake line – LH front and RH rear

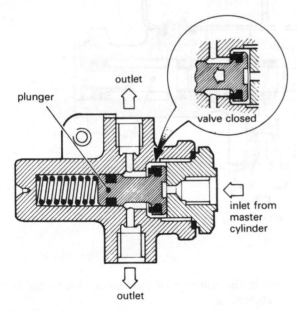

Figure 5.27 Pressure regulating valve

The valve consists of a spring-loaded plunger contained within a body. When the fluid pressure is relatively low, it will not overcome the spring, so the same pressure will act on all brakes.

When the brake is applied, fluid will initially pass to the rear brakes, but as the pressure is increased, and a predetermined pressure is reached, the valve will close. Any further increase of fluid pressure is only applied to the front brakes.

5.5.7 Brake pressure control valve (inertia valve)

The brake pressure control valve is a development of the pressure-regulating valve. The valve is particularly suited to overcome the problem of the large load variation between the front and rear wheels of front-wheel drive vehicles.

The valve, which is fitted in the rear brake line(s), is an inertia-sensitive, pressure-reducing valve that operates at a predetermined rate of vehicle deceleration. When the deceleration rate has been reached, the valve temporarily shuts off the rear line, and any additional brake pedal force increases the pressure in the front brake hydraulic circuit. After a given pressure is reached, the valve reinstates the fluid pressure supply to the rear brakes, but at a reduced rate (Figure 5.28).

The unit takes into account vehicle weight transfer and attitude during braking, and is also sensitive to vehicle loading and road conditions.

Figure 5.29 shows the construction of a valve suitable for a common rear brake circuit; a system having independent lines has two valves mounted side-by-side. The unit consists of a cylinder, mounted to the car body at a given angle, which contains a stepped piston and a steel ball.

At low vehicle deceleration rates, fluid enters the inlet port, passes around the ball and through the piston-drilling to the rear brakes. The fluid pressure is equal in the front and rear brake lines.

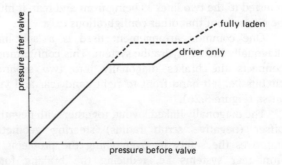

Figure 5.28 Control valve performance

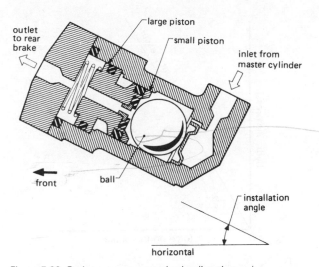

Figure 5.29 Brake pressure control valve (inertia type)

When the rate at which the vehicle slows down produces an inertia force sufficient to roll the ball up the sloping cylinder, the ball shuts off the fluid supply to the rear brakes. When this occurs, the difference in piston area causes the outlet pressure to remain constant even though the inlet pressure is being increased. At a given point, governed by the piston areas, an increase in inlet pressure starts to move the piston so as to give a proportional pressure to the rear brakes. Pressure in the two lines at this stage is given by:

$$\text{Inlet pressure} \times \text{Small area} = \frac{\text{Outlet}}{\text{pressure}} \times \frac{\text{Large}}{\text{area}}$$

5.5.8 The pressure differential warning actuator

This is a driver warning device to cause illumination of a 'brake failure warning lamp' if the pressure difference in the brake lines between two circuits differs by more than a given amount. Failure of one brake line causes the pistons (Figure 5.30) to move and operate the electrical switch. The switch then remains closed until the pistons are reset.

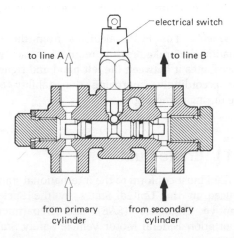

Figure 5.30 A brake pressure differential warning actuator

5.5.9 Load-apportioning valves

The purpose of this type of valve is to supply, within given limits, hydraulic pressure to the rear brakes in proportion to the load carried by the rear wheels.

The load-apportioning valve helps reduce the risk of a rear wheel skid at times when the rear of the vehicle is lightly loaded. The valve arrangement also ensures proportioning of the brake pressure when the rear wheels are heavily loaded.

Vehicles that frequently carry heavy loads, such as estate cars or light vans, are generally fitted with a braking system using a load-apportioning valve to vary the brake pressure to the rear brakes according to the load in the luggage area. Only one valve is required for a single line layout, but where a diagonal line system is used a separate valve must be fitted in each line.

The valve housing is bolted to a fixed part of the vehicle body and either a compression or tension spring is used to sense the load on the rear wheels. This spring connects the valve-operating lever to a part of the suspension system that moves in proportion to the vehicle load, e.g. the axle beam.

Figure 5.31 shows the construction of the valve. The operating lever acts directly on a piston, which incorporates a ball valve. When the brakes are off, the piston is at the bottom of the bore and the ball valve is held open by a push-rod fixed to the valve body. In this position the fluid can pass freely between the inlet and outlet ports. Upward piston movement takes place when hydraulic pressure is applied to the valve. This is achieved by making the area exposed to the fluid on the upper part of the piston larger than the area on the bottom part.

Operation under light loads

The force exerted by the external spring on the piston governs the hydraulic pressure that must be applied before the piston is raised and the ball valve is closed.

When the load is light, only a small force is exerted by the spring on the piston. As a result only a comparatively low pressure is needed to move the piston upwards so as to close the valve. When the pressure at this closure point is exceeded, full pressure cannot be applied to the rear brake. Any further increase in pedal force causes the piston to control the valve so as to supply a pressure that is lower and proportional to the pressure applied to the front brake.

Operation under heavy loads

As the load on the rear wheels is increased, a deflection of the suspension causes the external spring force to increase. To overcome the extra force exerted by this spring on the piston, a higher fluid pressure must be built up before the piston is able to rise. Consequently, full pressure on the rear brakes is maintained until a much higher pedal force is applied.

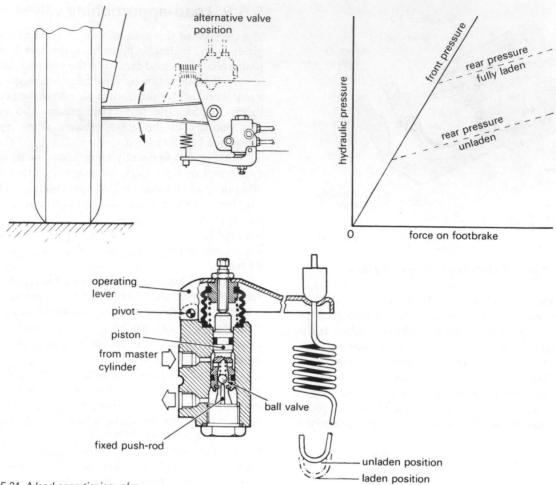

Figure 5.31 A load-apportioning valve

Load-apportioning valve faults

Besides possible leakage of the seals, fracture of the external spring is likely. This breakage will cause the valve to reduce the pressure supplied to the rear brakes considerably. When the valve is defective, the unit is usually replaced as a complete assembly.

The type of apportioning valve shown in Figure 5.31 has an adjusting screw between the lever and the piston. This controls the point at which the valve comes into operation, i.e. the front/rear braking ratio for a given rear wheel load. To set this adjusting screw correctly requires the use of specialized tools; these may include a brake pressure gauge and a set of vehicle scales. Refer to manufacturer's test procedures.

5.5.10 Electronically controlled proportioning

With improvements in electronic technology and the application of electronics to motor vehicles, many modern cars are now fitted with an anti-lock braking system (ABS). In addition to ABS control (preventing the wheels from locking when braking), the electronic control system may also be able to control the proportion of brake pressure applied to the brakes.

To achieve this proportioning of brake pressure, the ECU calculates from sensors which wheels (i.e. back or front) are on the verge of locking due to a transfer in vehicle weight during braking. The ECU limits the brake pressure to the front or rear brakes accordingly.

In addition to the proportioning of the brake pressure to the front and rear wheels, it is also possible to proportion the brake pressure to the brakes on each side of the vehicle while cornering.

During cornering, the centre of gravity causes the vehicle weight to transfer from the inside wheels to the outer wheels. The ECU calculates from the sensor information the brake pressure required at each wheel, and distributes it between the left-hand and right-hand wheels accordingly, improving the stability of the vehicle during cornering.

5.5.11 Brake fluid

Brake fluid must conform to the international standards introduced in the United States by the Society of Automotive Engineers (SAE) and Department of Transportation Federal Motor Vehicle Safety Standard (FMVSS).

The main requirements of a brake fluid include:

- Low viscosity – the fluid must flow easily over a wide temperature range and be able to operate in very cold conditions.
- Compatibility with rubber components – besides avoiding corrosion of metal parts, the fluid must not chemically react with the rubber seals etc.
- Lubricating properties – to reduce friction of moving parts, especially rubber seals.
- Resistance to chemical ageing – the fluid should have a long life when stored and must be stable when in use.
- Compatibility with other fluids – the fluid must mix with other fluids in its class.
- High boiling point – to avoid vapourization when in use and heated by brake action.

Most brake systems use a glycerine-alcohol (glycol) fluid with additives incorporated to allow it to meet the specifications.

A number of different fluids are available, some vegetable- and some mineral-based, so the manufacturer's recommendation should be consulted before a system is serviced. Checking the fluid recommended for the system is essential because if a minute quantity of mineral oil is introduced into a system designed to operate on vegetable-based fluid, the rubber seals will be severely damaged.

5.5.12 The boiling point of brake fluid

Glycol-based brake fluids are hygroscopic; this means they absorb moisture from the atmosphere over a period of time. As a result, the boiling point of the brake fluid is lowered and in extreme circumstances this causes complete failure of the brakes because of 'vapour lock'. The condition is produced when the fluid in a part of the system is heated above its boiling point sufficiently to vaporize the water in the fluid. Once this occurs, the elastic nature of the steam allows the pedal movement to reach its maximum travel (the pedal reaches the floor) before it can build up sufficient pressure to apply the brakes effectively.

In view of the hygroscopic nature of most brake fluids, the SAE and FMVSS specifications require the fluid to have a 'wet boiling point' and 'dry boiling point' in excess of the stated value. The wet boiling point is the temperature at which a fluid containing 3–3.5% water boils and produces steam bubbles.

In the case of a typical fluid such as SAE J 1703C, FMVSS 116 DOT 3, the wet boiling point must be above 140°C. To take account of the rising demands placed on brake fluids, especially with the use of disc brakes, the US Safety Regulations are continually being updated. Fluids that meet DOT 4, DOT 5 and DOT 5.1 standards are now available and some new fluids that have wet/dry boiling points of 190–270°C permit the fluid renewal interval to be extended to two years.

Some special silicone-based fluids have been developed to overcome the hygroscopic problem, but these are not commonly used because of their cost.

To prevent brake fluid from absorbing moisture from the air, brake fluids in common use should be stored in sealed containers and once opened, they should not be stored for long periods. The cap on the brake fluid reservoir should be replaced as soon as work on the braking system has been completed.

Brake fluid testers are available for use in a vehicle workshop; the tester is used to check the moisture content of the brake fluid. A brake fluid check is normally carried out by simply checking the fluid in the master cylinder reservoir. The test result is then analysed and used to determine if the vehicle's brake fluid requires changing.

Important note: Brake fluid can damage the vehicle's paintwork. Brake fluid should therefore not come into contact with the paintwork. If any brake fluid accidentally drips onto the paintwork, it should be washed off with water immediately.

5.6 POWER ASSISTANCE

5.6.1 The requirement for power assistance

To slow the vehicle down at the required rate the driver must exert a certain force on the footbrake. As well as driver comfort, it is also much safer if the driver is easily able to obtain high braking effort with relatively small pedal effort. When the driver cannot comfortably apply the level of force required to operate the footbrake and achieve good levels of braking force, some form of assistance must be given. The boosting force used to reinforce the driver's effort is referred to as 'servo assistance'.

In the past, the assistance was provided by the rotation of the brake drum and configuration of the brake shoes (self-servo), which kept the pedal force low. Disc brakes however have no self-servo assistance and therefore some other form of assistance is needed. Additionally, vehicle speeds have increased over the years and therefore improved braking has become necessary. Even disc brake systems provide substantially more braking force on modern cars than was the case for earlier disc systems. It therefore became unacceptable for the driver to apply the required effort to achieve necessary braking forces.

Servo assistance for light vehicle brakes is now normally provided by either pneumatic or hydraulic means. Vacuum assistance is used for small, medium and some larger cars, hydraulic assistance for heavy cars and light commercial vehicle, and compressed-air assistance for light trucks etc.

5.6.2 Vacuum assistance

The vacuum-operated servo is the most popular form of servo assistance. The term 'vacuum' is sometimes misleading because most systems use the depression formed in the induction manifold of the spark-ignition type of engine as a source of servo energy. In the case of a diesel engine, this energy is not available at the manifold, so an engine-driven 'vacuum' pump is used to provide the required assistance.

All servo systems must be fail-safe, so if for example a fault develops in the vacuum unit, the main braking system must still be able to operate, albeit with a pedal force considerably greater than normal.

Progressive operation of the servo is a further requirement; this means that for light pedal pressure, the assistance given by the servo is proportional to the pedal effort. Figure 5.32 shows the relationship between the hydraulic pressure that acts on the brake cylinders (both with and without servo assistance) and the pedal effort. The servo valves provide a gradual increase in the assistance up to the knee point; at this point maximum vacuum assistance is given. Any rise in output pressure beyond the knee point is a direct result of the increased pedal effort.

Vacuum servos in use today are called 'suspended vacuum types', because when the vehicle is in use and the brakes are off, 'vacuum conditions' exist on both sides of the servo piston. When the brake is applied, air

from the atmosphere is bled to the chamber on one side of the piston to give the pressure difference.

There are two main types of suspended-vacuum servo:

- indirect
- direct.

5.6.3 Indirect-acting servos

The indirect type is now not used, but it clearly demonstrates the principle of providing added effort to the pressure being applied to the wheel cylinders.

The, indirect type is sometimes referred to as a 'remote type' because it is located in the hydraulic line between the single master cylinder and the wheel cylinders and is therefore remote from the master cylinder. This enabled the servo to be added to a standard non-assisted braking system. Locating the servo was relatively easy which was an advantage on small vehicles that did not have much space under the bonnet.

Figure 5.33 shows an indirect servo suitable for a medium-sized car. It consists of three main items:

1 Vacuum cylinder containing a spring-loaded diaphragm.
2 Slave hydraulic cylinder.
3 Control valve actuated by hydraulic pressure.

With the engine running and the brake off, the unit is as shown in Figure 5.33a. The vacuum valve is open and equal 'vacuum' pressure is applied on both sides of the diaphragm.

Application of the brake pedal produces a hydraulic pressure on the brakes and also raises the valve piston in the servo (Figure 5.33b). This movement closes the vacuum control valve and opens the air valve to allow a breakdown of the 'vacuum' in the outer chamber of the vacuum cylinder. The outer chamber is therefore directly exposed to atmospheric pressure and this is allowed to pass through to the booster piston.

Air pressure is now acting on one side of the booster piston, but 'vacuum' is still applied to the other side. This pressure difference causes the booster piston (or booster diaphragm) to apply a thrust on the slave cylinder piston, which boosts the thrust given by the driver.

'Proportional' braking is obtained by allowing the difference in air pressure, felt by the booster diaphragm, to act on the control valve diaphragm: as the difference increases, the diaphragm overcomes the hydraulic pressure acting on the valve piston and closes the air valve (Figure 5.33c).

Release of the pedal drops the hydraulic pressure to allow the valve piston to return and open the vacuum control valve. Air is quickly evacuated from the outer chamber of the vacuum cylinder and a spring returns the diaphragm. A hole in the centre of the slave-cylinder piston ensures that the brake can still be operated if the servo fails.

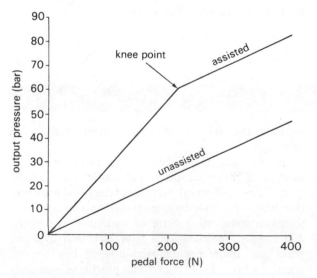

Figure 5.32 Servo assistance

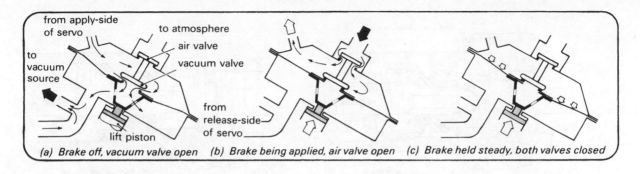

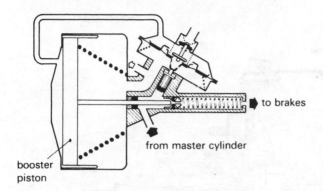

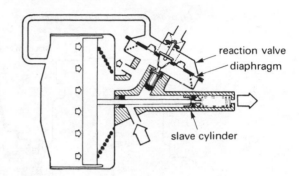

Figure 5.33 A suspended-vacuum servo – indirect type

Apart from general inspection of hoses etc., the only attention the unit requires is the periodic cleaning of its air filter.

Because the indirect servo forms part of the hydraulic circuit between the master cylinder and the wheel cylinders, it is not practical to use this type when modern tandem master cylinders are used, and a direct-type must be employed.

5.6.4 Direct-acting servos

Most cars are fitted with a direct-acting, suspended-vacuum servo, which is used with either single or tandem master cylinders. It gets its name from the fact that the brake pedal linkage and master cylinder assembly is directly connected to the servo.

Figure 5.34 (main picture) shows the position of the unit when the engine is running, the brakes are 'off' and the servo piston/diaphragm is 'suspended in vacuum'. Atmospheric air pressure has been removed from both servo compartments; the air pressure in the large vacuum chamber has effectively been drawn into the engine inlet manifold (petrol engine) due to engine vacuum. The pressure has passed through the pipe and non-return valve in the front of the vacuum chamber. Evacuation of air from the smaller rear chamber (behind the rubber diaphragm-seated piston) is through a control valve linked to the footbrake pedal (shown more clearly in Figures 5.34a and 5.34b).

Movement of the brake pedal initially closes the vacuum valve and then opens the air valve (Figure 5.34a). This allows air to flow through the filter and valve to the rear chamber. Atmospheric pressure is now acting on the rear chamber and the vacuum is acting on the front chamber. The difference in air pressure between the two chambers produces a force on the piston/diaphragm assembly, which boosts the effort applied by the driver.

As the servo piston starts to move, it exerts a force on the master cylinder push-rod through a rubber reaction disc. Pressure on this spongy disc causes it to squeeze back and close the air valve (Figure 5.34b). In this position the driver's efforts will be supplemented by a servo boost that is proportional to the effort applied; this feature enables the driver to 'feel' the load applied to the brake and also gives progressive operation.

Further movement of the pedal reopens the air valve and the previous events will be repeated up to the 'knee point' (Figure 5.32). Beyond this stage the driver keeps the air valve fully open, and this indicates the limit of servo assistance.

Releasing the brake pedal causes the air valve to close and the vacuum valve to open. This restores the vacuum suspension of the piston and allows the spring to return the piston to the 'off' position.

In the event of vacuum failure the brakes can still be applied without servo assistance.

The assistance given by a vacuum chamber is proportional to the area of the piston, i.e. the larger the area the greater the assistance. Accommodating a very large cylinder adjacent to the footbrake on a modern car is difficult and various mechanical linkages and systems have been used to overcome this problem.

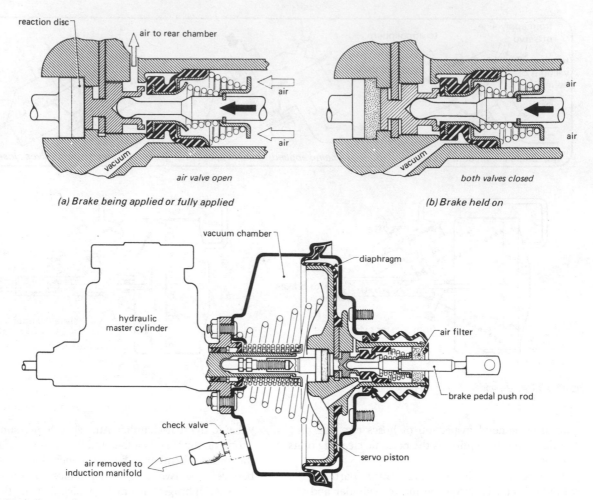

(a) Brake being applied or fully applied   *(b) Brake held on*

Figure 5.34 A direct-acting servo

5.6.5 Vacuum supply

Most servo units operate directly from the induction manifold (petrol engine). A few manufacturers have used a vacuum reservoir to 'store vacuum'; this can provide an improvement in performance, and extra safety. Figure 5.35 shows a typical system.

The manifold depression, if any, of most diesel engines cannot be used to operate a vacuum brake servo. A separate, engine-driven pump is fitted to create the required vacuum. This pump, or exhauster, produces a vacuum of about 500–600 mm (20–25 inch) of mercury.

5.6.6 Hydraulic assistance

Unless an effective servo is fitted, a considerable effort is required to stop a heavy motorcar or light truck. Because the pressure difference between atmospheric pressure and engine vacuum is limited, a system is needed that provides a much greater source of energy. This can be achieved with a hydraulic servo because this type of system operates using a pressure of 55–82 bar (800–1200 lbf/in²).

The hydraulic pressure can be produced by an engine-driven pump or an electrical motor-driven pump. Note that on some applications the hydraulic system can also be used to provide pressure for other requirements, e.g. power assisted steering, suspension, hydraulic lifts, etc.

Figure 5.36a shows a diagrammatic sketch of a continuous-flow hydraulic servo system.

Mounted behind the conventional master cylinder, the servo valve is supplied with pressurized fluid.

The diagram shows the brakes in the 'off' position. In this state the fluid can easily pass between the master-cylinder piston and servo valve to a drilling which leads back to the reservoir.

When the brake pedal is depressed, the conical servo valve closes initially and causes the pump to build up a pressure in region A, which will tend to force piston and valve apart. The piston has a larger area than the valve, and so the thrust exerted on the piston will be greater than that acting on the valve and brake pedal. The surface area ratio governs the assistance given to the driver. As soon as a given pressure, which will depend on the force applied to the pedal, has built up, the servo valve will partially open to maintain the pressure and give assistance. If the pedal force is

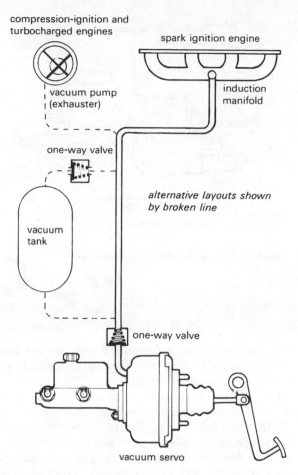

Figure 5.35 Vacuum servo layout

exceptionally high, a pressure relief valve opens and allows fluid to escape to the reservoir.

Releasing of the pedal returns and opens the servo valve, releases the brakes and restores uninterrupted flow of fluid from pump to reservoir.

Continuous-flow system with accumulator

The assistance given by the continuous-flow system depends on the pump speed, so a 'hard' pedal is felt when the pump is stationary or rotating slowly. To overcome this disadvantage, a hydraulic accumulator is normally incorporated into the system.

Figure 5.36b shows the layout of such a system, which uses the same pump and master cylinder as the previous example.

The accumulator (a pressure storage cylinder) contains a spring-loaded piston, which is acted upon by the fluid. The higher the fluid pressure in the accumulator, the more the spring is compressed. A cut-out valve maintains the accumulator pressure in the range 55–82 bar (800–1200 lbf/in²). A charging valve, activated by fluid pressure from the output or brake line side of the master cylinder, releases fluid from the accumulator to act on the servo valve, should the pump be incapable of supplying the necessary fluid.

Note: Whenever any part of this system is disconnected, it is essential that the pressure in the system and accumulator be discharged. This can normally be achieved by pumping the brake pedal many times with the engine or electrically driven pump switched off.

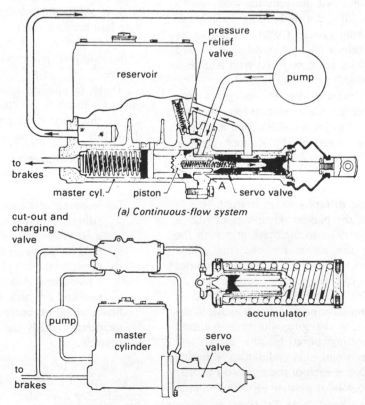

(a) Continuous-flow system

(b) Continuous-flow system with accumulator

Figure 5.36 Hydraulic servo system

5.6.7 Compressed-air assistance

An alternative to a hydraulic servo on light trucks and minibuses is a compressed-air servo. The system is generally referred to as an air/hydraulic (air-over hydraulic) or Airpac system, because compressed air is used to boost the force applied by the driver to a hydraulically operated brake.

The system is based on the layout shown in Figure 5.37. Air pressure, generated by an engine-driven compressor, is stored in a reservoir adjacent to the servo chamber; this houses a piston that operates another piston that controls the main hydraulic brake line. When the brake is applied, a valve directs compressed air into the servo cylinder to boost the pedal effort.

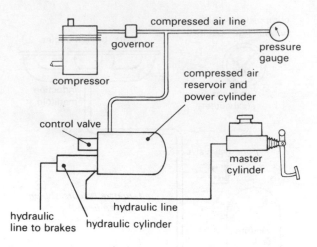

Figure 5.37 Basic layout of an air/hydraulic system

5.7 ANTI-LOCK BRAKING SYSTEMS

5.7.1 Requirement for an anti-lock braking system (ABS)

With a significant increase in the number of road users and traffic congestion, there is an increasing need for systems that provide greater safety for drivers and passengers. Vehicle and system manufacturers have developed several safety systems over the past few years to assist the driver of the vehicle, one of these being a braking system that prevents the road wheels from locking and skidding during braking. Referred to as an anti-lock braking system (ABS), it contributes towards additional vehicle safety, providing it is used correctly. Many vehicles are now fitted with ABS as a standard safety feature.

It is difficult for most drivers in emergency stop situations to quickly assess the maximum force that can be exerted on the brake pedal to make a controlled stop. Bringing the vehicle to rest in the shortest possible distance and with directional control being maintained is therefore difficult.

However, while ensuring that the vehicle can stop in the shortest possible distance in a straight line is obviously important, the biggest advantage of ABS is that the tyres can continue to maintain grip with the road surface when the car is manoeuvring. Many accidents can be avoided, or the damage and injuries reduced, if the driver can take avoiding action.

If a driver is trying to steer the vehicle to avoid an obstacle, and the tyres have no grip (such as when the road is icy) steering or changing direction is almost impossible. Any steering input by the driver will probably have little or no effect and also, differing levels of grip available at each of the tyres will usually cause the vehicle to take a path or direction that is totally undesirable.

ABS therefore ensures that the wheels do not lock during extreme braking thus allowing improved levels of grip to be achieved by the tyres. This enables the driver to have considerably increased control of the direction of the vehicle in these critical moments.

Any direct reduction in braking distance in a straight line should therefore be regarded as a bonus rather than as the objective, although it is true that braking distances in the wet and on slippery surfaces will be reduced due to the action of the ABS.

It is a difficult task for the driver of the vehicle to take into account the many varying factors that affect the tyre's grip, such as the type and frictional material of the road and tyre, together with the condition of the surface.

These factors generally mean the driver applies either too much or too little pressure on the brake pedal during this very short period of time. The effects of driver misjudgement are as follows:

1 **Brake pedal pressure too high.** One or more of the wheels lock and skid over the surface with the result that:
   (a) stopping distance is increased because the adhesion between a skidding wheel and the road is less than that given by a wheel that is held on the verge of locking
   (b) directional control is jeopardised; in the case of a rear-wheel skid, the vehicle turns from front to rear and a vehicle spin occurs.
2 **Brake pedal pressure too low.** Stopping distance is increased, which can result in impact with an obstacle.

The adhesion between the road wheel and road surface is governed by the coefficient of friction. This varies considerably depending on the condition of the road surface. As an example, the friction value of a dry asphalt road reduces from about 0.8 to 0.15 when it is covered with black ice.

If a vehicle is travelling at a constant speed, the speed of the vehicle is equal to the speed of its wheels.

If, when braking, the wheels slow down at a greater rate than the vehicle, a small amount of wheel slip occurs. The slip can be calculated by:

$$\text{Slip ratio} = \frac{\text{Vehicle speed} - \text{wheel speed}}{\text{Vehicle speed}} \times 100$$

On a dry surface the adhesion varies as the percentage of wheel slip ranges, from 0% (no slip) to 100% (locked wheel, sliding over the road surface).

Figure 5.38 shows how the longitudinal and transverse adhesion of a tyre changes as the amount of slip is increased. The curve representing longitudinal adhesion for a given condition shows that a braking force set to hold a wheel at about 15% slip provides the maximum retarding force.

Vehicle stability with respect to the tyres tendency to slide sideways, is indicated on the graph by the transverse adhesion curve. The adhesion in this direction falls as soon as the wheel starts to skid, so if any serious skidding occurs, this can quickly lead to loss of vehicle control, especially when the driver is making a steering correction, or when the vehicle is cornering.

By limiting the amount of wheel slip, vehicle stability and control is also maintained while the vehicle is braking.

ABS maximizes the braking of a vehicle by maintaining a slip ratio between 10 and 30%, which also allows the cornering force to be as high as possible under these conditions.

Although ABS functions on many road surfaces, the driver of the vehicle must still take care when driving on very slippery surfaces such as ice; stopping distances on these surfaces will increase significantly.

When driving conditions such as snow and gravel are encountered, the ABS may in fact not provide any advantage. When braking on these looser surfaces without ABS action, a build ip of snow or gravel in front of a skidding tyre actually acts as a brake to the movement of the vehicle. With ABS, the build-up would not occur thus increasing the braking distance.

It is therefore quite normal for rally drivers to not make use of ABS. As well as being experienced in the application of the brakes to suit the conditions, rally drivers also use the locking action of the brakes to promote skidding in a desired direction, which helps to set up the vehicle for the next corner. The rally driver may therefore be able to switch off ABS operation, if ABS is fitted to the vehicle.

Note: Drivers are sometimes concerned at the noise and vibrations felt through the brake pedal when the ABS is operating, but this is normal.

Since the 1970s ABS has been fitted during production to a few vehicles, usually as an option. Many of today's vehicles are fitted with ABS as a standard safety feature.

5.7.2 Types of ABS

Although various types of ABS have been fitted to vehicles, as previously mentioned, most systems are now electronically controlled. The various systems can be generally classed into two groups, the difference between the two types of system is the manner in which wheel slip is monitored. These systems are:

- electronic
- mechanical.

With advances in vehicle electronic technology, the mechanically sensed ABS is no longer fitted to vehicles. All ABS now fitted to vehicles is of the electronic-sensing type.

Mechanical as well as electronic systems are covered in full detail in Book 2.

Because safety is an inevitable priority with braking systems, ABS must allow braking to be maintained if the ABS should fail.

Most electronic ABS systems are designed in such a way that if a failure occurs, normal braking can be maintained. These ABS systems are fitted to the standard braking system as an add-on to the standard braking system.

Although ABS may visually appear to be an integrated part of the braking system, operation of ABS is achieved by intruding into the brake pressure lines and these systems are therefore referred to as 'intrusive systems'.

Some electronic systems did form part of the main braking system operation. Although these systems used the same basic principle of operation, they usually used a pressure pump to create braking pressure, with the driver providing a small part of the total pressure used to operate the brakes. In effect, the pump acted as a hydraulic servo system. If the pump failed, the driver was still able to operate the brakes but with a much reduced performance. These systems are usually referred to as 'integrated systems'.

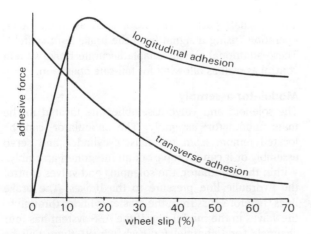

Figure 5.38 Adhesive force and wheel slip

5.7.3 Principle of ABS operation

Although there have been a number of types of ABS, which are dealt with in greater detail in Book 2, nearly all the systems now in use operate on a similar principle. These systems are usually electronically controlled.

The three phases of control

Most ABS systems now use a process of control that uses three operating phases:

Phase 1   Normal brake operation. Brake fluid pressure remains unaffected by ABS. ABS has no influence on the brake system operation because no wheel locking is detected or ABS has not detected any potential for wheel lock.

Phase 2   Pressure hold. ABS detects that the rotational speed of one or more wheels is slowing down at a rate that is greater than the other wheels. In effect, the grip from one or more tyres is lower than the others therefore the wheel speed is becoming slower than the other wheels, i.e. the wheel is about to lock up.

The ABS operation prevents the pressure of the brake fluid on the affected wheel(s) from increasing. Even if the driver applies greater pressure to the brake pedal, the pressure on the affected wheel brakes will not increase, although pressure on the other brakes will increase. The result should then be that all tyres end up with the same levels of grip.

Phase 3   Pressure reduction. If the affected wheel(s) is still slowing down at a greater rate than the other wheels, or is actually locking up, ABS reduces the pressure to the applicable brake(s). The affected wheels will now be able to speed up because there is less braking force being applied. The result will be that the slower wheel should increase speed to match the faster wheels.

When the speed of the affected wheel starts to increase, ABS allows pressure to be re-applied to the brake. In this way, ABS can maintain relatively consistent rates of deceleration for all four wheels.

ABS will implement the pressure hold and pressure reduction phases depending on the information supplied by the wheel speed sensors. The three phases of operation will be applied as necessary to help keep wheel speed deceleration consistent on all four wheels, which helps to maintain vehicle control and reduce braking distances on slippery surfaces.

5.7.4 Operation and components of intrusive electronic ABS

The following information relates to an intrusive electronic system, which is the most common type of ABS fitted to modern vehicles.

One common type of intrusive system makes use of speed sensors for each of the four wheels. The system is also able to control the brake line pressure separately to each of the four brakes. This system is referred to as a four-sensor, four-channel system i.e. one sensor for each wheel and one control valve for each wheel or brake.

Some systems can use three-wheel speed sensors (one sensor detecting prop shaft or differential pinion shaft speed on a rear-wheel drive vehicle) with one sensor on each of the front wheels; this would be a three-sensor system. Additionally, on the same system one valve may be used to control both of the rear brakes, with the front brakes retaining a valve for each brake; such systems would therefore be referred to as a three-channel, three-sensor system.

Wheel speed sensors

The wheel speed sensors provide an electrical signal to the computer or ECU. The sensors are located at each of the wheels, although on a three-sensor system, a single rear sensor would be usually located in the final-drive housing.

Adjacent to the wheel speed sensor is usually a toothed ring or disc (often referred to as a 'toothed rotor'). When the wheel is rotating, the sensor produces a small electrical pulse or signal as each tooth passes. The number of teeth on a rotor depends on the design, however it may typically have around 40 to 50 teeth. This would result in 40 to 50 individual pulses being produced by the sensor for each rotation of the wheel.

Electronic control unit (ECU)

Pulsed signals from the wheel speed sensors are passed to the ECU, which is then able to assess the speed of the wheels and also predict when one or more wheels is likely to lock up.

The ECU controls the operation of hydraulic valves by providing electrical control signals to solenoids. The solenoids cause valves in the hydraulic brake circuits to open and close, and so control the brake line pressure.

In this way the ECU is able to assess wheel speed, allowing it to control the valves as necessary to implement the three phases of ABS operation.

Other signals pass to the ECU, such as brake pedal operation (using a signal from the brake light switch). These additional signals enable accurate brake system control as well as allowing for fail-safe operation.

Modulator assembly

The solenoid and valve assemblies are located in the main modulator assembly. The modulator can be located remote from the master cylinder and servo assembly or it can form part of an integrated assembly. Within the modulator, the solenoids and valves control the hydraulic line pressure to the brakes. The brake lines therefore pass from the master cylinder through to the valves in the modulator. If the ABS system has four channels (one channel for each wheel) there will be four solenoids and valves. In this case, the hydraulic circuits passing from the master cylinder would be split within the modulator, so that each of the valves receives pressure from the master cylinder.

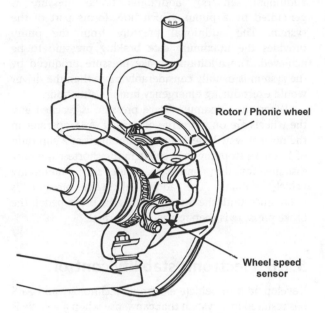

Figure 5.39 *Wheel speed sensors and a toothed rotor*

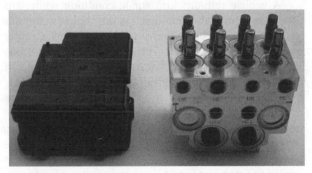

Figure 5.40 *ECU and modulator*

When the ECU intervenes the valves may be moved to different operating positions thus affecting the hydraulic pressure passing through each brake cylinder.

Note that with intrusive systems, the modulator cannot increase the brake line pressure but simply control the pressure created by the driver and the servo and master cylinder assembly. Pressure at the brake cylinder is therefore either the applied pressure, unmodified, or reduced (the three operating phases).

When the ECU detects that a particular wheel is about to lock up, it passes a control signal to the applicable solenoid, which in turn causes its valve to move to the appropriate operating position, thus reducing the pressure at the wheel cylinder.

5.7.5 Traction control system (TCS)

The electronic sensing arrangement that is used in ABS for the detection of road wheel speed and slip can be further utilized to control or limit the maximum traction force used to propel the vehicle. On roads that are slippery (i.e. ice and snow) the adhesion between the road surface and tyre is low. If during acceleration the power from the engine is too great, wheel slip will occur. Prevention of wheel slip, caused by the high torque of the driven wheels, was previously achieved by mechanical means using a 'limited slip differential' (LSD).

The slip-limiting action can also be achieved using ABS components to give either a braking action on the driven wheel that is slipping during acceleration, or to cause a reduction in engine power.

Brake application

Applying the brake to the slipping wheel transfers the power to the other driving wheel; this is a function of the differential unit within the final drive assembly (two-wheel drive vehicles).

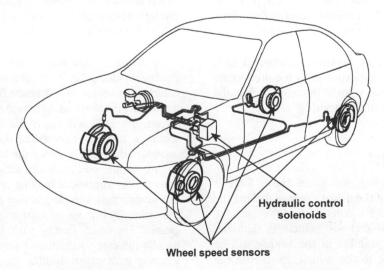

Figure 5.41 *Layout of intrusive ABS system with four sensors and four channels.*

Reducing engine power (torque control)

Because modern engines are computer controlled, when the ABS computer detects wheel spin via the wheel speed sensors, the ABS ECU can in fact pass an appropriate signal to the engine ECU.

Should one or more driving wheel display excessive slip, the engine ECU can impose a reduction in engine power or torque. This can be achieved by retarding the ignition timing, or reducing the amount of fuel delivered to the engine. An increasingly common method of reducing engine power is now possible using electronic throttle control. On such systems the ECU can close the throttle, thus reducing engine power.

Some vehicles use systems that achieve traction control by utilizing a reduction in engine power combined with application of a brake on the wheel that is spinning most.

5.7.6 Electronic brake apportioning

Brake apportioning, which was previously carried out on braking systems using mechanical brake-apportioning valves, can also be carried out electronically via ABS components. By altering the distribution of brake pressure applied to the wheels, the optimum brake pressure can be applied to the road wheels resulting in a higher level of grip.

To achieve this apportioning of brake pressure to the correct wheels, the ECU uses the wheel speed sensor signals to calculate which wheels (i.e. back or front) are on the verge of locking due to a transfer in vehicle weight during braking. The ECU limits the brake pressure to the front or rear brakes accordingly by controlling the hydraulic modulator valves.

In addition to the apportioning of the brake pressure between the front and rear road wheels, it is also possible to apportion the brake pressure to the brakes on each side of the vehicle while cornering.

During cornering, the centre of gravity causes the vehicle weight to transfer from the inside wheels to the outer wheels. The ECU receives information from various sensors that detect movement of the vehicle and other information; this information then enables the ECU to calculate the brake pressure required at each wheel. Brake pressure is apportioned as required to the left-hand and right-hand wheels thus improving the stability of the vehicle during cornering

5.7.7 Brake assist

During emergency braking, maximum brake force is rarely exerted because of the driver's fear of locking the road wheels. Experienced drivers know that once the road wheels are locked and the vehicle is skidding, directional control and stability of the vehicle will be lost. When ABS is fitted to the vehicle, even with the highest level of physical effort exerted by the driver on the brake pedal, wheel slip cannot occur during braking as the system prevents it.

Brake assist uses many of the ABS components. When emergency braking is detected (with the use of additional sensors), additional brake pressure is generated by a pump, which now forms part of the system. The additional pressure from the pump provides the maximum safe braking pressure to be achieved. The additional brake pressure produced by the system is usually considerably more than the driver would exert during emergency braking situations.

When the maximum brake pressure is reached and the wheels are on the verge of locking, ABS operates in the normal way. Wheel slip is maintained at a slip ratio of 10–30%, stopping the vehicle in the shortest stopping distance for the conditions, while still maintaining vehicle stability. The additional brake pressure is maintained until the driver releases the brake pedal; the brake pressure is then returned to normal.

5.7.8 Electronic stability control

Development in vehicle electronic technology and ABS has resulted in a system that can sense when a vehicle is being driven in a manner that would lead to vehicle instability and loss of control.

A vehicle remains in a stable condition while it is driven in a controlled manner, i.e. the vehicle maintains the direction in which the driver steers. However, under some conditions the vehicle becomes unstable, usually due to being driven too fast for the road conditions or because of the need for a sudden change of direction.

The stability control system is normally integrated into the ABS ECU because the system shares many of the components with ABS control. Additional sensors are required to monitor the direction in which the vehicle is travelling (yaw sensor) and also the angle at which the steering wheel is set (steering angle sensor). The ECU constantly monitors the information received by the sensors and assesses the stability of the vehicle. If the information received by the ECU indicates that the vehicle is in a stable condition, it does not interfere with the vehicle's braking system.

If the sensor information indicates that the vehicle is yawing, skidding or in an unstable condition (i.e. the vehicle is travelling in a direction that does not match the intended direction) as indicated by the steering angle sensor, the ECU will apply the brakes in a particular sequence and may also reduce the engine's torque. The actions of the ECU, applying the brakes and reducing the engine torque, will normally allow the driver to regain control. The control of braking and reduction of power can ensure that vehicle stability is maintained without the driver being aware that a stability problem had existed. However, during such control, the ECU will usually indicate to the driver (either via an instrument warning light or an audible signal), that the vehicle's stability is being controlled by the ECU.

5.8   BRAKE ROUTINE MAINTENANCE

5.8.1 Safety

For obvious reasons the braking system should be maintained to the highest levels at all times. Although some safety measures are built into the braking system, any decrease in the system's efficiency (or complete brake failure) may lead to an accident and personal injury or in extreme circumstances, death.

During routine maintenance the braking system should be checked and inspected for any defects that could result in its partial or complete failure. The components should also be checked for wear; special attention should be given to the frictional linings, i.e. brake pads and brake shoes.

Although the following section provides a guide for checking the brake system during routine maintenance, always refer to specific vehicle information for vehicle maintenance details and specifications. Routine maintenance of the braking system requires inspecting the underside of the vehicle, and the where necessary, the removal of the road wheels. A vehicle lift is ideal for carrying out these checks, although the maintenance checks can be carried out using a suitable vehicle jack and supports.

5.8.2 Handbrake

The handbrake and linkage should be checked to ensure it operates correctly and holds the vehicle stationary when parked.

The handbrake lever should be checked for the security of its mountings and the ratchet and pawl mechanism to ensure that the handbrake remains 'on' when applied.

The handbrake travel should be checked; too much travel and the brake force applied by the handbrake may be insufficient to hold the vehicle stationary. Too little travel and the handbrake may hold the brakes 'on' when fully released.

The handbrake linkage from the handbrake lever through to the brakes should be inspected for wear and seizure. A seized handbrake may cause brake shoe or pad binding, resulting in premature wear.

The handbrake efficiency can be checked with the use of a rolling road brake tester. The vehicle's handbrake efficiency is checked as part of the annual MOT test. This check provides an indication that the handbrake system is functioning with a specified efficiency but it does not confirm that the components of the handbrake operating system are in good condition or check whether any component is close to failure. A physical check is always advised.

5.8.3 Footbrake

The driver constantly uses the footbrake to slow down and stop the vehicle. The footbrake and brake components must be maintained to ensure they function correctly at all times.

The brake pedal should be set at the correct height. Too high and it will be uncomfortable for the driver to depress, too low and there may be insufficient travel for the brakes to be fully applied.

Pedal freeplay is necessary to ensure that the brakes are not held on, causing overheating and premature wearing of the brake linings.

It is necessary to check the function and level of servo assistance. Too little servo assistance and the driver may not be able to apply enough force to the brake pedal to stop the vehicle quickly. The servo assistance components should be inspected visually for any defects in the pipes and booster assembly.

5.8.4 Hydraulic system

Brake fluid

If any component or pipeline is disconnected from the hydraulic system it is necessary to remove the air from the system after refitting the component. The removal of the air from a hydraulic system is referred to as 'bleeding the system'.

During routine maintenance checks it may also be necessary to change the brake fluid in the hydraulic system. Changing the brake fluid in the system uses the same principle as bleeding the system, however when changing the fluid we must ensure that all of the fluid in the system is replaced with new fluid.

The main steps in the hydraulic fluid bleed procedure operation are:

1 Ensure that the reservoir is full.
2 Attach one end of a rubber tube to the bleeder valve and immerse the other end in a small volume of fluid contained in jar.
3 Open the bleeder valve and slowly depress the pedal; repeat the operation until air bubbles cease to appear. Close the bleeder valve when the pedal is fully depressed.
4 Repeat the procedure at all wheel cylinders.
5 Top up the reservoir with new brake fluid to the full mark.

There are many types of specialized equipment to assist the technician to bleed the air from the hydraulic system. The equipment used may allow the operation to be carried out by a single operative. Air pressure is normally used to force fluid through the hydraulic system.

Many vehicles today are fitted with anti-lock braking systems (ABS), which may require alternative procedures to bleed the air from the system or replace the brake fluid. These procedures may involve the use of test equipment to operate the electrical solenoids, allowing the fluid to pass through the ABS hydraulic modulator assembly.

The level of fluid in the reservoir should always be set to the maximum level. A very small lowering of the fluid level due to fluid loss caused by brake lining wear is acceptable, but any major fluid losses due to a fluid leak must be corrected.

A large loss of fluid occurring over a short period of time may provide an indication of a fluid leak. A warning light on the instrument panel may illuminate if the fluid drops to a dangerous level, warning the driver of a brake fault.

Brake fluid absorbs moisture from the atmosphere ('hygroscopic'). The absorption of moisture lowers the boiling point of the brake fluid, which can lead to vapour lock occurring in the hydraulic system during heavy braking. Many manufacturers recommend replacing of the brake fluid at specified service intervals, typically two years. Note that test equipment is available to check the moisture content in the brake fluid.

Hydraulic system components

The brake master cylinder should be inspected visibly for external leaks. The rubber seals within the master cylinder can also fail internally, usually identified by a brake pedal that slowly creeps downward when pressure is applied to the pedal.

The hydraulic brake pipelines transfer the hydraulic pressure from the master cylinder to the wheel cylinders. Most of the brake pipelines fitted to the vehicle are manufactured from metal, either of a non-ferrous type or coated in a material (plastic), which prevents corrosion. The metal brake pipelines should be checked for corrosion or damage, and replaced if defective. The security of the body fixings should be checked together with the installation. Flexible hoses are used to allow for suspension and steering movement; these flexible hoses should be checked for cracking, damage, swelling or twisting. If there are any visual defects, they should be replaced.

Each wheel cylinder should be inspected for leakage. The inspection of the disc caliper may require the removal of the road wheel to gain access to visibly check the caliper seals. The wheel cylinder fitted to the brake drum assembly will require the removal of the brake drum to visibly check for signs of leakage. If a wheel cylinder shows any sign of leakage it is necessary to replace the defective component.

5.8.5 Brake linings, discs and drums

Due to the application of the brakes, the frictional lining of the brake pad and the brake shoe will inevitably wear. The wear rate is dictated by the composition of the lining material and the manner in which the brakes are applied. Heavy braking will wear the brake linings at a faster rate than light braking. Some disc pads are fitted with a sensor that either activates a warning lamp or makes a loud metallic rubbing sound when the brake pads need replacing.

The thickness of the front and rear brake linings should be checked. It is usually necessary to remove the road wheels and possibly the brake drums to visibly inspect the brake shoe linings. If the thickness of the linings is less than 1 mm (or less than quoted by the vehicle or brake system manufacturer), the lining should be replaced, although it may be necessary to replace a lining before the next scheduled maintenance check if the lining is less than 25% of its original thickness. If the linings show any sign of uneven wear, cracks or contamination, they should be replaced.

The brakes disc and drum frictional surfaces also wear during the application of the brakes, although usually at a much slower rate than the lining. The manufacturer specifies the minimum acceptable thickness of each component. Components should be replaced if the disc or drum frictional surface is worn below this specification. It is also necessary to check the frictional surfaces for scoring and cracks.

5.8.6 Road testing

The vehicle should be road tested after routine maintenance has been carried out to ensure that the brakes are operating correctly. It should be driven along a flat road to check the efficiency of the brakes and that the vehicle brakes in a straight line. The footbrake travel should also be assessed at this time.

Ideally the vehicle should be parked on a slope to check the efficiency of the handbrake. When parked on a slope the handbrake should hold the vehicle stationary, and when the lever is released the vehicle should roll freely.

If possible, it is advisable to check brake operation using a roller brake tester such as the type used for MOT testing. The roller brake tester provides a clear indication of the efficiency of the brake operation and a guide as to whether the four brakes are working effectively in comparison to each other.

Chapter 6

BODY AND CHASSIS SYSTEMS

what is covered in this chapter . . .

- Heating and ventilation
- Air-conditioning
- Climate control
- Heating and ventilation – routine maintenance
- Heating and ventilation – fault diagnosis
- Passenger safety and restraint systems
- Passenger safety and restraint systems – routine maintenance and diagnosis

6.1 HEATING AND VENTILATION

6.1.1 Introduction

During the development of the motor vehicle, many systems have been produced to aid the comfort of the driver and passengers. For many years a heating and ventilation system was not thought a necessity, and the occupants of a vehicle had to suffer the extremes of temperature and exposure to the elements. Over the years, heating and ventilating systems have evolved from the days when the open window was the only source of cool air to the sophisticated climate control systems in use today.

As well as the cooling aspect, the occupants of a modern vehicle demand a heating system that maintains a comfortable temperature while still providing a steady supply of fresh air. The heating controls (i.e. temperature, airflow selection and fan speed) are usually located on the fascia or dashboard, which allows both driver and front-seat passenger access to the controls.

Until a few years ago, a basic heating and ventilation system was the common arrangement used on most vehicles; only luxury cars offered an air-conditioning system as an option. Today it is often fitted as standard equipment, with many smaller and less expensive vehicles also having air-conditioning as an option or as standard equipment. Although air-conditioning has been more popular in warmer climates, it is progressively becoming standard in the UK and many other cooler countries.

Systems in use today can be divided into three main categories; these are:

- basic heating and ventilating system
- air-conditioning
- climate control.

6.1.2 Heating and ventilating system design

The basic arrangement is normally a fresh air system combined with a heating system. The airflow is ducted to discharge at foot and face level, with additional airflow directed at the front windscreen and side windows to aid defrosting and demisting. It is also common for separate ducting to direct airflow to the rear passenger compartment.

The controls allow the setting of both temperature of the air and the discharge points to suit the conditions. These controls are connected to two or more flaps via either rods or cables. The flaps direct air through the appropriate ducts. An electrically driven fan is fitted in the system to speed up the airflow when necessary.

System layout

A fresh air circulation system is not effective unless the air can pass through the passenger compartment of the vehicle and flow out, allowing more space for fresh air to enter. Figure 6.1 shows the paths taken by the air as it flows through the intake ports at the front of the car and towards the various discharge vents in the body. Ideally these discharge points should be situated at points where the external air pressure is low to allow

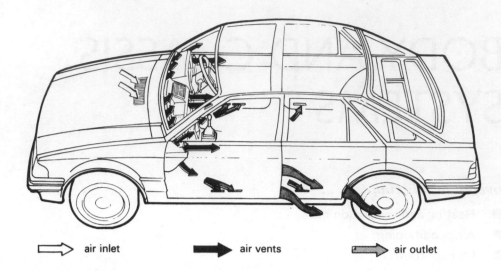

Figure 6.1 Air flow through a vehicle

natural circulation. In a similar way, the inlet point should be in a region of high pressure; the pressure increase at such points is normally caused by the combination of vehicle movement through the air and change in the airflow direction.

Typically, two or three main control functions are required to enable effective control of the heating and ventilation system.

Airflow control

The cut-away drawing in Figure 6.2 shows a typical ducting arrangement for a car. A manual control system allows the occupants to direct the air so that it is discharged from one or more outlets. These are:

- along the length of the front windscreen (for head level ventilation and defrost or demist) and two small side outlets (for side window demist)
- at independently controlled central and side vents
- in the foot-well region.

Discharging the air at the different outlets is achieved by altering the position of the flaps inside the heater assembly.

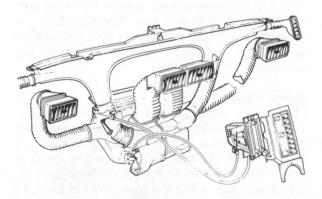

Figure 6.2 Air duct layout

Temperature control

The temperature control lever is used to select the temperature at which the air is discharged from the heater. The heat of the exhaust gas from the engine has occasionally been used as a heating source (via a heat exchanger which takes the heat from the exhaust system and passes it to the air circulating in the car). However, most manufacturers prefer to utilize the heat in the engine coolant because it is considered to be safer and produces a more stable temperature once the engine has reached the correct operating temperature. The engine coolant passes through a heat exchanger, often referred to as a heater matrix, similar to a small radiator.

The heater will obviously not function until the coolant reaches a sufficient temperature, but assuming the thermostat in the cooling system is serviceable and of the correct type, the heater should soon become effective after starting the engine from cold. To meet this requirement the coolant flow to the heater should be taken from the hottest part of the system – on the engine side of the thermostat.

The temperature is set by the occupants of the car using a control lever. Two different methods are used to control the temperature of the air discharged by the heater.

A water valve controls the flow of engine coolant through the heater matrix. When the control lever is set to hot, the water valve is open, the hot coolant can flow through the heater matrix and hot air is discharged from the heater. When the heater control is gradually moved from the hot setting through to the cold setting the valve restricts the flow of coolant through the heater matrix so the temperature of the air discharged reduces accordingly. When the valve is fully closed, cool air is discharged from the heater.

However, manufacturers often prefer not to use a water control valve, which can eventually wear or leak. Many heater systems therefore allow the hot engine coolant to constantly flow through the heater matrix. The temperature of the air is then controlled by mixing the cool incoming air with the warm air flowing through the heater matrix.

When the temperature control is set to hot, a temperature mixing flap within the heater directs all of the air through the heater matrix and therefore the temperature of the air discharged is hot. When the heater control is moved from the hot setting through to the cold setting, the mixing flap changes position progressively allowing cool air to mix with the hot air passing through the heater matrix. When the heater control is set to cool, the mixing flap prevents air passing through the heater matrix and only cool air is discharged into the interior of the car.

Figure 6.4 shows how the flaps control the air flow through the heater assembly; in the position shown part of the air flow is directed through the heater matrix. This provides warm air at the windscreen and from any vent that is opened by the front-seat occupants.

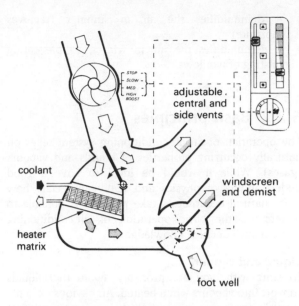

Figure 6.4 *A heating and ventilation system*

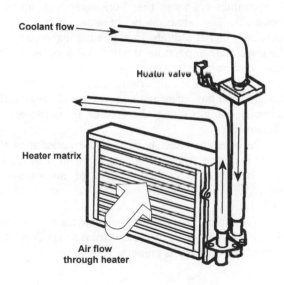

Figure 6.3 Temperature control – water tap-regulated

Heater fan control

A switch is used to control the speed of the heater fan motor; most vehicles are fitted with a fan that operates with three or more speeds or a continuously variable speed controller. Altering the resistance of the electrical circuit controls the speed of the permanent magnet-type motor (increasing the resistance in the circuit reduces the current flow through the motor).

Recirculated air control

Many heating and ventilation systems provide an additional control lever to prevent the outside air from entering the interior of the vehicle. A flap prevents fresh air from entering the vehicle and allows air already inside the passenger compartment to be drawn back into the heater assembly and recirculated into the passenger compartment. The recirculated-air setting is useful when the outside air is heavily polluted and it is used in conjunction with an air-conditioning system.

6.2   AIR-CONDITIONING

(Also refer to more detailed information in Book 2.)

6.2.1 Advantages of air-conditioning

Climatic conditions in hot countries forced vehicle manufacturers to offer cars with air-conditioning (AC) fitted as standard equipment. For many years the temperate conditions enjoyed in Northern Europe meant vehicle owners regarded an AC system as a luxury. However, more and more vehicle manufacturers are now fitting AC systems as standard on many cars for most markets. There are a number of reasons for this change but, because almost identical vehicles are now manufactured and sold across many

countries, by installing the systems on a larger number of each model, the cost of an AC system falls considerably. The reduced cost makes the AC system more affordable and therefore consumers are more likely to purchase AC, which helps to reduce costs even more.

If the vehicle is not fitted with an AC system as standard, an AC system is often offered as an option on even the most basic of vehicles. An AC system offers the following features:

- it maintains the passenger compartment at a comfortable temperature during hot weather

- it dehumidifies the air in summer (removes moisture)
- it dehumidifies the air in winter, so preventing misting of windows.

6.2.2 Basic principles

The operation of an air-conditioning system relies on naturally occurring properties of liquids and vapours (gases). While it would be ideal to have a good understanding of physics and really appreciate how these natural occurrences take place, it is possible to understand the basic operation of air-conditioning without such detailed knowledge.

Liquid and vapour

To start with, you are probably aware that liquids convert into vapours when heated. An obvious example is water turns into steam (which is a gas or vapour) when it is heated and it reaches a temperature of 100° C. When the water vapour loses the heat (to the atmosphere) and its temperature falls below 100° C, it condenses back into a liquid. So, when a kettle of water is boiled, the water turns to vapour. When the vapour cools below 100° C, it turns back to water.

It should be noted however that different substances turn from liquid to vapour at different temperatures; they do not all have to reach 100° C. Some substances will in fact 'boil' (turn to vapour) at quite low temperatures and then return to a liquid form at the same low temperature.

Heat transfer

When a warm can of beer is placed in a refrigerator, the can of beer becomes colder. What happens is that the heat contained within the can of beer transfers to the cold refrigerator; the can of beer does not absorb the lower temperature of the refrigerator, it simply loses its own heat until its temperature is the same as in the refrigerator. With any two substances, where one is hotter the other, heat will transfer to the colder substance, and not the other way round.

When you place your hand on a hot surface, the heat in the hot surface rapidly transfers to your (colder) hand; the speed at which it transfers causes the burn. Similarly, if a cold liquid were poured onto your hand, the heat of your hand would pass to the cold liquid, and if the liquid was very cold, the speed of the heat transfer could also cause a 'burn', even though the heat is passing the other way.

If the liquid poured onto your hand has a very low boiling point (lower than your body temperature), the heat from your hand will cause the liquid to turn to vapour (the same process as water turning to steam, but at a lower temperature). The liquid would feel cold, which is caused by the heat passing from your hand to evaporate the liquid; the greater the amount of heat transfer, the colder the liquid feels.

One important fact to grasp is that when a liquid changes into a vapour, the vapour stores a lot of heat which can quickly be transferred to another substance. When water turns to vapour (steam) and touches a colder surface, heat is very quickly transferred to the other substance. When steam from a kettle touches a wall, the heat is transferred to the wall. The water vapour temperature falls and the vapour then condenses (turns back to a liquid).

The heat transfer process (release of heat) is at its greatest at the exact moment that a liquid turns to vapour. This also means that when a liquid is very close to the boiling point, any heat that passes to the liquid (which would heat up the liquid to its boiling point) will be absorbed better at the exact moment that the liquid turns into a vapour.

Pressure, liquids and vapour

Another natural property of liquids is that the lower their pressure, the lower the temperature at which they boil or turn to vapour. An example of this is experienced by mountaineers when they boil water high up on a mountain. The atmospheric pressure is lower with increasing higher altitude, therefore the higher they are, the lower the temperature at which the water boils. The main complaint of mountaineers is that because the water boils at lower temperatures, hot drinks are not so hot, and the flavour of tea is not so good because the water is not absorbing the flavour from the tea so effectively.

The opposite effect is that, if the pressure of the water increases, then its boiling point also increases. This is why the cooling system of an engine is pressurized so that the water boils at a higher temperature.

So it is therefore possible to change the temperature at which a liquid boils (and turns from a vapour back to a liquid) by altering its pressure.

6.2.3 The principles applied to air-conditioning

Using the natural properties described above, it is possible to produce an air-conditioning system; it operates in much the same way as the household refrigerator.

To start with, a substance is required that is a vapour at normal daily temperatures: this substance is referred to as the 'refrigerant'.

The refrigerant is placed inside a long tube that has both ends joined together to form a complete circuit, i.e. It is a sealed tube. However, at various points along the tube there are various components which form important parts of the AC system. These are as follows:

Compressor

The first component is a compressor, which compresses the vapour into a high pressure vapour. As with any compressor, heat is generated during the compression

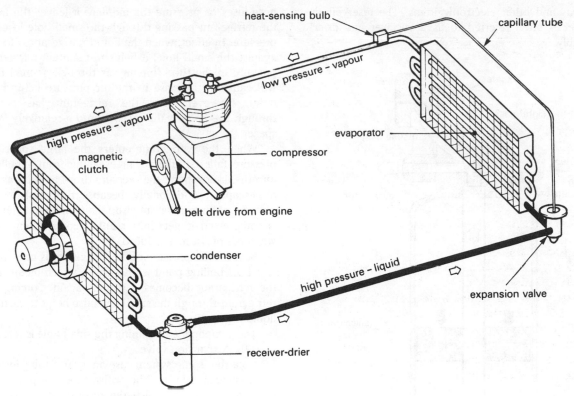

Figure 6.5 An air-conditioning system

process (the same as when a tyre is pumped up with a hand pump). Although the refrigerant is already at a temperature where it has turned from a liquid into a vapour, it absorbs some of the heat generated during compression and because the compressor forces the vapour around the tube, the vapour takes the heat along with it. The result is that high pressure and high temperature vapour are forced along the tube.

Condenser

The high pressure vapour, which is carrying a lot of heat, passes into a type of radiator called a condenser (similar in principle to the radiator or heater matrix used on a vehicle heating system). The condenser is constructed with many tubes and fins and is usually

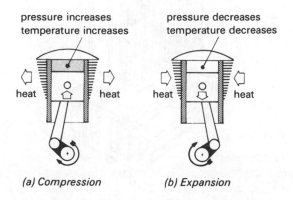

(a) Compression   (b) Expansion

Figure 6.6 Heat flow during compression and expansion

located in front of the main engine coolant radiator at the front of the vehicle. This location ensures that the condenser is exposed to the atmosphere. Because the condenser is exposed to the atmosphere and is therefore at a lower temperature than the refrigerant vapour, when the vapour passes into the top of the condenser, heat passes from the vapour to the condenser and then from the condenser to the atmosphere. In effect, the condenser functions as a heat exchanger by passing the heat from the vapour to the air in the atmosphere.

The vapour, which entered at the top of the condenser, progressively loses heat and therefore cools. Because hot gases rise and cold gases fall, the vapour progressively falls within the condenser. The vapour eventually loses a lot of heat and condenses into a liquid (the same as steam from the kettle turning back into water when it condenses on the surface wall). The liquid refrigerant now passes out of the bottom of the condenser (due to the flow of new refrigerant vapour passing into the top of the condenser). Importantly, the refrigerant is not only a liquid which is still under pressure, but it has also lost much of its heat.

Receiver/drier

The pressurized and cooled liquid refrigerant now passes to a reservoir or receiver. As well as being able to store the refrigerant in liquid form, the reservoir usually contains silica gel or crystals to absorb any water that may be contained in the refrigerant. These crystals are 'desiccant' crystals which absorb moisture; they are the same as those found in small bags included with new cameras and other electronic items. The reservoir or receiver is often referred to as a 'receiver and drier' assembly.

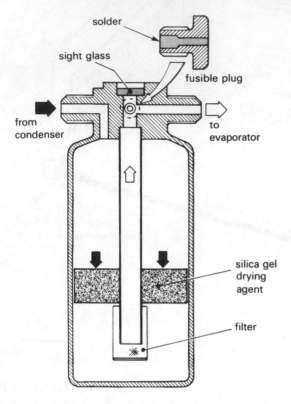

Figure 6.7 Receiver and drier assembly

Expansion valve

Assuming that the compressor is still operating, the liquid refrigerant will be forced along the tube away from the reservoir. The refrigerant will still be under pressure.

The liquid refrigerant then passes through a very small hole or orifice which has another important effect: in the same way that water coming out of the end of a

hose loses its pressure the moment it leaves the hose, the refrigerant passing through the small hole loses its pressure. In effect, when the liquid refrigerant is forced against the small hole, it helps to maintain refrigerant pressure in the tube (forcing air through a small tube will cause an increase in the air pressure behind the hole). However, once the refrigerant has passed through the hole, it then passes into a relatively large space.

When the refrigerant enters the large space, its pressure falls (similar to air escaping from a balloon into the atmosphere; the pressure drops as soon as the air escapes). Additionally, because the pressure has reduced, the temperature also falls (similarly, when air is compressed it gets hotter but it cools down again when the pressure is reduced).

Because the pressure of the refrigerant is now much lower, its boiling point is also lower, which means that the refrigerant becomes a vapour again. Forcing the refrigerant through the small hole also helps to turn the liquid into a vapour.

The component containing the small hole is referred to as the 'expansion valve'.

Note that some systems use an 'orifice tube' instead of an expansion valve. The orifice tube still provides a small hole through which the refrigerant sprays out, cooling down as it does so, however it does not vary the flow of refrigerant when the temperature changes. The flow of refrigerant is controlled by switching the compressor on and off.

Evaporator
The low pressure vapour now passes through to what is called an evaporator; effectively another radiator.

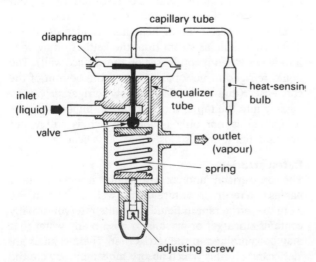

Figure 6.8 An expansion valve

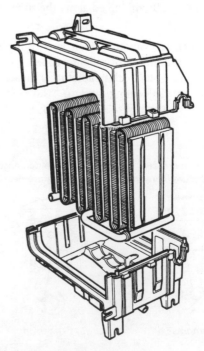

Figure 6.9 An evaporator

However, the evaporator is located in a warm or hot room, which in the case of a car would be the passenger compartment. The refrigerant vapour, which is relatively cool, passes through the evaporator and, because the evaporator is exposed to the hot air of the passenger compartment, heat passes from the air to the evaporator and into the refrigerant vapour. This process is the reverse of what occurred in the condenser.

In effect, heat in the passenger compartment is now passed to the refrigerant vapour reducing the temperature in the passenger compartment. Some of the heat in the passenger compartment is contained within the moisture of the air. When the heat passes to the evaporator and the refrigerant, the moisture in the air turns to water. The water collects around the evaporator and is ducted to the underside of the car (this is why vehicles with air-conditioning often have puddles of water beneath them when the vehicle is stopped).

As well as reducing the temperature inside the vehicle, the evaporator has also removed some of the moisture in the air; the humidity has been reduced. The lower moisture content of the air means that it more easily absorbs passengers' perspiration making them feel less 'hot and sticky'.

Repeat of the cycle

Having passed through the evaporator, the refrigerant is now a low pressure vapour which has absorbed a large amount of heat. The vapour passes back to the compressor and the whole cycle starts again.

Additional components and controls

Although the previous explanation of an air-conditioning system provides a basic understanding, there are additional components and controls which ensure more efficient operation.

Importantly, a means of regulating the flow of refrigerant is necessary and this is achieved using a heat sensor (heat-sensing bulb) which affects the size of the orifice in the expansion valve. When the temperature rises above the desired level, the orifice in the expansion valve opens to allow more refrigerant to flow, which then absorbs more heat thus lowering the temperature.

The compressor is also controlled using a clutch system. Because the compressor is usually driven by the engine, it is desirable to effectively switch off the compressor when the AC system is not required. The clutch mechanism (often a magnetic-type clutch) can connect and disconnect the drive from the engine to the compressor.

There are a number of variations of AC systems and more detailed information is provided in Book 2.

Refrigerant

The main requirements of a refrigerant are that it must change from a vapour to a liquid and back again at the appropriate temperatures and pressures.

Two main refrigerants have been used in light vehicle AC systems, R12 and R134a.

R12 (Freon gas 12) was in general use until the early- to mid-1990s but was banned in Europe because it is a CFC (chlorofluorocarbon) which contributes to the destruction of the ozone layer.

R134a, which is a HFC (hydrofluorocarbon), became the approved refrigerant for light vehicle AC systems, and although it is not quite so efficient as R12 for light vehicle use, it provides a much safer alternative.

Both refrigerants are non-toxic in small amounts and non-corrosive, but exposure to a naked flame can create toxic fumes.

Although they perform identical duties, the two refrigerants should not be mixed. A system that has been operating with one refrigerant should not be refilled with the other refrigerant unless some of the component parts are replaced and the system is totally flushed. Seals and components within the AC system are manufactured from materials that may react with one refrigerant and not the other, therefore components should be fitted to match the refrigerant.

A very small percentage of lubricating oil is added to the refrigerant to lubricate the compressor and other components. Again, the oils used are only compatible with one type of refrigerant and the correct oils must be selected.

6.3   CLIMATE CONTROL

6.3.1 Electronic control of the heating and cooling systems

Recent developments in electronic control have made it possible to use a combination of the heating and the air-conditioning systems to accurately control the temperature and humidity of the air in the passenger compartment. Additionally, by making use of sensors (to check the temperature at various places in the passenger compartment) and airflow control flaps (usually operated electrically), it is possible to maintain different temperatures in different parts of the passenger compartment.

Together these functions are known as a climate control system. It is usually controlled by an ECU (electronic control unit) which assesses the information from the sensors and adjusts the airflow flaps as necessary to achieve the desired conditions. The driver can select the desired temperature (or other requirements such as 'demist') and the climate control system automatically controls airflow flap positions to achieve the desired temperature.

Some systems allow different settings in the front and rear of the passenger compartment or different temperatures on the left- and right-hand sides.

Once the driver has selected a given temperature, an ECU automatically maintains the set temperature by controlling the path taken by the ventilating air as it flows to the interior of the car. Under hot or humid ambient conditions, the air is cooled or dehumidified by ducting it through an evaporator, whereas when the ambient temperature is low the air is heated.

On damp days misting up of the windows can seriously affect the driver's ability to see out. The cold glass condenses the moisture in the air within the car and a dangerous loss of visibility often results. A climate control system, (sometimes called an environmental control system) overcomes the problem by passing the ventilating air through the evaporator to remove excess moisture before heating it to the required temperature.

Figure 6.10 shows the layout of a full air-mix type of system, suitable for automatic temperature control. In this type, the temperature and air flow pattern are controlled by three flap valves. Movement of the valves is achieved using either electric motors or vacuum cylinders; the latter arrangement is controlled by small valves opened by electric solenoids.

6.3.2 Control systems

For fascia layout and ease of operation, electrical switches are provided to enable the driver to select the required temperature and distribution of air that enters the car interior. After the target temperature, which is often displayed in digital form, has been set by the driver, the ECU controls the heating and cooling sections of the system so that the air inside the car is kept at a temperature very close to the set value. The in-car temperature is constantly monitored by an electrical sensor, and by passing this information to the ECU, it is possible for the ECU to make the necessary airflow adjustments.

If a vehicle is fitted with a climate control system that allows individual temperature settings (e.g. For the driver and front passenger of the vehicle) the air temperature is monitored by sensors located in the two occupant areas and cool air is mixed separately within the heater to provide the two different temperature settings.

Natural heating of the car interior is either by the direct rays of the sun through the windows, or by the heat contained in the incoming air. Because the amount of heat entering the car governs the amount of cooling or heating required, additional sensors are fitted to measure these inputs.

Body and chassis systems on modern cars generally require little maintenance except for checking the operation of each system and inspecting components during the routine maintenance of the vehicle.

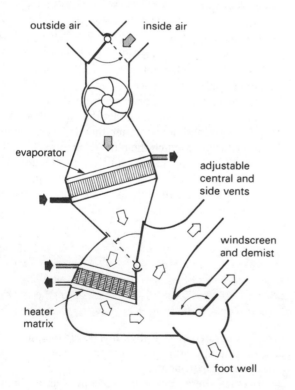

Figure 6.10 A 'full air-mix type' climate control system

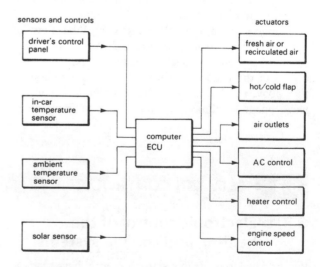

Figure 6.11 Climate control system

6.4.1 Heating and ventilation systems

The driver and passengers of the vehicle constantly use the heating and ventilation system to provide a comfortable environment in which to travel.

External air vents

The inlet points at which air enters the heating and ventilation system are normally covered with grilles that prevent objects such as leaves entering the system. Although these grilles are kept clear mainly by normal airflow and during the cleaning of the vehicle, a check should be made to ensure any grilles and drain holes remain free from blockages.

Filters

Many vehicles are fitted with a filter to prevent road pollution, bacteria and pollen entering the vehicle. These filters should be periodically inspected and replaced as per the vehicle manufacturer's service schedule. A blocked filter can restrict the mass of air entering the ventilation system.

Coolant hoses

During routine maintenance of the engine, the coolant hoses should be inspected for cracks, damage and swelling. The heater hoses through which the heater matrix coolant passes are usually inspected during these checks. The heater matrix is not often visible and cannot normally be inspected, but a coolant stain on the lower edge of the dash panel normally indicates a coolant leak from the heater.

General efficiency

The efficiency of the heater should be checked and all of the controls examined to make sure they operate correctly. A check should be made to each heater control, including altering the temperature setting, the airflow direction and the fan speed.

The maximum output temperature of the heater is affected by the temperature of the engine coolant. A low engine coolant temperature will lower the temperature of the heater. A check should be made during the routine maintenance of the engine to ensure that the engine is running at the correct operating temperature.

6.4.2 Air-conditioning/climate control

Although the air-conditioning system is filled with refrigerant, which during a routine maintenance schedule is not normally checked, additional checks should be made to ensure the system is operating correctly.

Filters and air vents

As with a standard heating system, pollen and particle filters are fitted to most AC and climate control systems. These filters should be inspected and replaced as recommended by the manufacturer.

Air vents should also be checked for blockage etc.

Compressor

The AC compressor is normally driven by the engine by means of an ancillary drive belt. The drive belt should be checked for cracks, damage and also for correct belt tension. The refrigerant pipes between the body of the vehicle and the engine are flexible to allow for engine movement. These flexible pipes should be checked for security and damage.

Condenser

The condenser, which is located directly in the air stream of the vehicle, should be checked for blockages between the tubes and fins, damage from debris and the security of its fixings.

Evaporator and water drain

An AC system removes moisture from the air drawn into the heating and ventilation system. When in use, a small quantity of water is usually seen dripping from underneath the vehicle. The moisture removed from the air during the cooling process is collected from under the evaporator on a drip tray and passes out of the vehicle via a pipe underneath. Although most of the moisture drains away, a small amount remains which provides an ideal breeding ground for bacteria and other micro-organisms. A musty smell is often detected after the use of the air-conditioning. If this musty smell continues after prolonged use of the air-conditioning, the evaporator and air vents should be de-fumigated with a suitable disinfectant.

General efficiency

To check the efficiency of the air-conditioning system it should have its temperature set to minimum. If the system does not cool the air sufficiently it indicates a probable fault. Manufacturers often quote specifications for the outlet temperature of the air vents when the air-conditioning is operating at its coldest setting. Referring to these specifications can provide an indication of efficiency.

To carry out further air-conditioning checks it is usually necessary to employ specialized test equipment to check the system for leaks and refrigerant.

Refrigerant

The AC refrigerant contains a small amount of lubricating oil; the correct amount is added when the system is recharged with refrigerant. The oil is held in suspension and lubricates the internal components of the system including the compressor. It is often recommended to periodically switch the air-conditioning on (even in winter), to allow the lubricating oil to circulate around the system.

Servicing

The AC system can only be serviced correctly with the use of specialized equipment. If such equipment is available, the following guidelines can be used in conjunction with the vehicle and equipment manufacturer's specific instructions:

- Reclaim used refrigerant.
- Drain the quantity of oil removed from the system.

- Renew the receiver drier.
- Evacuate the air from the system for 30 minutes, and check that the system retains a vacuum for 10 minutes after the vacuum pump has been switched off.
- Renew the interior filter
- Add the correct quantity of new oil to the system.
- Recharge the system with the correct amount of refrigerant.
- Check the efficiency of the system using a thermometer.
- Check for leaks using suitable leak-detecting equipment.

6.5 HEATING AND VENTILATION – FAULT DIAGNOSIS

6.5.1 The heating and ventilation system

The heating and ventilation systems fitted to many vehicles are often simple in operation. Most of the components are basic mechanical systems, generally located behind the dashboard. The heater matrix and engine coolant parts of the heating system can, however, cause problems.

Table 6.1 lists various faults that may be encountered.

6.5.2 The air-conditioning system

The AC system uses many of the heating and ventilation components described in the previous section. Faults in the heating and ventilation system that is fitted in conjunction with air-conditioning are similar to those in Table 6.1.

However, if a fault with the AC system occurs, it is often necessary to use specialized test equipment to diagnose the cause and repair or replace the component.

A relatively common problem relates to low refrigerant levels in the AC system. This results in poor performance. Topping up or replacing refrigerant requires the use of specialized equipment and procedures and these aspects are covered in Book 2.

Further information on the operation and diagnosis of faults in AC systems and climate control systems is provided in Book 2.

Table 6.1 Heating and ventilation faults

Fault	Possible cause
Engine coolant leaking from heater assembly	Heater hose or heater matrix leaking
Poor air flow through the heater	Restricted air intake/ intake filter blocked
Heater fan inoperative	Blown fuse (or faulty relay if part of the circuit); heater fan electrical circuit fault
Heater fan only operates on high speed	Heater fan electrical circuit resistor block fault
Heater will only blow cool air	Engine not reaching the correct operating temperature; heater coolant tap seized closed; airflow flaps not moving correctly
Heater will only blow hot air	Heat distribution flap fault; heater coolant tap seized fully open; airflow flaps not moving correctly
Distribution of air flow through heater incorrect	Air distribution flap incorrectly set

6.6.1 Introduction

In the very early days of motoring in the UK, a person walked in front of each vehicle waving a red flag to warn pedestrians and other road users of the impending danger. This inevitably restricted the speed of vehicles to a walking pace. In general terms, the red flag was the first safety system apart from that essential element, the vehicle brakes.

Modern motoring provides for driving on the roads with an enormous number of other vehicles that can all reach speeds well beyond those of the red-flag days. Not surprisingly, many 'accidents' occur, (although many accidents are avoidable) and these frequently result in injuries to the occupants of the vehicle.

Vehicle manufacturers design and construct modern cars with safety in mind, and many safety systems are now standard features of the cars we travel in. The construction of the vehicle is designed so that if involved in a severe accident, the structure of the vehicle protects the occupants of the car.

The front and rear sections of vehicles are designed to collapse in a controlled and progressive manner thus absorbing much of the impact caused by crashes. These collapsible sections are usually referred to as the safety cells, which effectively function as shock absorbers to the impact forces. They are also designed so that vehicle components and assemblies do not enter the passenger compartment due to impact.

The force of a vehicle impact also causes any unrestrained articles, including the occupants, to move around the interior of the vehicle. Personal injuries may occur to occupants when they strike solid objects within the interior of the vehicle. Manufacturers therefore often use softer, more impact absorbent materials within the vehicle (e.g. softer dashboards), to limit these types of injuries.

6.6.2 Primary restraint using seat belts

Seat belts are used to provide the primary restraint for the occupants of the vehicle. Both front and rear seat belts are a mandatory fitment to a vehicle and it is now law in many countries around the world that the seat

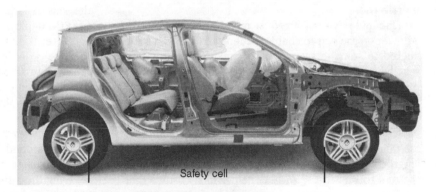

Figure 6.12 A safety cell

Safety cell

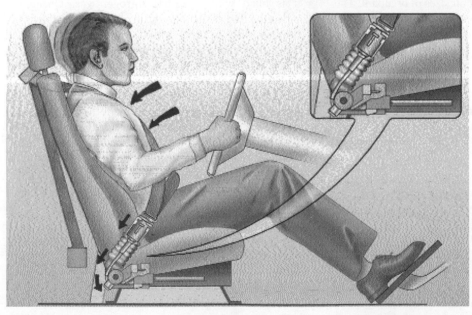

Figure 6.13 Seatbelt with pre-tensioner system to tighten belt

belts must be actually 'worn' by the occupants while the vehicle is being driven.

Most vehicle manufacturers fit three-point seat belts (seat belts having three fixing points). Although many manufacturers used to fit static seat belts, which had to be manually adjusted to suit the person, most seat belts today are of the 'automatic' type (inertia reel). The automatic type provides the occupant of the vehicle with an acceptable level of comfort and the freedom to move within limited space, but the seat belt restrains the occupant if the vehicle decelerates quickly.

For front-seat applications, the three-point seat belts have three mounting points: one at each side of the seat and one on the B-pillar. The mounting point at the side of the seat adjacent to the centre of the vehicle has a buckle assembly to enable belts to be easily connected and disconnected. When the buckle is connected, the belt passes across the lap of the occupant from the outside edge of the seat to the inside edge, then up across the chest of the occupant to the B-pillar. A similar arrangement is used for rear seat belts but the belt attaches to the C-pillar or to a convenient location. There are slightly different arrangements for those vehicles that do not have B- or C-pillars such as cars with convertible roof body styles.

Inertia reel

On the old style of fixed seat belts, there was an adjuster on the belt to enable the length of the belt to be altered to suit the size of the occupant. More modern seat belts make use of an automatic adjusting system that also functions as a means of keeping the belt tight during accidents or severe braking. Although these systems still use the three locating points, when the belt passes up to the B-pillar, it then passes down through the pillar to a spring-loaded reel onto which the surplus length of belt is wound. The spring loading will cause the reel to pull in the surplus belt, which ensures that the belt is a comfortable fit for all sizes of occupant. The tension in the spring-loaded reel is also weak enough to allow the occupant to move forward against the spring tension.

Within the reel is a mechanism that prevents the reel from unwinding if the belt is pulled rapidly or if the forward forces are too high. In effect, the reel locks if sudden braking forces occur or if severe forces are caused due to an accident. On most inertia reel systems, when the belt is pulled quickly, this is enough to lock the seat belts.

6.6.3 The supplementary restraint system (SRS)

The fitting of primary restraints (seat belts) reduces the movement of the occupants in the event of an accident. However, if the accident is severe it may still be possible for the occupants of the vehicle to strike the interior of the car. Supplementary restraint systems (SRS) are

therefore now fitted to vehicles to provide further protection from injuries in the event of an accident.

Airbags

In addition to the seat belts, airbags are now being fitted to vehicles as standard equipment, although they are not mandatory in most countries. Airbags are usually fitted to the front of the passenger compartment. A driver's side airbag is contained within the centre of the steering wheel assembly with the passenger airbags located within the dashboard. However, with additional safety equipment now being fitted to vehicles, it is common for additional airbags to be fitted, including side impact, rear passenger, side window protection (B-pillar), and driver's knee airbags.

Front airbags operate in conjunction with the seat belts. If the head of a driver were to strike the vehicle interior such as the steering wheel, the fascia or the windscreen, serious injury could occur. In the event of a severe frontal accident, the airbag inflates cushioning the front occupants from striking hard objects.

SRS systems are usually operated electronically, however, a few systems (primarily the earlier designs) are operated mechanically. Electronically operated systems are controlled by an electronic control module/unit (ECU). The ECU constantly monitors sensors which detect when a frontal impact occurs. If the sensors indicate that a severe impact has occurred, the ECU deploys the front airbags.

Note: If additional airbags are fitted to the vehicle such as side impact or B-pillar airbags, additional sensors are fitted in strategic areas of the vehicle to detect such impacts.

The front airbags are deployed if a severe frontal impact is sensed which would be caused by a vehicle colliding with solid object at an impact speed of typically around 20–32 km/h (12–20 mph). At the start of deployment, the airbag inflates and splits the trim covering the airbag. When the airbag is fully deployed, it is filled with non-toxic nitrogen gas. Once fully inflated a flap at the rear of the airbag allows the gas to progressively escape thus providing a gradual cushioning effect when an occupant strikes the airbag. When an occupant contacts the airbag, the energy is absorbed or cushioned thus protecting the occupants head and chest. The seat belt prevents further forward motion of the occupant and although the airbag quickly deflates, the occupants are retained in their seats by the seat belts. The inflation and deflation of the airbag takes place over a very short period of time, typically around 0.15 of a second.

6.6.4 Mechanical airbags

The original airbags fitted to vehicles (mainly in the USA) were mechanically operated and were generally fitted to the driver side of the vehicle only. The mechanical airbag mechanism is independent of other supplementary restraint systems although, as is the case

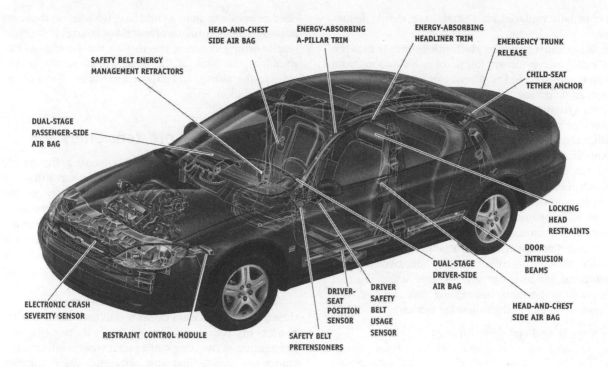

Figure 6.14 Advanced safety systems showing different airbag locations

with all airbags, it is more effective when seat belts are also worn by the occupants.

The airbag sensor, the deployment mechanism and airbag are contained within the centre of the steering wheel. A small detonator is contained within the assembly which, when detonated, ignites a gas generator (gas pellets). The rapid generation of the gas then inflates the airbag.

To achieve detonation, a small steel ball is positioned so that when an accident occurs, the ball overcomes spring tension and causes a trigger pin to strike the detonator.

The mechanical airbag system is generally regarded as less stable than the electronic systems that have replaced it. Additionally, more variation can be built into the electronic system to account for different speeds and types of accident thus making the electronic systems more adaptable and versatile.

6.6.5 Electronically controlled airbags

Electronic airbag systems differ from the mechanical systems in the way in which the airbag is triggered. Instead of a mechanical triggering system, the electronic systems make use of electronic sensors and an ECU.

When the sensors detect the impact caused by an accident, the information is received by the ECU which then sends an electrical pulse to the airbag igniter assembly. The igniter, when triggered, causes a propellant charge (the gas generator) to rapidly produce gas which inflates the airbag. The igniter and propellant charge assembly is referred to as the inflator

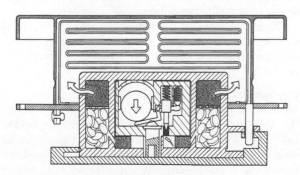

Figure 6.15 A mechanical airbag assembly

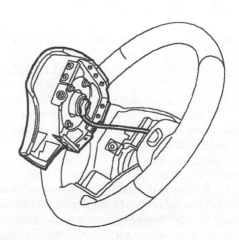

Figure 6.16 An electronic airbag assembly

and is usually replaced as a single unit should failure occur.

A big advantage of the electronic system is that the ECU can receive many items of information from different sensors, which allows for different control sequences or timing to be used. As an example, some modern systems assess the weight of the occupants, whether or not a passenger is sitting in the seat and whether seat belts are being worn.

Importantly, airbags operate in conjunction with the seat belts. Ideally, the seat belt is used to restrain the occupant, i.e. take the main strain of body weight. The airbag is then inflated just to prevent head and chest injuries which could occur when the occupant's head and possibly chest move forward slightly. The seat belts do not retain occupant's heads and therefore the airbag provides this protection. Airbag deployment can therefore be set to occur slightly later when the seat belts perform the many restraining task (refer to seat belt pre-tensioners in the following section).

Side impact and roll-over airbags

Many vehicles are now fitted with additional airbags that provide occupant protection against side impact and roll-over impact.

The airbags and inflatable curtains are located in various places around the passenger compartment. Locations include in the sides of seats and in door and roof pillars. The principle of operation is the same as for the frontal impact electronic airbags but using different sensors to detect different types of impact.

Safety and handling of airbag systems

Due to the explosive nature of airbag systems, extreme caution must be used when dealing with any part of the vehicle that may be in contact with an airbag. If anyone is directly in front of an airbag when it inflates, there is a very strong likelihood that it will cause injuries.

If any tasks are being performed, such as removing or working on the steering wheel or other relevant parts of the car, it is advisable to disable the airbag. The procedures for disabling airbags differ for each make and model, so reference should always be made to the manufacturer's recommendations and procedures. In most cases, a special electronic tool is required to perform the disabling process.

If an airbag deploys at the incorrect time due to a vehicle accident, or even when an accident has not occurred, it could result in injury to an occupant who is too close to the airbag. It is therefore important that any maintenance is carried out exactly as specified by the vehicle manufacturer.

Also, always refer to the instructions (often contained within the owner's handbook) with regard to the fitting of baby and child seats to a vehicle. Because the initial deployment of an airbag is created by what is effectively a small explosion, it can cause very serious injury or death to babies and small children if they are seated incorrectly, near to an airbag. For example, a child or baby sitting in a child seat (located on the front passenger seat) could receive serious injuries if the child seat is arranged facing the rear of the vehicle. In this situation, the back of the child's head would be too close to the airbag, and exposed to the full force of the airbag inflation.

6.6.6 Seat belt pre-tensioners

Although seat belts restrain the occupants in the vehicle in the event of an accident, the occupant can still move forward due to the small space that exists between the seat belt and the person's body, and of course the body will compress against the seat belt resulting in further forward movement. It is therefore possible for the occupant of the vehicle to make contact with the interior of the vehicle during a severe accident, even when correctly wearing a seat belt.

When an accident occurs, the occupant will still therefore move forward even though the vehicle itself is almost or completely stopped; it is this forward momentum of the occupant against what is effectively a stationary vehicle that can cause the worst injuries. Ideally, the occupant should be firmly held against the seat so that forward movement towards the steering wheel or dashboard is prevented.

To achieve this more effective restraint of the occupants, most modern seat belts have a pre-tensioning system. The system allows the belt to be worn in the normal way, allowing the occupant some freedom to move. However, when an accident occurs, the pre-tensioning system tightens the seat belt immediately the impact occurs. This process pulls the occupant tightly against the seat thus reducing continued forward movement.

Although the seat belts should restrain the occupant immediately on impact, the pre-tensioners should slacken off slightly at more or less the same time as the airbag deploys. This combination of seat belt and airbag deployment initially restrains the occupant and then allows the occupant to move forward in a controlled manner so that the inflated airbag absorbs the final momentum of the head and chest.

It can perhaps now be understood why an occupant who is not wearing a seat belt could be forced into the airbag just prior to inflation, which would result in the airbag causing further injuries.

Note that seat belt pre-tensioners are only designed to operate once. After the pre-tensioner has deployed, the mechanism and seat belt assemblies should be renewed.

Mechanical pre-tensioners

Mechanical pre-tensioners are normally located under the seat and are connected to the seat belt buckle assembly. A long, powerful spring is pre-tensioned (compressed) within a tube and is held in compression by a latching mechanism. When an accident occurs, if the impact is strong enough, the latching mechanism is forced to release the spring tension which pulls on the buckle assembly thus tightening the seat belt.

When a mechanical pre-tensioner has been deployed, it should be completely replaced by a new assembly. Care must also be taken when working on or around the seats to ensure that the pre-tensioner is not subjected to a substantial knock which could trigger the system.

Also note that mechanical pre-tensioners do not necessarily operate in conjunction with airbags. The mechanical pre-tensioners are normally totally independent devices and could therefore operate without airbag deployment or, may not in fact operate even if the airbag has been triggered.

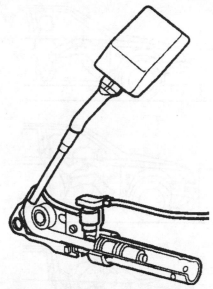

Figure 6.18 A pyrotechnic seat belt pre-tensioner

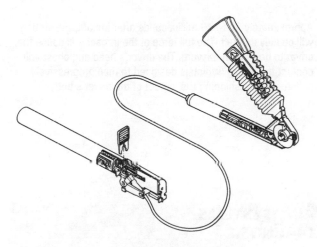

Figure 6.17 A mechanical seat belt pre-tensioner

Electronic/pyrotechnic seat belt pre-tensioners

Pyrotechnic pre-tensioners are generally located within the door pillar and are connected to the normal inertia reel mechanism or seat belt fixings. The principle of operation relies on a gas generator in much the same way as an airbag-triggering system. A detonator or igniter (explosive charge) when triggered, causes the gas generator to rapidly produce a volume of gas. The gas pressure is then used to activate a mechanical linkage which pulls on the seat belt or rotates the inertia reel, thus tightening the seat belt.

Different designs make use of different mechanisms to tighten the belts; two examples are shown in Figure 6.18.

Although some pyrotechnic pre-tensioners operate with a mechanical trigger, most systems utilize the airbag ECU as a trigger. As with the airbag triggering, an electrical signal is passed from the ECU to the igniter system, thus causing the gas to be produced.

ECU-triggered pre-tensioner systems can be controlled to operate just ahead of airbag deployment to provide a co-ordinated restraint and protection system. When a pyrotechnic pre-tensioner has been deployed, it should be replaced with a new assembly along with a new seat belt.

6.6.7 Deployment sequence of airbags and pre-tensioned seat belts

Figure 6.19 provides a guide to the sequence of events for airbag and seat belt deployment when an accident occurs.

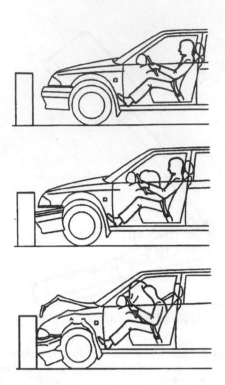

(a) Just prior to impact, the driver is braking hard and would be restrained by the action of the 3 point seatbelt, which would provide the initial protection.

(b) Approximately 15 milliseconds (15 thousandths of a second) after impact, the rapid deceleration of the vehicle is detected by the Supplementary Restraint System (SRS). The airbag system is therefore triggered, which progressively inflates the airbag using gas under pressure. At this stage, the driver remains in a relatively upright position because of the action of the seat belt pre-tensioning system, which tightens the belt on initial impact.

(c) Approximately 30 to 40 milliseconds after impact, the air bag will be fully inflated. The full force of the impact will cause the driver to be thrown forward. The driver's head and chest will contact the airbag, which is designed to then progressively deflate, thus cushioning the impact of the driver's body.

Figure 6.19 Deployment of airbags and pre-tensioned seat belts

6.7   PASSENGER SAFETY AND RESTRAINT SYSTEMS – ROUTINE MAINTENANCE AND DIAGNOSIS

Maintenance and repair

All seat belts should be checked for fraying or tears. Any damage or wear to the belt will cause a weakness that could lead to failure when the belt is placed under the stresses that occur in an accident.

The inertia reel mechanism should be checked for operation to ensure that it freely allows the occupant to move, but when any severe forward forces or rapid pulling of the belt occurs, the reel should lock.

Supplementary restraint systems require little maintenance except to check the condition of the components that are visible, such as the airbag trim covers.

Under no circumstances should any part of the restraint system be dismantled unless any specific instructions and procedures are provided by the manufacturer. The safety systems can contain explosive materials or strong springs which can cause very serious injury or death.

Most of the modern systems are ECU-controlled which usually means that some form of self-test system is built into the system. In these cases a warning light will normally be placed on the dashboard, and the light should illuminate if a system fault exists.

Operation of the warning light

When the ignition is initially switched on, the SRS warning light should illuminate: the ECU then monitors the system. The ECU checks the wiring through to each component, and if correct, the ECU will extinguish the warning light after 5–10 seconds.

If a fault is detected during these system self-checks, the warning light will remain illuminated. The ECU also constantly monitors the system while the vehicle is being driven and if it detects a fault during this time, it will again illuminate the warning light.

The illumination of the warning light provides an indication to the driver that a system fault exists and the SRS is disabled.

Diagnosis of faults

If the SRS warning light is constantly illuminated, it indicates that the ECU has detected a fault and disabled the system. The SRS ECU will record a fault code applicable to the fault, from a list of codes retained in the memory of the ECU. It is usually necessary to connect diagnostic test equipment to the vehicle to access this fault code information in the ECU memory. The fault code indicates the area in which ECU has detected the fault. Most vehicle workshop manuals detail the test procedures to check the applicable electrical circuit wiring and components necessary to repair the fault. Once the fault has been repaired it is necessary to erase the fault code from the ECU memory.

Chapter 7

VEHICLE ELECTRICAL SYSTEMS

what is covered in this chapter . . .

- **Introduction**
- **Basic principles of electricity**
- **Electrical circuits and calculations**
- **The battery**
- **The charging system**
- **The starter system**
- **The lighting system**
- **Auxiliary lighting and equipment**
- **Electrical systems – routine maintenance**

7.1 INTRODUCTION

As it is in most aspects of our daily lives today, electricity is a major part of the modern motor car. Almost since the motor car was invented, electricity has been used for lighting and many other functions including starting, battery charging and ignition. In addition to these fundamental systems, numerous auxiliary electrical systems are now fitted to provide safety and comfort aids for the driver and passengers of the vehicle.

Many of the vehicle's electrical systems are a mandatory requirement, such as the lighting, but drivers and passengers have also become accustomed to many non-essential systems, including electric windows, in-car entertainment (ICE), central locking, climate control systems.

These auxiliary systems often have the effect of reducing stress and fatigue on the driver and passengers. Many of them make use of electronic components or electronic control. This should make the systems more reliable and efficient, and reduce routine maintenance time and costs.

Over recent years the amount of electrical and electronic equipment fitted has increased considerably. This trend is destined to continue in the near and more distant future.

In view of the increased complexity of electrical and electronic equipment now fitted to modern motor vehicles, this electrical section should only provide the technician with a basic knowledge and understanding of these fundamental electrical systems.

In the past many workshops had access to an electrical specialist, or work would be passed on to a specialist. However, due to the amount of electrical systems and components fitted on modern vehicles, it is now increasingly difficult to function as a vehicle technician without having a good working knowledge of the systems and electricity. Although many electronic-based systems are also fitted to the modern vehicle, it is not actually necessary for the technician to be able to repair computers. However, a good understanding of computer-controlled systems is almost essential for technicians wishing to maintain, diagnose and repair the modern vehicle.

It should be noted that with the complexity of a modern motor vehicle, serious problems can arise if the technician undertaking a repair does not understand the basic construction and operation of both the mechanical and electrical/electronic systems.

The misunderstanding of such systems is particularly important when diagnosing faults; lack of basic knowledge in either mechanical or electrical areas can lead to component damage and costly repairs. Whereas in the past most repair activities on a motor vehicle could be divided into either mechanical or electrical tasks, the two technologies are now fully integrated into most vehicle systems.

In cases where further study of electrical/electronic topics is needed, the reader is referred to the companion book *Fundamentals of Automotive Electronics* and Book 2 in this series of *Fundamentals of Motor Vehicle Technology*.

7.1.1 Main electrical circuits

The battery, which is the electrical energy source when the engine is not running, is connected to a number of separate circuits. Although there are many electrical circuits used on a motor vehicle, these can be categorized into six main electrical circuits:

Charging circuit
This supplies the electrical energy for charging and maintaining the battery when the engine is running.

Starting circuit
This enables the engine to be cranked over (rotated) at a speed sufficient for it to 'start' and keep running.

Ignition circuit (earlier vehicles)
This provides a high voltage to the spark plug to ignite the air/fuel mixture in the engine cylinders (may be integrated into the engine management system).

Fuel injection circuit (earlier vehicles)
This provides the correct volume of fuel necessary to enable the engine to operate with the correct air/fuel mixture (may be integrated into the engine management system).

Engine management circuit (later vehicles)
This controls the ignition and fuel systems, also the emission systems.

Lighting circuit
This provides the necessary exterior/interior illumination and warning systems.

Auxiliary circuit
This includes various accessories such as windscreen wipers and washers, horn, in-car entertainment, etc. Additional functions include computer-controlled systems such as ABS, climate control, electronically controlled transmission, etc.

7.2   BASIC PRINCIPLES OF ELECTRICITY

7.2.1 Electricity – a fundamental part of the motor vehicle

Within the motor repair industry, it has been traditional that a specialist was employed to work on electrical problems. However, the modern vehicle is equipped with numerous electrical systems that often control or work alongside a mechanical system. Electricity is therefore a fundamental part of vehicle technology. The modern vehicle technician should understand and be competent with the electrical aspects of a motor vehicle.

Because many problems may arise due to a lack of knowledge and misunderstanding of the fundamentals of electricity, this chapter aims to dispel some of the mystery related to electricity and electrical systems. The following section provides a simplified explanation of the basic electrical units (volts, amps, and ohms) along with how they interrelate with each other and their importance when working on vehicle systems. A basic knowledge of electricity is essential before any fault finding is carried out on an electrical circuit using electrical test equipment, such as the multi-meter or oscilloscope.

In many ways electricity behaves similarly to water. The electric cables are like pipes and many electrical terms, expressions and components can be related to fluid flow. The difficulty in understanding electricity is that electricity cannot normally be seen passing through wires, whereas opening a water tap readily indicates the flow of the liquid.

The comparison between electricity and water is used in this section to introduce and describe the basic terms and principles of electricity.

Figure 7.1 compares the flow of water and electricity in their respective circuits and is used to introduce the main electrical terms.

Note: The following explanations are intentionally simplified to provide a basic understanding of electricity. Certain details need to be studied in greater depth for those who wish to gain a more accurate and complete understanding.

7.2.2 Comparison of an electrical circuit to a water circuit

Pressurized water circuit
Note: When a pressure gauge measures pressure, e.g. tyre or fuel pressure, it presents the measured value as compared with the atmospheric pressure, which is treated as being zero. The pressure measured in the tyres or fuel system is therefore a pressure value above atmospheric pressure, that is above zero. If the pressure gauge indicates a measured value of 12 bar, this means 12 bar above atmospheric pressure, or above zero.

Figure 7.1a shows water contained within tanks A and B. Tank A is vented to the atmosphere, so the pressure in this tank is the same as atmospheric pressure (which for this exercise, we will regard as zero).

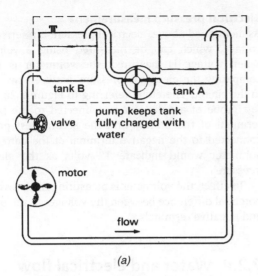
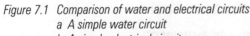
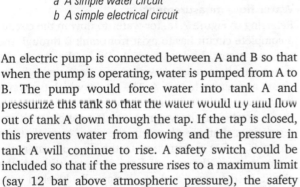

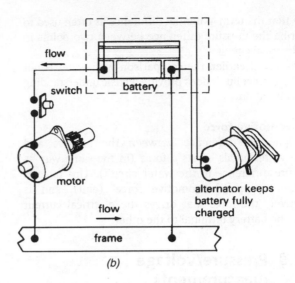

(a) *(b)*

Figure 7.1 Comparison of water and electrical circuits
  a A simple water circuit
  b A simple electrical circuit

An electric pump is connected between A and B so that when the pump is operating, water is pumped from A to B. The pump would force water into tank A and pressurize this tank so that the water would try and flow out of tank A down through the tap. If the tap is closed, this prevents water from flowing and the pressure in tank A will continue to rise. A safety switch could be included so that if the pressure rises to a maximum limit (say 12 bar above atmospheric pressure), the safety switch would cause the pump to switch off.

If, however, the tap is now opened, water will flow through the tap and pass through the motor. The flow of water (forced under a pressure of 12 bar) now turns the motor, which could then be used to drive a mechanical device.

While passing through the motor, the water will pass practically all of its energy to the motor (the energy stored in the water flow is used to drive the motor). However, because water is continuing to be forced round the system, it will flow from the motor back to tank A. When the water returns to tank A, it remains stored without any pressure (the pressure was effectively used to drive the motor). Any small residual pressure that may have existed on the return journey back to tank A will disappear as soon as the water reaches the open space of the tank, which is at atmospheric pressure (zero in this case).

The important fact is that water flows from tank B through the motor and back to tank A because the pressure in tank B is higher than that in tank A. If the pressures in the tanks were the same, water would not flow.

It is therefore the 'pressure difference' between the two tanks that causes the water to flow. In the example the pressure difference is 12 bar:

(12 bar in tank B) – (0 bar in tank A) = 12 bar

Electrical circuit

If we compare the electrical circuit in Figure 7.1b with the water circuit in Figure 7.1a, the battery could be regarded as taking the place of both water tanks; the positive terminal of the battery being equivalent to the outlet pipe at tank B and the negative terminal being the return pipe connection on tank A.

If we also accept that the battery is the storage device for electricity, then we can assume that the positive terminal of the battery is the high-pressure outlet and the negative terminal is the zero-pressure connection.

If the switch is 'on', then electricity will flow from the positive terminal through the switch and the motor and then return to the negative terminal. The process is virtually identical to the water circuit.

When the electricity passes through the motor, the energy is used to turn the motor, which can be used to drive a mechanical device. All of the energy in the electricity is used by the motor, so the electricity flowing back to the negative terminal has no effective energy or 'pressure'.

Again, by comparison with the water circuit the reason for the electricity to flow is that the pressure at the positive terminal is higher than at the negative terminal. This will therefore force the electricity to flow from the positive terminal through the circuit to the negative terminal. It is the 'pressure difference' between the positive and negative terminals that causes the electricity to flow.

The electrical pressure is expressed as a 'voltage' measured in volts, the abbreviation for which is V. In the example the pressure difference is 12 volts:

$$\left(\begin{array}{c} 12\,\text{V at the} \\ \text{positive terminal} \end{array} \right) - \left(\begin{array}{c} 0\,\text{V at the} \\ \text{negative terminal} \end{array} \right) = 12\,\text{V}$$

Note that the term 'potential difference' is often used to describe the pressure difference between two points in an electrical circuit.

As stated earlier, the comparison with water is not wholly correct but it does provide a basic understanding of electrical flow.

Electromotive force

The pressure difference between the positive and negative terminals exerts a force (in the same way as pressure difference in the water circuit). This force is referred to as 'electromotive force' (emf), and is effectively the force that drives the electrical current from one battery terminal to the other.

7.2.3 Pressure/voltage measurements

Water pressure measurement

If, in Figure 7.2a, a pressure gauge were attached to the outlet terminal at tank B, the gauge would indicate 12 bar. The gauge is in fact comparing the pressure at tank B with atmospheric pressure. Some gauges offer an attachment that could be connected to tank A which would then ensure that a true comparison of pressures was measured between tanks B and A.

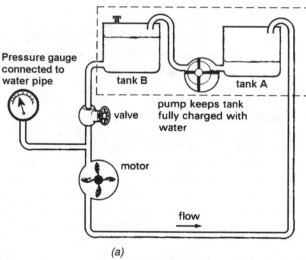

(a)

Electrical pressure measurement

As mentioned above, electrical pressure is referred to as voltage, which can be measured using a voltmeter. When voltage is measured, the voltmeter is in fact comparing the electrical 'pressure' between two points in the circuit. Therefore, referring to Figure 7.2b, if one test probe of a voltmeter is connected to the positive terminal of the battery and the second test probe is connected to the negative terminal of the battery, the voltmeter would indicate 12 volts as the electrical 'pressure'.

In effect, the voltmeter is measuring the 'pressure' or potential difference between the voltages at the positive and negative terminals.

7.2.4 Water and electrical flow measurement

Water flow measurement

Referring to Figure 7.1a, for water to flow in the circuit, a complete circuit has to exist from tank B through the tap and motor, back to tank A. When the tap in the water circuit is opened, water can flow through the circuit and return to tank A. The rate at which the water flows through the water circuit depends on the pressure that is exerted on the water at tank B, together with any restrictions that are placed in the pipe. Note that the motor is in fact a restriction to the flow of water; the motor reduces the rate of flow of water through the circuit in the same way as a partially blocked pipe would also act as a restriction.

Water flow could be measured at any point in the water circuit and could be quoted in 'litres per second'. Note that if 12 litres per second of water flowed out of tank B, then 12 litres per second of water would return to tank A. The flow of water is therefore the same at all points in this circuit.

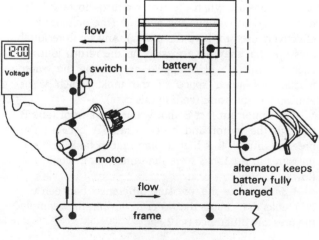

(b)

Figure 7.2 *Measuring 'pressure' in a water circuit and an electrical circuit.*
  a Pressure in a water circuit
  b Pressure in an electrical circuit

Electrical flow measurement

In the electrical circuit (Figure 7.1b), when the switch is 'on', electricity flows in the circuit. The electricity flows from the battery positive terminal, through the cable (wire) and components, to the battery negative terminal.

The amount of electricity flowing in a circuit depends on the voltage ('pressure') applied to the circuit, i.e. the pressure or potential difference between the positive and negative terminals. Additionally, the amount of electricity flowing will depend on any restrictions (called resistances) in the circuit. These restrictions are normally electrical components connected to the circuit. In the example shown in Figure 7.1b, an electric motor is a restriction to the flow of electricity in the same way as the motor in the water circuit restricted the flow of water.

The rate (amount per second) of electricity flowing through an electrical circuit is referred to as current flow, and is expressed in amperes, often abbreviated to 'amps' (the letter 'A' is also used to denote amperes). Amperes can be compared with the water flow measurement of litres per second.

Note that if 12 amps of electrical flow is passing out of the positive terminal, then 12 amps must pass back to the negative terminal. The flow of electricity (current) is therefore the same at any point in this circuit.

7.2.5 Measuring resistance to flow

In a water circuit, where the water flowed through the pipes, the size (or bore) of the pipe would affect the resistance to flow. If a large bore pipe were used, the resistance to flow would be very small, but if a very small bore pipe were used, this would represent a greater restriction to the flow of water. Similarly, if a piece of the pipe were crushed so that it almost blocked the flow completly, this would present a very severe restriction to flow.

In Figure 7.3a, the flow of water is driving a motor. If the motor is connected to a mechanical device (in this case a pulley-wheel with a rope and bucket connected to it) this would restrict the rotation of the motor. In effect, this forms a restriction or 'resistance' to the flow of water.

As described earlier, in an electrical circuit resistances affect the flow of electricity. Electrical resistances are generally created by electrical components such as motors or light bulbs. However, in some circuits, resistances are deliberately included to control or restrict electrical flow. A good example of a deliberate use of a resistance is a dimmer switch on a lighting circuit. A simple dimmer switch is effectively a resistance that can be adjusted to regulate the flow of electricity; the lower the flow the dimmer the light will be.

A dimmer switch can be compared directly with a tap in a water circuit (Figure 7.3b). As the tap is progressively closed, the flow of water reduces progressively. As a dimmer switch is progressively turned down, the resistance increases and the flow of electricity (current) is reduced.

Electrical resistance is measured in 'ohms'. (The omega symbol (Ω) is often used to denote ohms). The greater the number of ohms, the higher the resistance.

7.2.6 Relationships between volts, ohms and amps

The previous information in this chapter has identified three main elements of electricity, i.e. pressure, rate of flow and resistance. When working with electrical problems, it is always an advantage if the purpose or function of these three elements is remembered.

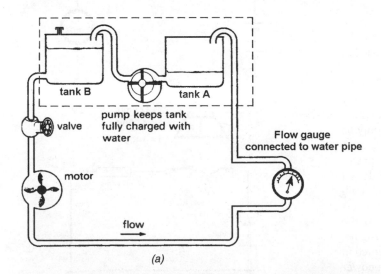

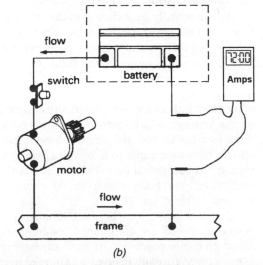

(a)

(b)

Figure 7.3 Measuring 'flow' in a water circuit and an electrical circuit.
   a Measuring 'flow' in a water circuit
   b Measuring 'flow' (current) in an electrical circuit

Volts = **Electrical pressure (potential difference)**
Creates the flow of electricity.

Amps = **Rate of flow (current).**
The rate at which electricity is flowing through the circuit.

Ohms = **Resistance to flow.**
A resistance is often an electrical component such as a light bulb; these components are referred to as 'electrical 'consumers'.

As with a water circuit:

- If the voltage (pressure) increases, it increases the rate of flow. If the voltage decreases, it reduces the rate of flow.
- If the ohms (resistance) increase, it reduces the rate of flow. If the ohms decrease, it increases the rate of flow.

So the rate of flow depends on the voltage (pressure) and the ohms (resistance) of a circuit.

7.2.7 Electrical power

Again, by comparing electrical circuits with water circuits, the greater the flow of water or electricity, the greater the energy or power that can be extracted. Therefore, if the rate of flow can be increased the power derived can also be increased.

Therefore, assuming that an electrical component such as a light bulb is fitted in a circuit, this represents the resistance (which itself cannot be altered). It is possible to fit a variable resistance which would be a dimmer switch, and by increasing the resistance of the dimmer switch, this will reduce the flow.

If however, we wanted to *increase* the brightness of the light bulb we would have to increase the current flow, and this would be achieved by increasing the pressure (voltage) in the circuit.

We can actually see a change in the brightness of the bulb when we adjust the dimmer switch or increase the voltage, but there is also a unit of measurement used to indicate the power output of the bulb.

Electrical power is quoted in 'watts', the higher the 'wattage' the brighter the bulb. Note that bulbs, and any other electrical component are usually designed with a certain wattage, which means that they should only be fitted to a circuit that provides this level of power. If a 12 volt bulb were fitted to a 24 volt circuit, the power from the circuit would be twice as much as the design capacity of the bulb, which would cause the bulb filament to 'blow' (melt).

Electrical power can be directly compared to the power produced by an internal-combustion engine. Although engine power has traditionally been quoted in 'horse power' (usually referred to as brake horsepower or BHP), engine power is often quoted in watts or kilowatts (1000 watts). One horsepower is equivalent to approximately 735 watts (or 0.735 kilowatts).

Electric motors are also described by their wattage rating, e.g. a 5 kilowatt motor. The power produced by this electric motor would be equivalent to approximately 6.8 horsepower.

7.2.8 Ohm's law

The relationship between the three electrical terms (volts, amps and ohms) is given by Ohm's law, which may be written as:

One volt is required to force a current of one ampere through a resistance of one ohm.

The law can also be expressed in the equations:

Voltage = Current × Resistance

or

$$V = I \times R$$

Where: V = voltage
I = current in amperes (A)
R = resistance in ohms (Ω)

If two of the values are known, the third value can be calculated. The following examples indicate how the third value can be calculated with the use of Ohm's law if two values are known.

Example 1
In the circuit in Figure 7.4, the resistance is 4 Ω and the current flowing is 3 A. Using Ohm's law, the voltage applied to the circuit can be calculated:

$$V = I \times R$$
$$= 3\,A \times 4\,\Omega$$
$$= 12\,V$$

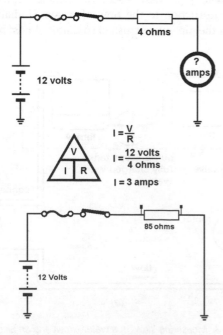

Figure 7.4 Using two of the three electrical values to calculate the third value

Example 2

In the circuit in Figure 7.4, the voltage applied to the circuit is 12 V and the current flowing is 3 A. Using Ohm's law, the resistance of the circuit can be calculated:

$$R = \frac{V}{I}$$

$$= \frac{12\,V}{3\,A}$$

$$= 4\,\Omega$$

Example 3

In the circuit in Figure 7.4, the voltage applied to the circuit is 12 V and the resistance in the circuit is 4 Ω. Using Ohm's law, the current flow (I in amps) in the circuit can be calculated:

$$I = \frac{V}{R}$$

$$= \frac{12\,V}{4\,\Omega}$$

$$= 3\,A$$

7.2.9 The effects of electrical energy

When current passes through a conductor, e.g. a cable or wire, the flow of electricity can provide three effects:

1 Heat,
2 Light
3 Magnetism.

Heat

When electricity flows through wire, it creates heat. Certain types of wire allow large amounts of heat to be produced.

Examples in the motor car are:
heated rear window, cigarette lighter.

Light

When electricity flows through certain types of wire, it glows and produces a bright light. Note that heat is also produced.

Examples in the motorcar are light bulbs.

Magnetism

When electricity passes through a wire, it produces a magnetic field around that wire. In effect, the magnetic field created is the same as that of a normal magnet, but it is the flow of electricity that creates the magnetic field. When this process is used, it produces an 'electromagnet'.

The magnetic fields produced this way are very weak but if the wire is longer, then more magnetism is produced. A long piece of wire is not a practical solution, so the next stage is to wind the long wire into a tight coil; this means that a long piece of wire can now

be fitted into a small space. The result is a strong magnetic field produced from a short coil of wire.

When such a magnetic field is created, it can be put to many uses. If an electromagnet is created, and placed next to another magnet (either a normal magnet or another electromagnet) the effect is that the two magnets repel or attract each other. This process can be used to produce movement of components. As an example, if one magnet is fitted to a rotating shaft, then when it is repelled by another magnet, it will cause the shaft to rotate, producing a simple electric motor.

Examples of electromagnets in the motor car are; ignition coil, alternator, starter motor, solenoids including relays, injectors.

7.2.10 Conductor and insulators

Conductors

A material which freely allows the flow of electrical current (i.e. has a very low resistance to current flow) is called a conductor.

Copper has a low resistance, which makes this metal suitable to use as an electrical cable. Other very good materials suitable for conducting electrical current are, platinum, gold, silver, and certain forms of carbon.

The type of cable used to connect the electrical components together will affect the resistance within the circuit. The cross-sectional area of the cable will affect the circuit resistance, as will the length of cable. In general terms, a thin cable has a higher resistance than a thicker cable, just as a small pipe has a greater resistance to water flow than a large pipe. The resistance of the wire also changes as the temperature of the wire changes.

A change in temperature of the conductors that make up an electrical circuit affects the resistance in that electrical circuit. The resistance of a conductor usually increases as temperature increases, although with some special types, the resistance may decrease as temperature increases.

Insulators

An insulator is a material that resists or opposes the flow of electricity. An insulator therefore has an extremely high resistance to the flow of electricity.

A cable is usually covered with an insulation material such as rubber or PVC. If the insulator around a piece of wire comes in contact with another piece of bare wire, the insulator prevents the electrical energy from passing across to the other piece of wire. When the insulation on a piece of wire fails, it can result in the electrical energy passing across to a piece of metal which may provide a shorter path or circuit back to the battery's negative terminal. This is referred to as a short circuit. Other materials suitable for insulating electrical currents are glass, plastics and porcelain. Each material has particular properties that make it suitable for specific applications.

Semiconductors

A semiconductor is a material that has a resistance value lower than an insulator but higher than that of a good conductor. However semiconductors have other properties that make them very useful in electronic components.

It is not necessary to provide a full explanation of how semiconductors work within this book, but Book 2 in this series and Hillier's *Fundamentals of Automotive Electronics* provide more detailed descriptions.

The two most widely used semiconductor materials are silicon and germanium; each has a different atomic structure to that of conductor materials and thus behaves differently. When these materials are in their pure state they will not conduct current, however, when they are mixed with very small amounts of impurities their atomic structure changes and allows current to pass through them.

A semiconductor has several properties:

- As the temperature of the semiconductor rises, so its resistance also changes, sometimes dramatically.
- When additional substances are mixed with the semiconductor, its ability to conduct electricity rises.

- The resistance of the semiconductor can change when exposed to a light source light, and it can produce light when a current is passed through it.
- In an electrical circuit, a semiconductor can be used to control the flow of current.
- Semiconductors are widely used in electronics. Examples include diodes, transistors and microchips.

Although there are many and varied uses of semiconductors, one of the simpler examples is as a temperature sensor. Because semiconductor resistance changes with temperature, this will affect current and voltage in a circuit, which provides an indication of the temperature change. Semiconductors also form an essential part of electronic switches; a semiconductor can be used as a switch, so that when the user switches a primary circuit with a semiconductor on it, the semiconductor acts as a switch to control one or more secondary circuits. Although mechanical switches can be used for these purposes (relays), semiconductor switches can switch many times faster than a mechanical switch and they can be made extremely small.

7.3   ELECTRICAL CIRCUITS AND CALCULATIONS

7.3.1 Electrical circuits: important note

When electricity was first discovered and investigated a convention was adopted that electricity flowed from positive to negative. This convention was accepted for many years and most rules of electrical theory were based on it. Eventually it was discovered that electricity was electron flow and that electrons actually pass from negative to positive. However, even now, for general discussion the flow of electricity is regarded as positive to negative.

For the purposes of this book and general motor vehicle work, the tradition of assuming electricity flows from positive to negative is quite acceptable. If we therefore assume that small particles are either positively charged or negatively charged (rather like the two poles of a magnet), then when a positively charged particle is free to move, it will be attracted to a negative charge.

The general principle can be demonstrated with two magnets. If the 'north' pole of one magnet is slowly moved towards the 'south' pole of the second magnet, the north pole will suddenly be attracted to the south pole.

In the example of a battery, we can assume that at the positive terminal, there are many positively charged particles. If a path is made for the particles to reach the negative terminal (negative particles), then the

positively charged particles will flow along the path to the negative terminal. This path could be created by connecting a piece of wire between the positive and negative terminals, in which case this path is a complete circuit.

The greater the number of positively charged particles at the positive terminal, the greater the flow around the circuit to the negative terminal (which has no positively charged particles). Therefore we could regard the number of positively charged particles as being the amount of 'pressure' or voltage at the positive terminal. More positively charged particles would equal more pressure or voltage.

A more detailed explanation of electricity is available in other *Fundamentals* titles.

7.3.2 A simple circuit

It should be noted that water will not flow around a hydraulic circuit (Figure 7.1) unless the pipe-work makes a complete path from the supply tank, around the system and back to the tank.

This principle also applies to an electrical circuit. An electric current will not flow, unless a complete circuit exists. When a battery is the power source, the circuit is only complete when a path exists between the battery positive terminal and the battery negative terminal.

The action of electrical flow around a circuit is the same as a pipe bent to form a loop and filled with water. No flow of water can take place in one part of the pipe unless there is a corresponding water movement in the remainder of the loop.

A simple electrical circuit is shown in Figure 7.5; the circuit is formed by connecting a lamp and switch to a battery. Figure 7.6 shows the same circuit but it is illustrated with commonly used electrical symbols.

In Figures 7.5 and 7.6, the flow of electricity is controlled by a simple on/off switch. The switch consists of a set of electrical contacts.

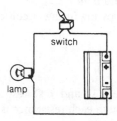

Figure 7.5 A simple circuit with a lamp and switch connected to a battery

When the switch is in the 'off' position, the contacts of the switch are open; the circuit is broken (often referred to as 'open circuit') which prevents current from flowing in the circuit. The bulb does not light up.

When the switch is moved to the 'on' position, the contacts close, which completes the circuit and allows current to flow. The current passes through the fine wire filament in the bulb, which causes it to glow (it becomes incandescent) and provides the illumination.

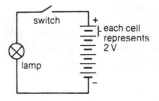

Figure 7.6 A simple circuit illustrated with electrical symbols

7.3.3 Earth return

When a lamp is connected to a battery by two cables, one cable is called the 'supply' and the other the 'return'.

However, nearly all vehicles use the metal body and frame of the vehicle as a part of the electrical circuit. By substituting the return cable with the body or frame of the vehicle, an 'earth return' system is formed (Figure 7.7).

The use of an earth return circuit reduces the overall length of cable required to create all of the electrical circuits, and in so doing reduces the weight and cost of the vehicle and simplifies the electrical wiring layout.

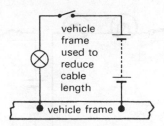

Figure 7.7 An earth return circuit

The frame is called earth (or ground) and is connected to one of the battery terminals.

Note: Normally the negative terminal is connected to the frame of the vehicle. In this case the polarity of the vehicle is described as 'negative earth'. The electrical illustrations show a negative earth circuit.

Use of the word 'return' is associated with the current flow in a circuit. The alternative two-wire arrangement, (called 'insulated return') is seldom used other than for special-purpose vehicles, for example, petrol tankers and military vehicles.

Note: It is essential that the battery terminals are connected so as to give the correct earth polarity. Electrical and electronic components can be damaged if the battery is incorrectly connected.

7.3.4 Types of circuit

Simple electrical circuits have only one resistance (electrical consumer) connected. However, many circuits, especially those used on modern vehicles, can have more than one resistance. Multiple resistances can be connected in a circuit using different methods. These are referred to as:

- series
- parallel.

7.3.5 Series circuits

In the example shown in Figure 7.8, the circuit is fitted with two bulbs. Because one bulb follows the other in the circuit, they are referred to as being 'in series'. For current to flow from the battery positive terminal to the battery negative terminal, the current only has one route, through both bulbs.

One disadvantage of using this circuit would be that if one bulb filament were to fail, the other bulb would also 'go out' as once it is broken no current can flow in the circuit.

Note that the current flow through the circuit is the same at any point in the circuit.

The total resistance (R_T) of the circuit is equal to the sum (addition) of the two resistance values in the circuit i.e. R_1 and R_2.

$$R_T = R_1 + R_2$$

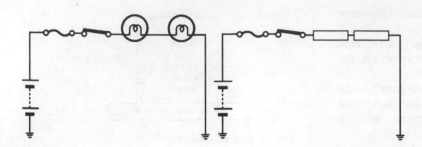

Figure 7.8 A series circuit (shown with bulbs and with resistor symbols)

Example:

If R_1 and R_2 are 2 Ω and 4 Ω respectively, then

$$R_T = 2\,\Omega + 4\,\Omega$$

$$= 6\,\Omega$$

The current flowing in the circuit can be calculated using Ohm's law, but note that the calculation must use the total resistance of the circuit.

Assuming the voltage applied to the circuit is 12 V, the current flow in the circuit is:

$$I\ (\text{current}) = \frac{V}{R_T}$$

$$= \frac{V}{R_1 + R_2}$$

$$= \frac{12\,\text{V}}{2\,\Omega + 4\,\Omega}$$

$$= \frac{12\,\text{V}}{6\,\Omega} = 2\,\text{A}$$

7.3.6 Parallel circuits

In the example shown in Figure 7.9, the circuit is fitted with two bulbs; the bulbs are effectively arranged in two parallel circuits. Each bulb is connected to the battery positive terminal and each bulb is also connected to the battery negative terminal. The supply voltage to each lamp is therefore equal to battery voltage.

An advantage of using a parallel circuit is that if one bulb filament were to fail, the other bulb would still remain lit. Therefore most lighting circuits used in motor vehicle applications are of the parallel type.

The total current flowing through the switch in Figure 7.9 will depend on the value of each resistance in the circuit, but note that there are effectively two

circuits, therefore the total current will be the current flowing through the first bulb plus the current flowing through the second bulb.

The current flowing in the circuit can be calculated by using Ohm's law:

$$I\ (\text{current}) = \frac{V}{R}$$

If R_1 and R_2 are 2 Ω and 6 Ω respectively then the current flow through each resistance is as follows:

$$\text{For } R_1 = \frac{12\,\text{V}}{2\,\Omega}$$

$$I\ (\text{current}) = 6\,\text{A}$$

$$\text{For } R_2 = \frac{12\,\text{V}}{6\,\Omega}$$

$$I\ (\text{current}) = 2\,\text{A}$$

The total current flowing through the circuit

$$= (\text{Current through } R_1)$$
$$+ (\text{current through } R_2)$$

$$= 6\,\text{A} + 2\,\text{A}$$

$$= 8\,\text{A}$$

The total resistance of the circuit can also be calculated by Ohm's law if the total current flow and the supply voltage are known:

$$R_T = \frac{V}{I}$$

$$= \frac{12\,\text{V}}{8\,\text{A}}$$

$$= 1.5\,\Omega$$

Note: The combined or total effective resistance value of a parallel circuit is always lower than the resistance value of the *smallest* resistor.

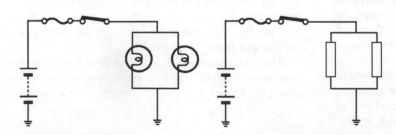

Figure 7.9 A parallel circuit (shown with bulbs and symbols)

Alternatively the total resistance of a parallel circuit can be calculated by using the following formula:

$$\frac{1}{R_T} = \frac{1}{R_1} + \frac{1}{R_2}$$

In this case: $\dfrac{1}{R_T} = \dfrac{1}{2} + \dfrac{1}{6}$

which is the same as $\dfrac{1}{R_T} = \dfrac{3}{6} + \dfrac{1}{6}$

or $\dfrac{1}{R_T} = \dfrac{4}{6}$

Therefore $\dfrac{R_T}{1} = \dfrac{6}{4} = 1.5 \ \Omega$

Note that, as stated earlier, the total resistance is *lower* than the value of the *smallest* resistor.

Although in most cases, a vehicle technician is unlikely to require the formula for general vehicle work, there are occasions when certain diagnostic problems are encountered where an understanding of parallel resistance calculations is an advantage.

7.3.7 Voltage drop

When current flows in a circuit, a resistance causes the voltage (potential difference) to fall as the current passes through the resistance.

So the voltage available at each side of a resistance will be different; the difference in the voltage is referred to as the 'voltage drop'.

Note: For a voltage drop to occur across a resistance, current must flow in the circuit.

Volt drop across a single resistance

If a single resistance exists in a circuit, Figure 7.10, it effectively uses up all of the energy (or voltage) in the circuit, so the voltage drop across a single resistor in a 12-volt circuit will equal 12 volts.

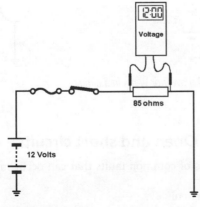

Figure 7.10 Voltage drop across a single resistance

The voltage applied to the start of the resistance is 12 volts but the resistance will use all of the available voltage and therefore the voltage at the end of the resistance will be zero volts. The voltage drop across this single resistance will be quoted as 12 volts.

Volt drop across resistances in series

If two resistances are connected in a series circuit, the total available voltage must drop across both the resistances R_1 and R_2. If both resistances are the same value (Figure 7.11), then these two resistances will share the available voltage equally, i.e. each resistance will use 6 volts. The voltage drop across *both* resistances would be quoted as 12 volts.

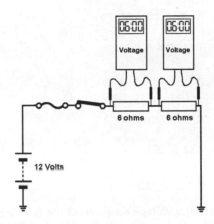

Figure 7.11 Voltage drop across two equal resistances in series

However, if two resistances are connected in a series circuit and the values of the resistances are *different*, then the voltage drop across each resistance will be different. Note however, that the total voltage drop across the two resistances will still equal total available voltage. In a 12-volt circuit therefore, it would not matter what the values of the two series resistances were; the total voltage drop would still be 12 volts. In effect, the two resistances are sharing all the available 12 volts.

The voltage drop across each resistance can be calculated by using Ohm's law. If the resistance is known and the total current is known then the voltage can be calculated thus:

$$\text{Vdrop}_1 = R_1 \times I \ \text{(current)}$$
$$\text{Vdrop}_2 = R_2 \times I \ \text{(current)}$$

Note: The sum of the voltage drops across the resistances in the circuit is equal to the supply voltage. With reference to Figure 7.12, to calculate the voltage drop across each resistance, the current flow in the circuit must first be calculated:

$$I = \frac{V}{R_T}$$

$$= \frac{V}{R_1 + R_2}$$

$$= \frac{12\,V}{2\,\Omega + 4\,\Omega}$$

$$= \frac{12\,V}{6\,\Omega}$$

$$= 2\,A$$

Again referring to Figure 7.12, the voltage drop across each resistance can be calculated:

$$V_1 = R_1 \times I \text{ (current)}$$

$$= 2\,\Omega \times 2\,A$$

$$= 4\,V$$

$$V_2 = R_2 \times I \text{ (current)}$$

$$= 4\,\Omega \times 2\,A$$

$$= 8\,V$$

The sum of the voltage drop across the two resistances is equal to the supply voltage (V_T), i.e. The battery voltage.

$$V_T = V_1 + V_2$$

$$= 4\,V + 8\,V$$

$$= 12\,V$$

Note: If the resistances in the circuit are of the same value, the supply voltage is divided equally between the resistances, e.g. if the supply voltage is 12 V and there are three resistances connected in a series circuit each

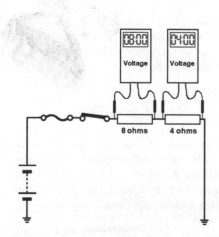

Figure 7.12 Voltage drop across two series resistances (with different values)

having a value of 2 Ω, the voltage drop across each resistance will be 4 V. In fact, it does not matter what the values are of the three resistances; assuming that they are all equal the three resistances will share the voltage equally and the voltage drop will still be 4 V across each resistance.

Volt drop across resistances in parallel

When two resistances are connected in parallel, it must be noted that each resistance is effectively independent and functions as a single resistance. This is because each resistance has the full available voltage applied from the battery positive terminal to one end and the battery negative terminal to its other end. Therefore the voltage drop at each resistance is calculated as if it was a single resistance.

7.3.8 Calculating power (watts)

As previously discussed in section 7.2.7, when electricity flows in a circuit, energy or power is produced. The various forms of this energy or power are heat, light, or creating movement (electric motors or solenoids).

Power is defined as work done in a given time, and is expressed in watts (W).

The power can be calculated from the expression:

Power = voltage × current

Or

Watts = volts × amperes

If two of the values are known, the third value can be calculated. The following example indicates how the third value can be calculated if two values are known.

$$W = V \times I$$

$$= 12\,V \times 0.5\,A$$

$$= 6\,W$$

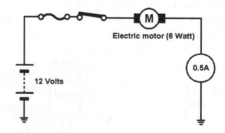

Figure 7.13 Power or watts in a circuit

7.3.9 Open and short circuits

Two types of common faults that can occur in a circuit are:

■ open circuit
■ short circuit.

Open circuit

The term open circuit is used to describe a break in a circuit which therefore prevents current from flowing.

A switch is usually connected to a circuit and provides an intentional means of making an open circuit. The switch is used to control the flow of current in the circuit.

However, an open circuit can also exist due to a fault as shown in Figure 7.14.

Current cannot flow and therefore the circuit will not function. In Figure 7.14, an ammeter (used to measure current or amps) forms part of the circuit to indicate the current in the circuit (effectively a flow rate measurement). In this case, there is an amp reading of zero because of the open circuit.

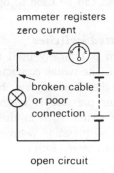

Figure 7.14 An open circuit

Short circuit

Electricity will always take the easiest route possible between the battery terminals. If the current flow has an option to either pass through a resistance, or to pass across a piece of wire which has little resistance, most of the flow will take the path of least resistance, i.e. the current will flow through the wire.

If the supply cable to an electrical component were to be accidentally connected to an earth connection (short circuit as shown in Figure 7.15), the current would mainly pass through the short circuit rather than taking the more difficult route through the component that acts as a resistance in the circuit.

In the illustration (Figure 7.15), the current is mostly not passing through the resistance and the flow is therefore not so restricted. This will result in the full

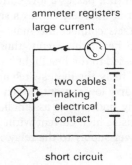

Figure 7.15 A short circuit

amperage or current flow from the battery, which is indicated by the ammeter. In such cases, the current flow will be so high that the wiring could melt and therefore some form of protection is required (discussed in the next section). A fuse would ideally be fitted to the circuit. The fuse is made with a specially selected wire that 'blows' or melts when the current is too high. This then protects the rest of the circuit and prevents a possible fire.

The thickness of the insulation on a cable is dictated by the voltage and current that the cable has to carry – the higher the voltage and current the thicker the insulation.

7.3.10 Fuses and other circuit protectors

A fuse is a short length of thin wire that is fitted into a holder. The fuse is designed to melt (commonly referred to as 'blow') and break the circuit (open the circuit) if the current exceeds the rated value (amps) marked on the fuse.

The fuse is generally connected in the circuit to the supply cable, usually as near as possible to the battery positive terminal (or the supply terminal from a switch). Provided it is of the correct rating, the fuse protects the circuit to which it is fitted from excessive current and therefore overheating, reducing the risk of fire in the event of a short circuit. If the fuse 'blows', it must be renewed.

Many fuses fitted to vehicles today are of the 'blade' type as shown in Figure 7.16. The blade fuse is slim and compact in design with the element protected by a

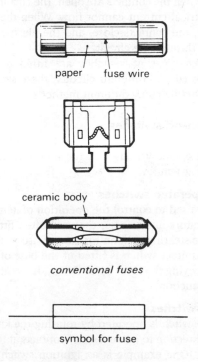

Figure 7.16 Types of fuse

plastic body. The various colours used for blade fuses easily identify different fuse ratings; the fuse rating is also printed on the top of the fuse.

Note: The maximum protection by a blade-type fuse is usually 30 amps.

The fuses for the vehicle's electrical systems are normally contained within a unit referred to as the 'fuse box'.

Fusible link

Some electrical components require a comparatively large current, so in these cases a fuse having a high amperage is specified. The protection for these high current circuits is often provided by a 'fusible link'. The fusible link is generally larger in size to allow for the thicker fusible wire. Fusible links provide protection for circuits from 30 amps to 100 amps. If the fusible link 'blows' the link should be renewed and the protected circuit checked for excessive current.

Circuit breakers

Some circuits (e.g. electric windows) are protected by circuit breakers. If the current exceeds the circuit breaker rating, it will interrupt the current (referred to as 'tripping'), preventing the circuit from functioning. The circuit breaker can either be reset manually, or in some cases the circuit breaker resets itself automatically when the current falls to an acceptable level.

7.3.11 Switches

The flow of electricity in a conventional circuit is normally controlled by means of a switch. The switch contains a set of contacts, which can be either open or closed. When the contacts are open, the circuit is broken and electrical current cannot flow. When the switch is operated, the contacts close, and the electrical current can flow through the circuit.

Various types of switches are fitted to a motor vehicle to control different circuits; these switches can be operated by many different methods.

Push – on/off switches

These simple switches are used to control many electrical circuits throughout the motor vehicle, e.g. a heated rear window.

Lever-operated switches

Typically used to control the operation of items such as the indicators and wipers, they are often fitted to the top of the steering column for ease of use by the driver. A multi-contact switch is fitted at the base of the lever and by moving the lever up or down, different electrical circuits function.

Rotary switches

A rotary switch is operated by rotating the knob in the desired direction to move a set of contacts at the base of the shaft. One example is an ignition switch (a key is used instead of a knob). At the base of the shaft is a multi-contact switch, and depending on the position to which the key is set, different electrical circuits will function.

Temperature/pressure switches

The operation of many components on a vehicle is controlled by the use of a set of contacts fitted within a switch unit that may be affected by temperature or pressure. Examples of such switches include:

Temperature-operated switches

A set of contacts is contained within the body of the switch (or sensor), which is placed in contact with a fluid. The contacts could be open when the fluid temperature is low, and when a pre-determined higher temperature is reached, the contacts then close. A switch such as this can be used to operate an electric cooling fan.

Pressure-operated switches

A pressure switch is typically used for detecting the pressure of a fluid. The switch contacts are closed when the pressure of the fluid is low, but when a pre-determined higher pressure is reached, the contacts open. A pressure switch such as this can be used to operate the 'low oil pressure' warning light, which is situated in the instrument cluster.

7.3.12 Relays

The use of a relay in a circuit allows an electrical circuit with a relatively low current flow to control the operation of a circuit that has a high current flow.

Example and advantages

As an example, Figure 7.17 shows a relay used to switch the headlight circuit (which would have a relatively high current demand and current flow). The relay could be located nearer to the headlights than the dashboard. Because the relay itself can be switched on using a very low current, this allows a very thin wire to be used between the headlight switch on the dashboard (or steering column switch) and the relay. The switch itself can be designed to deal with only low current values. However, the wire from the relay to the headlights which carries the high current needs to be much thicker.

The driver selects headlight operation via the switch, which in turn passes a low current to the relay. The low current at the relay causes a set of contacts to close. The contacts connect the main supply (battery positive) to the headlight circuit, thus enabling high current to be passed to the headlight bulbs.

By using the relay, the light switch and the wiring to the relay only carry low current, which means that less expensive wiring and switch assemblies can be used. The more expensive high current wiring is only used to connect the power supply to the relay, and the relay to the headlights.

As well as a cost reduction (because using a relay reduces the length of wiring that carries high current)

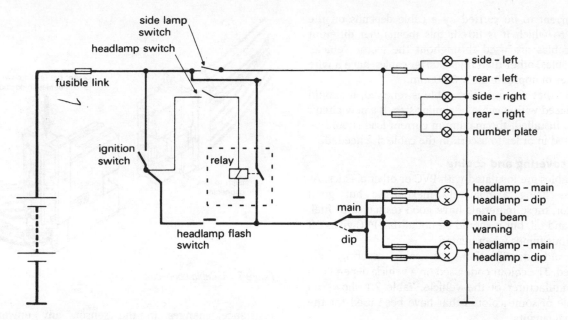

Figure 7.17 A relay as used in a simple headlight circuit

this also helps overcome the build-up of resistance that can occur in a long length of wire. The resistance in a long wire carrying a high current can result in an unacceptable voltage drop across the wire and reduced current flow, which would reduce the performance of the light bulbs or other electrical consumer.

There is also a safety issue with passing high current through long lengths of wire. The wire and switch contacts can get hot due to the current flow, which can result in switch contacts failing and wiring or switches causing fires. To overcome these problems, the wiring and switches need to be constructed in such a way that the costs are unacceptable compared with using a relay.

Basic operation of a relay

There are many different designs of relay, depending on the task that they have to perform; however, the basic principle of most relays is the same.

A relay contains a set of contacts (two contacts that form a switch), which are typically open when the relay is inactive. The contacts can however be made to close when a small magnetic field is created adjacent to the contacts.

The magnetic field is created by passing a current around a coil of wire (known as a winding); this is referred to as 'energizing' the coil or winding. The current required to energise the coil can be relatively small, which means that it can be switched on by a relatively inexpensive switch via thin wiring. When the magnetic field is created, it attracts one part of the contact assembly, which causes the two contacts' faces to touch (close the switch).

One of the contacts is connected to the power source (either direct to battery positive or a main power terminal). The other contact is connected to the electrical consumer, e.g. headlights or heated rear window. When the small current causes the contacts to

close, they then complete the high-current circuit from the battery to the electrical consumer.

In some cases, the reverse happens, so when the coil or winding is energized it actually causes the contacts to open which means that it switches *off* a circuit. It is therefore also possible to use a set of contacts to pass the high current through to one of two circuits, such as the dipped headlights or the main beam headlights. When the contacts are in their natural position they complete a circuit to the dipped headlights and when the driver selects main beam, the winding energizes causing the contacts to open the dipped beam circuit, but to close the main beam circuit. The dipped circuit is now off, but the main beam circuit has been turned on.

7.3.13 Cables

The various electrical components are connected to the supply by low-resistance cables (wires). Copper cables, which are usually stranded to give good flexibility, are generally used to connect components. Where several cables follow a common path they are taped together to form a 'loom' or wiring harness. The construction of a wiring harness reduces both the risk of chafing against the metal frame and breakage of the cable due to vibration. The harness is secured to the body of the vehicle using various securing clips, to prevent further movement and chaffing.

The quoted size of a cable refers to the diameter of the wire and the number of strands. If the cable is too small for its length or for the current it has to carry, it will overheat and produce a voltage drop, which affects the performance of the component which it connects, e.g. a light will not give its full brightness or a starter motor will not rotate at the correct speed.

The current to be carried by a cable depends on the circuit to which it is fitted; this means that different sized cables are used throughout the motor vehicle. Most cables, other than thick starter cables, have a wire diameter of approximately 0.30 mm.

Note that if a defective cable is renewed, it should be replaced with a cable of similar size. If a new circuit is to be installed, the maximum current load should be estimated in order to ascertain the cable size needed.

Cable covering and coding

Most cables are insulated with PVC or other plastics. As well as being a relatively inexpensive but good insulator, these materials have good resistance to fuel, petrol and oil, but it should be noted that PVC gives off dangerous fumes when heated.

To aid identification, the cable coverings are coloured. The colour code used on a vehicle depends on the manufacturer of the vehicle. Table 7.1 shows an example of some colours that have been used for the principal circuits.

In addition to the base colour, some cables have a thin 'tracer line' running along the cable. The colour of this tracer identifies the part of the circuit formed by this cable.

As an example, a cable shown as UW, has a blue base colour and a white tracer.

Table 7.1

Circuit	Cable colour	Abbreviation
Earth connections	Black	B
Ignition circuits	White	W
Main battery feed	Brown	N
Side lamps	Red	R
Auxiliaries controlled by ignition switch	Green	G
Auxiliaries not controlled by ignition switch	Purple	P
Headlamps	Blue	U

7.3.14 Connectors

Although connectors using traditional soldered and crimped terminals are still used to connect cables together, the need for greater terminal security and improved protection against the ingress of salt and moisture has demanded the use of more efficient connectors.

Figure 7.18 shows a typical plug-and-socket harness connector, which is used to join a number of cables. At the ends of the connector, the terminals are exposed; this provides a test point for meter checks.

It should be noted that on many vehicle systems where computer control and sensors are used, the sensor circuits use very low currents. These could be greatly affected by a poor connection that offers a high resistance. Because the sensors themselves may provide information to the computer that is dependent on

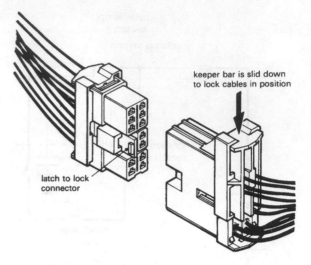

Figure 7.18 Cable connector

resistance changes in the sensor, any unwanted resistance due to poor connections could result in incorrect information to the computer and therefore incorrect system operation. For many systems therefore, terminal connections are gold plated, which provides a low resistance connection that is also relatively tolerant of moisture and other adverse elements.

7.3.15 Wiring diagrams

Wiring diagrams are used to illustrate the various electrical circuits fitted to a vehicle. These wiring diagrams may show the overall electrical circuit fitted to the vehicle or, due to the large number of electrical circuits fitted to a vehicle, a wiring diagram may only show a selected part of the overall wiring, e.g. a headlamp circuit.

Wiring diagrams can be used by a technician to help understand the operation of a relevant circuit and, should a fault occur, the diagnosis and repair of that electrical circuit.

Electrical symbols

Each wiring diagram is likely to show many wires and components. To simplify the wiring diagram, the electrical system is normally illustrated in a schematic (theoretical) format. The various electrical system components that make up the circuit are indicated as graphical symbols in such a schematic diagram.

Due to the large number of separate components that are used in an electrical system of a motor vehicle, a convention or standard format is needed to enable the technician to understand the various graphical symbols. Although each manufacturer uses a slightly different format in which to illustrate their wiring diagrams, many of the symbols used to represent the electrical components are similar. Familiarisation with these symbols will help the technician to understand wiring diagrams.

The British Standards Institution (BSI) recommends that the electrical symbols indicated in BS 3939-1: 1986 be used in wiring diagrams. Some of the main symbols are shown in Table 7.2. It should, however, be noted that European-based conventions may recommend different symbols, so reference should always be made to the relevant wiring diagram and any other references provided by the diagram supplier (such as the vehicle or part manufacturer, or publisher of the diagram).

Table 7.2 Examples of electrical symbols

Description	Symbol
Direct current / Alternating current	
Positive polarity / Negative polarity	
Current approaching / Current receding	
Battery 12V (Long line is positive)	
Earth, chassis frame / Earth, general	
Conductor (permanent) Thickness denotes importance / Conductor (temporary)	
Conductors crossing without connecting	
Conductors joining	
Junction, separable / Junction, inseparable / Plug and socket	
Variability: applied to other symbols	
Resistor (fixed value)	
Resistor (variable)	
General winding (inductor, coil)	
Winding with core	
Transformer	
Diode, rectifying junction	
Light emitting diode	
Diode, breakdown: Zener and avalanche	
Reverse blocking triode thyristor	
Transformer pnp / npn	

Description	Symbol
Lamp	
Fuse	
Switch ('make' contact, normally open)	
Switch ('break' contact, normally closed)	
Switch (maunally operated)	
Switch (two-way)	
Relay (single winding)	
Relay (thermal)	
Spark gap	
Generator ac and dc	
Motor dc	
Meters: ammeter, voltmeter, galvanometer	

Description	Symbol
Capacitor, general symbol	
Capacitor, polarised	
Amplifier	

Description	Symbol
Junction f.e.t. N-type channel / P-typer channel	
Photodiode	
Thyristor	

7.4   THE BATTERY

7.4.1 Introduction to the lead–acid battery

The purpose of a battery is to store the electrical energy that is needed to operate a vehicle's electrical systems. When the engine is not running or when the output from the electrical generator (alternator) is low, the battery functions as the storage device.

The battery stores the energy by converting the electrical energy supplied to it via the generator into chemical energy. When an electrical current is required, the energy flow is then reversed, i.e. the chemical energy is converted back into electrical energy.

Whenever the battery supplies electrical energy to the components, the energy consumed needs to be replaced. The electrical generator supplies further electrical energy, which the battery stores until required.

Lead–acid battery

Most vehicles use a lead–acid-type battery. This type of secondary (reversible in charge/discharge) battery has lead plates immersed in an electrolyte (a liquid solution) of sulphuric acid (H_2SO_4) and distilled water. The lead–acid battery is sometimes referred to as a 'wet-type' battery.

There are various types of lead–acid battery. These are:

- conventional
- low-maintenance
- maintenance-free.

7.4.2 Conventional lead–acid battery

Although widely used for many years, the conventional battery has been generally replaced by low maintenance or maintenance-free batteries. However, by understanding the basic principles of construction and operation of the conventional battery, technicians can appreciate the progression towards the newer low-maintenance and maintenance-free types.

The type of lead–acid battery shown in Figure 7.19 consists of a polypropylene or hard rubber container, which contains a number of separate cells (compartments), each with a nominal voltage of 2 volts. A 12-volt battery has six cells connected in series by lead strips.

The series arrangement means that the cells are interconnected with the positive terminal of each cell joined to the negative of the adjacent cell. Motor vehicles are usually fitted with batteries with six cells each of 2 volts, connected in series so the battery provides an output voltage of 12 volts. Note however that heavy vehicles may use a 24-volt system and that other voltage systems (e.g. 42 volts), are being developed for use in light vehicles.

Each cell is made up of two sets of lead plates, positive and negative, which are placed alternately and separated by a porous insulating material. The plates on the conventional type of battery consist of a lattice-type grid of lead/antimony alloy, which retains the active lead oxide paste material.

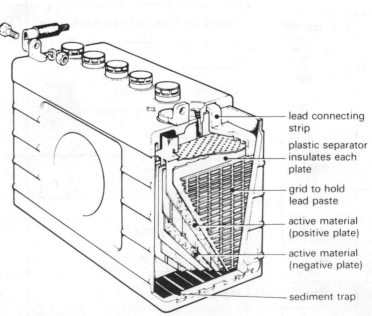

- lead connecting strip
- plastic separator insulates each plate
- grid to hold lead paste
- active material (positive plate)
- active material (negative plate)
- sediment trap

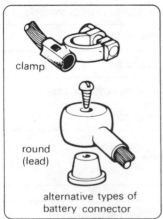

- clamp
- round (lead)

alternative types of battery connector

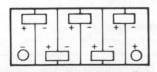

lead strips connect the cells in series – the positive plates in one cell are connected to the negative plates in the adjoining cell

Figure 7.19 Battery – conventional type

A moulded cover seals the cells and either individually screwed caps or a one-piece detachable cover allows the cells to be periodically topped up with distilled water. Vents in the cover permit the gas to escape; this is evident during the charging process and when the battery is used in a discharged state.

Various types of terminal post are used. Some batteries have a post with a hole to enable the connector to be clamped to it, others are fitted with a cylindrical post around which the connector is fitted.

It is essential that the battery be connected to the vehicle in a way that provides the correct earth polarity. Extensive damage to electrical components will occur if the polarity is incorrect.

Terminals are marked '+' (positive) and '–' (negative). If cylindrical battery terminal posts are used, the larger diameter is positive. Also the colours red (or brown) and black (or blue) are used to indicate the positive and negative terminals respectively.

Cell action

When the battery is discharging (the energy stored in the battery is used), the lead in the plates undergoes a chemical change and the acid becomes 'weaker', and its 'specific gravity' (density) decreases.

To reverse the action, an electrical charge is supplied from an alternator. The charge changes the lead plates back to their original chemical form and 'strengthens' the electrolyte; the acid becomes stronger and its specific gravity increases.

To charge the battery, the charge current must pass through the battery in one direction, so a direct current (DC) Must be used. To produce the chemical reversal of the plates, the charging current must flow in the opposite direction to the current given out by the battery. The connection between the battery and alternator (or bench charger) must be positive to positive (Figure 7.20).

Voltage variation

When the battery is 'taken off charge', the terminal voltage (potential difference) per cell is about 2.1 V.

The voltage quickly drops to 2.0 V, where it remains for the major part of the discharge period. Towards the end of the discharge period, the potential difference falls rapidly until a fully discharged value of 1.8 V is reached. These values represent potential difference, so current must be flowing at the normal discharge rate when the voltage reading is taken.

Towards the end of the charging period the terminal voltage rises to 2.5–2.7 V, but this quickly falls to about 2.1 V when the charging current ceases.

Capacity

The total surface area of the plates governs the amount of current which a battery will supply; this represents the capacity of a battery and is often expressed in ampere hours (Ah).

A battery rated at 38 Ah, based on a 10 hour rate, should supply a steady current of 3.8 A for 10 hours.

Reserve capacity is an alternative method of expressing the capacity of a battery. This rating indicates the time in minutes for which a battery will deliver a current of 25 A at 25°C before the cell voltage drops to 1.75 V. A typical 40 Ah battery having a reserve capacity of 45 minutes should keep the vehicle in operation for this time after the charging system has failed, provided that the electrical load is normal.

Maintenance of conventional-type batteries

Regular maintenance is needed to keep this type of battery in good condition. The maintenance of the battery includes the following tasks.

Battery fitting

Extensive damage to electrical components results if the earth polarity is accidentally reversed.

Mounting bolts and brackets are used to hold the battery firmly in place, but the bolts should not be over-tightened (damage to the casing and lead plates can occur).

When removing or refitting a battery, the earth lead should be removed first and fitted last. Using this procedure reduces the risk of the spanner arcing from the positive terminal to the vehicle body.

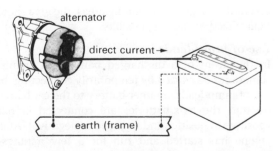

bench charging
(a)

battery charging by the vehicle alternator
(b)

Figure 7.20 Battery charging methods a) Bench charging b) Vehicle charging

For safety reasons, the battery earth terminal should be disconnected before work is carried out on engine or transmission, or any other components or vehicle systems that are likely to rotate or cause injury. The battery should also be disconnected before electric arc welding is carried out, as damage to electrical components can occur from the induced voltage resulting from the welding equipment and welding process.

Important note regarding disconnecting the battery

On many modern vehicles, disconnecting the battery can have a number of implications. An example is where a radio or in-car entertainment system is provided with an anti-theft device. In such cases, when the battery is re-connected it may be necessary to enter a code before the radio can be used.

It is also possible that the vehicle security system or immobiliser system may also require re-initialization after the battery has been disconnected and re-connected. Some other computers or ECUs such as the engine management ECU may also require re-initialisation after having their electrical power disconnected.

In most of the above cases, either the computer memory is lost when the power is disconnected or the ECU is designed so that it will not allow correct operation until the correct coding has been entered (this provides a measure of security for the vehicle owner).

Electrolyte level

The electrolyte should be maintained at the correct level (e.g. 6 mm above the plates) by topping up with distilled water. Frequent topping up indicates that the battery is being over-charged.

Terminal corrosion

Corrosion of the terminals is reduced by coating each terminal with petroleum jelly or silicone grease. A corroded terminal can be cleaned by immersing the terminal in ammoniated warm water or soda dissolved in water. This solution can also be used to neutralize acid spillage on vehicle body parts. If electrolyte is spilt on paintwork and surrounding areas, the area should be neutralized as soon as possible.

Use of jump-leads

In the event of a discharged battery, an engine can sometimes be started by temporarily connecting, by the use of jump-leads, another battery to the car battery. To do this, the two batteries are connected in parallel (positive to positive and negative to negative). After the engine has started and run for a few minutes, the engine must be allowed to slow-run before the jump-leads are disconnected, making sure that the earth lead is removed first.

It is however advisable to check with the vehicle manufacturer's recommendations since connecting and disconnecting jump leads has caused electronic component failures. This is due to the possibility of 'arcing' occurring when one of the jump leads is connected. In some cases this arcing causes a small voltage surge or spike that can damage electronic components.

Although most modern electronic components are protected against such problems, some vehicles could still be worked on that do not have full protection.

Battery hazards

A burn caused by battery acid should be treated immediately with sodium bicarbonate solution or, failing this, clean water. Acid splashed into the eye should be bathed immediately in clean water and medical attention sought as soon as possible.

For those organisations that re-fill batteries with acid, the acid supplied may need to be 'broken down' to weaken it before it is used. For safety reasons, the dilution must be carried out in a glass or earthenware container by adding acid to water and **not** water to acid.

Acid splashes on clothes must be neutralized with an alkali, such as ammonia, if holes are to be avoided. Gloves and goggles should be worn when handling or pouring acid; it is also advisable to wear an acid-proof apron.

Battery charging

Most battery charging equipment can charge the battery slowly or provide a fast-charge. A fast-charge is achieved by providing a higher current from the charger to the battery, but note that the life of the battery may be reduced if it is frequently fast-charged.

Ideally, therefore, batteries should be slow-charged.

If the battery is completely discharged, it may not accept a fast-charge, so an initial slow-charge may be necessary before a fast-charge can be used. The following precautions should be observed whenever charging a battery.

The battery electrolyte should be set at the correct level; add distilled water if incorrect. Remove all vent plugs from the battery. If charging the battery 'on the vehicle', disconnect the battery leads to prevent damage to the electronic components of the vehicle. Ensure that the battery terminals are clean before connecting the battery charger leads; clean them if necessary.

A quantity of explosive hydrogen gas is released from the cells when charging the battery. Always carry out the charging of a battery in a well-ventilated area. Ideally the vehicle workshop should have a specific area allocated for bench charging and provided with necessary ventilation.

Never over-charge the battery; damage to the battery will result. Many battery chargers will regulate the battery charging at the correct rate for the condition of the battery being charged. Refer to the battery charger instructions for the correct procedure. Ensure that the temperature of the electrolyte is below 45°C before and during charging; stop the charging if the temperature is too high.

There is a high risk of an explosion from the hydrogen when connecting the terminals; care must be taken to avoid a spark. Always switch off the battery charger main switch before disconnecting the charger leads from the battery.

After charging the battery, it should be left to stand for a period of time before fitting it to the vehicle, for hydrogen to disperse as a vehicle electrical system (e.g. central-locking door system) may cause the terminals to spark as the battery is reconnected.

Battery tests

The tests should be performed in accordance with the battery manufacturer's recommendations together with the relevant health and safety procedures. The following tests relate to a conventional battery and are intended as a guide only.

1 Hydrometer

The specific gravity (or relative density) of an electrolyte is measured by a hydrometer; the readings indicate the state of charge (Figure 7.21). Values quoted represent the weight of the electrolyte in relation to the weight of an equal volume of distilled water at 20°C. Note that the value will change with a change in temperature. Typical values are:

Fully charged	1.280
Half-charged	1.200
Fully discharged	1.150

2 Electrical load test

Also often referred to as a 'high-rate discharge' test or 'drop test', the equipment used indicates the ability of a battery to supply a large current, similar to that required to operate the starting motor. The test equipment displays the battery voltage during the time that a large current is being drawn from the battery.

The load test is severe and must not be prolonged beyond the recommended time. It should only be performed on a fully-charged battery.

A 30 Ah battery in good condition, tested against a load of about 100 A, should show a reading of 8–10 V for a period of 15 seconds. If lower than the reading specified, it indicates a high internal resistance in the battery and the battery should be replaced.

7.4.3 Low-maintenance batteries

Improved materials and new construction techniques have reduced the need for batteries to be periodically topped up with distilled water to replace losses caused by gassing. This type of battery is fitted to modern vehicles because it reduces maintenance time.

Use of these batteries has been made possible by the improved control of charging rate and voltage obtained from an alternator system as compared with old dynamo charging equipment used on older vehicles. The gas given off during the charging of the battery has been reduced by changing the grid material from lead/antimony to an alloy of lead and calcium.

When the low-maintenance battery operates together with an efficient charging system and at normal temperature, the electrolyte only has to be checked once per year or at 80,000 km intervals.

Other than in its grid material, the construction of a low-maintenance battery is similar to the conventional type. Since the performance characteristics are based on proven designs, it is normally possible to fit a low maintenance battery in place of a conventional battery.

7.4.4 Maintenance-free batteries

The maintenance-free battery shown in Figure 7.22 differs in several respects from the conventional battery. The most significant features are that the battery is sealed, except for a very small vent hole, and that it requires no service attention other than to be kept clean. A test indicator may be fitted in the top cover to register the state of charge. The indicator is a form of hydrometer which signals the battery condition by changing colour. The type illustrated shows green when the battery is charged and serviceable, and green/black or black when recharging is required. When a light yellow is signalled, it indicates that an internal fault is present; in this condition the battery must not be charged or tested. Furthermore, jump leads must not be used when this fault is indicated. Instead the battery should be replaced and the alternator output checked.

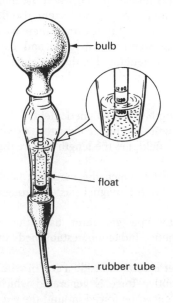

Figure 7.21 Use of a hydrometer

If the battery is discharged to a point where it cannot crank the engine and in consequence the engine has to be started either by jump-leads or by pushing the car, then it will be impossible for the vehicle's alternator to recharge the battery. When a battery is in this condition, it must be removed and bench charged. This is necessary because the voltage needed to recharge the battery is higher than that given by the charging system of the vehicle.

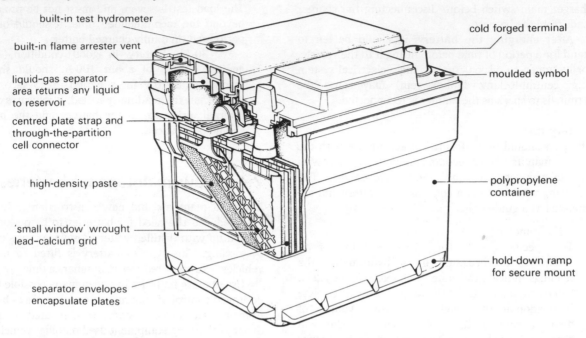

built-in test hydrometer

built-in flame arrester vent

liquid–gas separator area returns any liquid to reservoir

centred plate strap and through-the-partition cell connector

high-density paste

'small window' wrought lead–calcium grid

separator envelopes encapsulate plates

cold forged terminal

moulded symbol

polypropylene container

hold-down ramp for secure mount

Figure 7.22 Battery – maintenance-free type

7.5 THE CHARGING SYSTEM

7.5.1 Function of a generator

When the engine is running, the charging system provides the electrical energy for the operation of the vehicle's electrical components.

The charging system must also maintain the battery in a fully-charged state. To fulfil these duties, the generator of the charging system must convert mechanical energy into electrical energy.

There are two types of generator that can be fitted to a vehicle:

Dynamo – commonly used in the past but not used on modern motor vehicles
Alternator – fitted now to most vehicles.

7.5.2 Principle of the generator

The origin of the generator goes back many years. In 1831 Michael Faraday performed an experiment that showed that an electric current was generated when a magnet was moved in a coil of wire (Figure 7.23). He demonstrated that during the inward movement of the magnet, the needle on an ammeter (measuring amperes) moved; this showed that an electric current was flowing in the coil circuit. Withdrawal of the magnet caused the needle to move in the other direction. This indicated that when the magnet moved in the opposite direction, the current also flowed in the opposite direction. At times when there was no relative movement between the magnet and coil, electrical energy was not generated in the coil circuit.

The generation of electrical energy is dependent on three things:

1 The strength of the magnetic field.
2 The length of the conductor exposed to the magnetic field, i.e. the length of wire that forms the coil.
3 The speed at which the magnetic field is cut, i.e. how quickly the magnet passes through the coil of wire.

An alternator-type generator uses the principle of electromagnetic induction established in Faraday's experiment.

A magnet is rotated inside a coil of wire. In this coil an electromotive force is generated which causes an electric current to be forced around the circuit (refer to section 7.2.2).

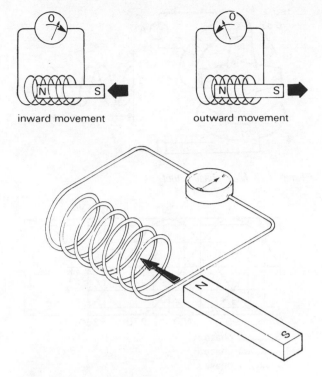

inward movement   outward movement

Figure 7.23 Generation of electric current

The function of each part of an alternator can be appreciated from the following sections.

Generation of an alternating current

Figure 7.24a shows a shaft-driven permanent magnet positioned in a soft iron C-shaped stationary member (stator). This stator provides an easy path for the magnetic flux between the N and S poles of the magnet.

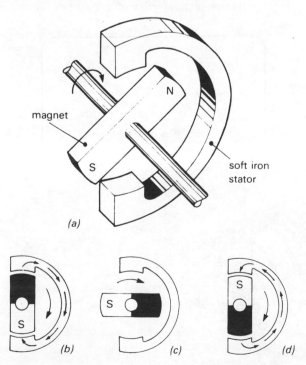

Figure 7.24 Path of magnetic flux

Figures. 7.24 b–d indicates how the magnetic lines of force (flux) vary in density and direction as the magnet is rotated.

In Figure 7.25 a voltmeter is placed across a coil of wire wound around the stator. Rotation of the magnet generates an electromotive force, which varies, as shown by the graph, with magnet position. The polarity of the magnetic flux in the stator changes as the magnet is rotated, so an alternating current (AC) is produced.

The amount of current depends on the three factors defined by Faraday: strength of magnetic field, length of conductor and speed at which magnetic field is cut. Since the only variable is the speed, the faster the magnet is rotated, the higher will be the output.

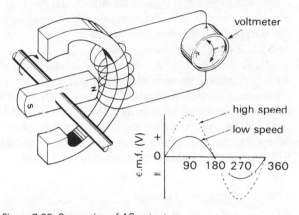

Figure 7.25 Generation of AC output

Space and weight are very important, so the alternator must be designed to give the highest possible output. One step towards improved efficiency is to use a multi-pole magnet arranged in the manner shown in Figure 7.26. In this case the magnet is placed coaxially with

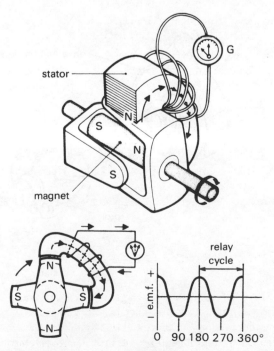

Figure 7.26 Output from a multi-pole magnet

the shaft and, by means of soft iron 'fingers', two extra poles are formed on the rotating member (rotor). This arrangement doubles the output and makes the unit more efficient.

As before, the output increases as the speed rises up to a point where the rapid changes in current flow prevent any further increase in output. This feature is advantageous because in this way the alternator protects itself from being overloaded.

Multi-phase output

To utilise more of the rotor poles, another stator winding is added in the position shown in Figure 7.27. This gives two independent outputs as shown in the graph. Stator winding B gives an output that peaks at a rotor position 45° after the output peak of winding A; the output from the two windings is 45° out of phase and this is called two phase output.

Similarly, if another stator winding is added and all three are spaced out around a multi-pole rotor, then a three-phase output is obtained (Figure 7.28). As the number of magnetic poles is increased, each individual cycle will be shorter, therefore the larger the number of AC cycles produced in one revolution of the rotor. This will produce a comparatively smooth peak output of current.

Control of magnet strength

When the engine is operating at high speed the alternator rotates rapidly and the very high electromotive force output from a permanent magnet-type alternator causes both damage to the alternator and overcharging of the battery. To overcome these problems, the permanent magnet on the rotor is replaced by an electromagnet. The use of the

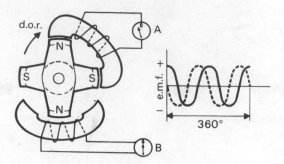

Figure 7.27 Multi-phase output

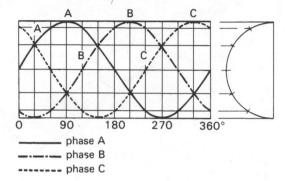

——— phase A
—·—·— phase B
-------- phase C

Figure 7.28 Three-phase output

electromagnet arrangement allows the strength of the magnetic field to be controlled by varying the current supplied to the winding; the greater the current passed to create the field, the stronger the magnet.

Figure 7.29 illustrates the components of a modern alternator that generates the electrical energy. The type shown is a three-phase, twelve-pole machine. Current is

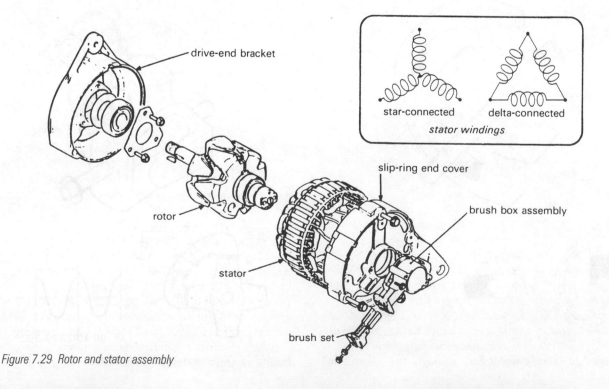

Figure 7.29 Rotor and stator assembly

delivered to the electromagnet rotor via slip rings; these are two rings of copper onto which rub two carbon brushes.

The three sets of stator windings, which are interconnected in a star or delta arrangement, have three output leads, one for each phase.

7.5.3 Rectification of alternating current to direct current

The alternating current (AC) produced by an alternator is unsuitable for battery charging because the current at the output terminals rapidly alternates from positive to negative. The current passing to either of the battery terminals would therefore also rapidly change from positive to negative and no complete positive charge could be passed to the battery positive terminal (the negative elements of the current would cancel the positive elements thus producing no charging effect at all). The output from the alternator must therefore be 'rectified' so that it becomes a direct current or DC output.

Rectification is now achieved by using a semiconductor device called a diode, which forms part of the rectifier assembly.

Semiconductors
Certain materials, such as silicon and germanium, are neither good electrical conductors nor insulators; they come in a borderline category. If semiconductor crystals are doped in a special way by adding traces of certain impurities and then arranged with other semiconductors, a range of solid-state electronic devices can be obtained. Common examples of semi-conductors are diodes and transistors.

The diode is an electronic 'one-way valve' that allows current to flow in one direction but not the other. It is represented by the symbol shown in Figure 7.30a. The arrowhead indicates the direction in which the diode freely conducts a conventional-flow current.

Note: The term 'conventional flow' is used when the current is assumed to flow from positive to negative.

Diode rectifier
Figure 7.30b shows how a diode can be used in a simple circuit to rectify AC to DC current. The one-way action of a single diode blocks the reverse current flow (negative flow) and therefore leaves only the positive flow. This provides an output called 'half-wave rectification', as shown in the graph.

The next stage is then to use four blocking diodes, set to form a bridge circuit (Figure 7.30c). With this arrangement, the four diodes not only allow the positive elements of the current to pass to the battery positive terminal, but also they allow negative elements of the current to pass to the negative battery terminal. This is, however, achieved irrespective of which way the current is flowing (polarity) through the alternator stator windings. This level of rectification is known as 'full wave rectification' as shown in Figure 7.30d.

A three-phase output from an alternator with three stator windings requires a rectifier having six output diodes arranged in the manner shown in Figure 7.31. This diode network ensures that the current output is always 'in one direction'. Irrespective of the position and direction of the current-flow arrow on the stator windings, terminal B+ will always be positive.

Battery reverse flow
When the engine is stationary (and at other times when the alternator output voltage is lower than the battery voltage) current would tend to flow from the battery to the alternator, thus discharging the battery. The one-way characteristic of the diodes in an alternator rectifier automatically prevents this.

Because the diodes prevent discharge of the battery when the alternator is not turning (engine switched off), there is no need for any cut out or switch to disconnect the battery positive terminal from the alternator. This inherent feature means that the main output terminal on the alternator is always connected directly to the positive battery terminal. It should be noted that this connection is permanently 'live' and this should be remembered when the alternator is either disconnected or removed.

7.5.4 Voltage output control

The output from an alternator must be limited to a voltage of about 14.2 V; this value equals the potential difference of a battery that is nearing its fully charged state. Ensuring that the alternator's maximum output voltage is also around 14.2 V allows it to charge at a high rate when the battery is discharged, but as the battery approaches its fully charged state, the charging rate will gradually reduce to zero.

It should, however, be remembered from Faraday's experiments, that the faster the magnetic field is cut, the greater the output. Because the alternator is driven by the engine, the faster the engine rotates, the faster the alternator rotates. This means that the magnetic fields within the alternator will be cut more quickly and higher voltage outputs will be produced. Alternator output must therefore be controlled (regulated) to ensure that overcharging of the battery does not occur, or that electrical consumers such as light bulbs are not damaged.

Alternator output is controlled by varying the current supplied to the rotor field (also part of Faraday's experiments) because lowering the current supplied to an electromagnet will reduce the strength of the magnetic field thus reducing the output generated. The regulator performs this current control function by using electronic devices in the form of diodes and transistors. These are retained in a 'micro' metal container, which is usually mounted under the alternator cover.

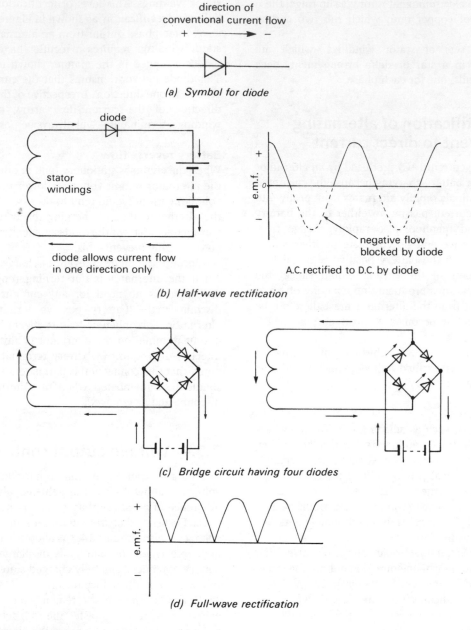

(a) *Symbol for diode*

(b) *Half-wave rectification*

(c) *Bridge circuit having four diodes*

(d) *Full-wave rectification*

Figure 7.30 *Current rectification*

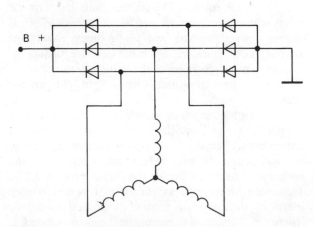

Figure 7.31 *Alternator diode arrangement*

Solid-state devices, such as diodes and transistors, are highly sensitive to heat and voltage surges, so during operation and repair, precautions need to be taken to ensure that the regulator (and rectifier pack) is protected from exposure to these conditions.

7.5.5 Alternator operation and construction

The alternator circuit shown in Figure 7.32 includes a charge-warning lamp to signal to the driver when the system is not operating. In addition to this duty, the warning lamp circuit is used initially to excite the field (initiating the rotor-winding magnetic field).

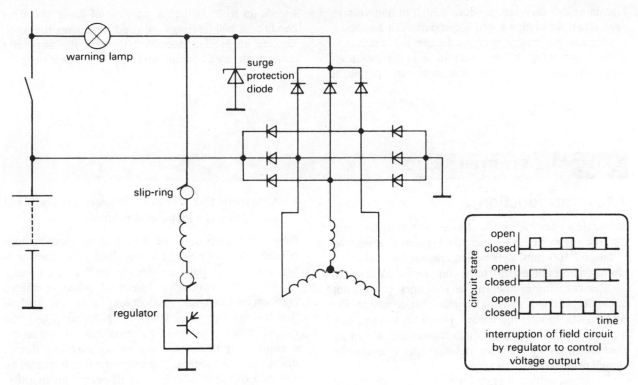

Figure 7.32 Regulator of field current surge protection

When the ignition is switched on, the small current needed to operate the warning lamp also passes through the rotor winding then through the regulator to earth. This current flow passing the rotor winding creates a weak magnetic field which is sufficient to enable the charging operation to begin when the alternator starts to rotate.

Naturally this operation will not occur if there is an open circuit because the bulb has 'blown'. Note that unless 12 V is obtained from the lead that supplies the 'IND' terminal, the alternator will not charge.

When the alternator is operating, three field diodes supply the field with a current as dictated by the regulator. As the engine speed rises from stationary, the output voltage at the field diodes also rises. The increase in output voltage reduces the current through the warning lamp circuit and causes the warning lamp to extinguish.

Surge protection diode
Breakdown of the main transistor in a regulator occurs if the alternator is charging and a fault such as a poor connection causes the output voltage to suddenly increase. To avoid damage to the electronic components, a surge protection diode is sometimes fitted between the 'IND' lead and earth. The special diode (referred to as a Zener diode) only conducts current when the surge voltage exceeds a given value.

Construction of the alternator
The construction of a modern alternator is shown in Figure 7.33. The engine crankshaft drives the alternator by a 'vee-belt' at a higher speed than the engine. An

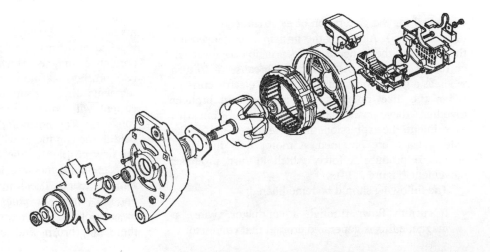

Figure 7.33 Exploded view of a modern alternator

alternator can therefore produce a high output voltage even when the engine speed is comparatively low.

Alternators require very good drive belt tension to prevent slip when a large current is being produced (high alternator load); the alternator can operate at speeds up to 15,000 rpm. In view of these operating conditions, ball bearings are used to support the rotor. Cooling air is also circulated through the alternator components by a cooling fan fixed to the rotor shaft.

7.6   THE STARTER SYSTEM

7.6.1 Introduction

To enable an internal-combustion engine to start up and run, the engine needs to be cranked (rotated) at a speed of around 100 rpm, which then enables the fuel to be atomised and the mixture to be compressed sufficiently.

The cranking of the engine was once carried out manually, using a starting handle (connected to the crankshaft), to turn the engine. However, modern cars use an electric starting system which makes use of an electrically operated starter motor to spin or crank the engine over to reach this speed.

To obtain sufficient cranking torque from the robust electric motor, a large current (amperage) is required. On a cold morning, this may be as high as 500 A although between 100 and 150 amps are more normal values for light vehicles. To carry such high amperages, suitable thick, short supply cables and a good battery capable of delivering this high current are required.

The complete system may be considered in three sections:

- electric starter motor
- starting circuit
- mechanical engagement systems.

7.6.2 Operating principles of electric starter motors

The motor converts electrical energy supplied from the battery into mechanical power. This is achieved by using an electromagnetic principle similar to that employed for the generation of electrical energy (refer to section 7.5). Although the principles employed are the same as the generator, the principle is reversed; current is passed to the motor which causes it to turn whereas a generator is turned to create electric current. When the 'like' poles of two magnets are brought together, they push each other apart. From this experiment, the expressions 'like poles repel' and 'unlike poles attract' are obtained. A motor uses the 'repel action' to produce a force, which in turn produces movement (Figure 7.34).

The following should be remembered:

- If current flows through a conductor (wire), a magnetic flux is generated around that conductor.

- A magnetic flux also exists between the north and south poles of a permanent magnet.

Note: Flux lines may be regarded as elastic bands between the two poles of the magnet; when the bands between the two poles are stretched a force is created.

When the conductor (piece of wire) is placed between the north and south poles of a magnet (such as the U-shaped magnet shown in Figure 7.34) the magnetic flux generated by the current flowing in the conductor interferes with the strong magnetic flux of the permanent magnet. The magnetic flux increases on one side of the conductor and decreases on its other side thus causing the conductor to move within the field of the permanent magnet.

By bending the conductor in the form of a loop, and placing the loop within the permanent magnet, the loop will start to rotate when current flows through the conductor (Figure 7.34, lower illustration). The movement occurs because when current flows through the loop, equal but opposing forces are applied to the magnetic flux of the permanent magnet. Carbon–copper brushes can be used to conduct the current (supplied by the battery) to the copper 'commutator' segments (two segments are shown on the illustration in Figure 7.34). The commutator segments are joined to the ends of the conductor, thus enabling current to flow around the conductor and produce the magnetic flux. The conductor loop will therefore rotate within the permanent magnet poles.

Note that when the conductor loop has partially rotated (i.e. slightly more than one quarter of a rotation from the position shown in the illustration) the magnetic field created by the loop will then not be repelled or attracted against the magnetic field of the permanent magnet. However, due to the rotation, the two brushes are now in contact with the opposite segments on the commutator, which means that the current will flow in the other direction around the conductor. The north and south poles of the magnetic field in the conductor will now be reversed and due to the new position of the loop against the poles of the permanent magnet the loop will rotate again in the same direction. Therefore, as the loop rotates and the opposing magnetic poles of the loop and permanent magnet lose their effect, the current flow is reversed in the loop (brush and commutator connections are

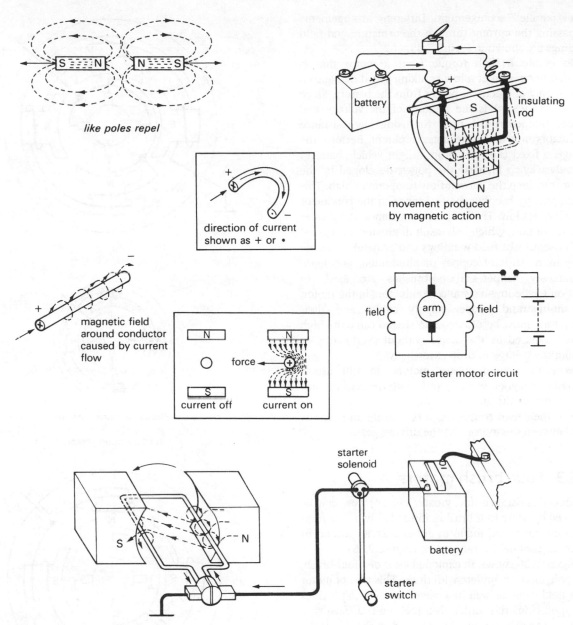

Figure 7.34 Principle of the starter motor

reversed) which causes the magnetic poles of the loop to be reversed. This means that the opposing magnetic fields now exist between the permanent magnet and the new position of the poles on the loop.

In reality, it is necessary to have more than one loop to ensure that the loops keep rotating. By adding a second loop at right angles to the first loop, a relatively smooth continuous rotation is achieved as the magnetic fields in the two loops are continuously reversed during rotation. In reality electric motors have a considerable number of conductor loops which results in high power and continuous, smooth rotation.

These loops are usually wound around a soft iron armature (or core) to concentrate the field and are joined to the various commutator segments so as to allow a current to flow to each individual loop as it passes through the densest part of the magnetic field.

Formation of the magnetic field

Although in the previous example an electromagnet formed the conductor loop, a permanent magnet was used to provide the second magnetic field. However, for many electric motors the permanent magnet is also replaced with an electromagnet, which means that two electromagnets are in use within the motor: one that forms the rotating conductor loops, and the other which is the stationary magnet.

It is common practice that the field windings (the stationary electromagnet coils or windings) and the armature windings (the rotating conductor loops), are connected in series, i.e. the current flows through each of the windings in turn. This arrangement produces a strong field because all of the current that is supplied to the motor must pass through the field windings. There is an alternative arrangement which is referred to as the 'series–parallel' arrangement. Different arrangements for passing the current through the armature and field windings are shown in Figure 7.35.

To obtain a high torque from a motor that is required to operate at a low cranking speed demands a large supply of electrical power from the battery. Since the power (watts) is the product of the voltage and current (amperes) the need for using low-resistance conductors in a motor becomes apparent. Because the voltage is fixed (i.e. 12 V from a light vehicle battery) the only way to increase the power developed by the motor is to keep the current flow (amperage) high. This is achieved by keeping the resistance in the conductor and windings low. The lower the resistance, the greater the current flow, which will result in greater wattage.

Consequently, field windings and armature coils are made from strips of copper or aluminium, and high-conductivity copper–carbon brushes are used. In addition to the low-resistance conductors in the motor, the multi-strand copper supply cables and their connectors, must be of adequate size to carry the high current required by the motor without overheating or causing the voltage to drop excessively.

Note that some starter motors do still use a permanent magnet, which significantly reduces the size and weight of the starter motor. These starter motors achieve their high torque output by using an epicyclic gear between the motor and the driving gear.

7.6.3 Four-brush motors

A reduced resistance and greater current flow can be achieved by using four brushes instead of two. The four-brush machines are made in either a series-wound or series–parallel field arrangement (Figure 7.35).

Figure 7.36 shows an exploded view of a four-brush, four-pole motor complete with drive. This type of motor has a field winding bent in a wave form, which provides four poles in the order N-S-N-S and a face-type commutator; this uses brushes situated on the side of the armature instead of the more common radial position associated with a cylindrically-shaped commutator.

7.6.4 Starter motor circuit and solenoid

Figure 7.37a shows a pictorial view of a typical cable layout for an 'inertia-type' starter motor circuit. The starter motor draws a high current when operating and therefore the cables supplying the starter motor have to be capable of carrying such high currents.

The use of a simple on/off switch situated on the dashboard would mean additional lengths of heavy-duty cable, and the switch would require exceptionally heavy-duty contacts to carry the current.

Starter circuits therefore normally use a set of heavy-duty contacts that are remote from the starter/ignition

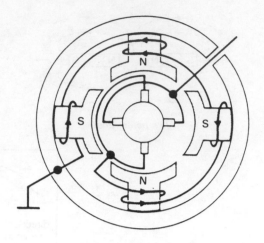

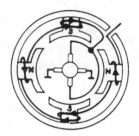

alternative construction

series-wound motor

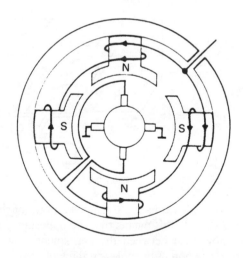

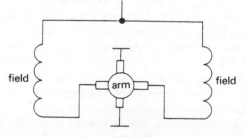

field   field

series–parallel motor

Figure 7.35 Field-winding arrangements

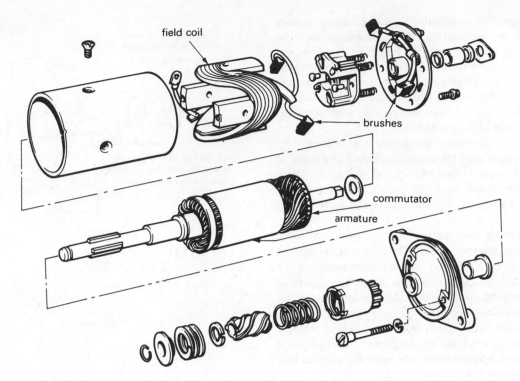

field coil

brushes

commutator

armature

Figure 7.36 A four-brush, four-pole starter motor and drive

switch; these contacts are located in a 'solenoid' assembly. The heavy-duty contacts within the solenoid are caused to close or connect in a similar manner to the contacts in a relay (refer to section 7.3.12). When the starter/ignition switch is set to the 'start' position, a small current passes from the starter switch to the solenoid. The small current is passed around a coil or winding within the solenoid, which creates a magnetic field which then causes a metal plunger to move (this is

the same principle as an electric motor, but the plunger moves in a straight line instead of rotating). The plunger is attached to the heavy-duty contacts, which means that when the plunger moves it causes the contacts to close thus connecting the battery supply to the starter motor.

The solenoid can be remotely located so that the cable between the battery and starter motor is a minimum length (as opposed to passing from the battery to the starter switch and then to the starter

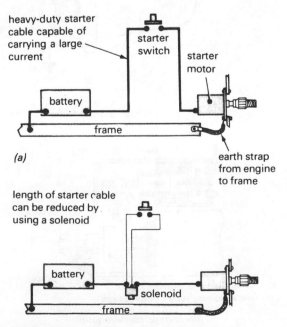

heavy-duty starter cable capable of carrying a large current

starter switch

starter motor

battery

frame

(a)

earth strap from engine to frame

length of starter cable can be reduced by using a solenoid

battery

solenoid

frame

(b) Solenoid – a remote-controlled switch

Figure 7.37 Starter motor circuits

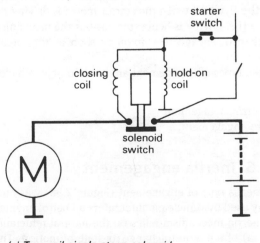

starter switch

closing coil

hold-on coil

solenoid switch

M

(c) Two-coil single-stage solenoid

motor). Note that solenoids on modern stator motors form part of the starter motor assembly. Because voltage drop increases with the length of the cable, the use of the shortest possible cable for the starter motor means that the voltage drop is kept to a minimum, thus ensuring that the current and voltage available for the starter motor are as high as possible (the potential difference is as high as possible).

The exact operation of a solenoid is as follows:

Switching of the high current is achieved by a pair of heavy-duty copper contacts in the solenoid. These contacts are closed by a low-current winding in the solenoid, energized by the starter/ignition switch (Figure 7.37b).

The solenoid has two windings: a closing coil and a hold-on coil (Figure 7.37c). These are connected in parallel with each other so they both operate when the remote switch is closed. When the motor is in operation only the hold-on coil is in use; this feature reduces the solenoid operating current.

The audible click given from the solenoid when it operates is a useful aid for diagnosis; for example, a repeated clicking sound from the solenoid suggests that the hold-on coil is defective.

7.6.5 Starter engagement with the engine

A low gear ratio between the starter motor and the engine enables sufficient torque to be developed to turn the crankshaft. This ratio is obtained by using a very small gear on the motor (referred to as the pinion) to drive a large gear (referred to as the ring gear) formed on the circumference of the engine flywheel.

Permanent engagement of the pinion causes the armature to over-speed when the engine is running, so a mechanism is used to ensure that the pinion engages with the flywheel when the starter motor is driving the engine (i.e. engine is being started) but the mechanism will then disengage the pinion as soon as the engine starts.

Two types of engagement are used on light vehicles; they are:

- inertia engagement
- pre-engagement.

7.6.6 Inertia engagement

The inertia type of engagement (Figure 7.38) was once widely used by vehicle manufacturers on petrol engines. The inertia mechanism relies on the natural reluctance (inertia) of a pinion to change its state of motion. This feature is utilized to move the pinion so that it engages with the teeth of the flywheel when the starter motor armature starts to rotate.

The pinion is mounted on a helix, which is splined to the motor armature. Sudden rotational movement of the

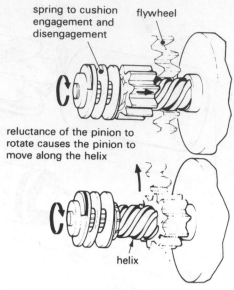

inertia engagement

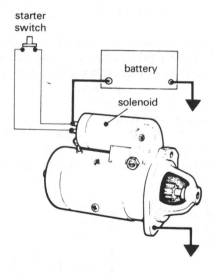

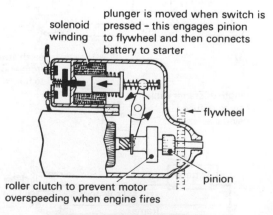

pre-engage starter motor

Figure 7.38 Starter motor engagement systems

armature rotates the helix, but owing to its inertia, the pinion tries to remain stationary; this causes the pinion to slide along the helix and engage with the flywheel teeth. A 'lead-in' (chamfer) is present on both the pinion and flywheel teeth to aid this initial engagement.

When the engine fires (starts) the increase in engine speed spins the pinion along the helix and causes it to disengage from the teeth of the flywheel.

The shock at the instant of engagement and disengagement is severe, so a large spring is fitted adjacent to the helix to act as a cushion.

One routine maintenance requirement of the inertia system was to ensure that the helix remained clean. Dirt, oil and grease as well as dust from the clutch can collect on the helix and prevents smooth or proper action of the pinion on the helix. Special types of lubricant were used for the pinion and helix but if unavailable, the helix should be left in a dry state after cleaning.

7.6.7 Pre-engagement

The pre-engagement arrangement is used with both petrol and diesel engines and is now the preferred type. The change from the inertia drive to a pre-engaged drive on petrol engines was due to the difficulty of maintaining pinion engagement with an inertia drive when the engine 'part-fires' during the cranking period.

The use of the pre-engagement drive starter motor takes into account the starting requirements of a compression ignition (diesel engine) and of the modern spark ignition petrol engine, these include:

- **Component inertia** – considerable torque is needed to rotate the crankshaft initially and accelerate it to the cranking speed.

- **Cranking speed** – the cranking speed of a diesel engine needs to be higher than that of a petrol engine to initiate combustion.

- **High compression pressure** – the compression ratio of a diesel engine and a modern petrol engine are high, resulting in a high cranking torque and an irregular engine speed during cranking.

Figure 7.39 shows constructional details of a pre-engaged-type starter motor.

A solenoid plunger is connected to an operating lever, which is pivoted at its centre to the casing. The lower end of the lever is forked to engage with a guide ring. The ring acts against a unidirectional roller clutch and pinion.

Helical splines, formed on the armature shaft, engage with the driving part of the unidirectional clutch. These splines cause the pinion to rotate slightly when the clutch and pinion are moved axially. A strong return spring in the solenoid retains the lever and pinion in the disengaged position.

Operation of a pre-engaged starter motor

When the starter switch is operated, the two-coil solenoid windings become energized and the plunger is drawn into the core.

The initial movement of the solenoid causes the lower end of the operating lever to move the guide ring and pinion assembly towards the flywheel teeth. This movement, aided by the slight rotation of the pinion, normally provides full engagement of the pinion and flywheel gears.

After this initial action, additional travel of the solenoid plunger causes the main contacts within the solenoid to close, connecting the battery positive terminal to the starter motor.

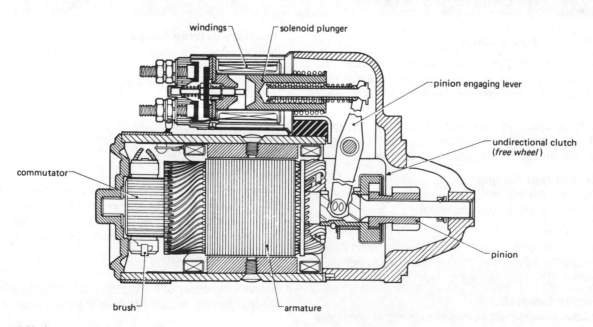

Figure 7.39 A pre-engaged starter motor

The motor starts to rotate. The rotation of the armature is transmitted to the unidirectional clutch and pinion by helical splines.

Sometimes the initial movement causes the pinion teeth to butt against the flywheel teeth; as a result engagement is prevented. If this occurs, a spring in the linkage flexes and allows the solenoid plunger sufficient movement to close the main contacts. As soon as the armature and pinion start to rotate, the teeth slip into mesh and the spring pushes the pinion to its driving position.

After the engine has started, the pinion speed will exceed the armature speed. If the motor is still in use, the rollers in the unidirectional clutch will unlock and the clutch will slip to protect the motor.

Release of the starter switch de-energizes the solenoid and allows the return spring to open the switch contacts. The opening of the electrical contacts occurs prior to the disengagement of the pinion and so avoids over-speeding of the motor. Further movement of the solenoid plunger causes the operating lever to withdraw the pinion fully from the flywheel.

7.6.8 Reduction-type starter motor

Many petrol engines are today fitted with a very compact, light-weight, reduction-type starter motor (Figure 7.40). The reduction-type starter motor is fitted with a high-speed motor, a set of reduction gears together with other conventional pre-engaged starter motor components, i.e. a unidirectional clutch and pinion.

The motor rotates at a much higher speed than the conventional type of pre-engaged starter motor. The use of the reduction gears reduces the speed of the pinion by approximately three times that of the motor.

The use of a high-speed motor increases the torque of the motor, allowing the engine to rotate at a greater rate from rest, thus improving the engine's ability to start. Note that the solenoid acts directly on the pinion, pushing the pinion into the flywheel ring gear.

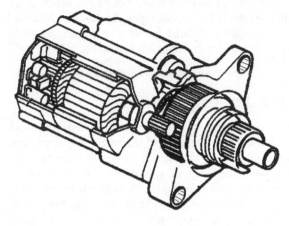

Figure 7.40 A reduction-type starter motor

7.7   THE LIGHTING SYSTEM

7.7.1 Introduction

Many types of lights are required to meet the regulations set by countries in which the vehicle is sold. Therefore, the modern vehicle is fitted with many different types of lights for safety and for driver/passenger comfort and convenience. Typically, each of these lights is grouped in one of a set of electrical circuits, which include the following:

Side and rear lamps
Including lamps for the number plate, glove compartment and instrument panel.

Headlamps
Including two sets of lamps, a 'dip beam' to avoid dazzle to oncoming drivers and a 'main beam' set to provide a powerful light while driving in dark conditions.

Rear fog lamp(s)
Used for 'guarding' the rear of the vehicle in conditions of poor visibility, e.g. fog, snow etc.

Auxiliary driving lamps
Including front fog lamps which provide additional light to the driver in adverse driving conditions (usually mounted below the front bumper).

Reversing lamps
Providing an indication to other road users that the vehicle is reversing while providing some light to aid the driver when reversing.

Brake lights
To warn following drivers that the vehicle is slowing down. An additional 'third' or centre brake light is now fitted to many vehicles to provide an additional warning to drivers when the vehicle is slowing down.

Directional indicators
Provide an indication to other road users in which direction the driver of the vehicle is intending to travel. The indictors are required to flash at a given rate.

Hazard warning lights

All of the indictors flash simultaneously to warn other road users of the impending danger of a parked vehicle (usually used when the vehicle has broken down). The warning lights must operate with the ignition in the off position.

Instrument panel lights

For illuminating the instrumentation and additional fascia-mounted components during dark conditions. The panel lights are normally connected so they illuminate whenever the sidelights are switched on.

7.7.2 Circuit arrangement

A very simple light circuit consists of the battery, a switch and a lamp. When a single switch controls more than one lamp, the lamps are connected in parallel. Connecting the lamps in parallel ensures that if one lamp fails, the remaining lamps remain illuminated (refer to sections 7.3.5 and 7.3.6).

To reduce the length of cable used, most lighting circuits use an earth return layout.

Note: Good, clean connections are required at the numerous body earth connection points. A 'dirty'

connection (i.e. poor earth) causes a high resistance. The high resistance reduces the current flow through the lamp circuit, which results in a dimmer light.

7.7.3 Circuit diagrams

Circuit diagrams shown in workshop manuals are normally in a compact schematic form. The use of this format makes the wiring diagram simpler to follow and understand the operation of the circuit. Figure 7.41 shows a simplified lighting circuit.

The parallel light circuit has lamps controlled by three switches, 1, 2 and 3:

- Switch 1 operates the side and rear lamps. It also supplies switch 2.

- Switch 2 operates the headlamps, and supplies switch 3.

- Switch 3 distributes the current to either the main beam or the dip-beam headlamp bulbs.

Note that there are established 'conventions' or standards, for symbols when creating wiring diagrams.

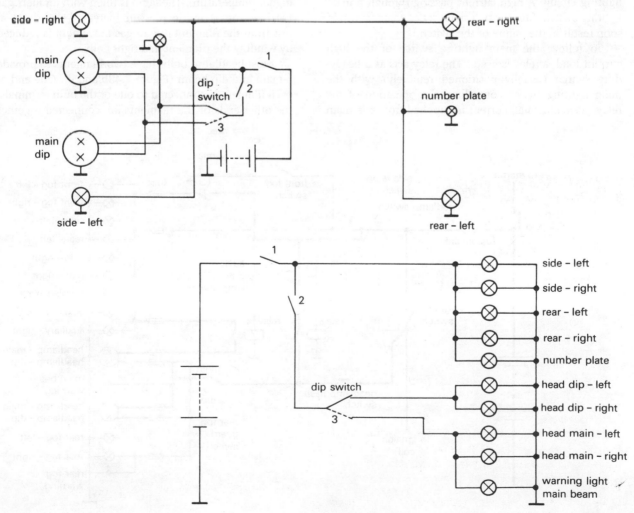

Figure 7.41 A lighting circuit simplified

In general these conventions are followed by vehicle manufacturers, but some diagrams may be created in specific formats that are developed by the manufacturers or the publishers of diagrams.

It is therefore necessary to refer to any additional information that is supplied with the diagrams that may indicate the meanings of symbols, etc.

Circuit protection (refer to section 7.3.10)

A single fuse, mounted in the main supply cable, protects a circuit in the event of a short circuit. However, the use of a single fuse to protect the entire external lighting circuit would result in the total loss of illumination if the fuse were to fail. This is a dangerous situation when the vehicle is travelling at speed along a dark road.

To avoid this danger, manufacturers usually fit separate fuses to protect each light circuit. Figure 7.42 shows a lighting system which incorporates a series of fuses.

Relay control (refer to section 7.3.12)

The use of brighter headlamps requires higher wattage bulbs, which in turn increases the current through the lighting circuit. A high current passing through a main lighting switch, fitted with a small set of contacts would soon result in the failure of the switch.

To relieve the main lighting switch of the high current load, a relay is used. The relay acts as a heavy-duty switch (usually positioned remotely) with the main lighting switch controlling the operation of the relay. When a small current is supplied from the main lighting switch to the relay, the relay switches on the high current and the headlamps function.

7.7.4 Filament lamps

Side lamp bulbs

The main details of a single centre contact (SCC) side lamp bulb are shown in Figure 7.43a. Enclosed in a glass container is a helically wound tungsten filament. The filament is held by two support wires, one attached to an insulated contact in a brass cup (supply) and the other soldered to the cap to form an earth connection. A low-wattage vacuum bulb of the type shown has the air removed to reduce heat loss and prevent oxidation of the filament. It is secured in its holder by a brass bayonet cap (BC). Alternative methods of bulb fitment are:

- miniature screw cap
- miniature edison screw (MES)
- capless-type bulb.

Headlamp bulbs

Driving lamps produce a brighter light and therefore the filaments of such lamps are made to operate at a much higher temperature. The lamp is filled with an inert gas (such as argon) and its pressure increased slightly. Heat loss from the filament due to gas movement is reduced by winding the filament in a tight helix.

Most headlamp bulbs have two filaments to provide a main and dip beam (Figure 7.43b and c). One end of each filament is connected to one of the bulb terminals, the other ends of the filaments are connected together

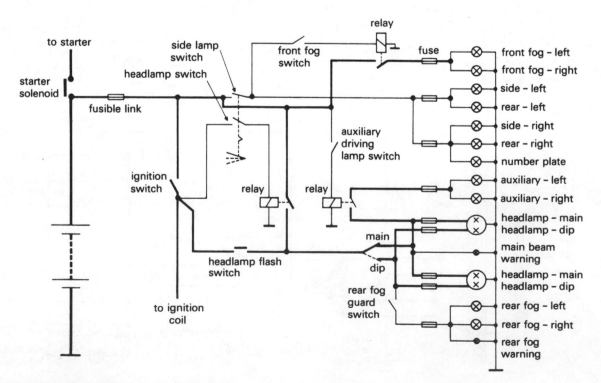

Figure 7.42 A lighting circuit incorporating fuse and relays

and then to the earth terminal on the bulb. With this type of dual filament bulb, the bulb fitting is usually designed so that the bulb will only fit into the holder in a specific way, this prevents incorrect fitment and therefore incorrect illumination of main and dip beams.

Tungsten–halogen bulbs

A tungsten–halogen bulb produces a high light output. Many headlamps are fitted with this type of bulb, which is also referred to as quartz–halogen bulb (Figure 7.43d). Quartz is used instead of glass and by filling the lamp with halogen gas, vaporization of the filament, which leads to blackening of the glass and filament

erosion, is reduced. Another advantage of this type is that its more compact form allows more precise focusing.

When replacing any bulb, and especially a tungsten–halogen type, a clean cloth should be used to avoid touching the glass of the bulb. Touching the glass of the bulb can lead to premature failure.

Sealed beam lamps

Accurate location of the filament at the focal point, as well as elimination of dirt and moisture on the reflector, are both achieved with a sealed beam lamp unit (Figure 7.44).

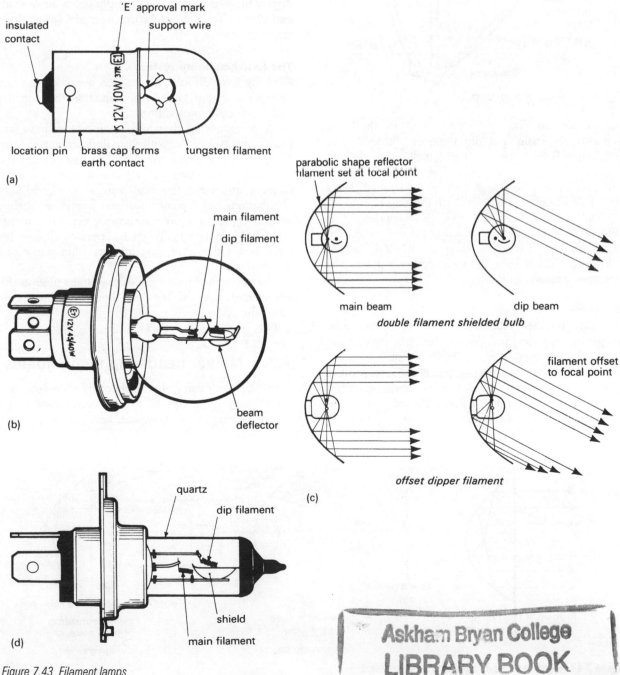

Figure 7.43 Filament lamps

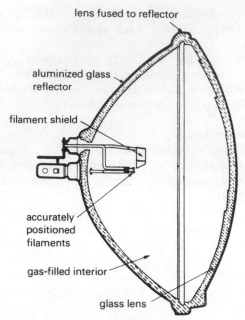

Figure 7.44 A sealed beam lamp unit

An aluminized glass reflector, fused to the lens, supports the main and dip tungsten filaments; the whole unit is filled with an inert gas. Because the bulb has no independent glass envelope, tungsten deposits are spread over a very large area, so the light efficiency of a sealed beam unit remains high for longer.

The sealed beam unit has disadvantages; it is difficult to manufacture a sealed beam unit to suit the body contours, it is costly to replace when a filament fails, and sudden light failure occurs when the lens becomes cracked.

Reflector

A highly polished aluminized reflector of parabolic shape concentrates and directs the light rays in the required direction (i.e. dipped or main beam). Positioning the main beam filament at the focal point of the reflector gives parallel rays and maximum illumination (Figure 7.45). This is achieved by siting the filament of the bulb accurately.

Some vehicles use a multi-segment reflector with several different focal lengths moulded together to form the light unit. These 'homofocular' plastic reflectors are very narrow, which allows them to blend in with the body contour.

Lens

A glass lens, consisting of several prismatic block sections, distributes the light to obtain the required illumination. The design of the lens pattern attempts to achieve good illumination for both main and dip positions; a concentrated, long-range illumination for the main beam, and a wide spread of light distributed just in front of the vehicle for the dip beam.

Regulations insist that to avoid dazzling oncoming drivers the lens must deflect the dip beam downwards and also offset it towards the nearside (away from oncoming cars).

The four-headlamp system

Optically it is difficult to produce a single lens and reflector unit that gives an illumination that satisfies both main and dip conditions.

To overcome this drawback some vehicles have four headlamps: two for long-distance illumination and two for lighting the area immediately in front of the car. Each one of the outer lamps has two filaments, a dip filament situated at the focal point to give good light distribution, and a second filament positioned slightly away from the focal point to provide near-illumination for main-beam lighting. When the lamps are dipped, the inner lamps that give long distance illumination are switched off.

For accommodation reasons the lamps used in this arrangement are smaller than those used on a two-headlamp system.

7.7.5 Newer headlamp technologies

With developments in technology, design and manufacturing processes, it has been possible for engineers, aided by computer design, to develop

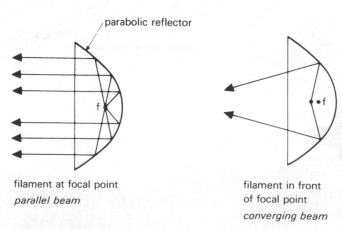
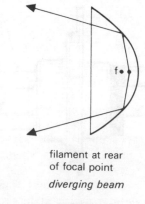

Figure 7.45 Headlamp filament position

headlamps that no longer require a lens to deflect the light source to the road surface when used as dipped headlights.

The reflector of many headlamps is geometrically designed and divided up into many complex segments; each segment deflects the light source onto a different section of the road surface. It is therefore possible to use the surface of the reflector to deflect the output from the bulb for dipped beam purposes.

The headlamp cover is generally made from a clear plastic material which can be made to follow the body contours, allowing the vehicle manufacturer to design the front section of the vehicle without having to compromise the design of the vehicle to accommodate the headlamps.

The output of light from this type of headlamp is unrestricted and therefore brighter than a headlamp fitted with a conventional reflector and lens. This headlamp design is widely used for motor cars.

Figure 7.46 Modern headlamp with a geometric type reflector

High intensity discharge headlamps (HIDs)

Although the tungsten–halogen bulb provides an improved light compared with an ordinary tungsten filament bulb, manufacturers are constantly researching new technologies and materials to improve the efficiency and light output of headlamps. Increasing the light output reduces the driver's tiredness and stress during dark driving conditions, and hazards in front of the vehicle are generally recognized more quickly with a brighter beam.

Powerful high intensity discharge (HID) headlamps are now being fitted to the dipped beam headlamp on many vehicles, ranging from medium-sized cars to commercial vehicles.

Conventional headlamps operate by passing a current through a tungsten filament; the filament then heats up to a very high temperature and produces light. HID (high intensity discharge) headlamps function by creating an electrical arc between two electrodes within a capsule containing a gas, typically xenon. The light that the HID unit produces is twice as intense as that of a tungsten–halogen bulb, and is of a higher 'colour temperature', producing a whiter colour, similar to that of daylight.

Tungsten–halogen bulbs make use of the 12 V supply; the current flow in the circuit, depending on the

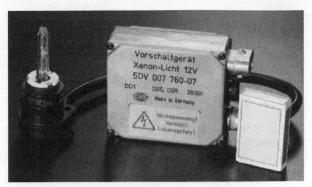

Figure 7.47 Xenon HID headlamps

wattage of the bulb, is approximately 10 A. However, the voltage required to initiate the arc between the two capsule electrodes of a HID lamp is approximately 25,000 V and a current flow of approximately 20 A is required. Once the arc is initiated, the voltage requirement reduces to approximately 75–80 V with a reduced current flow of only 3.5 A. To initiate and maintain the electric arc within the xenon capsule, an electronic control unit incorporating an electronic ballast unit produces the required voltage by effectively converting the original 12 V supply.

A conventional filament bulb suddenly fails when the filament breaks, normally due to excessive shocks, gas leaking from the bulb or burning of the filament. The HID lamp creates light by producing an arc, and therefore the life expectancy with the xenon capsule is considerably longer than that compared to a filament bulb. When the xenon capsule begins to fail, the light emitted gradually decays over a period of time allowing its replacement before complete failure of the headlamp.

Note: To prevent personal injury due to the high voltages and current levels created in a HID system, the technician should always ensure that all the necessary safety precautions, as detailed by the manufacturer, are taken into account before working on the system.

A disadvantage of the HID system is the additional glare that the xenon capsule produces due to the intense light emitted. Vehicles fitted with a HID system normally also use a headlamp self-levelling system, which maintains the headlamps at the correct level. Sensors are fitted between the suspension and the body to monitor the height of the body and the information is passed to an ECU, which alters the alignment of the headlamp beam setting using motors fitted to each headlamp.

7.7.6 Light-emitting diode (LED) lights

At the time of writing, LED light assemblies are being used for rear lights and other general lighting on the vehicle. However, LED-based headlights are due to be fitted to vehicles soon.

The LED system effectively combines a very large number of LED lights in one unit to achieve the total required light output. Book 2 provides additional information on these light systems.

7.7.7 Lamp marking

Regulations state that all bulbs, as well as other lighting components used on a vehicle, must be marked with the letter 'E' and a number that identifies the country where approval was given. The E mark indicates that the component conforms to the EU standard specified for a given application.

7.7.8 Additional vehicle lighting

Other lighting and auxiliary electrical equipment are discussed in section 7.8. However, side and rear lights also form part of the main lighting system.

Because there is not the same requirement for a high light output from the side and rear lights, (as is the case for the headlights) they generally use the less expensive filament-type bulbs.

Different wattage bulbs are used for side-light, rear-light and brake-light bulbs so care should be taken when fitting replacement units. Regulations apply to the wattage of many bulbs, which again means that checks should be made to ensure that the correct bulbs are fitted.

7.8	AUXILIARY LIGHTING AND EQUIPMENT

7.8.1 Introduction

The modern motor vehicle contains many items of electrically and electronically controlled equipment, some of which have already been described in this book. Other additional systems and components are classed as auxiliary equipment.

History shows that what was once a non-essential item becomes a statutory requirement, e.g. warning horns, windscreen wipers and washers, directional indicators and brake lamps. Nowadays all new vehicles must be fitted with these systems, and statutory regulations, framed by the EU, govern the construction and method of operation.

With advances in technology and customer demand, the vehicle manufacturer fits more and more electrical equipment to the vehicle. Some of these systems may be regarded as desirable but non-essential, whereas other items must be fitted to meet statutory requirements.

Auxiliary equipment fitted on a modern vehicle includes:

Horn
The law requires an audible warning device which emits a continuous note that is neither too loud nor harsh in sound.

Windscreen wipers
The law requires windscreen wipers that operate effectively.

Windscreen washers
The law requires a screen washer to be fitted to clean the driver's side of the windscreen.

Directional indicators
The law requires that three, coloured signal lamps are fitted in approved positions on *each* side of the vehicle, together with a tell-tale indicator in the instrument panel. The rating of each lamp is specified together with the flashing rate (60–120 flashes per minute).

Brake lamp
The law requires the fitting of a lamp which automatically lights up when the brake is applied.

Reversing lamp
The law states that no more than two white lamps may be used, the wattage of each lamp not being greater than 24 W. Regulations also cover the switching requirements of such lamps.

Note: Lighting regulations are revised periodically, and vary from one country to another, so when a bulb, or a lamp component is renewed, it is necessary to fit the type recommended by the manufacturer to comply with your local regulations.

Instrumentation systems
These include: fuel level, coolant temperature, and vehicle condition monitoring arrangements for detecting system faults such as failure warning lights.

Other auxiliary electrical equipment fitted to a vehicle may include:

- clock
- interior and courtesy lights
- fan and heater motor, air condition and climate control
- rear and front window heaters/demisters
- window winding motors
- central door locking and alarm/immobiliser systems
- in-car entertainment (ICE) systems
- door mirror adjustment and mirror heating systems
- sunroof control motors
- satellite navigation systems
- telephone systems
- seat position motors.

Most auxiliary systems are fused, either in groups or individually. Motor cars use a large number of fused circuits to provide maximum protection and minimum loss of component or system operation when a single fuse 'blows'. Normally the fuses, or other forms of circuit breaker, are mounted together on one or more fuse panels.

A circuit layout showing some of the main items of auxiliary equipment is shown in simplified form in Figure 7.48, together with typical fuse ratings. It will be

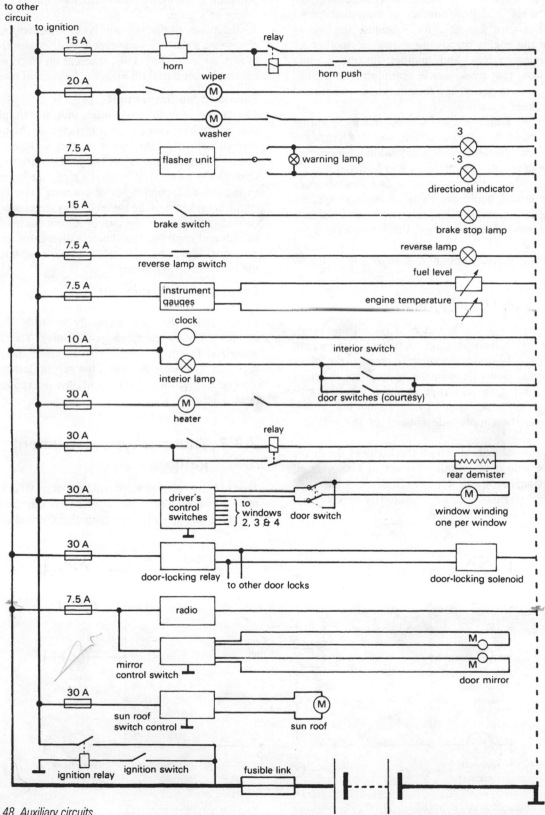

Figure 7.48 Auxiliary circuits

seen that each item of auxiliary equipment has its own individual circuit.

It is impossible for the vehicle manufacturer to publish the entire electrical system on one wiring diagram due to the large number of items of electrical equipment fitted to a modern vehicle. Instead, manufacturers publish a number of individual circuit wiring diagrams showing, for example, the wiring layout of the engine management system, another for the charging system, and another for the starting system. Note that most vehicle manufacturers publish this type of information in a format that can be viewed on a computer screen.

Whenever a fault has to be pin-pointed, the wiring diagram shows the interconnection, and location, of the various circuit elements. This information is necessary if the cause of a particular problem is to be diagnosed.

Due to the large subject area and limited space available in this book, the study of auxiliary systems will only provide information on simple instrumentation. For additional information on other systems, please refer to the companion book published in this series, *Fundamentals of Automotive Electronics*.

7.8.2 Directional indicators

Figure 7.49 shows the layout of a typical directional indicator circuit, incorporating the hazard warning light circuit. When the indicator switch is moved to the left or right, current flows through the appropriate indicator lamp circuit. Regular interruption of the current to give a flashing light is performed by the flasher unit; this is situated on the supply side (fused) of the indicator switch.

If a vehicle breaks down on the highway the driver should be able to warn other drivers by arranging all the directional indicator lamps to flash simultaneously. This hazard warning circuit is activated by an additional switch controlled by the driver.

Various types of flasher unit have been used to control the flashing of indicators: thermal, capacitor and electronic. These units all have three electrical connections: input, output and earth. A flasher unit has to meet international standards, which include the provision of an audible and visual system to signal the failure of a lamp.

Behaviour of the 'tell-tale' lamp varies with the type of system; a thermal vane-type flasher causes the lamp to stay on if one bulb fails, whereas an electronic type causes the lamp to flash at twice the normal rate.

Thermal-type flasher unit
The vane-type or thermal flasher unit, is a simple, low-cost unit which consists of a rectangular, snap-action, spring-steel strip. Operation of the indicator switch instantly activates the signal lamps. The current passing through the metal strip heats the strip causing the strip to expand and open a set of contacts. The indicator circuit is broken and the signal lights extinguish. A short time after this action, the lack of current causes the strip to cool and contract; the contacts then close again and the signal lights illuminate. The cycle is repeated until the indicator switch is turned off.

Electronic-type flasher unit
All cars today are fitted with an electronic type of flasher unit. The unit normally controls the lamp current with an electromagnetic relay. The relay is energized by an electronic circuit, which may use a capacitor as a timer to control the rate of flashing.

The flasher unit also controls the operation of the hazard lights.

7.8.3 Thermal-type instrument gauges

Thermal-type gauges were used on most vehicles until more advanced electronic systems were developed. The principles of operation for both the thermal-type fuel

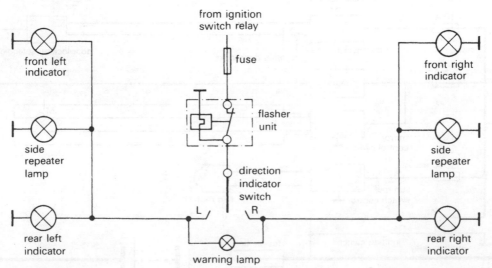

Figure 7.49 The indicator/hazard lamp circuit

gauge and temperature gauge are very similar. Gauge circuits are supplied with a constant voltage from a voltage stabilizer. The gauge indicators use the bending action of a bimetallic strip when it is heated.

Note: A bimetallic strip is a piece of metal made by laminating two different types of metal together, e.g. brass and steel. When the strip is heated, one metal expands at a greater rate than the other, so the strip bends, with the metal that expands at a greater rate on the outside.

Fuel gauge

In the case of the fuel gauge, the bimetallic strip has a winding of fine wire around it. When an electric current is passed through the winding it heats the bimetallic strip which then bends (Figure 7.50).

The amount that the strip bends depends on the current that flows through the heating coil; the greater the current, the greater the bending action.

Assuming that the voltage stabilizer provides a constant voltage to the gauge, the earth path from the gauge then passes through a variable resistor (potentiometer) through to the earth point.

The resistance of the potentiometer varies when a movable contact on the resistance track is moved (the same action is used on many volume controls and light dimmers). If the movable contact is connected to a float assembly in the fuel tank, when the fuel level changes, the float will rise and fall thus changing the resistance of the potentiometer. The change in resistance causes a change in the current flow which is sensed by the fuel gauge thus altering the position of the indicator needle on the gauge.

The lower the sender resistance the greater the electrical current flow in the fuel gauge circuit, which results in a larger deflection of the fuel gauge needle (gauge shows full). As the fuel is used, the resistance of the sender unit gradually increases, reducing the current flow through the circuit, which results in a smaller deflection of the gauge needle (gauge shows empty).

A false reading will occur unless the voltage applied to the circuit is kept constant; this is the duty of the voltage stabilizer. Modern vehicles are fitted with an electronic type of voltage stabilizer. Older vehicles had a bimetallic type of voltage stabilizer.

Note: Care must be taken to avoid an explosion when testing the operation of the system with the sensor. Checking the sensor requires its removal from the fuel tank. It is highly dangerous to generate sparks in an atmosphere where both oxygen and petrol vapour are present.

Engine temperature gauge

The principle of a conventional thermal-type gauge used to indicate engine temperature is similar to that used to indicate the contents of the fuel tank. Because the gauge reading is affected by supply voltage to the circuit, the supply voltage must be stabilized in the same way. In many cases, the same voltage stabilizer can be used.

The main difference in operation between the fuel gauge system and the engine temperature system is the type of resistance used to affect the flow of current.

The engine temperature sensor is the resistance used in this system. The temperature sensor is generally situated in the coolant system, on the engine side of the thermostat. The sensor construction includes a piece of semiconductor material which has the characteristic of

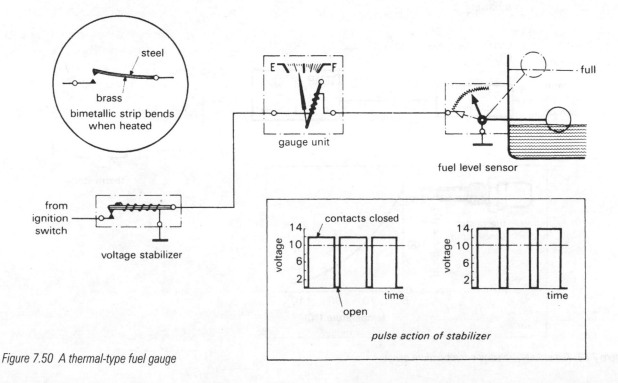

Figure 7.50 A thermal-type fuel gauge

changing its resistance with changes in temperature. This type of semiconductor is referred to as a 'thermistor' (a combination of the words thermal and resistor).

This thermistor varies its resistance in the opposite way to most metals: when the temperature of the thermistor increases, its resistance decreases. This characteristic is referred to as a 'negative temperature coefficient' (NTC).

The thermistor's NTC of resistance causes the resistance to vary from approximately 500 Ω at 30°C down to 20 Ω at 115°C.

On one end of the temperature sensor is a brass bulb. When the sensor is located on the engine (usually by screwing into a convenient part of the cylinder head adjacent to a coolant water passage), the brass bulb is in contact with the coolant and is therefore able to transfer the heat of the coolant to the thermistor.

The circuit for a bimetallic indicator gauge and thermistor is shown in Figure 7.51. As is the case with the fuel gauge system, the sensing resistance forms part of the earth circuit. In the case of the coolant temperature sensor, the current must flow through the thermistor to reach earth.

When the thermistor resistance is high, less electrical current will flow in the temperature gauge circuit, which results in a small deflection of the gauge needle (gauge shows cold). As the engine temperature increases, the resistance of the thermistor gradually decreases thus increasing the current flow through the circuit. The increase in current flow causes the bimetallic strip to heat up and therefore begin to bend, which results in a larger deflection of the gauge needle (gauge shows hot).

Note: Damage will occur if the thermistor is connected directly to a battery.

7.8.4 Electronic gauge systems

Many modern vehicles are fitted with an electronic control unit (ECU), which controls the operation of the gauges together with other instrumentation. The ECU monitors the information received from the various sensors, then controls the appropriate gauge from the relevant sensor signal.

During vehicle movement, the fuel is constantly surging around the fuel tank. A float will therefore constantly move up and down with the movement of the fuel which can result in continuous movement of the fuel gauge needle. However, most electronically-controlled fuel gauge systems dampen out the constantly varying fuel gauge sender signal. The ECU averages out the sensor signal over a short period of time, providing the driver with a steady gauge reading.

From the information received from the sensor signals, the ECU can also control the operation of a warning lamp in the instrument cluster to alert the driver to an impending danger (e.g. low fuel or high engine temperature.)

Note that many gauges and indicators for the driver are of the digital display type. Although the visual presentation to the driver is obviously different from the traditional analogue moving needle gauges, and the way in which the display is changed or controlled is also different, the principle of operation remains the same.

The electrical system requires routine maintenance to ensure that the electrical energy required by the vehicle systems (ignition, fuel, lighting etc.) is available at all times, and that the electrical systems are functioning correctly to meet the relevant regulations.

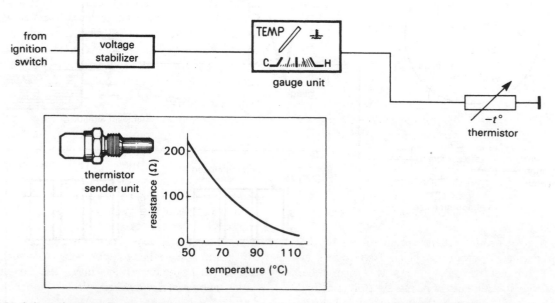

Figure 7.51 A thermal-type engine temperature gauge

7.9   ELECTRICAL SYSTEMS – ROUTINE MAINTENANCE

7.9.1 Batteries

The battery supplies electrical energy to the electrical components when the output from the generator is low, (engine not running or running slowly. It is therefore necessary to check the condition of the battery periodically to ensure that it can retain the stored energy and to allow the battery to be recharged.

To prevent the battery from moving around when the vehicle is being driven, it should be retained securely within the battery compartment by a clamp or other means. The battery case should be checked for cracks and leakage of electrolyte. The leakage of electrolyte will normally be indicated by corrosion near to the battery carrier and a low level of electrolyte in the battery. Because the electrolyte is corrosive, always clean corrosion from the bodywork of the vehicle, and use suitable materials to return the bodywork to its original state.

The battery terminals should be clean because dirty or corroded battery terminals can cause a high resistance and prevent the full available voltage and current being delivered to the electrical systems. If necessary, clean the terminals with neutralizing agent such sodium bicarbonate, together with a wire brush. Ensure the battery cables are securely fastened to the terminals.

The level of electrolyte in the battery should be checked (although this is not possible on many modern batteries). The casing of many batteries is made from a translucent plastic; the level of electrolyte in each cell can therefore easily be seen through the casing. If the battery has a non-translucent casing, it is necessary to remove the vent plug for each cell and check the electrolyte level through each hole. Ensure that the level of electrolyte in each cell is at the maximum.

Note: The electrolyte contains sulphuric acid. The acid can cause serious burns if contacting the body. If electrolyte contacts the skin, wash off immediately using water. If acid contacts the eyes, wash thoroughly for several minutes and seek urgent medical assistance.

If the electrolyte is low, it is necessary to add distilled water to top up the electrolyte to the correct level. If the level of electrolyte is too high, it can cause the electrolyte to overflow and corrode metal parts such as the battery terminals and bodywork of the vehicle.

Note: Always use distilled water to top up the electrolyte, never use water from a tap (sink or similar). The impurities that ordinary tap water contains will contaminate the plates and reduce the performance of the battery.

On those batteries where access to the cells is possible, the state of charge can be checked with the aid of a hydrometer (Figure 7.52). The hydrometer measures the specific gravity of the electrolyte. A high specific gravity (1.290) indicates a fully charged battery

while a low specific gravity (0.120) indicates a discharged battery. If the reading is low it will be necessary to recharge the battery and recheck the reading. Note that specific gravity cannot be checked directly after charging a battery or topping up a battery with distilled water, allow the battery to stand for a short time before the check is carried out.

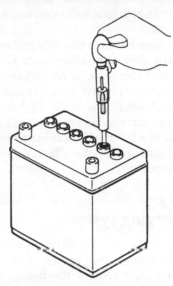

Figure 7.52 Checking the state of battery charge with a hydrometer

Disconnecting battery terminals

If it is necessary to remove the battery cables from the battery terminals, always disconnect the negative (earth) cable before the positive cable. When refitting the battery cables to the battery terminals, refit the positive cable first and then the negative cable.

If the positive cable were to be removed first and a metal tool (e.g. a spanner) were to accidentally touch the body of the vehicle while in contact with the terminal, a short circuit would be made by the spanner and excessive sparks would occur which could cause personal injury as well as damage to the vehicle systems.

Important note

On many modern vehicles, disconnecting the battery can have a number of implications. An example is where a radio or in-car entertainment system is provided with an anti-theft device; in such cases, when the battery is re-connected it may be necessary to enter a code before the radio can be used.

It is also possible that the vehicle security system or immobilizer system may also require re-initialization after the battery has been disconnected and re-connected. Some other computers or ECUs such as the engine management ECU may also require re-initialization after having the electrical power disconnected.

In most of these cases, either the computer memory is lost when the power is disconnected or the ECU is designed so that it will not allow correct operation until the correct coding has been entered (this provides a measure of security for the vehicle owner).

7.9.2 Starting systems

The starting system requires little maintenance except to ensure that the engine is being cranked at sufficient speed to start easily.

Checks can also be made for abnormal noises from the starter motor during the engagement of the pinion into the flywheel ring gear. If an abnormal noise is heard during use of the starter motor it could indicate a worn pinion or flywheel gear.

If the engine turns over slowly it could indicate a discharged battery, poor electrical connection in the starter circuit which will cause a high resistance, or a faulty starter motor.

7.9.3 Charging systems

The charging system supplies electrical energy to the electrical system while the engine is running. The charging system also charges the battery while the engine is running, thus maintaining the charge level of the battery so that it has sufficient stored electrical energy to operate the necessary electrical systems when the engine is not running. Importantly, there should be sufficient stored energy in the battery to re-start the engine.

The alternator is used to supply electrical energy to the vehicle's electrical system. The alternator is generally driven by the crankshaft front pulley via a rubber drive belt. It is therefore essential that during routine maintenance the condition of the drive belt is checked. Over a period of time the rubber and fibres from which the belt is constructed will deteriorate; if unnoticed this can lead to the failure of the belt. The condition of the belt should be checked for cracking, contamination from fluids such as coolant and oil and also wear, etc. The alignment of the belt should be checked because misalignment of the belt will increase wear and lead to premature failure.

The drive belt has to be sufficiently tensioned to prevent excessive slip when electrical loads are applied to the alternator. A belt that is too slack will slip and increase wear. A belt that is too tight will increase the load applied to the alternator bearings. The additional load on the pulley bearings will cause the bearings to become noisy and eventually wear.

Belt tension should be checked with a 'drive belt tension indicator gauge' (Figure 7.53); most vehicle manufacturers provide a specification to which the belt tension should be set. Note that the belt tension specification may differ between a new and a used belt.

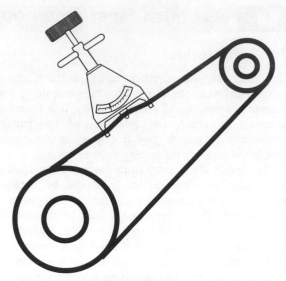

Figure 7.53 Checking drive belt tension with a tension gauge

The security of the alternator fixings should be checked together with the security of the electrical cables and connections. Note that some alternators are mounted in insulated bushes, to help reduce the vibrations that can influence the components of the alternator.

7.9.4 Additional electrical systems

Additional electrical systems fitted to the vehicle include the lights, horn, wipers, washers etc. Many of theses systems are mandatory and it is therefore necessary to check that they function during the routine maintenance checks on the vehicle. Although the driver of the vehicle may notice the failure of a system or a single light, if a system is not functioning correctly it may make the driving of the vehicle dangerous or the vehicle hazardous to other road users.

The lighting checks should include an inspection of the functionality of each light, together with a check on the condition of the light lens etc. Here is a checklist:

- Headlamps – 'dipped' and 'main beam' including tell-tale warning lamp for main beam operation
- Side lamps
- Indicators – including tell-tale warning lamp and the rate at which they flash
- Brake lamps – including centre brake lamp if fitted
- Hazard warning lamps – including tell-tale warning lamp
- Rear fog lamps
- Reversing lamps
- Rear number plate lamp
- Additional driving lamps.

Additional checks should be made to the following electrical systems:

- Horn – loudness and tone
- Wipers – including the condition of the blades

- Washers – including the alignment of the spray area and the level of the washer fluid.

Many vehicles include other electrical systems, many of which are specific to their vehicle manufacturer. The modern vehicle is fitted with many electronic systems, which are controlled by an ECU. Many of these systems feature a self-diagnostic system that constantly monitors the system for faults. If the system detects a fault, the driver is normally alerted with the illumination of a warning lamp situated with the instruments or in a similar area. If a warning lamp is illuminated it may be necessary to access the relevant ECU diagnostic system with the use of diagnostic test equipment (such as a fault code reader) to identify the fault.

7.9.5 Headlamp adjustment

With the increase in light intensity from modern headlamps, the alignment of the headlamps should be checked during routine maintenance to prevent dazzle to other road users, as well as to ensure that the driver has good visibility. Note that the MOT test includes headlamp alignment checks

When carrying out headlamp alignment checks, it is necessary to use special alignment equipment to check the horizontal and vertical aim of the headlamps. If the equipment is unavailable, an approximate check can usually be carried out with the use of a vertical screen.

Before checking the headlamp alignment, the vehicle should be at the correct height, so the tyre pressures should be set correctly. If the vehicle has been raised during the previous checks or during repairs etc. the suspension should be settled by driving the vehicle for a short distance.

Figure 7.54 Checking headlight alignment

Chapter 8

BEARINGS

what is covered in this chapter . . .

- **Plain bearings**
- **Ball and roller bearings**

8.1 PLAIN BEARINGS

8.1.1 Requirement for bearings

A bearing is a part of a mechanism that supports and guides a moving part. By far the commonest type of bearing is that used to support a rotating shaft, e.g. a crankshaft or camshaft.

Plain bearings are those in which the moving surfaces are in sliding contact with one another, apart from a film of lubricant, and nearly all engine bearings are of this type.

8.1.2 Bushes

The simplest type of bearing consists of a plain hole in the supporting component in which the shaft rotates. To provide a suitable combination of materials to minimize friction and wear, and to provide a simple and inexpensive way of repairing a worn or damaged bearing, a sleeve – called a 'bush' – is fitted in the hole.

Bushes are usually made an interference fit in the hole so that all movement and wear takes place between the bore of the bush and the shaft. Figure 8.1 shows three types of bush.

Type (a) is a plain bush and is used to support a shaft where radial loads only (i.e. loads acting at right angles to the shaft) are carried.

Type (b) has a flange at one end which, in conjunction with a collar or shoulder on the shaft, resists an end force – or axial load – on the shaft in *one* direction. It also has one end closed or blind, to prevent lubricant escaping or dirt getting in.

Type (c) is a popular and inexpensive type of bush made from metal strip bent into cylindrical shape. It is called a 'wrapped bush'.

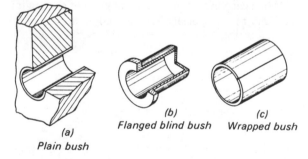

(a)
Plain bush

(b)
Flanged blind bush

(c)
Wrapped bush

Figure 8.1 Types of bush

Most bushes are an interference fit and therefore are fitted into the supporting component with a press.

8.1.3 Split bearings

A bush can only be used when the part of the shaft that runs in it can be inserted from one end. If the shaft is of such a shape that this is not possible (e.g. an engine crankshaft) the bearing must be split as illustrated in Figure 8.2 overleaf. The two halves of the bearing are held together by bolts, screws or studs and nuts. In this case the equivalent of the bush is known as 'a pair of bearing shells', or 'half bearings'.

The lower part (4) is the housing in which the bottom shell (3) is fitted. The top shell (2) fits in the cap (1). As in the case of a bush, the shells are prevented from turning in the housing by an interference fit. When a shell is pressed down into its housing, its edges should stand slightly proud of the housing faces, and similarly for the shell fitted in the cap. If the cap is now fitted in

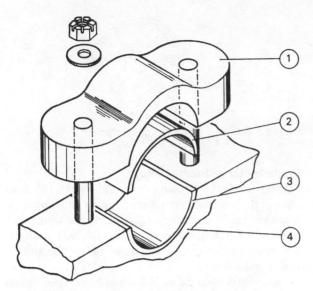

Figure 8.2 Split bearing with detachable shells

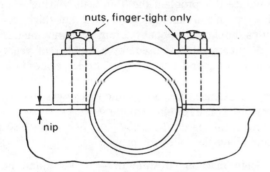

Figure 8.3 Bearing nip (greatly exaggerated)

place and the two nuts screwed down finger-tight, there will be a small clearance between the faces of the cap and housing, although the edges of the shells are touching, as shown (much exaggerated) in Figure 8.3. The gap (or 'nip') is actually only a few hundredths of a millimetre, the exact amount depending upon the size of the bearing and the materials from which the housing and cap are made. When the nuts are correctly tightened down, the nip disappears and the shells are tightly held.

Location devices

These are provided to ensure correct positioning of the shells during assembly. Two common types are illustrated in Figure 8.4. A dowel (a) is a short peg, one end of which is made a tight fit in a hole in the housing, the other (protruding) end being a clearance fit in a hole in the shell.

Commonly used on engine crankshaft and camshaft bearings are lugs (Figure 8.4b). The lugs are pressed out at one joint face of each shell and engage with corresponding notches cut in the housing and cap. One lug per shell is used, and the lugs of both shells of a pair are normally arranged at opposite ends of the same joint face, as shown in Figure 8.4c. It is most important

that there should be a clearance between the back of the lug and the notch to prevent the shell being pushed inwards and causing local metal-to-metal contact at this point. You can check this by pushing down on the joint face of the shell on the lug side. It should be possible to move it about 1 mm lower than the housing face before the lug touches the back of the notch.

It should be emphasized that the shells must be prevented from moving in the housing and cap by their interference fit alone. The dowels or lugs are purely for correct location during assembly and they must not be solely relied upon to prevent rotation of the shells, though they may contribute to it.

Oil holes and grooves

In most bearings, the oil for lubrication is supplied through a hole drilled through the housing, and there must be a corresponding hole in one of the shells. This hole should be placed at that part of the bearing where radial load is least, which is usually the centre of the upper shell. From this hole, oil is carried round by shaft rotation, and pressure causes the oil to spread towards the ends of the bearing. Oil grooves are unnecessary in most pressure-fed bearings and are undesirable in the areas supporting heavy loads, since not only do they reduce the surface area of the bearing but they also let the oil escape easily from the region where it is most important to retain it.

In order for the oil to lubricate the bearing, there must be a small clearance between the shaft and the bearing. In this clearance a film of oil forms which prevents the rubbing of metal surfaces. The clearance is generally 0.02 – 0.07 mm.

Certain bearings, such as the big-end bearing, are carried on moving parts (crankpin) and cannot conveniently be supplied with oil directly and independently. In such cases the oil is supplied through a drilling in the shaft via the main bearing, and therefore there is no need for an oil supply hole in the shells. To ensure a continuous supply of oil to the big-

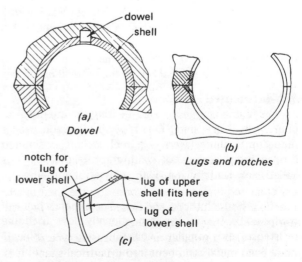

Figure 8.4 Methods of locating shells

ends, a circumferential groove is formed around the main bearing shells, into which the oil is fed from the main oil gallery (Figure 8.5). The main journal end of the hole through the crankshaft runs around this groove so that the big-end is in constant communication with the main oil gallery. The width and depth of this groove around the main bearing shells should be no more than is necessary to carry enough to the big-ends.

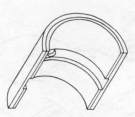

Figure 8.5 A bearing shell with transfer channel

8.1.4 Bearing materials

Shafts are almost invariably made of steel or iron, and the surface of the bearing should make a satisfactory combination with the shaft. Some materials used for the housing may be satisfactory in this respect: for instance both cast iron and aluminium are quite satisfactory for many conditions of operation and could be used without bushes or shells. But for operation at high speeds, or heavy loads, or both, some other material is generally preferred. A few are mentioned below.

Bronze

Bronzes are primarily alloys of copper and tin, the exact properties depending upon the proportions and also upon what other elements, if any, are included. A type commonly used contains a small amount of phosphorus and is known as 'phosphor bronze'.

Bronzes are fairly hard – though softer than steel – and have good load-carrying capacity, but are less suited than some other materials to high rubbing speeds.

In cases where the supply of lubricant is difficult, the plain bearing could be either pre-lubricated or self-lubricated.

Pre-lubricated

Powdered lead bronze can be compressed into a mould and heated to partially fuse the metal particles together; this process is called 'sintering'. The porous composition has the ability to absorb and retain a lubricant, which is applied either by soaking the bearing before fitting, or by occasional re-oiling. Some bushes are made with the bronze sintered to a steel backing and coated with a layer of acetal resin polymer. This surface gives a good bearing performance even when there is only a trace of lubricant. The bearing surface is often indented to give pockets to hold the oil or grease.

Self-lubricated

As the name suggests, this bearing is intended to operate in a dry state. One type, in common use, is made up of three layers – a steel backing, a sintered bronze interlayer and a coating (or overlay as it is called) of lead mixed with polytetrafluoroethylene (PTFE).

PTFE is a synthetic polymer (long-chain chemical compound), which has exceptionally low frictional resistance and complete immunity to most solvents including water, so it has many uses for rubbing surfaces on a vehicle.

White metal or Babbitt alloys

First introduced by Babbitt over a century ago, this is an alloy of tin and small amounts of copper and antimony. It has very good anti-friction properties and when used with a comparatively hard shaft, the soft material allows abrasive particles to embed below the surface and so reduce wear.

Softness is good for embeddability, but is poor when heavy loads have to be carried. Repeated heavy loads cause fatigue (break-up and flaking of the surface), so to reduce this problem the 'thin-wall bearing' is used. This type has a steel liner, about 2 mm thick, coated with a thin layer of about 0.1 mm of bearing metal.

White metal was used for a number of years for main and big-end bearings but the large inertia loads associated with modern engines is too great for this material. Camshaft bearings and thrust washers are the present-day uses of white metal.

An ideal material for big-ends and main bearings should have the following properties:

1 High mechanical strength – to withstand heavy loads and resist fatigue.
2 High melting point – to resist damage due to high oil temperature.
3 Resistance to corrosion.
4 Conformability – to yield easily when slight misalignment occurs.
5 Good surface properties – to prevent seizure or pick-up if the oil film breaks down momentarily (this property is also called 'compatability').

In practice no material meets the ideal requirements, so the alloy selected must match the properties that are special to the engine type, e.g. a compression-ignition engine requires a material of high strength, whereas in a spark-ignition engine the material has to withstand high oil temperatures (over 120 °C), extremely thin oil films and high rubbing speeds.

Aluminium-based alloys

A popular alloy used for car crankshaft and big-end bearings is 20% tin–aluminium. This material, formed in a thin-wall bearing, combines high fatigue strength with good surface properties and can be used without an overlay. When bonded together, the tin and aluminium form a network structure, so this material is sometimes called 'reticular tin–aluminium'.

Where higher loadings prevail, either 6% tin–aluminium or 11% aluminium–silicon alloys may be used. The former has a high fatigue strength and the latter a very high strength, but both materials require an overlay to improve compatibility and conformability.

Copper–lead and lead–bronze

These alloys have an exceptionally high fatigue strength and are used for heavily loaded bearings. Being harder and less able to embed abrasive particles, they generally require a harder shaft.

The materials have poor corrosion resistance: the lead is dissolved by acidic oil and this destroys the boundary and wear-resisting properties. To overcome this problem a very thin overlay (0.013–0.038 mm) of lead–tin or lead–indium is used. This overlay is soft so embeddability and conformability are also improved.

The life of these bearings is linked to the time it takes for abrasive particles in the oil to cut away the overlay. When the overlay is worn off the wear is extremely rapid, so attention to oil filtration is essential.

8.1.5 Thrust washers

Shafts usually need to be located endways, usually against a certain amount of end thrust. Bushes may be flanged (see Figure 8.1) in conjunction with shoulders or collars on the shaft, and shells may be flanged in a similar manner. In the case of wrapped bushes and thin-wall shells used as crankshaft bearings, it is more usual to use separate these thrust washers or half-washers. These have steel backs (faced with white metal, copper–lead or lead–bronze, and are located in a recess in the bearing housing (see Figure 8.6).

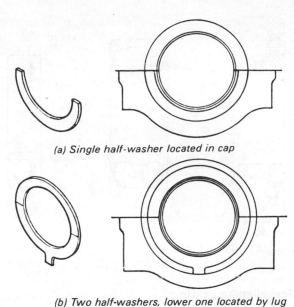

(a) Single half-washer located in cap

(b) Two half-washers, lower one located by lug

Figure 8.6 Thrust washers

In many cases only one half-washer is used, and it is prevented from rotating by letting its ends abut the unrecessed edge of the housing half (usually the main bearing cap) which does not have a half-washer. When a pair of half-washers is used, one has a lug, which engages a notch in the housing to prevent washer rotation.

Shafts are usually located endways by one bearing only, thrust washers being fitted at both ends of this bearing but omitted from all others.

8.2 BALL AND ROLLER BEARINGS

1 An inner race which is fixed on the shaft. In a few cases the shaft itself may form the inner race if it is made of suitable material, but replacement may then be more costly when excessively worn.
2 An outer race which is fixed in the housing. Similar to the inner race, it may sometimes be formed by the housing itself.
3 A suitable number of balls or rollers.
4 A cage to prevent adjacent balls or rollers from rubbing against one another and to space the elements equally around the circumference of the bearing.

8.2.2 Materials

The races and balls (or rollers) are made from a special quality steel, suitably hardened. There may be slight variations in the composition and heat treatment of the steel between different manufacturers and for different types of bearing. The cages may be made of bronze, aluminium or mild steel.

There are four main types of bearing, classified by the shape of the rolling elements as ball, cylindrical roller, spherical roller and taper roller.

8.2.3 Ball bearings

Figure 8.7 shows cross-sections of three examples of ball bearings.

A Single-row bearing

This has balls running in grooves in the races. This type is intended for carrying mainly radial loads, but can also support some axial load in both directions. Double-row bearings of this type are also made and are capable of carrying heavier loads.

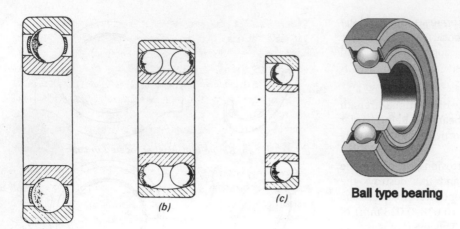

Ball type bearing

Figure 8.7 Types of ball bearing

Self-aligning bearing

The inner race has two ball tracks and both rows of balls run in an outer race whose inner surface forms a section of a sphere having its centre at the shaft centre. This allows the shaft axis to run at a small angle to the axis of the housing, and bearings of this type are used for applications where precise alignment of shaft and housing cannot be maintained.

Angular contact ball bearing

This type is capable of taking axial loads comparable with the radial loads, but in one direction only. Bearings of this type are generally used in pairs one at each end of a shaft, and care must be taken when fitting the bearings to ensure that they are fitted the correct way round.

8.2.4 Cylindrical roller bearings

An example of this type is shown in Figure 8.8. These are capable of carrying greater radial loads than ball bearings, but no axial load. The guiding flanges may be either on the inner or outer races.

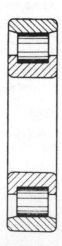

Figure 8.8 A cylindrical roller bearing

Where heavy radial loads have to be carried at low speeds, or where the motion is of an intermittent or oscillating nature, specially long rollers of small diameter – called 'needle rollers' – may be used.

8.2.5 Spherical roller bearings

As shown in Figure 8.9, this is the roller-bearing equivalent of the self-aligning ball bearing. It is constructed on similar principles and used for similar applications, but is capable of carrying greater loads.

Figure 8.9 A spherical roller bearing

8.2.6 Taper roller bearings

An example of this important and useful type of bearing is shown in Figure 8.10. The working surfaces of both races and rollers are conical, the taper being such that the cones, of which races and rollers form a part, each have their apex at a common point on the axis of the shaft.

They are always used in pairs facing opposite ways, and are capable of dealing with considerable axial loads as well as radial loads. Different taper angles may be used depending upon the amount of axial load to be carried. They are provided with some means of axial adjustment to control the amount of 'end play' or 'pre-load' allowed.

A single-row bearing as illustrated can only deal with thrust in one direction (hence the need for using two bearings), however, double-row types are also made, each row having its taper facing opposite ways, and are therefore capable of taking thrust in both directions.

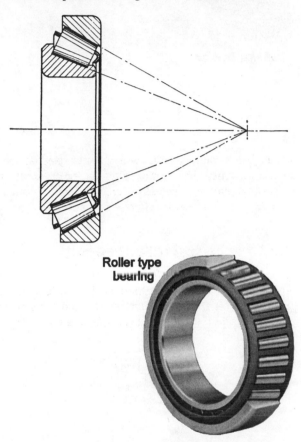

Roller type bearing

Figure 8.10 A taper roller bearing

8.2.7 Maintenance of bearings

Fitting bearings

Cleanliness is vitally important when fitting bearings of any type. Do not unwrap new bearings from their packaging until the bearing is ready to be fitted. Bearings are usually coated with a preservative to inhibit corrosion, and this need not be removed.

In most cases the races are an interference fit both in the housings and on the shafts. The correct method to fit the races into the housing or onto the shaft is usually with a press.

Note: Under no circumstances should pressure be applied to one race in order to press the other into place, i.e. the pressure must be applied directly to the race being fitted.

Where a press is not available, it may be possible to fit the races by carefully striking the tubular drifts with a suitably faced hammer. Always refer to the bearing/vehicle manufacturer's fitting instructions before installing a replacement bearing.

Removing bearings

Unless the bearing is to be scrapped, the same care must be exercised in removing one as in fitting one. In many cases, suitable extractors are available for this purpose. Again, force must be applied *directly* to the race being removed.

Bearing adjustment

Where adjustment is provided, it is usually possible with an adjusting nut, threaded rings or by distance pieces and shims.

The ideal adjustment for many applications is that there should be no end float and no pre-load, but that the bearing should not be over-tightened.

In certain applications, however, such as rear-axle pinion shafts, correct meshing of the gears demands complete elimination of play, and the bearings are generally 'pre-loaded', i.e. they are tightened slightly beyond the point of elimination of play. Specific installation instructions are given in workshop manuals on the fitment with this type of bearing installation.

Always ensure that the securing mechanism, usually a nut, is fastened correctly, e.g. if a split pin is used, that the tail of the pin is sufficiently bent over.

Bearing lubrication

Ball or roller bearings are lubricated with oil or grease depending upon the component into which they are fitted.

In engines, gearboxes and final-drive gears, oil is used and the design ensures a constant supply to each bearing.

If fitted to other areas of the vehicle, such as wheel hubs, the bearings are lubricated by grease. The bearings and the inside of the hub cavity are packed with grease, which is suitable for the purpose intended. Details of the type of grease to be used, and the amount to be put into the housing, are given in the workshop manual for the vehicle.

The lubricant (i.e. grease) is normally prevented from escaping from the bearing with some form of seal. Manufacturers normally use a lip-type synthetic rubber seal for this purpose.

INDEX